Introduction to Anthropology Student Reader

University of Connecticut

Annual Editions: Physical Anthropology 09/10, *Eighteenth Edition*

Editor: Elvio Angeloni
Pasadena City College

Annual Editions: Anthropology 09/10, *Thirty-Second Edition*

Editor: Elvio Angeloni
Pasadena City College

Annual Editions: Anthropology 07/08, *Thirtieth Edition*

Editor: Elvio Angeloni
Pasadena City College

Applying Cultural Anthropology: An Introductory Reader, *Seventh Edition*

Aaron Podolefsky
Central Missouri State University

Peter J. Brown
Emory University

Applying Anthropology: An Introductory Reader, *Eighth Edition*

Aaron Podolefsky
Central Missouri State University

Peter J. Brown
Emory University

McGraw Hill Learning Solutions

Boston Burr Ridge, IL Dubuque, IA New York San Francisco St. Louis
Bangkok Bogotá Caracas Lisbon London Madrid
Mexico City Milan New Delhi Seoul Singapore Sydney Taipei Toronto

The McGraw-Hill Companies

Introduction to Anthropology Student Reader
University of Connecticut

This book is a McGraw-Hill Learning Solutions textbook and contains select material from the following sources:
Annual Editions: Physical Anthropology 09/10, Eighteenth Edition by Elvio Angeloni. Copyright © 2009, previous edition(s) 1990-2008 by The McGraw-Hill Companies, Inc.
Annual Editions: Anthropology 09/10, Thirty-Second Edition by Elvio Angeloni. Copyright © 2009, previous edition(s) 1977-2008 by The McGraw-Hill Companies, Inc.
Annual Editions: Anthropology 07/08, Thirtieth Edition by Elvio Angeloni. Copyright © 2007 by The McGraw-Hill Companies, Inc.
Applying Cultural Anthropology: An Introductory Reader, Seventh Edition by Aaron Podolefsky and Peter J. Brown. Copyright © 2007, 2003, 2001, 1999, 1997, 1994, 1991 by The McGraw-Hill Companies, Inc.
Applying Anthropology: An Introductory Reader, Eighth Edition by Aaron Podolefsky and Peter J. Brown. Copyright © 2007, 2003, 2001, 1999, 1997, 1994, 1991 by The McGraw-Hill Companies, Inc.
All are reprinted with permission of the publisher. Many custom published texts are modified versions or adaptations of our best-selling textbooks. Some adaptations are printed in black and white to keep prices at a minimum, while others are in color.

1 2 3 4 5 6 7 8 9 0 QSR QSR 0 9

ISBN-13: 978-0-697-78453-7
ISBN-10: 0-697-78453-3

Learning Solutions Specialist: Thomas Weitz
Production Editor: Nina Meyer
Printer/Binder: Quebecor World

CONTENTS

Before: The Sixties

CONRAD PHILLIP KOTTAK

It Began by Accident

This is a story of change, but it didn't start out to be that. It began by accident. I first lived in Arembepe during the (North American) summer of 1962. That was between my junior and senior years at New York City's Columbia College (of Columbia University), where I was majoring in anthropology. I went to Arembepe as a participant in a now defunct program designed to give undergraduates an experience in ethnography—the firsthand study of local culture and social life. The program's cumbersome title, the Columbia-Cornell-Harvard-Illinois Summer Field Studies Program in Anthropology, reflected participation by four universities, each with a different field station. The other field sites were in Peru, Mexico, and Ecuador. The area around Salvador, Brazil, had just been chosen for the Columbia field station.

The field team leader was Professor Marvin Harris, who was later to become my adviser and doctoral dissertation committee chair during my graduate work in anthropology at Columbia University, which began in 1963. Also in Salvador that year was Professor Charles Wagley, another Columbia anthropologist, who had worked with Harris and others to establish the program. Through their links with Bahian social scientists, Harris and Wagley chose two villages that were anthropologically interesting but close enough to Salvador to maintain contact with the undergraduates. The two communities lay along the same road. Abrantes, the agricultural village, nearer to Salvador, was the district seat for Arembepe, the more remote fishing village. Liking the coast, I preferred Arembepe, where I was assigned, with fellow team member David Epstein. Harris arranged for us to rent the dilapidated summer house of a city man who sometimes vacationed in Arembepe.

Meanwhile, Professor Wagley's daughter, Betty, a Barnard College student also majoring in anthropology, arrived to spend the summer with her parents in Salvador. She went with us to visit Abrantes and Arembepe and decided she also wanted to do fieldwork in the latter. Betty arranged lodging with a local woman, but since David and I had hired a cook, she ate with us and shared the cost of food and supplies. Betty's mother was Brazilian, and Betty, herself born in Brazil, is bilingual in Portuguese (her first language). This made her more adept at fieldwork than either David or I was. She was also kind enough to translate for us many times.

Having taught anthropology now for more than 30 years, I realize how unusual my first field experience was. Most anthropologists begin fieldwork, which is required for the doctorate, after a few years of graduate study and not as undergraduates. They usually choose the part of the world they want to work in and the topic they will investigate there. For example, my own longest ethnographic project came just after graduate school. Having taken courses about several world areas, I became particularly interested in Madagascar, a large island off the southeast coast of Africa. I read as much as I could about the cultures of Madagascar. I focused on a problem—the social implications of an economic change, the expansion of irrigated agriculture—that I could investigate there.

With Arembepe, by contrast, someone else—the directors of the field program—selected the area, even the village, for me. I didn't have time to do the extensive background reading that normally precedes fieldwork. Nor did I have much time to study the language I would be using in the field.

Although I didn't control the initial choice of Arembepe, I *did* decide to keep on studying it, particularly when, by 1973, it was evident that Arembepe had changed more rapidly in less than two decades than some places change in centuries. Longitudinal (long-term, ongoing) fieldwork during that transformation is the basis of this book.

Most of my preparation for my 1962 fieldwork was in a prefield seminar that Harris offered at Columbia and another seminar about ethnographic field methods taught by Professor Lambros Comitas. In Harris's class, students talked about the kinds of research we planned to do when we got to Brazil. Harris urged us to do microprojects, focusing on limited aspects of community life that we could investigate easily in three months. The program's founders didn't intend our work to be traditional holistic ethnography—intensive study of all aspects of local life through long-term residence and participant observation. Comitas's seminar, on the other hand, had introduced me to techniques used in long-term, in-depth ethnography. One of my problems in doing fieldwork in Arembepe in 1962 was the conflict between my wish to do a holistic study and the program's preference for a microproject.

The program's goals were modest. I now realize that this was realistic, because we were novices. Harris and the other leaders wanted us to get our feet wet—to see if we liked fieldwork

(Conrad P. Kottak)

"We always got stuck at least once." The road to Arembepe, passing through the district seat, Abrantes, in 1964.

enough to pursue a career in cultural anthropology. Our experience would also prepare us for later, longer fieldwork. As training for our microprojects, our prefield seminar assignment was to write a library research paper on the topic we planned to investigate in Brazil.

Harris suggested I study race relations, which already had a large literature. Comparisons of race relations in Brazil and the United States are appropriate because both countries have a heritage of slavery. In both there has been considerable mixture of Europeans, Africans, and Native Americans. For the seminar, I read extensively. I learned the main differences between the role of race in Brazil and the United States and wrote a research paper on my findings. Harris and I later worked out a specific microproject on Brazilian racial classification, which I discuss later in this chapter.

Although I prepared myself to investigate Brazilian race relations, my preparation in Brazilian Portuguese was insufficient. Language was my biggest barrier in the field. I had never been abroad and had no experience speaking a foreign language: high school (Latin) and college (German) had barely taught me how to read one. As a result, I spent most of the summer of 1962 asking Brazilians to repeat everything they said to me. This led Arembepeiros to call me a *papagaio* (parrot)—because I could only echo words that someone else had originated. I discovered that it's difficult to gain much insight into native social life when you can't converse as well as a five-year-old can.

The Sixties

In June 1962, when I first set eyes on Arembepe, the 55-kilometer trip from Salvador was neither simple nor sure. It took three hours in a vehicle with four-wheel drive. Located about 13 degrees south of the equator and at sea level, Arembepe is never cold, but June and July are rainy, making travel difficult. The clay-surfaced road was usually muddy, and we always got stuck at least once in any round trip. The task of getting our heavy jeep station wagon unstuck usually required a work group of field team members and a dozen helpful onlookers.

Sand, lagoons, and more sand came after the mud. After heavy rains, crossing the freshwater lagoons that bordered Arembepe on the west made the jeep seem like a motorboat. High water washed onto the cabin floor and sometimes stalled the engine. After the lagoons came the dunes, with closely planted coconut trees—posing another traffic hazard. Making it into the village required finding another vehicle's tracks and flooring the accelerator. Once, as a frustrating drive out seemed over, I pulled up in front of the house I was renting to find that the brakes had failed. Frantic pumping kept me from crashing through the kitchen wall.

But Arembepe was worth the trip. I can't imagine a more beautiful field setting. The village was strung along a narrow strip of land (less than a kilometer) between ocean and lagoons. It was more spectacular than any South Sea island I later visited. Arembepe's houses—brightly painted in tones of blue, pink, purple, and orange—stood under lofty coconut palms. To the east, stretches of smooth white sand and protected swimming areas alternated with jagged rocks and churning Atlantic waves. On a sunny day in August, Arembepe was alive with color: the green-blue hues of ocean and lagoons, orange-red of brick and roof tiles, pinks and blues of houses, greens of palms, and white of sand. Colorful fishing boats anchored evenings and Sundays in the port, just east of the central square and the small, white Roman Catholic chapel. The harbor is formed by a rugged, partially submerged reef. Each morning the boats rowed through its narrow channels, then raised their sun-bleached sails to travel to their destinations for the day.

The conjunction of natural beauty with the middle-class appeal of a quaint fishing village had already drawn a handful of tourists and summer residents to Arembepe in 1962. Still, the poor quality of the road made it a hard trip even in summer, the dry season (December to February). Only a few residents of the capital—mainly middle-class and lower-middle-class people—had summer homes in Arembepe. Limited bus service began in 1965, but it brought few visitors until the road was improved in 1970.

Poverty and poor public health were blights that made Arembepe—despite the title of this book—something less than paradise. In theory, Arembepeiros got their drinking water from Big Well, a tiny settlement 2 kilometers away. An entrepreneur who lived there made money selling barrels of water in Arembepe. When well water wasn't readily available, villagers sometimes drank water from the freshwater lagoon. Some mothers even used lagoon water in the powdered milk they mixed for their children. Considering these traditional uses of water—and that the bushes where villagers relieved themselves were on the edge of the lagoon, which rose in the rainy season—it's easy to understand why children suffered from intestinal disorders and extreme malnutrition (the latter partly caused by parasites in their bodies).

(Conrad P. Kottak)

During the 1960s, as we approached Arembepe, the clay road yielded to sand.

Malinowski and Microprojects

I entered this romantic yet imperfect setting as a fledgling ethnographer with ambitious goals and a huge linguistic impediment. Two dimensions of my work in Arembepe bear discussion here. One involves my scientific and professional aims. The second has to do with my personal reactions to an alien setting. First the scientific goals.

As a conscientious anthropology major, I wanted to put the lessons from my classes into practice. I wanted to do the things that Bronislaw Malinowski describes as the ethnographer's work in the first chapter of his classic *Argonauts of the Western Pacific,* a field study of fishers and traders in Melanesia.

I often compared my experiences with Malinowski's. Even our field settings struck me as similar. He had also worked in a tropical South Sea setting (the Trobriand Islands). Though Arembepe is on the mainland, the phrase "South Sea island" kept running through my head. Reading Malinowski's description of the moment when the ethnographer set foot upon a beach reminded me of my own situation. I imagined myself in his sandals. Like me, Malinowski initially had trouble communicating with local people. "I was quite unable to enter any more detailed or explicit conversation with them at first. I knew well that the best remedy for this was to collect concrete data, and accordingly I took a village census, wrote down genealogies, drew up plans and collected the terms of kinship" (Malinowski 1961, p. 5).

I was eager to do those things that Malinowski had done, especially to census the village. But field leader Harris discouraged me, offering another lesson: Before I could gather the detailed and accurate data that ethnography demands, I needed to build rapport; people would have to get to know and trust me. I would have to convince them I wasn't dangerous and that it wouldn't be to their disadvantage to answer my questions. Furthermore, I didn't yet know enough about village life to devise pertinent questions to ask during a census. Accordingly, but regretfully, I put the census on hold and set about building rapport. David Epstein and Betty Wagley, my companions in the field, were doing the same thing.

How does one build rapport? "Get to know the men," Marvin told me. To do this I started joining the fishermen for their evening bath in the lagoon. I had my first doubts about the wisdom of this participant observation when I accidentally swatted a floating piece of donkey dung (I like to think I identified the correct mammal) during my third bath. I gave up lagoon bathing when I learned of the lagoon system's infestation by schistosomes—liver flukes. After that, I was careful to avoid the lagoon. I followed the advice of public health officials to rub exposed body parts with alcohol whenever I came into contact with lagoon water. Arembepeiros found these precautions laughable: Not to worry, they said—small fish in the lagoon ate the liver flukes (and germs in general).

If the lagoon was now off-limits, there was still the chapel stoop, where each evening, after the fleet had returned, baths had been taken, and the day's main meal consumed, men would gather to talk. This was male territory. Among females, only small girls and old women dared approach. David and I would sit and try to talk. My Portuguese was rudimentary. Still, villagers tossed questions my way. They were curious about the United States, but their questions were hardly scintillating: "Were there camels in the United States?" "Elephants?" "Monkeys?" They went through a litany of animals they had seen on the lottery tickets people brought back from Salvador. "Look! Up in the sky. It's a jet from the United States heading for Rio," they observed every other night, reflecting the airline's schedule. Whenever, after arduous mental rehearsal, I found the words to ask a question about Arembepe, I'd get an incomprehensible reply, followed by some such query as "Have you ever seen a bear, Conrado?"

"Bear, bear," I parroted.

"Parrot, parrot," they guffawed.

"Yes, I have seen a bear. I have seen a bear in a zoo."

Rapport building was fascinating indeed.

Visions of Malinowski danced in my head as I came to resent this kind of activity as a waste of time. I was eager to do something "more scientific." The microproject that Harris and I had planned involved testing a difference between race relations in Brazil and the United States. In the United States a rule of descent determines racial identity. If an American has one black (African-American) parent and one white one, he or she is assigned, automatically at birth and without regard for physical appearance, to the black race. In Brazil, it seemed that several factors determine racial identity and that no descent rule operates. Since, however, no one had systematically demonstrated that Brazil lacks such a rule, we decided that a genetically and phenotypically (physically) mixed community like Arembepe would be a good place to test it.

When an automatic descent rule operates, full siblings belong to the same group. Thus in the United States, full siblings can't belong to different races. In Arembepe, we set out to find full siblings who were physically very different, to see if they were assigned to different races. We found three sisters with widely varying skin shades, hair types, and facial features. After we photographed them, I finally got to do something more chal-

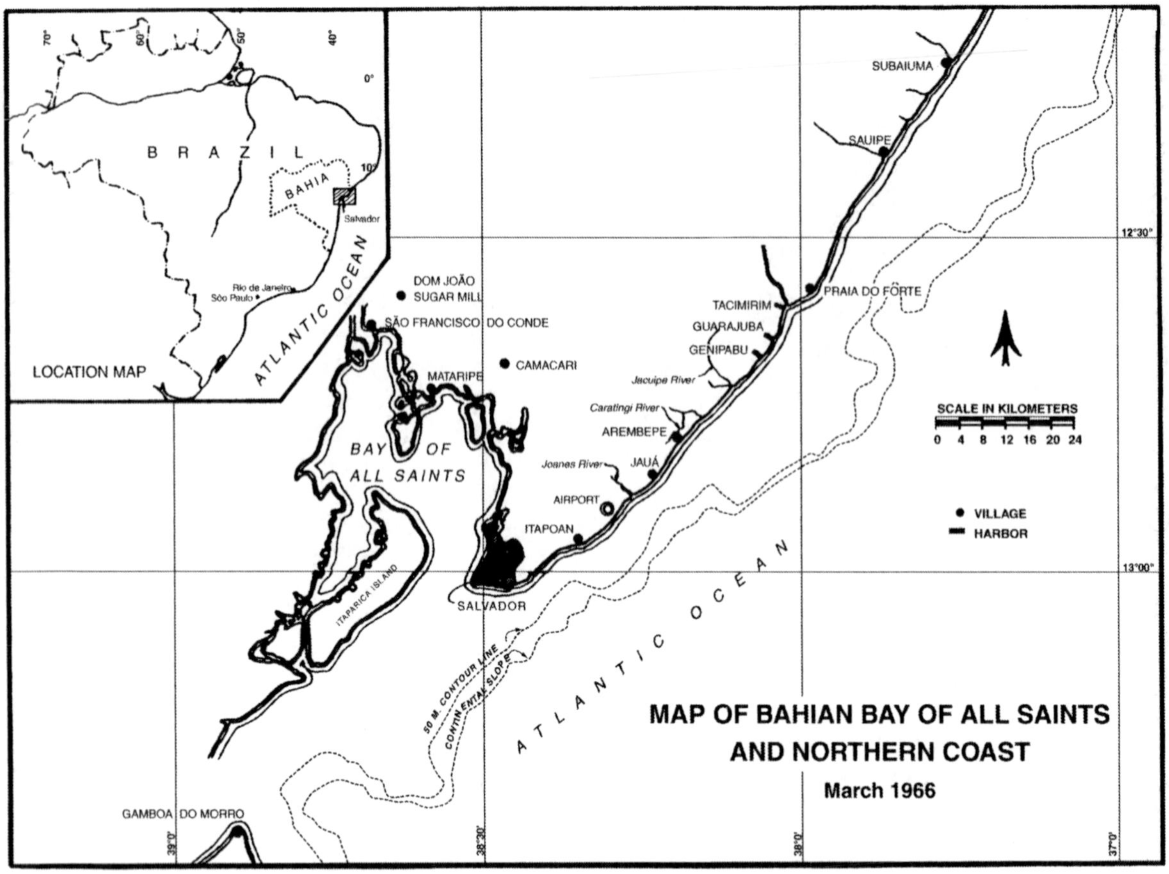

lenging than reporting on North American animals. I chose a sample of 100 villagers and showed the photo of the sisters to all, asking them to tell me each girl's race. Sure enough, I found that many different terms were used, that in Brazil full siblings could belong to different races.

New questions about race emerged from that first survey. We devised another set of questions, based on drawings of individuals who contrasted phenotypically. By questioning another sample of villagers, I found that Arembepeiros used many more racial terms (over 40) than had previously been reported for a Brazilian community. They also used them inconsistently, so that the racial term used for another person might vary from day to day, as might even self-identification. By the time my three months in Arembepe were up, I was fluent in Brazilian racial terminology, and Harris and I had the basis for a couple of journal articles. Although I still felt guilty that I hadn't managed to do a Malinowskian census, I did think I'd accomplished something in my first field experience.

To work again in Brazil, I knew I'd have to improve my Portuguese. I could get only so far talking about race relations. I spent the next summer (1963) taking an intensive course in Brazilian Portuguese at Columbia University while another field team lived in Arembepe. Also in the summer of 1963, Betty Wagley and I, whose romance had begun under Arembepe's full moon, got married; and I began graduate school in the fall.

I was delighted, the following spring, to be offered the job of assistant leader of the 1964 field team. I returned to Arembepe in June 1964 determined to do my census. And not just a census. By then I had studied more anthropology, and my Portuguese had improved dramatically. I felt I was ready to do a full-fledged interview schedule (a kind of questionnaire). Peter Gorlin, who now holds a Ph.D. in anthropology and an M.D. degree, was an undergraduate field team member stationed in Jauá, the next village south of Arembepe. Peter had read Malinowski, too; he was also eager to use Malinowski's "method of concrete, statistical documentation" (1961, p. 24), to satisfy the ethnographer's "fundamental obligation of giving a complete survey of the phenomena, and not of picking out the sensational [and] the singular" (1961, p. 11).

I was ready to do a survey of all the households in Arembepe, and Peter wanted to do the same thing in Jauá. But we needed an instrument. Our team leader, the renowned Bahian physician and anthropologist Thales de Azevedo, supplied us with one—an interview schedule that had been used in southern Bahia. We revised the schedule for the fishing villages and had it printed.

An *interview schedule* differs from a standard questionnaire in that the ethnographer talks directly, face to face, with informants, asks the questions, and writes down the answers. Questionnaire procedures, which sociologists routinely use, tend to be more indirect and impersonal; often the respondent fills

(Courtesy Jerald T. Milanich)

The beautiful, microbe-infested, freshwater lagoon that borders Arembepe to the west, at sundown.

in the form. Sociologists normally work with literate people, who can fill out the answer sheets or questionnaire forms themselves. Anthropologists, by contrast, haven't usually worked in places where most people are literate, so we have to record the answers ourselves.

Because we are in charge of pacing, we can choose to digress temporarily from the scheduled questions to follow up intriguing bits of information that emerge in the interview. Thus the ethnographer can keep interviews open-ended and exploratory while asking a basic set of questions, to gather comparable, quantifiable information. I learned as much about Arembepe from the open-ended questioning as I did from the formal queries.

Our interviews in Arembepe illustrate still another difference between the research techniques of anthropologists and sociologists. Because sociologists normally deal with large populations, such as the United States, they must use *sampling techniques,* which enable them to make inferences about a larger group from a detailed study of a smaller one. We didn't need to do sampling in Arembepe, because it was small enough for us to do a total sample—that is, to complete the schedule with all the households there—159 of them.

A final contrast between cultural anthropology and sociology is worth mentioning. Sociologists often distribute their questionnaires by mail or hire research assistants to administer, code, and analyze them. Ethnographers, by contrast, work right in the community, where they encounter a series of real-world obstacles. My main problem as I interviewed in Arembepe wasn't the few villagers who slammed doors in my face or even the droopy-nosed kids who used my pants as a handkerchief. My problem was fleas. I recall my third or fourth interview, in a sand-floored hut. Asking my questions to a dozen smiling members of an extended family, I began to itch in places I was embarrassed to scratch. I made it to the end of the form, but I didn't tarry for open-ended inquiry. Instead I ran home, through the house, out the back door, right into the harbor at high tide. I let the salt water burn into my flea wounds. Fleas bothered most of us, especially Betty, that summer. The remedy for the men was to wear pants and sprinkle our cuffs with flea powder. We managed to interview in almost all Arembepe's households, despite the predatory sand fleas.

Our interview schedule was eight pages long. We asked questions (for each household member) about age, gender, racial identity, diet, job, religious beliefs and practices, education, political preferences, possessions, consumption patterns, and ownership of livestock, boats, coconut trees, land, and farms. I encouraged Peter not to do a microproject but to follow the Malinowskian path I'd wanted to tread. He did it with gusto; in two months he'd finished the schedule with all the households in Jauá. He hiked up the beach to spend August helping Betty and me finish the interviewing in Arembepe.

There are advantages, I now realize, in both models for brief fieldwork. A microproject is easily manageable and holds out the promise of a modest research paper. The holistic Malinowskian approach is also valuable. I'm convinced my Portuguese would have improved much more if I'd done the interview schedule the first summer, rather than limiting my talk to rapport building and race relations. Peter Gorlin's work with the schedule in Jauá and Arembepe in 1964 helped him improve his Portuguese much more quickly than I had done in 1962.

Doing the schedule had an added benefit I didn't fully realize in 1964: It got at least one member of the field team into every home in Arembepe. Years later I was to hear from many villagers that they remembered those visits warmly. Our questions, asked in their homes, had communicated our personal interest and showed we didn't look down on Arembepeiros.

I found the people of Arembepe to be open, warm, and hospitable, much less wary of outsiders than the Betsileo of Madagascar, whom I studied for 14 months in 1966–1967. Most Arembepeiros welcomed us to their homes and gladly answered our questions. Only a handful played hard to get, slamming windows and doors as we approached, telling neighbors they wouldn't answer our questions. I had to settle for sketchier information about them and could only make estimates of their incomes and consumption patterns, using public information and behavior. Fortunately (since the 1964 data are the basis for much of the detailed comparison between Arembepe in the 1960s and later), fewer than a dozen households, scattered throughout the village, refused to let us do the schedule.

The interview schedule wasn't the only thing I did in Arembepe in 1964. Soon after my arrival, I met an excellent informant, Alberto, whose name figures prominently in the story that follows. Then a 40-year-old fisherman, Alberto was the eldest brother of our cook. He felt free to visit our house almost every night, and he was eager to teach me about the fishing industry. I also got information about fishing by talking to fishermen and fish marketers on the beach and by going out in several boats, including that of Tomé, Arembepe's most successful boat captain and owner. Tomé's name, too, is a prominent one in Arembepe's recent history.

(Conrad P. Kottak)

1964 field team members Peter Gorlin (second from left) and Erica Bressler with their host family in Jauá, the fishing village just south of Arembepe. Note the range of physical variation among the local people.

In 1965 I had my third chance to study Arembepe. The results of analyzing the interview schedules and my information on fishing had been so promising that both Marvin Harris and I felt that I might, with another summer of fieldwork, amass sufficient data to write my doctoral dissertation about Arembepe, which I did. This time Betty and I weren't part of a field team but on our own. A graduate fellowship and grant supported my work, and living was still cheap in cash-poor Arembepe. In summer 1965 I again followed the Malinowskian plan, but I already had much of the statistical and observational data needed for the "firm, clear outline" of my community's organization and the "anatomy of its culture" (Malinowski 1961, p. 24).

What I needed now was flesh for the skeleton. So I spent the summer of 1965 gathering data on the "imponderabilia of actual life . . . collected through minute, detailed observations . . . made possible by close contact with native life" (Malinowski 1961, p. 24). By this time, I didn't really have to harken back to Malinowski to know that although I had the bare bones, I still needed to find out more about local opinions, values, and feelings; to listen to stories, examine cases, and gather intimate, basic details about everyday life. Like Napoleon Chagnon, the principal ethnographer of the Yanomamo Indians of Venezuela, I knew "how much I enjoyed reading monographs that were sprinkled with real people, that described real events, and that had some sweat and tears, some smells and sentiments mingled with the words" (Chagnon 1977, p. xi). I wanted to add such dimensions—feeling tones—to my ethnography of Arembepe.

It Was an Alien Place

Those were some of my professional goals and research methods. Another part of ethnography is more personal. No matter how objective and scientific they fancy themselves, anthropologists are not mechanical measuring instruments. We are inevitably *participant* observers, taking part in—and by so doing modifying, no matter how slightly—the phenomena we are investigating and trying to understand. Not recording machines but people, anthropologists grow up in particular cultural traditions, possess idiosyncratic personality traits and experiences, have their own motivations, impressions, values, and reactions. Nor are our informants alike; we come to appreciate them differently. Some we never appreciate; an occasional one we detest.

Raised in one culture, curious about others, anthropologists still experience culture shock, especially on the first field trip. *Culture shock* refers to the whole set of feelings about being in an alien setting and the resulting reactions. It is a chilly, creepy feeling of alienation, of being without some of the most ordinary, trivial—and therefore basic—cues of one's culture of origin.

As I planned to set off for Brazil in 1962, I couldn't know how naked I would feel without the cloak of my language and culture. My sojourn in Arembepe would be my first trip outside the United States. I was an urban boy who had grown up in Atlanta, Georgia, and New York City. I had little experience with rural life in my country, none with Latin America, and I had received only minimal training in the Portuguese language.

New York City direct to Salvador, Bahia, Brazil. Just a brief stopover in Rio de Janeiro; a longer visit would be a reward at the end of fieldwork. As our plane approached tropical Salvador, I couldn't believe the whiteness of the sand. "That's not snow, is it?" I remarked to a fellow field team member. Marvin Harris had arranged our food and lodging at the Paradise Hotel, overlooking Bahia's magnificent, endlessly blue, All Saints' Bay. My first impressions of Bahia were of smells—alien odors of ripe and decaying mangoes, bananas, and passion fruit—and of swatting ubiquitous flies. There were strange concoctions of rice, black beans, and gobs of unidentified meats and floating pieces of skin. Coffee was strong and sugar crude. Every table top had containers for toothpicks and manioc (cassava) flour, to sprinkle, like parmesan cheese, on anything one might eat. I remember oatmeal soup and a slimy stew of beef tongue in tomatoes. At one meal a disintegrating fish head, eyes still attached, but barely, stared up at me as its body floated in a bowl of bright orange palm oil. Bearing my culture's don't-drink-the-water complex, it took me a few days to discover that plain mineral water quenched thirst better than the gaseous variety. Downstairs from the hotel was the Boite Clock, a nightclub whose rhythmic bossa nova music often kept us from sleeping.

I only vaguely remember my first day in Arembepe. Unlike ethnographers who have studied remote tribes in the tropical forests of South America or the highlands of New Guinea, I didn't hike or ride a canoe for days to arrive at my field site. Arembepe wasn't isolated compared with those places—only compared with every place *I*'d ever been. My first contact with Arembepe was just a visit, to arrange lodging. We found the crumbling summer house of a man who lived in Salvador and arranged to rent it and have it cleaned. We hired Dora, a 25-year-old unmarried mother of two, to cook for us, and another woman to clean house and do our laundry. My first visit to Arembepe didn't leave much of an impression. I knew I'd still have a few more days at the Paradise Hotel, with a real toilet and shower, before having to rough it in the field.

Back in the city, using her fluency in Brazilian language and culture, Betty Wagley bargained for our cots, pots, pans, flashlights, and other supplies. I don't remember our actual move to Arembepe or who accompanied us. Harris had employed a chauffeur; we stopped to deposit some field team members in Abrantes. I do recall what happened when we got to Arembepe. A crowd of children pursued our car through the sand and streets until we parked in front of our house, near the central square. We spent our first few days with children following us everywhere. For weeks we had little daytime privacy. Kids watched our every move through our living room window. Sometimes one made an incomprehensible remark. Usually they just stood there. Occasionally they would groom one another's hair, chewing on the lice they found.

Outcasts from an urban culture, David and I locked our doors. Once he went into Salvador while I stayed the night alone.

"Conrado's scared," said Dora, our cook. "He's afraid of the *bichos* [beasts, real and imaginary] outside." There was really nothing to be afraid of, she assured me. A dangerous *bicho* had never bothered anyone in Arembepe; most people didn't even have locks on their doors.

The sounds, sensations, sights, smells, and tastes of life in Arembepe slowly grew familiar. I grew accustomed to this world without Kleenex, where globs of mucus drooped from the noses of village children whenever a cold passed through. A world where, seemingly without effort, women with gracefully swaying hips carried 18-liter kerosene cans of water on their heads, where boys sailed kites and sported at catching houseflies in their bare hands, where old women smoked pipes, storekeepers offered *cachaça* (common rum) at nine in the morning, and men played dominoes on lazy afternoons when there was no fishing. I was in a world where life was oriented toward water—the sea, where men fished, and the lagoon, where women communally washed clothing, dishes, and their bodies.

Arembepe was a compact village, where the walls of most houses touched those of their neighbors. Privacy was a scarce commodity. No wonder villagers didn't lock their doors—who could steal anything and have it stay a secret? Young lovers found what privacy they could at night.

Even more dramatically than in other places without electricity, Arembepe's night life was transformed when the moon was full. Reflected everywhere by the sand and water, moonlight turned the village by night into almost day. Young people strolled in the streets and courted on the beach. Fishermen sought octopus and "lobster" (Atlantic crayfish) on the reef. Accustomed to the electrified, artificial pace of city life, I was enchanted by the moonlight and its effect on this remote village. Moonless nights impressed me, too. For the first time I could understand how the Milky Way got its name. Only in a planetarium had I seen a sky so crammed with stars. Looking south, distant Salvador's electric lights just barely dimmed the white stars against the coal-black sky, and for the first time I could view the Southern Cross in its magnificence.

Even a devout astrologer would have been impressed with the extent to which activities were governed by the phases of the moon. This was a slower and more natural epoch in Arembepe's history than the years that were to follow. People awakened near sunrise and went to bed early. Moonlight and a calm sea permitted occasional nighttime fishing, but the pattern was for the fleet to leave in the early morning and return in the late afternoon. Boats usually went out five or six days a week; as Christians, Arembepeiros took Sunday as a day of rest. But generally, life in Arembepe followed the availability of natural light and the passing of day and night.

Another force of nature, the weather, influenced the rhythm of life. My visits to Arembepe were during the season of rain and rough seas. Sailboats were vulnerable to high winds and stormy weather, and it was dangerous to negotiate the narrow channels in the rocky reef when racing home to escape a sudden squall. Storms usually lasted no more than a week, but I remember one three-week lull, in 1964. People speculated incessantly about when the weather would improve; they had no access to weather reports. Villagers lamented that they couldn't work. Eventually they began to complain of hunger. Cattle were brought in from farms to be butchered and sold, but many households were too poor to buy beef. Villagers said they were hungry for fish, for something with flesh to complement a diet of coffee, sugar, and manioc flour. The weather even forced us to let up on our interviewing. Our schedule had a whole section on diet—the quantities of various foods that people bought or ate per day, week, or month. We felt embarrassed asking people what they ate in normal or good times when they were starving for protein and, indeed, for all items whose purchase required cash.

The tropical rainy season meant constant high humidity, a perfect climate for molds. My black leather dress shoes turned white with mildew. Peter Gorlin had bought a navy blue drip-dry suit before his trip to Bahia in 1964. Since we attended few formal affairs in Salvador, Peter let his suit hang in a wardrobe in Jauá until he finally needed it. Discovering, a few hours before a party, that it was covered with mildew, Peter checked into a Salvador hotel, took a shower with his suit on, lathered and rinsed it, wore it to the party, and dripped dry for the next few hours.

The tile roofs of the houses we rented in Arembepe were never very effective in keeping the moisture (and bats) out. Whenever it rained, we had to avoid the large leaks, but there was no place we could be completely dry. One rainy day during the three-week fishing lull, Dora told us that lately, smelling the moist walls of her wattle-and-daub (stick-and-mud) hut, she had remembered her craving as a child to lick, even eat, dirt from the mud walls. Arembepeiros sometimes did eat earth, she told us. This geophagy may have been a symptom of iron deficiency in lean times.

I can summarize my feelings about living in Arembepe in the 1960s by saying that I had a profound sense of being away. In those days, almost no one except a fish buyer from Salvador ever drove a car into Arembepe. I felt cut off from the world. Only a few villagers owned radios, which rarely brought news

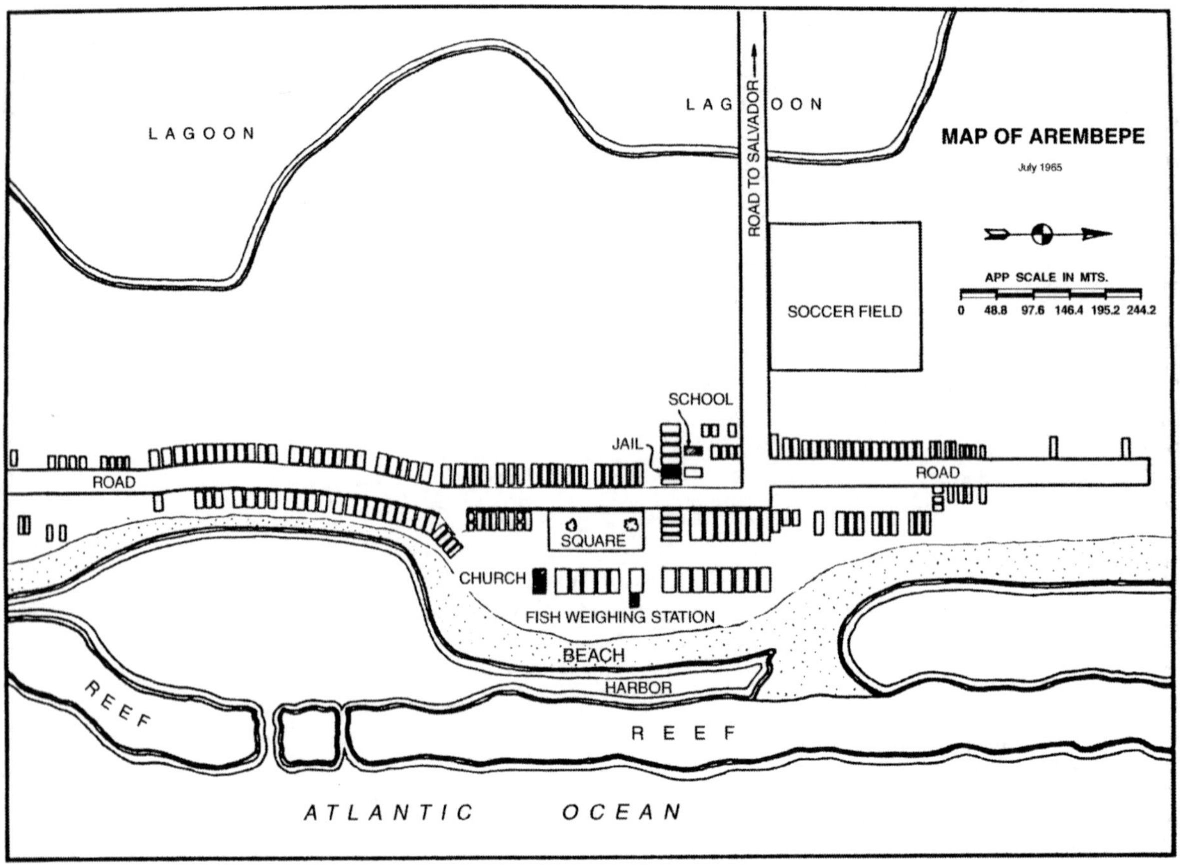

of the rest of the world anyway. I pored over every word of *Time*'s Latin American edition on each visit to Salvador. We sometimes planned our trips into Salvador to coincide with the day the new *Time* came out.

Even for Betty Wagley Kottak, a Brazilian (of dual nationality), Arembepe was unfamiliar. It was far removed from the sophistication, social stratification, and style consciousness of Rio de Janeiro and São Paulo, which she knew well. Betty had been exposed to much of Brazil's "Great Tradition" (to use Robert Redfield's term for the culture of literate, mainly urban, elites) but not the "little traditions" of its peasants and rural poor. For both of us, then, as for the other field team members, Arembepe provided a strong contrast with all previous settings in our lives.

I think that our work in Arembepe also gave us a better understanding of rural America as recently as the 1930s and 1940s. Then, in many isolated pockets, especially among the poor, night life still went on by candle and lantern. This was before business, government, and media had fully introduced rural folk to the industrial world's vast inventory of benefits and costs.

We learned firsthand about the habits and values of Arembepeiros, how they tried to make ends meet, how they dealt with fortune and adversity. We got to know many people as individuals and as friends. Characters like Alberto, Dora, and Tomé, whose words, stories, and experiences are laced through this chronicle of a changing Arembepe, are much more to me than informants. They are people I value as I do my friends and special colleagues in the United States. Yet they are the kind of people that few outsiders will ever have a chance to meet. The anthropologist's special obligation is to tell their story for them.

1

Teaching Theories

The Evolution-Creation Controversy

Robert Root-Bernstein and Donald L. McEachron

At the beginning of a book of readings on anthropology as a biosocial science, we can appropriately concern ourselves with defining science and scientific explanation. When asked, most people describe science by naming disciplines: "Oh, science, let's see, that's physics, chemistry, biology, and so on." However, science is more than a list of subjects or particular fields of study. Rather, it is a process for drawing conclusions. Stated differently, science is a particular way of knowing. We have, of course, many ways of knowing things. For example, one might see something in a dream and be convinced that it is true. One might be told some fact or theory by a teacher (such as what goes up must come down) and accept it based on the teacher's authority. In this case, the student has learned a scientific principle but has not participated in hypothesis testing or theory building.

In their work, scientists give special definitions to some common, everyday words. Words such as *validity, reliability, random, hypothesis,* and *theory* take on meanings that are precise and often significantly different from their everyday counterparts. These meanings can lead to serious misunderstandings as scientists try to communicate with the public.

In recent years, questions about the nature of science have been at the root of public debate over the teaching of human evolution in the public schools. As anthropologists, we respect and value the belief systems of other people, and we recognize that many of the cultures of the world have their own beliefs about creation. Yet the only scientific model that can explain the fossil and genetic record is evolution.

As you read this selection, ask yourself the following questions:

- How is the term *theory* used differently by scientists and nonscientists?
- Why is it so important that scientific theories be testable and correctable?
- What does the phrase "scientific skepticism" mean to you?
- Who do you think should decide what is science and what is not?
- Why has the evolution versus creationism debate been such an emotional issue in some sectors of American society?

The following terms discussed in this selection are included in the Glossary at the back of the book:

contingent truths
creationism
evolution
hypothesis
natural selection
religion
scientific theory

In recent years, a controversy has developed in the United States over the teaching of evolutionism and creationism in the public schools. The controversy, while nominally a scientific one, also has philosophical, historical, religious, and legal implications as well. Since some twenty state legislatures or courts are presently considering or have considered legislation and lawsuits concerning the controversy, we believe that it is in the best interest of the voting public to be informed of the issues.

We believe that there are four basic issues: (1) What is a scientific theory? (2) What is a religious belief? (3) Who has the right to decide these issues? (4) How do one's answers to the previous three questions affect one's view on whether evolutionism and creationism are scientific and should be taught in public schools?

Very briefly, a controversy has arisen between evolutionists and creationists because they disagree on

Root-Bernstein, Robert & McEachron, Donald L. "Teaching Theories: The Evolution-Creation Controversy." From The American Biology Teacher, October 1982. Reprinted with permission of the National Assoc. of Biology Teachers.

all four basic issues. Evolutionists generally believe: (1) that evolutionism is a valid scientific theory, whereas creationism is not; (2) that evolutionism is not a religious belief, whereas creationism is; and (3) that the validity of a religious belief should be decided by religious believers. In consequence, evolutionists conclude (4) that since evolutionism is a valid scientific theory, it should be taught in the public schools; whereas, since creationism is not a scientific theory, it should not be taught as science in the public schools.

Creationists disagree completely. Creationists generally believe (1) that evolutionism is not a valid scientific theory, whereas creationism is; (2) that evolutionism is a dogmatic, secular religion, whereas "scientific creationism" is not; and (3) that the state (that is, either the legislature or the courts) has the right to decide whether any theory is scientifically valid or not. Thus, creationists argue (4) that the state has the right to decide that evolutionism must be censored as a dogmatic religious belief and equal time given to creationism as a valid scientific theory. Creationists argue that either both should be taught in the public schools, or neither.

Clearly, to decide between these two positions, one must understand what a scientific theory is and how it differs from a religious belief. It is our purpose to explore these issues in this essay.

WHAT IS A SCIENTIFIC THEORY?

Begin by considering the question, "What is a scientific theory?" There is nothing mysterious about the answer; a scientific theory is a simple, *testable*, and *correctable* explanation of *observable* phenomena that yields *new information* about nature in answer to a set of pre-existing problems. While this definition may sound complicated or imposing, in practice it is not. All of us use scientific theories in our daily thinking. Consider the following situation as an example.

You come home one evening, open the front door, and turn on the light switch. The lights do not come on. This is an *observation*. One compares this observation to memories of observations made under similar circumstances: every other time you've turned on the light switch, the lights have come on. One has an *anomaly*—that is, something that should work the same as always, but doesn't. Why do the lights not come on? This is your *problem*.

How do you resolve your problem? First, it occurs to you that something about the electrical system is different tonight. You consider possible differences: perhaps the light switch isn't working properly. You've invented an *hypothesis*. Can you *test* it? Sure. You jiggle the switch. Nothing happens. Your hypothesis is probably wrong. You reject it. But you still have your problem. Can there be some other explanation? Yes. Maybe the fuse has burned out. Another hypothesis. Can it be tested? Easily. You go turn on the light switch in the next room and the lights in there go on. So your problem isn't the fuse. There must be some other explanation.

But wait a minute: you've made an *assumption* about the fuse that may not be correct! What if the two rooms are controlled by two different fuses? Then the fact that the lights work in the second room proves nothing at all about the first fuse. The manner in which you've tested your hypothesis about the fuse being burned out is not valid. If your *assumption* about both rooms being controlled by a single fuse is wrong, then the test is useless. Thus, one must be careful to test not only one's hypothesis, but the assumptions upon which it rests as well. This is a very important point to which we will return later.

Checking your fuses, you find that all are fine. So, still in the dark, you hypothesize that the bulb is burned out. You take out the bulb, put in a new one, throw the switch, and, lo and behold—light! So you conclude that your third hypothesis was correct. The reason the light would not go on was because it was burned out.

But wait! You've made another assumption, haven't you? You've assumed the light bulb is burned out, but have you tested the light bulb in another socket to see whether it really *is* burned out? If you are acting scientifically, you must not only test your hypothesis; you must also test your assumptions. So, you screw the light bulb into another socket and—much to your surprise—it lights! Your last hypothesis was wrong! And just think—if you hadn't bothered testing your assumption, you would never have known you were wrong. Indeed, you would have thrown away a perfectly good light bulb.

Now, how do you explain why the light bulb failed to light before? It wasn't burned out. The power was on. The fuse was fine. The switch works. Logically, there seems to be only one other likely explanation of all these observations: perhaps the light bulb wasn't screwed in properly. This is your new hypothesis.

As with any scientific hypothesis, you ask once again: Is it testable? But this time your answer is both yes and no. Yes, one may test the general hypothesis that an unscrewed light bulb won't light. That's easy to do: just loosen any light bulb in its socket and you can verify that it doesn't go on when you turn the switch. However, one cannot test the *particular* hypothesis that the cause of your problem tonight was a loose bulb; you've already removed the bulb from its socket. There is now no way to tell whether the bulb was loose or not. One concludes that it had to have been loose because one cannot think of any other *test hypothesis*.

Note that one accepts one's *particular* hypothesis only when *two* conditions are met: (1) that its corresponding *general* hypothesis is testable; and (2) when no other *testable* hypothesis is available to explain the problem. If one's explanation meets these criteria, then it is a scientific theory. But note also that one's theory is not actually *true*—it is only *probable.* It is only probable because there might be another testable hypothesis that might explain the collection of observations better; or there might be a test that demonstrates that one's theory is wrong. One might, for example, someday discover that one's lights go out sporadically because a mouse causes short circuits by gnawing on the wires in the wall. But, if you don't know you have a mouse then you are unlikely to think of this hypothesis and even less likely to test it by looking for the mouse. In consequence, theories are always tentative, even when tested and found correct. For, as you saw when you thought your problem was a burned-out bulb, it sometimes takes only one more simple test to reveal your error.

Now, we may draw several important conclusions about scientific theories from this example. Most important of these is the fact that scientific theories can never be proven absolutely. A mouse may always be hiding, unknown, in some wall waiting to be discovered, thereby disproving your loose-light-bulb theory. The same is true of *any* scientific theory. Science is not, therefore, truth—at best it is the unending *search* for truth. The conclusions reached by science are only *contingent* truths—truths contingent upon man's limited knowledge of himself and the world around him.[1]

Now, one may ask what good is a theory if it is not true? A theory is good because it is *useful* and it is *fruitful of new knowledge.* Scientific methods have explained more of the empirical world than any alternative approaches including religion. Science allows man to work in the universe as no other system of knowledge does. It allows one to do things that one could not otherwise do, and it allows one to learn things one would otherwise not learn. For example, Faraday's theory of electricity allowed him to invent the first electric motor. Pasteur's germ theory has allowed the control of innumerable diseases. The laws of thermodynamics allowed atomic power to be harnessed by mankind. The list could go on almost indefinitely. So, scientific theories are important because they give mankind knowledge of this world and the ability to act wisely in this world. In our case, it gave us knowledge of the electrical system and thus the ability to fix the light.

Man's ability to act usefully from the predictions of a theory, however, depend upon his ability to test the predictions made by the theory. The process of testing, as we saw with the light bulb, is more important than the theory itself. For even when the theory was wrong, the test yielded new information that was used to invent the next theory. Thus, right or wrong, a testable theory always yields new information about the problem it claims to resolve. This new information is *cumulative.* It adds up. First we tested the switch and found that it worked. So, we knew the problem was not the switch. Then we tested the fuse, and found that the fuse worked. So we knew the problem was not the fuse or the switch. Then we tested the light bub . . . and so on. The more we tested, the more we learned. And the more we learned, the fewer the possible explanations left to try. We knew more, and our ignorance was less. We were converging on the correct answer. All good scientific theories work this way. Thus, although scientific truths are always contingent ones, the method by which they are advanced and tested ensures their improvement.

In short, the power of scientific theories results from the fact that they are *correctable.* They may be tested. Whether the theory is right or wrong, these tests yield new information about the world. And, if the theory is wrong, then this new information can be used to invent a new and better theory. Thus, while scientific theories are never perfect, they become better and better with time. And, as theories become better, mankind knows more, can act more wisely, and can solve more problems.

CAN GOD BE USED IN A SCIENTIFIC THEORY?

One further explanation of our light problem remains to be discussed before considering whether evolutionism and creationism are scientific theories. One might explain the failure of the light by saying that "It was God's will." Indeed, it might have been. "God's will" cannot, however, be part of a *scientific* explanation.

Three reasons preclude the use of God, or other supernatural agencies, in scientific theories. First, scientific theories must be *bounded.* That is, they must apply only to a particular field of inquiry. A simple analogy can be made to sports. Each sport has its own rules that are valid only for that sport. And every sport is played within an area *bounded* by sidelines, goals, or a defined course. In this sense, science is the attempt to discover the rules by which nature plays its various "games" and the boundaries within which each different "game" is played. In our light bulb example, we concluded that a rule must exist that says: the light will not go on if the bulb is not screwed in properly. This is a *bounded* explanation that applies to all light bulbs, but which could not, for example, be used to explain other natural events such as a flood or a death. "God's will" is, on the other hand, an *unbounded* explanation. It can be used to explain the light problem, floods, deaths, and anything else imaginable. In consequence, "God's will" and other supernatural powers cannot be invoked in a scientific theory because they would make the theory *unbounded*. The rules of science would not apply, just as the rules of baseball do not apply to tennis.

Unbounded explanations have a second problem. They cannot be tested. As we stated above, all theories must be testable. Testability, in turn, is necessary if a theory is to be correctable. To be testable, and therefore correctable, a theory must state *how* an event occurs. Because God's actions are beyond man's knowledge, we cannot know *how* He works His will. The same is true of any supernatural explanation. Supernatural, by definition, means beyond man's comprehension. Since God's power is supernatural, He is capable of doing anything. Thus, there is no test imaginable that could disprove an hypothesis stating that an event occurred because of "God's will." In consequence, there would be no way to discover if one's hypothesis were wrong, and no way to correct one's error.

Untestable explanations present a third difficulty. They can neither be harnessed to useful ends nor to the discovery of new knowledge. Explaining the light bulb problem as "God's will," for example, does not enable us to correct the problem. On the contrary, it places the problem beyond our comprehension. By proposing that the light bulb failed to light because it was unscrewed, we could correct the problem immediately. Further, we would be able to recognize and solve that problem if it ever arose again. Thus, we have learned something new. We have acquired new knowledge. Invoking "God's will" does not yield the same sort of new and useful knowledge.

One must not conclude from the foregoing that science is anti-religious. On the contrary, scientific and religious explanations can be completely compatible. What the light bulb problem shows us is that scientific explanations are simply a very select subset of all possible explanations. Religious, or supernatural, explanations form another subset. Sometimes these two subsets overlap. Then, something may be "God's will" and also have a scientific explanation. In these cases, one should be able to explain *how* "God's will" was implemented. If one can do this, then science and religion are in harmony. If not, then they represent two irreconcilable views of the problem. On this point, Pope John Paul II recently quoted the following conclusion from the Vatican II Ecumenical Council: "research performed in a truly scientific manner can never be in contrast with faith because both profane and religious realities have their origin in the same God." Religious leaders of almost all religious denominations agree.

EVOLUTION: SCIENCE OR RELIGION?

Now, how does the light bulb example illuminate the question of whether evolution is a scientific explanation of nature? First of all, as in the light bulb example, one must have a *problem* to address. The problem evolutionists face is to explain *how* the living organisms that exist on the earth today developed through history, and *how* they achieved the forms and distributions characteristic of each species, alive or extinct. Many hypotheses have been proposed to resolve these problems during the 2,000 years of man's recorded history. Each has been found wanting. Perhaps the best known of these was Lamarck's idea that organisms could modify their structures by force of will. Lamarck's idea did not pass the test of observation and its assumptions were never verified. Thus, it, like our hypothesis concerning the fuses, was retired to scientific purgatory. Not until Darwin invented the concept of evolution by natural selection of the fittest organisms was an hypothesis suggested that explained all of the data accumulated during tests of previous hypotheses. It did so in a simple, harmonious, and verifiable way. Thus, if one looks at the history of science, one finds that Darwin's is neither the first nor the only theory to attempt to explain the history and development of life. It is the culmination of 2,000 years of theory building. In this, evolution is analogous to our loose-light-bulb hypothesis: it is the end product of a long chain of hypothesizing and testing. It is the best theory so far devised.

Darwin's basic hypothesis was that only the best-adapted organisms survive the competition for food, the ravages of disease, and the attacks of natural predators to reproduce themselves. The weeding out of weaker organisms creates a steady change in the adaptive characteristics of the individual organisms comprising each species. As the individual characteristics change, so does the profile of the whole species. Thus, evolution.

Is evolution a scientific theory? Just as with the light bulb example, the first question that must be asked about the Darwinian hypothesis is whether it is testable. In this case, as in the case of the loose-light-bulb hypothesis, one must answer both yes and no. Yes, the *general* mechanism of natural selection is testable because it is operating today. No, the specific application of natural selection to extinct species is not directly testable because they, like the light bulb in our analogy, have (metaphorically) already been taken out of the socket. Like the light bulb taken out of its socket, however, fossil remains provide enough information to disprove all hypotheses so far invented *other than* evolution by natural selection. Thus, just as in the light bulb example, one accepts evolution as a valid scientific theory for two reasons: (1) its corresponding *general* hypothesis is testable; and (2) no other *testable hypothesis* is available to explain the problem. It is, of course, always possible that a better theory will be invented in the future.

It was stated above that the general mechanism of natural selection is testable. Since many creationists have denied this conclusion, we present two examples here. Everyone knows that germs cause disease and that various insects, such as mosquitoes, can transmit diseases to man. Natural selection has been observed, occurring in both germs and insects. The selection process has even been controlled in the laboratory by means of antibiotics and pesticides. The invention of antibiotics has virtually allowed man to wipe out certain diseases. The few disease germs that have survived man's ingenuity, however, have developed into antibiotic-resistant strains which man can no longer easily control. The same thing has happened with insects sprayed repeatedly with insecticides. The hardiest have survived to reproduce new races of insects that are insecticide-resistant. Thus, in some areas of the world, diseases like yellow fever and malaria are once again becoming major health problems. Even in the United States, farmers are faced with crop-eating insects that are harder and harder to eliminate. Direct observation leaves no doubt that natural selection does occur. The fittest do survive, and they breed new populations of better-adapted individuals.

It is not sufficient to test just the hypothesis of natural selection. One must, as we pointed out repeatedly in our light bulb example, also test one's assumptions. Several assumptions underlie evolutionary theory. One assumption is that there is a mechanism for creating a spectrum of different individuals within a species so that natural selection can weed out the weakest. Another assumption is that some mechanism exists by which those individuals that survive can pass their adaptive traits on to future generations. And finally, evolution by natural selection assumes sufficient time for new species to be formed by the accumulation of adaptive traits. Each of these assumptions has been questioned, doubted, and tested. Each assumption is correct to the best of current scientific knowledge.

The primary mechanism for producing genetic variability in evolving organisms is mutation. Mutation theory has been given a firm experimental basis by numerous scientists including Nobel Laureates T. H. Morgan and J. H. Mueller. Geneticists, such as Barbara McClintock, have evidence that rearrangements of whole genes and even chromosomes may also play a role in creating genetic variability.

The mechanism of genetic inheritance of mutations and rearrangements is also well understood. Despite early fears by nineteenth-century biologists that adaptive variations would blend out of existence like a drop of ink in a gallon of paint, Gregor Mendel and his successors established that inheritance is not blending—it is particulate. The ink spot does not blend into the paint in genetics. Rather, it stays separate and definable, like a water drop in oil. If the water-based ink is better adapted than the oil-based paint, then the ink will reproduce faster than the paint and so come to dominate the mixture. Thus, beneficial mutations, while rare, are not lost from the population. Mendel's "laws" and the population genetics of R. A. Fisher, J. B. S. Haldane, and their colleagues explain the rules by which such populations evolve. James Watson and Sir Francis Crick, two more Nobel Laureates, have explained the details of the inheritance process itself at the molecular level of DNA.

Finally, astronomers, physicists, and geologists have established that the earth is definitely old enough to make evolution by natural selection plausible. One hundred years ago, scientific opinion was just the opposite. Physicists such as Lord Kelvin calculated that the age of the earth was only a few million years—too short to allow evolution. Even Darwin was worried by his arguments. But Kelvin's calculation turned out to be incorrect, for it was based on a faulty hypothesis. Kelvin *assumed* that there was no internal source of energy heating the earth because he knew of none. In fact, his assumption was incorrect. In this case there was a metaphorical "mouse in the wall" called radioactivity. Kelvin did not know about radioactivity because it was discovered after he died. Once other physicists took the heating effects of radioactivity into account in new calculations, it became clear that the earth was billions, not millions, of years old. Astronomers measuring the age of the solar system and geologists dating rocks and fossils have reached the same conclusion. There has been sufficient time for evolution to have occurred.

In short, evolution by natural selection is a valid scientific theory because it and its underlying assumptions have been tested and validated by observation or experiment. Further, anyone who has walked through a modern research library or flipped through a general science magazine will not fail to realize the amount of new knowledge this theory has evoked. Much of this new knowledge has even been useful, especially in the production of new breeds of farm animals and hybrid crops. Evolution by natural selection has thus fulfilled the requirements of a scientific theory superbly. To what degree it may someday need to be modified by new discoveries, only the future will tell.

CREATIONISM: SCIENCE OR RELIGION?

Now, is "scientific creationism" also a scientific theory? "Scientific" creationists claim to be interested in solving the same problems that evolutionists address: how does one explain the forms of living organisms and their geological and geographical distribution? In place of evolution by natural selection, creationists postulate the existence of a supernatural "God," "Creator" or "Intelligence" who created the earth and all of the living organisms on it and in it. They claim that this supernatural agent produced the earth and its life within a period of thousands of years. The question we must address is whether or not the "creation explanation" is a scientific one. In other words, is it testable? Is it correctable? Have its assumptions been tested and verified? And is it fruitful of new or useful information concerning nature?

It is important to point out that our criteria for evaluating scientific theories are identical to those used by creationists such as Robert Kofahl, Kelly Segraves, Duane Gish, and Henry Morris in the course of this controversy. We are not, therefore, asking of "creation science" any more than the creationists ask of science itself.

Can "scientific" or "special" creationism be tested? Creationist scientists themselves admit that it cannot be. Gish, for example, writes in his book *Evolution? The Fossils Say No!* that

> . . . we do not know how God created, what processes He used, for God used processes which are not now operating anywhere in the natural universe. This is why we refer to divine creation as special creation. We cannot discover by scientific investigations anything about the creative processes used by God.

Instead, creationists maintain that the Creator used catastrophic or supernatural means to His end. The Noahic Flood is an example of such a supernatural catastrophe. But, Morris, Director of the Institute for Creation Research (ICR), has written in his book *Biblical Cosmology and Modern Science,* "the main trouble with catastrophist theories is that there is no way of subjecting them to empirical test." Thus, the scientific methods of hypothesis followed by testing, which were so useful in solving our light bulb problem, are totally useless for solving the problems addressed by creationists.

The second characteristic of a theory is that it is correctable. Once again, creationist scientists admit that the creation explanation fails to possess this characteristic. Morris, for example, lists 23 predictions from Genesis 1–11 in his book. His own conclusion is that all 23 predictions are contradicted by the past century of geological research. Does he therefore treat Genesis 1–11 as a scientific hypothesis in need of correction? No. On the contrary, Morris states that "no geological difficulties, *real or imagined,* can be allowed to take precedence over the clear statements and necessary inferences of Scriptures." In short, creationism is uncorrectable.

Indeed, another creationist scientist, John N. Moore of the ICR, has written in several pamphlets that the major advantage creationism has over evolution is that creationism is "the *only unchanging* explanation of origins." It is so unchanging that "scientific creationism" is essentially identical to the prescientific form of Biblical creationism espoused by Jews over 2,000 years ago. This makes creationism one of the oldest surviving explanations for anything. No doubt this intellectual stability is comforting in these times of rapid change, but is stability, in and of itself, necessarily good?

Think back a moment to our light bulb analogy. Would an unchanging, uncorrectable explanation of our problem have been an advantage to us there? Certainly not. Just imagine the depths of our ignorance had we stuck with our first light bulb hypothesis no matter what the evidence indicated. Instead of accumulating new knowledge through the testing of new hypotheses until we discovered that the light bulb was loose, we would still be standing at the light switch wondering what in Heaven's name could be wrong. After a while, no doubt, we would conclude that whatever it is, it is beyond our comprehension. Unfortunately, this is exactly what the creationists have concluded.

All creationist literature falls back, at some point, upon the assumption that a supernatural, omniscient, omnipotent God, Creator, or Intelligence must exist to direct the creative process. Some creationists make this assumption explicit. Others, especially those writing public school texts, do not. These others believe that if they leave God out of the text, then it will be "less religious" and "more scientific." Their belief is unfounded. As we have demonstrated with examples both from the light bulb analogy and from evolutionary theory, all assumptions must be tested whether they are stated explicitly or not. Failure to state an assumption simply makes the explanation less scientific because it is then harder to test it. In this case, whether one explicitly states that God is the Creator or one leaves the Creator unidentified, Someone or Something must cause Creation. These assumed causes (or mechanisms) have been identified and tested for evolution. They must also be identified and tested for creationism if it is to be considered scientific.

Unfortunately, creation scientists are on the horns of a scientific dilemma. If they leave the Creator out of their explanations, they provide no testable mechanism for creation. This form of the creation explanation is therefore unscientific. On the other horn, if they identify the Creator with God or other supernatural powers, then they are also being unscientific. As the great and pious astronomer Sir Isaac Newton said more than a century before Darwin was born, the use of any final cause such as God automatically takes the explanation out of the realm of science. Morris and A. E. Wilder-Smith of ICR and Kofahl and Segraves of the Creation Research Center (CRC) consistently and blatantly identify the Creator as a final cause in their textbooks. But, "God's will," as we discussed with regard to our light bulb analogy, cannot be used as a *scientific* explanation of anything.

Nonetheless, the "scientific creationists" attempt to do just that. Morris and Gish of ICR, Kofahl and Segraves of CRC, and the hundreds of members of the Creation Research Society have all stated that the Creator is the God of the Bible and that the Creation itself occurred exactly as described in Genesis. These same individuals also admit that, to use Morris' words from his textbook *Scientific Creationism,*

> . . . it is impossible to devise a scientific experiment to describe the creation process, or even to ascertain whether such a process can take place. The Creator does not create at the whim of a scientist.

So we come to the crux of the evolution-creation debate. Science depends upon observation, testing, and control. Religion depends upon faith in the existence of an unobservable, untestable, uncontrollable God. As scientists, we can turn off and on a light at will; we can create mutations and breed new varieties of plants and animals at will; we can observe the natural processes of evolution in fossils, fields, forests, and laboratories—at will. How different is creationism. No one can turn off or on the Creator at will. No one can cause Him to create new varieties of plants or animals at will. No one can observe any of the processes by which He creates. Creationism, because it depends upon the existence of such an unobservable, untestable, uncorrectable Creator can not be a scientific theory.

Indeed, the attempt to use a Creator as a scientific explanation only promotes *scientific* ignorance. Invoking "God's will" did not help us to understand or fix our light problem. Invoking "God's will" as the cause of Creation is no more enlightening. "God's will," because it is not testable or correctable, yields no new or useful knowledge concerning nature. Thus, creationism fails to possess the final characteristic required of all scientific theories: that it be fruitful of new scientific knowledge. Creationism is not *scientifically* fruitful.

There are two ways of demonstrating this. The first is to search the historical record since Darwin to determine whether creationism has been used in the formulation of any major scientific discovery. The history of science shows that it has not. On the contrary, almost all important discoveries made during the last century in biology and geology either stem from or add to our understanding of evolution.

This conclusion may be verified in a second manner. Reference to the numerous sources cited by the creationists themselves demonstrates that their conclusions are almost entirely dependent upon research carried out by evolutionists. Only in the rarest instances have the creationist scientists created any of their own data. This is a sorry state of affairs for an explanation that is hundreds and thousands of years older than evolutionary theory. Yet, it makes sense when you think about it. Science, as we pointed out initially, is based upon recognizing and answering new questions or problems. Creationists have no new problems. Accepting the Biblical account of Creation as the True Word of God, creationists can assert, as Kofahl and Segraves have done in their book *The Creation Explanation,* that "the Genesis record [already] provides the answers." For creationists, nothing more can be known; nothing more needs to be known.

CONCLUSION: SCIENCE AND RELIGION

In summary, we have argued that evolution qualifies as a valid scientific theory while creationism does not. We have also argued that evolutionary theory is not a religious explanation while creationism is. We do not conclude thereby that evolution is "true" and creationism "false," nor can the opposite conclusion be maintained. We conclude only that evolution and creationism are two totally different sorts of explanations of nature. They should not be confused.

It is also clear to us that evolution, as the best available scientific explanation of nature, deserves to be taught as a scientific theory in science classes. Creationism, since it is not a scientific theory, should not be taught as science in science classes. On the other hand, we have no objection to seeing creationism taught as a *religious* explanation of nature. Although religion is constitutionally banned from the public schools, perhaps some time could be made available for the teaching of creationism in its proper historical and philosophical context. Such an arrangement would teach students the differences between scientific and religious explanations that have been summarized here.

We believe that it is particularly important that students do learn the differences between scientific and religious beliefs. Indeed, we believe that it is the confusion between the two that has caused the present controversy. Despite the rhetoric used by the creationists, their view is not scientific, nor is science a religion. Yet "scientific creationists" have made both claims. Historically, this is nothing new. Fundamentalists have created the same confusion ever since Darwin first published *On the Origin of Species* in 1859. Harvey Cox, Professor of Divinity at the Harvard Divinity School, has recently written that

> . . . the notorious nineteenth century "Warfare Between Science and Religion" arose from mistaken notions of what religion and science are. Although there are still occasional border skirmishes, most theologians and scientists now recognize that religion overstepped its boundaries when—at least in the West—it tried to make geological and biological history into matters of revelation.

We can only regret that a small group of fundamentalists believe it necessary once again to overstep the boundaries differentiating science from religion. The result is needless confusion, confusion that could be eliminated by proper teaching of what science is, what religion is, and how they differ.

Science and religion, as Cox pointed out, need not be at war. They can be, as we pointed out initially, complementary. It is only when science poses as religion or religion as science that controversy erupts. Otherwise faith and reason are compatible. In fact, the English clergyman Charles Kingsley pointed this compatibility out to Darwin in a letter written in 1860. Kingsley wrote:

> I have gradually learnt to see that it is just as noble a conception of Deity to believe that He created animal forms capable of self-development into all forms needful . . . as to believe that He required a fresh act of intervention to supply the lacunae which He Himself made. I question whether the former be not the loftier thought.

Whether one agrees with Kingsley's view or not, it illustrates an important point. There are many possible conceptions of the relationship between science and religion. It does not seem appropriate to us that any group, such as the creationists, should attempt to legislate their particular view of this relationship into law. Our Constitution guarantees freedom of religious choice. We believe that an equal guarantee exists for all intellectual choices, including those involving science. Thus, just as the courts and legislatures may not judge the validity of various religious beliefs or impose one in preference to another, neither should courts and legislatures be involved in determining the validity of scientific ideas nor should they impose one in preference to another. Just as religious practice is left to the individual religious practitioner, so should scientific research be left to the individual scientist. To do otherwise infringes upon the rights of individuals to decide for themselves the relationship between scientific ideas and religious beliefs. To do otherwise is thus not only an abridgment of intellectual freedom, but of religious freedom as well.

It may strike some people as odd that we equate protection of religion with protection of science. There is good reason for the equation. Several governments in the past have usurped to themselves the control of science. They are not commendable examples to follow: Nazi Germany, Soviet Russia, and Communist Red China. Science, religion, and liberty suffered hand-in-hand in these countries. Let us not begin the journey down their road by harnessing science to legislatures and courts. On the other hand, let us learn from the evolutionism-creationism controversy that dogmatism, be it scientific or religious, is best left out of the classroom. Dogmatism teaches only narrow-mindedness at a time when it is clear that better understanding of the issues is what is needed. We must teach the best of man's knowledge to the best of our ability. But we must also teach how we can recognize it as best. And we must always remain humbly aware that we may be ignorant of something better. That is the lesson of science.

NOTE

1. The authors of this article used the term *man* to refer to humanity in general. This term is not used by modern anthropologists because, to many people, it reflects an unconscious sexist bias in language and rhetoric. At the time that this article was written, however, the generalized *man* was a common convention in writing. In the interest of historical accuracy we have not changed the wording in this article, but students should be aware that nonsexist terms (*humans, people, Homo sapiens,* and so on) are preferred.—The Editors.

REFERENCES

Barbour, I. 1966. *Issues in science and religion.* New York: Harper and Row.

Baum, R. M. 1982. Science confronts creationist assault. *Chemical and Engineering News* 12(26):19.

Beckner, M. 1968. *The biological way of thought.* Berkeley and Los Angeles: University of California Press.

Clark, H. W. 1968. *Fossils, flood and fire.* Escondido, Calif.: Outdoor Picture Press.

Colloms, B. 1975. *Charles Kingsley.* London: Constable; New York: Barnes and Noble.

Cox, H. 1981. Religion. In Villoldo, A., and Dychtwald, K. (eds.). *Millennium: Glimpses into the 21st century.* Los Angeles: J. P. Tarcher.

Eldredge, N. 1981. The elusive eureka. *Natural History* August 24–26.

Gillispie, C. C. 1959. *Genesis and geology.* New York: Harper and Row.

Gish, D. T. 1978. *Evolution? The fossils say no!* San Diego: Creation-Life Publishers.

______. n.d. *Have you been brainwashed?* San Diego: Creation-Life Publishers.

______. 1981. Letter to the editor. *Science Teacher* 48: 20.

Gould, S. J. 1982. On paleontology and prediction. *Discover* July 56–57.

Hardin, G. 1959. *Nature and man's fate.* New York: Holt, Rinehart and Winston.

Huxley, T. H. 1892. *Essays on controverted questions.* London and New York: Macmillan and Co.

Kofahl, R. E., and Segraves, K. L. 1975. *The creation explanation.* Wheaton, Ill.: Shaw.

Lammerts, W. (ed.) 1970. *Why not creation?* Phillipsburg, NJ Presbyterian and Reformed Publishing Co.

______. 1971. *Scientific studies in special creation.* Phillipsburg, NJ Presbyterian and Reformed Publishing Co.

Lewin, R. 1982. Where is the science in creation science? *Science* 215: 142–146.

Moore, J. R. 1979. *The post-Darwinian controversies.* Cambridge and New York: Cambridge University Press.

Morris, H. M. 1975. *Introducing scientific creationism into the public schools.* San Diego: Institute for Creation Research.

______. 1970. *Biblical cosmology and modern science.* Nutley, N.J.: Craig Press.

Overton, W. R. 1982. Creationism in schools: The decision in *McLean versus the Arkansas Board of Education* [Text of 5 January 1982 Judgment]. *Science* 215: 934–943.

Peacocke, A. R. 1979. *Creation and the world of science.* Oxford: The Clarendon Press.

Pupin, M. (ed.) 1969. *Science and religion.* Freeport, N.Y.: Books for Libraries Press.

Root-Bernstein, R. S. 1982. On defining a scientific theory: Creationism considered. In Montagu, A. (ed.) *Evolution and creationism.* Oxford: The University Press.

______. 1982. Ignorance versus knowledge in the evolutionist creationist controversy. Paper presented June 22 at the symposium, "Evolutionists Confront Creationists," American Association for the Advancement of Science, Pacific Division, Santa Barbara, Calif.

Ruse, M. 1982. A philosopher at the monkey trial. *New Scientist* 317–319.

Skoog, G. 1980. The textbook battle over creationism. *Christian Century* 97: 974–976.

______. 1982. We must not succumb to specious arguments for equal time. *Education Week* 1(18): 19.

Zimmerman, P. A. (ed.) 1970. *Rock strata and the Bible record.* St. Louis: Concordia Publishing House.

Evolution in Action

Finches, monkeyflowers, sockeye salmon, and bacteria are changing before our eyes.

JONATHAN WEINER

Charles Darwin's wife, Emma, was terrified that they would be separated for eternity, because she would go to heaven and he would not. Emma confessed her fears in a letter that Charles kept and treasured, with his reply to her scribbled in the margin: "When I am dead, know that many times, I have kissed and cryed over this."

Close as they were, the two could hardly bear to talk about Darwin's view of life. And today, those of us who live in the United States, by many measures the world's leading scientific nation, find ourselves in a house divided. Half of us accept Darwin's theory, half of us reject it, and many people are convinced that Darwin burns in hell. I find that old debate particularly strange, because I've spent some of the best years of my life as a science writer peering over the shoulders of biologists who actually watch Darwin's process in action. What they can see casts the whole debate in a new light—or it should.

Darwin himself never tried to watch evolution happen. "It may metaphorically be said," he wrote in the *Origin of Species,*

> that natural selection is daily and hourly scrutinizing, throughout the world, the slightest variations; rejecting those that are bad, preserving and adding up all that are good; silently and insensibly working, whenever and wherever opportunity offers. . . . We see nothing of these slow changes in progress, until the hand of time has marked the lapse of ages.

Darwin was a modest man who thought of himself as a plodder (one of his favorite mottoes was, "It's dogged as does it"). He thought evolution plodded too. If so, it would be more boring to watch evolution than to watch drying paint. As a result, for several generations after Darwin's death, almost nobody tried. For most of the twentieth century the only well-known example of evolution in action was the case of peppered moths in industrial England. The moth had its picture in all the textbooks, as a kind of special case.

Then, in 1973, a married pair of evolutionary biologists, Peter and Rosemary Grant, now at Princeton University, began a study of Darwin's process in Darwin's islands, the Galápagos, watching Darwin's finches. At first, they assumed that they would have to infer the history of evolution in the islands from the distribution of the various finch species, varieties, and populations across the archipelago. That is pretty much what Darwin had done, in broad strokes, after the *Beagle's* five-week survey of the islands in 1835. But the Grants soon discovered that at their main study site, a tiny desert island called Daphne Major, near the center of the archipelago, the finches were evolving rapidly. Conditions on the island swung wildly back and forth from wet years to dry years, and finches on Daphne adapted to each swing, from generation to generation. With the help of a series of graduate students, the Grants began to spend a good part of every year on Daphne, watching evolution in action as it shaped and reshaped the finches' beaks.

At the same time, a few biologists began making similar discoveries elsewhere in the world. One of them was John A. Endler, an evolutionary biologist at the University of California, Santa Barbara, who studied Trinidadian guppies. In 1986 Endler published a little book called *Natural Selection in the Wild,* in which he collected and reviewed all of the studies of evolution in action that had been published to that date. Dozens of new field projects were in progress. Biologists finally began to realize that Darwin had been too modest. Evolution by natural selection can happen rapidly enough to watch.

Now the field is exploding. More than 250 people around the world are observing and documenting evolution, not only in finches and guppies, but also in aphids, flies, grayling, monkeyflowers, salmon, and sticklebacks. Some workers are even documenting pairs of species—symbiotic insects and plants—that have recently found each other, and observing the pairs as they drift off into their own world together like lovers in a novel by D.H. Lawrence.

The Grants' own study gets more sophisticated every year. A few years ago, a group of molecular biologists working with the Grants nailed down a gene that plays a key role in shaping the beaks of the finches. The gene codes for a signaling molecule called bone morphogenic protein 4 (BMP4). Finches with bigger beaks tend to have more BMP4, and finches with smaller beaks have less. In the laboratory, the biologists demonstrated that they could sculpt the beaks themselves by adding or subtracting BMP4. The same gene that shapes the beak of the finch in the egg also shapes the human face in the womb.

Some of the most dramatic stories of evolution in action result from the pressures that human beings are imposing on the planet. As Stephen Palumbi, an evolutionary biologist at Stanford University, points out, we are changing the course of evolution for virtually every living species everywhere, with consequences that are sometimes the opposite of what we might have predicted, or desired.

Take trophy hunting. Wild populations of bighorn mountain sheep are carefully managed in North America for hunters who want a chance to shoot a ram with a trophy set of horns. Hunting permits can cost well into the six figures. On Ram Mountain, in Alberta, Canada, hunters have shot the biggest of the bighorn rams for more than thirty years. And the result? Evolution has made the hunters' quarry scarce. The runts have had a better chance than the giants of passing on their genes. So on Ram Mountain the rams have gotten smaller, and their horns are proportionately smaller yet.

Or take fishing, which is economically much more consequential. The populations of Atlantic cod that swam for centuries off the coasts of Labrador and Newfoundland began a terrible crash in the late 1980s. In the years leading up to the crash, the cod had been evolving much like the sheep on Ram Mountain. Fish that matured relatively fast and reproduced relatively young had the better chance of passing on their genes; so did the fish that stayed small. So even before the population crashed, the average cod had been shrinking.

We often seem to lose out wherever we fight hardest to control nature. Antibiotics drive the evolution of drug-resistant bacteria at a frightening pace. Sulfonamides were introduced in the 1930s, and resistance to them was first observed a decade later. Penicillin was deployed in 1943, and the first penicillin resistance was observed in 1946. In the same way, pesticides and herbicides create resistant bugs and weeds.

Palumbi estimates that the annual bill for such unintended human-induced evolution runs to more than $100 billion in the U.S. alone. Worldwide, the pressure of global warming, fragmented habitats, heightened levels of carbon dioxide, acid rain, and the other myriad perturbations people impose on the chemistry and climate of the planet—all change the terms of the struggle for existence in the air, in the water, and on land. Biologists have begun to worry about those perturbations, but global change may be racing ahead of them.

To me, the most interesting news in the global evolution watch concerns what Darwin called "that mystery of mysteries, the origin of species."

The process whereby a population acquires small, inherited changes through natural selection is known as microevolution. Finches get bigger, fish gets smaller, but a finch is still a finch and a fish is still a fish. For people who reject Darwin's theory, that's the end of the story: no matter how many small, inherited changes accumulate, they believe, natural selection can never make a new kind of living thing. The kinds, the species, are eternal.

Darwin argued otherwise. He thought that many small changes could cause two lines of life to diverge. Whenever animals and plants find their way to a new home, for instance, they suffer, like emigres in new countries. Some individuals fail, others adapt and prosper. As the more successful individuals reproduce, Darwin maintained, the new population begins to differ from the ancestral one. If the two populations diverge widely enough, they become separate species. Change on that scale is known as macroevolution.

In *Origin,* Darwin estimated that a new species might take between ten thousand and fourteen thousand generations to arise. Until recently, most biologists assumed it would take at least that many, or maybe even millions of generations, before microevolutionary changes led to the origin of new species. So they assumed they could watch evolution by natural selection, but not the divergence of one species into separate, reproductively isolated species. Now that view is changing too.

Not long ago, a young evolution-watcher named Andrew Hendry, a biologist at McGill University in Montreal, reported the results of a striking study of sockeye salmon. Sockeye tend to reproduce either in streams or along lake beaches. When the glaciers of the last ice age melted and retreated, about ten thousand years ago, they left behind thousands of new lakes. Salmon from streams swam into the lakes and stayed. Today their descendants tend to breed among themselves rather than with sockeyes that live in the streams. The fish in the lakes and streams are reproductively isolated from each other. So how fast did that happen?

In the 1930s and 1940s, sockeye salmon were introduced into Lake Washington, in Washington State. Hundreds of thousands of their descendants now live and breed in Cedar River, which feeds the lake. By 1957 some of the introduced sockeye also colonized a beach along the lake called Pleasure Point, about four miles from the mouth of Cedar River.

Hendry could tell whether a full-grown, breeding salmon had been born in the river or at the beach by examining the rings on its otoliths, or ear stones. Otolith rings reflect variations in water temperature while a fish embryo is developing. Water temperatures at the beach are relatively constant compared with the river temperatures. Hendry and his colleagues checked the otoliths and collected DNA samples from the fish—and found that more than a third of the sockeye breeding at Pleasure Point had grown up in the river. They were immigrants.

With such a large number of immigrants, the two populations at Pleasure Point should have blended back together. But they hadn't. So at breeding time many of the river sockeye that swam over to the beach must have been relatively unsuccessful at passing on their genes.

Hendry could also tell the stream fish and the beach fish apart just by looking at them. Where the sockeye's breeding waters are swift-flowing, such as in Cedar River, the males tend to be slender. Their courtship ritual and competition with other males requires them to turn sideways in strong current—an awkward maneuver for a male with a deep, roundish body. So in strong current, slender males have the better chance of passing on their genes. But in still waters, males with the deepest bodies have the best chance of getting mates. So beach males tend to be rounder—their dimensions greater from the top of the back to the bottom of the belly—than river males.

What about females? In the river, where currents and floods are forever shifting and swirling the gravel, females have to dig deep nests for their eggs. So the females in the river tend to be bigger than their lake-dwelling counterparts, because bigger females can dig deeper nests. Where the water is calmer, the gravel stays put, and shallower nests will do.

So all of the beachgoers, male and female, have adapted to life at Pleasure Point. Their adaptations are strong enough that reproductive isolation has evolved. How long did the evolution take? Hendry began studying the salmon's reproductive isolation in 1992. At that time, the sockeyes in the stream and the ones at Pleasure Point had been breeding in their respective habitats for at most thirteen generations. That is so fast that, as Hendry and his colleagues point out, it may be possible someday soon to catch the next step, the origin of a new species.

And it's not just the sockeye salmon. Consider the three-spined stickleback. After the glaciers melted at the end of the last ice age, many sticklebacks swam out of the sea and into new glacial lakes—just as the salmon did. In the sea, sticklebacks wear heavy, bony body armor. In a lake they wear light armor. In a certain new pond in Bergen, Norway, during the past century, sticklebacks evolved toward the lighter armor in just thirty-one years. In Loberg Lake, Alaska, the same kind of change took only a dozen years. A generation for sticklebacks is two years. So that dramatic evolution took just six generations.

Dolph Schluter, a former finch-watcher from the Galapagos and currently a biologist at the University of British Columbia in Vancouver, has shown that, along with the evolution of new body types, sticklebacks also evolve a taste for mates with the new traits. In other words, the adaptive push of sexual selection is going hand-in-hand with natural selection. Schluter has built experimental ponds in Vancouver to observe the phenomenon under controlled conditions, and the same patterns he found in isolated lakes repeat themselves in his ponds. So adaptation can sometimes drive sexual selection and accelerate reproductive isolation.

There are other developments in the evolution watch, too many to mention in this small space. Some of the fastest action is microscopic. Richard Lenski, a biologist at Michigan State University in East Lansing, watches the evolution of *Escherichia coli.* Because one generation takes only twenty minutes, and billions of *E. coli* can fit in a petri dish, the bacteria make ideal subjects for experimental evolution. Throw some *E. coli* into a new dish, for instance, with food they haven't encountered before, and they will evolve and adapt—quickly at first and then more slowly, as they refine their fit with their new environment.

And then there are the controversies. Science progresses and evolves by controversy, by internal debate and revision. In the United States these days one almost hates to mention that there are arguments among evolutionists. So often, they are taken out of context and hyperamplified to suggest that nothing about Darwinism is solid—that Darwin is dead. But research is messy because nature is messy, and fieldwork is some of the messiest research of all. It is precisely here at its jagged cutting edge that Darwinism is most vigorously alive.

Not long ago, one of the most famous icons of the evolution watch toppled over: the story of the peppered moths, familiar to anyone who remembers biology 101. About half a century ago, the British evolutionist Bernard Kettlewell noted that certain moths in the British Isles had evolved into darker forms when the trunks of trees darkened with industrial pollution. When the trees lightened again, after clean air acts were passed, the moths had evolved into light forms again. Kettlewell claimed that dark moths resting on dark tree trunks were harder for birds to see; in each decade, moths of the right color were safer.

But in the past few years, workers have shown that Kettlewell's explanation was too simplistic. For one thing, the moths don't normally rest on tree trunks. In forty years of observation, only twice have moths been seen resting there. Nobody knows where they do rest. The moths did evolve rapidly, but no one can be certain why.

To me what remains most interesting is the light that studies such as Hendry's, or the Grants', may throw on the origin of species. It's extraordinary that scientists are now examining the very beginnings of the process, at the level of beaks and fins, at the level of the genes. The explosion of evolution-watchers is a remarkable development in Darwin's science. Even as the popular debate about evolution in America is reaching its most heated moment since the trial of John Scopes, evolutionary biologists are pursuing one of the most significant and surprising voyages of discovery since the young Darwin sailed into the Galápagos Archipelago aboard Her Majesty's ship *Beagle.*

Not long ago I asked Hendry if his studies have changed the way he thinks about the origin of species. "Yes," he replied without hesitation, "I think it's occurring all over the place."

Jonathan Weiner began writing about evolution in 1990, when he met Peter and Rosemary Grant, who observe evolution firsthand in finch populations in the Galápagos. Weiner's book *The Beak of the Finch* (Alfred A. Knopf) won a Pulitzer Prize in 1994. He is a professor in the Graduate School of Journalism at Columbia University, in New York City. He is also working on a book about human longevity for Ecco Press.

Dim Forest, Bright Chimps

In the rain forest of Ivory Coast, chimpanzees meet the challenge of life by hunting cooperatively and using crude tools.

CHRISTOPHE BOESCH AND HEDWIGE BOESCH-ACHERMANN

Taï National Park, Ivory Coast, December 3, 1985. Drumming, barking, and screaming, chimps rush through the undergrowth, little more than black shadows. Their goal is to join a group of other chimps noisily clustering around Brutus, the dominant male of this seventy-member chimpanzee community. For a few moments, Brutus, proud and self-confident, stands fairly still, holding a shocked, barely moving red colobus monkey in his hand. Then he begins to move through the group, followed closely by his favorite females and most of the adult males. He seems to savor this moment of uncontested superiority, the culmination of a hunt high up in the canopy. But the victory is not his alone. Cooperation is essential to capturing one of these monkeys, and Brutus will break apart and share this highly prized delicacy with most of the main participants of the hunt and with the females. Recipients of large portions will, in turn, share more or less generously with their offspring, relatives, and friends.

In 1979, we began a long-term study of the previously unknown chimpanzees of Taï National Park, 1,600 square miles of tropical rain forest in the Republic of the Ivory Coast (Côte d'Ivoire). Early on, we were most interested in the chimps' use of natural hammers—branches and stones—to crack open the five species of hard-shelled nuts that are abundant here. A sea otter lying on its back, cracking an abalone shell with a rock, is a familiar picture, but no primate had ever before been observed in the wild using stones as hammers. East Africa's savanna chimps, studied for decades by Jane Goodall in Gombe, Tanzania, use twigs to extract ants and termites from their nests or honey from a bees' nest, but they have never been seen using hammerstones.

As our work progressed, we were surprised by the many ways in which the life of the Taï forest chimpanzees differs from that of their savanna counterparts, and as evidence accumulated, differences in how the two populations hunt proved the most intriguing. Jane Goodall had found that chimpanzees hunt monkeys, antelope, and wild pigs, findings confirmed by Japanese biologist Toshida Nishida, who conducted a long-term study 120 miles south of Gombe, in the Mahale Mountains. So we were not surprised to discover that the Taï chimps eat meat. What intrigued us was the degree to which they hunt cooperatively. In 1953 Raymond Dart proposed that group hunting and cooperation were key ingredients in the evolution of *Homo sapiens.* The argument has been modified considerably since Dart first put it forward, and group hunting has also been observed in some social carnivores (lions and African wild dogs, for instance), and even some birds of prey. Nevertheless, many anthropologists still hold that hunting cooperatively and sharing food played a central role in the drama that enabled early hominids, some 1.8 million years ago, to develop the social systems that are so typically human.

We hoped that what we learned about the behavior of forest chimpanzees would shed new light on prevailing theories of human evolution. Before we could even begin, however, we had to habituate a community of chimps to our presence. Five long years passed before we were able to move with them on their daily trips through the forest, of which "our" group appeared to claim some twelve square miles. Chimpanzees are alert and shy animals, and the limited field of view in the rain forest—about sixty-five feet at best—made finding them more difficult. We had to rely on sound, mostly their vocalizations and drumming on trees. Males often drum regularly while moving through the forest: pant-hooting, they draw near a big buttress tree; then, at full speed they fly over the buttress, hitting it repeatedly with their hands and feet. Such drumming may resound more than half a mile in the forest. In the beginning, our ignorance about how they moved and who was drumming led to failure more often than not, but eventually we learned that the dominant males drummed during the day to let other group members know the direction of travel. On some days, however, intermittent drumming about dawn was the only signal for the whole day. If we were out of earshot at the time, we were often reduced to guessing.

During these difficult early days, one feature of the chimps' routine proved to be our salvation: nut cracking is a noisy business. So noisy, in fact, that in the early days of French colonial rule, one officer apparently even proposed the theory that some unknown tribe was forging iron in the impenetrable and dangerous jungle.

Guided by the sounds made by the chimps as they cracked open nuts, which they often did for hours at a time, we were gradually able to get within sixty feet of the animals. We still seldom saw the chimps themselves (they fled if we came too close), but even so, the evidence left after a session of nut cracking taught us a great deal about what types of nuts they were eating, what sorts of hammer and anvil tools they were using, and—thanks to the very distinctive noise a nut makes when it finally splits open—how many hits were needed to crack a nut and how many nuts could be opened per minute.

After some months, we began catching glimpses of the chimpanzees before they fled, and after a little more time, we were able to draw close enough to watch them at work. The chimps gather nuts from the ground. Some nuts are tougher to crack than others. Nuts of the *Panda oleosa* tree are the most demanding, harder than any of the foods processed by present-day hunter-gatherers and breaking open only when a force of 3,500 pounds is applied. The stone hammers used by the Taï chimps range from stones of ten ounces to granite blocks of four to forty-five pounds. Stones of any size, however, are a rarity in the forest and are seldom conveniently placed near a nut-bearing tree. By observing closely, and in some cases imitating the way the chimps handle hammerstones, we learned that they have an impressive ability to find just the right tool for the job at hand. Taï chimps could remember the positions of many of the stones scattered, often out of sight, around a panda tree. Without having to run around rechecking the stones, they would select one of appropriate size that was closest to the tree. These mental abilities in spatial representation compare with some of those of nine-year-old humans.

To extract the four kernels from inside a panda nut, a chimp must use a hammer with extreme precision. Time and time again, we have been impressed to see a chimpanzee raise a twenty-pound stone above its head, strike a nut with ten or more powerful blows, and then, using the same hammer, switch to delicate little taps from a height of only four inches. To finish the job, the chimps often break off a small piece of twig and use it to extract the last tiny fragments of kernel from the shell. Intriguingly, females crack panda nuts more often than males, a gender difference in tool use that seems to be more pronounced in the forest chimps than in their savanna counterparts.

After five years of fieldwork, we were finally able to follow the chimpanzees at close range, and gradually, we gained insights into their way of hunting. One morning, for example, we followed a group of six male chimps on a three-hour patrol that had taken them into foreign territory to the north. (Our study group is one of five chimpanzee groups more or less evenly distributed in the Taï forest.) As always during these approximately monthly incursions, which seem to be for the purpose of territorial defense, the chimps were totally silent, clearly on edge and on the lookout for trouble. Once the patrol was over, however, and they were back within their own borders, the chimps shifted their attention to hunting. They were after monkeys, the most abundant mammals in the forest. Traveling in large, multi-species groups, some of the forest's ten species of monkeys are more apt than others to wind up as a meal for the chimps. The relatively sluggish and large (almost thirty pounds) red colobus monkeys are the chimps' usual fare. (Antelope also live in the forest, but in our ten years at Taï, we have never seen a chimp catch, or even pursue, one. In contrast, Gombe chimps at times do come across fawns, and when they do, they seize the opportunity—and the fawn.)

The six males moved on silently, peering up into the vegetation and stopping from time to time to listen for the sound of monkeys. None fed or groomed; all focused on the hunt. We followed one old male, Falstaff, closely, for he tolerates us completely and is one of the keenest and most experienced hunters. Even from the rear, Falstaff set the pace; whenever he stopped, the others paused to wait for him. After thirty minutes, we heard the unmistakable noises of monkeys jumping from branch to branch. Silently, the chimps turned in the direction of the sounds, scanning the canopy. Just then, a diana monkey spotted them and gave an alarm call. Dianas are very alert and fast; they are also about half the weight of colobus monkeys. The chimps quickly gave up and continued their search for easier, meatier prey.

Shortly after, we heard the characteristic cough of a red colobus monkey. Suddenly Rousseau and Macho, two twenty-year-olds, burst into action, running toward the cough. Falstaff seemed surprised by their precipitousness, but after a moment's hesitation, he also ran. Now the hunting barks of the chimps mixed with the sharp alarm calls of the monkeys. Hurrying behind Falstaff, we saw him climb up a conveniently situated tree. His position, combined with those of Schubert and Ulysse, two mature chimps in their prime, effectively blocked off three of the monkeys' possible escape routes. But in another tree, nowhere near any escape route and thus useless, waited the last of the hunters, Kendo, eighteen years old and the least experienced of the group. The monkeys, taking advantage of Falstaff's delay and Kendo's error, escaped.

The six males moved on and within five minutes picked up the sounds of another group of red colobus. This time, the chimps approached cautiously, nobody hurrying. They screened the canopy intently to locate the monkeys, which were still unaware of the approaching danger. Macho and Schubert chose two adjacent trees, both full of monkeys, and started climbing very quietly, taking care not to move any branches. Meanwhile, the other four chimps blocked off anticipated escape routes. When Schubert was halfway up, the monkeys finally detected the two chimps. As we watched the colobus monkeys take off in literal panic, the appropriateness of the chimpanzees' scientific name—*Pan* came to mind: with a certain stretch of the imagination, the fleeing monkeys could be shepherds and shepherdesses frightened at the sudden appearance of Pan, the wild Greek god of the woods, shepherds, and their flocks.

Taking off in the expected direction, the monkeys were trailed by Macho and Schubert. The chimps let go with loud hunting barks. Trying to escape, two colobus monkeys jumped into smaller trees lower in the canopy. With this, Rousseau and Kendo, who had been watching from the ground, sped up into the trees and tried to grab them. Only a third of the weight of the chimps, however, the monkeys managed to make it to the next tree along branches too small for their pursuers. But Falstaff had anticipated this move and was waiting for them. In the following confusion, Falstaff seized a juvenile and killed it with a bite to the neck. As the chimps met in a rush on the ground, Falstaff began to eat, sharing with Schubert and Rousseau. A juvenile colobus does not provide much meat, however, and this time, not all the chimps got a share. Frustrated individuals soon started off on another hunt, and relative calm returned fairly quickly: this sort of hunt, by a small band of chimps acting on their own at the edge of their territory, does not generate the kind of high excitement that prevails when more members of the community are involved.

So far we have observed some 200 monkey hunts and have concluded that success requires a minimum of three motivated hunters acting cooperatively. Alone or in pairs, chimps succeed less than 15 percent of the time, but when three or four act as a group, more than half the hunts result in a kill. The chimps seem well aware of the odds; 92 percent of all the hunts we observed were group affairs.

Gombe chimps also hunt red colobus monkeys, but the percentage of group hunts is much lower: only 36 percent. In addition, we learned from Jane Goodall that even when Gombe chimps do hunt in groups, their strategies are different. When Taï chimps arrive under a group of monkeys, the hunters scatter, often silently, usually out of sight of one another but each aware of the others' positions. As the hunt progresses, they gradually close in, encircling the quarry. Such movements require that each chimp coordinate his movements with those of the other hunters, as well as with those of the prey, at all times.

Coordinated hunts account for 63 percent of all those observed at Taï but only 7 percent of those at Gombe. Jane Goodall says that in a Gombe group hunt, the chimpanzees typically travel together until they arrive at a tree with monkeys. Then, as the chimps begin climbing nearby trees, they scatter as each pursues a different target. Goodall gained the impression that Gombe chimps boost their success by hunting independently but simultaneously, thereby disorganizing their prey; our impression is that the Taï chimps owe their success to being organized themselves.

Just why the Gombe and Taï chimps have developed such different hunting strategies is difficult to explain, and we plan to spend some time at Gombe in the hope of finding out. In the meantime, the mere existence of differences is interesting enough and may perhaps force changes in our understanding of human evolution. Most currently accepted theories propose that some three million years ago, a dramatic climate change in Africa east of the Rift Valley turned dense forest into open, drier habitat. Adapting to the difficulties of life under these new conditions, our ancestors supposedly evolved into cooperative hunters and began sharing food they caught. Supporters of this idea point out that plant and animal remains indicative of dry, open environments have been found at all early hominid excavation sites in Tanzania, Kenya, South Africa, and Ethiopia. That the large majority of apes in Africa today live west of the Rift Valley appears to many anthropologists to lend further support to the idea that a change in environment caused the common ancestor of apes and humans to evolve along a different line from those remaining in the forest.

Our observations, however, suggest quite another line of thought. Life in dense, dim forest may require more sophisticated behavior than is commonly assumed: compared with their savanna relatives, Taï chimps show greater complexity in both hunting and tool use. Taï chimps use tools in nineteen different ways and have six different ways of making them, compared with sixteen uses and three methods of manufacture at Gombe.

Anthropologist colleagues of mine have told me that the discovery that some chimpanzees are accomplished users of hammerstones forces them to look with a fresh eye at stone tools turned up at excavation sites. The important role played by female Taï chimps in tool use also raises the possibility that in the course of human evolution, women may have been decisive in the development of many of the sophisticated manipulative skills characteristic of our species. Taï mothers also appear to pass on their skills by actively teaching their offspring. We have observed mothers providing their young with hammers and then stepping in to help when the inexperienced youngsters encounter difficulty. This help may include carefully showing how to position the nut or hold the hammer properly. Such behavior has never been observed at Gombe.

Similarly, food sharing, for a long time said to be unique to humans, seems more general in forest than in savanna chimpanzees. Taï chimp mothers share with their young up to 60 percent of the nuts they open, at least until the latter become sufficiently adept, generally at about six years old. They also share other foods acquired with tools, including honey, ants, and bone marrow. Gombe mothers share such foods much less often, even with their infants. Taï chimps also share meat more frequently than do their Gombe relatives, sometimes dividing a chunk up and giving portions away, sometimes simply allowing beggars to grab pieces.

Any comparison between chimpanzees and our hominid ancestors can only be suggestive, not definitive. But our studies lead us to believe that the process of hominization may have begun independently of the drying of the environment. Savanna life could even have delayed the process; many anthropologists have been struck by how slowly hominid-associated remains, such as the hand ax, changed after their first appearance in the Olduvai age.

Will we have the time to discover more about the hunting strategies or other, perhaps as yet undiscovered abilities of these forest chimpanzees? Africa's tropical rain forests, and their inhabitants, are threatened with extinction by extensive logging, largely to provide the Western world with tropical timber and such products as coffee, cocoa, and rubber. Ivory Coast has lost 90 percent of its original forest, and less than 5 percent of the remainder can be considered pristine. The climate has changed dramatically. The harmattan, a cold, dry wind from the Sahara previously unknown in the forest, has now swept through the Taï forest every year since 1986. Rainfall has diminished; all the rivulets in our study region are now dry for several months of the year.

In addition, the chimpanzee, biologically very close to humans, is in demand for research on AIDS and hepatitis vaccines. Captive-bred chimps are available, but they cost about twenty times more than wild-caught animals. Chimps taken from the wild for these purposes are generally young, their mothers having been shot during capture. For every chimp arriving at its sad destination, nine others may well have died in the forest or on the way. Such priorities—cheap coffee and cocoa and chimpanzees—do not do the economies of Third World countries any good in the long run, and they bring suffering and death to innocent victims in the forest. Our hope is that Brutus, Falstaff, and their families will survive, and that we and others will have the opportunity to learn about them well into the future. But there is no denying that modern times work against them and us.

4

What Are Friends For?

Barbara Smuts

In tracing the evolution of humanity, anthropologists are concerned with both biological features and socio-cultural forms. Some people believe that a prerequisite for culture was the emergence of more permanent relationships between men and women and the formation of families. How this actually occurred in evolution has been the subject of controversy. The traditional view centered on dominant males who, as mighty hunters, put the proverbial meat on the table, selected females, and, through protection of the helpless females and their offspring, ensured the transmission of their genes to future generations. The conventional wisdom left little room for the role of women in human adaptation. This is no longer the case.

In recent years, much research has helped to revise and refine our understanding of ancestral lifeways. In this selection, Barbara Smuts examines sex and friendship among baboons. The implications for the origin of male–female relations and the role of female choice are fascinating.

As you read this selection, ask yourself the following questions:

- Why do some anthropologists study monkeys and apes to better understand human behavior?
- Why do females prefer some males over others?
- Who forms the core membership of a baboon troop?
- What criteria does the author use to determine friendship?
- Do the bonds between adult male baboons and infants arise from paternity or from a relationship with the infant's mother?
- In what three ways does this article challenge the conventional wisdom about the origin of the nuclear family?

The following terms discussed in this selection are included in the Glossary at the back of the book:

aggression	*grooming*
dominance	*paternity*
estrus	*primatology*

Virgil, a burly adult male olive baboon, closely followed Zizi, a middle-aged female easily distinguished by her grizzled coat and square muzzle. On her rump Zizi sported a bright pink swelling, indicating that she was sexually receptive and probably fertile. Virgil's extreme attentiveness to Zizi suggested to me—and all rival males in the troop—that he was her current and exclusive mate.

Zizi, however, apparently had something else in mind. She broke away from Virgil, moved rapidly through the troop, and presented her alluring sexual swelling to one male after another. Before Virgil caught up with her, she had managed to announce her receptive condition to several of his rivals. When Virgil tried to grab her, Zizi screamed and dashed into the bushes with Virgil in hot pursuit. I heard sounds of chasing and fighting coming from the thicket. Moments later Zizi emerged from the bushes with an older male named Cyclops. They remained together for several days, copulating often. In Cyclops's presence, Zizi no longer approached or even glanced at other males.

Primatologists describe Zizi and other olive baboons (*Papio cynocephalus anubis*) as promiscuous, meaning that both males and females usually mate with several members of the opposite sex within a short period of time. Promiscuous mating behavior characterizes many of the larger, more familiar primates, including chimpanzees, rhesus macaques, and gray langurs, as well as olive, yellow, and chacma baboons, the three subspecies of savanna baboon. In colloquial usage, promiscuity often connotes wanton and random sex, and several early studies of primates supported this

Smuts, Barbara. "What Are Friends For" from Natural History (Feb. 1987):36, 38–44.

stereotype. However, after years of laboriously recording thousands of copulations under natural conditions, the Peeping Toms of primate fieldwork have shown that, even in promiscuous species, sexual pairings are far from random.

Some adult males, for example, typically copulate much more often than others. Primatologists have explained these differences in terms of competition: the most dominant males monopolize females and prevent lower-ranking rivals from mating. But exceptions are frequent. Among baboons, the exceptions often involve scruffy, older males who mate in full view of younger, more dominant rivals.

A clue to the reason for these puzzling exceptions emerged when primatologists began to question an implicit assumption of the dominance hypothesis—that females were merely passive objects of male competition. But what if females were active arbiters in this system? If females preferred some males over others and were able to express these preferences, then models of mating activity based on male dominance alone would be far too simple.

Once researchers recognized the possibility of female choice, evidence for it turned up in species after species. The story of Zizi, Virgil, and Cyclops is one of hundreds of examples of female primates rejecting the sexual advances of particular males and enthusiastically cooperating with others. But what is the basis for female choice? Why might they prefer some males over others?

This question guided my research on the Eburru Cliffs troop of olive baboons, named after one of their favorite sleeping sites, a sheer rocky outcrop rising several hundred feet above the floor of the Great Rift Valley, about 100 miles northwest of Nairobi, Kenya. The 120 members of Eburru Cliffs spent their days wandering through open grassland studded with occasional acacia thorn trees. Each night they retired to one of a dozen sets of cliffs that provided protection from nocturnal predators such as leopards.

Most previous studies of baboon sexuality had focused on females who, like Zizi, were at the peak of sexual receptivity. A female baboon does not mate when she is pregnant or lactating, a period of abstinence lasting about eighteen months. The female then goes into estrus, and for about two weeks out of every thirty-five-day cycle, she mates. Toward the end of this two-week period she may ovulate, but usually the female undergoes four or five estrous cycles before she conceives. During pregnancy, she once again resumes a chaste existence. As a result, the typical female baboon is sexually active for less than 10 percent of her adult life. I thought that by focusing on the other 90 percent, I might learn something new. In particular, I suspected that routine, day-to-day relationships between males and pregnant or lactating (nonestrous) females might provide clues to female mating preferences.

Nearly every day for sixteen months, I joined the Eburru Cliffs baboons at their sleeping cliffs at dawn and traveled several miles with them while they foraged for roots, seeds, grass, and occasionally, small prey items, such as baby gazelles or hares (see "Predatory Baboons of Kekopey," *Natural History,* March 1976). Like all savanna baboon troops, Eburru Cliffs functioned as a cohesive unit organized around a core of related females, all of whom were born in the troop. Unlike the females, male savanna baboons leave their natal troop to join another where they may remain for many years, so most of the Eburru Cliffs adult males were immigrants. Since membership in the troop remained relatively constant during the period of my study, I learned to identify each individual. I relied on differences in size, posture, gait, and especially facial features. To the practiced observer, baboons look as different from one another as human beings do.

As soon as I could recognize individuals, I noticed that particular females tended to turn up near particular males again and again. I came to think of these pairs as friends. Friendship among animals is not a well-documented phenomenon, so to convince skeptical colleagues that baboon friendship was real, I needed to develop objective criteria for distinguishing friendly pairs.

I began by investigating grooming, the amiable simian habit of picking through a companion's fur to remove dead skin and ectoparasites (see "Little Things That Tick Off Baboons," *Natural History,* February 1984). Baboons spend much more time grooming than is necessary for hygiene, and previous research had indicated that it is a good measure of social bonds. Although eighteen adult males lived in the troop, each nonestrous female performed most of her grooming with just one, two, or occasionally three males. For example, of Zizi's twenty-four grooming bouts with males, Cyclops accounted for thirteen, and a second male, Sherlock, accounted for all the rest. Different females tended to favor different males as grooming partners.

Another measure of social bonds was simply who was observed near whom. When foraging, traveling, or resting, each pregnant or lactating female spent a lot of time near a few males and associated with the others no more often than expected by chance. When I compared the identities of favorite grooming partners and frequent companions, they overlapped almost completely. This enabled me to develop a formal definition of friendship: any male that scored high on both grooming and proximity measures was considered a friend.

Virtually all baboons made friends; only one female and the three males who had most recently joined the troop lacked such companions. Out of more than 600 possible adult female–adult male pairs in the troop, however, only about one in ten qualified as friends; these really were special relationships.

Several factors seemed to influence which baboons paired up. In most cases, friends were unrelated to each other, since the male had immigrated from another troop. (Four friendships, however, involved a female and an adolescent son who had not yet emigrated. Unlike other friends, these related pairs never mated.) Older females tended to be friends with older males; younger females with younger males. I witnessed occasional May–December romances, usually involving older females and young adult males. Adolescent males and females were strongly rule-bound, and with the exception of mother–son pairs, they formed friendships only with one another.

Regardless of age or dominance rank, most females had just one or two male friends. But among males, the number of female friends varied greatly from none to eight. Although high-ranking males enjoyed priority of access to food and sometimes mates, dominant males did not have more female friends than low-ranking males. Instead it was the older males who had lived in the troop for many years who had the most friends. When a male had several female friends, the females were often closely related to one another. Since female baboons spend a lot of time near their kin, it is probably easier for a male to maintain bonds with several related females at once.

When collecting data, I focused on one nonestrous female at a time and kept track of her every movement toward or away from any male; similarly, I noted every male who moved toward or away from her. Whenever the female and a male moved close enough to exchange intimacies, I wrote down exactly what happened. When foraging together, friends tended to remain a few yards apart. Males more often wandered away from females than the reverse, and females, more often than males, closed the gap. The female behaved as if she wanted to keep the male within calling distance, in case she needed his protection. The male, however, was more likely to make approaches that brought them within actual touching distance. Often, he would plunk himself down right next to his friend and ask her to groom him by holding a pose with exaggerated stillness. The female sometimes responded by grooming, but more often, she exhibited the most reliable sign of true intimacy: she ignored her friend and simply continued whatever she was doing.

In sharp contrast, when a male who was not a friend moved close to a female, she dared not ignore him. She stopped whatever she was doing and held still, often glancing surreptitiously at the intruder. If he did not move away, she sometimes lifted her tail and presented her rump. When a female is not in estrus, this is a gesture of appeasement, not sexual enticement. Immediately after this respectful acknowledgement of his presence, the female would slip away. But such tense interactions with nonfriend males were rare, because females usually moved away before the males came too close.

These observations suggest that females were afraid of most of the males in their troop, which is not surprising: male baboons are twice the size of females, and their canines are longer and sharper than those of a lion. All Eburru Cliffs males directed both mild and severe aggression toward females. Mild aggression, which usually involved threats and chases but no body contact, occurred most often during feeding competition or when the male redirected aggression toward a female after losing a fight with another male. Females and juveniles showed aggression toward other females and juveniles in similar circumstances and occasionally inflicted superficial wounds. Severe aggression by males, which involved body contact and sometimes biting, was less common and also more puzzling, since there was no apparent cause.

An explanation for at least some of these attacks emerged one day when I was watching Pegasus, a young adult male, and his friend Cicily, sitting together in the middle of a small clearing. Cicily moved to the edge of the clearing to feed, and a higher-ranking female, Zora, suddenly attacked her. Pegasus stood up and looked as if he were about to intervene when both females disappeared into the bushes. He sat back down, and I remained with him. A full ten minutes later, Zora appeared at the edge of the clearing; this was the first time she had come into view since her attack on Cicily. Pegasus instantly pounced on Zora, repeatedly grabbed her neck in his mouth and lifted her off the ground, shook her whole body, and then dropped her. Zora screamed continuously and tried to escape. Each time, Pegasus caught her and continued his brutal attack. When he finally released her five minutes later she had a deep canine gash on the palm of her hand that made her limp for several days.

This attack was similar in form and intensity to those I had seen before and labeled "unprovoked." Certainly, had I come upon the scene after Zora's aggression toward Cicily, I would not have understood why Pegasus attacked Zora. This suggested that some, perhaps many, severe attacks by males actually represented punishment for actions that had occurred some time before.

Whatever the reasons for male attacks on females, they represent a serious threat. Records of fresh injuries indicated that Eburru Cliffs adult females received canine slash wounds from males at the rate of one for every female each year, and during my study, one female died of her injuries. Males probably pose an even greater threat to infants. Although only one infant was killed during my study, observers in Botswana and Tanzania have seen recent male immigrants kill several young infants.

Protection from male aggression, and from the less injurious but more frequent aggression of other females and juveniles, seems to be one of the main advantages of friendship for a female baboon. Seventy times I observed an adult male defend a female or her offspring against aggression by another troop member, not infrequently a high-ranking male. In all but six of these cases, the defender was a friend. Very few of these confrontations involved actual fighting; no male baboon, subordinate or dominant, is anxious to risk injury by the sharp canines of another.

Males are particularly solicitous guardians of their friends' youngest infants. If another male gets too close to an infant or if a juvenile female plays with it too roughly, the friend may intervene. Other troop members soon learn to be cautious when the mother's friend is nearby, and his presence provides the mother with a welcome respite from the annoying pokes and prods of curious females and juveniles obsessed with the new baby. Male baboons at Gombe Park in Tanzania and Amboseli Park in Kenya have also been seen rescuing infants from chimpanzees and lions. These several forms of male protection help to explain why females in Eburru Cliffs stuck closer to their friends in the first few months after giving birth than at any other time.

The male–infant relationship develops out of the male's friendship with the mother, but as the infant matures, this new bond takes on a life of its own. My co-worker Nancy Nicolson found that by about nine months of age, infants actively sought out their male friends when the mother was a few yards away, suggesting that the male may function as an alternative caregiver. This seemed to be especially true for infants undergoing unusually early or severe weaning. (Weaning is generally a gradual, prolonged process, but there is tremendous variation among mothers in the timing and intensity of weaning. See "Mother Baboons," *Natural History,* September 1980.) After being rejected by the mother, the crying infant often approached the male friend and sat huddled against him until its whimpers subsided. Two of the infants in Eburru Cliffs lost their mothers when they were still quite young. In each case, their bond with the mother's friend subsequently intensified, and—perhaps as a result—both infants survived.

A close bond with a male may also improve the infant's nutrition. Larger than all other troop members, adult males monopolize the best feeding sites. In general, the personal space surrounding a feeding male is inviolate, but he usually tolerates intrusions by the infants of his female friends, giving them access to choice feeding spots.

Although infants follow their male friends around rather than the reverse, the males seem genuinely attached to their tiny companions. During feeding, the male and infant express their pleasure in each other's company by sharing spirited, antiphonal grunting duets. If the infant whimpers in distress, the male friend is likely to cease feeding, look at the infant, and grunt softly, as if in sympathy, until the whimpers cease. When the male rests, the infants of his female friends may huddle behind him, one after the other, forming a "train," or, if feeling energetic, they may use his body as a trampoline.

When I returned to Eburru Cliffs four years after my initial study ended, several of the bonds formed between males and the infants of their female friends were still intact (in other cases, either the male or the infant or both had disappeared). When these bonds involved recently matured females, their long-time male associates showed no sexual interest in them, even though the females mated with other adult males. Mothers and sons, and usually maternal siblings, show similar sexual inhibitions in baboons and many other primate species.

The development of an intimate relationship between a male and the infant of his female friend raises an obvious question: Is the male the infant's father? To answer this question definitely we would need to conduct genetic analysis, which was not possible for these baboons. Instead, I estimated paternity probabilities from observations of the temporary (a few hours or days) exclusive mating relationships, or consortships, that estrous females form with a series of different males. These estimates were apt to be fairly accurate, since changes in the female's sexual swelling allow one to pinpoint the timing of conception to within a few days. Most females consorted with only two or three males during this period, and these males were termed likely fathers.

In about half the friendships, the male was indeed likely to be the father of his friend's most recent infant, but in the other half he was not—in fact, he had never been seen mating with the female. Interestingly, males who were friends with the mother but not likely fathers nearly always developed a relationship with her infant, while males who had mated with the female but were not her friend usually did not. Thus friendship with the mother, rather than paternity, seems to mediate the development of male–infant bonds. Recently, a similar pattern was documented for South American capuchin monkeys in a laboratory study in which paternity was determined genetically.

These results fly in the face of a prominent theory that claims males will invest in infants only when they are closely related. If males are not fostering the survival of their own genes by caring for the infant, then why do they do so? I suspected that the key was female choice. If females preferred to mate with males who had already demonstrated friendly behavior, then friendships with mothers and their infants might pay off in the future when the mothers were ready to mate again.

To find out if this was the case, I examined each male's sexual behavior with females he had befriended before they resumed estrus. In most cases, males consorted considerably more often with their friends than with other females. Baboon females typically mate with several different males, including both friends and nonfriends, but prior friendship increased a male's probability of mating with a female above what it would have been otherwise.

This increased probability seemed to reflect female preferences. Females occasionally overtly advertised their disdain for certain males and their desire for others. Zizi's behavior, described above, is a good example. Virgil was not one of her friends, but Cyclops was. Usually, however, females expressed preferences and aversions more subtly. For example, Delphi, a petite adolescent female, found herself pursued by Hector, a middle-aged adult male. She did not run away or refuse to mate with him, but whenever he wasn't watching, she looked around for her friend Homer, an adolescent male. When she succeeded in catching Homer's eye, she narrowed her eyes and flattened her ears against her skull, the friendliest face one baboon can send another. This told Homer she would rather be with him. Females expressed satisfaction with a current consort partner by staying close to him, initiating copulations, and not making advances toward other males. Baboons are very sensitive to such cues, as indicated by an experimental study in which rival hamadryas baboons rarely challenged a male–female pair if the female strongly preferred her current partner. Similarly, in Eburru Cliffs, males were less apt to challenge consorts involving a pair that shared a long-term friendship.

Even though females usually consorted with their friends, they also mated with other males, so it is not surprising that friendships were most vulnerable during periods of sexual activity. In a few cases, the female consorted with another male more often than with her friend, but the friendship survived nevertheless. One female, however, formed a strong sexual bond with a new male. This bond persisted after conception, replacing her previous friendship. My observations suggest that adolescent and young adult females tend to have shorter, less stable friendships than do older females. Some friendships, however, last a very long time. When I returned to Eburru Cliffs six years after my study began, five couples were still together. It is possible that friendships occasionally last for life (baboons probably live twenty to thirty years in the wild), but it will require longer studies, and some very patient scientists, to find out.

By increasing both the male's chances of mating in the future and the likelihood that a female's infant will survive, friendship contributes to the reproductive success of both partners. This clarifies the evolutionary basis of friendship-forming tendencies in baboons, but what does friendship mean to a baboon? To answer this question we need to view baboons as sentient beings with feelings and goals not unlike our own in similar circumstances. Consider, for example, the friendship between Thalia and Alexander.

The affair began one evening as Alex and Thalia sat about fifteen feet apart on the sleeping cliffs. It was like watching two novices in a singles bar. Alex stared at Thalia until she turned and almost caught him looking at her. He glanced away immediately, and then she stared at him until his head began to turn toward her. She suddenly became engrossed in grooming her toes. But as soon as Alex looked away, her gaze returned to him. They went on like this for more than fifteen minutes, always with split-second timing. Finally, Alex managed to catch Thalia looking at him. He made the friendly eyes-narrowed, ears-back face and smacked his lips together rhythmically. Thalia froze, and for a second she looked into his eyes. Alex approached, and Thalia, still nervous, groomed him. Soon she calmed down, and I found them still together on the cliffs the next morning. Looking back on this event months later, I realized that it marked the beginning of their friendship. Six years later, when I returned to Eburru Cliffs, they were still friends.

If flirtation forms an integral part of baboon friendship, so does jealousy. Overt displays of jealousy, such as chasing a friend away from a potential rival, occur occasionally, but like humans, baboons often express their emotions in more subtle ways. One evening a colleague and I climbed the cliffs and settled down near Sherlock, who was friends with Cybelle, a middle-aged female still foraging on the ground below the cliffs. I observed Cybelle while my colleague watched Sherlock, and we kept up a running commentary. As long as Cybelle was feeding or interacting with females, Sherlock was relaxed, but each time she approached another male, his body would stiffen, and he would stare intently at the scene below. When Cybelle presented politely to a male who had recently tried to befriend her, Sherlock even made threatening sounds under his breath. Cybelle was not in estrus at the time, indicating that male baboon jealousy extends beyond the sexual arena to include affiliative interactions between a female friend and other males.

Because baboon friendships are embedded in a network of friendly and antagonistic relationships, they inevitably lead to repercussions extending beyond the pair. For example, Virgil once provoked his weaker rival Cyclops into a fight by first attacking Cyclops's friend Phoebe. On another occasion, Sherlock chased Circe, Hector's best friend, just after Hector had chased Antigone, Sherlock's friend.

In another incident, the prime adult male Triton challenged Cyclops's possession of meat. Cyclops grew increasingly tense and seemed about to abandon the prey to the younger male. Then Cyclops's friend Phoebe appeared with her infant Phyllis. Phyllis wandered over to Cyclops. He immediately grabbed her, held her close, and threatened Triton away from the prey. Because any challenge to Cyclops now involved a threat to Phyllis as well, Triton risked being mobbed by Phoebe and her relatives and friends. For this reason, he backed down. Males frequently use the infants of their female friends as buffers in this way. Thus, friendship involves costs as well as benefits because it makes the participants vulnerable to social manipulation or redirected aggression by others.

Finally, as with humans, friendship seems to mean something different to each baboon. Several females in Eburru Cliffs had only one friend. They were devoted companions. Louise and Pandora, for example, groomed their friend Virgil and no other male. Then there was Leda, who, with five friends, spread herself more thinly than any other female. These contrasting patterns of friendship were associated with striking personality differences. Louise and Pandora were unobtrusive females who hung around quietly with Virgil and their close relatives. Leda seemed to be everywhere at once, playing with infants, fighting with juveniles, and making friends with males. Similar differences were apparent among the males. Some devoted a great deal of time and energy to cultivating friendships with females, while others focused more on challenging other males. Although we probably will never fully understand the basis of these individual differences, they contribute immeasurably to the richness and complexity of baboon society.

Male–female friendships may be widespread among primates. They have been reported for many other groups of savanna baboons, and they also occur in rhesus and Japanese macaques, capuchin monkeys, and perhaps in bonobos (pygmy chimpanzees). These relationships should give us pause when considering popular scenarios for the evolution of male–female relationships in humans. Most of these scenarios assume that, except for mating, males and females had little to do with one another until the development of a sexual division of labor, when, the story goes, females began to rely on males to provide meat in exchange for gathered food. This, it has been argued, set up new selection pressures favoring the development of long-term bonds between individual males and females, female sexual fidelity, and as paternity certainty increased, greater male investment in the offspring of these unions. In other words, once women began to gather and men to hunt, presto—we had the nuclear family.

This scenario may have more to do with cultural biases about women's economic dependence on men and idealized views of the nuclear family than with the actual behavior of our hominid ancestors. The nonhuman primate evidence challenges this story in at least three ways.

First, long-term bonds between the sexes can evolve in the absence of a sexual division of labor or food sharing. In our primate relatives, such relationships rest on exchanges of social, not economic, benefits.

Second, primate research shows that highly differentiated, emotionally intense male–female relationships can occur without sexual exclusivity. Ancestral men and women may have experienced intimate friendships long before they invented marriage and norms of sexual fidelity.

Third, among our closest primate relatives, males clearly provide mothers and infants with social benefits even when they are unlikely to be the fathers of those infants. In return, females provide a variety of benefits to the friendly males, including acceptance into the group and, at least in baboons, increased mating opportunities in the future. This suggests that efforts to reconstruct the evolution of hominid societies may have overemphasized what the female must supposedly do (restrict her mating to just one male) in order to obtain male parental investment.

Maybe it is time to pay more attention to what the male must do (provide benefits to females and young) in order to obtain female cooperation. Perhaps among our ancestors, as in baboons today, sex and friendship went hand in hand. As for marriage—well, that's another story.

3

The Human Family Tree Has Become a Bush with Many Branches

John Noble Wilford

Approximately three and a half million years ago, two human ancestors and a small child took a stroll through what is now northern Tanzania. Shortly after, a volcano named Sadiman erupted, spreading a layer of ash over the landscape. Then, when a light rain turned this ash into a cement-like substance, it preserved the footprints of these bipedal hominins leaving a fossil record of this prehistoric walk. Several million years later, Paleoanthropologist Andrew Hill stumbled upon these fossilized footprints while working with a group of researchers led by Meave Leakey.

Hill discovered the footprints in 1976, just two years after Donald Johanson unearthed the historic remains of Lucy, an *Australopithecus afarensis* whose partial skeleton represents one of the earliest hominins found in the known fossil record. After dating these fossil remains, the way we think of early human history was drastically changed; we revised our earliest estimates of when the human lineage diverged from the other apes.

Today, new discoveries continue to shed light on the history and timeline of our prehistoric ancestors. In this selection, John Noble Wilford explains how the ever-increasing fossil record, along with the development of molecular biology continue to reveal and push back the timeline of the divergence of humankind from our common ancestry with other apes.

As you read this selection, ask yourself the following questions:

- What is the primary difference between the work of paleoanthropologists and biologists in terms of their contributions to our understanding of our early hominid ancestors?
- How has our knowledge about our earliest human ancestors changed since the 1990s, and what evidence supports this new understanding?
- What does the author mean when he states that the human family tree is more like a bush with many branches?
- According to recent molecular research and the fossil record, how long ago did humans split from other primates? Why is it difficult to pinpoint the exact point of divergence of the human lineage from a common ape ancestor?

The following terms discussed in this selection are included in the Glossary at the back of the book:

African Eve | *Australopithecus anamensis*
Homo floresiensis | *morphology*

Time was, fossils and a few stone artifacts were about the only means scientists had of tracing the lines of early human evolution. And gaps in such material evidence were frustratingly wide.

When molecular biologists joined the investigation some 30 years ago, their techniques of genetic analysis yielded striking insights. DNA studies pointed to a common maternal ancestor of all anatomically modern humans in Africa by at least 130,000 years. She inevitably became known as the African Eve.

Other genetic research plotted ancestral migration patterns and the extremely close DNA relationship between humans and chimpanzees, our nearest living relatives. Genetic clues also set the approximate time of the divergence of the human lineage from a common ancestor with apes: between six million and eight million years ago.

Fossil researchers were skeptical at first, a reaction colored perhaps by their dismay at finding scientific poachers on their turf. These paleoanthropologists contended that the biologists' "molecular clocks" were unreliable, and in some cases they were, though apparently not to a significant degree.

Now paleoanthropologists say they accept the biologists as allies triangulating the search for human origins from different angles. As much as anything, a rapid succession of fossil discoveries since the early 1990s has restored the confidence of paleoanthropologists in the relevance of their approach to the study of early hominids, those fossil ancestors and related species in human evolution.

The new finds have filled in some of the yawning gaps in the fossil record. They have doubled the record's time span from 3.5 million back almost to 7 million years ago and more than doubled the number of earliest known hominid species. The teeth and bone fragments suggest the form—the morphology—of these ancestors that lived presumably just this side of the human-ape split.

"The amount of discord between morphology and molecules is actually not that great anymore," said Frederick E. Grine, a paleoanthropologist at the State University of New York at Stony Brook.

With more abundant data, Dr. Grine said, scientists are, in a sense, fleshing out the genetic insights with increasingly earlier fossils. It takes the right bones to establish that a species walked upright, which is thought to be a defining trait of hominids after the split with the ape lineage.

"All biology can tell you is that my nearest relative is a chimpanzee and about when we had a common ancestor," he said. "But biology can't tell us what the common ancestor looked like, what shaped that evolutionary change or at what rate that change took place."

Although hominid species were much more apelike in their earliest forms, Tim D. White of the University of California, Berkeley, said: "We've come to appreciate that you cannot simply extrapolate from the modern chimp to get a picture of the last common ancestor. Humans and chimps have been changing down through time."

But Dr. White, one of the most experienced hominid hunters, credits the genetic data with giving paleoanthropologists a temporal framework for their research. Their eyes are always fixed on a time horizon for hominid origins, which now appears to be at least seven million years ago.

Ever since its discovery in 1973, the species *Australopithecus afarensis*, personified by the famous Lucy skeleton, has been the continental divide in the exploration of hominid evolution. Donald Johanson, the Lucy discoverer, and Dr. White determined that the apelike individual lived 3.2 million years ago, walked upright and was probably a direct human ancestor. Other afarensis specimens and some evocative footprints showed the species existed for almost a million years, down to three million years ago.

In the 1990s, scientists finally crossed the Lucy divide. In Kenya, Meave G. Leakey of the celebrated fossil-hunting family came up with *Australopithecus anamensis*, which lived about four million years ago and appeared to be an afarensis precursor. Another discovery by Dr. Leakey challenged the prevailing view that the **family tree** had a more or less single trunk rising from ape roots to a pinnacle occupied by *Homo sapiens*. Yet here was evidence that the new species *Kenyanthropus platyops* co-existed with Lucy's afarensis kin.

The **family tree** now looks more like a **bush** with many branches. "Just because there's only one human species around now doesn't mean it was always that way," Dr. Grine said.

Few hominid fossils have turned up from the three-million- to two-million-year period, during which hominids began making stone tools. The first *Homo* species enter the fossil record sometime before two million years ago, and the transition to much larger brains began with *Homo erectus*, about 1.7 million years ago.

Other recent discoveries have pushed deeper in time, closer to the hominid origins predicted by molecular biologists.

Dr. White was involved in excavations in Ethiopia of many specimens that lived 4.4 million years ago and were more primitive and apelike than Lucy. The species was named *Ardipithecus ramidus*. Later, a related species from 5.2 million to 5.8 million years ago was classified *Ardipithecus kadabba*.

At that time, six years ago, C. Owen Lovejoy of Kent State University said, "We are indeed coming very close to that point in the fossil record where we simply will not be able to distinguish ancestral hominid from ancestral" chimpanzees, because, he said, "They were so anatomically similar."

Two even earlier specimens are even harder to interpret. One found in Kenya by a French team has been dated to six million years and named *Orrorin tugenensis*. The teeth and bone pieces are few, though the discoverers think a thigh fragment suggests that the individual was a biped—a walker on two legs.

Another French group then uncovered 6.7-million-year-old fossils in Chad. Named *Sahelanthropus tchadensis*, the sole specimen includes only a few teeth, a jawbone and a crushed cranium. Scientists said the head appeared to have perched atop a biped.

"These are clearly the earliest hominids we have," said Eric Delson, a human-origins scientist at the American Museum of Natural History. "But we still know rather little about any of these specimens. The farther back we go toward the divergence point, the more similar specimens will look on both sides of the split."

Other challenges arise from human evolution in more recent epochs. Just who were the "little people" found a few years ago in a cave on the island of Flores in Indonesia? The Australian and Indonesian discoverers concluded that one partial skeleton and other bones belonged to a now-extinct separate human species, *Homo floresiensis*, which lived as recently as 18,000 years ago.

The apparent diminutive stature and braincase of the species prompted howls of dispute. Critics contended that this was not a distinct species, but just another dwarf-size *Homo sapiens*, possibly with a brain disorder. Several prominent scientists, however, support the new-species designation.

The tempest over the Indonesian find is nothing new in a field known for controversy. Some scholars counsel patience, recalling that it was years after the discovery of the first Neanderthal skull, in 1856, before it was accepted as an ancient branch of the human family. Critics had at first dismissed the find as only the skull of a degenerate modern human or a Cossack who died in the Napoleonic wars.

Perhaps the analogy is not as encouraging as intended. Scientists to this day are arguing about Neanderthals, their exact relationship to us and the cause of their extinction 30,000 years ago, not long after the arrival in Europe of the sole surviving hominid that is so curious about its origins.

Hunting the First Hominid

PAT SHIPMAN

Self-centeredly, human beings have always taken an exceptional interest in their origins. Each discovery of a new species of hominid—both our human ancestors and the near-relatives arising after the split from the gorilla-chimp lineage—is reported with great fanfare, even though the First Hominid remains elusive. We hope that, when our earliest ancestor is finally captured, it will reveal the fundamental adaptations that make us *us*.

There is no shortage of ideas about the essential nature of the human species and the basic adaptations of our kind. Some say hominids are fundamentally thinkers; others favor tool-makers or talkers; still others argue that hunting, scavenging or bipedal walking made hominids special. Knowing what the First Hominid looked like would add some meat to a soup flavored with speculation and prejudice.

Genetic and molecular studies provide one sort of insight, showing what sort of *stuff* we are made of, and that it is only slightly different stuff from that which makes up the apes (gorillas, chimps, orangutans and gibbons). From the molecular differences among the genes of humans and apes, geneticists estimate the time when each of the various ape and hominid lineages diverged from the common stem. The result is a sort of hairy Y diagram, with multiple branches instead of simply two as is usual on a Y. Each terminus represents a living species; each branching point or node represents the appearance of some new evolutionary trait, such as new molecules, new genes, new shapes or new proportions of limb, skull and tooth. Unfortunately, this way of diagramming the results tends to lull us into thinking (falsely) that all the evolutionary changes occurred at those nodes, and none along the branches.

Such studies omit a crucial part of our history: the extinct species. Only the fossil record contains evidence, in context, of the precise pathway that evolution took. In this technological age, when sophisticated instrumentation and gee-whiz algorithms seem downright necessary, the most basic information about the evolution of our lineage still comes from branches of science that operate in rather old-fashioned ways. The primary discoveries in paleontology (the study of old things), pale oanthropology (the study of old humans) and archaeology (the study of the old stuff that old humans leave around) still rely on the efforts of handful of investigators who slog around on foot or excavate in desolate landscapes. Fancy equipment can't replace eyes and brains, although instrumentation plays a crucial role in the dating an analysis of fossil remains.

Finding the evolutionary origin of hominids is little like stalking big game. Paleoanthropologist struggle to establish when and where their quarry was last seen and what it was like—hoping to follow its tracks backward in time. (*Why* hominids or any other group arose is such a metaphysical question that most paleoanthropologists run away screaming when it is asked.)

When the first hominid slinked through the underbush has been estimated from molecular clock and confirmed by radiometric dates. These line of evidence converge on a period between 5 million and 7 million years ago as the time when primitive, perhaps vaguely apelike species evolved some definitive new adaptation that transformed it into the First Hominid. But like the point of inflection on a line graph, the first species in any new lineage is only readily apparent after the fact. The emergence of the first hominid was probably not obvious in prospect but only now, in retrospect—in the context of the entire evolutionary record of the hominids—when the long-term evolutionary trends can be seen.

Where this dangerous creature once lived has to be Africa, since both our closest living relatives (chimpanzees and gorillas) and all early hominids (older than about 2 million years ago) are African.

What to Look For?

What happened, exactly, and to *whom,* remain to be discovered. Two newly discovered fossil species have each been proposed to be the First Hominid. This circumstance raises a significant issue: How would we know the First Hominid if we saw it?

Making a list of key features that differentiate apes from people is not difficult, but misleading. It is absurd to expect that all of these differences arose simultaneously during a single evolutionary event represented by the final fork on the hairy Y diagram. The first ape on the gorilla-chimp lineage was neither a gorilla nor a chimpanzee, for modem gorillas and chimps have had at least 5 million years to evolve in isolation before arriving at their modem form. In the same way the First Hominid on our lineage was not a human and did not possess all of the characteristics of modem humans.

Using a hairy Y diagram, we can limit the number of contenders for the essential or basal hominid adaptation:

- Hominids might be essentially bipeds. All known hominids are bipedal; no apes are.
- Wishful thinking aside, hominids are not simply brainy apes. Alas, until about 2 million years ago no hominid had a brain larger than an ape's relative to its body size.
- Hominids might be apelike creatures that have lost their sexual dimorphism. Sexual dimorphism is exhibited as male-female differences that are not related to reproduction. For example, male orangs are typically much larger than females and have longer canine teeth that hone sharper with wear. The fossil record shows that hominids lost their dental sexual dimorphism first, since all known hominids have small and flat-wearing canines. In contrast, sexual dimorphism in body size persisted in hominids until about 2 million years ago, when the genus *Homo* first appeared.
- Thick dental enamel may be a key hominid trait. All hominids have thick enamel, whereas all fossil and living apes (except those in the orangutan lineage) have thin enamel. Because the fossil record of apes is so poor, we do not know whether the primitive condition for apes and hominids was thick or thin enamel. Indeed, how enamel thickness is to be measured and evaluated has generated many pages of debate.
- Hominids are hand-graspers or manipulators (from the Latin for hand, *manus*), whereas apes are foot-graspers. These differences are reflected in the sharp contrasts in the hand and foot anatomy of apes and humans. Apes have divergent big toes and long, curved toe bones for holding onto branches; their thumbs are short and cannot be opposed to the other fingers for skillful manipulation. Human beings are the opposite, with long, opposable thumbs and big toes that are closely aligned with the remaining short, straight toes. Human feet are nearly useless for grasping but are well adapted to bipedalism. An intermediate condition occurs in early hominids such as Lucy (the best-known individual of *Australopithecus afarensis*), who had opposable thumbs and numerous adaptations to bipedalism, and yet retained rather long and curved toes. Lucy and probably other types of *Australopithecus* were walkers, hand-graspers *and* somewhat compromised foot-graspers.

A description of our desired prey, then, might read like this:

An ape-brained and small-canined creature, with dental enamel of unknown thickness. Large if male but smaller if female. May be spotted climbing adeptly in trees or walking bipedally on the ground. Last seen in Africa between 5 million and 7 million years ago.

From this description, can we identify the First Hominid? Well, no—not yet.

A Tale of Two Trophies

Yohannes Haile-Selassie of the University of California, Berkeley, described a likely contender from Ethiopia in July of 2001. His material comes from Ethiopian sediments between 5.2 million and 5.8 million years old and is called *Ardipithecus ramidus kadabba,* a new subspecies. *Ardipithecus* means "root ape" in the Mar language, and the species has been explicitly proposed to be a "root species" ancestral to all later hominids.

Haile-Selassie's specimens include more than 20 teeth, some associated with a mandible or lower jaw; substantial pieces of two left humeri, or upper arm bones; a partial ulna from the same forearm as one humerus; a partial clavicle or collarbone; a half of one finger bone; and a complete toe bone.

No ironclad evidence of bipedality in any *Ardipithecus* specimen has yet been published. In this collection, the only evidence about habitual patterns of locomotion comes from the single toe bone. Its weight-bearing surface faces downward as in bipeds, not inward as in apes. Any jury might be suspicious that *Ardipithecus* was bipedal, but none of the really telltale body parts—pelvis, complete femur, tibia, or ankle bones—has yet been recovered. The preserved bones of the arm, finger and shoulder closely resemble those of Lucy and may have been used in grasping and tree-climbing. *Ardipithecus* is as yet too poorly known for its relative brain size or sexual dimorphism in body size to be assessed.

The other candidate that has already been bagged is a 6 million-year-old find from the Tugen Hills of Kenya called *Orrorin tugenensis.* Its generic name is derived from the Tugen language and means "original man"—a claim as bold as "root ape." Found by a joint French-Kenyan team headed by Brigitte Senut of the Centre nationale de la recherche scientifique, the *Orrorin* fossils include a few teeth, some embedded in a jaw fragment; a partial humerus; a finger bone; and substantial parts of three femurs, or thigh bones.

The femurs, which might provide definitive evidence of bipedality, are incomplete. The sole evidence for bipedality lies in the head of the femur in *Orrorin,* which is proportionately larger than Lucy's. One reason to evolve a large-headed femur is to dissipate the forces produced by bipedalism. The team concludes that *Orrorin* evolved bipedalism separately from Lucy (and from other species of *Australopithecus*), making *Orrorin* the only known ancestor of *Homo. Australopithecus* is displaced to an extinct side-branch of the hominid lineage.

Their surprising conclusion is not universally accepted. Skeptics reply that the femoral differences between *Orrorin* and *Australopithecus* might disappear if *Orrorin*'s femur were compared with that of a large male individual rather than with the diminutive Lucy.

As in *Ardipithecus,* the bones from the upper limb of *Orrorin* show tree-climbing adaptations. Neither relative brain size nor body size dimorphism can be evaluated in *Orrorin.*

Where *Orrorin* and *Ardipithecus* differ are in their teeth. *Orrorin* appears to have thick enamel, like a hominid or an orangutan, and *Ardipithecus* seems to have thin enamel, like other apes. This dental comparison might resolve the question "Who is the First Hominid?" in favor of *Orrorin,* except that *Orrorin*'s canine teeth imply the opposite conclusion. *Orrorin*'s single known canine is sizable and pointed and wears like an ape's canine. In contrast, the several known canines of *Ardipithecus* are all small-crowned and flat-wearing, like a hominid's canines.

Puzzlingly, *Ardipithecus* and *Orrorin* show different mosaics of hominid and ape features. Both may be bipeds, although *Ardipithecus* is a biped in the manner of *Australopithecus* and *Orrorin* is not. If one of these two newly announced species is the First Hominid, then the other must be banished to the ape lineage. The situation is deliciously complex and confusing.

It is also humbling. We thought we knew an ape from a person; we thought we could even identify a man in an ape suit or an ape in a tuxedo for what they were. Humans have long prided themselves on being very different from apes—but pride goeth before a fall. In this case, embarrassingly, we can't tell the ape from the hominid even though we have teeth, jaws, and arm and leg bones.

Paleoanthropologists must seriously reconsider the defining attributes of apes and hominids while we wait for new fossils. In the meantime, we should ponder our complicity, too, for we have been guilty of expecting evolution to be much simpler than it ever is.

PAT SHIPMAN is an adjunct professor of anthropology at the Pennsylvania State University. Address: Department of Anthropology, 315 Carpenter Building, Pennsylvania State University, University Park, PA 16801. Internet:pls10@psu.edu

Man the Hunted

Just Another Item on the Menu

Donna Hart and Robert W. Sussman

On the second day of January 2001 something occurred that has happened uncountable times before . . . something that has been happening, in fact, for millions of years . . . something that has influenced the way we humans act and the way we evolved.

A woman was cross-country skiing along a popular lake trail near her home in Alberta, Canada. Rangers say a 132-pound cougar lay hidden under an evergreen. It watched her pass, then stealthily zigzagged behind her for nearly 150 feet. The woman was probably totally unaware of the cat until just moments before it killed her.

Man-eater! The word conjures up a latent human nightmare. It shocks us; it scares us badly. It seems to frighten us down to some deep collective subconscious. It's gruesome . . . macabre . . . downright ghoulish when a human being is killed by a predator. Newspapers report the event, books are written, movies are made, eyewitnesses are interviewed for more snippets about such an aberrant deed.

A quick browse of the Internet comes up with over a hundred Web sites connected to the word "man-eater." There is even a book entitled *Maneaters* that "explores the wide world of man-eaters—creatures who regard *Homo sapiens* as just another noon-day snack."

During the relatively short period of written human history—with weapons ever more efficient and living areas secured behind barriers to the natural world—we have come to think we should be exempt from attacks by carnivores, birds of prey, and reptiles. Those of us living within the rarified atmosphere of Western civilization presume that our superior position in the hierarchy of the animal kingdom is unquestionable. And, truth be told, modern humans in the industrial world have suffered relatively little at the claws and teeth of predators.

The human species excels in duality of thought. This comes as no surprise to anyone who has read the work of the famous anthropologist Claude Lévi-Strauss. He theorized that all human cognition was based on dealing with binary contrasts or oppositions—left versus right, low versus high, night versus day, them versus us. We also seem to carry this duality into our feelings about predators. On the one hand, we humans—or at least those of us in Western cultures—have a conception of ourselves as superior entities who exist on a plane above the rest of the animal inhabitants of our world. And yet—and here is the duality—we worry ceaselessly that inferior beings, such as predators, may harm us.

Modern humans, with the help of technology, are able to ward off predation effectively, and mask our vulnerability as a species. As cited at the beginning of this chapter, there are times when people meet their demise from predators: The solitary jogger or cross-country skier attacked by a cougar . . . a tiger or leopard that preys on villagers in India . . . the two lions, made famous in the film *The Ghost and the Darkness,* that savaged railway workers . . . newspaper reports of crocodiles consuming humans from West Africa to Indonesia.

The bizarre realization that humans get eaten comes hard to the Western mind. However, much current ethnographic evidence points to the fact that large predators are often a major and well-recognized problem in regions of the world where villagers are in near contact with big cats or large reptiles. Perhaps there's more truth than we in the Western world would like to acknowledge that "the ultimate horror of being eaten alive is very real [by] sharks, lions, leopards, tigers, bears, wolves . . . jaguar and puma."

In South Asia—India and Bangladesh, in particular—there is a long history of dealing on a daily basis with predation by tigers and leopards. Before World War II and prior to independence for India, British colonial records listed 1,500 human deaths from tigers *per year,* and these statistics excluded the numerous Princely States. One tigress was responsible for an incredible 436 human predations.

The Sundarbans delta of the Ganges and Brahmaputra Rivers—a huge area of over 3,800 square miles of mangrove forest and islands that spans both India and Bangladesh—is notorious for its man-eating tigers. John Seidensticker, tiger expert at the Smithsonian Institution, commented in a speech he made at an academic meeting: "Tigers kill people. They don't kill people in every part of their range and that might be interpreted as great restraint on the part of the tiger considering the abundance of this very vulnerable potential prey species. One area where tigers do eat people on a regular basis is the Sundarbans."

During one decade near the end of the twentieth century (between 1975 and 1985) 425 people were killed by tigers on the Indian portion of the delta and another 187 on the Bangladesh side. Plastic face masks—constructed to be worn on the *back* of the head—have been distributed by the Indian authorities. Locals wear them as a deterrent to tiger predation while they are boating through the swamps in the Sundarbans delta. These masks help reduce tiger attacks because big cats like to stalk prey that are unaware of impending danger. The wide-eyed, staring mask on the back of a human head is interpreted by the tiger as a fully *aware* prey and, therefore, not a potential meal. Dummy humans set in boats and wired with electric shocks are also used to deter tigers from the enticement of human flesh. The theory is that once a tiger has been literally and figuratively shocked by pouncing on an electrified "human," that particular item will no longer be so appealing. Some of the other, more traditional Indian and Bangladeshi means to counter tiger attacks include fireworks, special shrines, and priests.

Why specific animals become predators on humans is complex. Predators are after the simplest avenue to a meal, and modern humans—even those in the undeveloped world—are usually dwelling *in* villages, *inside* houses, *with* weapons, and seldom make a simple target. We do not in any way want to portray carnivores (or reptiles, or birds of prey) as rapacious fiends that must be eliminated for the good of humankind. All predators are critical and necessary parts of healthy ecosystems. If we are going to save any of the wild places on earth, predators are the keystone species that must be protected.

Fossil Evidence and Living Primates

Having noted that (outside the West) predation on humans happens—and not all that infrequently—we are confronted with a number of questions: Was this always the case? What about the 99% of human evolution from which we have no written records? Does the occasional unsettling instance of an attack by a predator accentuate the long history of humans as simply one more link in the food chain?

Were early humans bold hunters or were they fearful prey? Has *Homo sapiens'* evolution been molded by hunting ability or by survival techniques developed to avoid being eaten?

We only have two sources to draw on if we want to fill in the millions of years before historical times. These are the *paleontological remains*—a sparse but fascinating fossil record—and the *living primates*—who are our closest relatives.

There are caves in South Africa where bones of early hominids (humans and their ancestors) lie in piles. Researchers study how bones came to be buried in the earth and preserved as fossils, thus shedding light on how these ancient humans lived. Early hominids, using rocks and branches as weapons the way many living primate species do, had (presumably) the same ability as other primates to ward off predation—that is, not much except a slightly larger brain-body ratio than other mammals and the ability to communicate between group members when danger was sighted. These were not superb weapons if the predator managed a surprise ambush or just outran or outclimbed its hominid prey.

Paleontological evidence supports the conclusion that both hominids and other primates, such as baboons, were frequent meals for ancient predators. Both australopithecines (one of the groups of early hominids) and baboons are found together in the prey-remain assemblages of true saber-toothed cats, false saber-toothed cats, hunting hyenas, spotted hyenas, and leopards. Fossil evidence from South Africa supports theories of extensive predation by leopards on both early hominids and baboons between 1 and 2 million years ago.

One skull of a fossil hominid found in a South African cave has a set of puncture marks. Two round holes about the size of dimes are spaced several inches apart on the skull. If a leopard caught one of the australo-pithecines and dragged the prize up a tree for eating, the cat's upper canines would have drilled deep into the frontal part of the brain directly above the eyes, and the lower canines would have grasped the prey on the back of the skull. When paleontologists reunited a fossil of this ancient cat with the fossil hominid skull, there was a perfect matchup between the two puncture holes in the skull and the two huge lower fangs of the cat.

The famous "Taung child," a two-million-year-old *Australopithecus africanus* skull, was discovered in 1924 by Raymond Dart, an early and influential paleontologist. Dart had an arrangement with a limestone quarry in South Africa; all intriguing fossils were extracted intact and shipped to him. One of these boxes of limestone rubble contained a veritable jewel of paleontology—the skull and mineralized brain of a very young child, a child that died 2 million years ago. Were violent circumstances involved in the child's death? Unlike the other skull from a different site in South Africa, the Taung child did not bear the marks of carnivore teeth but instead exhibited deep rakings. More oddly, the mandible, or lower jaw, of the Taung child was still attached. (The remains of carnivore meals most often have detached mandibles. Big-cat fangs tearing away at small hominid skulls would rarely result in a still-attached jaw.)

What was going on? If not ancient cats, then what might have caused the death of the Taung child? It took another 70 years for an answer to this mystery. In 1995 paleontologists Lee Berger and Ron Clarke published their detailed findings about the predator who killed the Taung child. Birds of prey, technically called raptors, include living species of eagles with enormously robust feet and talons. These adaptations enable the eagles to kill antelopes and monkeys many times the birds' own weight. Berger and Clarke found that marks on the Taung child were identical to the marks that modern African eagles leave on the bones of *their* prey. The Taung child was no doubt the prey of a very large and very strong extinct eagle.

The most exciting fossils of early *true* humans—individuals who can be classified in our own genus, *Homo*—were uncovered beneath a medieval town called Dmanisi in the Republic of Georgia within the past few years. Besides astounding the world of science with the age of *Homo* specimens found *outside* of Africa—a whopping 1.75 million years old!— the remains of six individuals include another verification of hominids as prey. Again, telltale round holes were found in one of the skulls. This time saber-toothed cat fangs fit neatly and perfectly into the two punctures.

David Lordkipanidze is the Georgian scientist who worked the Dmanisi site. He has speculated that simple chopping and scraping tools unearthed with the fossils may indicate that these ancient humans sometimes scavenged off kills of the big cats. The idea of early hominids as scavengers, rather than the more traditional vignette of humans as biggame hunters, also has been advanced by Pat Shipman at Johns Hopkins University. Shipman suggests that Man the Scavenger is not nearly as attractive an image as Man the Hunter, but hominid-made cut marks that overlay carnivore-made tooth marks occur on the same fossil bones.

We propose that a choice lies not between *hunting* man and *scavenging* man at all—the reality is more likely that *hunted* man took advantage of predator kills. Recent research by John Cavallo suggests that early hominids (adults, at least) were able to protect themselves from predators fairly capably during the daylight hours. But when nightfall came, it was a different story altogether. Leopards, especially, ruled the night. Early hominids may have been in competition with leopards to scavenge tree-stored kills during the day, while they themselves became leopard prey at night.

If we look at the behavior of other primates today, such as baboons, we see the same phenomenon of day-night shifts in primate-predator clashes. Male savanna baboons bare their teeth and rush at predators during the day. Actually, there are even quite a few cases in which male baboons have killed predators. Out of eleven aggressive retaliations against leopards by baboons that are written up in scientific papers, the leopard was killed in four instances. One scientist even observed a single dominant male baboon malm or kill four large dogs when they attacked his troop.

But baboons retreat to trees and cliffs at night where they are virtually helpless after dark to protect themselves and their young when lions or leopards are on the prowl. After primatologist Curt Busse switched to nocturnal observations in his study of baboon populations at Moremi, Botswana, he saw an entirely different picture of primate defensive skills. Based on night observation hours during which Busse followed the screams of his terrified baboon subjects, he calculated that at least 8% of the baboon population was killed annually due to predation by lions and leopards.

Predation and Primate Studies

Busse feels strongly that primatologists may get a skewed and misinformed representation of predation by studying primate behavior and ecology only during daylight hours. To accomplish an accurate appraisal of predation, Busse has challenged his fellow researchers to make significant changes in field methods, such as including night observations, as well as studies of the predators of primates (along with the primates themselves).

Predation is acknowledged to be an issue of fundamental importance in the study of primates. However, while predation has been discussed in broad theoretical terms, little quantified data have existed on the subject. There has been little attempt to recruit research carried out on various predators as an aid to understanding the impact of predation on primates. In this book we have combined the research of primatologists with the findings of their colleagues who study large and small predatory mammals, raptors, and reptiles to assemble both empirical and anecdotal overviews of primate deaths due to predation. Perhaps combining these data may sound like a natural, very standard process. However, the multidisciplinary approach had not been extended previously to merge the world of primatology with the world of predator research. When we did combine data from both primatologists and predator researchers, we found that a clear picture emerged of primates as prey.

Current examples of predation on primates can be used to infer the rates of predation on our hominid ancestors. Because paleoanthropologists have been unaware of the extent of predation on living primates, they have tended to analyze hominid fossils and construct theories without integrating predation as an important factor in human adaptations. Some of the past analyses of fossil assemblages require reinterpretation using this approach.

An Accurate Appraisal of Predation

A continuing academic debate concerns whether primates, in general, are important as prey species. Furthermore, the debate has now entered into the scientific literature on hominid evolution. Our premise is that primates, including early humans, have been the prey of many carnivores, reptiles, and even birds of prey and that being *hunted* is integral to our hominid lineage. In this book we propose that much of human evolution has to do with the fact that we—along with other primates—are prey species.

This aspect of human evolution and its implications for modern humans is a controversial departure from more traditional theories. We are not the first nor the only ones to arrive at this theory. Well-known paleoanthropologists have drawn the same conclusions as we have about early humans and predation, for example C. K. Brain, Lewis Binford, and Matt Cartmill. (Brain, in fact, coined the phrase "Man the Hunted.") But combining the fossil evidence regarding levels of predation on early hominids with comparisons to predation on living primates has not yet been done. By merging the two kinds of evidence, we hope to accomplish a long-overdue synthesis of the theory we call Man the Hunted.

Man the Hunter?

The question "Why is man man?" has been posed since literal biblical origins gave way to scientific inquiries. "Because man evolved as a meat eater" is one answer to the question. Robert Ardrey stated in one of his series of immensely popular books of the 1970s, *The Hunting Hypothesis:*

> If among all the members of our primate family the human being is unique, even in our noblest aspirations, it is because we alone through untold millions of years were continuously dependent on killing to survive.

There are several misconceptions included in this proposal of human hunting singularity. First, we are not the only primate that hunts for living prey. Hunting is a common feeding strategy throughout the primate order. Baboons are adept at capturing infant antelope; chimpanzees, especially, excel in hunting and eating monkeys. Even different methods and approaches toward hunting have been observed in different chimpanzee populations. At Jane Goodall's field site, Gombe Reserve in Tanzania, the male chimps hunt as lions do—the more individuals involved the greater the success rate, but no coordinated team effort is manifested. In the Tai Forest of Côte d'Ivoire the chimps hunt like wolves, each individual playing a key role in a team effort.

Whether hunting could have been the main food-procurement venture for early hominids is also subject to anatomical constraints. We need to look carefully at teeth and digestive systems, the critical parts of human anatomy that lend themselves to answers about early hominid dependence on hunted meat. Intestines do not fossilize, but teeth make up a good portion of the fossil remains of australopithecines and their dentition is not that of a carnivore.

So, where did the Man the Hunter idea come from? When did the certitude that humans were too busy *killing* to *be killed* arise? Who were the proponents of the myth of fierce and dangerous hominids? When you consider the reality, what a public-relations coup!—a fangless, clawless, smallish bipedal primate gets a reputation for being Godzilla wielding an antelope jawbone!

In some sense the Taung child is the key to the Man the Hunter theme. Taung child was the first fossil in a series of australopithecine finds. It is somewhat ironic that Raymond Dart's painstaking reclamation of this fossil—probably the young victim of a predator—was so instrumental in creating a trend toward "killer-ape" status for human ancestors.

To view the inception of Man the Hunter's forceful accession and acceptance, we need to go back and fill in the people who inhabited the rather small and esoteric world of paleoanthropology in the 1920s. As emphasized earlier, Africa was not then the important arena for fossil humans. The English had their Piltdown Man, reassuring the white European experts that large brains came before flat faces. The Neanderthal finds in Europe were augmented by Java Man and Peking Man from the Far East. What did it matter if an obscure anatomy professor in South Africa had found a skull and fossilized brain that didn't look like a chimp but whose brain was way, way too small to be considered human?

In the atmosphere of the day it is no wonder that the Piltdown Man, with its ape-like jaw and large cranium, was immediately accepted as the earliest hominid ancestor, while the small-skulled, ape-like australopithecine discovered by Raymond Dart was considered a pathological specimen or a mere ape. While Piltdown supporters were busy explaining the intellectual endowments of our large-brained ancestors, Dart was convinced his small-brained creature was the first ape-man, and he developed a theoretical picture of the behavior of this transitional form. At first Dart believed that australopithecines were scavengers barely eking out an existence in the harsh savanna environment; a primate that did not live to kill large animals but scavenged small animals in order to live.

Few cared what Dart believed, however, because few took his ape-man seriously. In fact it was not until a quarter of a century later, with the unearthing of many more australopithecines and the discovery in 1953 that Piltdown was a fraud, that students of human evolution realized our earliest ancestors were more ape-like than they were modern-human-like. This led to a great interest in using primates to understand human evolution and the evolutionary basis of human nature. With these discoveries began a long list of theories attempting to re-create the behavior and often the basic morality of the earliest hominids.

By 1950 Dart had developed a wholly new and different view from his former scavenger model. His ponderings about strange depressions in the crania of fossil australopithecines eventually flowered into a full-blown theory about killers who murdered their own kind. Given the game animals with which australopithecine fossils were associated and the dents and holes in the skulls of the australopithecines themselves, Dart became convinced that the mammals had been killed, butchered, and eaten by the ape-men, and that these early hominids had even been killing one another.

Dart once believed that the australopithecines had been forced to scratch out a meager existence on the savanna once they abandoned the trees of the African forest. But Dart now saw that hunting, and a carnivorous lust for blood, actively drew man-apes out of the forest and were together a main force in human evolution. He stated more than once that "the ancestors of *Australopithecus* left their fellows in the trees of Central Africa through a spirit of adventure and the more attractive fleshy food that lay in the vast savannas of the southern plains." Dart was himself influenced by a University of London professor, Carveth Read, who suggested in 1925 that human ancestors were similar to wolves; they hunted in packs and lived off the meat of large game. Read suggested that the name *Lycopithecus* (literally, "wolf-ape") would be descriptive of early hominids.

The discovery of baboon skulls mysteriously bashed in on the left side of the skull inspired Dart to conclude that only the australopithecine ancestor of humans could have killed with such precision. Since no stone weapons or tools were found in the South African sites, Dart postulated that the unusually high frequency of thigh bones and jawbones from antelopes must have been the weapons of choice. His "osteodontokeratic" culture—that early man had used the bones, teeth, and horns of his prey to kill even more prey—provided the means by which these killer apes accomplished their bloody work.

In 1953 Dart published a paper entitled "The Predatory Transition from Ape to Man." In it he hypothesized that the dentition and geography of australopithecines precluded any type of diet other than heavy reliance on meat. And not only did they eat meat but they armed themselves with weapons to hunt large prey. None of the well-known journals would accept the article, so readership within the scientific community was sparse. Robert Ardrey, a successful playwright, visited Dart in South Africa and was convinced that this theory would revolutionize the science of anthropology. Ardrey spent 5 years between 1955 and 1960 researching and writing *African Genesis*—a popular account of our beginnings as killer apes. The book was a best-seller and had tremendous influence both on the general public and the scientific community.

By the mid-1970s Dart's claim that a hominid with a brain no larger than our ape cousins expertly fashioned weapons and went on the hunt because it was easier than scavenging was fully accepted. But, Dart's *evidence* for Man the Hunter was not good, and his particular vision of the human hunter/killer hypothesis did not stand up to rigorous scrutiny. C. K. Brain, a South African specialist in how fossils are formed by natural forces, was skeptical of the baboon-killing theory from the first. Upon examination of the evidence, Brain noted that the bones associated with the man-apes were exactly like fragments left by leopards and hyenas. He saw the holes in the baboon skulls and the similar indentations in *A. africanus* as oddly similar to the tooth patterns of living African carnivores. He set about measuring the distance between the lower canines of African big cats and found that the space between the lower fangs of leopards fit precisely into the fossil skull holes.

Round holes that match perfectly with fangs of leopards. It seems that the australopithecines were likely the hunted and not the hunters. Fossil bones of early hominid origin were found with baboon remains in South African cave excavations at Swartkrans, Kromdraii, and Sterkfontein, places that have become famous for their australopithecine remains. Brain hypothesized that baboons and early hominids slept in caves, providing an excellent opportunity for leopards to kill them and drag the carcasses farther into the caves for feeding. The Mt. Suswa lava caves in Kenya provide a current analogy to the paleontological record in South Africa and lend significant credibility to the hypotheses. Mt. Suswa is a favorite sleeping site for baboons, and leopards in the area subsist almost entirely on these primates.

Man the Dancer!

The next widely accepted version of the recurring Man the Hunter theme was presented in the late 1960s by Sherwood Washburn (the father of American field primatology) and his colleagues. They claimed that many of the features that define *men* as hunters (more about why the other 50% of the species was not defined will be discussed later in this book) again separated the earliest humans from their primate relatives.

> To assert the biological unity of mankind is to affirm the importance of the hunting way of life. It is to claim that, however much conditions and customs may have varied locally, the main selection pressures that forged the species were the same. The biology, psychology, and customs that separate us from the apes—these we owe to the hunters of time past. And, for those who would understand the origin and nature of human behavior there is no choice but to try to understand "Man the Hunter."

Like Dart, Washburn related human hunting to human morality, both of which had their biological basis in our evolutionary past. What he termed the "carnivorous psychology" of the australopithecines resulted in a human species that takes pleasure not just in the chasing, hunting, and killing of other animals, but in dark depredations on fellow humans. The public spectacles of torture and suffering in "most" cultures are for the *enjoyment* of all humans. This interpretation led him to the conclusion that only careful *un*training of our natural drives can lay a veneer of compassion for others on top of naturally human "carnivorous curiosity and aggression."

Again, much like Dart before him, Washburn did not amass a large amount of evidence to support his theory and seemed to have recognized that evidence to the contrary existed. Rather, he relied upon a nineteenth-century anthropological concept of cultural "survivals." These are behaviors that are no longer useful in society but that persist as leftover survival mechanisms from a time when they *were* adaptive. Washburn saw a connection between the ease with which modern sports (including hunting) are learned and the pleasures they confer, and the survival mechanisms of a bygone age. Because successful ancestral humans were those who hunted best, their genetic legacy is an easy and pleasurable acquisition of hunting-like behaviors.

Using a similar logic, we have developed an alternative (sarcastic, yes—but no less feasible) theory to challenge Man the Hunter. We call our theory "Man the Dancer." After all, men *and* women love to dance, it is a behavior found in all cultures, and it has less obvious function in most cultures than does hunting.

Although it takes two to tango, a variety of social systems could develop from various types of dance: square dancing, line dancing, riverdance, or the funky chicken. The footsteps at Laetoli might not represent two individuals going out for a hunt but the Afarensis shuffle, one of the earliest dances. In the movie *2001: A Space Odyssey,* it was wrong to depict the first tool as a weapon. It could easily have been a drumstick, and the first battle may not have involved killing at all but a battle of the bands. Other things such as face-to-face sex, cooperation, language and singing, and bipedalism (it's difficult to dance on all fours), even moving out of the trees and onto the ground might all be better explained by our propensity to dance than by our desire to hunt. Although we are being facetious with our Man the Dancer hypothesis, the evidence for dancing is certainly as good and no more preposterous than that for hunting.

We Were Not "Cat Food"!

Between 1961 and 1976, the playwright Robert Ardrey popularized the then-current version of the Man the Hunter myth with a number of best-sellers. Ardrey believed that it was the competitive spirit, as acted out in warfare, that made humans what they are today: "the mentality of the single Germanic tribe under Hitler differed in no way from that of early man or late baboon." Because of a lack of a competitive territorial instinct, gorillas—Ardrey believed—had lost the will to live and with it the drive for sex. He argued that gorillas defend no territory and copulate rarely. And their story "will end, one day, not with a bang but with a whimper."

African Genesis may well have been the starting point for the public popularity of Man the Hunter, but the prominence brought to paleoanthropology by the patriarch of the Leakey family was the strong suit that clinched the public's acceptance. The great Dr. Louis S. B. Leakey, a larger-than-life personality, was the premier paleoanthropologist of the mid-twentieth century and the personification of the fossil-hunting field scientist. His dynamic personality and exciting ideas took the quest for human origins to the heights of media coverage, catching the public's imagination. Inquiring minds finally *did* want to know about our origins! Along with his wife, Mary, who accomplished much of the actual discovery and reconstruction of the fossils, the Leakeys became worldwide celebrities. From their home base at the Kenya Museum of Natural History, they made Olduvai Gorge in Tanzania synonymous with human origins. Leakey also gave the world an eventual look at our closest relatives through his support for Jane Goodall's research on chimpanzees, Dian Fossey's work on mountain gorillas, and Birute Galdikas' study of orangutans. He was particularly thrilled when Goodall identified hunting and meat-eating in chimpanzees.

And Leakey's endorsement of Man the Hunter gave it the academic credentials that Ardrey's popular books lacked. In a famous defense of Man the Hunter as fearless and bellicose, Leakey stated that we were *not* "cat food," and the ramification was a change in perception of human origins for the entire Western world.

The designation of early humans as Man the Hunter rapidly attained axiomatic status. Our ancestry as fearless hunters and remorseless killers of our own and other species has been the generally accepted perception now for nearly 50 years. And not just the layperson, but academics as well, fall easily into using this paradigm. Here's a common example from an evolutionary psychologist, Charles Crawford of Simon Fraser University in Burnaby, British Columbia. Crawford lamented in an article about human evolutionary adaptations gone awry in modern times: "I used to hunt saber-toothed tigers all the time, thousands of years ago. Now I sit in front of a computer and don't get exercise."

We think it's time to put this particular myth to rest. Tweaking Charles Crawford's theme, our hominid ancestors probably got plenty of exercise from desperately trying to *avoid* saber-toothed cats, not from blatantly suicidal attempts to hunt them. Instead of Man the Hunter, we contend that Man the Hunted is a more accurate snapshot. For smallish bipedal primates, we envision a whole host of predators were licking their chops with anticipation.

Scavenger Hunt

As paleoanthropologists close in on their quarry, it may turn out to be a different beast from what they imaged.

Pat Shipman

In both textbooks and films, ancestral humans (hominids) have been portrayed as hunters. Small-brained, big-browed, upright, and usually mildly furry, early hominid males gaze with keen eyes across the gold savanna, searching for prey. Skillfully wielding a few crude stone tools, they kill and dismember everything from small gazelles to elephants, while females care for young and gather roots, tubers, and berries. The food is shared by group members at temporary camps. This familiar image of Man the Hunter has been bolstered by the finding of stone tools in association with fossil animal bones. But the role of hunting in early hominid life cannot be determined in the absence of more direct evidence.

I discovered one means of testing the hunting hypothesis almost by accident. In 1978, I began documenting the microscopic damage produced on bones by different events. I hoped to develop a diagnostic key for identifying the post-mortem history of specific fossil bones, useful for understanding how fossil assemblages were formed. Using a scanning electron microscope (SEM) because of its excellent resolution and superb depth of field, I inspected high-fidelity replicas of modern bones that had been subjected to known events or conditions. (I had to use replicas, rather than real bones, because specimens must fit into the SEM's small vacuum chamber.) I soon established that such common events as weathering, root etching, sedimentary abrasion, and carnivore chewing produced microscopically distinctive features.

In 1980, my SEM study took an unexpected turn. Richard Potts (now of Yale University), Henry Bunn (now of the University of Wisconsin at Madison), and I almost simultaneously found what appeared to be stone-tool cut marks on fossils from Olduvai Gorge, Tanzania, and Koobi Fora, Kenya. We were working almost side by side at the National Museums of Kenya, in Nairobi, where the fossils are stored. The possibility of cut marks was exciting, since both sites preserve some of the oldest known archaeological materials. Potts and I returned to the United States, manufactured some stone tools, and started "butchering" bones and joints begged from our local butchers. Under the SEM, replicas of these cut marks looked very different from replicas of carnivore tooth scratches, regardless of the species of carnivore or the type of tool involved. By comparing the marks on the fossils with our hundreds of modern bones of known history, we were able to demonstrate convincingly that hominids using stone tools had processed carcasses of many different animals nearly two million years ago. For the first time, there was a firm link between stone tools and at least some of the early fossil animal bones.

This initial discovery persuaded some paleoanthropologists that the hominid hunter scenario was correct. Potts and I were not so sure. Our study had shown that many of the cut-marked fossils also bore carnivore tooth marks and that some of the cut marks were in places we hadn't expected—on bones that bore little meat in life. More work was needed.

In addition to more data about the Olduvai cut marks and tooth marks, I needed specific information about the patterns of cut marks left by known hunters performing typical activities associated with hunting. If similar patterns occurred on the fossils, then the early hominids probably behaved similarly to more modern hunters; if the patterns were different, then the behavior was probably also different. Three activities related to hunting occur often enough in peoples around the world and leave consistent enough traces to be used for such a test.

First, human hunters systematically disarticulate their kills, unless the animals are small enough to be eaten on the spot. Disarticulation leaves cut marks in a predictable pattern on the skeleton. Such marks cluster near the major joints of the limbs: shoulder, elbow, carpal joint (wrist), hip, knee, and hock (ankle). Taking a carcass apart at the joints is much easier than breaking or cutting through bones. Disarticulation enables hunters to carry food back to a central place or camp, so that they can share it with others or cook it or even store it by placing portions in trees, away from the reach of carnivores. If early hominids were hunters who transported and shared their kills, disarticulation marks would occur near joints in frequencies comparable to those produced by modern human hunters.

Second, human hunters often butcher carcasses, in the sense of removing meat from the bones. Butchery marks are usually found on the shafts of bones from the upper part of the front or hind limb, since this is where the big muscle masses lie. Butchery may be carried out at the kill site—especially if the animal is very large and its bones very heavy—or it may take place at the base camp, during the process of sharing food with others. Compared with disarticulation, butchery leaves relatively few marks. It is hard for a hunter to locate an animal's joints without leaving cut marks on the bone. In contrast, it is easier to cut the meat away from the midshaft of the bone without making such marks. If early hominids shared their food, however, there ought to be a number of cut marks located on the midshaft of some fossil bones.

Finally, human hunters often remove skin or tendons from carcasses, to be used for clothing, bags, thongs, and so on. Hide or tendon must be separated from the bones in many areas where there is little flesh, such as the lower limb bones of pigs, giraffes, antelopes, and zebras. In such cases, it is difficult to cut the skin without leaving a cut mark on the bone. Therefore, one expects to find many more cut marks on such bones than on the flesh-covered bones of the upper part of the limbs.

Unfortunately, although accounts of butchery and disarticulation by modern human hunters are remarkably consistent, quantitative studies are rare. Further, virtually all modern hunter-gatherers use metal tools, which leave more cut marks than stone tools. For these reasons I hesitated to compare the fossil evidence with data on modern hunters. Fortunately, Diane Gifford of the University of California, Santa Cruz, and her colleagues had recently completed a quantitative study of marks and damage on thousands of antelope bones processed by Neolithic (Stone Age) hunters in Kenya some 2,300 years ago. The data from Prolonged Drift, as the site is called, were perfect for comparison with the Olduvai material.

Assisted by my technician, Jennie Rose, I carefully inspected more than 2,500 antelope bones from Bed I at Olduvai Gorge, which is dated to between 1.9 and 1.7 million years ago. We made high-fidelity replicas of every mark that we thought might be either a cut mark or a carnivore tooth mark. Back in the United States, we used the SEM to make positive identifications of the marks. (The replication and SEM inspection was time consuming, but necessary: only about half of the marks were correctly identified by eye or by light microscope.) I then compared the patterns of cut mark and tooth mark distributions on Olduvai fossils with those made by Stone Age hunters at Prolonged Drift.

By their location, I identified marks caused either by disarticulation or meat removal and then compared their frequencies with those from Prolonged Drift. More than 90 percent of the Neolithic marks in these two categories were from disarticulation, but to my surprise, only about 45 percent of the corresponding Olduvai cut marks were from disarticulation. This difference is too great to have occurred by chance; the Olduvai bones did not show the predicted pattern. In fact, the Olduvai cut marks attributable to meat removal and disarticulation showed essentially the same pattern of distribution as the carnivore tooth marks. Apparently, the early hominids were not regularly disarticulating carcasses. This finding casts serious doubt on the idea that early hominids carried their kills back to camp to share with others, since both transport and sharing are difficult unless carcasses are cut up.

When I looked for cut marks attributable to skinning or tendon removal, a more modern pattern emerged. On both the Neolithic and Olduvai bones, nearly 75 percent of all cut marks occurred on bones that bore little meat; these cut marks probably came from skinning. Carnivore tooth marks were much less common on such bones. Hominids were using carcasses as a source of skin and tendon. This made it seem more surprising that they disarticulated carcasses so rarely.

A third line of evidence provided the most tantalizing clue. Occasionally, sets of overlapping marks occur on the Olduvai fossils. Sometimes, these sets include both cut marks and carnivore tooth marks. Still more rarely, I could see under the SEM which mark had been made first, because its features were overlaid by those of the later mark, in much the same way as old tire tracks on a dirt road are obscured by fresh ones. Although only thirteen such sets of marks were found, in eight cases the hominids made the cut marks after the carnivores made their tooth marks. This finding suggested a new hypothesis. Instead of hunting for prey and leaving the remains behind for carnivores to scavenge, perhaps hominids were scavenging from the carnivores. This might explain the hominids' apparently unsystematic use of carcasses: they took what they could get, be it skin, tendon, or meat.

Man the Scavenger is not nearly as attractive an image as Man the Hunter, but it is worth examining. Actually, although hunting and scavenging are different ecological strategies, many mammals do both. The only pure scavengers alive in Africa today are vultures; not one of the modern African mammalian carnivores is a pure scavenger. Even spotted hyenas, which have massive, bone-crushing teeth well adapted for eating the bones left behind by others, only scavenge about 33 percent of their food. Other carnivores that scavenge when there are enough carcasses around include lions, leopards, striped hyenas, and jackals. Long-term behavioral studies suggest that these carnivores scavenge when they can and kill when they must. There are only two nearly pure predators, or hunters—the cheetah and the wild dog—that rarely, if ever, scavenge.

What are the costs and benefits of scavenging compared with those of predation? First of all, the scavenger avoids the task of making sure its meal is dead: a predator has already endured the energetically costly business of chasing or stalking animal after animal until one is killed. But while scavenging may be cheap, it's risky. Predators rarely give up their prey to scavengers without defending it. In such disputes, the larger animal, whether a scavenger or a predator, usually wins, although smaller animals in a pack may defeat a lone, larger animal. Both predators and scavengers suffer the dangers inherent in fighting for possession of a carcass. Smaller scavengers such as jackals or striped hyenas avoid disputes to some extent by specializing in darting in and removing a piece of a carcass without trying to take possession of the whole thing. These two strategies can be characterized as that of the bully or that of the sneak: bullies need to be large to be successful, sneaks need to be small and quick.

Because carcasses are almost always much rarer than live prey, the major cost peculiar to scavenging is that scavengers must survey much larger areas than predators to find food. They can travel slowly, since their "prey" is already dead, but endurance is important. Many predators specialize in speed at the expense of endurance, while scavengers do the opposite.

The more committed predators among the East African carnivores (wild dogs and cheetahs) can achieve great top speeds when running, although not for long. Perhaps as a consequence, these "pure" hunters enjoy a much higher success rate in hunting (about three-fourths of their chases end in kills) than any of the scavenger-hunters do (less than half of their chases are successful). Wild dogs and cheetahs are efficient hunters, but they are neither big enough nor efficient enough in their locomotion to make good scavengers. In fact, the cheetah's teeth are so specialized for meat slicing that they probably cannot withstand the stresses of bone crunching and carcass dismembering carried out by scavengers. Other carnivores are less successful at hunting, but have specializations of size, endurance, or (in the case of the hyenas) dentition that make successful scavenging possible. The small carnivores seem to have a somewhat higher hunting success rate than the large ones, which balances out their difficulties in asserting possession of carcasses.

In addition to endurance, scavengers need an efficient means of locating carcasses, which, unlike live animals, don't move or make noises. Vultures, for example, solve both problems by flying. The soaring, gliding flight of vultures expends much less energy than walking or cantering as performed by the part-time mammalian scavengers. Flight enables vultures to maintain a foraging radius two to three times larger than that of spotted hyenas, while providing a better vantage point. This explains why vultures can scavenge all of their food in the same habitat in which it is impossible for any mammal to be a pure scavenger. (In fact, many mammals learn where carcasses are located from the presence of vultures.)

Since mammals can't succeed as full-time scavengers, they must have another source of food to provide the bulk of their diet. The large carnivores rely on hunting large animals to obtain food when scavenging doesn't work. Their size enables them to defend a carcass against others. Since the small carnivores—jackals and striped hyenas—often can't defend carcasses successfully, most of their diet is composed of fruit and insects. When they do hunt, they usually prey on very small animals, such as rats or hares, that can be consumed in their entirety before the larger competitors arrive.

The ancient habitat associated with the fossils of Olduvai and Koobi Fora would have supported many herbivores and carnivores. Among the latter were two species of large saber-toothed cats, whose teeth show extreme adaptations for meat slicing. These were predators with primary access to carcasses. Since their teeth were unsuitable for bone crushing, the saber-toothed cats must have left behind many bones covered with scraps of meat, skin, and tendon. Were early hominids among the scavengers that exploited such carcasses?

All three hominid species that were present in Bed I times (*Homo habilis, Australopithecus africanus, A. robustus*) were adapted for habitual, upright bipedalism. Many anatomists see evidence that these hominids were agile tree climbers as well. Although upright bipedalism is a notoriously peculiar mode of locomotion, the adaptive value of which has been argued for years (See Matt Cartmill's article, "Four Legs Good, Two Legs Bad," *Natural History*, November 1983), there are three general points of agreement.

First, bipedal running is neither fast nor efficient compared to quadrupedal gaits. However, at moderate speeds of 2.5 to 3.5 miles per hour, bipedal *walking* is more energetically efficient than quadrupedal walking. Thus, bipedal walking is an excellent means of covering large areas slowly, making it an unlikely adaptation for a hunter but an appropriate and useful adaptation for a scavenger. Second, bipedalism elevates the head, thus improving the hominid's ability to spot items on the ground—an advantage both to scavengers and to those trying to avoid becoming a carcass. Combining bipedalism with agile tree climbing improves the vantage point still further. Third, bipedalism frees the hands from locomotive duties, making it possible to carry items. What would early hominids have carried? Meat makes a nutritious, easy-to-carry package; the problem is that carrying meat attracts scavengers. Richard Potts suggests that carrying stone tools or unworked stones for toolmaking to caches would be a more efficient and less dangerous activity under many circumstances.

In short, bipedalism is compatible with a scavenging strategy. I am tempted to argue that bipedalism evolved because it provided a substantial advantage to scavenging hominids. But I doubt hominids could scavenge effectively without tools, and bipedalism predates the oldest known stone tools by more than a million years.

Is there evidence that, like modern mammalian scavengers, early hominids had an alternative food source, such as either hunting or eating fruits and insects? My husband, Alan Walker, has shown that the microscopic wear on an animal's teeth reflects its diet. Early hominid teeth wear more like that of chimpanzees and other modern fruit eaters than that of carnivores. Apparently, early hominids ate mostly fruit, as the smaller, modern scavengers do. This accords with the estimated body weight of early hominids, which was only about forty to eighty pounds—less than that of any of the modern carnivores that combine scavenging and hunting but comparable to the striped hyena, which eats fruits and insects as well as meat.

Would early hominids have been able to compete for carcasses with other carnivores? They were too small to use a bully strategy, but if they scavenged in groups, a combined bully-sneak strategy might have been possible. Perhaps they were able to drive off a primary predator long enough to grab some meat, skin, or marrow-filled bone before relinquishing the carcass. The effectiveness of this strategy would have been vastly improved by using tools to remove meat or parts of limbs, a task at which hominid teeth are poor. As agile climbers, early hominids may have retreated into the trees to eat their scavenged trophies, thus avoiding competition from large terrestrial carnivores.

In sum, the evidence on cut marks, tooth wear, and bipedalism, together with our knowledge of scavenger adaptation in general, is consistent with the hypothesis that two million years ago hominids were scavengers rather than accomplished hunters. Animal carcasses, which contributed relatively little to the hominid diet, were not systematically cut up and transported for sharing at base camps. Man the Hunter may not have appeared until 1.5 to 0.7 million years ago, when we do see a shift toward omnivory, with a greater proportion of meat in the diet. This more heroic ancestor may have been *Homo erectus,* equipped with Acheulean-style stone tools and, increasingly, fire. If we wish to look further back, we may have to become accustomed to a less flattering image of our heritage.

Pat Shipman is an assistant professor in the Department of Cell Biology and Anatomy at The Johns Hopkins University School of Medicine.

The Scavenging of "Peking Man"

New evidence shows that a venerable cave was neither hearth nor home.

Noel T. Boaz and Russell L. Ciochon

China is filled with archaeological wonders, but few can rival the Peking Man Site at Zhoukoudian, which has been inscribed on UNESCO's World Heritage List. Located about thirty miles southwest of Beijing, the town of Zhoukoudian boasts several attractions, including ruins of Buddhist monasteries dating from the Ming Dynasty (1368–1644). But the town's main claim to fame is Longgushan, or Dragon Bone Hill, the site of the cave that yielded the first (and still the largest) cache of fossils of *Homo erectus pekinensis,* historically known as Peking man—a human relative who walked upright and whose thick skull bones and beetling brow housed a brain three-quarters the size of *H. sapiens*'s.

The remains of about forty-five individuals—more than half of them women and children—along with thousands of stone stools, debris from tool manufacturing, and thousands of animal bones, were contained within the hundred-foot-thick deposits that once completely filled the original cave. The task of excavation, initiated in 1921, was not completed until 1982. Some evidence unearthed at the site suggested that these creatures, who lived from about 600,000 to 300,000 years ago, had mastered the use of fire and practiced cannibalism. But despite years of excavation and analysis, little is certain about what occurred here long ago. In the past two years we have visited the cave site, reexamined the fossils, and carried out new tests in an effort to sort out the facts.

To most of the early excavators, such as anatomist Davidson Black, paleontologist Pierre Teilhard de Chardin, and archaeologist Henri Breuil, the likely scenario was that these particular early humans lived in the cave where their bones and stone tools were found and that the animal bones were the remains of meals, proof of their hunting expertise. Excavation exposed ash in horizontal patches within the deposits or in vertical patches along the cave's walls; these looked very much like the residue of hearths built up over time.

A more sensational view, first advanced by Breuil in 1929, was that the cave contained evidence of cannibalism. If the animal bones at the site were leftovers from the cave dwellers' hunting forays, he argued, why not the human bones as well? And skulls were conspicuous among the remains, suggesting to him that these might be the trophies of headhunters. Perhaps, Breuil even proposed, the dull-witted *H. erectus* had been prey to a contemporary, advanced cousin, some ancestral form of *H. sapiens.* Most paleoanthropologists rejected this final twist, but the cannibalism hypothesis received considerable support.

In the late 1930s Franz Weidenreich, an eminent German paleoanthropologist working at Peking Union Medical College, described the *H. erectus* remains in scientific detail. A trained anatomist and medical doctor, he concluded that some of the skulls showed signs of trauma, including scars and fresh injuries from attacks with both blunt and sharp instruments, such as clubs and stone tools. Most convincing to him and others was the systematic destruction of the skulls, apparently at the hands of humans who had decapitated the victims and then broken open the skull bases to retrieve the brains. Weidenreich also believed that the large longitudinal splits seen, for example, in some of the thighbones could only have been caused by humans and were probably made in an effort to extract the marrow.

Others held dissenting views. Chinese paleoanthropologist Pei Wenzhong, who codirected the early Zhoukoudian excavations, disagreed with Breuil and suggested in 1929 that the skulls had been chewed by hyenas. Some Western scientists also had doubts. In 1939 German paleontologist Helmuth Zapfe published his findings on the way hyenas at the Vienna zoo fed on cow bones. Echoing Pei's earlier observations, of which he was aware, Zapfe convincingly argued that many of the bones found at sites like Longgushan closely resembled modern bones broken up by hyenas. In fact, a new term, taphonomy, was coined shortly thereafter for the field Zapfe pioneered: the study of how, after death, animal and plant remains become modified, moved, buried, and fossilized. Franz Weidenreich soon revised his prior interpretation of several *H. erectus* bones whose condition he had attributed to human cannibalistic activity, but he continued to argue that the long-bone splinters and broken skull bases must have resulted from human action.

Following disruptions in fieldwork during World War II (including the loss of all the *H. erectus* fossils collected at Longgushan up to that time, leaving only the casts that had been made of them), Chinese paleoanthropologists resumed investigation of the site. While rejecting the idea of cannibalism, they continued to look upon the cave as a shelter used by early humans equipped with stone tools and fire, as reflected in the title of paleoanthropologist Jia Lampo's book *The Cave Home of Peking Man,* published in 1975.

About this time, Western scientists began to appreciate and develop the field of taphonomy. A few scholars, notably U.S. archaeologist Lewis R. Binford, then reexamined the Longgushan evidence, but only from a distance, concluding that the burning of accumulated bat or bird guano may have accounted for the ash in the cave. With the founding in 1993 of the Zhoukoudian International Paleoanthropological Research Center at Beijing's Institute of Vertebrate Paleontology and Paleoanthropology, a new era of multidisciplinary and international research at Longgushan began. At the institute, we have been able to collaborate with paleontologists Xu Qinqi and Liu Jinyi and with other scholars in a reassessment of the excavations.

It looked as if *H. erectus* had smashed open the skulls to cannibalize the brains.

One of taphonomy's maxims is that the most common animals at a fossil site and/or the animals whose remains there are the most complete are most likely the ones to have inhabited the area in life. Standing in the Beijing institute amid row after row of museum cases filled with mammal fossils from the cave, we were immediately struck by how few belonged to *H. erectus*—perhaps only 0.5 percent. This suggests that most of the time, this species did not live in the cave. Furthermore, none of the *H. erectus* skeletons is complete. There is a dearth of limb bones, especially of forearms, hands, lower leg bones, and feet—indicating to us that these individuals died somewhere else and that their partial remains were subsequently brought to the cave. But how?

The answer was suggested by the remains of the most common and complete animal skeletons in the cave deposit: those of the giant hyena, *Pachycrocuta brevirostris.* Had *H. erectus,* instead of being the mighty hunters of anthropological lore, simply met the same ignominious fate as the deer and other prey species in the cave? This possibility, which had been raised much earlier by Pei and Zapfe, drew backing from subsequent studies by others. In 1970, for example, British paleontologist Anthony J. Sutcliffe reported finding a modern hyena den in Kenya that contained a number of human bones, including skulls, which the animals had apparently obtained from a nearby hospital cemetery. In the same year, South African zoologist C. K. Brain published the findings of his extensive feeding experiments with captive carnivores, akin to those of Zapfe three decades earlier. One of Brain's conclusions was that carnivores tend to chew up and destroy the ends of the extremities, leaving, in the case of primates, very little of the hands and feet.

To test the giant hyena hypothesis, we examined all the fossil casts and the few actual fossils of *H. erectus* from Longgushan. We looked for both carnivore bite marks and the shallow, V-shaped straight cuts that would be left by stone tools (although we realized that cut marks would probably not be detectable on the casts). We also analyzed each sample's fracture patterns. Breaks at right angles indicate damage long after death, when the bone is fossilized or fossilizing; fractures in fresh bone tend to be irregular, following natural structural lines. Breakage due to crushing by cave rocks is usually massive, and the fracture marks characteristically match rock fragments pushed into the bone.

We were surprised by our findings. Two-thirds of Longgushan's *H. erectus* fossils display what we are convinced are one or more of the following kinds of damage: puncture marks from a carnivore's large, pointed front teeth, most likely the canines of a hyena; long, scraping bite marks, typified by U-shaped grooves along the bone; and fracture patterns comparable to those created by modern hyenas when they chew bone. Moreover, we feel that the longitudinal splitting of large bones—a feature that Weidenreich considered evidence of human activity—can also be attributed to a hyena, especially one the size of the extinct *Pachycrocuta,* the largest hyena known, whose preferred prey was giant elk and woolly rhinoceros. One of the *H. erectus* bones, part of a femur, even reveals telltale surface etchings from stomach acid, indicating it was swallowed and then disgorged.

The pattern of damage on some of the skulls sheds light on how hyenas may have handled them. Bite marks on the brow ridge above the eyes indicate that this protrusion had been grasped and bitten by an animal in the course of chewing off the face. Most animals' facial bones are quite thin, and modern hyenas frequently attack or bite the face first; similarly, their ancient predecessors would likely have discovered this vulnerable region in *H. erectus.* Practically no such facial bones, whose structure is known to us from discoveries at other sites, have been found in the Longgushan cave.

The rest of the skull is a pretty tough nut to crack, however, even for *Pachycrocuta,* since it consists of bones half again as thick as those of a modern human, with massive mounds called tori above the eyes and ears and around the back of the skull. Puncture marks and elongated bite marks around the skulls reveal that the hyenas gnawed at and grappled with them, probably in an effort to crack open the cranium and consume the tasty, lipid-rich brain. We concluded that the hyenas probably succeeded best by chewing through the face, gaining a purchase on the bone surrounding the foramen magnum (the opening in the cranium where the spinal cord enters), and then gnawing away until the skull vault cracked apart or the opening was large enough to expose the brain. This is how we believe the skull bases were destroyed—not by the actions of cannibalistic *H. erectus.*

Two-thirds of the fossils show bite marks or fractures inflicted by carnivores.

We know from geological studies of the cave that the animal bones found there could not have been washed in by rains or carried in by streams: the sediments in which the bones are found are either very fine-grained—indicating gradual deposition by wind or slow-moving water—or they contain angular, sharp-edged shards that would not have survived in a stream or flood. Some of the bones may have belonged to animals that died inside the cave during the course of living in it or frequenting it. Other bones were probably brought in and chewed on by hyenas and other carnivores.

Cut marks we observed on several mammal bones from the cave suggest that early humans did sometimes make use of Longgushan, even if they were not responsible for accumulating most of the bones. Stone tools left near the cave entrance also attest to their presence. Given its long history, the cave may have served a variety of occupants or at times have been configured as several separate, smaller shelters. Another possibility is that, in a form of time-sharing, early humans ventured partway into the cave during the day to scavenge on what the hyenas had not eaten and to find temporary shelter. They may not have realized that the animals, which roamed at twilight and at night, were sleeping in the dark recesses a couple of hundred feet away.

What about the ash in the cave, which has been taken as evidence that *H. erectus* used fire? Recently published work by geochemist Steve Weiner and his team at the Weizmann Institute of Science in Israel suggests that the fires were not from hearths. In detailed studies of the ash levels, they discovered no silica-rich layers, which would be left by the burning of wood. Wood (as well as grass and leaves) contains silica particles known as phytoliths—heat-resistant residues that are ubiquitous in archaeological hearth sites. The results indicate that fire was present in the cave but that its controlled use in hearths was not part of the story.

Still, a human hand may somehow be implicated in these fires. One possibility we are exploring in the next phase of our research is that Longgushan was a place where *Pachycrocuta* and *H. erectus* confronted each other as the early humans sought to snatch some of the meat brought back to the cave by the large hyenas. *Pachycrocuta* would have had the home court advantage, but *H. erectus,* perhaps using fire to hold the carnivore at bay, could have quickly sliced off slivers of meat. Although today we might turn up our noses at such carrion, it may have been a dependable and highly prized source of food during the Ice Age.

Hard Times Among the Neanderthals

Although life was difficult, these prehistoric people may not have been as exclusively brutish as usually supposed.

ERIK TRINKAUS

Throughout the century that followed the discovery in 1856 of the first recognized human fossil remains in the Neander Valley (*Neanderthal* in German) near Düsseldorf, Germany, the field of human paleontology has been beset with controversies. This has been especially true of interpretations of the Neanderthals, those frequently maligned people who occupied Europe and the Near East from about 100,000 years ago until the appearance of anatomically modern humans about 35,000 years ago.

During the last two decades, however, a number of fossil discoveries, new analyses of previously known remains, and more sophisticated models for interpreting subtle anatomical differences have led to a reevaluation of the Neanderthals and their place in human evolution.

This recent work has shown that the often quoted reconstruction of the Neanderthals as semierect, lumbering caricatures of humanity is inaccurate. It was based on faulty anatomical interpretations that were reinforced by the intellectual biases of the turn of the century. Detailed comparisons of Neanderthal skeletal remains with those of modern humans have shown that there is nothing in Neanderthal anatomy that conclusively indicates locomotor, manipulative, intellectual, or linguistic abilities inferior to those of modern humans. Neanderthals have therefore been added to the same species as ourselves—*Homo sapiens*—although they are usually placed in their own subspecies, *Homo sapiens neanderthalensis.*

Despite these revisions, it is apparent that there are significant anatomical differences between the Neanderthals and present-day humans. If we are to understand the Neanderthals, we must formulate hypotheses as to why they evolved from earlier humans about 100,000 years ago in Europe and the Near East, and why they were suddenly replaced about 35,000 years ago by peoples largely indistinguishable from ourselves. We must determine, therefore, the behavioral significance of the anatomical differences between the Neanderthals and other human groups, since it is patterns of successful behavior that dictate the direction of natural selection for a species.

In the past, behavioral reconstructions of the Neanderthals and other prehistoric humans have been based largely on archeological data. Research has now reached the stage at which behavioral interpretations from the archeological record can be significantly supplemented by analyses of the fossils themselves. These analyses promise to tell us a considerable amount about the ways of the Neanderthals and may eventually help us to determine their evolutionary fate.

One of the most characteristic features of the Neanderthals is the exaggerated massiveness of their trunk and limb bones. All of the preserved bones suggest a strength seldom attained by modern humans. Furthermore, not only is this robustness present among the adult males, as one might expect, but it is also evident in the adult females, adolescents, and even children. The bones themselves reflect this hardiness in several ways.

First, the muscle and ligament attachment areas are consistently enlarged and strongly marked. This implies large, highly developed muscles and ligaments capable of generating and sustaining great mechanical stress. Secondly, since the skeleton must be capable of supporting these levels of stress, which are frequently several times as great as body weight, the enlarged attachments for muscles and ligaments are associated with arm and leg bone shafts that have been reinforced. The shafts of all of the arm and leg bones are modified tubular structures that have to absorb stress from bending and twisting without fracturing. When the habitual load on a bone increases, the bone responds by laying down more bone in those areas under the greatest stress.

In addition, musculature and body momentum generate large forces across the joints. The cartilage, which covers joint surfaces, can be relatively easily overworked to the point where it degenerates, as is indicated by the prevalence of arthritis in joints subjected to significant wear and tear over the years. When the surface area of a joint is increased, the force per unit area of cartilage is reduced, decreasing the pressure on the cartilage.

Most of the robustness of Neanderthal arm bones is seen in muscle and ligament attachments. All of the muscles that go

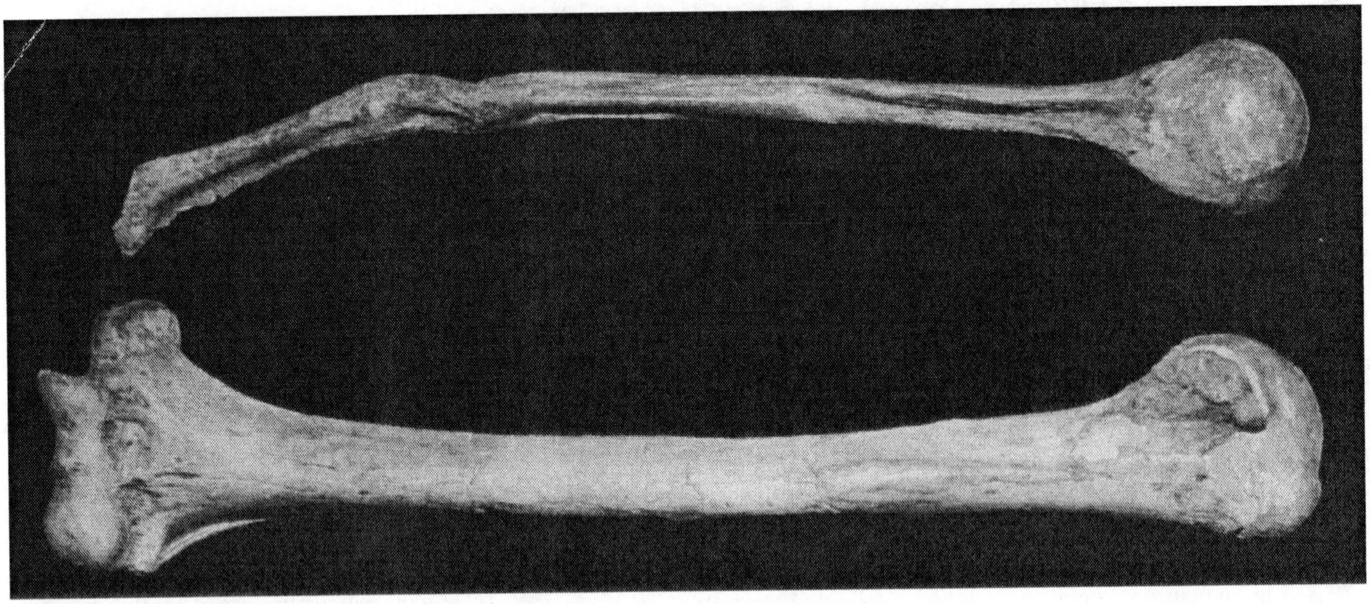

Photograph by Erik Trinkaus

Diagonal lines on these two arm bones from Shanidar 1 are healed fractures. The bottom bone is normal. That on the top is atrophied and has a pathological tip, caused by either amputation or an improperly healed elbow fracture.

from the trunk or the shoulder blade to the upper end of the arm show massive development. This applies in particular to the muscles responsible for powerful downward movements of the arm and, to a lesser extent, to muscles that stabilize the shoulder during vigorous movements.

Virtually every major muscle or ligament attachment on the hand bones is clearly marked by a large roughened area or a crest, especially the muscles used in grasping objects. In fact, Neanderthal hand bones frequently have clear bony crests, where on modern human ones it is barely possible to discern the attachment of the muscle on the dried bone.

In addition, the flattened areas on the ends of the fingers, which provide support for the nail and the pulp of the finger tip, are enormous among the Neanderthals. These areas on the thumb and the index and middle fingers are usually two to three times as large as those of similarly sized modern human hands. The overall impression is one of arms to rival those of the mightiest blacksmith.

Neanderthal legs are equally massive; their strength is best illustrated in the development of the shafts of the leg bones. Modern human thigh and shin bones possess characteristic shaft shapes adapted to the habitual levels and directions of the stresses acting upon them. The shaft shapes of the Neanderthals are similar to those in modern humans, but the cross-sectional areas of the shafts are much greater. This implies significantly higher levels of stress.

Further evidence of the massiveness of Neanderthal lower limbs is provided by the dimensions of their knee and ankle joints. All of these are larger than in modern humans, especially with respect to the overall lengths of the bones.

The development of their limb bones suggests that the Neanderthals frequently generated high levels of mechanical stress in their limbs. Since most mechanical stress in the body is produced by body momentum and muscular contraction, it appears that the Neanderthals led extremely active lives. It is hard to conceive of what could have required such exertion, especially since the maintenance of vigorous muscular activity would have required considerable expenditure of energy. That level of energy expenditure would undoubtedly have been maladaptive had it not been necessary for survival.

The available evidence from the archeological material associated with the Neanderthals is equivocal on this matter. Most of the archeological evidence at Middle Paleolithic sites concerns stone tool technology and hunting activities. After relatively little change in technology during the Middle Paleolithic (from about 100,000 years to 35,000 years before the present), the advent of the Upper Paleolithic appears to have brought significant technological advances. This transition about 35,000 years ago is approximately coincident with the replacement of the Neanderthals by the earliest anatomically modern humans. However, the evidence for a significant change in hunting patterns is not evident in the animal remains left behind. Yet even if a correlation between the robustness of body build and the level of hunting efficiency could be demonstrated, it would only explain the ruggedness of the Neanderthal males. Since hunting is exclusively or at least predominantly a male activity among humans, and since Neanderthal females were in all respects as strongly built as the males, an alternative explanation is required for the females.

Some insight into why the Neanderthals consistently possessed such massiveness is provided by a series of partial skeletons of Neanderthals from the Shanidar Cave in northern Iraq. These fossils were excavated between 1953 and 1960 by anthropologist Ralph Solecki of Columbia University and have

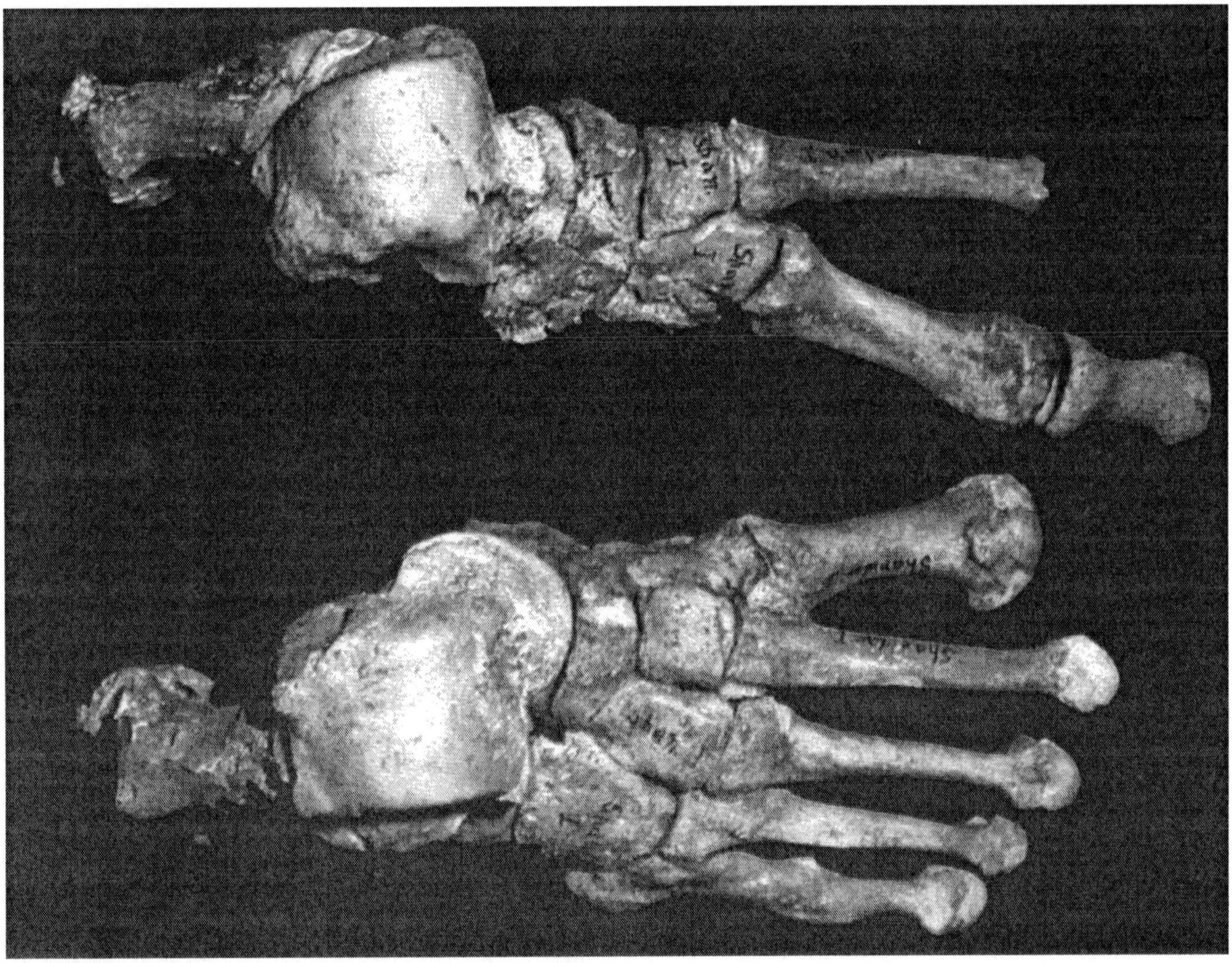

Photograph by Erik Trinkaus

The ankle and big toe of Shanidar 1's bottom foot show evidence of arthritis, which suggests an injury to those parts. The top foot is normal though incomplete.

been studied principally by T. Dale Stewart, an anthropologist at the Smithsonian Institution, and myself. The most remarkable aspect of these skeletons is the number of healed injuries they contain. Four of the six reasonably complete adult skeletons show evidence of trauma during life.

The identification of traumatic injury in human fossil remains has plagued paleontologists for years. There has been a tendency to consider any form of damage to a fossil as conclusive evidence of prehistoric violence between humans if it resembles the breakage patterns caused by a direct blow with a heavy object. Hence a jaw with the teeth pushed in or a skull with a depressed fracture of the vault would be construed to indicate blows to the head.

The central problem with these interpretations is that they ignore the possibility of damage after death. Bone is relatively fragile, especially as compared with the rock and other sediment in which it is buried during fossilization. Therefore when several feet of sediment caused compression around fossil remains, the fossils will almost always break. In fact, among the innumerable cases of suggested violence between humans cited over the years, there are only a few exceptional examples that cannot be readily explained as the result of natural geologic forces acting after the death and burial of the individual.

One of these examples is the trauma of the left ninth rib of the skeleton of Shanidar 3, a partially healed wound inflicted by a sharp object. The implement cut obliquely across the top of the ninth rib and probably pierced the underlying lung. Shanidar 3 almost certainly suffered a collapsed left lung and died several days or weeks later, probably as a result of secondary complications. This is deduced from the presence of bony spurs and increased density of the bone around the cut.

The position of the wound on the rib, the angle of the incision, and the cleanness of the cut make it highly unlikely that the injury was accidentally inflicted. In fact, the incision is almost exactly what would have resulted if Shanidar 3 had been stabbed in the side by a right-handed adversary in face-to-face

Photograph by Erik Trinkaus

The scar on the left ninth rib of Shanidar 3 is a partially healed wound inflicted by a sharp object. This wound is one of the few examples of trauma caused by violence.

conflict. This would therefore provide conclusive evidence of violence between humans, the *only* evidence so far found of such violence among the Neanderthals.

In most cases, however, it is impossible to determine from fossilized remains the cause of an individual's death. The instances that can be positively identified as prehistoric traumatic injury are those in which the injury was inflicted prior to death and some healing took place. Shortly after an injury to bone, whether a cut or a fracture, the damaged bone tissue is resorbed by the body and new bone tissue is laid down around the injured area. As long as irritation persists, new bone is deposited, creating a bulge or spurs of irregular bone extending into the soft tissue. If the irritation ceases, the bone will slowly re-form so as to approximate its previous, normal condition. However, except for superficial injuries or those sustained during early childhood, some trace of damage persists for the life of the individual.

In terms of trauma, the most impressive of the Shanidar Neanderthals is the first adult discovered, known as Shanidar 1. This individual suffered a number of injuries, some of which may be related. On the right forehead there are scars from minor surface injuries, probably superficial scalp cuts. The outside of the left eye socket sustained a major blow that partially collapsed that part of the bony cavity, giving it a flat rather than a rounded contour. This injury possibly caused loss of sight in the left eye and pathological alterations of the right side of the body.

Shanidar 1's left arm is largely preserved and fully normal. The right arm, however, consists of a highly atrophied but otherwise normal collarbone and shoulder blade and a highly abnormal upper arm bone shaft. That shaft is atrophied to a fraction of the diameter of the left one but retains most of its original length. Furthermore, the lower end of the right arm bone has a healed fracture of the atrophied shaft and an irregular, pathological tip. The arm was apparently either intentionally amputated just above the elbow or fractured at the elbow and never healed.

This abnormal condition of the right arm does not appear to be a congenital malformation, since the length of the bone is close to the estimated length of the normal left upper arm bone. If, however, the injury to the left eye socket also affected the left side of the brain, directly or indirectly, by disrupting the blood supply to part of the brain, the result could have been partial paralysis of the right side. Motor and sensory control areas for the right side are located on the left side of the brain, slightly behind the left eye socket. This would explain the atrophy of the whole right arm since loss of nervous stimulation will rapidly lead to atrophy of the affected muscles and bone.

The abnormality of the right arm of Shanidar 1 is paralleled to a lesser extent in the right foot. The right ankle joint shows extensive arthritic degeneration, and one of the major joints of the inner arch of the right foot has been completely reworked by arthritis. The left foot, however, is totally free of pathology. Arthritis from normal stress usually affects both lower limbs equally; this degeneration therefore suggests that the arthritis in the right foot is a secondary result of an injury, perhaps a sprain, that would not otherwise be evident on skeletal remains. This conclusion is supported by a healed fracture of the right fifth instep bone, which makes up a major portion of the outer arch of the foot. These foot pathologies may be tied into the damage to the left side of the skull; partial paralysis of the right side would certainly weaken the leg and make it more susceptible to injury.

The trauma evident on the other Shanidar Neanderthals is relatively minor by comparison. Shanidar 3, the individual who died of the rib wound, suffered debilitating arthritis of the right ankle and neighboring foot joints, but lacks any evidence of pathology on the left foot; this suggests a superficial injury similar to the one sustained by Shanidar 1. Shanidar 4 had a healed broken rib. Shanidar 5 received a transverse blow across the left forehead that left a large scar on the bone but does not appear to have affected the brain.

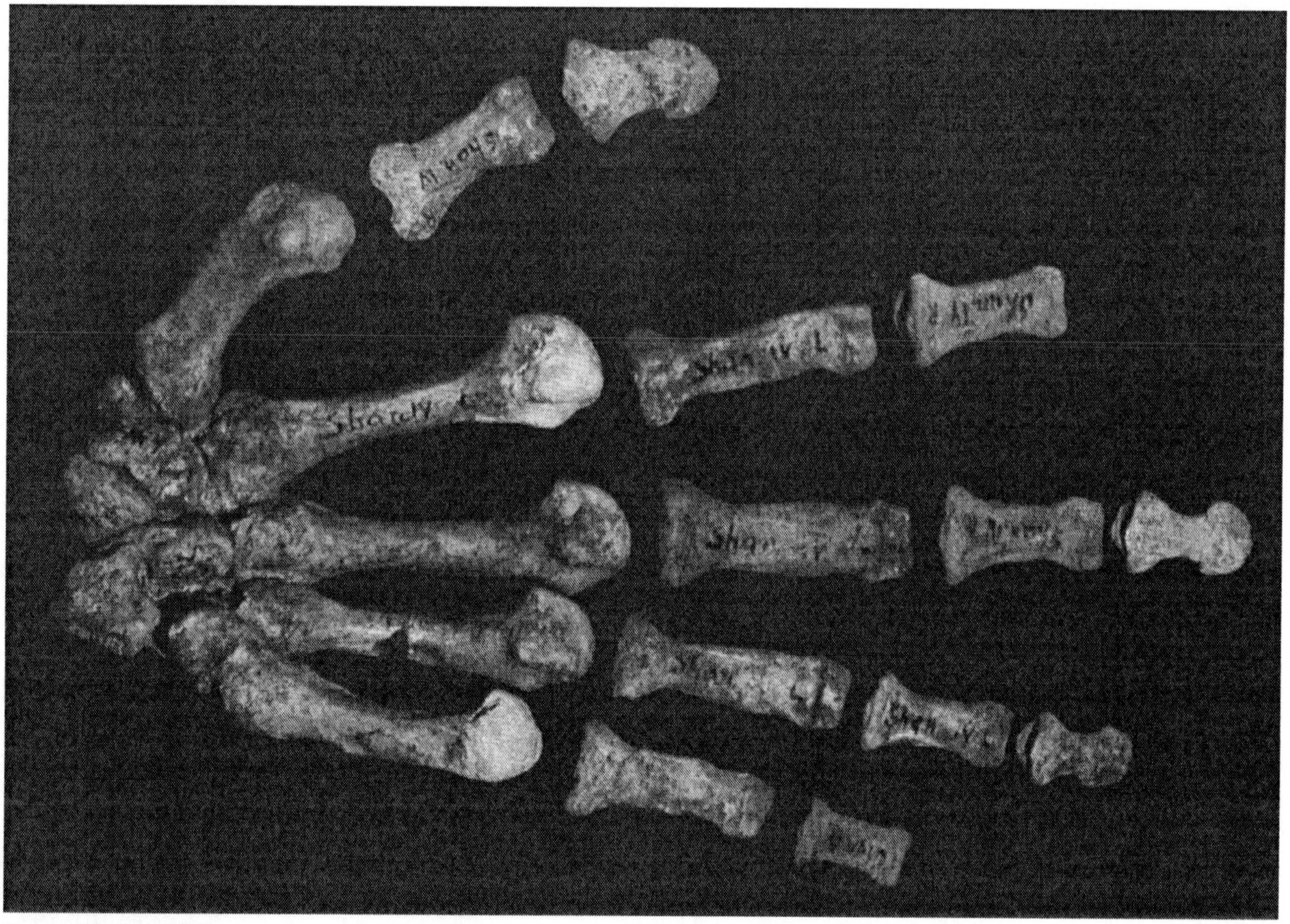

Photograph by Erik Trinkaus

The right hand of Shanidar 4 demonstrates the enlarged finger tips and strong muscle markings characteristic of Neanderthal hands.

None of these injuries necessarily provides evidence of deliberate violence among the Neanderthals; all of them could have been accidentally self-inflicted or accidentally caused by another individual. In either case, the impression gained of the Shanidar Neanderthals is of a group of invalids. The crucial variable, however, appears to be age. All four of these individuals died at relatively advanced ages, probably between 40 and 60 years (estimating the age at death for Neanderthals beyond the age of 25 is extremely difficult); they therefore had considerable time to accumulate the scars of past injuries. Shanidar 2 and 6, the other reasonably complete Shanidar adults, lack evidence of trauma, but they both died young, probably before reaching 30.

Other Neanderthal remains, all from Europe, exhibit the same pattern. Every fairly complete skeleton of an elderly adult shows evidence of traumatic injuries. The original male skeleton from the Neander Valley had a fracture just below the elbow of the left arm, which probably limited movement of that arm for life. The "old man" from La Chapelle-aux-Saints, France, on whom most traditional reconstructions of the Neanderthals have been based, suffered a broken rib. La Ferrassi 1, the old adult male from La Ferrassie, France, sustained a severe injury to the right hip, which may have impaired his mobility.

In addition, several younger specimens and ones of uncertain age show traces of trauma. La Quina 5, the young adult female from La Quina, France, was wounded on her right upper arm. A young adult from Sala, Czechoslovakia, was superficially wounded on the right forehead just above the brow. And an individual of unknown age and sex from the site of Krapina, Yugoslavia, suffered a broken forearm, in which the bones never reunited after the fracture.

The evidence suggests several things. First, life for the Neanderthals was rigorous. If they lived through childhood and early adulthood, they did so bearing the scars of a harsh and dangerous life. Furthermore, this incident of trauma correlates with the massiveness of the Neanderthals; a life style that so consistently involved injury would have required considerable strength and fortitude for survival.

There is, however, another, more optimistic side to this. The presence of so many injuries in a prehistoric human group, many of which were debilitating and sustained years before death, shows that individuals were taken care of long after their economic usefulness to the social group had ceased. It is perhaps no accident that among the Neanderthals, for the first time in human history, people lived to a comparatively old age. We also find among the Neanderthals the first intentional burials of the dead, some of which involved offerings. Despite the hardships of their life style, the Neanderthals apparently had a deep-seated respect and concern for each other.

Taken together, these different pieces of information paint a picture of life among the Neanderthals that, while harsh and dangerous, was not without personal security. Certainly the hardships the Neanderthals endured were beyond those commonly experienced in the prehistoric record of human caring and respect as well as of violence between individuals. Perhaps for these reasons, despite their physical appearance, the Neanderthals should be considered the first modern humans.

The Gift *of* Gab

Grooves and holes in fossil skulls may reveal when our ancestors began to speak. The big question, though, is what drove them to it?

MATT CARTMILL

People can talk. Other animals can't. They can all communicate in one way or another—to lure mates, at the very least—but their whinnies and wiggles don't do the jobs that language does. The birds and beasts can use their signals to attract, threaten, or alert each other, but they can't ask questions, strike bargains, tell stories, or lay out a plan of action.

Those skills make *Homo sapiens* a uniquely successful, powerful, and dangerous mammal. Other creatures' signals carry only a few limited kinds of information about what's happening at the moment, but language lets us tell each other in limitless detail about what used to be or will be or might be. Language lets us get vast numbers of big, smart fellow primates all working together on a single task—building the Great Wall of China or fighting World War II or flying to the moon. It lets us construct and communicate the gorgeous fantasies of literature and the profound fables of myth. It lets us cheat death by pouring out our knowledge, dreams, and memories into younger people's minds. And it does powerful things for us inside our own minds because we do a lot of our thinking by talking silently to ourselves. Without language, we would be only a sort of upright chimpanzee with funny feet and clever hands. With it, we are the self-possessed masters of the planet.

How did such a marvelous adaptation get started? And if it's so marvelous, why hasn't any other species come up with anything similar? These may be the most important questions we face in studying human evolution. They are also the least understood. But in the past few years, linguists and anthropologists have been making some breakthroughs, and we are now beginning to have a glimmering of some answers.

Could Neanderthals talk? They seem to have had nimble tongues, but some scientists think the geometry of their throats prevented them from making many clear vowel sounds.

We can reasonably assume that by at least 30,000 years ago people were talking—at any rate, they were producing carvings, rock paintings, and jewelry, as well as ceremonial graves containing various goods. These tokens of art and religion are high-level forms of symbolic behavior, and they imply that the everyday symbol-handling machinery of human language must have been in place then as well.

Language surely goes back further than that, but archeologists don't agree on just how far. Some think that earlier, more basic human behaviors—hunting in groups, tending fires, making tools—also demanded language. Others think these activities are possible without speech. Chimpanzees, after all, hunt communally, and with human guidance they can learn to tend fires and chip flint.

Paleontologists have pored over the fossil bones of our ancient relatives in search of evidence for speech abilities. Because the most crucial organ for language is the brain, they have looked for signs in the impressions left by the brain on the inner surfaces of fossil skulls, particularly impressions made by parts of the brain called speech areas because damage to them can impair a person's ability to talk or understand language. Unfortunately, it turns out that you can't tell whether a fossil hominid was able to talk simply by looking at brain impressions on the inside of its skull. For one thing, the fit between the brain and the bony braincase is loose in people and other large mammals, and so the impressions we derive from fossil skulls are disappointingly fuzzy. Moreover, we now know that language functions are not tightly localized but spread across many parts of the brain.

Faced with these obstacles, researchers have turned from the brain to other organs used in speech, such as the throat and tongue. Some have measured the fossil skulls and jaws of early hominids, tried to reconstruct the shape of their vocal tracts, and then applied the laws of acoustics to them to see whether they might have been capable of producing human speech.

All mammals produce their vocal noises by contracting muscles that compress the rib cage. The air in the lungs is driven out through the windpipe to the larynx, where it flows between

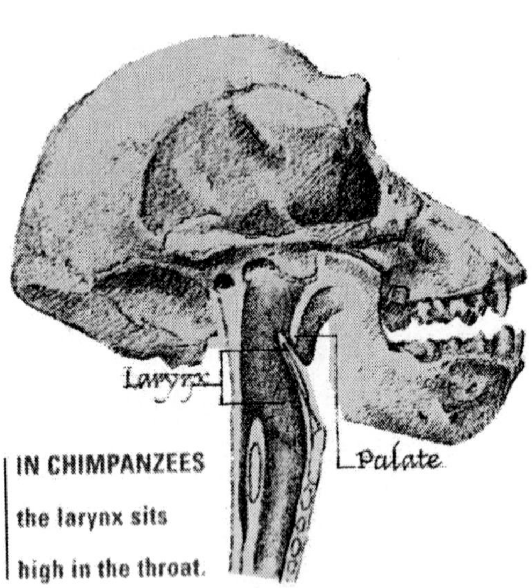

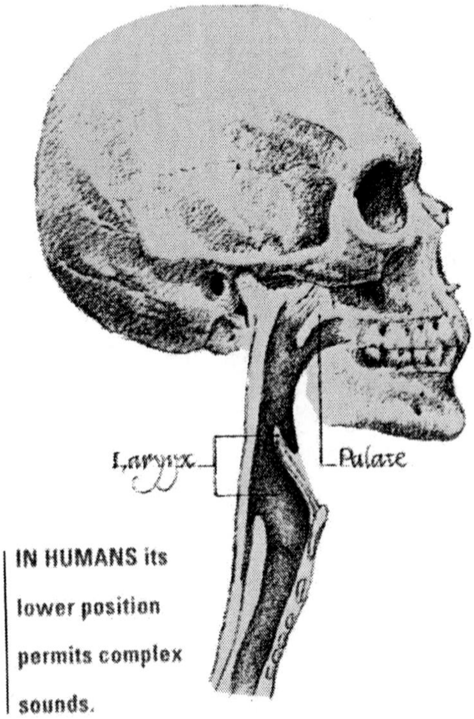

Illustrations by Dugald Stermer

the vocal cords. More like flaps than cords, these structures vibrate in the breeze, producing a buzzing sound that becomes the voice. The human difference lies in what happens to the air after it gets past the vocal cords.

In people, the larynx lies well below the back of the tongue, and most of the air goes out through the mouth when we talk. We make only a few sounds by exhaling through the nose—for instance, nasal consonants like *m* or *n,* or the so-called nasal vowels in words like the French *bon* and *vin.* But in most mammals, including apes, the larynx sticks farther up behind the tongue, into the back of the nose, and most of the exhaled air passes out through the nostrils. Nonhuman mammals make mostly nasal sounds as a result.

At some point in human evolution the larynx must have descended from its previous heights, and this change had some serious drawbacks. It put the opening of the windpipe squarely in the path of descending food, making it dangerously easy for us to choke to death if a chunk of meat goes down the wrong way—something that rarely happens to a dog or a cat. Why has evolution exposed us to this danger?

Some scientists think that the benefits outweighed the risks, because lowering the larynx improved the quality of our vowels and made speech easier to understand. The differences between vowels are produced mainly by changing the size and shape of the airway between the tongue and the roof of the mouth. When the front of the tongue almost touches the palate, you get the *ee* sound in *beet;* when the tongue is humped up high in the back (and the lips are rounded), you get the *oo* sound in *boot,* and so on. We are actually born with a somewhat apelike throat, including a flat tongue and a larynx lying high up in the neck, and this arrangement makes a child's vowels sound less clearly separated from each other than an adult's.

Philip Lieberman of Brown University thinks that an apelike throat persisted for some time in our hominid ancestors. His studies of fossil jaws and skulls persuade him that a more modern throat didn't evolve until some 500,000 years ago, and that some evolutionary lines in the genus *Homo* never did acquire modern vocal organs. Lieberman concludes that the Neanderthals, who lived in Europe until perhaps 25,000 years ago, belonged to a dead-end lineage that never developed our range of vowels, and that their speech—if they had any at all—would have been harder to understand than ours. Apparently, being easily understood wasn't terribly important to them—not important enough, at any rate, to outweigh the risk of inhaling a chunk of steak into a lowered larynx. This suggests that vocal communication wasn't as central to their lives as it is to ours.

Many paleoanthropologists, especially those who like to see Neanderthals as a separate species, accept this story. Others have their doubts. But the study of other parts of the skeleton in fossil hominids supports some of Lieberman's conclusions. During the 1980s a nearly complete skeleton of a young *Homo* male was recovered from 1.5-million-year-old deposits in northern Kenya. Examining the vertebrae attached to the boy's rib cage, the English anatomist Ann MacLarnon discovered that his spinal cord was proportionately thinner in this region than it is in people today. Since that part of the cord controls most of the muscles that drive air in and out of the lungs, MacLarnon concluded that the youth may not have had the kind of precise neural control over breathing movements that is needed for speech.

This year my colleague Richard Kay, his student Michelle Balow, and I were able to offer some insights from yet another part of the hominid body. The tongue's movements are controlled almost solely by a nerve called the hypoglossal. In its course from the brain to the tongue, this nerve passes through a hole in the skull, and Kay, Balow, and I found that this bony canal is relatively big in modern humans—about twice as big in cross section as that of a like-size chimpanzee. Our larger canal presumably reflects a bigger hypoglossal nerve, giving us the precise control over tongue movements that we need for speech.

We also measured this hole in the skulls of a number of fossil hominids. Australopithecines have small canals like those of apes, suggesting that they couldn't talk. But later *Homo* skulls, beginning with a 400,000-year-old skull from Zambia, all have big, humanlike hypoglossal canals. These are also the skulls that were the first to house brains as big as our own. On these counts our work supports Lieberman's ideas. We disagree only on the matter of Neanderthals. While he claims their throats couldn't have produced human speech, we find that their skulls also had human-size canals for the hypoglossal nerve, suggesting that they could indeed talk.

The verdict is still out on the language abilities of Neanderthals. I tend to think they must have had fully human language. After all, they had brains larger than those of most humans.

In short, several lines of evidence suggest that neither the australopithecines nor the early, small-brained species of *Homo* could talk. Only around half a million years ago did the first big-brained *Homo* evolve language. The verdict is still out on the language abilities of Neanderthals. I tend to think that they must have had fully human language. After all, they had brains larger than those of most modern humans, made elegant stone tools, and knew how to use fire. But if Lieberman and his friends are right about those vowels, Neanderthals may have sounded something like the Swedish chef on *The Muppet Show.*

We are beginning to get some idea of when human language originated, but the fossils can't tell us how it got started, or what the intermediate stages between animal calls and human language might have been like. When trying to understand the origin of a trait that doesn't fossilize, it's sometimes useful to look for similar but simpler versions of it in other creatures living today. With luck, you can find a series of forms that suggest how simple primitive makeshifts could have evolved into more complex and elegant versions. This is how Darwin attacked the problem of the evolution of the eye. Earlier biologists had pointed to the human eye as an example of a marvelously perfect organ that must have been specially created all at once in its final form by God. But Darwin pointed out that animal eyes exist in all stages of complexity, from simple skin cells that can detect only the difference between light and darkness, to pits lined with such cells, and so on all the way to the eyes of people and other vertebrates. This series, he argued, shows how the human eye could have evolved from simpler precursors by gradual stages.

Can we look to other animals to find simpler precursors of language? It seems unlikely. Scientists have sought experimental evidence of language in dolphins and chimpanzees, thus far without success. But even if we had no experimental studies, common sense would tell us that the other animals can't have languages like ours. If they had, we would be in big trouble because they would organize against us. They don't. Outside of Gary Larson's *Far Side* cartoons and George Orwell's *Animal Farm,* farmers don't have to watch their backs when they visit the cowshed. There are no conspiracies among cows, or even among dolphins and chimpanzees. Unlike human slaves or prisoners, they never plot rebellions against their oppressors.

Even if language as a whole has no parallels in animal communication, might some of its peculiar properties be foreshadowed among the beasts around us? If so, that might tell us something about how and in what order these properties were acquired. One such property is reference. Most of the units of human languages refer to things—to individuals (like *Fido*), or to types of objects (*dog*), actions (*sit*), or properties (*furry*). Animal signals don't have this kind of referential meaning. Instead, they have what is called instrumental meaning: this is, they act as stimuli that trigger desired responses from others. A frog's mating croak doesn't *refer* to sex. Its purpose is to get some, not to talk about it. People, too, have signals of this purely animal sort—for example, weeping, laughing, and screaming—but these stand outside language. They have powerful meanings for us but not the kind of meaning that words have.

Some animal signals have a focused meaning that looks a bit like reference. For example, vervet monkeys give different warning calls for different predators. When they hear the "leopard" call, vervets climb trees and anxiously look down; when they hear the "eagle" call, they hide in low bushes or look up. But although the vervets' leopard call is in some sense about leopards, it isn't a word for leopard. Like a frog's croak or human weeping, its meaning is strictly instrumental; it's a stimulus that elicits an automatic response. All a vervet can "say" with it is "*Eeek!* A leopard!"—not "I really hate leopard!" or "No leopards here, thank goodness" or "A leopard ate Alice yesterday."

Australopithecus Africanus and other early hominids couldn't speak.

In these English sentences, such referential words as *leopard* work their magic through an accompanying framework of nonreferential, grammatical words, which set up an empty web of meaning that the referential symbols fill in. When Lewis Carroll tells us in "Jabberwocky" that "the slithy toves did gyre and gimble in the wabe," we have no idea what he is talking about, but we do know certain things—for instance, that all this happened in the past and that there was more than one tove but only one wabe. We know these things because of the grammatical structure of the sentence, a structure that linguists call syntax. Again, there's nothing much like it in any animal signals.

But if there aren't any intermediate stages between animal calls and human speech, then how could language evolve? What

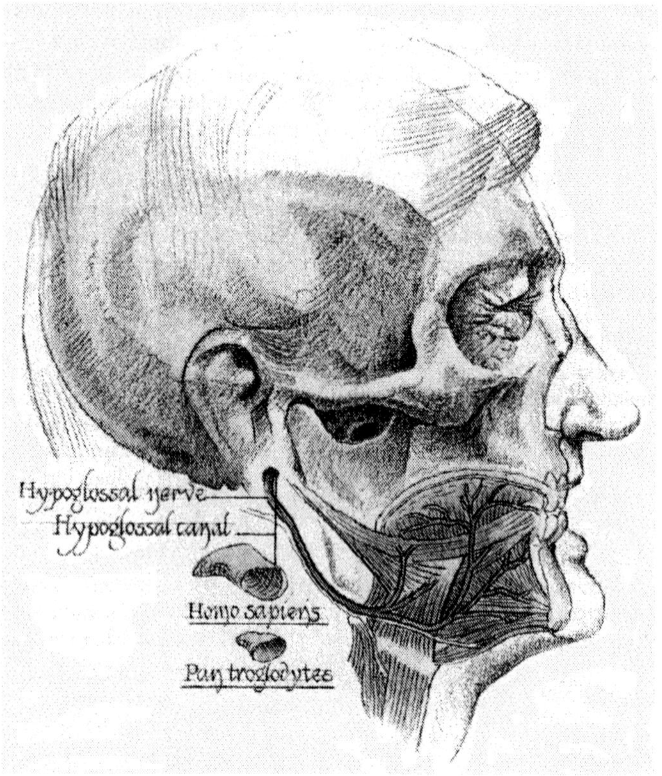

The Tongue-Controlling hypoglossal nerve is larger in humans than in chimps.

was there for it to evolve from? Until recently, linguists have shrugged off these questions—or else concluded that language didn't evolve at all, but just sprang into existence by accident, through some glorious random mutation. This theory drives Darwinians crazy, but the linguists have been content with it because it fits neatly into some key ideas in modern linguistics.

Forty years ago most linguists thought that people learn to talk through the same sort of behavior reinforcement used in training an animal to do tricks: when children use a word correctly or produce a grammatical sentence, they are rewarded. This picture was swept away in the late 1950s by the revolutionary ideas of Noam Chomsky. Chomsky argued that the structures of syntax lie in unconscious linguistic patterns—so-called deep structures—that are very different from the surface strings of words that come out of our mouths. Two sentences that look different on the surface (for instance, "A leopard ate Alice" and "Alice was eaten by a leopard") can mean the same thing because they derive from a single deep structure. Conversely, two sentences with different deep structures and different meanings can look exactly the same on the surface (for example, "Fleeing leopards can be dangerous"). Any models of language learning based strictly on the observable behaviors of language, Chomsky insisted, can't account for these deep-lying patterns of meaning.

Chomsky concluded that the deepest structures of language are innate, not learned. We are all born with the same fundamental grammar hard-wired into our brains, and we are preprogrammed to pick up the additional rules of the local language, just as baby ducks are hard-wired to follow the first big animal they see when they hatch. Chomsky could see no evidence of other animals' possessing this innate syntax machinery. He concluded that we can't learn anything about the origins of language by studying other animals and they can't learn language from us. If language learning were just a matter of proper training, Chomsky reasoned, we ought to be able to teach English to lab rats, or at least to apes.

As we have seen, apes aren't built to talk. But they can be trained to use sign language or to point to word-symbols on a keyboard. Starting in the 1960s, several experimenters trained chimpanzees and other great apes to use such signs to ask for things and answer questions to get rewards. Linguists, however, were unimpressed. They said that the apes' signs had a purely instrumental meaning: the animals were just doing tricks to get a treat. And there was no trace of syntax in the random-looking jumble of signs the apes produced; an ape that signed "You give me cookie please" one minute might sign "Me cookie please you cookie eat give" the next.

Duane Rumbaugh and Sue Savage-Rumbaugh set to work with chimpanzees at the Yerkes Regional Primate Research Center in Atlanta to try to answer the linguists' criticisms. After many years of mixed results, Sue made a surprising break-through with a young bonobo (or pygmy chimp) named Kanzi. Kanzi had watched his mother, Matata, try to learn signs with little success. When Sue gave up on her and started with Kanzi, she was astonished to discover that he already knew the meaning of 12 of the keyboard symbols. Apparently, he had learned them without any training or rewards. In the years that followed, he learned new symbols quickly and used them referentially, both to answer questions and to "talk" about things that he intended to do or had already done. Still more amazingly, he had a considerable understanding of spoken English—including its syntax. He grasped such grammatical niceties as case structures ("Can you throw a potato to the turtle?") and if-then implication ("You can have some cereal if you give Austin your monster mash to play with"). Upon hearing such sentences, Kanzi behaved appropriately 72 percent of the time—more than a 30-month-old human child given the same tests.

Kanzi is a primatologist's dream and a linguist's nightmare. His language-learning abilities seem inexplicable. He didn't need any rewards to learn language, as the old behaviorists would have predicted; but he also defies the Chomskyan model, which can't explain why a speechless ape would have an innate tendency to learn English. It looks as though some animals can develop linguistic abilities for reasons unrelated to language itself.

Brain enlargement in hominids may have been the result of evolutionary pressures that favored intelligence. As a side effect, human evolution crossed a threshold at which language became possible.

Neuroscientist William Calvin of the University of Washington and linguist Derek Bickerton of the University of Hawaii have a suggestion as to what those reasons might be. In their forthcoming book, *Lingua ex Machina,* they argue that the ability to create symbols—signs that refer to things—is potentially present in any animal that can learn to interpret natural signs, such as a trail of footprints. Syntax, meanwhile, emerges from the abstract thought required for a social life. In apes and some other mammals with complex and subtle social relationships, individuals make alliances and act altruistically towards others, with the implicit understanding that their favors will be returned. To succeed in such societies, animals need to choose trustworthy allies and to detect and punish cheaters who take but never give anything in return. This demands fitting a shifting constellation of individuals into an abstract mental model of social roles (debtors, creditors, allies, and so on) connected by social expectations ("If you scratch my back, I'll scratch yours"). Calvin and Bickerton believe that such abstract models of social obligation furnished the basic pattern for the deep structures of syntax.

These foreshadowings of symbols and syntax, they propose, laid the groundwork for language in a lot of social animals but didn't create language itself. That had to wait until our ancestors evolved brains big enough to handle the large-scale operations needed to generate and process complex strings of signs. Calvin and Bickerton suggest that brain enlargement in our ancestry was the result of evolutionary pressures that favored intelligence and motor coordination for making tools and throwing weapons. As a side effect of these selection pressures, which had nothing to do with communication, human evolution crossed a threshold at which language became possible. Big-brained, nonhuman animals like Kanzi remain just on the verge of language.

Fossils hint that language dawned 500,000 years ago.

This story reconciles natural selection with the linguists' insistence that you can't evolve language out of an animal communication system. It is also consistent with what we know about language from the fossil record. The earliest hominids with modern-size brains also seem to be the first ones with modern-size hypoglossal canals. Lieberman thinks that these are also the first hominids with modern vocal tracts. It may be no coincidence that all three of these changes seem to show up together around half a million years ago. If Calvin and Bickerton are right, the enlargement of the brain may have abruptly brought language into being at this time, which would have placed new selection pressures on the evolving throat and tongue.

This account may be wrong in some of its details, but the story in its broad outlines solves so many puzzles and ties up so many loose ends that something like it must surely be correct. It also promises to resolve our conflicting views of the boundary between people and animals. To some people, it seems obvious that human beings are utterly different from any beasts. To others, it's just as obvious that many other animals are essentially like us, only with fewer smarts and more fur. Each party finds the other's view of humanity alien and threatening. The story of language origins sketched above suggests that both parties are right: the human difference is real and profound, but it is rooted in aspects of psychology and biology that we share with our close animal relatives. If the growing consensus on the origins of language can join these disparate truths together, it will be a big step forward in the study of human evolution.

Matt Cartmill is a professor at Duke, where he teaches anatomy and anthropology and studies animal locomotion. Cartmill is also the author of numerous articles and books on the evolution of people and other animals, including an award-winning book on hunting, *A View to a Death in the Morning.* He is the president of the American Association of Physical Anthropologists.

Mysterious Migrations

Our prehistoric ancestors journeyed out of Africa on contested roads.

BRUCE BOWER

It was the most momentous immigration ever, a population realignment that marked a startling departure for our species, Homo sapiens. After emerging in eastern Africa close to 200,000 years ago, anatomically modern people stayed on one continent for roughly 140,000 years before spreading out in force around the world. Then, from 40,000 to 35,000 years ago, our forerunners advanced into areas stretching from what is now France to southeastern Asia and Australia. For the past century, scientists have tried to retrace the intercontinental paths followed by ancient human pioneers and to reconstruct what happened when these intrepid travelers encountered other humanlike species, such as Neandertals, or Homo neanderthalensis. Neandertals originated in Europe around 130,000 years ago, having evolved from ancestors who had already lived there for hundreds of thousands of years. Researchers fiercely debate how H. sapiens came to dominate. Some propose that modern people drove related species to extinction and replaced them, thanks to mental and social advantages. Others say that the African emigrants interbred with their northern kin as intellectual equals and assimilated into their cultures before genetically overpowering them with larger populations. A third idea, known as multiregional evolution, posits that modern humans evolved simultaneously in Africa, Asia, and Europe through periodic population movements and interbreeding. From this minority perspective, modern people originated as early as 2 million years ago, not 200,000 years ago. Two new studies, both published in the Jan. 12 Science, inject new elements into the replacement-versus-interbreeding dispute. One investigation focuses on the South African "Hofmeyr" skull, recently dated to 36,000 years ago. The investigators conclude that modern humans emigrated from sub-Saharan Africa in the late Stone Age and produced European and western Asian populations that made rapid cultural strides. A second paper describes evidence for the presence of modern H. sapiens in western Russia more than 40,000 years ago. That would have been several thousand years before their spread across the rest of Europe. The authors of both studies suspect that modern humans advanced speedily out of Africa in various directions, out competing and hastening the demise of Neandertals and others. "The new discoveries . . . reinforce the argument that the break between the Neandertals and modern humans is a sharp one," says archaeologist John F. Hoffecker of the University of Colorado at Boulder.

Archaeologist João Zilhão of the University of Bristol in England contests that conclusion. He says that Hoffecker and other scientists have twisted the new findings to accommodate their preconceived notion that modern humans swarmed out of Africa, wiped out and replaced the Neandertals more than 30,000 years ago, and spread a uniquely advanced culture. More likely, in Zilhão's view, these species interbred, and their two complex cultures intermingled. "The [replacement] model has become an obstacle to modern-human-origins research," he says.

Southern Link In 1952, archaeologists working in a dry river channel near the town of Hofmeyr, South Africa, unearthed a partial H. sapiens skull, filled with hardened sediment. They tried to obtain a radiocarbon age for a piece of the fossil, but it was unsuitable for such measurement. A team led by anthropologist Frederick E. Grine of Stony Brook (N.Y.) University has now taken a different approach to gauge the Hofmeyr skull's age. After measuring the rate of decay of radioactive material in the sediment packed into the skull, the researchers concluded that the specimen dates to about 36,000 years ago, a time when modern humans were leaving Africa in droves. In a series of anatomical comparisons, Grine and his coworkers have also found that the Hofmeyr skull looks more like European H. sapiens skulls from 30,000 to 20,000 years ago than like the skulls of Africans, Asians, or Europeans from the past few centuries. Moreover, the Hofmeyr skull's relatively long head and flat face contrasts with Neandertals' shorter heads and sloping faces, the researchers say.

Grine's data fit a scenario in which "36,000 years ago, modern [human] populations of sub-Saharan Africa and Europe shared a very recent common ancestor, one that likely expanded from eastern Africa 60,000 years ago," remarks anthropologist Ted Goebel of Texas A&M University in College Station. Migrating groups of modern humans spread out in separate directions, Goebel asserts. Some headed south into what's now South Africa; others forged east into Asia, reaching Australia by around 50,000 years ago. Populations represented by the Hofmeyr skull then waited awhile before heading north. They needed to become capable of surviving Europe's cold, dry climate and dealing with Neandertals, in Goebel's view. DNA studies suggest that sets of genes carried by the first modern humans spread into Europe and western Asia by 45,000 years ago. After "a short period of interaction," modern humans' northern thrust led to the Neandertals' demise, in Goebel's view. Recent advances in radiocarbon dating show that the overlap of modern humans with Neandertals in Europe lasted only 1,000 to 2,000 years, according to archaeologist Paul Mellars of the University of Cambridge in England. Incoming H. sapiens populations were better equipped and better organized to deal with severe cold than resident Neandertals were, Mellars argues in the Feb. 23, 2006 Nature. "This could have delivered the coup de grâce to the Neandertals in many parts of western and central Europe," Mellars says.

Mosaic Skulls When Zilhão peruses the Hofmeyr skull, he envisions a far different evolutionary scenario than Grine's team does. For now, Zilhão says, 36,000 years represents a minimum estimate of how long ago sediment clogged the South African fossil. The skull's large proportions and thick bones suggest that that it could be up to 100,000 years old, he notes. Only measurements of the decay of radioactive uranium in the skull itself—which have yet to be conducted—can narrow down its age, in his opinion. If the age estimate made by Grine and his colleagues holds up, then fossil evidence not mentioned in their report challenges their notion of southern Africans moving into Europe and setting off cultural fireworks, Zilhão says. Those fossil finds suggest that the Hofmeyr individual belonged to a group that arrived in southern Africa long after other modern humans had settled there. The group then stayed put rather than relocating to Europe, Zilhão speculates. For instance, the new data reveal an anatomical gulf between the Hofmeyr individual and present-day hunter-gatherers in South Africa. In the same vein, other researchers have reported that modern hunter-gatherers display skeletal links to human fossils at Border Cave, a 70,000-year-old South African site.

The Hofmeyr skull also differs in many respects from the skulls of H. sapiens previously discovered at two 100,000-year-old sites in Israel, further cementing its status as an African latecomer, Zilhão says. Most researchers regard the Israeli fossils as evidence of an early human migration from eastern Africa that never approached the scale of later population thrusts. "These facts should lead to the conclusion that the Hofmeyr fossil documents a migration of early modern Europeans into sub-Saharan Africa between 40,000 and 30,000 years ago," Zilhão concludes. He proposes that large numbers of modern humans, nurtured in the bounty of Africa's tropical savannas, entered Europe around 40,000 years ago and encountered relatively small numbers of Neandertals. Europe's harsh glacial conditions slowed Neandertal population growth, but Neandertals' mental and cultural capabilities matched those of H. sapiens, in Zilhão's view.

The two species then interbred, producing offspring with an unusual mosaic of skeletal traits, Zilhão says. Within a few thousand years, the genetic contributions of modern humans overwhelmed those of Neandertals, erasing all traces of the smaller population's DNA. Anthropologist Erik Trinkaus of Washington University in St. Louis concurs. Fossil evidence indicates that, after leaving eastern Africa, the earliest modern humans interbred with other Homo species that they encountered, Trinkaus holds. This phenomenon would have occurred most often in geographically dead-end regions, including southern Africa and western Europe, where various immigrant populations accumulated.

This would explain why the Hofmeyr skull exhibits not only modern-human traits but also so-called primitive characteristics, such as a brow ridge and large cheek teeth, Trinkaus says. Similarly, a 40,000-year-old H. sapiens skull found in Romania 2 years ago contains a mix of modern-human and Neandertal features. Trinkaus and his colleagues describe the skull in the Jan. 23 Proceedings of the National Academy of Sciences. He mentions that other finds, such as a 25,000-year-old skeleton of a youth found in Portugal, also include a montage of H. sapiens and Neandertal traits suggestive of interbreeding. "Far more-complex population interactions occurred as modern humans dispersed into southern Africa and Europe than many researchers have recognized," Trinkaus says.

Eastern Pioneers Researchers have long focused on western Europe as a destination for modern humans leaving Africa. But Colorado's Hoffecker says that new evidence puts H. sapiens in what's now southern Russia between 45,000 and 42,000 years ago, a few millennia prior to any incursions into the rest of Europe. In his view, the Russian discoveries underscore unique cultural advances achieved by modern humans but not by Neandertals. This idea serves as a linchpin of the replacement model of human evolution. Hoffecker and an international team of coworkers base this conclusion on work at ancient sites clustered near the town of Kostenki, about 250 miles south of Moscow. Russian investigators first discovered Stone Age material at Kostenki in 1872. Twenty-one prehistoric locations have now been identified there.

Hoffecker's group dated the oldest Kostenki occupations by radiocarbon measurements of burned wood and assessments of the decay of radioactive substances in the soil. Also, artifacts in these deposits lie just beneath ash that was created in a massive volcanic eruption dated elsewhere in Europe to 40,000 years ago. In the oldest parts of Kostenki, the researchers uncovered tools and other objects that they consider remnants of a unique late Stone Age culture. Modern humans probably fashioned all the artifacts discovered so far, Hoffecker says. Remains include bone points and narrow, sharpened stone implements, which might have been used to carve bone. The team also found a piece of carved ivory that might represent a person's head, and shells with holes punched in them. Much of the stone used for tools came from areas about 100 miles from Kostenki, the scientists hold. They say that shells at Kostenki were probably imported from the Black Sea, more than 300 miles away.

Some artifacts found below the ancient ash consist of relatively simple stone tools typical of those used by H. sapiens and Neandertals more than 50,000 years ago. Such artifacts, along with the bones of reindeer and other large animals, also turn up in Kostenki sediment from about 30,000 years ago. Hoffecker regards these finds as modern-human tools for butchering game after hunting expeditions. Similar prehistoric implements have been unearthed inside the Arctic Circle in northern Russia, where only H. sapiens could have survived the brutal cold, he contends. Moreover, two teeth uncovered among Kostenki's oldest artifacts appear to have come from modern humans, Hoffecker adds.

Hoffecker suspects that modern humans who arrived at Kostenki more than 40,000 years ago came from further east, perhaps central Asia. H. sapiens emigrating to southern Russia at that time probably avoided any extensive dealings with Neandertals that already inhabited the only direct route north from the Near East. Wherever Kostenki's ancient residents came from, Goebel agrees that they were "a pioneering group of modern humans."

Site Fight Efforts to portray Stone Age Kostenki as the exclusive preserve of modern humans—apparently because they wielded cultural advances that allowed them to adapt to a harsh locale avoided by Neandertals—rankle other researchers. "No one has a realistic idea of which biological group, Homo sapiens or Neandertals, was responsible for the Kostenki material," Trinkaus says. Since modern humans and Neandertals made comparable tools beginning around 40,000 years ago, only the discovery of substantial skeletal remains at Kostenki will reveal who first settled the region, he asserts. The two teeth found at Kostenki could have come from either species, in his opinion.

Anthropologist John Hawks of the University of Wisconsin-Madison suggests on his blog (http://www.johnhawks.net/weblog) that people and Neandertals simultaneously inhabited Kostenki more than 40,000 years ago. Basic stone tools found at the Russian sites resemble those already attributed to central European Neandertals, whereas other ancient-Kostenki finds have more in common with European H. sapiens material, he says. In contrast, Zilhão suspects that Neandertals monopolized Kostenki at first. The oldest remains uncovered by Hoffecker's group "represent a Russian example of the northward extension of the Neandertal range," he says.

Neandertal sites in England, France, and Poland contain artifacts similar to those that Hoffecker attributes to modern humans at Kostenki, Zilhão contends. These Neandertal finds include small, sharpened stone blades, decorated bone tools, and bone ornaments that apparently held symbolic significance for their makers. After hosting Neandertals for a few thousand years, Kostenki shows no sign of occupation between 36,000 and 32,000 years ago, Zilhão notes. After that, stone and bone implements like those made by European modern humans began to appear. This pattern fits with his view that Neandertals and modern humans developed comparably complex cultures, with Neandertals eventually getting absorbed by larger H. sapiens populations. To make a long, ancient story short, the Hofmeyr skull and the Kostenki remains won't resolve quarrels over how modern humans spread from Africa to all corners of the world. But they may encourage scientific clashes along some intriguing new routes.

The Littlest Human

A spectacular find in Indonesia reveals that a strikingly different hominid shared the earth with our kind in the not so distant past.

KATE WONG

On the island of Flores in Indonesia, villagers have long told tales of a diminutive, upright-walking creature with a lopsided gait, a voracious appetite, and soft, murmuring speech.

They call it *ebu gogo,* "the grandmother who eats anything." Scientists' best guess was that macaque monkeys inspired the *ebu gogo* lore. But last October, an alluring alternative came to light. A team of Australian and Indonesian researchers excavating a cave on Flores unveiled the remains of a lilliputian human—one that stood barely a meter tall—whose kind lived as recently as 13,000 years ago.

The announcement electrified the paleoanthropology community. *Homo sapiens* was supposed to have had the planet to itself for the past 25 millennia, free from the company of other humans following the apparent demise of the Neandertals in Europe and *Homo erectus* in Asia. Furthermore, hominids this tiny were known only from fossils of australopithecines (Lucy and the like) that lived nearly three million years ago—long before the emergence of *H. sapiens.* No one would have predicted that our own species had a contemporary as small and primitive-looking as the little Floresian. Neither would anyone have guessed that a creature with a skull the size of a grapefruit might have possessed cognitive capabilities comparable to those of anatomically modern humans.

Overview/Mini Humans

- Conventional wisdom holds that *Homo sapiens* has been the sole human species on the earth for the past 25,000 years. Remains discovered on the Indonesian island of Flares have upended that view.
- The bones are said to belong to a dwarf species of *Homo* that lived as recently as 13,000 years ago.
- Although the hominid is as small in body and brain as the earliest humans, it appears to have made sophisticated stone tools, raising questions about the relation between brain size and intelligence.
- The find is controversial, however—some experts wonder whether the discoverers have correctly diagnosed the bones and whether anatomically modern humans might have made those advanced artifacts.

Isle of Intrigue

This is not the first time Flores has yielded surprises. In 1998 archaeologists led by Michael J. Morwood of the University of New England in Armidale, Australia, reported having discovered crude stone artifacts some 840,000 years old in the Soa Basin of central Flores. Although no human remains turned up with the tools, the implication was that *H. erectus,* the only hominid known to have lived in Southeast Asia during that time, had crossed the deep waters separating Flores from Java. To the team, the find showed *H. erectus* to be a seafarer, which was startling because elsewhere *H. erectus* had left behind little material culture to suggest that it was anywhere near capable of making watercraft. Indeed, the earliest accepted date for boat-building was 40,000 to 60,000 years ago, when modern humans colonized Australia. (The other early fauna on Flores probably got there by swimming or accidentally drifting over on flotsam. Humans are not strong enough swimmers to have managed that voyage, but skeptics say they may have drifted across on natural rafts).

Hoping to document subsequent chapters of human occupation of the island, Morwood and Radien P. Soejono of the Indonesian Center for Archaeology in Jakarta turned their attention to a large limestone cave called Liang Bua located

> Dwarfs and giants tend to evolve on islands, with animals larger than rabbits shrinking and animals smaller than rabbits growing. The shifts appear to be adaptive responses to the limited food supplies available in such environments. *Stegodon,* an extinct proboscidean, colonized Flores several times, dwindling from elephant to water buffalo proportions. Some rats, in contrast, became rabbit-sized over time. *H. floresiensis* appears to have followed the island rule as well. It is thought to be a dwarfed descendant of *H. erectus,* which itself was nearly the size of a modern human.

> Shared features between LB1 and members of our own genus led to the classification of the Flores hominid as *Homo,* despite its tiny brain size. Noting that the specimen most closely resembles *H. erectus,* the researchers posit that it is a new species, *H. floresiensis,* that dwarfed from a *H. erectus* ancestor. *H. floresiensis* differs from *H. sapiens* in having, among other characteristics, no chin, a relatively projecting face, a prominent brow and a low braincase.

in western Flores. Indonesian archaeologists had been excavating the cave intermittently since the 1970s, depending on funding availability, but workers had penetrated only the uppermost deposits. Morwood and Soejono set their sights on reaching bedrock and began digging in July 2001. Before long, their team's efforts turned up abundant stone tools and bones of a pygmy version of an extinct elephant relative known as *Stegodon.* But it was not until nearly the end of the third season of fieldwork that diagnostic hominid material in the form of an isolated tooth surfaced. Morwood brought a cast of the tooth back to Armidale to show to his department colleague Peter Brown. "It was clear that while the premolar was broadly humanlike, it wasn't from a modern human," Brown recollects. Seven days later Morwood received word that the Indonesians had recovered a skeleton. The Australians boarded the next plane to Jakarta.

Peculiar though the premolar was, nothing could have prepared them for the skeleton, which apart from the missing arms was largely complete. The pelvis anatomy revealed that the individual was bipedal and probably a female, and the tooth eruption and wear indicated that it was an adult. Yet it was only as tall as a modern three-year-old, and its brain was as small as the smallest australopithecine brain known. There were other primitive traits as well, including the broad pelvis and the long neck of the femur. In other respects, however, the specimen looked familiar. Its small teeth and narrow nose, the overall shape of the braincase and the thickness of the cranial bones all evoked *Homo.*

Brown spent the next three months analyzing the enigmatic skeleton, catalogued as LB1 and affectionately nicknamed the Hobbit by some of the team members, after the tiny beings in J.R.R. Tolkien's *The Lord of the Rings* books. The decision about how to classify it did not come easily. Impressed with the characteristics LB1 shared with early hominids such as the australopithecines, he initially proposed that it represented a new genus of human. On further consideration, however, the similarities to *Homo* proved more persuasive. Based on the 18,000-year age of LB1, one might have reasonably expected the bones to belong to *H. sapiens,* albeit a very petite representative. But when Brown and his colleagues considered the morphological characteristics of small-bodied modern humans—including normal ones, such as pygmies, and abnormal ones, such as pituitary dwarfs—LB1 did not seem to fit any of those descriptions. Pygmies have small bodies and large brains—the result of delayed growth during puberty, when the brain has already attained its full size. And individuals with genetic disorders that produce short stature and small brains have a range of distinctive features not seen in LB1 and rarely reach adulthood, Brown says. Conversely, he notes, the Flores skeleton exhibits archaic traits that have never been documented for abnormal small-bodied *H. sapiens.*

What LB1 looks like most, the researchers concluded, is a miniature *H. erectus.* Describing the find in the journal *Nature,* they assigned LB1 as well as the isolated tooth and an arm bone from older deposits to a new species of human, *Homo floresiensis.* They further argued that it was a descendant of *H. erectus* that had become marooned on Flores and evolved in isolation into a dwarf species, much as the elephant-like *Stegodon* did.

Biologists have long recognized that mammals larger than rabbits tend to shrink on small islands, presumably as an adaptive response to the limited food supply. They have little to lose by doing so, because these environments harbor few predators. On Flores, the only sizable predators were the Komodo dragon and another, even larger monitor lizard. Animals smaller than rabbits, on the other hand, tend to attain brobdingnagian proportions—perhaps because bigger bodies are more energetically efficient than small ones. Liang Bua has yielded evidence of that as well, in the form of a rat as robust as a rabbit.

But attributing a hominid's bantam size to the so-called island rule was a first. Received paleoanthropological wisdom holds that culture has buffered us humans from many of the selective pressures that mold other creatures—we cope with cold, for example, by building fires and making clothes, rather than evolving a proper pelage. The discovery of a dwarf hominid species indicates that, under the right conditions, humans can in fact respond in the same, predictable way that other large mammals do when the going gets tough. Hints that *Homo* could deal with resource fluxes in this manner came earlier in 2004 from the discovery of a relatively petite *H. erectus* skull from Olorgesailie in Kenya, remarks Richard Potts of the Smithsonian Institution, whose team recovered the bones. "Getting small is one of the things *H. erectus* had in its biological tool kit," he says, and the Flores hominid seems to be an extreme instance of that.

Curiouser and Curiouser

H. floresiensis's teeny brain was perplexing. What the hominid reportedly managed to accomplish with such a modest organ was nothing less than astonishing. Big brains are a hallmark of human evolution. In the space of six million to seven million years, our ancestors more than tripled their cranial capacity, from some 360 cubic centimeters in *Sahelanthropus,* the earliest putative hominid, to a whopping 1,350 cubic centimeters on average in modern folks. Archaeological evidence indicates that behavioral complexity increased correspondingly. Experts were thus fairly certain that large brains are a prerequisite for advanced cultural practices. Yet whereas the pea-brained australopithecines left behind only crude stone tools at best (and most seem not to have done any stone working at all), the comparably gray-matter-impoverished *H. floresiensis* is said to have manufactured implements that exhibit a level of sophistication elsewhere associated exclusively with *H. sapiens.*

The bulk of the artifacts from Liang Bua are simple flake tools struck from volcanic rock and chert, no more advanced than the implements made by late australopithecines and early *Homo.* But mixed in among the pygmy *Stegodon* remains excavators found a fancier set of tools, one that included finely worked points, large blades, awls and small blades that may have been hafted for use as spears. To the team, this association suggests that *H. floresiensis* regularly hunted *Stegodon.* Many of the *Stegodon* bones are those of young individuals that one *H. floresiensis* might have been able to bring down alone. But some belonged to adults that weighed up to half a ton, the hunting and transport of which must have been a coordinated group activity—one that probably required language, surmises team member Richard G. ("Bert") Roberts of the University of Wollongong in Australia.

The discovery of charred animal remains in the cave suggests that cooking, too, was part of the cultural repertoire of *H. floresiensis.* That a hominid as cerebrally limited as this one might have had control of fire gives pause. Humans are not thought to have tamed flame until relatively late in our collective cognitive development: the earliest unequivocal evidence of fire use comes from 200,000-year-old hearths in Europe that were the handiwork of the large-brained Neandertals.

If the *H. floresiensis* discoverers are correct in their interpretation, theirs is one of the most important paleoanthropological finds in decades. Not only does it mean that another species of human coexisted with our ancestors just yesterday in geological terms, and that our genus is far more variable than expected, it raises all sorts of questions about brain size and intelligence. Perhaps it should come as no surprise, then, that controversy has accompanied their claims.

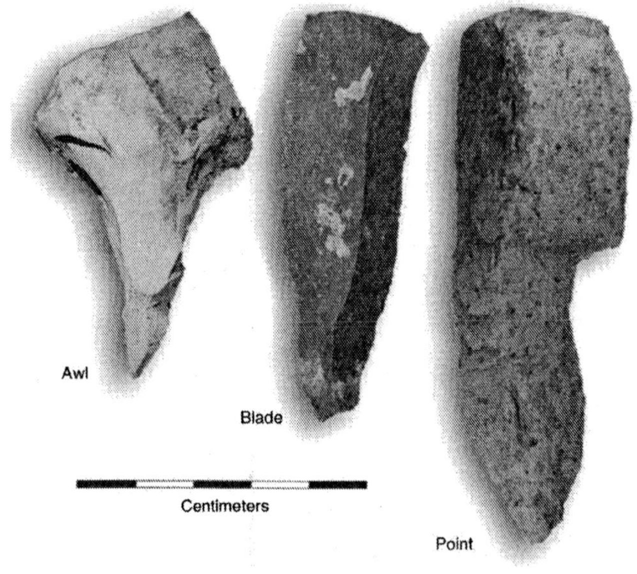

H. *floresiensis.* Earlier hominids with brains similar in size to that of H. floresiensis made only simple flake tools at most. But in the same stratigraphic levels as the hominid remains at Liang Bua, researchers found a suite of sophisticated artifacts—including awls, blades and points—exhibiting a level of complexity previously thought to be the sole purview of *H. sapiens.*

Classification Clash

It did not take long for alternative theories to surface. In a letter that ran in the October 31 edition of Australia's *Sunday Mail,* just three days after the publication of the *Nature* issue containing the initial reports, paleoanthropologist Maciej Henneberg of the University of Adelaide countered that a pathological condition known as microcephaly (from the Greek for "small brain") could explain LB1's unusual features. Individuals afflicted with the most severe congenital form of microcephaly, primordial microcephalic dwarfism, die in childhood. But those with milder forms, though mentally retarded, can survive into adulthood. Statistically comparing the head and face dimensions of LB1 with those of a 4,000-year-old skull from Crete that is known to have belonged to a microcephalic, Henneberg found no significant differences between the two. Furthermore, he argued, the isolated forearm bone found deeper in the deposit corresponds to a height of 151 to 162 centimeters—the stature of many modern women and some men, not that of a dwarf—suggesting that larger-bodied people, too, lived at Liang Bua. In Henneberg's view, these findings indicate that LB1 is more likely a microcephalic *H. sapiens* than a new branch of *Homo*.

Susan C. Antón of New York University disagrees with that assessment. "The facial morphology is completely different in microcephalic [modern] humans," and their body size is normal, not small, she says. Antón questions whether LB1 warrants a new species, however. "There's little in the shape that differentiates it from *Homo erectus*," she notes. One can argue that it's a new species, Antón allows, but the difference in shape between LB1 and *Homo erectus* is less striking than that between a Great Dane and a Chihuahua. The possibility exists that the LB1 specimen is a *H. erectus* individual with a pathological growth condition stemming from microcephaly or nutritional deprivation, she observes.

But some specialists say the Flores hominid's anatomy exhibits a more primitive pattern. According to Colin P. Groves of the Australian National University and David W. Cameron of the University of Sydney, the small brain, the long neck of the femur and other characteristics suggest an ancestor along the lines of *Homo habilis*, the earliest member of our genus, rather than the more advanced *H. erectus*. Milford H. Wolpoff of the University of Michigan at Ann Arbor wonders whether the Flores find might even represent an offshoot of *Australopithecus*. If LB1 is a descendant of *H. sapiens* or *H. erectus*, it is hard to imagine how natural selection left her with a brain that's even smaller than expected for her height, Wolpoff says. Granted, if she descended from *Australopithecus*, which had massive jaws and teeth, one has to account for her relatively delicate jaws and dainty dentition. That, however, is a lesser evolutionary conundrum than the one posed by her tiny brain, he asserts. After all, a shift in diet could explain the reduced chewing apparatus, but why would selection downsize intelligence?

Finding an australopithecine that lived outside of Africa—not to mention all the way over in Southeast Asia—18,000 years ago would be a first. Members of this group were thought to have died out in Africa one and a half million years ago, never having left their mother continent. Perhaps, researchers reasoned, hominids needed long, striding limbs, large brains and better technology before they could venture out into the rest of the Old World. But the recent discovery of 1.8 million-year-old *Homo* fossils at a site called Dmanisi in the Republic of Georgia refuted that explanation—the Georgian hominids were primitive and small and utilized tools like those australopithecines had made a million years before. Taking that into consideration, there is no a priori reason why australopithecines (or habilines, for that matter) could not have colonized other continents.

Troubling Tools

Yet if *Australopithecus* made it out of Africa and survived on Flores until quite recently, that would raise the question of why no other remains supporting that scenario have turned up in the region. According to Wolpoff, they may have: a handful of poorly studied Indonesian fossils discovered in the 1940s have been variously classified as *Australopithecus*, *Meganthropus* and, most recently, *H. erectus*. In light of the Flores find, he says, those remains deserve reexamination.

Many experts not involved in the discovery back Brown and Morwood's taxonomic decision, however. "Most of the differences [between the Flores hominid and known members of *Homo*], including apparent similarities to australopithecines, are almost certainly related to very small body mass," declares David R. Begun of the University of Toronto. That is, as the Flores people dwarfed from *H. erectus*, some of their anatomy simply converged on that of the likewise little australopithecines. Because LB1 shares some key derived features with *H. erectus* and some with other members of *Homo*, "the most straightforward option is to call it a new species of *Homo*," he remarks. "It's a fair and reasonable interpretation," *H. erectus* expert G. Philip Rightmire of Binghamton University agrees. "That was quite a little experiment in Indonesia."

Even more controversial than the position of the half-pint human on the family tree is the notion that it made those advanced-looking tools. Stanford University paleoanthropologist Richard Klein notes that the artifacts found near LB1 appear to include few, if any, of the sophisticated types found elsewhere in the cave. This brings up the possibility that the modern-looking tools were produced by modern humans, who could have occupied the cave at a different time. Further excavations are necessary to determine the stratigraphic relation between the implements and the hominid remains, Klein opines. Such efforts may turn up modern humans like us. The question then, he says, will be whether there were two species at the site or whether modern humans alone occupied Liang Bua—in which case LB1 was simply a modern who experienced a growth anomaly.

Stratigraphic concerns aside, the tools are too advanced and too large to make manufacture by a primitive, diminutive hominid likely, Groves contends. Although the Liang Bua implements allegedly date back as far as 94,000 years ago, which the team argues makes them too early to be the handiwork of *H. sapiens*, Groves points out that 67,000-year-old tools have turned up in Liujiang, China, and older indications of a modern human presence in the Far East might yet emerge. "*H. sapiens*, once it was out of Africa, didn't take long to spread into eastern Asia," he comments.

"At the moment there isn't enough evidence" to establish that *H. floresiensis* created the advanced tools, concurs Bernard Wood of George Washington University. But as a thought experiment, he says, "let's pretend that they did." In that case, "I don't have a clue about brain size and ability," he confesses. If a hominid with no more gray matter than a chimp has can create a material culture like this one, Wood contemplates, "why did it take people such a bloody long time to make tools" in the first place?

"If *Homo floresiensis* was capable of producing sophisticated tools, we have to say that brain size doesn't add up to much," Rightmire concludes. Of course, humans today exhibit considerable variation in gray matter volume, and great thinkers exist at both ends of the spectrum. French writer Jacques Anatole Francois Thibault (also known as Anatole France), who won the 1921 Nobel Prize for Literature, had a cranial capacity of only about 1,000 cubic centimeters; England's General Oliver Cromwell had more than twice that. "What that means is that once you get the brain to a certain size, size no longer matters, it's the organization of the brain," Potts states. At some point, he adds, "the internal wiring of the brain may allow competence even if the brain seems small."

LB1's brain is long gone, so how it was wired will remain a mystery. Clues to its organization may reside on the interior of the braincase, however. Paleontologists can sometimes obtain latex molds of the insides of fossil skulls and then create plaster endocasts that reveal the morphology of the organ. Because LBI's bones are too fragile to withstand standard casting procedures, Brown is working on creating a virtual endocast based on CT scans of the skull that he can then use to generate a physical endocast via stereolithography, a rapid prototyping technology.

"If it's a little miniature version of an adult human brain, I'll be really blown away," says paleoneurologist Dean Falk of the University of Florida. Then again, she muses, what happens if the convolutions look chimplike? Specialists have long wondered whether bigger brains fold differently simply because they are bigger or whether the reorganization reflects selection for increased cognition. "This specimen could conceivably answer that," Falk observes.

Return to the Lost World

Since submitting their technical papers to *Nature,* the Liang Bua excavators have reportedly recovered the remains of another five or so individuals, all of which fit the *H. floresiensis* profile. None are nearly so complete as LB1, whose long arms turned up during the most recent field season. But they did unearth a second lower jaw that they say is identical in size and shape to LB1's. Such duplicate bones will be critical to their case that they have a population of these tiny humans (as opposed to a bunch of scattered bones from one person). That should in turn dispel concerns that LB1 was a diseased individual.

Additional evidence may come from DNA: hair samples possibly from *H. floresiensis* are undergoing analysis at the University of Oxford, and the hominid teeth and bones may contain viable DNA as well. "Tropical environments are not the best for long-term preservation of DNA, so we're not holding our breath," Roberts remarks, "but there's certainly no harm in looking."

The future of the bones (and any DNA they contain) is uncertain, however. In late November, Teuku Jacob of the Gadjah Mada University in Yogyakarta, Java, who was not involved in the discovery or the analyses, had the delicate specimens transported from their repository at the Indonesian Center for Archaeology to his own laboratory with Soejono's assistance. Jacob, the dean of Indonesian paleoanthropology, thinks LB1 was a microcephalic and allegedly ordered the transfer of it and the new, as yet undescribed finds for examination and safekeeping, despite strong objections from other staff members at the center. At the time this article was going to press, the team was waiting for Jacob to make good on his promise to return the remains to Jakarta by January 1 of this year, but his reputation for restricting scientific access to fossils has prompted pundits to predict that the bones will never be studied again.

Efforts to piece together the *H. floresiensis* puzzle will proceed, however. For his part, Brown is eager to find the tiny hominid's large-bodied forebears. The possibilities are three-fold, he notes. Either the ancestor dwarfed on Flores (and was possibly the maker of the 840,000-year-old Soa Basin tools), or it dwindled on another island and later reached Flores, or the ancestor was small before it even arrived in Southeast Asia. In fact, in many ways, LB1 more closely resembles African *H. erectus* and the Georgian hominids than the geographically closer Javan *H. erectus,* he observes. But whether these similarities indicate that *H. floresiensis* arose from an earlier *H. erectus* foray into Southeast Asia than the one that produced Javan *H. erectus* or are merely coincidental results of the dwarfing process remains to be determined. Future excavations may connect the dots. The team plans to continue digging on Flores and Java and will next year begin work on other Indonesian islands, including Sulawesi to the north.

The hominid bones from Liang Bua now span the period from 95,000 to 13,000 years ago, suggesting to the team that the little Floresians perished along with the pygmy *Stegodon* because of a massive volcanic eruption in the area around 12,000 years ago, although they may have survived later farther east. If *H. erectus* persisted on nearby Java until 25,000 years ago, as some evidence suggests, and *H. sapiens* had arrived in the region by 40,000 years ago, three human species lived cheek by jowl in Southeast Asia for at least 15,000 years. And the discoverers of *H. floresiensis* predict that more will be found. The islands of Lombok and Sumbawa would have been natural stepping-stones for hominids traveling from Java or mainland Asia to Flores. Those that put down roots on these islands may well have set off on their own evolutionary trajectories.

t has been proposed, some of these offshoots of eage survived until historic times. Maybe they ...note pockets of Southeast Asia's dense rain forests, awaiting (or avoiding) discovery. On Flores, oral histories hold that the *ebu gogo* was still in existence when Dutch colonists settled there in the 19th century. And Malay folklore describes another small, humanlike being known as the *orang pendek* that supposedly dwells on Sumatra to this day.

"Every country seems to have myths about these things," Brown reflects. "We've excavated a lot of sites around the world, and we've never found them. But then [in September 2003] we found LB1." Scientists may never know whether tales of the *ebu gogo* and *orang pendek* do in fact recount actual sightings of other hominid species, but the newfound possibility will no doubt spur efforts to find such creatures for generations to come.

Kate Wong is editorial director of ScientificAmerican.com.

Skin Deep

Throughout the world, human skin color has evolved to be dark enough to prevent sunlight from destroying the nutrient folate but light enough to foster the production of vitamin D.

Nina G. Jablonski and George Chaplin

Among primates, only humans have a mostly naked skin that comes in different colors. Geographers and anthropologists have long recognized that the distribution of skin colors among indigenous populations is not random: darker peoples tend to be found nearer the equator, lighter ones closer to the poles. For years, the prevailing theory has been that darker skins evolved to protect against skin cancer. But a series of discoveries has led us to construct a new framework for understanding the evolutionary basis of variations in human skin color. Recent epidemiological and physiological evidence suggests to us that the worldwide pattern of human skin color is the product of natural selection acting to regulate the effects of the sun's ultraviolet (UV) radiation on key nutrients crucial to reproductive success.

From Hirsute to Hairless

The evolution of skin pigmentation is linked with that of hairlessness, and to comprehend both these stories, we need to page back in human history. Human beings have been evolving as an independent lineage of apes since at least seven million years ago, when our immediate ancestors diverged from those of our closest relatives, chimpanzees. Because chimpanzees have changed less over time than humans have, they can provide an idea of what human anatomy and physiology must have been like. Chimpanzees' skin is light in color and is covered by hair over most of their bodies. Young animals have pink faces, hands, and feet and become freckled or dark in these areas only as they are exposed to sun with age. The earliest humans almost certainly had a light skin covered with hair. Presumably hair loss occurred first, then skin color changed. But that leads to the question, When did we lose our hair?

The skeletons of ancient humans—such as the well-known skeleton of Lucy, which dates to about 3.2 million years ago—give us a good idea of the build and the way of life of our ancestors. The daily activities of Lucy and other hominids that lived before about three million years ago appear to have been similar to those of primates living on the open savannas of Africa today. They probably spent much of their day foraging for food over three to four miles before retiring to the safety of trees to sleep.

By 1.6 million years ago, however, we see evidence that this pattern had begun to change dramatically. The famous skeleton of Turkana Boy—which belonged to the species *Homo ergaster*—is that of a long-legged, striding biped that probably walked long distances. These more active early humans faced the problem of staying cool and protecting their brains from overheating. Peter Wheeler of John Moores University in Liverpool, England, has shown that this was accomplished through an increase in the number of sweat glands on the surface of the body and a reduction in the covering of body hair. Once rid of most of their hair, early members of the genus *Homo* then encountered the challenge of protecting their skin from the damaging effects of sunlight, especially UV rays.

Built-In Sunscreen

In chimpanzees, the skin on the hairless parts of the body contains cells called melanocytes that are capable of synthesizing the dark-brown pigment melanin in response to exposure to UV radiation. When humans became mostly hairless, the ability of the skin to produce melanin assumed new importance. Melanin is nature's sunscreen: it is a large organic molecule that Overview/ Skin Color Evolution serves the dual purpose of physically and chemically filtering the harmful effects of UV radiation; it absorbs UV rays, causing them to lose energy, and it neutralizes harmful chemicals called free radicals that form in the skin after damage by UV radiation.

Anthropologists and biologists have generally reasoned that high concentrations of melanin arose in the skin of peoples in tropical areas because it protected them against skin cancer. James E. Cleaver of the University of California at San Francisco, for instance, has shown that people with the disease xeroderma pigmentosum, in which melanocytes are destroyed by exposure to the sun, suffer from significantly higher than normal rates

Overview/Skin Color Evolution

- After losing their hair as an adaptation for keeping cool, early hominids gained pigmented skins. Scientists initially thought that such pigmentation arose to protect against skin-cancer-causing ultraviolet [UV] radiation.
- Skin cancers tend to arise after reproductive age, however. An alternative theory suggests that dark skin might have evolved primarily to protect against the breakdown of folate, a nutrient essential for fertility and for fetal development.
- Skin that is too dark blocks the sunlight necessary for catalyzing the production of vitamin D, which is crucial for maternal and fetal bones. Accordingly, humans have evolved to be light enough to make sufficient vitamin B yet dark enough to protect their stores of folate.
- As a result of recent human migrations, many people now live in areas that receive more [or less] UV radiation than is appropriate for their skin color.

of squamous and basal cell carcinomas, which are usually easily treated. Malignant melanomas are more frequently fatal, but they are rare (representing 4 percent of skin cancer diagnoses) and tend to strike only light-skinned people. But all skin cancers typically arise later in life, in most cases after the first reproductive years, so they could not have exerted enough evolutionary pressure for skin protection alone to account for darker skin colors. Accordingly, we began to ask what role melanin might play in human evolution.

The Folate Connection

In 1991 one of us (Jablonski) ran across what turned out to be a critical paper published in 1978 by Richard F. Branda and John W. Eaton, now at the University of Vermont and the University of Louisville, respectively. These investigators showed that light-skinned people who had been exposed to simulated strong sunlight had abnormally low levels of the essential B vitamin folate in their blood. The scientists also observed that subjecting human blood serum to the same conditions resulted in a 50-percent loss of folate content within one hour.

The significance of these findings to reproduction—and hence evolution—became clear when we learned of research being conducted on a major class of birth defects by our colleagues at the University of Western Australia. There Fiona J. Stanley and Carol Bower had established by the late 1980s that folate deficiency in pregnant women is related to an increased risk of neural tube defects such as spina bifida, in which the arches of the spinal vertebrae fail to close around the spinal cord. Many research groups throughout the world have since confirmed this correlation, and efforts to supplement foods with folate and to educate women about the importance of the nutrient have become widespread.

We discovered soon afterward that folate is important not only in preventing neural tube defects but also in a host of other processes. Because folate is essential for the synthesis of DNA in dividing cells, anything that involves rapid cell proliferation, such as spermatogenesis (the production of sperm cells), requires folate. Male rats and mice with chemically induced folate deficiency have impaired spermatogenesis and are infertile. Although no comparable studies of humans have been conducted, Wai Yee Wong and his colleagues at the University Medical Center of Nijmegen in the Netherlands have recently reported that folic acid treatment can boost the sperm counts of men with fertility problems.

Such observations led us to hypothesize that dark skin evolved to protect the body's folate stores from destruction. Our idea was supported by a report published in 1996 by Argentine pediatrician Pablo Lapunzina, who found that three young and otherwise healthy women whom he had attended gave birth to infants with neural tube defects after using sun beds to tan themselves in the early weeks of pregnancy. Our evidence about the breakdown of folate by UV radiation thus supplements what is already known about the harmful (skin-cancer-causing) effects of UV radiation on DNA.

Human Skin on the Move

The earliest members of *Homo sapiens,* or modern humans, evolved in Africa between 120,000 and 100,000 years ago and had darkly pigmented skin adapted to the conditions of UV radiation and heat that existed near the equator. As modern humans began to venture out of the tropics, however, they encountered environments in which they received significantly less UV radiation during the year. Under these conditions their high concentrations of natural sunscreen probably proved detrimental. Dark skin contains so much melanin that very little UV radiation, and specifically very little of the shorter-wavelength UVB radiation, can penetrate the skin. Although most of the effects of UVB are harmful, the rays perform one indispensable function: initiating the formation of vitamin D in the skin. Dark-skinned people living in the tropics generally receive sufficient UV radiation during the year for UVB to penetrate the skin and allow them to make vitamin D. Outside the tropics this is not the case. The solution, across evolutionary time, has been for migrants to northern latitudes to lose skin pigmentation.

The connection between the evolution of lightly pigmented skin and vitamin D synthesis was elaborated by W. Farnsworth Loomis of Brandeis University in 1967. He established the importance of vitamin D to reproductive success because of its role in enabling calcium absorption by the intestines, which in turn makes possible the normal development of the skeleton and the maintenance of a healthy immune system. Research led by Michael Holick of the Boston University School of Medicine has, over the past 20 years, further cemented the significance of vitamin D in development and immunity. His team also showed that not all sunlight contains enough UVB to stimulate vitamin D production. In Boston, for instance, which is located at about 42 degrees north latitude, human skin cells begin to produce vitamin D only after mid-March. In the wintertime there isn't enough UVB to do the job. We realized that this was another piece of evidence essential to the skin color story.

During the course of our research in the early 1990s, we searched in vain to find sources of data on actual UV radiation levels at the earth's surface. We were rewarded in 1996, when we contacted Elizabeth Weatherhead of the Cooperative Institute for Research in Environmental Sciences at the University of Colorado at Boulder. She shared with us a database of measurements of UV radiation at the earth's surface taken by NASA's Total Ozone Mapping Spectrophotometer satellite between 1978 and 1993. We were then able to model the distribution of UV radiation on the earth and relate the satellite data to the amount of UVB necessary to produce vitamin D.

We found that the earth's surface could be divided into three vitamin D zones: one comprising the tropics, one the subtropics and temperate regions, and the last the circumpolar regions north and south of about 45 degrees latitude. In the first, the dosage of UVB throughout the year is high enough that humans have ample opportunity to synthesize vitamin D all year. In the second, at least one month during the year has insufficient UVB radiation, and in the third area not enough UVB arrives on average during the entire year to prompt vitamin D synthesis. This distribution could explain why indigenous peoples in the tropics generally have dark skin, whereas people in the subtropics and temperate regions are lighter-skinned but have the ability to tan, and those who live in regions near the poles tend to be very light skinned and burn easily.

One of the most interesting aspects of this investigation was the examination of groups that did not precisely fit the predicted skin-color pattern. An example is the Inuit people of Alaska and northern Canada. The Inuit exhibit skin color that is somewhat darker than would be predicted given the UV levels at their latitude. This is probably caused by two factors. The first is that they are relatively recent inhabitants of these climes, having migrated to North America only roughly 5,000 years ago. The second is that the traditional diet of the Inuit is extremely high in foods containing vitamin D, especially fish and marine mammals. This vitamin D-rich diet offsets the problem that they would otherwise have with vitamin D synthesis in their skin at northern latitudes and permits them to remain more darkly pigmented.

Our analysis of the potential to synthesize vitamin D allowed us to understand another trait related to human skin color: women in all populations are generally lighter-skinned than men. (Our data show that women tend to be between 3 and 4 percent lighter than men.) Scientists have often speculated on the reasons, and most have argued that the phenomenon stems from sexual selection—the preference of men for women of lighter color. We contend that although this is probably part of the story, it is not the original reason for the sexual difference. Females have significantly greater needs for calcium throughout their reproductive lives, especially during pregnancy and lactation, and must be able to make the most of the calcium contained in food. We propose, therefore, that women tend to be lighter-skinned than men to allow slightly more UVB rays to penetrate their skin and thereby increase their ability to produce vitamin D. In areas of the world that receive a large amount of UV radiation, women are indeed at the knife's edge of natural selection, needing to maximize the photoprotective function of their skin on the one hand and the ability to synthesize vitamin D on the other.

Where Culture and Biology Meet

As modern humans moved throughout the Old World about 100,000 years ago, their skin adapted to the environmental conditions that prevailed in different regions. The skin color of the indigenous people of Africa has had the longest time to adapt because anatomically modern humans first evolved there. The skin-color changes that modern humans underwent as they moved from one continent to another—first Asia, then Austro-Melanesia, then Europe and, finally, the Americas—can be reconstructed to some extent. It is important to remember, however, that those humans had clothing and shelter to help protect them from the elements. In some places, they also had the ability to harvest foods that were extraordinarily rich in vitamin D, as in the case of the Inuit. These two factors had profound effects on the tempo and degree of skin-color evolution in human populations.

Africa is an environmentally heterogeneous continent. A number of the earliest movements of contemporary humans outside equatorial Africa were into southern Africa. The descendants of some of these early colonizers, the Khoisan (previously known as Hottentots), are still found in southern Africa and have significantly lighter skin than indigenous equatorial Africans do—a clear adaptation to the lower levels of UV radiation that prevail at the southern extremity of the continent.

Interestingly, however, human skin color in southern Africa is not uniform. Populations of Bantu-language speakers who live in southern Africa today are far darker than the Khoisan. We know from the history of this region that Bantu speakers migrated into this region recently—probably within the past 1,000 years—from parts of West Africa near the equator. The skin-color difference between the Khoisan and Bantu speakers such as the Zulu indicates that the length of time that a group has inhabited a particular region is important in understanding why they have the color they do.

Cultural behaviors have probably also strongly influenced the evolution of skin color in recent human history. This effect can be seen in the indigenous peoples who live on the eastern and western banks of the Red Sea. The tribes on the western side, which speak so-called Nilo-Hamitic languages, are thought to have inhabited this region for as long as 6,000 years. These individuals are distinguished by very darkly pigmented skin and long, thin bodies with long limbs, which are excellent biological adaptations for dissipating heat and intense UV radiation. In contrast, modern agricultural and pastoral groups on the eastern bank of the Red Sea, on the Arabian Peninsula, have lived there for only about 2,000 years. These earliest Arab people, of European origin, have adapted to very similar environmental conditions by almost exclusively cultural means—wearing heavy protective clothing and devising portable shade in the form of tents. (Without such clothing, one would have expected their skin to have begun to darken.) Generally speaking, the more recently a group has migrated into an area, the more extensive its cultural, as opposed to biological, adaptations to the area will be.

Perils of Recent Migrations

Despite great improvements in overall human health in the past century, some diseases have appeared or reemerged in populations that had previously been little affected by them. One of these is skin cancer, especially basal and squamous cell carcinomas, among light-skinned peoples. Another is rickets, brought about by severe vitamin D deficiency, in dark-skinned peoples. Why are we seeing these conditions?

As people move from an area with one pattern of UV radiation to another region, biological and cultural adaptations have not been able to keep pace. The light-skinned people of northern European origin who bask in the sun of Florida or northern Australia increasingly pay the price in the form of premature aging of the skin and skin cancers, not to mention the unknown cost in human life of folate depletion. Conversely, a number of dark-skinned people of southern Asian and African origin now living in the northern U.K., northern Europe or the northeastern U.S. suffer from a lack of UV radiation and vitamin D, an insidious problem that manifests itself in high rates of rickets and other diseases related to vitamin D deficiency.

The ability of skin color to adapt over long periods to the various environments to which humans have moved reflects the importance of skin color to our survival. But its unstable nature also makes it one of the least useful characteristics in determining the evolutionary relations between human groups. Early Western scientists used skin color improperly to delineate human races, but the beauty of science is that it can and does correct itself. Our current knowledge of the evolution of human skin indicates that variations in skin color, like most of our physical attributes, can be explained by adaptation to the environment through natural selection. We look ahead to the day when the vestiges of old scientific mistakes will be erased and replaced by a better understanding of human origins and diversity. Our variation in skin color should be celebrated as one of the most visible manifestations of our evolution as a species.

More to Explore

The Evolution of Human Skin Coloration. Nina G. Jablonski and George Chaplin in *Journal of Human Evolution,* Vol. 39, No. 1, pages 57–106; July 1, 2000. An abstract of the article is available online at **www.idealibrary.com/links/doi/10.1006/jhev.2000.0403**

Why Skin Comes in Colors. Blake Edgar in *California Wild,* Vol. 53, No. 1, pages 6–7; Winter 2000. The article is also available at **www.calacademy.org/calwild/winter2000/html/horizons.html**

The Biology of Skin Color: Black and White. Gina Kirchweger in *Discover,* Vol. 22, No. 2, pages 32–33; February 2001. The article is also available at **www.discover.com/feb_01/featbiology.html**

Nina G. Jablonski and **George Chaplin** work at the California Academy of Sciences in San Francisco, where Jablonski is Irvine Chair and curator of anthropology, and Chaplin is a research associate in the department of anthropology. Jablonski's research centers on the evolutionary adaptations of monkeys, apes and humans. She is particularly interested in how primates have responded to changes over time in the global environment. Chaplin is a private geographic information systems consultant who specializes in describing and analyzing geographic trends in biodiversity. In 2001 he was awarded the Student of the Year prize by the Association of Geographic Information in London for his master's thesis on the environmental correlates of skin color.

Does Race Exist?

A Proponent's Perspective

GEORGE W. GILL

Slightly over half of all biological/physical anthropologists today believe in the traditional view that human races are biologically valid and real. Furthermore, they tend to see nothing wrong in defining and naming the different populations of *Homo sapiens*. The other half of the biological anthropology community believes either that the traditional racial categories for humankind are arbitrary and meaningless, or that at a minimum there are better ways to look at human variation than through the "racial lens."

Are there differences in the research concentrations of these two groups of experts? Yes, most decidedly there are. As pointed out in a recent 2000 edition of a popular physical anthropology textbook, forensic anthropologists (those who do skeletal identification for law-enforcement agencies) are overwhelmingly in support of the idea of the basic biological reality of human races, and yet those who work with blood-group data, for instance, tend to reject the biological reality of racial categories.

I happen to be one of those very few forensic physical anthropologists who actually does research on the particular traits used today in forensic racial identification (i.e., "assessing ancestry," as it is generally termed today). Partly this is because for more than a decade now U.S. national and regional forensic anthropology organizations have deemed it necessary to quantitatively test both traditional and new methods for accuracy in legal cases. I volunteered for this task of testing methods and developing new methods in the late 1980s. What have I found? Where do I now stand in the "great race debate?" Can I see truth on one side or the other—or on both sides—in this argument?

Findings

First, I have found that forensic anthropologists attain a high degree of accuracy in determining geographic racial affinities (white, black, American Indian, etc.) by utilizing both new and traditional methods of bone analysis. Many well-conducted studies were reported in the late 1980s and 1990s that test methods objectively for percentage of correct placement. Numerous individual methods involving midfacial measurements, femur traits, and so on are over 80 percent accurate alone, and in combination produce very high levels of accuracy. No forensic anthropologist would make a racial assessment based upon just *one* of these methods, but in combination they can make very reliable assessments, just as in determining sex or age. In other words, multiple criteria are the key to success in all of these determinations.

I have a respected colleague, the skeletal biologist C. Loring Brace, who is as skilled as any of the leading forensic anthropologists at assessing ancestry from bones, yet he does not subscribe to the concept of race. Neither does Norman Sauer, a board-certified forensic anthropologist. My students ask, "How can this be? They can identify skeletons as to racial origins but do not believe in race!" My answer is that we can often *function* within systems that we do not believe in.

As a middle-aged male, for example, I am not so sure that I believe any longer in the chronological "age" categories that many of my colleagues in skeletal biology use. Certainly parts of the skeletons of some 45-year-old people look older than corresponding portions of the skeletons of some 55-year-olds. If, however, law enforcement calls upon me to provide "age" on a skeleton, I can provide an answer that will be proven sufficiently accurate should the decedent eventually be identified. I may not believe in society's "age" categories, but I can be very effective at "aging" skeletons. The next question, of course, is how "real" is age biologically? My answer is that if one can use biological criteria to assess age with reasonable accuracy, then age has some basis in biological reality even if the particular "social construct" that defines its limits might be imperfect. I find this true not only for age and stature estimations but for sex and race identification.

The "reality of race" therefore depends more on the definition of reality than on the definition of race. If we choose to accept the system of racial taxonomy that physical anthropologists have traditionally established—major races: black, white, etc.—then one can classify human skeletons within it just as well as one can living humans. The bony traits of the nose, mouth, femur, and cranium are just as revealing to a good osteologist as skin color, hair form, nose form, and lips to the perceptive observer of living humanity. I have been able to prove to myself over the years, in actual legal cases, that I am *more* accurate at assessing race from skeletal remains than from looking at living people standing before me. So those of us in forensic anthropology know that the skeleton reflects race, whether "real" or not, just as well if not better than superficial soft tissue does. The idea that race is "only skin deep" is simply not true, as any experienced forensic anthropologist will affirm.

Position on Race

Where I stand today in the "great race debate" after a decade and a half of pertinent skeletal research is clearly more on the side of the reality of race than on the "race denial" side. Yet I do see why many other physical anthropologists are able to ignore or deny the race concept. Blood-factor analysis, for instance, shows many traits that cut across racial boundaries in a purely *clinal* fashion with very few if any "breaks" along racial boundaries. (A cline is a gradient of change, such as from people with a high frequency of blue eyes, as in Scandinavia, to people with a high frequency of brown eyes, as in Africa.)

Morphological characteristics, however, like skin color, hair form, bone traits, eyes, and lips tend to follow geographic boundaries coinciding often with climatic zones. This is not surprising since the selective forces of climate are probably the primary forces of nature that have shaped human races with regard not only to skin color and hair form but also the underlying bony structures of the nose, cheekbones, etc. (For example, more prominent noses humidify air better.) As far as we know, blood-factor frequencies are *not* shaped by these same climatic factors.

So, serologists who work largely with blood factors will tend to see human variation as clinal and races as not a valid construct, while skeletal biologists, particularly forensic anthropologists, will see races as biologically real. The common person on the street who sees only a person's skin color, hair form, and face shape will also tend to see races as biologically real. They are not incorrect. Their perspective is just different from that of the serologist.

So, yes, I see truth on both sides of the race argument.

Those who believe that the concept of race is valid do not discredit the notion of clines, however. Yet those with the clinal perspective who believe that races are not real do try to discredit the evidence of skeletal biology. Why this bias from the "race denial" faction? This bias seems to stem largely from sociopolitical motivation and not science at all. For the time being at least, the people in "race denial" are in "reality denial" as well. Their motivation (a positive one) is that they have come to believe that the race concept is socially dangerous. In other words, they have convinced themselves that race promotes racism. Therefore, they have pushed the politically correct agenda that human races are not biologically real, no matter what the evidence.

Consequently, at the beginning of the 21st century, even as a majority of biological anthropologists favor the reality of the race perspective, not one introductory textbook of physical anthropology even presents that perspective as a possibility. In a case as flagrant as this, we are not dealing with science but rather with blatant, politically motivated censorship. But, you may ask, are the politically correct actually correct? Is there a relationship between thinking about race and racism?

Race and Racism

Does discussing human variation in a framework of racial biology promote or reduce racism? This is an important question, but one that does not have a simple answer. Most social scientists over the past decade have convinced themselves that it runs the risk of promoting racism in certain quarters. Anthropologists of the 1950s, 1960s, and early 1970s, on the other hand, believed that they were combating racism by openly discussing race and by teaching courses on human races and racism. Which approach has worked best? What do the intellectuals among racial minorities believe? How do students react and respond?

Three years ago, I served on a NOVA-sponsored panel in New York, in which panelists debated the topic "Is There Such a Thing as Race?" Six of us sat on the panel, three proponents of the race concept and three antagonists. All had authored books or papers on race. Loring Brace and I were the two anthropologists "facing off" in the debate. The ethnic composition of the panel was three white and three black scholars. As our conversations developed, I was struck by how similar many of my concerns regarding racism were to those of my two black teammates. Although recognizing that embracing the race concept can have risks attached, we were (and are) more fearful of the form of racism likely to emerge if race is denied and dialogue about it lessened. We fear that the social taboo about the subject of race has served to suppress open discussion about a very important subject in need of dispassionate debate. One of my teammates, an affirmative-action lawyer, is afraid that a denial that races exist also serves to encourage a denial that racism exists. He asks, "How can we combat racism if no one is willing to talk about race?"

Who Will Benefit?

In my experience, minority students almost invariably have been the strongest supporters of a "racial perspective" on human variation in the classroom. The first-ever black student in my human variation class several years ago came to me at the end of the course and said, "Dr. Gill, I really want to thank you for changing my life with this course." He went on to explain that, "My whole life I have wondered about why I am black, and if that is good or bad. Now I know the reasons why I am the way I am and that these traits are useful and good."

A human-variation course with another perspective would probably have accomplished the same for this student if he had ever noticed it. The truth is, innocuous contemporary human-variation classes with their politically correct titles and course descriptions do not attract the attention of minorities or those other students who could most benefit. Furthermore, the politically correct "race denial" perspective in society as a whole suppresses dialogue, allowing ignorance to replace knowledge and suspicion to replace familiarity. This encourages ethnocentrism and racism more than it discourages it.

Dr. George W. Gill is a professor of anthropology at the University of Wyoming. He also serves as the forensic anthropologist for Wyoming law-enforcement agencies and the Wyoming State Crime Laboratory.

13

The Worst Mistake in the History of the Human Race

Jared Diamond

What we eat and how we eat are important both nutritionally and culturally. This selection suggests that how we get what we eat—through gathering and hunting versus agriculture, for example—has dramatic consequences. This seems pretty obvious. We all imagine what a struggle it must have been before the development of agriculture. We think of our ancestors spending their days searching for roots and berries to eat or, out at the crack of dawn, hunting wild animals. In fact, this was not quite the case. Nevertheless, isn't it really better simply to go to the refrigerator, open the door, and reach for a container of milk to pour into a bowl of flaked grain for your regular morning meal? What could be simpler and more nutritious?

There are many things that we seldom question; the truth seems so evident and the answers obvious. One such sacred cow is the tremendous prosperity brought about by the agricultural revolution. This selection is a thought-provoking introduction to the connection between culture and agriculture. The transition from food foraging to farming (what archaeologists call the Neolithic revolution) may have been the worst mistake in human history or its most important event. You be the judge. But for better or worse, this cultural evolution has occurred, and the world will never be the same again.

As you read this selection, ask yourself the following questions:

- What is the fundamental difference between the progressivist view and the revisionist interpretation?
- How did the development of agriculture affect people's health?
- What three reasons explain the changes brought about by the development of agriculture?
- How did the development of agriculture affect social equality, including gender equality?

The following terms discussed in this selection are included in the Glossary at the back of the book:

agricultural development
civilization
domestication of plants and animals
hunter-gatherers
Neolithic
paleontology
paleopathology
social stratification

To science we owe dramatic changes in our smug self-image. Astronomy taught us that our earth isn't the center of the universe but merely one of billions of heavenly bodies. From biology we learned that we weren't specially created by God but evolved along with millions of other species. Now archaeology is demolishing another sacred belief: that human history over the past million years has been a long tale of progress. In particular, recent discoveries suggest that the adoption of agriculture, supposedly our most decisive step toward a better life, was in many ways a catastrophe from which we have never recovered. With agriculture came the gross social and sexual inequality, the disease and despotism, that curse our existence.

At first, the evidence against this revisionist interpretation will strike twentieth-century Americans as irrefutable. We're better off in almost every respect than the people of the Middle Ages, who in turn had it easier than cavemen, who in turn were better off than apes. Just count our advantages. We enjoy the most abundant and varied foods, the best tools and material goods, some of the longest and healthiest lives, in history. Most of us are safe from starvation and predators. We get our energy from oil and machines, not

Diamond, Jared. "The Worst Mistake in the History of the Human Race." Discover Magazine. (May 1987):64–66. Reprinted with permission of the author.

from our sweat. What neo-Luddite among us would trade his life for that of a medieval peasant, a caveman, or an ape?

For most of our history we supported ourselves by hunting and gathering: we hunted wild animals and foraged for wild plants. It's a life that philosophers have traditionally regarded as nasty, brutish, and short. Since no food is grown and little is stored, there is (in this view) no respite from the struggle that starts anew each day to find wild foods and avoid starving. Our escape from this misery was facilitated only 10,000 years ago, when in different parts of the world people began to domesticate plants and animals. The agricultural revolution gradually spread until today it's nearly universal, and few tribes of hunter-gatherers survive.

From the progressivist perspective on which I was brought up, to ask "Why did almost all our hunter-gatherer ancestors adopt agriculture?" is silly. Of course they adopted it because agriculture is an efficient way to get more food for less work. Planted crops yield far more tons per acre than roots and berries. Just imagine a band of savages, exhausted from searching for nuts or chasing wild animals, suddenly gazing for the first time at a fruit-laden orchard or a pasture full of sheep. How many milliseconds do you think it would take them to appreciate the advantages of agriculture?

The progressivist party line sometimes even goes so far as to credit agriculture with the remarkable flowering of art that has taken place over the past few thousand years. Since crops can be stored, and since it takes less time to pick food from a garden than to find it in the wild, agriculture gave us free time that hunter-gatherers never had. Thus it was agriculture that enabled us to build the Parthenon and compose the B-minor Mass.

While the case for the progressivist view seems overwhelming, it's hard to prove. How do you show that the lives of people 10,000 years ago got better when they abandoned hunting and gathering for farming? Until recently, archaeologists had to resort to indirect tests, whose results (surprisingly) failed to support the progressivist view. Here's one example of an indirect test: Are twentieth-century hunter-gatherers really worse off than farmers? Scattered throughout the world, several dozen groups of so-called primitive people, like the Kalahari Bushmen, continue to support themselves that way. It turns out that these people have plenty of leisure time, sleep a good deal, and work less hard than their farming neighbors. For instance, the average time devoted each week to obtaining food is only 12 to 19 hours for one group of Bushmen, 14 hours or less for the Hadza nomads of Tanzania. One Bushman, when asked why he hadn't emulated neighboring tribes by adopting agriculture, replied, "Why should we, when there are so many mongongo nuts in the world?"

While farmers concentrate on high-carbohydrate crops like rice and potatoes, the mix of wild plants and animals in the diets of surviving hunter-gatherers provides more protein and a better balance of other nutrients. In one study, the Bushmen's average daily food intake (during a month when food was plentiful) was 2,140 calories and 93 grams of protein, considerably greater than the recommended daily allowance for people of their size. It's almost inconceivable that Bushmen, who eat 75 or so wild plants, could die of starvation the way hundreds of thousands of Irish farmers and their families did during the potato famine of the 1840s.

So the lives of at least the surviving hunter-gatherers aren't nasty and brutish, even though farmers have pushed them into some of the world's worst real estate. But modern hunter-gatherer societies that have rubbed shoulders with farming societies for thousands of years don't tell us about conditions before the agricultural revolution. The progressivist view is really making a claim about the distant past: that the lives of primitive people improved when they switched from gathering to farming. Archaeologists can date that switch by distinguishing remains of wild plants and animals from those of domesticated ones in prehistoric garbage dumps.

How can one deduce the health of the prehistoric garbage makers, and thereby directly test the progressivist view? That question has become answerable only in recent years, in part through the newly emerging techniques of paleopathology, the study of signs of disease in the remains of ancient peoples.

In some lucky situations, the paleopathologist has almost as much material to study as a pathologist today. For example, archaeologists in the Chilean deserts found well preserved mummies whose medical conditions at time of death could be determined by autopsy. And feces of long-dead Indians who lived in dry caves in Nevada remain sufficiently well preserved to be examined for hookworm and other parasites.

Usually the only human remains available for study are skeletons, but they permit a surprising number of deductions. To begin with, a skeleton reveals its owner's sex, weight, and approximate age. In the few cases where there are many skeletons, one can construct mortality tables like the ones life insurance companies use to calculate expected life span and risk of death at any given age. Paleopathologists can also calculate growth rates by measuring bones of people of different ages, examining teeth for enamel defects (signs of childhood malnutrition), and recognizing scars left on bones by anemia, tuberculosis, leprosy, and other diseases.

One straightforward example of what paleopathologists have learned from skeletons concerns historical changes in height. Skeletons from Greece and Turkey show that the average height of hunter-gatherers toward the end of the ice ages was a generous 5'9" for men, 5'5" for women. With the adoption of agriculture, height crashed, and by 3000 B.C. had reached a low of only 5'3" for men, 5' for women. By classical times heights were very slowly on the rise again, but modern Greeks and Turks have still not regained the average height of their distant ancestors.

Another example of paleopathology at work is the study of Indian skeletons from burial mounds in the Illinois and Ohio river valleys. At Dickson Mounds, located near the confluence of the Spoon and Illinois Rivers, archaeologists have excavated some 800 skeletons that paint a picture of the health changes that occurred when a hunter-gatherer culture gave way to intensive maize farming around A.D. 1150. Studies by George Armelagos and his colleagues then at the University of Massachusetts show these early farmers paid a price for their new-found livelihood. Compared to the hunter-gatherers who preceded them, the farmers had a nearly 50 percent increase in enamel defects indicative of malnutrition, a fourfold increase in iron-deficiency anemia (evidenced by a bone condition called porotic hyperostosis), a threefold rise in bone lesions reflecting infectious disease in general, and an increase in degenerative conditions of the spine, probably reflecting a lot of hard physical labor. "Life expectancy at birth in the pre-agricultural community was about twenty-six years," says Armelagos, "but in the post-agricultural community it was nineteen years. So these episodes of nutritional stress and infectious disease were seriously affecting their ability to survive."

The evidence suggests that the Indians at Dickson Mounds, like many other primitive peoples, took up farming not by choice but from necessity in order to feed their constantly growing numbers. "I don't think most hunter-gatherers farmed until they had to, and when they switched to farming they traded quality for quantity," says Mark Cohen of the State University of New York at Plattsburgh, co-editor, with Armelagos, of one of the seminal books in the field, *Paleopathology at the Origins of Agriculture.* "When I first started making that argument ten years ago, not many people agreed with me. Now it's become a respectable, albeit controversial, side of the debate."

There are at least three sets of reasons to explain the findings that agriculture was bad for health. First, hunter-gatherers enjoyed a varied diet, while early farmers obtained most of their food from one or a few starchy crops. The farmers gained cheap calories at the cost of poor nutrition. (Today just three high-carbohydrate plants—wheat, rice, and corn—provide the bulk of the calories consumed by the human species, yet each one is deficient in certain vitamins or amino acids essential to life.) Second, because of dependence on a limited number of crops, farmers ran the risk of starvation if one crop failed. Finally, the mere fact that agriculture encouraged people to clump together in crowded societies, many of which then carried on trade with other crowded societies, led to the spread of parasites and infectious disease. (Some archaeologists think it was crowding, rather than agriculture, that promoted disease, but this is a chicken-and-egg argument, because crowding encourages agriculture and vice versa.) Epidemics couldn't take hold when populations were scattered in small bands that constantly shifted camp. Tuberculosis and diarrheal disease had to await the rise of farming, measles and bubonic plague the appearance of large cities.

Besides malnutrition, starvation, and epidemic diseases, farming helped bring another curse upon humanity: deep class divisions. Hunter-gatherers have little or no stored food, and no concentrated food sources, like an orchard or a herd of cows: they live off the wild plants and animals they obtain each day. Therefore, there can be no kings, no class of social parasites who grow fat on food seized from others. Only in farming populations could a healthy, non-producing elite set itself above the disease-ridden masses. Skeletons from Greek tombs at Mycenae *c.* 1500 B.C. suggest that royals enjoyed a better diet than commoners, since the royal skeletons were two or three inches taller and had better teeth (on the average, one instead of six cavities or missing teeth). Among Chilean mummies from *c.* A.D. 1000, the élite were distinguished not only by ornaments and gold hair clips but also by a fourfold lower rate of bone lesions caused by disease.

Similar contrasts in nutrition and health persist on a global scale today. To people in rich countries like the U.S., it sounds ridiculous to extol the virtues of hunting and gathering. But Americans are an élite, dependent on oil and minerals that must often be imported from countries with poorer health and nutrition. If one could choose between being a peasant farmer in Ethiopia or a Bushman gatherer in the Kalahari, which do you think would be the better choice?

Farming may have encouraged inequality between the sexes, as well. Freed from the need to transport their babies during a nomadic existence, and under pressure to produce more hands to till the fields, farming women tended to have more frequent pregnancies than their hunter-gatherer counterparts—with consequent drains on their health. Among the Chilean mummies, for example, more women than men had bone lesions from infectious disease.

Women in agricultural societies were sometimes made beasts of burden. In New Guinea farming communities today I often see women staggering under loads of vegetables and firewood while the men walk empty-handed. Once while on a field trip there studying birds, I offered to pay some villagers to carry supplies from an airstrip to my mountain camp. The heaviest item was a 110-pound bag of rice, which I lashed to a pole and assigned to a team of four men to shoulder together. When I eventually caught up with the villagers, the men were carrying light loads, while one small woman weighing less than the bag of rice was bent under it, supporting its weight by a cord across her temples.

As for the claim that agriculture encouraged the flowering of art by providing us with leisure time, modern hunter-gatherers have at least as much free time as do farmers. The whole emphasis on leisure time as a critical factor seems to me misguided. Gorillas have had ample free time to build their own Parthenon, had they wanted to. While post-agricultural technological advances did make new art forms possible and preservation of art easier, great paintings and sculptures were already being produced by hunter-gatherers 15,000 years ago, and were still being produced as recently as the last century by such hunter-gatherers as some Eskimos and the Indians of the Pacific Northwest.

Thus with the advent of agriculture an élite became better off, but most people became worse off. Instead of swallowing the progressivist party line that we chose agriculture because it was good for us, we must ask how we got trapped by it despite its pitfalls.

One answer boils down to the adage "Might makes right." Farming could support many more people than hunting, albeit with a poorer quality of life. (Population densities of hunter-gatherers are rarely over one person per ten square miles, while farmers average 100 times that.) Partly, this is because a field planted entirely in edible crops lets one feed far more mouths than a forest with scattered edible plants. Partly, too, it's because nomadic hunter-gatherers have to keep their children spaced at four-year intervals by infanticide and other means, since a mother must carry her toddler until it's old enough to keep up with the adults. Because farm women don't have that burden, they can and often do bear a child every two years.

As population densities of hunter-gatherers slowly rose at the end of the ice ages, bands had to choose between feeding more mouths by taking the first steps toward agriculture, or else finding ways to limit growth. Some bands chose the former solution, unable to anticipate the evils of farming, and seduced by the transient abundance they enjoyed until population growth caught up with increased food production. Such bands outbred and then drove off or killed the bands that chose to remain hunter-gatherers, because a hundred malnourished farmers can still outfight one healthy hunter. It's not that hunter-gatherers abandoned their life style, but that those sensible enough not to abandon it were forced out of all areas except the ones farmers didn't want.

At this point it's instructive to recall the common complaint that archaeology is a luxury, concerned with the remote past, and offering no lessons for the present. Archaeologists studying the rise of farming have reconstructed a crucial stage at which we made the worst mistake in human history. Forced to choose between limiting population or trying to increase food production, we chose the latter and ended up with starvation, warfare, and tyranny.

Hunter-gatherers practiced the most successful and longest-lasting life style in human history. In contrast, we're still struggling with the mess into which agriculture has tumbled us, and it's unclear whether we can solve it. Suppose that an archaeologist who had visited us from outer space were trying to explain human history to his fellow spacelings. He might illustrate the results of his digs by a 24-hour clock on which one hour represents 100,000 years of real past time. If the history of the human race began at midnight, then we would now be almost at the end of our first day. We lived as hunter-gatherers for nearly the whole of that day, from midnight through dawn, noon, and sunset. Finally, at 11:54 p.m., we adopted agriculture. As our second midnight approaches, will the plight of famine-stricken peasants gradually spread to engulf us all? Or will we somehow achieve those seductive blessings that we imagine behind agriculture's glittering façade, and that have so far eluded us?

16

Disease and Death at Dr. Dickson's Mounds

Alan H. Goodman and George J. Armelagos

In a popular book, *The Third Wave*, Alvin Toffler identified three major "transformations" of global consequence. The first of these was the agricultural revolution, the second was the industrial revolution, and the third is the present-day technological revolution. The impacts of these events and processes are far-reaching and generally assumed to be quite positive. However, it is possible that there have been subtle, but exceedingly important, unintended consequences that have gone undetected. One of the best ways to raise awareness of these problems is to reexamine history. Of course, the agricultural revolution, which some anthropologists think may have been the most important event in human history, occurred during the prehistoric period. No written records were left, and it is therefore up to archaeologists to provide insights into the changes the agricultural revolution brought.

We do not need to go to the Near East, Asia, or Mesoamerica to study the transformation from hunting and gathering to agriculture. You can find it right in your own backyard. In this selection, Alan Goodman and George Armelagos examine the health consequences of the rise of agriculture. The paleopathological study of bones can be an important supplement to traditional archaeological description and analysis. Like the conclusions of Eaton and Konner on Paleolithic diet (Selection 9), cultural evolution does not always mean progress.

As you read this selection, ask yourself the following questions:

- What happened to the population density around Dickson's Mounds during the first fifty years of agriculture?
- What social changes seem to accompany the rise of agriculture?
- What three factors made possible the tracing of changing health patterns from preagricultural to postagricultural subsistence patterns?
- Did agriculture lead to a better diet and improved health conditions?
- Why did prehistoric people become farmers?

The following terms discussed in this selection are included in the Glossary at the back of the book:

dental anthropology
Mississippian tradition
paleopathology
population pressure
sickle-cell anemia

Clustered in west-central Illinois, atop a bluff near the confluence of the Illinois and Spoon rivers, are twelve to thirteen poorly defined earthen mounds. The mounds, which overlap each other to some extent, cover a crescent-shaped area of about an acre. Since at least the middle of the nineteenth century, local residents have known that prehistoric Native Americans built these mounds to bury their dead. But it was not until the late 1920s that Don Dickson, a chiropractor, undertook the first systematic excavation of the mounds located on farmland owned by his father. Barely into his thirties at the time, Dickson became so involved in the venture that he never returned to his chiropractic practice. Apparently, he was intrigued by the novel undertaking of unearthing skeletons and trying to diagnose the maladies of long-dead individuals. Later on, he became more concerned with the patterns of disease and death in this extinct group in order to understand how these people lived and why they often died at an early age.

The "Dickson Mounds" (the site also includes two early, unmounded burial grounds) quickly attracted the attention of professional anthropologists. In the early

Goodman, Alan H. & George J. Armelagos, "Disease and Death at Dr. Dickson's Mounds" from Natural History (Sept. 1985):12–18.

1930s, a team of University of Chicago archeologists exposed about 200 of the estimated 3,000 burials and identified a number of settlement sites in a 100-square-mile area. A second phase of excavation at Dickson began in the 1960s under the direction of Alan Harn, an archeologist working for the state of Illinois, whose crew excavated many of the local living sites and more than 800 additional burials. The archeological research revealed that these prehistoric people had taken part in an important transition, from hunting and gathering to an agricultural way of life.

About A.D. 950, hunter-gatherers lived along the Illinois River valley area near Dickson, subsisting on a wide range of local plants and animals, including grasses and seeds, fruits and berries, roots and tubers, vines, herbs, large and small mammals, migratory waterfowl and riverine birds, and fish. The moderate climate, copious water supply, and rich soil made this a bountiful and attractive area for hunter-gatherers. Groups occupied campsites that consisted of a few small structures, and the debris scattered around these sites suggests seasonal use. The population density was low, perhaps on the order of two to three persons per square mile. Then, about 1050, broken hoes and other agricultural tools, as well as maize, began to form part of village refuse, evidence of the introduction of maize agriculture. At the same time, the population grew. By 1200 the population density may have increased by a factor of ten, to about twenty-five persons per square mile. Living sites became larger and more permanent. The largest settlement in the area, Larson, was a residential and ceremonial center where some 1,000 inhabitants lived, many behind a palisaded wall.

Trade also flourished. Dickson became part of what archeologists call the Mississippian tradition, a network of maize-growing, mound-building societies that spread throughout most of the eastern United States. More and more, items used at the village sites or deposited as grave offerings were not of local origin. Some, such as marine shell necklaces, came from as far away as the Gulf of Mexico and Florida, one thousand miles to the south. Everyday objects such as spoons and jars were received from peoples of the eastern plains and the western prairies, while luxury items of ceremonial or decorative value arrived in trade from the south, probably coming upriver to Dickson through Cahokia, a Mississippian center some 110 miles away. Cahokia is a massive site that includes some 120 mounds within a six-square-mile area. As many as 30,000 persons lived at Cahokia and in the surrounding villages.

What we know about Dickson might have ended at this point, but continues because the skeletal remains that Harn excavated have been used to evaluate how the health of these prehistoric people fared following the adoption of agriculture and other changes in their life style. Interest in this issue stems from the writings of the eminent British archeologist V. Gordon Childe (1892–1957), who believed that the development of agriculture prompted the first great revolution in human technology, ushering in fundamental changes in economy, social organization, and ideology. Archeologists continue to debate the causes of agricultural revolutions. For example, some believe that in various regions of the world, increased population pressure, leading to food shortages and declining health, spurred the switch to agricultural food production. Others believe population increase was one of the consequences of agricultural revolutions. More important to us are the effects of an agricultural revolution on the health of people who lived at the time of such change.

Three circumstances have made it possible to test the effects agriculture had upon health at Dickson. First, Harn and those working with him valued the potential information to be gained from skeletons and therefore paid close attention to their excavation. Ultimately, the skeletal remains were sent to the University of Massachusetts at Amherst for analysis by George Armelagos and many of his graduate students (this is how we became involved). Second, the recovered remains include both individuals who lived before the development of maize agriculture (Late Woodland, or pre-Mississippian) and after (Mississippian). The two groups of individuals could be distinguished according to the mounds they were buried in, their placement within each mound, and their burial position (in earlier burials the bodies tend to be in a flexed or semiflexed position; in later burials they tend to be extended). The third enabling condition was provided by Janice Cohen, one of Armelagos's graduate students. Her analysis of highly heritable dental traits showed that although Dickson was in contact with persons from outside the central Illinois River valley area during the period of rapid cultural change, outside groups did not replace or significantly merge with the local groups. It is therefore possible to follow the health over time of a single population that, for all intents and purposes, was genetically stable.

As a doctoral student working under Armelagos in the early 1970s, John Lallo, now at Cleveland State University, set out to test whether health at Dickson improved, got worse, or remained the same with the advent of agriculture and its accompanying changes. Lallo argued that intensification of maize agriculture most likely resulted in a poorer diet. Although a common assumption is that the adoption of agriculture should have provided a prehistoric people with a better diet, there are good reasons to predict just the opposite. Heavy reliance on a single crop may lead to nutritional problems. Maize, for example, is deficient in lysine, an essential amino acid. Furthermore, agricultural societies that subsist on a few foodstuffs are more vulnerable to famines brought about by drought and other disasters. Finally, increased population density, a more sedentary life style, and greater trade, all of which are associated with agriculture, provide conditions for the spread and maintenance of infectious diseases.

The skeletons of individuals who lived before and after the introduction of maize agriculture were examined for a number of different health indicators, in order to provide a balanced picture of the pattern of stress, disease, and death that affected the Dickson population. The indicators that proved most sensitive to health differences were: bone lesions (scars) due to infection, nutritional deficiencies, trauma, and degenerative conditions; long bone growth; dental developmental defects; and age at death. To avoid unconscious bias, we and the other researchers involved measured these seven traits without knowing in advance which skeletons came from each of the two cultural periods.

Persistent bacterial infection leaves its mark on the outer, or periosteal, layer of bone. Tibias (shinbones) are the most frequently affected bones because they have relatively poor circulation and therefore tend to accumulate bacteria. Toxins produced by bacteria kill some of the bone cells; as new bone is produced, the periosteal bone becomes roughened and layered. Lallo and his co-workers found that following the introduction of agriculture there was a threefold increase in the percentage of individuals with such lesions. Eighty-four percent of the Mississippian tibias had these "periosteal reactions," as compared with only 26 percent of pre-Mississippian tibias. The lesions also tended to be more severe and to show up in younger individuals in the Mississippian population.

A second type of lesion, more easily seen in the thinner bones of the body (such as those of the skull), is a sign of anemia. In response to anemia, the body steps up its production of red blood cells, which are formed in the bone marrow. To accomplish this the marrow must expand at the expense of the outer layer of bone. In severe cases, this expansion may cause the outer layer of bone to disappear, exposing the porous, sieve-like inner bone. This lesion, called porotic hyperostosis, can occur with any kind of anemia. In the Dickson Mounds populations, the lesions are not severe, are restricted to the eye sockets and crania, and occur mainly in children and young adult females. This pattern suggests anemia resulting from a nutritional deficiency, specifically an iron deficiency. (A hereditary anemia, such as sickle-cell anemia, would have been more severe in its manifestation and would have affected all ages and both sexes in the population.)

There is a significant increase in the frequency of porotic hyperostosis during the Mississippian period. Half the Mississippian infants and children had porotic hyperostosis, twice the rate found for pre-Mississippian infants and children. Individuals with both periosteal reactions and porotic hyperostosis tend to have suffered more severely from each condition. This may be evidence of a deadly synergism of malnutrition and infection, like that often reported among contemporary populations.

Traumatic lesions were measured by diagnosis of healed fractures of the long bones of the legs and arms. Adult males had the highest frequency of such fractures. Approximately one out of three Mississippian males had at least one fracture, twice the frequency of their predecessors. These fractures often occurred at the midshaft of the ulna and radius, the bones of the lower arm. Fractures at this location are called parry fractures because they are typically the result of efforts to ward off a blow.

The frequency of degenerative pathologies, including arthritic conditions found on joints and the contacting surfaces of the vertebral column, also increased through time. One or more degenerative conditions were diagnosed in 40 percent of pre-Mississippian adults but in more than 70 percent of Mississippian adults.

In addition to the studies of the changing pattern of disease and trauma, we, along with Lallo and Jerome Rose, now at the University of Arkansas, assessed differences in skeletal growth and developmental timing. Skeletal growth and development are susceptible to a wide variety of stressful conditions and therefore reflect overall health. We found that in comparison to pre-Mississippians of the same age, Mississippian children between the ages of five and ten had significantly shorter and narrower tibias and femurs (the major long bones of the legs). This difference may be explained by a decreased rate of growth before the age of five. The Mississippians apparently were able to catch up in growth after age ten, however, since adult Mississippians are only slightly smaller than pre-Mississippians.

A more detailed exploration of developmental changes came from studying defects in enamel, the hard white coating of the crowns of teeth. Ameloblasts, the enamel-forming cells, secrete enamel matrix in ringlike fashion, starting at the biting surface and ending at the bottom of the crown. A deficiency in enamel thickness, called a hypoplasia, may result if the individual suffers a systemic physiological stress during enamel formation. Since the timing of enamel secretion is well known and relatively stable, the position of such a lesion on a tooth corresponds to an individual's age at the time of stress.

We examined the permanent teeth—teeth that form between birth and age seven. For skeletons with nearly complete sets of permanent teeth, 55 percent of pre-Mississippians had hypoplasias, while among Mississippians the figure rose to 80 percent. In both groups, hypoplasias were most frequently laid down between the ages of one and one-half and four. However, the hypoplasias in the Mississippian group peak at age two and one-half, approximately one-half year earlier than the pre-Mississippian peak. The peak is also more pronounced. This pattern of defects may indicate both an earlier age at weaning and the use of cereal products as weanling foods.

The repeated occurrence of hypoplasias within individuals revealed an annual cycle of stress. Most likely there was a seasonal food shortage. This seems to have worsened in the period just before the population becomes completely "Mississippianized," suggesting that it provided a rationale for intensifying agriculture.

All the above six indicators point toward a decrease in health associated with cultural change at Dickson. However, they are not meaningful apart from an analysis of the pattern of death in these populations. Healthy-looking skeletons, for example, may be the remains of young individuals who died outright because their bodies were too weak to cope in the face of disease, injury, and other forms of stress. Conversely, skeletons that show wear and tear may be those of individuals who survived during stressful times and lived to a ripe old age.

At Dickson, however, the trend is unambiguous. Individuals whose skeletons showed more signs of stress and disease (for example, enamel hypoplasias) also lived shorter lives, on average, than individuals with fewer such indications. For the population as a whole, life expectancy at birth decreased from twenty-six years in the pre-Mississippian to nineteen years in the Mississippian. The contrast in mortality is especially pronounced during the infant and childhood years. For example, 22 percent of Mississippians died during their first year as compared to 13 percent of the pre-Mississippians. Even for those who passed through the dangerous early years of childhood, there is a differential life expectancy. At fifteen years of age, pre-Mississippians could expect to live for an average of twenty-three more years, while Mississippians could expect to live for only eighteen more years.

What caused this decline in health? A number of possibilities have been proposed. Lallo and others have emphasized the effect of agriculture on diet. Most of the health trends may be explained by a decline in diet quality. These include the trends in growth, development, mortality, and nutritional disease, all four of which have obvious links to nutrition. The same explanation may be offered for the increase in infectious diseases, since increased susceptibility may be due to poor nutrition. Furthermore, a population subject to considerable infectious disease would be likely to suffer from other conditions, including increased rates of anemia and mortality and decreased growth rates.

The link between diet and infectious disease is bolstered by an analysis of trace elements from tibial bone cores. Robert Gilbert found that the Mississippian bones contain less zinc, an element that is limited in maize. Building on this research, Wadia Bahou, now a physician in Ann Arbor, Michigan, showed that the skeletons with the lowest levels of zinc had the highest frequency of infectious lesions. This is strong evidence that a diet of maize was relied on to a point where health was affected.

The population increase associated with the changeover to agriculture probably also contributed to the decline in health. We do not believe that the population ever threatened to exceed the carrying capacity of the bountiful Dickson area (and there are no signs of the environmental degradation one would expect to find if resources were overexploited). However, increased population density and sedentariness, coupled with intensification of contact with outsiders, create opportunities for the spread of infectious disease. George Milner of the University of Kentucky, while still a graduate student at Northwestern University, argued this point in comparing Dickson with the Kane Mounds populations. Kane is located near Cahokia, the major center south of Dickson. Despite Kane's proximity to this large center, its population density was much lower than at Larson, the major agricultural village of the Dickson population. Of the two, Kane had the lower rate of infectious diseases.

While the "agricultural hypothesis," including the effects of population pressure, offers an explanation for much of the health data, it doesn't automatically account for the two remaining measures: degenerative and traumatic pathologies. Poor nutrition and infectious disease may make people more susceptible to degenerative disease. However, the arthritic conditions found in the Dickson skeletons, involving movable joints, were probably caused by strenuous physical activity. The link, then, is not with the consumption of an agricultural diet but, if anything, with the physically taxing work of agricultural production. An explanation for the increase in traumatic injuries is harder to imagine. Possibly, the increased population density caused social tension and strife to arise within communities, but why should this have happened?

A curious fact makes us think that explanations based only on agricultural intensification and population increase are missing an important contributing factor. Recent archeological research at Dickson suggests that hunting and gathering remained productive enterprises and were never completely abandoned. Many of the local Mississippian sites have a great concentration of animal bones and projectile points used for hunting. A balanced diet apparently was available. The health and trace element data, however, suggest that the Mississippian diet was deficient. There is a disparity between what was available and what was eaten.

At present our search for an explanation for this paradox centers on the relationship between Dickson and the Cahokia population. The builders of the Dickson Mounds received many items of symbolic worth from the Cahokia region, such as copper-covered ear spools and marine shell necklaces. Much of the health data would be explained if Dickson had been trading perishable foodstuffs for these luxury items. In particular, the diversion of meat or fish to Cahokia would explain the apparent discrepancy between diet and resources.

To have a food surplus to trade, individuals from the Dickson area may have intensified their agricultural production while continuing to hunt and gather. The increase in degenerative conditions could have resulted from such a heavy workload. The system may also have put social strain on the community, leading to internal strife. And the accumulation of wealth in terms of ceremonial or other luxury items may have necessitated protection from outside groups. This would explain why the Larson site was palisaded. Both internal and external strain may have led to the increase in traumatic pathologies.

To test the validity of this scenario, we are hoping to gather additional evidence, concentrating on an analysis of trade. The flow of perishable goods such as meat is hard to trace, but we can study the sets of animal bones found at Cahokia and at Dickson village and butchering sites. The distribution of animal bones at the archeological sites can then be compared with examples of bone distributions in areas where trading has been ethnographically recorded. Further evidence is provided by data such as Milner's, which showed that health at Kane—a community that shared in Cahokia's power—was better than at Dickson.

The trading of needed food for items of symbolic value, to the point where health is threatened, may not seem to make sense from an objective outsider's perspective. But it is a situation that has been observed in historic and modern times. An indigenous group learns that it can trade something it has access to (sugar cane, alpacas, turtles) for something it greatly admires but can only obtain from outside groups (metal products, radios, alcohol). The group's members do not perceive that the long-term health and economic results of such trade are usually unfavorable. Nor are all such arrangements a result of voluntary agreement. The pattern of health observed at Dickson is seen in most situations where there is a decline in access to, and control over, resources. For example, lower classes in stratified societies live shorter lives and suffer more from nearly all major diseases.

Agriculture is not invariably associated with declining health. A recent volume edited by Mark N. Cohen and George J. Armelagos, *Paleopathology and the Origins of Agriculture,* analyzed health changes in twenty-three regions of the world where agriculture developed. In many of these regions there was a clear, concurrent decline in health, while in others there was little or no change or slight improvements in health. Perhaps a decline is more likely to occur when agriculture is intensified in the hinterland of a political system. Groups living far away from the centers of trade and power are apt to be at a disadvantage. They may send the best fruits of their labors to market and receive little in return. And during times of economic hardship or political turmoil, they may be the ones to suffer the most, as resources are concentrated on maintaining the central parts of the system.

14

Uncovering America's Pyramid Builders

Karen Wright

Travelers who pass through Collinsville, Illinois may know this Midwestern city as the "Horseradish Capital of the World" or as the home of a water tower in the shape of the world's largest ketchup bottle, but these superlatives are not what put this city on the list of United Nations World Heritage Sites. An earthen mound within city limits once served as the foundation of a 5,000 square foot temple bigger than any of the Egyptian pyramids at Giza. This mound, now known as Monks Mound, sat at the center of a thriving civilization that disappeared approximately 700 years ago.

The Cahokian civilization that built Monks Mound established their early city at the confluence of the Mississippi, Missouri, and Illinois rivers, creating an urban center that was a hub for regional trade. Many mysteries remain about Cohokia and its downfall, largely because this civilization did not use a written language and they used building materials that do not leave an enduring archaeological record. In this selection, Karen Wright presents conflicting interpretations about the size, nature, and collapse of what may have been the largest prehistoric settlement north of Mexico.

As you read this selection, ask yourself the following questions:

- How do the mounds of Cahokia and the civilization that built them compare with Pharaonic Egypt and the Great Pyramids of Giza?
- Why did migrants come to Cahokia in such great numbers?
- What factors may have contributed to the downfall of Cahokia?
- How and when were the Cahokian mounds re-discovered?
- How were Cahokia and Monks Mound named?

The following terms discussed in this selection are included in the Glossary at the back of the book:

chiefdom	*matriarchal*
United Nations World Heritage Site	*woodhenge*

When U.S. 40 reaches Collinsville, Illinois, the land is flat and open. Seedy storefronts line the highway: a pawnshop, a discount carpet warehouse, a taco joint, a bar. Only the Indian Mound Motel gives any hint that the road bisects something more than underdeveloped farmland. This is the Cahokia Mounds State Historic Site, a United Nations World Heritage Site on a par with the Great Wall of China, the Egyptian pyramids, and the Taj Mahal. The 4,000-acre complex preserves the remnants of the largest prehistoric settlement north of Mexico, a walled city that flourished on the floodplain of the Mississippi River 10 centuries ago. Covering an area more than five miles square, Cahokia dwarfs the ancient pueblos of New Mexico's Chaco Canyon and every other ruin left by the storied Anasazi of the American Southwest. Yet despite its size and importance, archaeologists still don't understand how this vast, lost culture began, how it ended, and what went on in between.

A thousand years ago, no one could have missed Cahokia—a complex, sophisticated society with an urban center, satellite villages, and as many as 50,000 people in all. Thatched-roof houses lined the central plazas. Merchants swapped copper, mica, and seashells from as far away as the Great Lakes and the Gulf of Mexico. Thousands of cooking fires burned night and day. And between A.D. 1000 and 1300, Cahokians built more than 120 earthen mounds as landmarks, tombs, and ceremonial platforms. The largest of these monuments, now called Monks Mound, still dominates the site. It is a flat-topped pyramid of dirt that covers more than 14 acres and once supported a 5,000-square-foot temple. Monks

Wright, Karen. "Uncovering America's Pyramid Builders."
This article first appeared in Discover Magazine (Feb. 2004):50–55.

Mound is bigger than any of the three great pyramids at Giza outside Cairo. "This is the third or fourth biggest pyramid in the world, in terms of volume," says archaeologist Tim Pauketat of the University of Illinois at Urbana-Champaign. It towers 100 feet over a 40-acre plaza that was surrounded by lesser mounds and a two-mile-long stockade. The monument was the crowning achievement of a mound-building culture that began thousands of years earlier and was never duplicated on this continent.

Why Cahokia crumbled and its people vanished is unknown. Malnutrition, overcrowding, a dwindling resource base, the raids of jealous trade partners—any or all of these reasons may have contributed to the city's demise. No one knows whether the populace cleared out all at once or dispersed gradually, but by A.D. 1300 Cahokia was a ghost town. By the time Europeans arrived in the Mississippi bottomland, the region was only sparsely settled, and none of the native residents could recount what had happened there centuries before. So far, archaeologists have uncovered no evidence of invasion, rampant disease, overpopulation, deforestation, or any of the other hallmarks of the decline and fall of civilization. Cahokia abounds in artifacts, but archaeologists have not yet made sense of them in a meaningful way. "It actually becomes quite scary," says John Kelly of Washington University in St. Louis. "After a while you begin to realize that you're dealing with rituals that had a great deal of meaning 800 years ago and that you're kind of clueless."

Intellectual frustration is not the only reason for Cahokia's obscurity. Pauketat complains that the region is geographically challenged. It has the look and feel of a place "like Buffalo, except warmer," he says. Cahokia doesn't exactly lure others away from more exotic digs in Turkey, Mexico, or Peru, he says. "That's the problem with this site." Another reason for its lack of popularity is the ordinary, perishable building materials used by the residents. "Cahokians are discounted because they built with dirt—dirt and wood, things they valued," says Pauketat. "I get tired of hearing people say, 'We have civilization and you guys don't.'"

Meanwhile, developers see Cahokia as ripe for expansion; strip malls and subdivisions threaten on every side. "It's developing faster than we can survey," Pauketat says. "We don't know what we're losing out there." Although a good portion of the central city is now protected, archaeologists are discovering related sites throughout a six-county region on both sides of the nearby Mississippi—an area 3,600 miles square. Indeed, digs are under way in such unlikely places as a railroad yard eight miles west in East St. Louis, where a new bridge is scheduled. "If you want to find out the archaeology of an area," says Brad Koldehoff of the Illinois Department of Transportation's archaeology team, "build a road through it."

One Morning last September, a warm red sun rose behind Monks Mound, inching above the level terrace where a tribal palace once stood, burning the mist off the flat green expanses of former plazas. To the west of the mound, in a circle more than 400 feet in diameter, several dozen cedar posts rise to the height of telephone poles. The woodhenge, as the structure is known, is a reconstruction of a series of circles found in the 1960s and '70s when excavations to build a mammoth clover-leaf joining three interstate highways unearthed the remains of several hundred houses and dozens of post pits. (The findings persuaded the Federal Highway Administration to relocate the cloverleaf a few miles north.)

At the autumnal equinox, the rising sun aligns exactly with one post when viewed from the center of the circle, just as it does at the spring equinox and the solstices. William Iseminger, assistant site manager for the Cahokia Mounds State Historic Society, takes these alignments as evidence that the posts may have functioned as a kind of calendar, marking the turn of the seasons. Other woodhenges may have been part of lesser mounds, but, says Iseminger, they are nearly impossible to find because the post pits are so far apart, and wood rarely survives centuries underground.

Many archaeologists point to the size and ambition of structures like the woodhenge as evidence of Cahokia's sophistication. The construction of Monks Mound, for example, used between 15 billion and 20 billion pounds of soil, which were lugged to the site in woven baskets that held 50 to 60 pounds of dirt each. Grading and draining the 40-acre plaza in front of it meant moving just as much earth. The stockade walls consumed 20,000 trees. Subsidiary mounds in the city "grid" seem to be placed according to a rational design. These accomplishments imply organized feats of labor and planning enacted by a central authority.

In many excavations, the number of artifacts and the amount of refuse indicate the population spiked sharply around A.D. 1100, jumping from hundreds to perhaps tens of thousands of people. Large homes and mounds appeared where villages of small houses had existed just a generation before. In the mid-1990s, excavations by Pauketat, Kelly, and others showed that the hills east of Cahokia were far more populous than anyone had suspected. A wooded rise among farmhouses in the city of O'Fallon marks the site of an ancient acropolis that probably served more than 500 people. At a site south of O'Fallon, Pauketat found remnants of 80 houses, three temples, clay pots, hoe blades, ax heads, and carved redstone statues. On a tree-lined street in Lebanon, a flagpole is planted in the center of a former platform mound marking another temple center.

Based on these findings, Pauketat estimates that as many as 50,000 people may have lived in Cahokia's greater metropolitan area at the settlement's peak. They seem to have appeared as if from nowhere. "Cahokia had to be created by large-scale migration from other places," says Tom Emerson, director of the state transportation department's archaeological program. "Nobody can breed that fast."

Why did migrants come to Cahokia? Past theories suggested that the dual forces of nature and commerce drove the city's rapid growth. The fertile bottomland was ripe for cultivation by farmers skilled in raising corn, squash, and sunflowers. The nearby confluence of the Illinois, Missouri, and Mississippi rivers could have put Cahokia at the nexus of trade networks that spanned much of the continent. But American Indians had been building modest mounds in the Mississippi River valley since 3500 B.C.; they'd been growing corn with much the same tools for hundreds of years, and the rivers and flood-plains had been there for thousands. Economic and geographic felicities alone cannot account for the sudden concentration of people in the area at a particular moment.

Pauketat has come to believe that charismatic leaders created a dynamic social movement with Cahokia at the epicenter, luring inhabitants of far-flung communities away from their home-steads to the fast urban action. Pauketat resists the term *cult*, but it evokes the phenomenon he envisions. "There were certainly individuals who were movers and shakers, but they weren't consciously, deliberately exploiting people," he asserts.

"Cahokia is a political construct," Emerson adds. "It's not due to some massive change in subsistence, it's not archaeological, it's not technological. It's the kind of place that results from changes in how you conduct yourself socially and politically. What happened at Cahokia is politics, probably in the guise of religion."

Not all scholars see a burgeoning statehood in Cahokia's remains. Anthropologist George Milner of Pennsylvania State University believes there were at most 8,000 people at Cahokia, and he calculates that with even half that population one person per household working just a few weeks a year could have built Monks Mound. The construction would have proceeded at a desultory pace, he concedes; it may have required hundreds of years to complete. Only if the woodhenges and mounds were rapidly constructed would they require full-time laborers or engineers. And he is skeptical that the ecology of the region, abundant as it was, could have supported a community as vast as that supposed by Pauketat and others.

The trump card for Milner and other minimalists is the fact that, unlike the ancient Mesopotamians, Maya, Egyptians, and Chinese, Cahokians never developed a written counterpart to their spoken language. Writing is generally considered a prerequisite for the kind of record keeping typical of organized governments. (The names "Cahokia" and "Monks Mound" were applied long after the fact: Cahokia was the name of an Illini tribe that occupied the area in the 1600s, and Monks Mound was named for French Trappists who settled on one of its terraces in the 1800s.)

But champions of an advanced Cahokian civilization would rather make their case with numbers than with language anyway. Even Milner admits that if Cahokia was as populous or expansive as some claim, it would have exerted statelike control over its citizens. To support his theory, Pauketat is looking for evidence that the settlements outside of Cahokia follow a planned pattern—a support network of communities allied with the power center, perhaps communicating with the capital using runners and smoke signals. He found traces of buildings at the intersection of Routes 159 and 64, now home to a Toys 'R' Us and a Ramada Inn, and he believes they may have faced Cahokia, a six-hour walk away. That orientation would bolster his contention that the outlying villages were all part of one big polity.

Early in his career at the state department of transportation, Tom Emerson found an eight-inch statuette at the site of a temple two or three miles from Cahokia. Five pounds of distinctive redstone called flint clay had been carved into a kneeling female figure sinking a hoe into the back of a serpent. The serpent's tail climbs up the woman's back, bearing squash and gourds like a vine. The images echo familiar pre-Columbian themes of reproductive and agricultural fertility. As similar figures were discovered in the Cahokian environs, a pattern emerged. Around A.D. 1100, Emerson says, the elite of Cahokia seem to have co-opted or codified the fertility symbol, raising it to an unprecedented stature that became a kind of brand identity for the budding metropolis. "They're taking a symbolism that exists across the entire hemisphere and selectively emphasizing parts of it to their own benefit," Emerson says.

Some archaeologists have taken the emphasis on the bucolic feminine as a sign that Cahokian society was peaceful, egalitarian, and possibly matriarchal. There is, in fact, no evidence that the city was ever invaded, and no indication of bellicose tendencies other than the robust stockade surrounding the city center. But Emerson warns against this interpretation.

For one thing, he says, war wasn't necessary, because it would have been clear from the city's size alone that it could mount raiding parties with more members than the total of men, women, and children in any of the surrounding villages. "Nobody could stand against Cahokia. I don't know that they had to do much actual conflict. It was mostly intimidation."

Cahokia's downfall has been blamed on a variety of culprits. A corn-based, protein-poor diet might have sent urban dwellers west in search of buffalo. A centuries-long cold spell could have crippled the region's agricultural productivity. Deforestation of the uplands would have choked downstream water supplies with silt and exacerbated flooding. Or the cause could have been those same intangibles invoked by latter-day theorists to describe Cahokia's rise: a shift in belief systems or the balance of power. Certainly the sprawling pacts that Cahokian chiefs may have forged with nearby villages would have challenged any lasting centralization of power.

"The typical life history of a chiefdom is that it comes together, it has its heyday, and it falls apart, all within a couple of generations," says Emerson. "The interesting thing about Cahokia is that it managed to hang together. The fact that it didn't go on forever isn't unusual at all."

One of Cahokia's chiefs appears to be buried in Mound 72, which lies a half mile south of Monks Mound. It is a modest hillock by comparison, but the site holds far grimmer implications about Cahokian society. During excavations there in the late 1960s, Melvin Fowler of the University of Wisconsin at Milwaukee uncovered the remains of more than 250 people. One middle-aged male had been laid on a shelf of 20,000 seashell beads arranged in the shape of a bird. Near him were the bones of six other people, a cache of more than 800 flint arrowheads, a rolled-up sheet of copper, and several bushels of unprocessed mica—all seemingly placed in tribute to the Beaded Birdman.

In other parts of the mound, skeletons of more than 100 young women clearly indicate human sacrifice, and another grouping of four men with no hands or heads denotes the same. Another 40 bodies seemed to have been tossed into a grave hap-hazardly. Other mass burials in Mound 72 show varying degrees of respect and carelessness—and seem to reflect some sort of social hierarchy as yet undeciphered. Human sacrifice, for example, can be a sign of a coercive society or of a cultlike mentality. "Mound 72 is an ancient text with its own set of Rosetta stones and is slow to give up its secrets," Fowler wrote in *Cahokia*, a book he coauthored with Biloine Whiting Young.

The cause of Cahokia's demise is no more certain, but at least one expert links it to the Toltec civilization of south-central Mexico some 1,400 miles away. Although no Mexican artifacts have ever been found at Cahokia, similarities in the monumental and ornamental styles are conspicuous—and far from accidental, according to anthropologist Stephen Lekson of the University of Colorado at Boulder. Lekson and anthropologist Peter Peregrine of Lawrence University in Wisconsin believe that the mound cultures of the American East, the pueblo cultures of the American Southwest, and the pyramid cultures of the Mexican highlands were not only familiar but possibly even integrated with one another. There's plenty of evidence for such an exchange at Chaco Canyon, where copper bells, macaw feathers, pyrite mirrors, and other Mexican goods turn up. But Chaco was a wannabe compared with Cahokia—much smaller, far less populous, and without a centuries-long tradition preceding its development. Cahokia, with its central location, entrenched culture, and extensive trade network, didn't need Mexican trinkets to bolster its stature, Lekson says. "If someone from Cahokia showed up in any major town in Mexico, he'd be taken seriously," says Lekson. "But if someone from Chaco wandered in, they'd ask him if he had an appointment."

The Toltec, Chaco, and Cahokian societies all collapsed at very nearly the same moment, and Lekson believes that that, too, is no accident. Events in Mexico may have rippled up the Gulf Coast to the Mississippi and thence to Cahokia. "I'm not saying that Mexico is pulling everybody's strings," says Lekson. "But [the cultures] are more alike than not, and it's interesting to ask why."

Interesting as it might be, a continental perspective doesn't yield an explanation, because no one's sure what caused the Toltec regime to fall, either. It may be that if scientists ever determine why Cahokia fell, they may be able to help explain what happened elsewhere in the Americas. At present it's still anyone's guess. "We are telling stories that will fall apart in the future," says Pauketat. "But we can't ignore the evidence, either. You could make the mistake of saying this is a coercive society, based on Mound 72. Or you could look at the outlying villages and say, 'This is a peaceful community.' They must have *wanted* to build Cahokia. The truth may be somewhere in between. We don't really know what happened here."

Shakespeare in the Bush

Laura Bohannan

Just before I left Oxford for the Tiv in West Africa, conversation turned to the season at Stratford. "You Americans," said a friend, "often have difficulty with Shakespeare. He was, after all, a very English poet, and one can easily misinterpret the universal by misunderstanding the particular."

I protested that human nature is pretty much the same the whole world over; at least the general plot and motivation of the greater tragedies would always be clear—everywhere—although some details of custom might have to be explained and difficulties of translation might produce other slight changes. To end an argument we could not conclude, my friend gave me a copy of *Hamlet* to study in the African bush: it would, he hoped, lift my mind above its primitive surroundings, and possibly I might, by prolonged meditation, achieve the grace of correct interpretation.

It was my second field trip to that African tribe, and I thought myself ready to live in one of its remote sections—an area difficult to cross even on foot. I eventually settled on the hillock of a very knowledgeable old man, the head of a homestead of some hundred and forty people, all of whom were either his close relatives or their wives and children. Like the other elders of the vicinity, the old man spent most of his time performing ceremonies seldom seen these days in the more accessible parts of the tribe. I was delighted. Soon there would be three months of enforced isolation and leisure, between the harvest that takes place just before the rising of the swamps and the clearing of new farms when the water goes down. Then, I thought, they would have even more time to perform ceremonies and explain them to me.

I was quite mistaken. Most of the ceremonies demanded the presence of elders from several homesteads. As the swamps rose, the old men found it too difficult to walk from one homestead to the next, and the ceremonies gradually ceased. As the swamps rose even higher, all activities but one came to an end. The women brewed beer from maize and millet. Men, women, and children sat on their hillocks and drank it.

People began to drink at dawn. By midmorning the whole homestead was singing, dancing, and drumming. When it rained, people had to sit inside their huts: there they drank and sang or they drank and told stories. In any case, by noon or before, I either had to join the party or retire to my own hut and my books. "One does not discuss serious matters when there is beer. Come, drink with us." Since I lacked their capacity for the thick native beer, I spent more and more time with *Hamlet.* Before the end of the second month, grace descended on me. I was quite sure that *Hamlet* had only one possible interpretation, and that one universally obvious.

Early every morning, in the hope of having some serious talk before the beer party, I used to call on the old man at his reception hut—a circle of posts supporting a thatched roof above a low mud wall to keep out wind and rain. One day I crawled through the low doorway and found most of the men of the homestead sitting huddled in their ragged cloths on stools, low plank beds, and reclining chairs, warming themselves against the chill of the rain around a smoky fire. In the center were three pots of beer. The party had started.

The old man greeted me cordially. "Sit down and drink." I accepted a large calabash full of beer, poured some into a small drinking gourd, and tossed it down. Then I poured some more into the same gourd for the man second in seniority to my host before I handed my calabash over to a young man for further distribution. Important people shouldn't ladle beer themselves.

"It is better like this," the old man said, looking at me approvingly and plucking at the thatch that had caught in my hair. "You should sit and drink with us more often. Your servants tell me that when you are not with us, you sit inside your hut looking at a paper."

The old man was acquainted with four kinds of "papers": tax receipts, bride price receipts, court fee receipts, and letters. The messenger who brought him letters from the chief used them mainly as a badge of office, for he always knew what was in them and told the old man. Personal letters for the few who had relatives in the government or mission stations were kept until someone went to a large market where there was a letter writer and reader. Since my arrival, letters were brought to me to be read. A few men also brought me bride price receipts, privately, with requests to change the figures to a higher sum. I found moral arguments were of no avail, since in-laws are fair game, and the technical hazards of forgery difficult to explain to an illiterate people. I did not wish them to think me silly enough to look at any such papers for days on end, and I hastily explained that my "paper" was one of the "things of long ago" of my country.

"Ah," said the old man. "Tell us."

I protested that I was not a storyteller. Story telling is a skilled art among them; their standards are high, and the audiences critical—and vocal in their criticism. I protested in vain. This morning they wanted to hear a story while they drank. They threatened to tell me no more stories until I told them one of mine. Finally, the old man promised that no one would criticize my style "for we know you are struggling with our language." "But," put in one of the elders, "you must explain what we do not understand, as we do when we tell you our stories." Realizing that here was my chance to prove *Hamlet* universally intelligible, I agreed.

The old man handed me some more beer to help me on with my storytelling. Men filled their long wooden pipes and knocked coals from the fire to place in the pipe bowls; then, puffing contentedly, they sat back to listen. I began in the proper style, "Not yesterday, not yesterday, but long ago, a thing occurred. One night three men were keeping watch outside the homestead of the great chief, when suddenly they saw the former chief approach them."

"Why was he no longer their chief?"

"He was dead," I explained. "That is why they were troubled and afraid when they saw him."

"Impossible," began one of the elders, handing his pipe on to his neighbor, who interrupted, "Of course it wasn't the dead chief. It was an omen sent by a witch. Go on."

Slightly shaken, I continued. "One of these three was a man who knew things"—the closest translation for scholar, but unfortunately it also meant witch. The second elder looked triumphantly at the first. "So he spoke to the dead chief saying, 'Tell us what we must do so you may rest in your grave,' but the dead chief did not answer. He vanished, and they could see him no more. Then the man who knew things—his name was Horatio—said this event was the affair of the dead chief's son, Hamlet."

There was a general shaking of heads round the circle. "Had the dead chief no living brothers? Or was this son the chief?"

"No," I replied. "That is, he had one living brother who became the chief when the elder brother died."

The old men muttered: such omens were matters for chiefs and elders, not for youngsters; no good could come of going behind a chief's back; clearly Horatio was not a man who knew things.

"Yes, he was," I insisted, shooing a chicken away from my beer. "In our country the son is next to the father. The dead chief's younger brother had become the great chief. He had also married his elder brother's widow only about a month after the funeral."

"He did well," the old man beamed and announced to the others, "I told you that if we knew more about Europeans, we would find they really were very like us. In our country also," he added to me, "the younger brother marries the elder brother's widow and becomes the father of his children. Now, if your uncle, who married your widowed mother, is your father's full brother, then he will be a real father to you. Did Hamlet's father and uncle have one mother?"

His question barely penetrated my mind; I was too upset and thrown too far off balance by having one of the most important elements of *Hamlet* knocked straight out of the picture. Rather uncertainly I said that I thought they had the same mother, but I wasn't sure—the story didn't say. The old man told me severely that these genealogical details made all the difference and that when I got home I must ask the elders about it. He shouted out the door to one of his younger wives to bring his goatskin bag.

Determined to save what I could of the mother motif, I took a deep breath and began again. "The son Hamlet was very sad because his mother had married again so quickly. There was no need for her to do so, and it is our custom for a widow not to go to her next husband until she has mourned for two years."

"Two years is too long," objected the wife, who had appeared with the old man's battered goatskin bag. "Who will hoe your farms for you while you have no husband?"

"Hamlet," I retorted without thinking, "was old enough to hoe his mother's farms himself. There was no need for her to remarry." No one looked convinced. I gave up. "His mother and the great chief told Hamlet not to be sad, for the great chief himself would be a father to Hamlet. Furthermore, Hamlet would be the next chief: therefore he must stay to learn the things of a chief. Hamlet agreed to remain, and all the rest went off to drink beer."

While I paused, perplexed at how to render Hamlet's disgusted soliloquy to an audience convinced that Claudius and Gertrude had behaved in the best possible manner, one of the younger men asked me who had married the other wives of the dead chief.

"He had no other wives," I told him.

"But a chief must have many wives! How else can he brew beer and prepare food for all his guests?"

I said firmly that in our country even chiefs had only one wife, that they had servants to do their work, and that they paid them from tax money.

It was better, they returned, for a chief to have many wives and sons who would help him hoe his farms and feed his people; then everyone loved the chief who gave much and took nothing—taxes were a bad thing.

I agreed with the last comment, but for the rest fell back on their favorite way of fobbing off my questions: "That is the way it is done, so that is how we do it."

I decided to skip the soliloquy. Even if Claudius was here thought quite right to marry his brother's widow, there remained the poison motif, and I knew they would disapprove of fratricide. More hopefully I resumed, "That night Hamlet kept watch with the three who had seen his dead father. The dead chief again appeared, and although the others were afraid, Hamlet followed his dead father off to one side. When they were alone, Hamlet's dead father spoke."

"Omens can't talk!" The old man was emphatic.

"Hamlet's dead father wasn't an omen. Seeing him might have been an omen, but he was not." My audience looked as confused as I sounded. "It *was* Hamlet's dead father. It was a thing we call a 'ghost.'" I had to use the English word, for unlike many of the neighboring tribes, these people didn't believe in the survival after death of any individuating part of the personality.

"What is a 'ghost?' An omen?"

"No, a 'ghost' is someone who is dead but who walks around and can talk, and people can hear him and see him but not touch him."

They objected. "One can touch zombis."

"No, no! It was not a dead body the witches had animated to sacrifice and eat. No one else made Hamlet's dead father walk. He did it himself."

"Dead men can't walk," protested my audience as one man.

I was quite willing to compromise. "A 'ghost' is the dead man's shadow."

But again they objected. "Dead men cast no shadows."

"They do in my country," I snapped.

The old man quelled the babble of disbelief that arose immediately and told me with that insincere, but courteous, agreement one extends to the fancies of the young, ignorant, and superstitious, "No doubt in your country the dead can also walk without being zombis." From the depths of his bag he produced a withered fragment of kola nut, bit off one end to show it wasn't poisoned, and handed me the rest as a peace offering.

"Anyhow," I resumed, "Hamlet's dead father said that his own brother, the one who became chief, had poisoned him. He wanted Hamlet to avenge him. Hamlet believed this in his heart, for he did not like his father's brother." I took another swallow of beer. "In the country of the great chief, living in the same homestead, for it was a very large one, was an important elder who was often with the chief to advise and help him. His name was Polonius. Hamlet was courting his daughter, but her father and her brother . . . [I cast hastily about for some tribal analogy] warned her not to let Hamlet visit her when she was alone on her farm, for he would be a great chief and so could not marry her."

"Why not?" asked the wife, who had settled down on the edge of the old man's chair. He frowned at her for asking stupid questions and growled, "They lived in the same homestead."

"That was not the reason," I informed them. "Polonius was a stranger who lived in the homestead because he helped the chief, not because he was a relative."

"Then why couldn't Hamlet marry her?"

"He could have," I explained, "but Polonius didn't think he would. After all, Hamlet was a man of great importance who ought to marry a chief's daughter, for in his country a man could have only one wife. Polonius was afraid that if Hamlet made love to his daughter, then no one else would give a high price for her."

"That might be true," remarked one of the shrewder elders, "but a chief's son would give his mistress's father enough presents and patronage to more than make up the difference. Polonius sounds like a fool to me."

"Many people think he was," I agreed. "Meanwhile Polonius sent his son Laertes off to Paris to learn the things of that country, for it was the homestead of a very great chief indeed. Because he was afraid that Laertes might waste a lot of money on beer and women and gambling, or get into trouble by fighting, he sent one of his servants to Paris secretly, to spy out what Laertes was doing. One day Hamlet came upon Polonius's daughter Ophelia. He behaved so oddly he frightened her. Indeed"—I was fumbling for words to express the dubious quality of Hamlet's madness—"the chief and many others had also noticed that when Hamlet talked one could understand the words but not what they meant. Many people thought that he had become mad." My audience suddenly became much more attentive. "The great chief wanted to know what was wrong with Hamlet, so he sent for two of Hamlet's age mates [school friends would have taken long explanation] to talk to Hamlet and find out what troubled his heart. Hamlet, seeing that they had been bribed by the chief to betray him, told them nothing. Polonius, however, insisted that Hamlet was mad because he had been forbidden to see Ophelia, whom he loved."

"Why," inquired a bewildered voice, "should anyone bewitch Hamlet on that account?"

"Bewitch him?"

"Yes, only witchcraft can make anyone mad, unless, of course, one sees the beings that lurk in the forest."

I stopped being a storyteller, took out my notebook and demanded to be told more about these two causes of madness. Even while they spoke and I jotted notes, I tried to calculate the effect of this new factor on the plot. Hamlet had not been exposed to the beings that lurk in the forests. Only his relatives in the male line could bewitch him. Barring relatives not mentioned by Shakespeare, it had to be Claudius who was attempting to harm him. And, of course, it was.

For the moment I staved off questions by saying that the great chief also refused to believe that Hamlet was mad for the love of Ophelia and nothing else. "He was sure that something much more important was troubling Hamlet's heart."

"Now Hamlet's age mates," I continued, "had brought with them a famous storyteller. Hamlet decided to have this man tell the chief and all his homestead a story about a man who had poisoned his brother because he desired his brother's wife and wished to be chief himself. Hamlet was sure the great chief could not hear the story without making a sign if he was indeed guilty, and then he would discover whether his dead father had told him the truth."

The old man interrupted, with deep cunning, "Why should a father lie to his son?" he asked.

I hedged: "Hamlet wasn't sure that it really was his dead father." It was impossible to say anything, in that language, about devil-inspired visions.

"You mean," he said, "it actually was an omen, and he knew witches sometimes send false ones. Hamlet was a fool not to go to one skilled in reading omens and divining the truth in the first place. A man-who-sees-the-truth could have told him how his father died, if he really had been poisoned, and if there was witchcraft in it; then Hamlet could have called the elders to settle the matter."

The shrewd elder ventured to disagree. "Because his father's brother was a great chief, one-who-sees-the-truth might therefore have been afraid to tell it. I think it was for that reason that a friend of Hamlet's father—a witch and an elder—sent an omen so his friend's son would know. Was the omen true?"

"Yes," I said, abandoning ghosts and the devil; a witch-sent omen it would have to be. "It was true, for when the storyteller was telling his tale before all the homestead, the great chief rose in fear. Afraid that Hamlet knew his secret he planned to have him killed."

The stage set of the next bit presented some difficulties of translation. I began cautiously. "The great chief told Hamlet's mother to find out from her son what he knew. But because a woman's children are always first in her heart, he had the important elder Polonius hide behind a cloth that hung against the wall of Hamlet's mother's sleeping hut. Hamlet started to scold his mother for what she had done."

There was a shocked murmur from everyone. A man should never scold his mother.

"She called out in fear, and Polonius moved behind the cloth. Shouting, 'A rat!' Hamlet took his machete and slashed through the cloth." I paused for dramatic effect. "He had killed Polonius!"

The old men looked at each other in supreme disgust. "That Polonius truly was a fool and a man who knew nothing! What child would not know enough to shout, 'It's me!' " With a pang, I remembered that these people are ardent hunters, always armed with bow, arrow, and machete; at the first rustle in the grass an arrow is aimed and ready, and the hunter shouts "Game!" If no human voice answers immediately, the arrow speeds on its way. Like a good hunter Hamlet had shouted, "A rat!"

I rushed in to save Polonius's reputation. "Polonius did speak. Hamlet heard him. But he thought it was the chief and wished to kill him earlier that evening. . . ." I broke down, unable to describe to these pagans, who had no belief in individual afterlife, the difference between dying at one's prayers and dying "unhousell'd, disappointed, unaneled."

This time I had shocked my audience seriously. "For a man to raise his hand against his father's brother and the one who has become his father—that is a terrible thing. The elders ought to let such a man be bewitched."

I nibbled at my kola nut in some perplexity, then pointed out that after all the man had killed Hamlet's father.

"No," pronounced the old man, speaking less to me than to the young men sitting behind the elders. "If your father's brother has killed your father, you must appeal to your father's age mates; *they* may avenge him. No man may use violence against his senior relatives." Another thought struck him. "But if his father's brother had indeed been wicked enough to bewitch Hamlet and make him mad that would be a good story indeed, for it would be his fault that Hamlet, being mad, no longer had any sense and thus was ready to kill his father's brother."

There was a murmur of applause. *Hamlet* was again a good story to them, but it no longer seemed quite the same story to me. As I thought over the coming complications of plot and motive, I lost courage and decided to skim over dangerous ground quickly.

"The great chief," I went on, "was not sorry that Hamlet had killed Polonius. It gave him a reason to send Hamlet away, with his two treacherous mates, with letters to a chief of a far country, saying that Hamlet should be killed. But Hamlet changed the writing on their papers, so that the chief killed his age mates instead." I encountered a reproachful glare from one of the men whom I had told undetectable forgery was not merely immoral but beyond human skill. I looked the other way.

"Before Hamlet could return, Laertes came back for his father's funeral. The great chief told him Hamlet had killed Polonius. Laertes swore to kill Hamlet because of this, and because his sister Ophelia, hearing her father had been killed by the man she loved, went mad and drowned in the river."

"Have you already forgotten what we told you?" The old man was reproachful. "One cannot take vengeance on a madman; Hamlet killed Polonius in his madness. As for the girl, she not only went mad, she was drowned. Only witches can make people drown. Water itself can't hurt anything. It is merely something one drinks and bathes in."

I began to get cross. "If you don't like the story, I'll stop."

The old man made soothing noises and himself poured me some more beer. "You tell the story well, and we are listening. But it is clear that the elders of your country have never told you what the story really means. No, don't interrupt! We believe you when you say your marriage customs are different, or your clothes and weapons. But people are the same everywhere; therefore, there are always witches and it is we, the elders, who know how witches work. We told you it was the great chief who wished to kill Hamlet, and now your own words have proved us right. Who were Ophelia's male relatives?"

"There were only her father and her brother." *Hamlet* was clearly out of my hands.

"There must have been many more; this also you must ask of your elders when you get back to your country. From what you tell us, since Polonius was dead, it must have been Laertes who killed Ophelia, although I do not see the reason for it."

We had emptied one pot of beer, and the old men argued the point with slightly tipsy interest. Finally one of them demanded of me, "What did the servant of Polonius say on his return?"

With difficulty I recollected Reynaldo and his mission. "I don't think he did return before Polonius was killed."

"Listen," said the elder, "and I will tell you how it was and how your story will go, then you may tell me if I am right. Polonius knew his son would get into trouble, and so he did. He had many fines to pay for fighting, and debts from gambling. But he had only two ways of getting money quickly. One was to marry off his sister at once, but it is difficult to find a man who will marry a woman desired by the son of a chief. For if the chief's heir commits adultery with your wife, what can you do? Only a fool calls a case against a man who will someday be his judge. Therefore Laertes had to take the second way: he killed his sister by witchcraft, drowning her so he could secretly sell her body to the witches."

I raised an objection. "They found her body and buried it. Indeed Laertes jumped into the grave to see his sister once more—so, you see, the body was truly there. Hamlet, who had just come back, jumped in after him."

"What did I tell you?" The elder appealed to the others. "Laertes was up to no good with his sister's body. Hamlet prevented him, because the chief's heir, like a chief, does not wish any other man to grow rich and powerful. Laertes would be angry, because he would have killed his sister without benefit to himself. In our country he would try to kill Hamlet for that reason. Is this not what happened?"

"More or less," I admitted. "When the great chief found Hamlet was still alive, he encouraged Laertes to try to kill Hamlet and arranged a fight with machetes between them. In the fight both the young men were wounded to death. Hamlet's mother drank the poisoned beer that the chief meant for Hamlet in case he won the fight. When he saw his mother die of poison, Hamlet, dying, managed to kill his father's brother with his machete."

"You see, I was right!" exclaimed the elder.

"That was a very good story," added the old man, "and you told it with very few mistakes. There was just one more error, at the very end. The poison Hamlet's mother drank was obviously meant for the survivor of the fight, whichever it was. If Laertes had won, the great chief would have poisoned him, for no one would know that he arranged Hamlet's death. Then, too, he need not fear Laertes' witchcraft; it takes a strong heart to kill one's only sister by witchcraft.

"Sometime," concluded the old man, gathering his ragged toga about him, "you must tell us some more stories of your country. We, who are elders, will instruct you in their true meaning, so that when you return to your own land your elders will see that you have not been sitting in the bush, but among those who know things and who have taught you wisdom."

Laura Bohannan is a former professor of anthropology at the University of Illinois, at Chicago.

Anthropology and Counterinsurgency

The Strange Story of Their Curious Relationship

MONTGOMERY MCFATE

Something mysterious is going on inside the U.S. Department of Defense (DOD). Over the past 2 years, senior leaders have been calling for something unusual and unexpected—cultural knowledge of the adversary. In July 2004, retired Major General Robert H. Scales, Jr., wrote an article for the Naval War College's Proceedings magazine that opposed the commonly held view within the U.S. military that success in war is best achieved by overwhelming technological advantage. Scales argues that the type of conflict we are now witnessing in Iraq requires "an exceptional ability to understand people, their culture, and their motivation."[1] In October 2004, Arthur Cebrowski, Director of the Office of Force Transformation, concluded that "knowledge of one's enemy and his culture and society may be more important than knowledge of his order of battle."[2] In November 2004, the Office of Naval Research and the Defense Advanced Research Projects Agency (DARPA) sponsored the Adversary Cultural Knowledge and National Security Conference, the first major DOD conference on the social sciences since 1962.

Why has cultural knowledge suddenly become such an imperative? Primarily because traditional methods of warfighting have proven inadequate in Iraq and Afghanistan. U.S. technology, training, and doctrine designed to counter the Soviet threat are not designed for low-intensity counterinsurgency operations where civilians mingle freely with combatants in complex urban terrain.

The major combat operations that toppled Saddam Hussein's regime were relatively simple because they required the U.S. military to do what it does best—conduct maneuver warfare in flat terrain using overwhelming firepower with air support. However, since the end of the "hot" phase of the war, coalition forces have been fighting a complex war against an enemy they do not understand. The insurgents' organizational structure is not military, but tribal. Their tactics are not conventional, but asymmetrical. Their weapons are not tanks and fighter planes, but improvised explosive devices (IEDs). They do not abide by the Geneva Conventions, nor do they appear to have any informal rules of engagement.

Countering the insurgency in Iraq requires cultural and social knowledge of the adversary. Yet, none of the elements of U.S. national power—diplomatic, military, intelligence, or economic—explicitly take adversary culture into account in the formation or execution of policy. This cultural knowledge gap has a simple cause—the almost total absence of anthropology within the national-security establishment.

Once called "the handmaiden of colonialism," anthropology has had a long, fruitful relationship with various elements of national power, which ended suddenly following the Vietnam War. The strange story of anthropology's birth as a warfighting discipline, and its sudden plunge into the abyss of postmodernism, is intertwined with the U.S. failure in Vietnam. The curious and conspicuous lack of anthropology in the national-security arena since the Vietnam War has had grave consequences for countering the insurgency in Iraq, particularly because political policy and military operations based on partial and incomplete cultural knowledge are often worse than none at all.

A Lack of Cultural Awareness

In a conflict between symmetric adversaries, where both are evenly matched and using similar technology, understanding the adversary's culture is largely irrelevant. The Cold War, for all its complexity, pitted two powers of European heritage against each other. In a counterinsurgency operation against a non-Western adversary, however, culture matters. U.S. Department of the Army Field Manual (FM) (interim) 3-07.22, Counterinsurgency Operations, defines insurgency as an "organized movement aimed at the overthrow of a constituted government through use of subversion and armed conflict. It is a protracted politico-military struggle designed to weaken government control and legitimacy while increasing insurgent control. Political power is the central issue in an insurgency [emphasis added]." Political considerations must therefore circumscribe military action as a fundamental matter of strategy. As British Field Marshall Gerald Templar explained in 1953, "The answer lies not in pouring more troops into the jungle, but rests in the hearts and minds of the . . . people." Winning hearts and minds requires understanding the local culture.[3]

Aside from Special Forces, most U.S. soldiers are not trained to understand or operate in foreign cultures and societies. One U.S. Army captain in Iraq said, "I was never given classes on how to sit down with a sheik. . . . He is giving me the traditional dishdasha and the entire outfit of a sheik because he claims that

I am a new sheik in town so I must be dressed as one. I don't know if he is trying to gain favor with me because he wants something [or if it is] something good or something bad." In fact, as soon as coalition forces toppled Saddam Hussein, they became de facto players in the Iraqi social system. The young captain had indeed become the new sheik in town and was being properly honored by his Iraqi host.[4]

As this example indicates, U.S. forces frequently do not know who their friends are, and just as often they do not know who their enemies are. A returning commander from the 3d Infantry Division observed: "I had perfect situational awareness. What I lacked was cultural awareness. I knew where every enemy tank was dug in on the outskirts of Tallil. Only problem was, my soldiers had to fight fanatics charging on foot or in pickups and firing AK-47s and RPGs [rocket-propelled grenades]. Great technical intelligence. Wrong enemy."[5]

While the consequences of a lack of cultural knowledge might be most apparent (or perhaps most deadly) in a counterinsurgency, a failure to understand foreign cultures has been a major contributing factor in multiple national-security and intelligence failures. In her 1962 study, Pearl Harbor: Warning and Decision, Roberta Wohlstetter demonstrated that although the U.S. Government picked up Japanese signals (including conversations, decoded cables, and ship movements), it failed to distinguish signals from noise—to understand which signals were meaningful—because it was unimaginable that the Japanese might do something as "irrational" as attacking the headquarters of the U.S. Pacific fleet.[6]

Such ethnocentrism (the inability to put aside one's own cultural attitudes and imagine the world from the perspective of a different group) is especially dangerous in a national-security context because it can distort strategic thinking and result in assumptions that the adversary will behave exactly as one might behave. India's nuclear tests on 11 and 13 May 1998 came as a complete surprise because of this type of "mirror-imaging" among CIA analysts. According to the internal investigation conducted by former Vice Chairman of the Joint Chiefs of Staff David Jeremiah, the real problem was an assumption by intelligence analysts and policymakers that the Indians would not test their nuclear weapons because Americans would not test nuclear weapons in similar circumstances. According to Jeremiah, "The intelligence and the policy communities had an underlying mind-set going into these tests that the B.J.P [Bharatiya Janata Party] would behave as we [would] behave."[7]

The United States suffers from a lack of cultural knowledge in its national-security establishment for two primary, interrelated reasons. First, anthropology is largely and conspicuously absent as a discipline within our national-security enterprise, especially within the intelligence community and DOD. Anthropology is a social science discipline whose primary object of study has traditionally been non-Western, tribal societies. The methodologies of anthropology include participant observation, fieldwork, and historical research. One of the central epistemological tenets of anthropology is cultural relativism—understanding other societies from within their own framework.

The primary task of anthropology has historically been translating knowledge gained in the "field" back to the West. While it might seem self-evident that such a perspective would be beneficial to the national-security establishment, only one of the national defense universities (which provide master's degree-level education to military personnel) currently has an anthropologist on its faculty. At West Point, which traditionally places a heavy emphasis on engineering, anthropology is disparagingly referred to by cadets as "nuts and huts." And, although political science is well represented as a discipline in senior policymaking circles, there has never been an anthropologist on the National Security Council.

The second and related reason for the current lack of cultural knowledge is the failure of the U.S. military to achieve anything resembling victory in Vietnam. Following the Vietnam War, the Joint Chiefs of Staff collectively put their heads in the sand and determined they would never fight an unconventional war again. From a purely military perspective, it was easier for them to focus on the threat of Soviet tanks rolling through the Fulda Gap, prompting a major European land war—a war they could easily fight using existing doctrine and technology and that would have a clear, unequivocal winner.[8]

The preference for the use of overwhelming force and clear campaign objectives was formalized in what has become known as the Weinberger doctrine. In a 1984 speech, Secretary of Defense Caspar Weinberger articulated six principles designed to ensure the Nation would never become involved in another Vietnam. By the mid-1980s, there was cause for concern: deployment of troops to El Salvador seemed likely and the involvement in Lebanon had proved disastrous following the bombing of the U.S. Marine barracks in Beirut. Responding to these events, Weinberger believed troops should be committed only if U.S. national interests were at stake; only in support of clearly defined political and military objectives; and only "with the clear intention of winning."[9]

In 1994, Chairman of the Joint Chiefs of Staff Colin Powell (formerly a military assistant to Weinberger) rearticulated the Weinberger doctrine's fundamental elements, placing a strong emphasis on the idea that force, when used, should be overwhelming and disproportionate to the force used by the enemy. The Powell-Weinberger doctrine institutionalized a preference for "major combat operations"—big wars—as a matter of national preference. Although the Powell-Weinberger doctrine was eroded during the Clinton years; during operations other than war in Haiti, Somali, and Bosnia; and during the second Bush Administration's pre-emptive strikes in Afghanistan and Iraq, no alternative doctrine has emerged to take its place.[10]

We have no doctrine for "nationbuilding," which the military eschews as a responsibility because it is not covered by Title 10 of the U.S. Code, which outlines the responsibilities of the military as an element of national power. Field Manual 3-07, Stability Operations and Support Operations, was not finalized until February 2003, despite the fact the U.S. military was already deeply engaged in such operations in Iraq. Field Manual 3-07.22—meant to be a temporary document—is still primarily geared toward fighting an enemy engaged in Maoist revolutionary warfare, a type of insurgency that has little application to the situation in Iraq where multiple organizations are competing for multiple, confusing objectives.[11]

Since 1923, the core tenet of U.S. warfighting strategy has been that overwhelming force deployed against an equally powerful state will result in military victory. Yet in a counterinsurgency situation such as the one the United States currently faces in Iraq, "winning" through overwhelming force is often inapplicable as a concept, if not problematic as a goal. While negotiating in Hanoi a few days before Saigon fell, U.S. Army Colonel Harry Summers, Jr., said to a North Vietnamese colonel, "You know, you never defeated us on the battlefield." The Vietnamese colonel replied, "That may be so, but it is also irrelevant."[12] The same could be said of the conflict in Iraq.

Winning on the battlefield is irrelevant against an insurgent adversary because the struggle for power and legitimacy among competing factions has no purely military solution. Often, the application of overwhelming force has the negative, unintended effect of strengthening the insurgency by creating martyrs, increasing recruitment, and demonstrating the "brutality" of state forces.

The alternative approach to fighting insurgency, such as the British eventually adopted through trial and error in Northern Ireland, involves the following: A comprehensive plan to alleviate the political conditions behind the insurgency; civil-military cooperation; the application of minimum force; deep intelligence; and an acceptance of the protracted nature of the conflict. Deep cultural knowledge of the adversary is inherent to the British approach.[13]

Although cultural knowledge of the adversary matters in counterinsurgency, it has little importance in major combat operations. Because the Powell-Weinberger doctrine meant conventional, large-scale war was the only acceptable type of conflict, no discernable present or future need existed to develop doctrine and expertise in unconventional war, including counterinsurgency. Thus, there was no need to incorporate cultural knowledge into doctrine, training, or warfighting. Until now, that is.

On 21 October 2003, the House Armed Services Committee held a hearing to examine lessons learned from Operation Iraqi Freedom. Scales' testimony at the hearing prompted U.S. Representative "Ike" Skelton to write a letter to Secretary of Defense Donald Rumsfeld in which he said: "In simple terms, if we had better understood the Iraqi culture and mindset, our war plans would have been even better than they were, the plan for the postwar period and all of its challenges would have been far better, and we [would have been] better prepared for the 'long slog' . . . to win the peace in Iraq."[14]

Even such DOD luminaries as Andrew Marshall, the mysterious director of the Pentagon's Office of Net Assessment, are now calling for "anthropology-level knowledge of a wide range of cultures" because such knowledge will prove essential to conducting future operations. Although senior U.S. Government officials such as Skelton are calling for "personnel in our civilian ranks who have cultural knowledge and understanding to inform the policy process," there are few anthropologists either available or willing to play in the same sandbox with the military.[15]

. . . The Perils of Incomplete Knowledge

DOD yearns for cultural knowledge, but anthropologists en masse, bound by their own ethical code and sunk in a mire of post-modernism, are unlikely to contribute much of value to reshaping national-security policy or practice. Yet, if anthropologists remain disengaged, who will provide the relevant subject matter expertise? As Anna Simons, an anthropologist who teaches at the Naval Postgraduate School, points out: "If anthropologists want to put their heads in the sand and not assist, then who will the military, the CIA, and other agencies turn to for information? They'll turn to people who will give them the kind of information that should make anthropologists want to rip their hair out because the information won't be nearly as directly connected to what's going on the local landscape."[16]

Regardless of whether anthropologists decide to enter the national-security arena, cultural information will inevitably be used as the basis of military operations and public policy. And, if anthropologists refuse to contribute, how reliable will that information be? The result of using incomplete "bad" anthropology is, invariably, failed operations and failed policy. In a May 2004 New Yorker article, "The Gray Zone: How a Secret Pentagon Program Came to Abu Ghraib," Seymour Hersh notes that Raphael Patai's 1973 study of Arab culture and psychology, The Arab Mind, was the basis of the military's understanding of the psychological vulnerabilities of Arabs, particularly to sexual shame and humiliation.[17]

Patai says: "The segregation of the sexes, the veiling of the women . . . , and all the other minute rules that govern and restrict contact between men and women, have the effect of making sex a prime mental preoccupation in the Arab world." Apparently, the goal of photographing the sexual humiliation was to blackmail Iraqi victims into becoming informants against the insurgency. To prevent the dissemination of photos to family and friends, it was believed Iraqi men would do almost anything.[18]

As Bernard Brodie said of the French Army in 1914, "This was neither the first nor the last time that bad anthropology contributed to bad strategy." Using sexual humiliation to blackmail Iraqi men into becoming informants could never have worked as a strategy since it only destroys honor, and for Iraqis, lost honor requires its restoration through the appeasement of blood. This concept is well developed in Iraqi culture, and there is even a specific Arabic word for it: al-sharaf, upholding one's manly honor. The alleged use of Patai's book as the basis of the psychological torment at Abu Ghraib, devoid of any understanding of the broader context of Iraqi culture, demonstrates the folly of using decontextualized culture as the basis of policy.[19]

Successful counterinsurgency depends on attaining a holistic, total understanding of local culture. This cultural understanding must be thorough and deep if it is to have any practical benefit at all. This fact is not lost on the Army. In the language of interim FM 3-07.22: "The center of gravity in counterinsurgency operations is the population. Therefore, understanding the local society and gaining its support is critical to success. For U.S. forces to operate effectively among a local population and gain and maintain their support, it is important to develop a thorough understanding of the society and its culture, including its history, tribal/family/social structure, values, religions, customs, and needs."[20]

To defeat the insurgency in Iraq, U.S. and coalition forces must recognize and exploit the underlying tribal structure of the country; the power wielded by traditional authority figures; the use of Islam as a political ideology; the competing interests of the Shia, the Sunni, and the Kurds; the psychological effects of totalitarianism; and the divide between urban and rural, among other things.

Interim FM 3-07.22 continues: "Understanding and working within the social fabric of a local area is initially the most influential factor in the conduct of counterinsurgency operations. Unfortunately, this is often the factor most neglected by U.S. forces."[21]

And, unfortunately, anthropologists, whose assistance is urgently needed in time of war, entirely neglect U.S. forces. Despite the fact that military applications of cultural knowledge might be distasteful to ethically inclined anthropologists, their assistance is necessary.

Notes

1. MG Robert H. Scales, Jr., "Culture-Centric Warfare," Proceedings (October 2004).
2. Megan Scully, "'Social Intel' New Tool For U.S. Military," Defense News, 26 April 2004, 21.
3. U.S. Department of the Army Field Manual (FM) (Interim) 3-07.22, Counterinsurgency Operations (Washington, DC: U.S. Government Printing Office [GPO], 1 October 2004), sec. 1-1; David Charters, "From Palestine to Northern Ireland: British Adaptation to Low-Intensity Operations," in Armies in Low-Intensity Conflict." A Comparative Analysis, eds., D. Charters and M. Tugwell (London: Brassey's Defence Publishers, 1989), 195.
4. Leonard Wong, "Developing Adaptive Leaders: The Crucible Experience of Operation Iraqi Freedom," Strategic Studies Institute, U.S. Army War College, Carlisle Barracks, Pennsylvania, July 2004, 14.
5. Scales, "Army Transformation: Implications for the Future," testimony before the House Armed Services Committee, Washington, D.C., 15 July 2004.
6. Roberta Wohlstetter, Pearl Harbor: Warning and Decision (California: Stanford University Press, 1962).
7. Jeffrey Goldberg, "The Unknown: The C.I.A. and the Pentagon take another look at Al Qaeda and Iraq," The New Yorker, 10 February 2003.
8. See Max Boot, The Savage Wars of Peace: Small Wars and the Rise of American Power (New York: Basic Books, 2003).
9. Casper W. Weinberger, "The Uses of Military Power," speech at the National Press Club, Washington, D.C., 28 November 1984.
10. Jeffrey Record, "Weinberger-Powell Doctrine Doesn't Cut It," Proceedings (October 2000) The Powell doctrine also "translates into a powerful reluctance to engage in decisive combat, or to even risk combat, and an inordinate emphasis at every level of command on force protection." Stan Goff, "Full-Spectrum Entropy: Special Operations in a Special Period," Freedom Road Magazine, on-line at www.freedom.read.org/fr/03/english/07_entropy.html, accessed 18 February 2005.
11. U.S. Code, Title 10, "Armed Forces," on-line at www.access.gpo.gov/uscode/ title10/title10.html, accessed 18 February 2005; FM 3-07, Stability Operations and Support Operations (Washington, DC: GPO, February, 2003); FM 3-07.22, Interim.
12. The 1923 Field Service Regulations postulate that the ultimate objective of all military operations is the destruction of the enemy's armed forces and that decisive results are obtained only by the offensive. The Regulations state that the Army must prepare to tight against an "opponent organized for war on modern principles and equipped with all the means of modern warfare. . . ." The preference for use of offensive force is found continuously in U.S. military thought, most recently in FM 3-0, Operations (Washington, DC: GPO, 2001), which says: "The doctrine holds warfighting as the Army's primary focus and recognizes that the ability of Army forces to dominate land warfare also provide the ability to dominate any situation in military operations other than war"; Richard Darilek and David Johnson, "Occupation of Hostile Territory: History, Theory, Doctrine; Past and Future Practice, "conference presentation, Future Warfare Seminar V. Carlisle, Pennsylvania, 18 January 2005; Peter Grier, "Should US Fight War in Bosnia? Question Opens an Old Debate," Christian Science Monitor, 14 September 1992, 9.
13. For a full discussion of British principles of counterinsurgency, see Thomas Mockaitis, British Counterinsurgency, 1919–1960 (New York: St. Martin's Press, 1990); Ian Beckett and John Pimlott, eds., Armed Forces and modern Counter-Insurgency (London: Croom Helm, 1985)
14. Office of Congressman Ike Skelton, "Skelton Urges Rumsfeld To Improve Cultural Awareness Training," press release, 23 October 2003, on-line at www.house.gov/skelton/pr031023.html, accessed 18 February 2005.
15. Jeremy Feller, "Marshall US Needs To Sustain Long-Distance Power Projection," Inside The Pentagon, 4 March 2004, 15.
16. Renee Montagne, "Interview: Anna Simons and Catherine Lutz on the involvement of anthropologists in war," National Public Radio's Morning Edition, 14 August 2002.
17. Raphael Patai in Seymour M. Hersh, "The Gray Zone: How a secret Pentagon program came to Abu Ghraib," The New Yorker, 24 May 2004; Patai, The Arab Mind (Now York: Scribner's 1973).
18. Patai.
19. Bernard Brodie, Strategy in the Missile Age (New Jersey: Princeton University Press, 1959), 52.
20. Amatzia Baram, "Victory in Iraq, One Tribe at a Time," New York Times, 28 October 2003; FM (Interim) 3-07.22, sec 4–11.
21. FM (Interim) 3-07.22, sec. 4–13.

Montgomery McFate, JD, PhD, is an American Association for the Advancement of Science Defense Policy Fellow at the Office of Naval Research, Arlington, Virginia. She received a BA from the University of California at Berkeley, an MA, M Phil, and a PhD from Yale University, and a JD from Harvard Law School. She was formerly at RAND's Intelligence Policy Center.

From *Military Review,* March/April 2005. Published in 2005 by Military Review, a publication of the U.S. Army.

Tricking and Tripping

Fieldwork on Prostitution in the Era of AIDS

CLAIRE E. STERK

Students often think of anthropological fieldwork as requiring travel to exotic tropical locations, but that is not necessarily the case. This reading is based on fieldwork in the United States—on the streets in New York City as well as Atlanta. Claire Sterk is an anthropologist who works in a school of public health and is primarily interested in issues of women's health, particularly as it relates to sexual behavior. In this selection, an introduction to a recent book by the same title, she describes the basic fieldwork methods she used to study these women and their communities. Like most cultural anthropologists, Sterk's primary goal was to describe "the life" of prostitution from the women's own point of view. To do this, she had to be patient, brave, sympathetic, trustworthy, curious, and nonjudgmental. You will notice these characteristics in this selection; for example, Sterk begins her book with a poem written by one of her informants. Fieldwork is a slow process, because it takes time to win people's confidence and to learn their language and way of seeing the world. In this regard, there are probably few differences between the work of a qualitative sociologist and that of a cultural anthropologist (although anthropologists would not use the term "deviant" to describe another society or a segment of their own society).

Throughout the world, HIV/AIDS is fast becoming a disease found particularly in poor women. Sex workers or prostitutes have often been blamed for AIDS, and they have been further stigmatized because of their profession. In reality, however, entry into prostitution is not a career choice; rather, these women and girls are themselves most often victims of circumstances such as violence and poverty. Public health officials want to know why sex workers do not always protect their health by making men wear condoms. To answer such questions, we must know more about the daily life of these women. The way to do that, the cultural anthropologist would say, is to ask and to listen.

As you read this selection, ask yourself the following questions:

- What happens when Sterk says, "I'm sorry for you" to one of her informants? Why?
- Why do you think fieldwork might be a difficult job?
- Do you think that the fact that Sterk grew up in Amsterdam, where prostitution is legal, affected her research?
- Which of the six themes of this work, described at the end of the article, do you think is most important?

One night in March of 1987 business was slow. I was hanging out on a stroll with a group of street prostitutes. After a few hours in a nearby diner/coffee shop, we were kicked out. The waitress felt bad, but she needed our table for some new customers. Four of us decided to sit in my car until the rain stopped. While three of us chatted about life, Piper wrote this poem. As soon as she read it to us, the conversation shifted to more serious topics—pimps, customers, cops, the many hassles of being a prostitute, to name a few. We decided that if I ever finished a book about prostitution, the book would start with her poem.

This book is about the women who work in the lower echelons of the prostitution world. They worked in the streets and other public settings as well as crack houses. Some of these women viewed themselves primarily as prostitutes, and a number of them used drugs to cope with the pressures of the life. Others identified themselves more as drug users, and their main reason for having sex for money or other goods was to support their own drug use and often the habit of their male partner. A small group of women interviewed for this book had left prostitution, and most of them were still struggling to integrate their past experiences as prostitutes in their current lives.

The stories told by the women who participated in this project revealed how pimps, customers, and others such as police officers and social and health service providers treated them as "fallen" women. However, their accounts also showed their strengths and the many strategies they developed to challenge these others. Circumstances, including their drug use, often forced them to sell sex, but they all resisted the notion that they might be selling themselves. Because they engaged in an illegal profession, these women had little status: their working conditions were poor, and their work was physically and mentally exhausting. Nevertheless, many women described the ways in which they gained a sense of control over their lives. For instance, they learned how to manipulate pimps, how to control the types of services and length of time bought by their customers, and how to select customers. While none of these schemes explicitly enhanced their working conditions, they did make the women feel stronger and better about themselves.

In this book, I present prostitution from the point of view of the women themselves. To understand their current lives, it was necessary to learn how they got started in the life, the various processes involved in their continued prostitution careers, the link between prostitution and drug use, the women's interactions with their pimps and customers, and the impact of the AIDS epidemic and increasing violence on their experiences. I also examined the implications for women. Although my goal was to present the women's thoughts, feelings, and actions in their own words, the final text is a sociological monograph compiled by me as the researcher. Some women are quoted more than others because I developed a closer relationship with them, because they were more able to verbalize and capture their circumstances, or simply because they were more outspoken.

The Sample

The data for this book are qualitative. The research was conducted during the last ten years in the New York City and Atlanta metropolitan areas. One main data source was participant observation on streets, in hotels and other settings known for prostitution activity, and in drug-use settings, especially those that allowed sex-for-drug exchanges. Another data source was in-depth, life-history interviews with 180 women ranging in age from 18 to 59 years, with an average age of 34. One in two women was African-American and one in three white; the remaining women were Latina. Three in four had completed high school, and among them almost two-thirds had one or more years of additional educational training. Thirty women had graduated from college.

Forty women worked as street prostitutes and did not use drugs. On average, they had been prostitutes for 11 years. Forty women began using drugs an average of three years after they began working as prostitutes, and the average time they had worked as prostitutes was nine years. Forty women used drugs an average of five years before they became prostitutes, and on the average they had worked as prostitutes for eight years. Another forty women began smoking crack and exchanging sex for crack almost simultaneously, with an average of four years in the life. Twenty women who were interviewed were ex-prostitutes.

Comments on Methodology

When I tell people about my research, the most frequent question I am asked is how I gained access to the women rather than what I learned from the research. For many, prostitution is an unusual topic of conversation, and many people have expressed surprise that I, as a woman, conducted the research. During my research some customers indeed thought I was a working woman, a fact that almost always amuses those who hear about my work. However, few people want to hear stories about the women's struggles and sadness. Sometimes they ask questions about the reasons why women become prostitutes. Most of the time, they are surprised when I tell them that the prostitutes as well as their customers represent all layers of society. Before presenting the findings, it seems important to discuss the research process, including gaining access to the women, developing relationships, interviewing, and then leaving the field.[1]

Locating Prostitutes and Gaining Entree

One of the first challenges I faced was to identify locations where street prostitution took place. Many of these women worked on strolls, streets where prostitution activity is concentrated, or in hotels known for prostitution activity. Others, such as the crack prostitutes, worked in less public settings such as a crack house that might be someone's apartment.

I often learned of well-known public places from professional experts, such as law enforcement officials and health care providers at emergency rooms and sexually transmitted disease clinics. I gained other insights from lay experts, including taxi drivers, bartenders, and community representatives such as members of neighborhood associations. The contacts universally mentioned some strolls as the places where many women worked, where the local police focused attention, or where residents had organized protests against prostitution in their neighborhoods.

As I began visiting various locales, I continued to learn about new settings. In one sense, I was developing ethnographic maps of street prostitution. After several visits to a specific area, I also was able to expand these maps by adding information about the general atmosphere on the stroll, general characteristics of the various people present, the ways in which the women and customers connected, and the overall flow of action. In addition, my visits allowed the regular actors to notice me.

I soon learned that being an unknown woman in an area known for prostitution may cause many people to notice you, even stare at you, but it fails to yield many verbal interactions. Most of the time when I tried to make eye contact with one of the women, she quickly averted her eyes. Pimps, on the other hand, would stare at me straight on and I ended up being the one to look away. Customers would stop, blow their horn, or wave me over, frequently yelling obscenities when I ignored them. I realized that gaining entree into the prostitution world was not going to be as easy as I imagined it. Although I lacked such training in any of my qualitative methods classes, I decided to move slowly and not force any interaction. The most I said during the initial weeks in a new area was limited to "how are you" or "hi." This strategy paid off during my first visits to one of the strolls in Brooklyn, New York. After several appearances, one of the women walked up to me and sarcastically asked if I was looking for something. She caught me off guard, and all the answers I had practiced did not seem to make sense. I mumbled something about just wanting to walk around. She did not like my answer, but she did like my accent. We ended up talking about the latter and she was especially excited when I told her I came from Amsterdam. One of her friends had gone to Europe with her boyfriend, who was in the military. She understood from her that prostitution and drugs were legal in the Netherlands. While explaining to her that some of her friend's impressions were incorrect, I was able to show off some of my knowledge about prostitution. I mentioned that I was interested in prostitution and wanted to write a book about it.

Despite the fascination with my background and intentions, the prostitute immediately put me through a Streetwalker 101 test, and apparently I passed. She told me to make sure to come back. By the time I left, I not only had my first conversation but also my first connection to the scene. Variations of this entry process occurred on the other strolls. The main lesson I learned in these early efforts was the importance of having some knowledge of the lives of the people I wanted to study, while at the same time refraining from presenting myself as an expert.

Qualitative researchers often refer to their initial connections as gatekeepers and key respondents. Throughout my fieldwork I learned that some key respondents are important in providing initial access, but they become less central as the research evolves. For example, one of the women who introduced me to her lover, who was also her pimp, was arrested and disappeared for months. Another entered drug treatment soon after she facilitated my access. Other key respondents provided access to only a segment of the players on a scene. For example, if a woman worked for a pimp, [she] was unlikely . . . to introduce me to women working for another pimp. On one stroll my initial contact was with a pimp whom nobody liked. By associating with him, I almost lost the opportunity to meet other pimps. Some key respondents were less connected than promised—for example, some of the women who worked the street to support their drug habit. Often their connections were more frequently with drug users and less so with prostitutes.

Key respondents tend to be individuals central to the local scene, such as, in this case, pimps and the more senior prostitutes. Their function as gatekeepers often is to protect the scene and to screen outsiders. Many times I had to prove that I was not an undercover police officer or a woman with ambitions to become a streetwalker. While I thought I had gained entree, I quickly learned that many insiders subsequently wondered about my motives and approached me with suspicion and distrust.

Another lesson involved the need to proceed cautiously with self-nominated key respondents. For example, one of the women presented herself as knowing everyone on the stroll. While she did know everyone, she was not a central figure. On the contrary, the other prostitutes viewed her as a failed streetwalker whose drug use caused her to act unprofessionally. By associating with me, she hoped to regain some of her status. For me, however, it meant limited access to the other women because I affiliated myself with a woman who was marginal to the scene. On another occasion, my main key respondent was a man who claimed to own three crack houses in the neighborhood. However, he had a negative reputation, and people accused him of cheating on others. My initial alliance with him delayed, and almost blocked, my access to others in the neighborhood. He intentionally tried to keep me from others on the scene, not because he would gain something from that transaction but because it made him feel powerful. When I told him I was going to hang out with some of the other people, he threatened me until one of the other dealers stepped in and told him to stay away. The two of them argued back and forth, and finally I was free to go. Fortunately, the dealer who had spoken up for me was much more central and positively associated with the local scene. Finally, I am unsure if I would have had success in gaining entrance to the scene had I not been a woman.

Developing Relationships and Trust

The processes involved in developing relationships in research situations amplify those involved in developing relationships in general. Both parties need to get to know each other, become aware and accepting of each other's roles, and engage in a reciprocal relationship. Being supportive and providing practical assistance were the most visible and direct ways for me as the researcher to develop a relationship. Throughout the years, I have given countless rides, provided child care on numerous occasions, bought groceries, and listened for hours to stories that were unrelated to my initial research questions. Gradually, my role allowed me to become part of these women's lives and to build rapport with many of them.

Over time, many women also realized that I was uninterested in being a prostitute and that I genuinely was interested in learning as much as possible about their lives. Many felt flattered that someone wanted to learn from them and that they had knowledge to offer. Allowing women to tell their stories and engaging in a dialogue with them probably were the single most important techniques that allowed me to develop relationships with them. Had I only wanted to focus on the questions I had in mind, developing such relationships might have been more difficult.

At times, I was able to get to know a woman only after her pimp endorsed our contact. One of my scariest experiences occurred before I knew to work through the pimps, and one such man had some of his friends follow me on my way home one night. I will never know what plans they had in mind for me because I fortunately was able to escape with only a few bruises. Over a year later, the woman acknowledged that her pimp had gotten upset and told her he was going to teach me a lesson.

On other occasions, I first needed to be screened by owners and managers of crack houses before the research could continue. Interestingly, screenings always were done by a man even if the person who vouched for me was a man himself. While the women also were cautious, the ways in which they checked me out tended to be much more subtle. For example, one of them would tell me a story, indicating that it was a secret about another person on the stroll. Although I failed to realize this at the time, my field notes revealed that frequently after such a conversation, others would ask me questions about related topics. One woman later acknowledged that putting out such stories was a test to see if I would keep information confidential.

Learning more about the women and gaining a better understanding of their lives also raised many ethical questions. No textbook told me how to handle situations in which a pimp abused a woman, a customer forced a woman to engage in unwanted sex acts, a customer requested unprotected sex from a woman who knew she was HIV infected, or a boyfriend had realistic expectations regarding a woman's earnings to support his drug habit. I failed to know the proper response when asked to engage in illegal activities such as holding drugs or money a woman had stolen from a customer. In general, my response was to explain that I was there as a researcher. During those occasions when pressures became too severe, I decided to leave a scene. For example, I never returned to certain crack houses because pimps there continued to ask me to consider working for them.

Over time, I was fortunate to develop relationships with people who "watched my back." One pimp in particular intervened if he perceived other pimps, customers, or passersby harassing me. He also was the one who gave me my street name: Whitie (indicating my racial background) or Ms. Whitie for those who disrespected me. While this was my first street name, I subsequently had others. Being given a street name was a symbolic gesture of acceptance. Gradually, I developed an identity that allowed me to be both an insider and an outsider. While hanging out on the strolls and other gathering places, including crack houses, I had to deal with some of the same uncomfortable conditions as the prostitutes, such as cold or warm weather, lack of access to a rest room, refusals from owners for me to patronize a restaurant, and of course, harassment by customers and the police.

I participated in many informal conversations. Unless pushed to do so, I seldom divulged my opinions. I was more open with my feelings about situations and showed empathy. I learned quickly that providing an opinion can backfire. I agreed that one of the women was struggling a lot and stated that I felt sorry for her. While I meant to indicate my "genuine concern for her, she heard that I felt sorry for her because she was a failure. When she finally, after several weeks, talked with me again, I was able to explain to her that I was not judging her, but rather felt concerned for her. She remained cynical and many times asked me for favors to make up for my mistake. It took me months before I felt comfortable telling her that I felt I had done enough and that it was time to let go. However, if she was not ready, she needed to know that I would no longer go along. This was one of many occasions when I learned that although I wanted to facilitate my work as a researcher, that I wanted people to like and trust me, I also needed to set boundaries.

Rainy and slow nights often provided good opportunities for me to participate in conversations with groups of women. Popular topics included how to work safely, what to do about condom use, how to make more money. I often served as a health educator and a supplier of condoms, gels, vaginal douches, and other feminine products. Many women were very worried about the AIDS epidemic. However, they also were worried about how to use a condom when a customer refused to do so. They worried particularly about condom use when they needed money badly and, consequently, did not want to propose that the customer use one for fear of rejection. While some women became experts at "making" their customers use a condom—for example, "by hiding it in their mouth prior to beginning oral sex—others would carry condoms to please me but never pull one out. If a woman was HIV positive and I knew she failed to use a condom, I faced the ethical dilemma of challenging her or staying out of it.

Developing trusting relationships with crack prostitutes was more difficult. Crack houses were not the right environment for informal conversations. Typically, the atmosphere was tense and everyone was suspicious of each other. The best times to talk with these women were when we bought groceries together, when I helped them clean their homes, or when we shared a meal. Often the women were very different when they were not high than they were when they were high or craving crack. In my conversations with them, I learned that while I might have observed their actions the night before, they themselves might not remember them. Once I realized this, I would be very careful to omit any detail unless I knew that the woman herself did remember the event.

In-Depth Interviews

All interviews were conducted in a private setting, including women's residences, my car or my office, a restaurant of the women's choice, or any other setting the women selected. I did not begin conducting official interviews until I developed relationships with the women. Acquiring written informed consent prior to the interview was problematic. It made me feel awkward. Here I was asking the women to sign a form after they had begun to trust me. However, often I felt more upset about this technicality than the women themselves. As soon as they realized that the form was something the university required, they seemed to understand. Often they laughed about the official statements, and some asked if I was sure the form was to protect them and not the school.[2] None of the women refused to sign the consent form, although some refused to sign it right away and asked to be interviewed later.

In some instances the consent procedures caused the women to expect a formal interview. Some of them were disappointed when they saw I only had a few structured questions about demographic characteristics, followed by a long list of open-ended questions. When this disappointment occurred, I reminded the women that I wanted to learn from them and that the best way to do so was by engaging in a dialogue rather than interrogating them. Only by letting the women identify their salient issues and the topics they wanted to address was I able to gain an insider's perspective. By being a careful listener and probing for additional information and explanation, I as the interviewer, together with the women, was able to uncover the complexities of their lives. In addition, the nature of the interview allowed me to ask questions about contradictions in a woman's story. For example, sometimes a woman would say that she always used a condom. However, later on in the conversation she would indicate that if she needed drugs she would never use one. By asking her to elaborate on this, I was able to begin developing insights into condom use by type of partner, type of sex acts, and social context.

The interviewer becomes much more a part of the interview when the conversations are in-depth than when a structured questionnaire is used. Because I was so integral to the process, the way the women viewed me may have biased their answers. On the one hand, this bias might be reduced because of the extent to which both parties already knew each other; on the other, a woman might fail to give her true opinion and reveal her actions if she knew that these went against the interviewer's opinion. I suspected that some women played down the ways in which their pimps manipulated them once they knew that I was not too fond of these men. However, some might have taken more time to explain the relationship with their pimp in order to "correct" my image.

My background, so different from that of these women, most likely affected the nature of the interviews. I occupied a higher socioeconomic status. I had a place to live and a job. In contrast to the nonwhite women, I came from a different racial background. While I don't know to what extent these differences played a role, I acknowledge that they must have had some effect on this research.

Leaving the Field

Leaving the field was not something that occurred after completion of the fieldwork, but an event that took place daily. Although I sometimes stayed on the strolls all night or hung out for several days, I always had a home to return to. I had a house with electricity, a warm shower, a comfortable bed, and a kitchen. My house sat on a street where I had no fear of being shot on my way there and where I did not find condoms or syringes on my doorstep.

During several stages of the study, I had access to a car, which I used to give the women rides or to run errands together. However, I will never forget the cold night when everyone on the street was freezing, and I left to go home. I turned up the heat in my car, and tears streamed down my cheeks. I appreciated the heat, but I felt more guilty about that luxury than ever before. I truly felt like an outsider, or maybe even more appropriate, a betrayer.

Throughout the years of fieldwork, there were a number of times when I left the scene temporarily. For example, when so many people were dying from AIDS, I was unable to ignore the devastating impact of this disease. I needed an emotional break.

Physically removing myself from the scene was common when I experienced difficulty remaining objective. Once I became too involved in a woman's life and almost adopted her and her family. Another time I felt a true hatred for a crack house owner and was unable to adhere to the rules of courteous interactions. Still another time, I got angry with a woman whose steady partner was HIV positive when she failed to ask him to use a condom when they had sex.

I also took temporary breaks from a particular scene by shifting settings and neighborhoods. For example, I would invest most of my time in women from a particular crack house for several weeks. Then I would shift to spending more time on one of the strolls, while making shorter and less frequent visits to the crack house. By shifting scenes, I was able to tell people why I was leaving and to remind all of us of my researcher role.

While I focused on leaving the field, I became interested in women who had left the life. It seemed important to have an understanding of their past and current circumstances. I knew some of them from the days when they were working, but identifying others was a challenge. There was no gathering place for ex-prostitutes. Informal networking, advertisements in local newspapers, and local clinics and community settings allowed me to reach twenty of these women. Conducting interviews with them later in the data collection process prepared me to ask specific questions. I realized that I had learned enough about the life to know what to ask. Interviewing ex-prostitutes also prepared me for moving from the fieldwork to writing.

It is hard to determine exactly when I left the field. It seems like a process that never ends. Although I was more physically removed from the scene, I continued to be involved while analyzing the data and writing this book. I also created opportunities to go back, for example, by asking women to give me feedback on parts of the manuscript or at times when I experienced writer's block and my car seemed to automatically steer itself to one of the strolls. I also have developed other research projects in some of the same communities. For example, both a project on intergenerational drug use and a gender-specific intervention project to help women remain HIV negative have brought me back to the same population. Some of the women have become key respondents in these new projects, while others now are members of a research team. For example, Beth, one of the women who has left prostitution, works as an outreach worker on another project.

Six Themes in the Ethnography of Prostitution

The main intention of my work is to provide the reader with a perspective on street prostitution from the point of view of the women themselves. There are six fundamental aspects of the women's lives as prostitutes that must be considered. The first concerns the women's own explanations for their involvement in prostitution and their descriptions of the various circumstances that led them to become prostitutes. Their stories include justifications such as traumatic past experiences, especially sexual abuse, the lack of love they experienced as children, pressures by friends and pimps, the need for drugs, and most prominently, the economic forces that pushed them into the life. A number of women describe these justifications as excuses, as reflective explanations they have developed after becoming a prostitute.

The women describe the nature of their initial experiences, which often involved alienation from those outside the life. They also show the differences in the processes between women who work as prostitutes and use drugs and women who do not use drugs.

Although all these women work either on the street or in drug-use settings, their lives do differ. My second theme is a typology that captures these differences, looking at the women's prostitution versus drug-use identities. The typology distinguishes among (a) streetwalkers, women who work strolls and who do not use drugs; (b) hooked prostitutes, women who identify themselves mainly as prostitutes but who upon their entrance into the life also began using drugs; (c) prostituting addicts, women who view themselves mainly as drug users and who became prostitutes to support their drug habit; and (d) crack prostitutes, women who trade sex for crack.

This typology explains the differences in the women's strategies for soliciting customers, their screening of customers, pricing of sex acts, and bargaining for services. For example, the streetwalkers have the most bargaining power, while such power appears to be lacking among the crack prostitutes.

Few prostitutes work in a vacuum. The third theme is the role of pimps, a label that most women dislike and for which they prefer to substitute "old man" or "boyfriend." Among the pimps, one finds entrepreneur lovers, men who mainly employ streetwalkers and hooked prostitutes and sometimes prostituting addicts. Entrepreneur lovers engage in the life for business reasons. They treat the women as their employees or their property and view them primarily as an economic commodity. The more successful a woman is in earning them money, the more difficult it is for that woman to leave her entrepreneur pimp.

Most prostituting addicts and some hooked prostitutes work for a lover pimp, a man who is their steady partner but who also lives off their earnings. Typically, such pimps employ only one woman. The dynamics in the relationship between a prostitute and her lover pimp become more complex when both partners use drugs. Drugs often become the glue of the relationship.

For many crack prostitutes, their crack addiction serves as a pimp. Few plan to exchange sex for crack when they first begin using; often several weeks or months pass before a woman who barters sex for crack realizes that she is a prostitute.

Historically, society has blamed prostitutes for introducing sexually transmitted diseases into the general population. Similarly, it makes them scapegoats for the spread of HIV/AIDS. Yet their pimps and customers are not held accountable. The fourth theme in the anthropological study of prostitution is the impact of the AIDS epidemic on the women's lives. Although most are knowledgeable about HIV risk behaviors and the ways to reduce their risk, many misconceptions exist. The women describe the complexities of condom use, especially with steady partners but also with paying customers. Many women have mixed feelings about HIV testing, wondering how to cope with a positive test result while no cure is available. A few of the women already knew their HIV-infected status, and the discussion touches on their dilemmas as well.

The fifth theme is the violence and abuse that make common appearances in the women's lives. An ethnography of prostitution must allow the women to describe violence in their neighborhoods as well as violence in prostitution and drug-use settings. The most common violence they encounter is from customers. These men often assume that because they pay for sex they buy a woman. Apparently, casual customers pose more of a danger than those who are regulars. The types of abuse the women encounter are emotional, physical, and sexual. In addition to customers, pimps and boyfriends abuse the women. Finally, the women discuss harassment by law enforcement officers.

When I talked with the women, it often seemed that there were no opportunities to escape from the life. Yet the sixth and final theme must be the escape from prostitution. Women who have left prostitution can describe the process of their exit from prostitution. As ex-prostitutes they struggle with the stigma of their past, the challenges of developing a new identity, and the impact of their past on current intimate relationships. Those who were also drug users often view themselves as ex-prostitutes and recovering addicts, a perspective that seems to create a role conflict. Overall, most ex-prostitutes find that their past follows them like a bad hangover.

Notes

1. For more information about qualitative research methods, see, for example, Patricia Adler and Peter Adler, *Membership Roles in Field Research* (Newbury Park: Sage, 1987); Michael Agar, *The Professional Stranger* (New York: Academic Press, 1980) and *Speaking of Ethnography* (Beverly Hills: Sage, 1986); Howard Becker and Blanche Geer, "Participant Observation and Interviewing: A Comparison," *Human Organization* 16 (1957): 28–32; Norman Denzin, *Sociological Methods: A Sourcebook* (Chicago: Aldine, 1970); Barney Glaser and Anselm Strauss, *The Discovery of Grounded Theory: Strategies for Qualitative Research* (Chicago: Aldine, 1967); Y. Lincoln and E. Guba, *Naturalistic Inquiry* (Beverly Hills: Sage, 1985); John Lofland, "Analytic Ethnography: Features, Failings, and Futures," *Journal of Contemporary Ethnography* 24 (1996): 30–67; and James Spradley, *The Ethnographic Interview* (New York: Holt, Rinehart and Winston, 1979) and *Participant Observation* (New York: Holt, Rinehart and Winston, 1980).
2. For a more extensive discussion of informed consent procedures and related ethical issues, see Bruce L. Berg, *Qualitative Research Methods for the Social Sciences,* 3rd edition, Chapter 3: "Ethical Issues" (Boston: Allyn and Bacon, 1998).

Doing Fieldwork among the Yanomamö [1]

NAPOLEON A. CHAGNON

Vignette

The Yąnomamö are thinly scattered over a vast and verdant tropical forest, living in small villages that are separated by many miles of unoccupied land. They have no writing, but they have a rich and complex language. Their clothing is more decorative than protective. Well-dressed men sport nothing more than a few cotton strings around their wrists, ankles, and waists. They tie the foreskins of their penises to the waist string. Women dress about the same. Much of their daily life revolves around gardening, hunting, collecting wild foods, collecting firewood, fetching water, visiting with each other, gossiping, and making the few material possessions they own: baskets, hammocks, bows, arrows, and colorful pigments with which they paint their bodies. Life is relatively easy in the sense that they can 'earn a living' with about three hours' work per day. Most of what they eat they cultivate in their gardens, and most of that is plantains—a kind of cooking banana that is usually eaten green, either roasted on the coals or boiled in pots. Their meat comes from a large variety of game animals, hunted daily by the men. It is usually roasted on coals or smoked, and is always well done. Their villages are round and open—and very public. One can hear, see, and smell almost everything that goes on anywhere in the village. Privacy is rare, but sexual discreetness is possible in the garden or at night while others sleep. The villages can be as small as 40 to 50 people or as large as 300 people, but in all cases there are many more children and babies than there are adults. This is true of most primitive populations and of our own demographic past. Life expectancy is short.

The Yąnomamö fall into the category of Tropical Forest Indians called 'foot people.' They avoid large rivers and live in interfluvial plains of the major rivers. They have neighbors to the north, Carib-speaking Ye'kwana, who are true 'river people': They make elegant, large dugout canoes and travel extensively along the major waterways. For the Yąnomamö, a large stream is an obstacle and can be crossed only in the dry season. Thus, they have traditionally avoided larger rivers and, because of this, contact with outsiders who usually come by river.

They enjoy taking trips when the jungle abounds with seasonally ripe wild fruits and vegetables. Then, the large village—the *shabono*—is abandoned for a few weeks and everyone camps out for from one to several days away from the village and garden. On these trips, they make temporary huts from poles, vines, and leaves, each family making a separate hut.

Two major seasons dominate their annual cycle: the wet season, which inundates the low-lying jungle, making travel difficult, and the dry season—the time of visiting other villages to feast, trade, and politic with allies. The dry season is also the time when raiders can travel and strike silently at their unsuspecting enemies. The Yąnomamö are still conducting intervillage warfare, a phenomenon that affects all aspects of their social organization, settlement pattern, and daily routines. It is not simply 'ritualistic' war: At least one-fourth of all adult males die violently in the area I lived in.

Social life is organized around those same principles utilized by all tribesmen: kinship relationships, descent from ancestors, marriage exchanges between kinship/descent groups, and the transient charisma of distinguished headmen who attempt to keep order in the village and whose responsibility it is to determine the village's relationships with those in other villages. Their positions are largely the result of kinship and marriage patterns; they come from the largest kinship groups within the village. They can, by their personal wit, wisdom, and charisma, become autocrats, but most of them are largely 'greaters' among equals. They, too, must clear gardens, plant crops, collect wild foods, and hunt. They are simultaneously peacemakers and valiant warriors. Peacemaking often requires the threat or actual use of force, and most headmen have an acquired reputation for being *waiteri*: fierce.

The social dynamics within villages are involved with giving and receiving marriageable girls. Marriages are arranged by older kin, usually men, who are brothers, uncles, and the father. It is a political process, for girls are promised in marriage while they are young, and the men who do this attempt to create alliances with other men via marriage exchanges. There is a shortage of women due in part to a sex-ratio imbalance in the younger age categories, but also complicated by the fact that some men have multiple wives. Most fighting within the village stems from sexual affairs or failure to deliver a promised woman—or out-and-out seizure of a married woman by some other man. This can lead to internal fighting and conflict of such an intensity that villages split up and fission, each group then becoming a new village and, often, enemies to each other.

But their conflicts are not blind, uncontrolled violence. They have a series of graded forms of violence that ranges from chest-pounding and club-fighting duels to out-and-out shooting to kill. This gives them a good deal of flexibility in settling disputes without immediate resort to lethal violence. In addition, they have developed patterns of alliance and friendship that serve to limit violence—trading and feasting with others in order to become friends. These alliances can, and often do, result in intervillage exchanges of marriageable women, which leads to additional amity between villages. No good thing lasts forever, and most alliances crumble. Old friends become hostile and, occasionally, treacherous. Each village must therefore be keenly aware that its neighbors are fickle and must behave accordingly. The thin line between friendship and animosity must be traversed by the village leaders, whose political acumen and strategies are both admirable and complex.

Each village, then, is a replica of all others in a broad sense. But each village is part of a larger political, demographic, and ecological process, and it is difficult to attempt to understand the village without knowing something of the larger forces that affect it and its particular history with all its neighbors.

Collecting the Data in the Field

I have now spent over 60 months with Yąnomamö, during which time I gradually learned their language and, up to a point, submerged myself in their culture and way of life.[2] As my research progressed, the thing that impressed me most was the importance that aggression played in shaping their culture. I had the opportunity to witness a good many incidents that expressed individual vindictiveness on the one hand and collective bellicosity on the other hand. These ranged in seriousness from the ordinary incidents of wife beating and chest pounding to dueling and organized raids by parties that set out with the intention of ambushing and killing men from enemy villages. One of the villages was raided approximately twenty-five times during my first 15 months of fieldwork—six times by the group among whom I was living. And, the history of every village I investigated, from 1964 to 1991, was intimately bound up in patterns of warfare with neighbors that shaped its politics and determined where it was found at any point in time and how it dealt with its current neighbors.

The fact that the Yąnomamö have lived in a chronic state of warfare is reflected in their mythology, ceremonies, settlement pattern, political behavior, and marriage practices. Accordingly, I have organized this case study in such a way that students can appreciate the effects of warfare on Yąnomamö culture in general and on their social organization and political relationships in particular.

I collected the data under somewhat trying circumstances, some of which I will describe to give a rough idea of what is generally meant when anthropologists speak of 'culture shock' and 'fieldwork.' It should be borne in mind, however, that each field situation is in many respects unique, so that the problems I encountered do not necessarily exhaust the range of possible problems other anthropologists have confronted in other areas. There are a few problems, however, that seem to be nearly universal among anthropological fieldworkers, particularly those having to do with eating, bathing, sleeping, lack of privacy, loneliness, or discovering that the people you are living with have a lower opinion of you than you have of them or you yourself are not as culturally or emotionally 'flexible' as you assumed.

The Yąnomamö can be difficult people to live with at times, but I have spoken to colleagues who have had difficulties living in the communities they studied. These things vary from society to society, and probably from one anthropologist to the next. I have also done limited fieldwork among the Yąnomamö's northern neighbors, the Carib-speaking Ye'kwana Indians. By contrast to many experiences I had among the Yąnomamö, the Ye'kwana were very pleasant and charming, all of them anxious to help me and honor bound to show any visitor the numerous courtesies of their system of etiquette. In short, they approached the image of 'primitive man' that I had conjured up in my mind before doing fieldwork, a kind of 'Rousseauian' view, and it was sheer pleasure to work with them. Other anthropologists have also noted sharp contrasts in the people they study from one field situation to another. One of the most startling examples of this is in the work of Colin Turnbull, who first studied the Ituri Pygmies (1965, 1983) and found them delightful to live with, but then studied the Ik (1972) of the desolate outcroppings of the Kenya/Uganda/Sudan border region, a people he had difficulty coping with intellectually, emotionally, and physically. While it is possible that the anthropologist's reactions to a particular people are personal and idiosyncratic, it nevertheless remains true that there are enormous differences between whole peoples, differences that affect the anthropologist in often dramatic ways.

Hence, what I say about some of my experiences is probably equally true of the experiences of many other fieldworkers. I describe some of them here for the benefit of future anthropologists—because I think I could have profited by reading about the pitfalls and field problems of my own teachers. At the very least I might have been able to avoid some of my more stupid errors. In this regard there is a growing body of excellent descriptive work on field research. Students who plan to make a career in anthropology should consult these works, which cover a wide range of field situations in the ethnographic present.[3]

The Longest Day: The First One

My first day in the field illustrated to me what my teachers meant when they spoke of 'culture shock.' I had traveled in a small, aluminum rowboat propelled by a large outboard motor for two and a half days. This took me from the territorial capital, a small town on the Orinoco River, deep into Yąnomamö country. On the morning of the third day we reached a small mission settlement, the field 'headquarters' of a group of Americans who were working in two Yąnomamö villages. The missionaries had come out of these villages to hold their annual conference on the progress of their mission work and were conducting their meetings when I arrived. We picked up a passenger at the mission station, James P. Barker, the first non-Yąnomamö to make a sustained, permanent contact with the tribe (in 1950). He had just returned from a year's furlough in the United States, where I had earlier visited him before leaving for Venezuela. He agreed to accompany me to the village I had selected for my base of operations to introduce me to the Indians. This village was also his own home base, but he had not been there for over a year and did not plan to join me for another three months. Mr. Barker had been living with this particular group about five years.

We arrived at the village, Bisaasi-teri, about 2:00 P.M. and docked the boat along the muddy bank at the terminus of the path used by Yąnomamö to fetch their drinking water. It was hot and muggy, and my clothing was soaked with perspiration. It clung uncomfortably to my body, as it did thereafter for the remainder of the work. The small biting gnats, *bareto*, were out in astronomical numbers, for it was the beginning of the dry season. My face and hands were swollen from the venom of their numerous stings. In just a few moments I was to meet my first Yąnomamö, my first primitive man. What would he be like? I had visions of entering the village and seeing 125 social facts running about altruistically calling each other kinship terms and sharing food, each waiting and anxious to have me collect his genealogy. I would wear them out in turn. Would they like me? This was important to me; I wanted them to be so fond of me that they would adopt me into their kinship system and way of life. I had heard that successful anthropologists always get adopted by their people. I had learned during my seven years of anthropological training at the University of Michigan that kinship was equivalent to society in primitive tribes and that it was a moral way of life, 'moral' being something 'good' and 'desirable.' I was determined to work my way into their moral system of kinship and become a member of their society—to be 'accepted' by them.

How Did They Accept You?

My heart began to pound as we approached the village and heard the buzz of activity within the circular compound. Mr. Barker commented that he was anxious to see if any changes had taken place while he was away and wondered how many of them had died during his absence. I nervously felt my back pocket to make sure that my notebook was still there and felt personally more secure when I touched it.

The entrance to the village was covered over with brush and dry palm leaves. We pushed them aside to expose the low opening to the village. The excitement of meeting my first Yąomamö was almost unbearable as I duck-waddled through the low passage into the village clearing.

I looked up and gasped when I saw a dozen burly, naked, sweaty, hideous men staring at us down the shafts of their drawn arrows! Immense wads of green tobacco were stuck between their lower teeth and lips making them look even more hideous, and strands of dark-green slime dripped or hung from their nostrils—strands so long that they clung to their pectoral muscles or drizzled down their chins. We arrived at the village while the men were blowing a hallucinogenic drug up their noses. One of the side effects of the drug is a runny nose. The mucus is always saturated with the green powder and they usually let it run freely from their nostrils. My next discovery was that there were a dozen or so vicious, underfed dogs snapping at my legs, circling me as if I were to be their next meal. I just stood there holding my notebook, helpless and pathetic. Then the stench of the decaying vegetation and filth hit me and I almost got sick. I was horrified. What kind of welcome was this for the person who came here to live with you and learn your way of life, to become friends with you? They put their weapons down when they recognized Barker and returned to their chanting, keeping a nervous eye on the village entrances.

We had arrived just after a serious fight. Seven women had been abducted the day before by a neighboring group, and the local men and their guests had just that morning recovered five of them in a brutal club fight that nearly ended in a shooting war. The abductors, angry because they had lost five of their seven new captives, vowed to raid the Bisaasi-teri. When we arrived and entered the village unexpectedly, the Indians feared that we were the raiders. On several occasions during the next two hours the men in the village jumped to their feet, armed themselves, nocked their arrows and waited nervously for the noise outside the village to be identified. My enthusiasm for collecting ethnographic facts diminished in proportion to the number of times such an alarm was raised. In fact, I was relieved when Barker suggested that we sleep across the river for the evening. It would be safer over there.

As we walked down the path to the boat, I pondered the wisdom of having decided to spend a year and a half with these people before I had even seen what they were like. I am not ashamed to admit that had there been a diplomatic way out, I would have ended my fieldwork then and there. I did not look forward to the next day—and months—when I would be left alone with the Yąnomamö; I did not speak a word of their language, and they were decidedly different from what I had imagined them to be. The whole situation was depressing, and I wondered why I ever decided to switch from physics and engineering in the first place. I had not eaten all day, I was soaking wet from perspiration, the *bareto* were biting me, and I was covered with red pigment, the result of a dozen or so complete examinations I had been given by as many very pushy Yąnomamö men. These examinations capped an otherwise grim day. The men would blow their noses into their hands, flick as much of the mucus off that would separate in a snap of the wrist, wipe the residue into their hair, and then carefully examine my face, arms, legs, hair, and the contents of my pockets. I asked Barker how to say, 'Your hands are dirty'; my comments were met by the Yąnomamö in the following way: They would 'clean' their hands by spitting a quantity of slimy tobacco juice into them, rub them together, grin, and then proceed with the examination.

Mr. Barker and I crossed the river and slung our hammocks. When he pulled his hammock out of a rubber bag, a heavy disagreeable odor of mildewed cotton and stale wood smoke came with it. 'Even the missionaries are filthy,' I thought to myself. Within two weeks, everything I owned smelled the same way, and I lived with that odor for the remainder of the fieldwork. My own habits of personal cleanliness declined to such levels that I didn't even mind being examined by the Yąnomamö, as I was not much cleaner than they were after I had adjusted to the circumstances. It is difficult to blow your nose gracefully when you are stark naked and the invention of handkerchiefs is millenia away.

Life in the Jungle: Oatmeal, Peanut Butter, and Bugs

It isn't easy to plop down in the Amazon Basin for a year and get immediately into the anthropological swing of things. You have been told about horrible diseases, snakes, jaguars, electric eels, little spiny fish that will swim up your urine into your penis, quicksand, and getting lost. Some of the dangers are real, but your imagination makes them more real and threatening than many of them really are. What my teachers never bothered to advise me about, however, was the mundane, nonexciting, and trivial stuff—like eating, defecating, sleeping, or keeping clean. These turned out to be the bane of my existence during the first several months of field research. I set up my household in Barker's abandoned mud hut, a few yards from the village of Bisaasi-teri, and immediately set to work building my own mud/thatch hut with the help of the Yąnomamö. Meanwhile, I had to eat and try to do my 'field research.' I soon discovered that it was an enormously time-consuming task to maintain my own body in the manner to which it had grown accustomed in the relatively antiseptic environment of the northern United States. Either I could be relatively well fed and relatively comfortable in a fresh change of clothes and do very little fieldwork, or I could do considerably more fieldwork and be less well fed and less comfortable.

It is appalling how complicated it can be to make oatmeal in the jungle. First, I had to make two trips to the river to haul the water. Next, I had to prime my kerosene stove with alcohol to get it burning, a tricky procedure when you are trying to mix powdered milk and fill a coffee pot at the same time. The alcohol prime always burned out before I could turn the kerosene on, and I would have to start all over. Or, I would turn the kerosene on, optimistically hoping that the Coleman element was still hot enough to vaporize the fuel, and start a small fire in my palm-thatched hut as the liquid kerosene squirted all over the table and walls and then ignited. Many amused Yąnomamö onlookers quickly learned the English phrase 'Oh, Shit!' and, once they discovered that the phrase offended and irritated the missionaries, they used it as often as they could in their presence. I usually had to start over with the alcohol. Then I had to boil the oatmeal and pick the bugs out of it. All my supplies, of course, were carefully stored in rat-proof, moisture-proof, and insect-proof containers, not one of which ever served its purpose adequately. Just taking things out of the multiplicity of containers and repacking them afterward was a minor project in itself. By the time I had hauled the water to cook with, unpacked my food, prepared the oatmeal, milk, and coffee, heated water for dishes, washed and dried the dishes, repacked the food in the containers, stored the containers in locked trunks, and cleaned up my mess, the ceremony of preparing breakfast had brought me almost up to lunch time!

Eating three meals a day was simply out of the question. I solved the problem by eating a single meal that could be prepared in a single container, or, at most, in two containers, washed my dishes only when there were no clean ones left, using cold river water, and wore each change of clothing at least a week to cut down on my laundry problem—a courageous undertaking in the tropics. I reeked like a jockstrap that had been left to mildew in the bottom of some dark gym locker. I also became less concerned about sharing my provisions with the rats, insects, Yąnomamö, and the elements, thereby eliminating the need for my complicated storage process. I was able to last most of the day on *café con leche*, heavily sugared espresso coffee diluted about five to one with hot milk. I would prepare this in the evening and store it in a large thermos. Frequently, my single meal was no more complicated than a can of sardines and a package of soggy crackers. But at least two or three times a week I would do something 'special' and sophisticated, like make a batch of oatmeal or boil rice and add a can of tuna fish or tomato paste to it. I even saved time by devising a water system that obviated the trips to the river. I had a few sheets of tin roofing brought in and made a rain water trap; I caught the water on the tin surface, funneled it into an empty gasoline drum, and then ran a plastic hose from the drum to my hut. When the drum was exhausted in the dry season, I would get a few Yąnomamö boys to fill it with buckets of water from the river, 'paying' them with crackers, of which they grew all too fond all too soon.

I ate much less when I traveled with the Yąnomamö to visit other villages. Most of the time my travel diet consisted of roasted or boiled green plantains (cooking bananas) that I obtained from the Yąnomamö, but I always carried a few cans of sardines with me in case I got lost or stayed away longer than I had planned. I found peanut butter and crackers a very nourishing 'trail' meal, and a simple one to prepare. It was nutritious and portable, and only one tool was required to make the meal: a hunting knife that could be cleaned by wiping the blade on a convenient leaf. More importantly, it was one of the few foods the Yąnomamö would let me eat in relative peace. It looked suspiciously like animal feces to them, an impression I encouraged. I referred to the peanut butter as the feces of babies or 'cattle.' They found this disgusting and repugnant. They did not know what 'cattle' were, but were increasingly aware that I ate several canned products of such an animal. Tin cans were thought of as containers made of 'machete skins,' but how the cows got inside was always a mystery to them. I went out of my way to describe my foods in such a way as to make them sound unpalatable to them, for it gave me some peace of mind while I ate: They wouldn't beg for a share of something that was too horrible to contemplate. Fieldworkers develop strange defense mechanisms and strategies, and this was one of my own forms of adaptation to the fieldwork. On another occasion I was eating a can of frankfurters and growing very weary of the demands from one of the onlookers for a share in my meal. When he finally asked what I was eating, I replied: 'Beef.' He then asked: 'Shaki![4] What part of the animal are you eating?' To which I replied, 'Guess.' He muttered a contemptuous epithet, but stopped asking for a share. He got back at me later, as we shall see.

Meals were a problem in a way that had nothing to do with the inconvenience of preparing them. Food sharing is important to the Yąnomamö in the context of displaying friendship. 'I am hungry!' is almost a form of greeting with them. I could not possibly have brought enough food with me to feed the entire village, yet they seemed to overlook this logistic fact as they begged for my food. What became fixed in their minds was the fact that I did not share my food with whomsoever was present—usually a small crowd—at each and every meal. Nor could I easily enter their system of reciprocity with respect to food. Every time one of them 'gave' me something 'freely,' he would dog me for months to 'pay him back,' not necessarily with food but with knives, fishhooks, axes, and so on. Thus, if I accepted a plantain from someone in a different village while I was on a visit, he would most likely visit me in the future and demand a machete as payment for the time that he 'fed' me. I usually reacted to these kinds of demands by giving a banana, the customary reciprocity in their culture—food for food—but this would be a disappointment for the individual who had nursed visions of that single plantain growing into a machete over time. Many years after beginning my fieldwork, I was approached by one of the prominent men who demanded a machete for a piece of meat he claimed he had given me five or six years earlier.

Despite the fact that most of them knew I would not share my food with them at their request, some of them always showed up at my hut during mealtime. I gradually resigned myself to this and learned to ignore their persistent demands while I ate. Some of them would get angry because I failed to give in, but most of them accepted it as just a peculiarity of the subhuman foreigner who had come to live among them. If or when I did accede to a request for a share of my food, my hut quickly filled with Yąnomamö, each demanding their share of the food that I had just given to one of them. Their begging for food was not provoked by hunger, but by a desire to try something new and to attempt to establish a coercive relationship in which I would accede to a demand. If one received something, all others would immediately have to test the system to see if they, too, could coerce me.

A few of them went out of their way to make my meals downright unpleasant—to spite me for not sharing, especially if it was a food that they had tried before and liked, or a food that was part of their own cuisine. For example, I was eating a cracker with peanut butter and honey one day. The Yąnomamö will do almost anything for honey, one of the most prized delicacies in their own diet. One of my cynical onlookers—the fellow who had earlier watched me eating frankfurters—immediately recognized the honey and knew that I would not share the tiny precious bottle. It would be futile to even ask. Instead, he glared at me and queried icily, 'Shaki! What kind of animal semen are you pouring onto your food and eating?' His question had the desired effect and my meal ended.

Finally, there was the problem of being lonely and separated from your own kind, especially your family. I tried to overcome this by seeking personal friendships among the Yąnomamö. This usually complicated the matter because all my 'friends' simply used my confidence to gain privileged access to my hut and my cache of steel tools and trade goods—and looted me when I wasn't looking. I would be bitterly disappointed that my erstwhile friend thought no more of me than to finesse our personal relationship exclusively with the intention of getting at my locked up possessions, and my depression would hit new lows every time I discovered this. The loss of the possessions bothered me much less than the shock that I was, as far as most of them were concerned, nothing more than a source of desirable items. No holds were barred in relieving me of these, since I was considered something subhuman, a non-Yąomamö.

The hardest thing to learn to live with was the incessant, passioned, and often aggressive demands they would make. It would become so unbearable at times that I would have to lock myself in my hut periodically just to escape from it. Privacy is one of our culture's most satisfying achievements, one you never think about until you suddenly have none. It is like not appreciating how good your left thumb feels until someone hits it with a hammer. But I did not want privacy for its own sake; rather, I simply had to get away from the begging. Day and night for almost the entire time I lived with the Yąnomamö, I was plagued by such demands as: 'Give me a knife, I am poor!'; 'If you don't take me with you on your next trip to Widokaiya-teri, I'll chop a hole in your canoe!'; 'Take us hunting up the Mavaca River with your shotgun or we won't help you!'; 'Give me some matches so I can trade with the Reyaboböwei-teri, and be quick about it or I'll hit you!'; 'Share your food with me, or I'll burn your hut!'; 'Give me a flashlight so I can hunt at night!'; 'Give me all your medicine, I itch all over!'; 'Give me an ax or I'll break into your hut when you are away and steal all of them!' And so I was bombarded by such demands day after day, month after month, until I could not bear to see a Yąomamö at times.

It was not as difficult to become calloused to the incessant begging as it was to ignore the sense of urgency, the impassioned tone of voice and whining, or the intimidation and aggression with which many of the demands were made. It was likewise difficult to adjust to the fact that the Yąnomamö refused to accept 'No' for an answer until or unless it seethed with passion and intimidation—which it did after a few months. So persistent and characteristic is the begging that the early 'semi-official' maps made by the Venezuelan Malaria Control Service *(Malarialogía)* designated the site of their first permanent field station, next to the village of Bisaasi-teri, as *Yababuhii:* 'Gimme.' I had to become like the Yąnomamö to be able to get along with them on their terms: somewhat sly, aggressive, intimidating, and pushy.

It became indelibly clear to me shortly after I arrived there that had I failed to adjust in this fashion I would have lost six months of supplies to them in a single day or would have spent most of my time ferrying them around in my canoe or taking them on long hunting trips. As it was, I did spend a considerable amount of time doing these things and did succumb often to their outrageous demands for axes and machetes, at least at first, for things changed as I became more fluent in their language and learned how to defend myself socially as well as verbally. More importantly, had I failed to demonstrate that I could not be pushed around beyond a certain point, I would have been the subject of far more ridicule, theft, and practical jokes than was the actual case. In short, I had to acquire a certain proficiency in their style of interpersonal politics and to learn how to imply subtly that certain potentially undesirable, but unspecified, consequences might follow if they did such and such to me. They do this to each other incessantly in order to establish precisely the point at which they cannot goad or intimidate an individual any further without precipitating some kind of retaliation. As soon as I realized this and gradually acquired the self-confidence to adopt this strategy, it became clear that much of the intimidation was calculated to determine my flash point or my 'last ditch' position—and I got along much better with them. Indeed, I even regained some lost ground. It was sort of like a political, interpersonal game that everyone had to play, but one in which each individual sooner or later had to give evidence that his bluffs and implied threats could be backed up with a sanction. I suspect that the frequency of wife beating is a component in this syndrome, since men can display their *waiteri* (ferocity) and 'show' others that they are capable of great violence. Beating a wife with a club is one way of displaying ferocity, one that does not expose the man to much danger—unless the wife has concerned, aggressive brothers in the village who will come to her aid. Apparently an important thing in wife beating is that the man has displayed his presumed potential for violence and the intended message is that other men ought to treat him with circumspection, caution, and even deference.

After six months, the level of Yąnomamö demand was tolerable in Bisaasi-teri, the village I used for my base of operations. We had adjusted somewhat to each other and knew what to expect with regard to demands for food, trade goods, and favors. Had I elected to remain in just one Yąnomamö village for the entire duration of my first 15 months of fieldwork, the experience would have been far more enjoyable than it actually was. However, as I began to understand the social and political dynamics of this village, it became patently obvious that I would have to travel to many other villages to determine the demographic bases and political histories that lay behind what I could understand in the village of Bisaasi-teri. I began making regular trips to some dozen neighboring Yąnomamö villages as my language fluency improved. I collected local genealogies there, or rechecked and cross-checked those I had collected elsewhere. Hence, the intensity of begging was relatively constant and relatively high for the duration of my fieldwork, for I had to establish my personal position in each village I visited and revisited.

For the most part, my own 'fierceness' took the form of shouting back at the Yąnomamö as loudly and as passionately as they shouted at me, especially at first, when I did not know much of the language. As I became more fluent and learned more about their political tactics, I became more sophisticated in the art of bluffing and brinksmanship. For example, I paid one young man a machete (then worth about $2.50) to cut a palm tree and help me make boards from the wood. I used these to fashion a flooring in the bottom of my dugout canoe to keep my possessions out of the water that always seeped into the canoe and sloshed around. That afternoon I was working with one of my informants in the village. The long-awaited mission supply boat arrived and most of the Yąnomamö ran out of the village to see the supplies and try to beg items from the crew. I continued to work in the village for another hour or so and then went down to the river to visit with the men on the supply boat. When I reached the river I noticed, with anger and frustration, that the Yąnomamö had chopped up all my new floor boards to use as crude paddles to get their own canoes across the river to the supply boat.[5] I knew that if I ignored this abuse I would have invited the Yąnomamö to take even greater liberties with my possessions in the future. I got into my canoe, crossed the river, and docked amidst their flimsy, leaky craft. I shouted loudly to them, attracting their attention. They were somewhat sheepish, but all had mischievous grins on their impish faces. A few of them came down to the canoe, where I proceeded with a spirited lecture that revealed my anger at their audacity and license. I explained that I had just that morning paid one of them a machete for bringing me the palmwood, how hard I had worked to shape each board and place it in the canoe, how carefully and painstakingly I had tied each one in with vines, how much I had perspired, how many *bareto* bites I had suffered, and so on. Then, with exaggerated drama and finality, I withdrew my hunting knife as their grins disappeared and cut each one of their canoes loose and set it into the strong current of the Orinoco River where it was immediately swept up and carried downstream. I left without looking back and huffed over to the other side of the river to resume my work.

They managed to borrow another canoe and, after some effort, recovered their dugouts. Later, the headman of the village told me, with an approving chuckle, that I had done the correct thing. Everyone in the village, except, of course, the culprits, supported and defended my actions—and my status increased as a consequence.

Whenever I defended myself in such ways I got along much better with the Yąnomamö and gradually acquired the respect of many of them. A good deal of their demeanor toward me was directed with the forethought of establishing the point at which I would draw the line and react defensively. Many of them, years later, reminisced about the early days of my fieldwork when I was timid and *mohode* ("stupid") and a little afraid of them, those golden days when it was easy to bully me into giving my goods away for almost nothing.

Theft was the most persistent situation that required some sort of defensive action. I simply could not keep everything I owned locked in trunks, and the Yąnomamö came into my hut and left at will. I eventually developed a very effective strategy for recovering almost all the stolen items: I would simply ask a child who took the item and then I would confiscate that person's hammock when he was not around, giving a spirited lecture to all who could hear on the antisociality of thievery as I stalked off in a faked rage with the thief's hammock slung over my shoulder. Nobody ever attempted to stop me from doing this, and almost all of them told me that my technique for recovering my possessions was ingenious. By nightfall the thief would appear at my hut with the stolen item or send it over with someone else to make an exchange to recover his hammock. He would be heckled by his covillagers for having got caught and for being embarrassed into returning my item for his hammock. The explanation was usually, 'I just borrowed your ax! I wouldn't think of stealing it!'

Collecting Yanomamö Genealogies and Reproductive Histories

My purpose for living among Yąnomamö was to systematically collect certain kinds of information on genealogy, reproduction, marriage practices, kinship, settlement patterns, migrations, and politics. Much of the fundamental data was genealogical—who was the parent of whom, tracing these connections as far back in time as Yąnomamö knowledge and memory permitted. Since 'primitive' society is organized largely by kinship relationships, figuring out the social organization of the Yąnomamö essentially meant collecting extensive data on genealogies, marriage, and reproduction. This turned out to be a staggering and very frustrating problem. I could not have deliberately picked a more difficult people to work with in this regard. They have very stringent name taboos and eschew mentioning the names of prominent living people as well as all deceased friends and relatives. They attempt to name people in such a way that when the person dies and they can no longer use his or her name, the loss of the word in their language is not inconvenient. Hence, they name people for specific and minute parts of things, such as 'toenail of sloth,' 'whisker of howler monkey,' and so on, thereby being able to retain the words 'toenail' or 'whisker' but somewhat handicapped in referring to these anatomical parts of sloths and monkeys respectively. The taboo is maintained even for the living, for one mark of prestige is the courtesy others show you by not using your name publicly. This is particularly true for men, who are much more competitive for status than women in this culture, and it is fascinating to watch boys grow into young men, demanding to be called either by a kinship term in public, or by a teknonymous reference such as 'brother of Himotoma.' The more effective they are at getting others to avoid using their names, the more public acknowledgment there is that they are of high esteem and social standing. Helena Valero, a Brazilian woman who was captured as a child by a Yąnomamö raiding party, was married for many years to a Yąnomamö headman before she discovered what his name was (Biocca, 1970; Valero, 1984). The sanctions behind the taboo are more complex than just this, for they involve a combination of fear, respect, admiration, political deference, and honor.

At first I tried to use kinship terms alone to collect genealogies, but Yąnomamö kinship terms, like the kinship terms in all systems, are ambiguous at some point because they include so many possible relatives (as the term 'uncle' does in our own kinship system). Again, their system of kin classification merges many relatives that we 'separate' by using different terms: They call both their actual father and their father's brother by a single term, whereas we call one 'father' and the other 'uncle.' I was forced, therefore, to resort to personal names to collect unambiguous genealogies or 'pedigrees.' They quickly grasped what I was up to and that I was determined to learn everyone's 'true name,' which amounted to an invasion of their system of prestige and etiquette, if not a flagrant violation of it. They reacted to this in a brilliant but devastating manner: They invented false names for everybody in the village and systematically learned them, freely revealing to me the 'true' identities of everyone. I smugly thought I had cracked the system and enthusiastically constructed elaborate genealogies over a period of some five months. They enjoyed watching me learn their names and kinship relationships. I naively assumed that I would get the 'truth' to each question and the best information by working in public. This set the stage for converting my serious project into an amusing hoax of the grandest proportions. Each 'informant' would try to outdo his peers by inventing a name even more preposterous or ridiculous than what I had been given by someone earlier, the explanations for discrepancies being 'Well, he has two names and this is the other one.' They even fabricated devilishly improbable genealogical relationships, such as someone being married to his grandmother, or worse yet, to his mother-in-law, a grotesque and horrifying prospect to the Yąnomamö. I would collect the desired names and relationships by having my informant whisper the name of the person softly into my ear, noting that he or she was the parent of such and such or the child of such and such, and so on. Everyone who was observing my work would then insist that I repeat the name aloud, roaring in hysterical laughter as I clumsily pronounced the name, sometimes laughing until tears streamed down their faces. The 'named' person would usually react with annoyance and hiss some untranslatable epithet at me, which served to reassure me that I had the 'true' name. I conscientiously checked and rechecked the names and relationships with multiple informants, pleased to see the inconsistencies disappear as my genealogy sheets filled with those desirable little triangles and circles, thousands of them.

My anthropological bubble was burst when I visited a village about 10 hours' walk to the southwest of Bisaasi-teri some five months after I had begun collecting genealogies on the Bisaasi-teri. I was chatting with the local headman of this village and happened to casually drop the name of the wife of the Bisaasi-teri headman. A stunned silence followed, and then a village-wide roar of uncontrollable laughter, choking, gasping, and howling followed. It seems that I thought the Bisaasi-teri headman was married to a woman named "hairy cunt." It also seems that the Bisaasi-teri headman was called 'long dong' and his brother 'eagle shit.' The Bisaasi-teri headman had a son called "asshole" and a daughter called 'fart breath.' And so on. Blood welled up my temples as I realized that I had nothing but nonsense to show for my five months' of dedicated genealogical effort, and I had to throw away almost all the information I had collected on this the most basic set of data I had come there to get. I understood at that point why the Bisaasi-teri laughed so hard when they made me repeat the names of their covillagers, and why the 'named' person would react with anger and annoyance as I pronounced his 'name' aloud.

I was forced to change research strategy—to make an understatement to describe this serious situation. The first thing I did was to begin working in private with my informants to eliminate the horseplay and distraction that attended public sessions. Once I did this, my informants, who did not know what others were telling me, began to agree with each other and I managed to begin learning the 'real' names, starting first with children and gradually moving to adult women and then, cautiously, adult men, a sequence that reflected the relative degree of intransigence at revealing names of people. As I built up a core of accurate genealogies and relationships—a core that all independent informants had verified repetitiously—I could 'test' any new informant by soliciting his or her opinion and knowledge about these 'core' people whose names and relationships I was confident were accurate. I was, in this fashion, able to immediately weed out the mischievous informants who persisted in trying to deceive me. Still, I had great difficulty getting the names of dead kinsmen, the only accurate way to extend genealogies back in time. Even my best informants continued to falsify names of the deceased, especially closely related deceased. The falsifications at this point were not serious and turned out to be readily corrected as my interviewing methods improved (see below). Most of the deceptions were of the sort where the informant would give me the name of a living man as the father of some child whose actual father was dead, a response that enabled the informant to avoid using the name of a deceased kinsman or friend.

The quality of a genealogy depends in part on the number of generations it embraces, and the name taboo prevented me from making any substantial progress in learning about the deceased ancestors of the present population. Without this information, I could not, for example, document marriage patterns and interfamilial alliances through time. I had to rely on older informants for this information, but these were the most reluctant informants of all for this data. As I became more proficient in the language and more skilled at detecting fabrications, any informants became better at deception. One old man was particularly cunning and persuasive, following a sort of Mark Twain policy that the most effective lie is a sincere lie. He specialized in making a ceremony out of false names for dead ancestors. He would look around nervously to make sure nobody was listening outside my hut, enjoin me never to mention the name again, become very anxious and spooky, and grab me by the head to whisper a secret name into my ear. I was always elated after a session with him, because I managed to add several generations of ancestors for particular members of the village. Others steadfastly refused to give me such information. To show my gratitude, I paid him quadruple the rate that I had been paying the others. When word got around that I had increased the pay for genealogical and demographic information, volunteers began pouring into my hut to 'work' for me, assuring me of their changed ways and keen desire to divest themselves of the 'truth.'

Enter Rerebawä: Inmarried Tough Guy

I discovered that the old man was lying quite by accident. A club fight broke out in the village one day, the result of a dispute over the possession of a woman. She had been promised to a young man in the village, a man named Rerebawä, who was particularly aggressive. He had married into Bisaasi-teri and was doing his 'bride service'—a period of several years during which he had to provide game for his wife's father and mother, provide them with wild foods he might collect, and help them in certain gardening and other tasks. Rerebawä had already been given one of the daughters in marriage and was promised her younger sister as his second wife. He was enraged when the younger sister, then about 16 years old, began having an affair with another young man in the village, Bäkotawä, making no attempt to conceal it. Rerebawä challenged Bäkotawä to a club fight. He swaggered boisterously out to the duel with his 10-foot-long club, a roof-pole he had cut from the house on the spur of the moment, as is the usual procedure. He hurled insult after insult at both Bäkotawä and his father, trying to goad them into a fight. His insults were bitter and nasty. They tolerated them for a few moments, but Rerebawä's biting insults provoked them to rage. Finally, they stormed angrily out of their hammocks and ripped out roof-poles, now returning the insults verbally, and rushed to the village clearing. Rerebawä continued to insult them, goading them into striking him on the head with their equally long clubs. Had either of them struck his head—which he held out conspicuously for them to swing at—he would then have the right to take his turn on their heads with his club. His opponents were intimidated by his fury, and simply backed down, refusing to strike him, and the argument ended. He had intimidated them into submission. All three retired pompously to their respective hammocks, exchanging nasty insults as they departed. But Rerebawä had won the showdown and thereafter swaggered around the village, insulting the two men behind their backs at every opportunity. He was genuinely angry with them, to the point of calling the older man by the name of his long-deceased father. I quickly seized on this incident as an opportunity to collect an accurate genealogy and confidentially asked Rerebawä about his adversary's ancestors. Rerebawä had been particularly 'pushy' with me up to this point, but we soon became warm friends and staunch allies: We were both 'outsiders' in Bisaasi-teri and, although he was a Y̨anomamö, he nevertheless had to put up with some considerable amount of pointed teasing and scorn from the locals, as all inmarried 'sons-in-law' must. He gave me the information I requested of his adversary's deceased ancestors, almost with devilish glee. I asked about dead ancestors of other people in the village and got prompt, unequivocal answers: He was angry with everyone in the village. When I compared his answers to those of the old man, it was obvious that one of them was lying. I then challenged his answers. He explained, in a sort of 'you damned fool, don't you know better?' tone of voice that everyone in the village knew the old man was lying to me and gloating over it when I was out of earshot. The names the old man had given to me were names of dead ancestors of the members of a village so far away that he thought I would never have occasion to check them out authoritatively. As it turned out, Rerebawä knew most of the people in that distant village and recognized the names given by the old man.

I then went over all my Bisaasi-teri genealogies with Rerebawä, genealogies I had presumed to be close to their final form. I had to revise them all because of the numerous lies and falsifications they contained, much of it provided by the sly old man. Once again, after months of work, I had to recheck everything with Rerebawä's aid. Only the living members of the nuclear families turned out to be accurate; the deceased ancestors were mostly fabrications.

Discouraging as it was to have to recheck everything all over again, it was a major turning point in my fieldwork. Thereafter, I began taking advantage of local arguments and animosities in selecting my informants, and used more extensively informants who had married into the village in the recent past. I also began traveling more regularly to other villages at this time to check on genealogies, seeking out villages whose members were on strained terms with the people about whom I wanted information. I would then return to my base in the village of Bisaasi-teri and check with local informants the accuracy of the new information. I had to be careful in this work and scrupulously select my local informants in such a way that I would not be inquiring about *their* closely related kin. Thus, for each of my local informants, I had to make lists of names of certain deceased people that I dared not mention in their presence. But despite this precaution, I would occasionally hit a new name that would put some informants into a rage, or into a surly mood, such as that of a dead 'brother' or 'sister'[6] whose existence had not been indicated to me by other informants. This usually terminated my day's work with that informant, for he or she would be too touchy or upset to continue any further, and I would be reluctant to take a chance on accidentally discovering another dead close kinsman soon after discovering the first.

These were unpleasant experiences, and occasionally dangerous as well, depending on the temperament of my informant. On one occasion I was planning to visit a village that had been raided recently by one of their enemies. A woman, whose name I had on my census list for that village, had been killed by the raiders. Killing women is considered to be bad form in Yąnomamö warfare, but this woman was deliberately killed for revenge. The raiders were unable to bushwhack some man who stepped out of the village at dawn to urinate, so they shot a volley of arrows over the roof into the village and beat a hasty retreat. Unfortunately, one of the arrows struck and killed a woman, an accident. For that reason, her village's raiders *deliberately* sought out and killed a woman in retaliation—whose name was on my list. My reason for going to the village was to update my census data on a name-by-name basis and estimate the ages of all the residents. I knew I had the name of the dead woman in my list, but nobody would dare to utter her name so I could remove it. I knew that I would be in very serious trouble if I got to the village and said her name aloud, and I desperately wanted to remove it from my list. I called on one of my regular and usually cooperative informants and asked him to tell me the woman's name. He refused adamantly, explaining that she was a close relative—and was angry that I even raised the topic with him. I then asked him if he would let me whisper the names of *all* the women of that village in his ear, and he would simply have to nod when I hit the right name. We had been 'friends' for some time, and I thought I was able to predict his reaction, and thought that our friendship was good enough to use this procedure. He agreed to the procedure, and I began whispering the names of the women, one by one. We were alone in my hut so that nobody would know what we were doing and nobody could hear us. I read the names softly, continuing to the next when his response was a negative. When I ultimately hit the dead woman's name, he flew out of his chair, enraged and trembling violently, his arm raised to strike me: 'You son-of-a-bitch!' he screamed. 'If you say her name in my presence again, I'll kill you in an instant!' I sat there, bewildered, shocked, and confused. And frightened, as much because of his reaction, but also because I could imagine what might happen to me should I unknowingly visit a village to check genealogy accuracy without knowing that someone had just died there or had been shot by raiders since my last visit. I reflected on the several articles I had read as a graduate student that explained the 'genealogical method,' but could not recall anything about its being a potentially lethal undertaking. My furious informant left my hut, never again to be invited back to be an informant. I had other similar experiences in different villages, but I was always fortunate in that the dead person had been dead for some time, or was not very closely related to the individual into whose ear I whispered the forbidden name. I was usually cautioned by one of the men to desist from saying any more names lest I get people 'angry.'[7]

Kaobawä: The Bisaasi-teri Headman Volunteers to Help Me

I had been working on the genealogies for nearly a year when another individual came to my aid. It was Kaobawä, the headman of Upper Bisaasi-teri. The village of Bisaasi-teri was split into two components, each with its own garden and own circular house. Both were in sight of each other. However, the intensity and frequency of internal bickering and argumentation was so high that they decided to split into two separate groups but remain close to each other for protection in case they were raided. One group was downstream from the other; I refer to that group as the 'Lower' Bisaasi-teri and call Kaobawä's group 'Upper' (upstream) Bisaasi-teri, a convenience they themselves adopted after separating from each other. I spent most of my time with the members of Kaobawä's group, some 200 people when I first arrived there. I did not have much contact with Kaobawä during the early months of my work. He was a somewhat retiring, quiet man, and among the Yąnomamö, the outsider has little time to notice the rare quiet ones when most everyone else is in the front row, pushing and demanding attention. He showed up at my hut one day after all the others had left. He had come to volunteer to help me with the genealogies. He was 'poor,' he explained, and needed a machete. He would work only on the condition that I did not ask him about his own parents and other very close kinsmen who had died. He also added that he would not lie to me as the others had done in the past.

This was perhaps the single most important event in my first 15 months of field research, for out of this fortuitous circumstance evolved a very warm friendship, and among the many things following from it was a wealth of accurate information on the political history of Kaobawä's village and related villages, highly detailed genealogical information, sincere and useful advice to me, and hundreds of valuable insights into the Yąnomamö way of life. Kaobawä's familiarity with his group's history and his candidness were remarkable. His knowledge of details was almost encyclopedic, his memory almost photographic. More than that, he was enthusiastic about making sure I learned the truth, and he encouraged me, indeed, *demanded that* I learn all details I might otherwise have ignored. If there were subtle details he could not recite on the spot, he would advise me to wait until he could check things out with someone else in the village. He would often do this clandestinely, giving me a report the next day, telling me who revealed the new information and whether or not he thought they were in a position to know it. With the information provided by Kaobawä and Rerebawä, I made enormous gains in understanding village interrelationships based on common ancestors and political histories and became lifelong friends with both. And both men knew that

I had to learn about his recently deceased kin from the other one. It was one of those quiet understandings we all had but none of us could mention.

Once again I went over the genealogies with Kaobawä to recheck them, a considerable task by this time. They included about two thousand names, representing several generations of individuals from four different villages. Rerebawä's information was very accurate, and Kaobawä's contribution enabled me to trace the genealogies further back in time. Thus, after nearly a year of intensive effort on genealogies, Yąnomamö demographic patterns and social organization began to make a good deal of sense to me. Only at this point did the patterns through time begin to emerge in the data, and I could begin to understand how kinship groups took form, exchanged women in marriage over several generations, and only then did the fissioning of larger villages into smaller ones emerge as a chronic and important feature of Yąnomamö social, political, demographic, economic, and ecological adaptation. At this point I was able to begin formulating more sophisticated questions, for there was now a pattern to work from and one to flesh out. Without the help of Rerebawä and Kaobawä it would have taken much longer to make sense of the plethora of details I had collected from not only them, but dozens of other informants as well.

I spent a good deal of time with these two men and their families, and got to know them much better than I knew most Yą nomamö. They frequently gave their information in a way which related themselves to the topic under discussion. We became warm friends as time passed, and the formal 'informant/anthropologist' relationship faded into the background. Eventually, we simply stopped 'keeping track' of work and pay. They would both spend hours talking with me, leaving without asking for anything. When they wanted something, they would ask for it no matter what the relative balance of reciprocity between us might have been at that point....

For many of the customary things that anthropologists try to communicate about another culture, these two men and their families might be considered to be 'exemplary' or 'typical.' For other things, they are exceptional in many regards, but the reader will, even knowing some of the exceptions, understand Yąnomamö culture more intimately by being familiar with a few examples.

Kaobawä was about 40 years old when I first came to his village in 1964. I say "about 40" because the Yąnomamö numeration system has only three numbers: one, two, and more-than-two. It is hard to give accurate ages or dates for events when the informants have no means in their language to reveal such detail. Kaobawä is the headman of his village, meaning that he has somewhat more responsibility in political dealings with other Yąnomamö groups, and very little control over those who live in his group except when the village is being raided by enemies. We will learn more about political leadership and warfare in a later chapter, but most of the time men like Kaobawä are like the North American Indian 'chief' whose authority was characterized in the following fashion: "One word from the chief, and each man does as he pleases." There are different 'styles' of political leadership among the Yąnomamö. Some leaders are mild, quiet, inconspicuous most of the time, but intensely competent. They act parsimoniously, but when they do, people listen and conform. Other men are more tyrannical, despotic, pushy, flamboyant, and unpleasant to all around them. They shout orders frequently, are prone to beat their wives, or pick on weaker men. Some are very violent. I have met headmen who run the entire spectrum between these polar types, for I have visited some 60 Yąnomamö villages. Kaobawä stands at the mild, quietly competent end of the spectrum. He has had six wives thus far—and temporary affairs with as many more, at least one of which resulted in a child that is publicly acknowledged as his child. When I first met him he had just two wives: Bahimi and Koamashima. Bahimi had two living children when I first met her; many others had died. She was the older and enduring wife, as much a friend to him as a mate. Their relationship was as close to what we think of as 'love' in our culture as I have seen among the Yąnomamö. His second wife was a girl of about 20 years, Koamashima. She had a new baby boy when I first met her, her first child. There was speculation that Kaobawä was planning to give Koamashima to one of his younger brothers who had no wife; he occasionally allows his younger brother to have sex with Koamashima, but only if he asks in advance. Kaobawä gave another wife to one of his other brothers because she was *beshi* ("horny"). In fact, this earlier wife had been married to two other men, both of whom discarded her because of her infidelity. Kaobawä had one daughter by her. However, the girl is being raised by Kaobawä's brother, though acknowledged to be Kaobawä's child.

Bahimi, his oldest wife, is about five years younger than he. She is his cross-cousin—his mother's brother's daughter. Ideally, all Yąnomamö men should marry a cross-cousin.... Bahimi was pregnant when I began my field work, but she destroyed the infant when it was born—a boy in this case—explaining tearfully that she had no choice. The new baby would have competed for milk with Ariwari, her youngest child, who was still nursing. Rather than expose Ariwari to the dangers and uncertainty of an early weaning, she chose to terminate the newborn instead. By Yąnomamö standards, this has been a very warm, enduring marriage. Kaobawä claims he beats Bahimi only 'once in a while, and only lightly' and she, for her part, never has affairs with other men.

Kaobawä is a quiet, intense, wise, and unobtrusive man. It came as something of a surprise to me when I learned that he was the headman of his village, for he stayed at the sidelines while others would surround me and press their demands on me. He leads more by example than by coercion. He can afford to be this way at his age, for he established his reputation for being forthright and as fierce as the situation required when he was younger, and the other men respect him. He also has five mature brothers or half-brothers in his village, men he can count on for support. He also has several other mature 'brothers' (parallel cousins, whom he must refer to as 'brothers' in his kinship system) in the village who frequently come to his aid, but not as often as his 'real' brothers do. Kaobawä has also given a number of his sisters to other men in the village and has promised his young (8-year-old) daughter in marriage to a young man who, for that reason, is obliged to help him. In short, his 'natural' or 'kinship' following is large, and partially because of this support, he does not have to display his aggressiveness to remind his peers of his position.

Rerebawä is a very different kind of person. He is much younger—perhaps in his early twenties. He has just one wife, but they have already had three children. He is from a village called Karohi-teri, located about five hours' walk up the Orinoco, slightly inland off to the east of the river itself. Kaobawä's village enjoys amicable relationships with Rerebawä's, and it is for this reason that marriage alliances of the kind represented by Rerebawä's marriage into Kaobawä's village occur between the two groups. Rerebawä told me that he came to Bisaasi-teri because there were no eligible women from him to marry in his own village, a fact that I later was able to document when I did a census of his village and a preliminary analysis of its social organization. Rerebawä is perhaps more typical than Kaobawä in the sense that he is chronically concerned about his personal reputation for aggressiveness and goes out of his way to be noticed, even if he has to act tough. He gave me a hard time during my early months of fieldwork, intimidating, teasing, and insulting me frequently. He is, however, much braver than the other men his age and is quite prepared to back up his threats with immediate action—as in the club fight incident just described above. Moreover, he is fascinated with political relationships and knows the details of intervillage relationships over a large area of the tribe. In this respect he shows all the attributes of being a headman, although he has too many competent brothers in his own village to expect to move easily into the leadership position there.

He does not intend to stay in Kaobawä's group and refuses to make his own garden—a commitment that would reveal something of an intended long-term residence. He feels that he has adequately discharged his obligations to his wife's parents by providing them with fresh game, which he has done for several years. They should let him take his wife and return to his own village with her, but they refuse and try to entice him to remain permanently in Bisaasi-teri to continue to provide them with game when they are old. It is for this reason that they promised to give him their second daughter, their only other child, in marriage. Unfortunately, the girl was opposed to the marriage and ultimately married another man, a rare instance where the woman in the marriage had this much influence on the choice of her husband.

Although Rerebawä has displayed his ferocity in many ways, one incident in particular illustrates what his character can be like. Before he left his own village to take his new wife in Bisaasi-teri, he had an affair with the wife of an older brother. When it was discovered, his brother attacked him with a club. Rerebawä responded furiously: He grabbed an ax and drove his brother out of the village after soundly beating him with the blunt side of the single-bit ax. His brother was so intimidated by the thrashing and promise of more to come that he did not return to the village for several days. I visited this village with Kabawä shortly after this event had taken place; Rerebawä was with me as my guide. He made it a point to introduce me to this man. He approached his hammock, grabbed him by the wrist, and dragged him out on the ground: 'This is the brother whose wife I screwed when he wasn't around!' A deadly insult, one that would usually provoke a bloody club fight among more valiant Yąnomamö. The man did nothing. He slunk sheepishly back into his hammock, shamed, but relieved to have Rerebawä release his grip.

Even though Rerebawä is fierce and capable of considerable nastiness, he has a charming, witty side as well. He has a biting sense of humor and can entertain the group for hours with jokes and clever manipulations of language. And, he is one of few Yąnomamö that I feel I can trust. I recall indelibly my return to Bisaasi-teri after being away a year—the occasion of my second field trip to the Yąnomamö. When I reached Bisaasi-teri, Rerebawä was in his own village visiting his kinsmen. Word reached him that I had returned, and he paddled downstream immediately to see me. He greeted me with an immense bear hug and exclaimed, with tears welling up in his eyes, 'Shaki! Why did you stay away so long? Did you not know that my will was so cold while you were gone that I could not at times eat for want of seeing you again?' I, too, felt the same way about him—then, and now.

Of all the Yąnomamö I know, he is the most genuine and the most devoted to his culture's ways and values. I admire him for that, although I cannot say that I subscribe to or endorse some of these values. By contrast, Kaobawä is older and wiser, a polished diplomat. He sees his own culture in a slightly different light and seems even to question aspects of it. Thus, while many of his peers enthusiastically accept the 'explanations' of things given in myths, he occasionally reflects on them—even laughing at some of the most preposterous of them.... Probably more of the Yąnomamö are like Rerebawä than like Kaobawä , or at least try to be....

NOTES

1. The word Yąnomamö is nasalized through its entire length, indicated by the diacritical mark '¸'. When this mark appears on any Yąnomamö word, the whole word is nasalized. The vowel 'ö' represents a sound that does not occur in the English language. It is similar to the umlaut 'ö' in the German language or the 'oe' equivalent, as in the poet Goethe's name. Unfortunately, many presses and typesetters simply eliminate diacritical marks, and this has led to multiple spellings of the word Yąnomamö—and multiple mispronunciations. Some anthropologists have chosen to introduce a slightly different spelling of the word Yąnomamö since I began writing about them, such as Yąnomami, leading to additional misspellings as their diacriticals are characteristically eliminated by presses, and to the *incorrect* pronunciation 'Yąnomameee.' Vowels indicated as 'ä' are pronounced as the 'uh' sound in the word 'duck'. Thus, the name Kaobawä would be pronounced 'cow-ba-wuh,' but entirely nasalized.
2. I spent a total of 60 months among the Yąnomamö between 1964 and 1991. The first edition of this case study was based on the first 15 months I spent among them in Venezuela. I have, at the time of this writing, made 20 field trips to the Yąnomamö and this edition reflects the new information and understandings I have acquired over the years. I plan to return regularly to continue what has now turned into a lifelong study.
3. See Spindler (1970) for a general discussion of field research by anthropologists who have worked in other cultures. Nancy How-

ell has recently written a very useful book (1990) on some of the medical, personal, and environmental hazards of doing field research, which includes a selected bibliography on other fieldwork programs.

4. They could not pronounce "Chagnon." It sounded to them like their name for a pesky bee, shaki, and that is what they called me: pesky, noisome bee.
5. The Yąnomamö in this region acquired canoes very recently. The missionaries would purchase them from the Ye'kwana Indians to the north for money, and then trade them to the Yąnomamö in exchange for labor, produce, or 'informant' work in translating. It should be emphasized that those Yąnomamö who lived on navigable portions of the Upper Orinoco River moved there recently from the deep forest in order to have contact with the missionaries and acquire the trade goods the missionaries (and their supply system) brought.
6. Rarely were there actual brothers or sisters. In Yąnomamö kinship classifications, certain kinds of cousins are classified as siblings. See Chapter 4.
7. Over time, as I became more and more 'accepted' by the Yą nomamö, they became less and less concerned about my genealogical inquiries and now, provide me with this information quite willingly because I have been very discrete with it. Now, when I revisit familiar villages I am called aside by someone who whispers to me things like, "Don't ask about so-and-so's father."

24

A Cultural Approach to Male-Female Miscommunication

Daniel N. Maltz and Ruth A. Borker

Of the 60,000 or so words in the English language, the typical educated adult uses about 2,000. Five hundred of these words alone can convey over 14,000 meanings. But even with all these alternatives, this is not the central problem of miscommunication in North America. Rather, interethnic and cross-sex conversations are the central problem, because the participants possess different subcultural rules for speaking.

Conversation is a negotiated activity. Within a given culture, conversations rely on unspoken understandings about tone of voice, visual cues, silence, minimal responses (such as "mm hmm"), and a variety of other subtle conventions. A cultural approach to male-female conversation highlights unconscious meanings that can lead members of one group to misinterpret the intent of others. Evidence suggests, for example, that women use the response "mm hmm" to indicate they are listening, whereas men use the same response to indicate they are agreeing. Thus, a man who does not provide such cues may indicate to a female conversation partner that he is not listening, whereas a woman may appear to keep changing her mind when giving the same cue. This and similar insights are found throughout this selection and indicate the need for paying attention to communication across cultural and subcultural boundaries.

As you read this selection, ask yourself the following questions:

- What are some of the differences in the ways men and women talk to each other that have been noted in earlier research?
- How do differences between men and women in conversational style reflect differences in power in the larger society?
- If men and women exist in different linguistic subcultures, how and when were these subcultures learned? How does the world of girls differ from the world of boys?
- What kinds of miscommunications occur in cross-sex conversation?
- Can you think of situations that have occurred in your own life that can be better understood after reading this cultural analysis of cross-sex conversation?

The following terms discussed in this selection are included in the Glossary at the back of the book:

gender	*social networks*
metalinguistics	*sociolinguistics*
sex roles	*subculture*

INTRODUCTION

This chapter presents what we believe to be a useful new framework for examining differences in the speaking patterns of American men and women. It is based not on new data, but on a reexamination of a wide variety of material already available in the scholarly literature. Our starting problem is the nature of the different roles of male and female speakers in informal cross-sex conversations in American English. Our attempts to think about this problem have taken us to preliminary examination of a wide variety of fields often on or beyond the margins of our present competencies: children's speech, children's play, styles and patterns of friendship, conversational turn-taking, discourse analysis, and interethnic communication. The research which most influenced the development of our present model includes John Gumperz's work on problems in interethnic communication (1982) and

Maltz, Daniel N. & Ruth A. Borker. "A Cultural Approach to Male-Female Miscommunication." From Language and Identity, pp. 196–216, John Gumperz, ed. © 1982 Cambridge University Press. Reprinted with permission of Cambridge University Press.

Marjorie Goodwin's study of the linguistic aspects of play among black children in Philadelphia (1978, 1980a, 1980b).

Our major argument is that the general approach recently developed for the study of difficulties in cross-ethnic communication can be applied to cross-sex communication as well. We prefer to think of the difficulties in both cross-sex and cross-ethnic communication as two examples of the same larger phenomenon: cultural difference and miscommunication.

THE PROBLEM OF CROSS-SEX CONVERSATION

Study after study has shown that when men and women attempt to interact as equals in friendly cross-sex conversations they do not play the same role in interaction, even when there is no apparent element of flirting. We hope to explore some of these differences, examine the explanations that have been offered, and provide an alternative explanation for them.

The primary data on cross-sex conversations come from two general sources: social psychology studies from the 1950s such as Soskin and John's (1963) research on two young married couples and Strodbeck and Mann's (1956) research on jury deliberations, and more recent sociolinguistic studies from the University of California at Santa Barbara and the University of Pennsylvania by Candace West (Zimmerman and West 1975; West and Zimmerman 1977; West 1979), Pamela Fishman (1978), and Lynette Hirschman (1973).

WOMEN'S FEATURES

Several striking differences in male and female contributions to cross-sex conversation have been noticed in these studies.

First, women display a greater tendency to ask questions. Fishman (1978:400) comments that "at times I felt that all women did was ask questions," and Hirschman (1973:10) notes that "several of the female-male conversations fell into a question-answer pattern with the females asking the males questions."

Fishman (1978:408) sees this question-asking tendency as an example of a second, more general characteristic of women's speech, doing more of the routine "shitwork" involved in maintaining routine social interaction, doing more to facilitate the flow of conversation (Hirschman 1973:3). Women are more likely than men to make utterances that demand or encourage responses from their fellow speakers and are therefore, in Fishman's words, "more actively engaged in insuring interaction than the men" (1978:404). In the earlier social psychology studies, these features have been coded under the general category of "positive reactions" including solidarity, tension release, and agreeing (Strodbeck and Mann 1956).

Third, women show a greater tendency to make use of positive minimal responses, especially "mm hmm" (Hirschman 1973:8), and are more likely to insert "such comments throughout streams of talk rather than [simply] at the end" (Fishman 1978:402).

Fourth, women are more likely to adopt a strategy of "silent protest" after they have been interrupted or have received a delayed minimal response (Zimmerman and West 1975; West and Zimmerman 1977:524).

Fifth, women show a greater tendency to use the pronouns "you" and "we," which explicitly acknowledge the existence of the other speaker (Hirschman 1973:6).

MEN'S FEATURES

Contrasting contributions to cross-sex conversations have been observed and described for men.

First, men are more likely to interrupt the speech of their conversational partners, that is, to interrupt the speech of women (Zimmerman and West 1975; West and Zimmerman 1977; West 1979).

Second, they are more likely to challenge or dispute their partners' utterances (Hirschman 1973:11).

Third, they are more likely to ignore the comments of the other speaker, that is, to offer no response or acknowledgment at all (Hirschman 1973:11), to respond slowly in what has been described as a "delayed minimal response" (Zimmerman and West 1975:118), or to respond unenthusiastically (Fishman 1978).

Fourth, men use more mechanisms for controlling the topic of conversation, including both topic development and the introduction of new topics, than do women (Zimmerman and West 1975).

Finally, men make more direct declarations of fact or opinion than do women (Fishman 1978:402), including suggestions, opinions, and "statements of orientation" as Strodbeck and Mann (1956) describe them, or "statements of focus and directives" as they are described by Soskin and John (1963).

EXPLANATIONS OFFERED

Most explanations for these features have focused on differences in the social power or in the personalities of men and women. One variant of the social power argument, presented by West (Zimmerman and West 1975; West and Zimmerman 1977), is that men's dominance in conversation parallels their dominance in society. Men enjoy power in society and also in conversation. The two levels are seen as part of a single social-political system. West sees interruptions and topic control as male displays of power—a power based in the larger social order but reinforced and expressed in face-to-face interaction with women. A second variant of this argument, stated by Fishman (1978), is that while the differential power of men and women is crucial, the specific mechanism through which it enters conversation is sex-role definition. Sex roles serve to obscure the issue of power for participants, but the fact is, Fishman argues, that norms of appropriate behavior for women and men serve to give power and interactional control to men while keeping it from women. To be socially acceptable as women, women cannot exert control and must actually support men in their control. In this casting of the social power argument, men are not necessarily seen to be consciously flaunting power, but simply reaping the rewards given them by the social system. In both variants, the link between macro and micro levels of social life is seen as direct and unproblematic, and the focus of explanation is the general social order.

Sex roles have also been central in psychological explanations. The primary advocate of the psychological position has been Robin Lakoff (1975). Basically, Lakoff asserts that, having been taught to speak and act like "ladies," women become as unassertive and insecure as they have been made to sound. The impossible task of trying to be both women and adults, which Lakoff sees as culturally incompatible, saps women of confidence and strength. As a result, they come to produce the speech they do, not just because it is how women are supposed to speak, but because it fits with the personalities they develop as a consequence of sex-role requirements.

The problem with these explanations is that they do not provide a means of explaining why these specific features appear as opposed to any number of others, nor do they allow us to differentiate between various types of male-female interaction. They do not really tell us why and how these specific interactional phenomena are linked to the general fact that men dominate within our social system.

AN ALTERNATIVE EXPLANATION: SOCIOLINGUISTIC SUBCULTURES

Our approach to cross-sex communication patterns is somewhat different from those that have been previously proposed. We place the stress not on psychological differences or power differentials, although these may make some contribution, but rather on a notion of cultural differences between men and women in their conceptions of friendly conversation, their rules for engaging in it, and, probably most important, their rules for interpreting it. We argue that American men and women come from different sociolinguistic subcultures, having learned to do different things with words in a conversation, so that when they attempt to carry on conversations with one another, even if both parties are attempting to treat one another as equals, cultural miscommunication results.

The idea of distinct male and female subcultures is not a new one for anthropology. It has been persuasively argued again and again for those parts of the world such as the Middle East and southern Europe in which men and women spend most of their lives spatially and interactionally segregated. The strongest case for sociolinguistic subcultures has been made by Susan Harding from her research in rural Spain (1975).

The major premise on which Harding builds her argument is that speech is a means for dealing with social and psychological situations. When men and women have different experiences and operate in different social contexts, they tend to develop different genres of speech and different skills for doing things with words. In the Spanish village in which she worked, the sexual division of labor was strong, with men involved in agricultural tasks and public politics while women were involved in a series of networks of personal relations with their children, their husbands, and their female neighbors. While men developed their verbal skills in economic negotiations and public political argument, women became more verbally adept at a quite different mode of interactional manipulation with words: gossip, social analysis, subtle information gathering through a carefully developed technique of verbal prying, and a kind of second-guessing the thoughts of others (commonly known as "women's intuition") through a skillful monitoring of the speech of others. The different social needs of men and women, she argues, have led them to sexually differentiated communicative cultures, with each sex learning a different set of skills for manipulating words effectively.

The question that Harding does not ask, however, is, if men and women possess different subcultural rules for speaking, what happens if and when they try to interact with each other? It is here that we turn to the research on interethnic miscommunication.

INTERETHNIC COMMUNICATION

Recent research (Gumperz 1977, 1978a, 1978b, 1979; Gumperz and Tannen 1978) has shown that systematic problems develop in communication when speakers of different speech cultures interact and that these problems are the result of differences in systems of conversational inference and the cues for signalling speech acts and speaker's intent. Conversation is a negotiated activity. It progresses in large part because of shared assumptions about what is going on.

Examining interactions between English-English and Indian-English speakers in Britain (Gumperz 1977, 1978a, 1979; Gumperz et al. 1977), Gumperz found that differences in cues resulted in systematic miscommunication over whether a question was being asked, whether an argument was being made, whether a person was being rude or polite, whether a speaker was relinquishing the floor or interrupting, whether and what a speaker was emphasizing, whether interactants were angry, concerned, or indifferent. Rather than being seen as problems in communication, the frustrating encounters that resulted were usually chalked up as personality clashes or interpreted in the light of racial stereotypes which tended to exacerbate already bad relations.

To take a simple case, Gumperz (1977) reports that Indian women working at a cafeteria, when offering food, used a falling intonation, e.g., "gra̖vy," which to them indicated a question, something like "do you want gravy?" Both Indian and English workers saw a question as an appropriate polite form, but to English-English speakers a falling intonation signalled not a question, which for them is signalled by a rising intonation such as "gra̖vy," but a declarative statement, which was both inappropriate and extremely rude.

A major advantage of Gumperz's framework is that it does not assume that problems are the result of bad faith, but rather sees them as the result of individuals wrongly interpreting cues according to their own rules.

THE INTERPRETATION OF MINIMAL RESPONSES

How might Gumperz's approach to the study of conflicting rules for interpreting conversation be applied to the communication between men and women? A simple example will illustrate our basic approach: the case of positive minimal responses. Minimal responses such as nods and comments like "yes" and "mm hmm" are common features of conversational interaction. Our claim, based on our attempts to understand personal experience, is that these minimal responses have significantly different meanings for men and women, leading to occasionally serious miscommunication.

We hypothesize that for women a minimal response of this type means simply something like "I'm listening to you; please continue," and that for men it has a somewhat stronger meaning such as "I agree with you" or at least "I follow your argument so far." The fact that women use these responses more often than men is in part simply that women are listening more often than men are agreeing.

But our hypothesis explains more than simple differential frequency of usage. Different rules can lead to repeated misunderstandings. Imagine a male speaker who is receiving repeated nods or "mm hmm"s from the woman he is speaking to. She is merely indicating that she is listening, but he thinks she is agreeing with everything he says. Now imagine a female speaker who is receiving only occasional nods and "mm hmm"s from the man she is speaking to. He is indicating that he doesn't always agree; she thinks he isn't always listening.

What is appealing about this short example is that it seems to explain two of the most common complaints in male-female interaction: (1) men who think that women are always agreeing with them and then conclude that it's impossible to tell what a woman really thinks, and (2) women who get upset with men who never seem to be listening. What we think we have here are two separate rules for conversational maintenance which come into conflict and cause massive miscommunication.

SOURCES OF DIFFERENT CULTURES

A probable objection that many people will have to our discussion so far is that American men and women interact with one another far too often to possess different subcultures. What we need to explain is how it is that men and women can come to possess different cultural assumptions about friendly conversation.

Our explanation is really quite simple. It is based on the idea that by the time we have become adults we possess a wide variety of rules for interacting in different situations. Different sets of these rules were learned at different times and in different contexts. We have rules for dealing with people in dominant or subordinate social positions, rules which we first learned as young children interacting with our parents and teachers. We have rules for flirting and other sexual encounters which we probably started learning at or near adolescence. We have rules for dealing with service personnel and bureaucrats, rules we began learning when we first ventured into the public domain. Finally, we have rules for friendly interaction, for carrying on friendly conversation. What is striking about these last rules is that they were learned not from adults but from peers, and that they were learned during precisely that time period, approximately age 5 to 15, when boys and girls interact socially primarily with members of their own sex.

The idea that girls and boys in contemporary America learn different ways of speaking by the age of five or earlier has been postulated by Robin Lakoff (1975), demonstrated by Andrea Meditch (1975), and more fully explored by Adelaide Haas (1979). Haas's research on school-age children shows the early appearance of important male-female differences in patterns of language use, including a male tendency toward direct requests and information giving and a female tendency toward compliance (1979:107).

But the process of acquiring gender-specific speech and behavior patterns by school-age children is more complex than the simple copying of adult "genderlects" by preschoolers. Psychologists Brooks-Gunn and Matthews (1979) have labelled this process the "consolidation of sex roles;" we call it learning of gender-specific "cultures."

Among school-age children, patterns of friendly social interaction are learned not so much from adults as from members of one's peer group, and a major feature of most middle-childhood peer groups is homogeneity; "they are either all-boy or all-girl" (Brooks-Gunn and Matthews 1979). Members of each sex are learning self-consciously to differentiate their behavior from that of the other sex and to exaggerate these differences. The process can be profitably compared to accent divergence in which members of two groups that wish to become clearly distinguished from one another socially acquire increasingly divergent ways of speaking.[1]

Because they learn these gender-specific cultures from their age-mates, children tend to develop stereotypes and extreme versions of adult behavior patterns. For a boy learning to behave in a masculine way, for example, Ruth Hartley (1959, quoted in Brooks-Gunn and Matthews 1979:203) argues that:

> both the information and the practice he gets are distorted. Since his peers have no better sources of information than he has, all they can do is pool the impressions and anxieties they derived from their early training. Thus, the picture they draw is oversimplified and overemphasized. It is a picture drawn in black and white, with little or no modulation and it is incomplete, including a few of the many elements that go to make up the role of the mature male.

What we hope to argue is that boys and girls learn to use language in different ways because of the very different social contexts in which they learn how to carry on friendly conversation. Almost anyone who remembers being a child, has worked with school-age children, or has had an opportunity to observe school-age children can vouch for the fact that groups of girls and groups of boys interact and play in different ways. Systematic observations of children's play have tended to confirm these well-known differences in the ways girls and boys learn to interact with their friends.

In a major study of sex differences in the play of school-age children, for example, sociologist Janet Lever (1976) observed the following six differences between the play of boys and that of girls: (1) girls more often play indoors; (2) boys tend to play in larger groups; (3) boys' play groups tend to include a wider age range of participants; (4) girls play in predominantly male games more often than vice versa; (5) boys more often play competitive games, and (6) girls' games tend to last a shorter period of time than boys' games.

It is by examining these differences in the social organization of play and the accompanying differences in the patterns of social interaction they entail, we argue, that we can learn about the sources of male-female differences in patterns of language use. And it is these same patterns, learned in childhood and carried over into adulthood as the bases for patterns of single-sex friendship relations, we contend, that are potential sources of miscommunication in cross-sex interaction.

THE WORLD OF GIRLS

Our own experience and studies such as Goodwin's (1980b) of black children and Lever's (1976, 1978) of white children suggest a complex of features of girls' play and the speech within it. Girls play in small groups, most often in pairs (Lever 1976; Eder and Hallinan 1978; Brooks-Gunn and Matthews 1979), and their play groups tend to be remarkably homogeneous in terms of age. Their play is often in private or semi-private settings that require participants be invited in. Play is cooperative and activities are usually organized in noncompetitive ways (Lever 1976; Goodwin 1980b). Differentiation between girls is not made in terms of power, but relative closeness. Friendship is seen by girls as involving intimacy, equality, mutual commitment, and loyalty. The idea of "best friend" is central for girls. Relationships between girls are to some extent in opposition to one another, and new relationships are often formed at the expense of old ones. As Brooks-Gunn and Matthews (1979:280) observe, "friendships tend to be exclusive, with a few girls being exceptionally close to one another. Because of this breakups tend to be highly emotional," and Goodwin (1980a:172) notes that "the non-hierarchical framework of the girls provides a fertile ground for rather intricate processes of alliance formation between equals against some other party."

There is a basic contradiction in the structure of girls' social relationships. Friends are supposed to be equal and everyone is supposed to get along, but in fact they don't always. Conflict must be resolved, but a girl cannot assert social power or superiority as an individual to resolve it. Lever (1976), studying fifth-graders, found that girls simply could not deal with quarrels and that when conflict arose they made no attempt to settle it; the group just broke up. What girls learn to do with speech is cope with the contradiction created by an ideology of equality and cooperation and a social reality that includes differences and conflict. As they grow up they learn increasingly subtle ways of balancing the conflicting pressures created by a female social world and a female friendship ideology.

Basically girls learn to do three things with words: (1) to create and maintain relationships of closeness and equality, (2) to criticize others in acceptable ways, and (3) to interpret accurately the speech of other girls.

To a large extent friendships among girls are formed through talk. Girls need to learn to give support, to recognize the speech rights of others, to let others speak, and to acknowledge what they say in order to establish and maintain relationships of equality and closeness. In activities they need to learn to create cooperation through speech. Goodwin (1980a) found that inclusive forms such as "let's," "we gonna," "we could," and "we gotta" predominated in task-oriented activities. Furthermore, she found that most girls in the group she studied made suggestions and that the other girls usually agreed to them. But girls also learn to exchange information and confidences to create and maintain relationships of closeness. The exchange of personal thoughts not only expresses closeness but mutual commitment as well. Brooks-Gunn and Matthews (1979:280) note of adolescent girls:

> much time is spent talking, reflecting, and sharing intimate thought. Loyalty is of central concern to the 12- to 14-year-old girl, presumably because, if innermost secrets are shared, the friend may have "dangerous knowledge" at her disposal.

Friendships are not only formed through particular types of talk, but are ended through talk as well. As Lever (1976:4) says of "best friends," "sharing secrets binds the union together, and 'telling' the secrets to outsiders is symbolic of the 'break-up.'"

Secondly, girls learn to criticize and argue with other girls without seeming overly aggressive, without being perceived as either "bossy" or "mean," terms girls use to evaluate one another's speech and actions. Bossiness, ordering others around, is not legitimate because it denies equality. Goodwin (1980a) points out that girls talked very negatively about the use of commands to equals, seeing it as appropriate only in role play or in unequal relationships such as those with younger siblings. Girls learn to direct things without seeming bossy, or they learn not to direct. While disputes are common, girls learn to phrase their arguments in terms of group needs and situational requirements rather than personal power or desire (Goodwin 1980a). Meanness is used by girls to describe nonlegitimate acts of exclusion, turning on someone, or withholding friendship. Excluding is a frequent occurrence (Eder and Hallinan 1978), but girls learn over time to discourage or even drive away other girls in ways that don't seem to be just personal whim. Cutting someone is justified in terms of the target's failure to meet group norms and a girl often rejects another using speech that is seemingly supportive on the surface. Conflict and criticism are risky in the world of girls because they can both rebound against the critic and can threaten social relationships. Girls learn to hide the source of criticism; they present it as coming from someone else or make it indirectly through a third party (Goodwin 1980a, 1980b).

Finally, girls must learn to decipher the degree of closeness being offered by other girls, to recognize what is being withheld, and to recognize criticism. Girls who don't actually read these cues run the risk of public censure or ridicule (Goodwin 1980a). Since the currency of closeness is the exchange of secrets which can be used against a girl, she must learn to read the intent and loyalty of others and to do so continuously, given the system of shifting alliances and indirect expressions of conflict. Girls must become increasingly sophisticated in reading the motives of others, in determining when closeness is real, when conventional, and when false, and to respond appropriately. They must learn who to confide in, what to confide, and who not to approach. Given the indirect expression of conflict, girls must learn to read relationships and situations sensitively. Learning to get things right is a fundamental skill for social success, if not just social survival.

THE WORLD OF BOYS

Boys play in larger, more hierarchically organized groups than do girls. Relative status in this ever-fluctuating hierarchy is the main thing that boys learn to manipulate in their interactions with their peers. Nondominant boys are rarely excluded from play but are made to feel the inferiority of their status positions in no uncertain terms. And since hierarchies fluctuate over time and over situation, every boy gets his chance to be victimized and must learn to take it. The social world of boys is one of posturing and counterposturing. In this world, speech is used in three major ways: (1) to assert one's position of dominance, (2) to attract and maintain an audience, and (3) to assert oneself when other speakers have the floor.

The use of speech for the expression of dominance is the most straightforward and probably the best-documented sociolinguistic pattern in boys' peer groups. Even ethological studies of human dominance patterns have made extensive use of various speech behaviors as indices of dominance. Richard Savin-Williams (1976), for example, in his study of dominance patterns among boys in a summer camp uses the following speech interactions as measures of dominance: (1) giving of verbal commands or orders, such as "Get up," "Give it to me," or "You go over there;" (2) name calling and other forms of verbal ridicule, such as "You're a dolt;" (3) verbal threats or boasts of authority, such as "If you don't shut up, I'm gonna come over and bust your teeth in;" (4) refusals to obey orders; and (5) winning a verbal argument as in the sequence: "I was here first"/"Tough," or in more elaborate forms of verbal duelling such as the "dozens."[2]

The same patterns of verbally asserting one's dominance and challenging the dominance claims of others form the central element in Goodwin's (1980a) observations of boys' play in Philadelphia. What is easy to forget in thinking about this use of words as weapons, however, is that the most successful boy in such interaction is not the one who is most aggressive and uses the most power-wielding forms of speech, but the boy who uses these forms most successfully. The simple use of assertiveness and aggression in boys' play is the sign not of a leader but of a bully. The skillful speaker in a boys' group is considerably more likeable and better liked by his peers than is a simple bully. Social success among boys is based on knowing both how and when to use words to express power as well as knowing when not to use them. A successful leader will use speech to put challengers in their place and to remind followers periodically of their nondominant position, but will not browbeat unnecessarily and will therefore gain the respect rather than the fear of less dominant boys.

A second sociolinguistic aspect of friendly interaction between boys is using words to gain and maintain an audience. Storytelling, joke telling, and other narrative performance events are common features of the social interaction of boys. But actual transcripts of such storytelling events collected by Harvey Sacks (Sacks 1974; Jefferson 1978) and Goodwin (1980a), as opposed to stories told directly to interviewers, reveal a suggestive feature of storytelling activities among boys: audience behavior is not overtly supportive. The storyteller is frequently faced with mockery, challenges, and side comments on his story. A major sociolinguistic skill which a boy must apparently learn in interacting with his peers is to ride out this series of challenges, maintain his audience, and successfully get to the end of his story. In Sacks's account (1974) of some teenage boys involved in the telling of a dirty joke, for example, the narrator is challenged for his taste in jokes (an implication that he doesn't know a dirty joke from a non-dirty one) and for the potential ambiguity of his opening line "Three brothers married three sisters," not, as Sacks seems to imply, because audience members are really confused, but just to hassle the speaker. Through catches,[3] put-downs, the building of suspense, or other interest-grabbing devices, the speaker learns to control his audience. He also learns to continue when he gets no encouragement whatever, pausing slightly at various points for possible audience response but going on if there is nothing but silence.

A final sociolinguistic skill which boys must learn from interacting with other boys is how to act as audience members in the types of storytelling situations just discussed. As audience member as well as storyteller, a boy must learn to assert himself and his opinions. Boys seem to respond to the storytelling of other boys not so much with questions on deeper implications or with minimal-response encouragement as with side comments and challenges. These are not meant primarily to interrupt, to change topic, or to change the direction of the narrative itself, but to assert the identity of the individual audience member.

WOMEN'S SPEECH

The structures and strategies in women's conversation show a marked continuity with the talk of girls. The key logic suggested by Kalčik's (1975) study of women's rap groups, Hirschman's (1973) study of students and Abrahams's (1975) work on black women is that women's conversation is interactional. In friendly talk, women are negotiating and expressing a relationship, one that should be in the form of support and closeness, but which may also involve criticism and distance. Women orient themselves to the person they are talking to and expect such orientation in return. As interaction, conversation requires participation from those involved and back-and-forth movement between participants. Getting the floor is not seen as particularly problematic; that should come about automatically. What is problematic is getting people engaged and keeping them engaged—maintaining the conversation and the interaction.

This conception of conversation leads to a number of characteristic speech strategies and gives a particular dynamic to women's talk. First, women tend to use personal and inclusive pronouns, such as "you" and "we" (Hirschman 1973). Second, women give off and look for signs of engagement such as nods and minimal response (Kalčik 1975; Hirschman 1973). Third, women give more extended signs of interest and attention, such as interjecting comments or questions during a speaker's discourse. These sometimes take the form of interruptions. In fact, both Hirschman (1973) and Kalčik (1975) found that interruptions were extremely common, despite women's concern with politeness and decorum (Kalčik 1975). Kalčik (1975) comments that women often asked permission to speak but were concerned that each speaker be allowed to finish and that all present got a chance to speak. These interruptions were clearly not seen as attempts to grab the floor but as calls for elaboration and development, and were taken as signs of support and interest. Fourth, women at the beginning of their utterances explicitly acknowledge and respond to what has been said by others. Fifth, women attempt to link their utterance to the one preceding it by building on the previous utterance or talking about something parallel or related to it. Kalčik (1975) talks about strategies of tying together, filling in, and serializing as signs of women's desire to create continuity in conversation, and Hirschman (1973) describes elaboration as a key dynamic of women's talk.

While the idiom of much of women's friendly talk is that of support, the elements of criticism, competition, and conflict do occur in it. But as with girls, these tend to take forms that fit the friendship idiom. Abrahams (1975) points out that while "talking smart" is clearly one way women talk to women as well as to men, between women it tends to take a more playful form, to be more indirect and metaphoric in its phrasing and less prolonged than similar talk between men. Smartness, as he points out, puts distance in a relationship (Abrahams 1975). The target of criticism, whether present or not, is made out to be the one violating group norms and values (Abrahams 1975). Overt competitiveness is also disguised. As Kalčik (1975) points out, some stories that build on preceding ones are attempts to cap the original speaker, but they tend to have a form similar to supportive ones. It is the intent more than the form that differs. Intent is a central element in the concept of "bitchiness," one of women's terms for evaluating their talk, and it relates to this contradiction between form and intent, whether putting negative messages in overtly positive forms or acting supportive face to face while not being so elsewhere.

These strategies and the interactional orientation of women's talk give their conversation a particular dynamic. While there is often an unfinished quality to particular utterances (Kalčik 1975), there is a progressive development to the overall conversation. The conversation grows out of the interaction of its participants, rather than being directed by a single individual or series of individuals. In her very stimulating discussion, Kalčik (1975) argues that this is true as well for many of the narratives women tell in conversation. She shows how narrative "kernels" serve as conversational resources for individual women and the group as a whole. How and if a "kernel story" is developed by the narrator and/or audience on a particular occasion is a function of the conversational context from which it emerges (Kalčik 1975:8), and it takes very different forms at different tellings. Not only is the dynamic of women's conversation one of elaboration and continuity, but the idiom of support can give it a distinctive tone as well. Hannerz (1969:96), for example, contrasts the "tone of relaxed sweetness, sometimes bordering on the saccharine," that characterizes approving talk between women, to the heated argument found among men. Kalčik (1975:6) even goes so far as to suggest that there is an "underlying esthetic or organizing principle" of "harmony" being expressed in women's friendly talk.

MEN'S SPEECH

The speaking patterns of men, and of women for that matter, vary greatly from one North American subculture to another. As Gerry Philipsen (1975:13) summarizes it, "talk is not everywhere valued equally; nor is it anywhere valued equally in all social contexts." There are striking cultural variations between subcultures in whether men consider certain modes of speech appropriate for dealing with women, children, authority figures, or strangers; there are differences in performance rules for storytelling and joke telling; there are differences in the context of men's speech; and there are differences in the rules for distinguishing aggressive joking from true aggression.

But more surprising than these differences are the apparent similarities across subcultures in the patterns of friendly interaction between men and the resemblances between these patterns and those observed for boys. Research reports on the speaking patterns of men among urban blacks (Abrahams 1976; Hannerz 1969), rural Newfoundlanders (Faris 1966; Bauman 1972), and urban blue-collar whites (Philipsen 1975; LeMasters 1975) point again and again to the same three features: storytelling, arguing and verbal posturing.

Narratives such as jokes and stories are highly valued, especially when they are well performed for an audience. In Newfoundland, for example, Faris (1966:242) comments that "the reason 'news' is rarely passed between two men meeting in the road—it is simply not to one's advantage to relay information to such a small audience." Loud and aggressive argument is a second common feature of male-male speech. Such arguments, which may include shouting, wagering, name-calling, and verbal threats (Faris 1966:245), are often, as Hannerz (1969:86) describes them, "debates over minor questions of little direct import to anyone," enjoyed for their own sake and not taken as signs of real conflict. Practical jokes, challenges, put-downs, insults, and other forms of verbal aggression are a third feature of men's speech, accepted as normal among friends. LeMasters (1975:140), for example, describes life in a working-class tavern in the Midwest as follows:

> It seems clear that status at the Oasis is related to the ability to "dish it out" in the rapid-fire exchange called "joshing": you have to have a quick retort, and preferably one that puts you "one up" on your opponent. People who can't compete in the game lose status.

Thus challenges rather than statements of support are a typical way for men to respond to the speech of other men.

WHAT IS HAPPENING IN CROSS-SEX CONVERSATION

What we are suggesting is that women and men have different cultural rules for friendly conversation and that these rules come into conflict when women and men attempt to talk to each other as friends and equals in casual conversation. We can think of at least five areas, in addition to that of minimal responses already discussed, in which men and women probably possess different conversational rules, so that miscommunication is likely to occur in cross-sex interaction.

1. There are two interpretations of the meaning of questions. Women seem to see questions as a part of conversational maintenance, while men seem to view them primarily as requests for information.
2. There are two conventions for beginning an utterance and linking it to the preceding utterance. Women's rules seem to call for an explicit acknowledgment of what has been said and making a connection to it. Men seem to have no such rule and in fact some male strategies call for ignoring the preceding comments.
3. There are different interpretations of displays of verbal aggressiveness. Women seem to interpret overt aggressiveness as personally directed, negative, and disruptive. Men seem to view it as one conventional organizing structure for conversational flow.
4. There are two understandings of topic flow and topic shift. The literature on storytelling in particular seems to indicate that men operate with a system in which topic is fairly narrowly defined and adhered to until finished and in which shifts between topics are abrupt, while women have a system in which topic is developed progressively and shifts gradually. These two systems imply very different rules for and interpretations of side comments, with major potential for miscommunication.
5. There appear to be two different attitudes towards problem sharing and advice giving. Women tend to discuss problems with one another, sharing experiences and offering reassurances. Men, in contrast, tend to hear women, and other men, who present them with problems as making explicit requests for solutions. They respond by giving advice, by acting as experts, lecturing to their audiences.[4]

CONCLUSIONS

Our purpose in this paper has been to present a framework for thinking about and tying together a number of strands in the analysis of differences between male and female conversational styles. We hope to prove the intellectual value of this framework by demonstrating its ability to do two things: to serve as a model both of and for sociolinguistic research.

As a model *of* past research findings, the power of our approach lies in its ability to suggest new explanations of previous findings on cross-sex communication while linking these findings to a wide range of other fields, including the study of language acquisition, of play, of friendship, of storytelling, of cross-cultural miscommunication, and of discourse analysis. Differences in the social interaction patterns of boys and girls appear to be widely known but rarely utilized in examinations of sociolinguistic acquisition or in explanations of observed gender differences in patterns of adult speech. Our proposed framework should serve to link together these and other known facts in new ways.

As a model *for* future research, we hope our framework will be even more promising. It suggests to us a number of potential research problems which remain to be investigated. Sociolinguistic studies of school-age children, especially studies of the use of speech in informal peer interaction, appear to be much rarer than studies of young children, although such studies may be of greater relevance for the understanding of adult patterns, particularly those related to gender. Our framework also suggests the need for many more studies of single-sex conversations among adults, trying to make more explicit some of the differences in conversational rules suggested by present research. Finally, the argument we have been making suggests a number of specific problems that appear to be highly promising lines for future research:

1. A study of the sociolinguistic socialization of "tomboys" to see how they combine male and female patterns of speech and interaction;
2. An examination of the conversational patterns of lesbians and gay men to see how these relate to the sex-related patterns of the dominant culture;
3. An examination of the conversational patterns of the elderly to see to what extent speech differences persist after power differences have become insignificant;
4. A study of children's cultural concepts for talking about speech and the ways these shape the acquisition of speech styles (for example, how does the concept of "bossiness" define a form of behavior which little girls must learn to recognize, then censure, and finally avoid?);
5. An examination of "assertiveness training" programs for women to see whether they are really teaching women the speaking skills that politically skillful men learn in boyhood or are merely teaching women how to act like bossy little girls or bullying little boys and not feel guilty about it.

We conclude this paper by reemphasizing three of the major ways in which we feel that an anthropological perspective on culture and social organization can prove useful for further research on differences between men's and women's speech.

First, an anthropological approach to culture and cultural rules forces us to reexamine the way we interpret what is going on in conversations. The rules for interpreting conversations are, after all, culturally determined. There may be more than one way of understanding what is happening in a particular conversation and we must be careful about the rules we use for interpreting cross-sex conversations, in which the two participants may not fully share their rules of conversational inference.

Second, a concern with the relation between cultural rules and their social contexts leads us to think seriously about differences in different kinds of talk, ways of categorizing interactional situations, and ways in which conversational patterns may function as strategies for dealing with specific aspects of one's social world. Different types of interaction lead to different ways of speaking. The rules for friendly conversation between equals are different from those for service encounters, for flirting, for teaching, or for polite formal interaction. And even within the apparently uniform domain of friendly interaction, we argue that there are systematic differences between men and women in the way friendship is defined and thus in the conversational strategies that result.

Third and finally, our analysis suggests a different way of thinking about the connection between the gender-related behavior of children and that of adults. Most discussions of sex-role socialization have been based on the premise that gender differences are greatest for adults and that these adult differences are learned gradually throughout childhood. Our analysis, on the other hand, would suggest that at least some aspects of behavior are most strongly gender-differentiated during childhood and that adult patterns of friendly interaction, for example, involve learning to overcome at least partially some of the gender-specific cultural patterns typical of childhood.

NOTES

1. The analogy between the sociolinguistic processes of dialect divergence and genderlect divergence was pointed out to us by Ron Macaulay.
2. In the strict sense of the term, "dozens" refers to a culturally specific form of stylized argument through the exchange of insults that has been extensively documented by a variety of students of American black culture and is most frequently practiced by boys in their teens and pre-teens. Recently folklorist Simon Bronner (1978) has made a convincing case for the existence of a highly similar but independently derived form of insult exchange known as "ranking," "mocks," or "cutting" among white American adolescents. What we find striking and worthy of note is the tendency for both black and white versions of the dozens to be practiced primarily by boys.
3. "Catches" are a form of verbal play in which the main speaker ends up tricking a member of his or her audience into a vulnerable or ridiculous position. In an article on the folklore of black children in South Philadelphia, Roger Abrahams (1963) distinguishes between catches which are purely verbal and tricks in which the second player is forced into a position of being not only verbally but also physically abused, as in the following example of a catch which is also a trick:

   A. Adam and Eve and Pinch-Me-Tight
   Went up the hill to spend the night.

Adam and Eve came down the hill.
Who was left?

B: Pinch-Me-Tight

[A pinches B]

What is significant about both catches and tricks is that they allow for the expression of playful aggression and that they produce a temporary hierarchical relation between a winner and loser, but invite the loser to attempt to get revenge by responding with a counter-trick.

4. We thank Kitty Julien for first pointing out to us the tendency of male friends to give advice to women who are not necessarily seeking it and Niyi Akinnaso for pointing out that the sex difference among Yoruba speakers in Nigeria in the way people respond verbally to the problems of others is similar to that among English speakers in the U.S.

REFERENCES

Abrahams, R. D. 1963. The "Catch" in negro Philadelphia. *Keystone Folklore Quarterly* 8(3): 107–116.

Abrahams, R. D. 1975. Negotiating respect: Patterns of presentation among black women. In *Women in Folklore,* ed. C. R. Farrat, Austin: University of Texas Press.

Abrahams, R. D. 1976. *Talking Black.* Rowley, Mass.: Newbury House.

Bauman, R. 1972. The La Have Island General Store: Sociability and verbal art in a Nova Scotia community. *Journal of American Folklore* 85: 330–343.

Bronner, S. J. 1978. A Re-examining of white dozens. *Western Folklore* 37(2): 118–128.

Brooks-Gunn, J. and Matthews, W. S. 1979. *He and She: How Children Develop Their Sex-Role Identity.* Englewood Cliffs, NJ: Prentice Hall.

Eder, D. and Hallinan, M. T. 1978. Sex differences in children's friendships. *American Sociological Review* 43: 237–250.

Faris, J. C. 1966. The dynamics of verbal exchange: A Newfoundland example. *Anthropologica* (Ottawa) 8(2): 235–248.

Fishman, P. M. 1978. Interaction: The work women do. *Social Problems* 25(4): 397–406.

Goodwin, M. 1978. Conversational practices in a peer group of urban black children. Doctoral dissertation. University of Pennsylvania, Philadelphia.

Goodwin, M. 1980a. Directive-response speech sequences in girls' and boys' task activities. In *Women and Language in Literature and Society,* eds. S. McConnell-Ginet, R. Borker, and N. Furman. New York: Praeger.

Goodwin, M. 1980b. He-said-she-said: Formal cultural procedures for the construction of a gossip dispute activity. *American Ethnologist* 7(4): 674–695.

Gumperz, J. J. 1977. Sociocultural knowledge in conversational inference. In *Linguistics and Anthropology,* ed. M. Saville-Troike. Washington, DC: Georgetown University Press (Georgetown University Round Table on Languages and Linguistics), 1977.

Gumperz, J. J. 1978a. The conversational analysis of interethnic communication. In *Interethnic Communication,* ed. E. Lamar Ross. Athens, Ga.: University of Georgia Press.

Gumperz, J. J. 1978b. Dialect and conversational inference in urban communication. *Language in Society* 7(3): 393–409.

Gumperz, J. J. 1979. The sociolinguistic basis of speech act theory. In *Speech Act Ten Years After,* eds. J. Boyd and S. Fertara. Milan: Versus.

Gumperz, J. J. 1982. *Discourse Strategies.* Cambridge: Cambridge University Press.

Gumperz, J. J., Agrawal, A., and Aulakh, G. 1977. Prosody, paralinguistics and contextualization in Indian English. Language Behavior Research Laboratory, typescript. University of California, Berkeley.

Gumperz, J. J. and Tannen, D. 1978. Individual and social differences in language use. In *Individual Differences in Language Ability and Language Behavior,* eds. W. Wang and C. Fillmore. New York: Academic Press.

Haas, A. 1979. The acquisition of genederlect. In Language, Sex and Gender: Does La Différence Make a Difference? eds. J. Orasnu, M. Slater, and L. Adler. *Annals of the New York Academy of Sciences* 327: 101–113.

Hannerz, U. 1969. *Soulside.* New York: Columbia University Press.

Harding, S. 1975. Women and words in a Spanish village. In *Towards an Anthropology of Women,* ed. R. Reiter. New York: Monthly Review Press.

Hirschman, L. 1973. Female–male differences in conversational interaction. Paper presented at Linguistic Society of America, San Diego.

Jefferson, G. 1978. Sequential aspects of storytelling in conversation. In *Studies in the Organization of Conversation Interaction,* ed. J. Schenker. New York: Academic Press.

Kalčik, S. 1975. ". . . Like Anne's gynecologist or the time I was almost raped": Personal narratives in women's rap groups. In *Women and Folklore,* ed. C. R. Farrar. Austin: University of Texas Press.

Lakoff, R. 1975. *Language and Women's Place.* New York: Harper and Row.

LeMasters, E. E. 1975. *Blue Collar Aristocrats: Life-Styles at a Working-Class Tavern.* Madison: University of Wisconsin Press.

Lever, J. 1976. Sex differences in the games children play. *Social Problems* 23: 478–483.

Lever, J. 1978. Sex differences in the complexity of children's play and games. *American Sociological Review* 43: 471–483.

Meditch, A. 1975. The development of sex-specific speech patterns in young children. *Anthropological Linguistics* 17: 421–433.

Philipsen, G. 1975. Speaking "like a man" in Teamsterville: Cultural patterns of role enactment in an urban neighborhood. *Quarterly Journal of Speech* 61: 13–22.

Sacks, H. 1974. An analysis of the course of a joke's telling in conversation. In *Explorations in the Ethnography of Speaking*, eds. R. Bauman and J. Scherzer. Cambridge: Cambridge University Press.

Savin-Williams, R. C. 1976. The ethological study of dominance formation and maintenance in a group of human adolescents. *Child Development* 47: 972–979.

Soskin, W. F. and John, V. P. 1963. The study of spontaneous talk. In *The Stream of Behavior*, ed. R. G. Barker. New York: Appleton-Century-Croft.

Strodbeck, F. L. and Mann, R. D. 1956. Sex role differentiation in jury deliberations. *Sociometry* 19: 3–11.

West, C. 1979. Against our will: Male interruptions of females in cross-sex conversation. In *Language, Sex and Gender: Does La Différence Make a Difference?* eds. J. Oranzanu, M. Slater and L. Adler. *Annals of the New York Academy of Sciences* 327: 81–100.

West, C. and Zimmerman, D. H. 1977. Women's place in everyday talk: Reflections on parent–child interaction. *Social Problems* 24(5): 521–529.

Zimmerman, D. H. and West, C. 1975. Sex roles, interruptions, and silences in conversation. In *Language and Sex: Differences and Dominance*, eds. B. Thorne and N. Henley. Rowley, Mass.: Newbury House.

Do You Speak American?

"Well, butter my butt and call me a biscuit"; a documentary on the English language, as spoken in the U.S., is airing on PBS.

ROBERT MACNEIL

On Columbus Avenue in New York, a young waitress approaches our table and asks, "How are you guys doin'?" My wife and I are old enough to be her grandparents, but we are "you guys" to her. Today, in American English, guys can be guys, girls, or grandmothers. Girls call themselves guys, even dudes. For a while, young women scorned the word girls, but that is cool again, probably because African-American women use it and it can be real cool—even empowering—to whites to borrow black talk, like the word cool. It is empowering to gay men to call themselves queer, once a hated homophobic term, but now used to satirize the whole shifting scene of gender attitudes in the TV reality show, "Queer Eye for the Straight Guy." As society changes, so does language, and American society has changed enormously in recent decades. Moreover, when new norms are resented or feared, language often is the target of that fear or resentment.

How we use the English language became a hot topic during the 1960s, and it remains so today—a charged ingredient in the culture wars, as intensely studied and disputed as any other part of our society. That is appropriate because nothing is more central to our identity and sense of who we are and where we belong. "Aside from a person's physical appearance, the first thing someone will be judged by is how he or she talks," maintains linguist Dennis Baron.

Many feel that the growing informality of American life, the retreat from fixed standards, ("the march of casualization," *The New York Times* recently called it)—in clothing, manners, sexual mores—is reflected in our language and is corrupting it. They see schools lax about teaching grammar and hear nonstandard forms accepted in broadcasting, newspapers, politics, and advertising. They believe the slogan "Winston tastes good like a cigarette should" is so embedded in the national psyche that few Americans would now balk at the use of "like" (instead of "as") because that usage is fast becoming the new standard. They hate such changes in the language and they despair for our culture.

Others, however, believe language is thriving—as inventive and vigorous as English was in the time of the Elizabethans—and they see American English as the engine driving what is now a global language.

This deep disagreement is one of the issues explored in a survey producer William Cran and I recently completed and a three-hour documentary, "Do You Speak American?"

We address the controversies, issues, anxieties, and assumptions swirling around language today—some highly emotional and political. Why are black and white Americans speaking less and less like each other? We explain. Does Hispanic immigration threaten the English language? We do not think so. Is our exposure to national media wiping out regional differences and causing us all to speak the same? We think not. Is the language really in serious decline? Well, we have quite a debate about that.

The people who believe so are known as prescriptivists: those who want us to obey prescribed rules of grammar. They do not mind being called curmudgeons and they alternate between pleasure and despair—pleasure in correcting their fellow citizens: despair that they cannot stop the language from going to hell in our generation.

The Prince of Prescriptivists

One of the leading curmudgeons of our time—he has been called the Prince of Prescriptivists—is John Simon, theater critic for *New York Magazine,* and he comes to do battle in "Do You Speak American?" Simon sees the language today as "unhealthy, poor, sad, depressing, and probably fairly hopeless." In the foreword to a new book, *The Dictionary of Disagreeable English,* he writes: "No damsel was ever in such distress, no drayhorse more flogged, no defenseless child more drunkenly abused than the English language today."

The enemies for Simon are the descriptivists, those content to describe language as it actually is used. They include the editors of great dictionaries who, Simon charges, have grown dangerously permissive, abandoning advice on what is correct and what is not. He calls descriptivist linguists "a curse on their race."

One such individual is Jesse Sheidlower, American editor of the august *Oxford English Dictionary.* Does he believe the language is being ruined by the great informality of American life? "No, it is not being ruined at all," he replies. Sheidlower believes that Simon and other language conservatives actually are complaining that linguists and dictionary writers no longer are focused on the language of the elite. They look at the old days and say, "Well, everything used to be very proper, and now we have all these bad words and people are being careless, and so forth." In fact, he insists people always have spoken that way. "It's just that you didn't hear them because the media would only report on the language of the educated upper middle class," Sheidlower points out. "Nowadays . . . we see the language of other groups, of other social groups, of other income levels, in a way that we never used to.

"Language change happens and there's nothing you can do about it." To which Simon replies, "Maybe change is inevitable—maybe. Maybe dying from cancer is also inevitable, but I don't think we should help it along."

Helping it along, to Simon, would mean surrendering to the word "hopefully," one of his pet peeves. "To say, 'Hopefully it won't rain tomorrow'—who, or what, is filled with hope? Nothing. So you have to say, 'I hope it won't rain tomorrow.' But you can say, 'I enter a room hopefully,' because you are the vessel for that hopefulness."

Sheidlower replies that modern computer databases make it possible to check texts back over the centuries: "We see that 'hopefully' is not in fact very new. . . . It goes back hundreds of years, and it has been very common even in highly educated speech for much of the time."

This battle—the stuff of angry skirmishes in books, magazines, and seminars—is only one part of what makes our language news today. Other findings may surprise many people because they challenge widely held popular conceptions, or misconceptions, about the language.

Our study took the form of a journey starting in the Northeast, down to the mid-Atlantic states, west to the Great Lakes, Midwest, Appalachia, then toward the South, through Louisiana, Texas, and California into the Pacific Northwest. In linguistic terms, we traveled through the main dialect areas of the nation. Professional linguists, students of the science of language, were the key to our understanding of the forces changing the language as rapidly as the society has changed in the past 50 years.

While computers, information technology, globalization, digital communications, and satellites have revolutionized how we work, equally potent revolutions have occurred concerning the home, family structure and marriage, sexual mores, the role of women, race relations, and the rise of teenagers as a major consumer and marketing force. With this has come alterations in our public manners, eating habits, clothing, and tolerance of different lifestyles—all of which have been swept by a tide of informality.

Linguists Spring into Action

Observing how these rapid social changes have altered our language have been the linguists, whose new branch of the social sciences really came into its own in the 1960s, followed more recently by sociolinguistics, the study of how language and society interact. They have produced a body of fascinating research that usually is couched in technical language difficult for non-linguists to understand. Dozens of linguists have lent their skills to help us translate their findings, and marry their scholarship to our sampling of the actual speech of ordinary Americans in all its variety, vitality, and humor, drawn from the widest social spectrum. They include waitresses, cowboys, hip-hop artists, Marine drill sergeants, Border Patrol agents, Mexican immigrants, Cajun musicians, African-American and Hispanic broadcasters, and Silicon Valley techies (who try to make computers talk like real people), as well as writers and editors, teachers and teenagers, surfers and snowboarders, actors and screenwriters, and presidents and politicians.

Did they all sound the same? One of the most common assumptions is that our total immersion in the same mass media is making us all speak in a similar manner. Not true, claim the linguists. We are not talking more alike, but less.

One of the enduring themes in American life is the pull of national against regional interests and regret for local distinctiveness erased in the relentless march of uniformity. It surfaced in the song "Little Boxes" by Pete Seeger, about people put into little boxes of identical houses made of "ticky tacky" and who all come out the same. Today, with more and more national franchising of basic elements—food, mobile homes, clothing, hotels, recreation—the U.S. can seem like one giant theme park endlessly reduplicated, the triumph of the cookie cutter culture and its distinctive art form, the national TV commercial.

Paradoxically, however, language is one fundamental aspect of our cultural identity in which growing homogenization is a myth. While some national trends are apparent, regional speech differences not only thrive, in some places they are becoming more distinctive. Local differences, pride, and identity with place are asserting themselves strongly, perhaps as instinctive resistance to the homogenizing forces of globalization. One remarkable example is the speech of urban African-Americans, which is diverging from standard mainstream English. After decades of progress in civil rights, and the growth of a large and successful black middle class, African-American speech in our big cities dramatically is going its own way.

Two linguists, Guy Bailey, provost of the University of Texas at San Antonio, and Patricia Cukor-Avila of the University of North Texas at Denton have documented this. For 18 years, they have studied a small community in East Central Texas they named "Springville," which appears to live in a time warp from a century ago, when it was the center for local cotton sharecroppers, black and white. Little remains now but the original general store. During the late 1930s, the Works Progress Administration recorded the voices of elderly blacks, some former slaves, some the children of slaves.

One of them, Laura Smalley, was born to a slave mother. She was nine at the time of Emancipation in 1863. She told how the slave owner kept them ignorant of Lincoln's Proclamation for six months. "An' I thought ol' master was dead, but he wasn'. . . . He'd been off to the war an' come back. All the niggers gathered aroun' to see ol' master again. You know, an' ol' master didn' tell, you know, they was free. . . . They worked there, I think now they say they worked them six months after that, six months. And turn them loose on the 19th of June. That's why, you know, they celebrate that day. Colored folks celebrates that day."

Black and White Dialects

Reviewing the speech of Smalley and others, the linguists were taken by how similar it was to the speech of rural whites of that time and place, but now dissimilar to the speech of blacks today. Features characteristic of modern black speech, what linguists call African-American vernacular English—such as the invariant "be," as in "they 'be' working," or the deleted copular, leaving out the auxiliary verb in "they working"—were absent.

Here are samples of modern speech of African-Americans in large cities:

> "When the baby be sleep, and the othe' kids be at school, and my husband be at work, then . . . I might can finally sit down."
>
> "She told David they Mama had went to Chicago to see her sister and her sister's new baby."

These examples show the invariant "be," and the construction "had went." Bailey and Cukor-Avila say that these features did not exist in black speech before World War II. They conclude that, after the great migration to the North from World War I to the 1970s, blacks were segregated in urban ghettoes, had less contact with whites than they had in places like Springville, and their speech began to develop new features, as all human speech does when people are separated culturally and have little communication.

This has serious consequences in efforts to reduce the school dropout rate among blacks. Not only white teachers, but many African-American instructors, despise the "street talk" or "slang" as they call it, and often treat the children as if they were stupid or uneducable. In 1979, a Federal judge in Detroit ruled that an Ann Arbor, Mich., school, ironically named after Martin Luther King, Jr., was discriminating against black kids because of their language and ordered the school to remedy it. Yet, the prejudice lives on elsewhere. In 1997, Oakland schools tried to get black speech recognized not as a dialect of English but a separate language, Ebonics, to qualify for Federal money to teach English as a second language. That backfired amid furious protests nationally from black and white educators.

What is shocking to linguists is the manner in which many newspaper columnists excoriate black English, using terms such as "gibberish." In the linguistic community, black English is recognized as having its own internal consistency and grammatical forms. It certainly is not gibberish (which means something unintelligible) because it works effectively for communication within the urban community.

One of the first to give black English this measure of respect was William Labov of the University of Pennsylvania, who testified at a Senate hearing during the Ebonics furor in 1997: "This African-American vernacular English . . . is not a set of slang words, or a random set of grammatical mistakes, but a well-formed set of rules of grammar and pronunciation that is capable of conveying complex logic and reasoning."

To linguists, the fault lies not in a particular dialect, but in what attitudes others bring to it. Steve Harvey, an African-American who hosts the most popular morning radio show in Los Angeles, told us: "I speak good enough American. You know, I think there's variations of speaking American. I don't think there's any one set way, because America's so diverse." He added, "You do have to be bilingual in this country, which means you can be very adept at slang, but you also have to be adept at getting through the job interview."

Now, without fanfare, some Los Angeles schools have been trying a more sympathetic approach to help minority students become bilingual—by teaching them the differences between African-American Language, as they call it, and Mainstream American English. We visited PS 100 in Watts to watch fifth-graders play a "Jeopardy"-like game in which they won points for "translating" such sentences as "Last night we bake cookies."

Teacher: "What language is it in?"

Student: "AAL."

Teacher: "It is in African-American Language. What linguistic feature is in AAL?"

Student: "Past-tense marker-ed."

Teacher: "Past-tense marker-ed. That's cool! And how do you code-switch it to Mainstream American English?"

Student: "Last night we baked cookies."

Teacher: "You got five hundred more points." Big cheers from the kids.

So, four decades after the passage of landmark legislation outlawing racial discrimination, the news is that it blatantly survives in language. Columnists would not dream of describing other attributes of being African-American with epithets like "gibberish." They could, however, get away with it in writing about black language, which remains a significant barrier to success in school and ultimately in the job market and housing—pathways to the American dream.

Ironically, as much as it is despised, black English is embraced and borrowed by whites, especially young whites in thrall to the appeal of hip hop music. There are divergences just as dramatic within the English of white Americans. Around the Great Lakes, people are making what Labov believes are "revolutionary changes in the pronunciation of short vowels that have remained relatively stable in the language for a thousand years."

Labov is director of an effort to determine the boundaries of different dialects within American speech. Traditionally, that was achieved by comparing distinctive local or regional words people used for every day things. One surviving example is the different terms for the long sandwich that contains cold cuts, cheese, and lettuce—a grinder in some parts of New England; a wedge in Rhode Island: a spuky in Boston; a hero in New York; a hoagie in Philadelphia; a submarine in Ohio and farther west. By drawing lines around places where each term is used, linguists can form maps of dialect areas. Many such regional terms are dying out because old craft skills are replaced by products marketed nationally. Labov leads a new method in which the different ways people pronounce words are recorded with colored dots on a map of the U.S. Connecting the dots produces the Atlas of North American English.

Labov and his colleagues found startling pronunciation changes in cities such as Chicago, Cleveland, and Detroit and New York State's Rochester and Syracuse. On a computer in his office in Philadelphia, we heard a woman say the word "black," then the complete phrase: "Old senior citizens living on one 'black,' and it was apparent that she was pronouncing "block" like "black." Similarly, another woman mentions what sounds like "bosses." The full sentence reveals she means "buses:" "I can vaguely remember when we had 'bosses' with the antennas on top."

When one vowel changes, so do the neighboring ones: "caught" shifts toward "cot," "cot" toward "cat," "cat" toward "kit" or "keeyat." Labov thinks these changes are quite important. "From our point of view as linguists, we want to understand why people should become more different from each other. We're all watching the same radio and television; we live side by side. And it's important to recognize that people don't always want to behave in the same way."

Labov has a theory that, behind changes like these, are women, the primary transmitters of language. Traditionally enjoying less economic power than men, women rely on the symbolic power offered by words. Labov believes women are more apt than men to adopt "prestige forms" of language and symbols of nonconformism—new or "stigmatized forms" that can acquire a kind of "covert prestige." Labov writes that women are quicker and more forceful in employing the new social symbolism, whatever it may be. Working on his landmark study, "The Principles of Linguistic Change," he identifies a particular type of woman—working class, well-established in her community—who takes pleasure in being nonconformist and is strong enough to influence others. He sees parallels between leadership in fashion and language change. Most young women are alert to novelty in fashion; some have the confidence to embrace it and the natural authority to induce others to follow.

These are mysterious forces working on our language from underneath, as it were, and producing startling changes that, far from homogenizing our speech, actually create more diversity. Despite all the forces of global and national uniformity in products and trends, Americans clearly still want to do their own thing linguistically. An example is Pittsburgh, where the local dialect, or Pittsburghese, is celebrated, constantly talked about, and made a commodity. They know themselves as "Yinzers," from "yinz," the plural of "you," or "you ones." They use "slippy" for "slippery"; "red up" means to "tidy up"; and "anymore" as in "'Anymore,' there's so many new buildings you can't tell which is which." In downtown Pittsburgh—pronounced "dahntahn"—the question, "Did you eat yet?" sounds like "Jeet jet?" If you haven't, the response is, "No, 'jew?'"

Barbara Johnstone, a linguist from Pittsburgh, thinks the pride in their local speech is a way for Pittsburghers to talk about who they are and what it means to live there. People treasure their local accents, because where they come from, or where they feel they belong, still does matter. In the words of California linguist, Carmen Fought, "People want to talk like the people they want to be like." This contradicts the common assumption that media exposure is making everyone sound the same.

Local Accents Prevail

Yet, amusingly, people often are quite unaware of how their own speech sounds to others. Linguists we met were full of stories about people in Texas or coastal North Carolina with strong local accents who were convinced they sounded like Walter Cronkite. It happened to me. I grew up in the Canadian province of Nova Scotia, so fascinated with words that I called a memoir of my childhood *Wordstruck*. Even in my own family, I often heard the same words said differently. My grandfather, from Nova Scotia's south shore, said "garridge" while his daughter, my mother, said "gar-aghe."

Until I first came to the U.S. in 1952, I was unaware how different my speech was even from that of neighboring New England. I was 21 and (briefly, thank God!) an aspiring actor, thrilled to be working in a summer theater in Massachusetts. The first time I stepped on to the stage and opened my mouth, the director said, "You can't talk like that." I was stunned, not knowing until that moment that I was pronouncing "out" to rhyme with "oat," and "about" with "aboat"—still the common Nova Scotian pronunciation. Anxious not to close any career doors, I immediately began trying to modify the "oat" sound, but 50 years later, when I am tired or back with my brothers in Canada, I still slip into the pronunciations I grew up with.

What appears to be the determining force in whether regional dialects survive or disappear is not media influence, but rather the movements of people. We talked to John Coffin, a lobsterman in South Freeport, Me. Once a quiet fishing and ship-building harbor but now a bustling outlet shopping center, the town has attracted so many new visitors and residents that Coffin fears the Maine way of speaking—with its characteristic "ayeh" for "yes"—is disappearing: "I think in this area it's going to be a lost thing," and that makes him sad. "I'd like to think my children and grandchildren talk that way, whether people laugh at you, wherever we go—whatever." Do people laugh at his Maine accent? "Oh, yes, lots of times. When I was in the military, they made fun of me wicked."

"Wicked" is a typical Maine word, meaning "very," as in" "wicked' good."

This homogenizing trend is obvious on some of the islands, like Ocrakoke, off the coast of North Carolina, home of the Hoi Toiders, people who pronounce "high tide" as "hoi toid." These islands have become meccas for individuals from elsewhere building vacation homes, displacing locals and their dialect.

Still, the national media are having some effect: Labov notes two sound changes that have spread nationally, probably from California. One is the vowel in "do," which increasingly sounds like "dew." Labov calls it "oo-fronting"; the sound is produced more to the front of the mouth. You also hear it in the word "so," which sounds like "so-ew." Another trend, more noticeable among young women, but also some men, is a rising inflection at the ends of sentences, making statements such as "The bus station is around *the corner*" sound like a query. One of the regions where "oo-fronting" is common is the South, where there are changes just as dramatic as those in the North. Southern ghosts do not say "boo," but "bew."

The most prevalent shift is that Southerners increasingly are pronouncing the "r" at the ends of words such as father. In part, this is due to the large migration of Northerners to Southern cities. Partly it is the historic decline in influence of the coastal Southern areas that once boasted the great slave-holding plantation culture, and the kind of r-less pronunciation we associated with languid belles posing in hoop skirts on the porches of antebellum houses. This advancing "r" marks the growing prestige of what linguists call Inland Southern, the speech deriving from Appalachia. That pattern goes back to the earliest days of British settlement, when people from parts of England who did not pronounce "r" settled the coastal areas, while the Scots-Irish, settlers from Northern Ireland who spoke with a strong "r," moved into the hills of Appalachia because the easily-cultivated coastal land already was taken.

Their speech has been given a huge boost by the rise of country music, no longer a regional craze, but a national phenomenon. Those who "sing country," wherever they come from, "talk country" and "talkin' country" has become a kind of default way of speaking informal American. It is considered easygoing and friendly. Pres. George W. Bush has made it his trademark, with no disadvantage politically because, like him, a great many Americans say, "Howya doin'? Doin' fine!" and they are not more particular than he is about making subject agree with verb in sentences such as, "There's no negotiations with North Korea."

The economic rise of the South has had another startling result. So many Americans have moved into the South and Southwest and happily adopted Southernisms—such as "y'all" and "fixin' to" and pronouncing "I" as "all," not the Northern "eye-ee"—that more Americans now speak some variety of Southern than any other dialect. That is the conclusion of linguist John Fought, who believes that, as the population shift to the Sun Belt continues, "In time, we should expect 'r-full' southern to become accepted as standard American speech."

That news will come as a shock to Northerners conditioned over generations to despise Southern talk, considering it evidence of stupidity and backwardness. In the film "Sweet Home Alabama," the good ol' boy played by Josh Lucas says to his Northernized wife, Reese Witherspoon, "Just because I talk slow, doesn't mean I'm stupid." The context leads the audience to believe him.

The comedian Jeff Foxworthy still fills huge theaters North and South with his hilarious routine ridiculing Southern speech and Northern attitudes towards it. He kills them with his list of Southern "words:'"

> "May-o-naise. Man, a's a lotta people here tonight,"
>
> "Urinal. I told my brother, 'You're in a lotta trouble when Daddy gets home."
>
> "Wichadidja. Hey, you didn't bring your track with you, did you?"

Northern attitudes to Southerners may be ameliorating slightly, possibly because it no longer is uncool in Northern cities to like country music and the culture that goes with it. Yet, an ingrained sense of the prestige of some dialects and scorn for others is very much alive. Linguist Dennis Preston of Michigan State University has spent years studying the prejudices Americans have concerning speech different from their own. He joined us on a train west from Philadelphia, demonstrating his regular technique. Establishing quick rapport with other passengers, he got them to mark on a map of the U.S. where they thought people spoke differently. Almost without exception, they circled the South and New York to locate the worst English. Referring to New York, a Pennsylvania woman told Preston contemptuously, "They say waader!" Preston asked, "What do you say?" "Water!" she declared proudly.

A Distinct New York Voice

Preston, though, detects another emotion creeping in beneath the scorn, and that is pleasure. People may think Southern or New York speech is not good, but they find them charming, and that must be partly an effect of media exposure, for instance, to the sympathetic New York characters in the TV series "Law and Order." Linguists believe that broadcasting and the movies help all Americans understand different dialects, perhaps appreciating the diversity in our culture. Moreover, no matter how they themselves speak, Americans learn to understand the language of network broadcasters, which is the closest thing to an overall American standard. That standard coincides with the speech that Preston's subjects inevitably identify as the best American speech—that of the Midwest—because it has the fewest regional features.

That Midwest standard is relevant to the cutting edge of computer research in Silicon Valley. There is heavy investment in efforts to make computers speak like us and understand us. The researchers believe they will achieve that in 10 to 15 years but it is an incredible challenge.

What these efforts demonstrate is how infinitely complex our language and understanding of it is, how meaning turns on the subtlest changes in intonation, how vast any computer data base must be to catch all the nuances we take for granted. How do you program a computer to avoid those charming errors in context which foreigners make in perfectly grammatical sentences? For instance, a sign in an Egyptian hotel states: "Patrons need have no anxiety about the water. It has all been passed by the management." Or, this in a Swiss hotel: "Due to the impropriety of entertaining guests of the opposite sex in the bedrooms, it is suggested that the lobby be used for this purpose."

The effort to make computers understand speech raises other questions about the future of language. Will the technology, and the business imperatives behind it, create an irresistible drive toward more standard speech? If so, which accents or varieties of American speech will that leave out? Whom will it disenfranchise because of their dialect—African-Americans, Hispanics, Cajuns in Louisiana'? A couple of years ago, the police chief of Shreveport, La., complained that the computer voice-recognition system used to route nonemergency calls did not understand the local accent. Researchers point out, however, that if you speak like someone from the Midwest, computers will understand you.

The emerging technology is irresistible for business. When United Airlines introduced a computerized voice-recognition system for flight information–replacing live bodies—it saved a reported $25,000,000. As these systems become more sophisticated, a lot of companies will want them to replace expensive warm bodies. Inevitably, more and more of our lives will involve talking to and being understood by computers. Being understood will be increasingly important. Will the technology work to reinforce existing linguistic stereotypes—about your race, ethnicity, gender, or where you live—or help to break them down? Will we have to talk as computers would like us to in order for them to obey us?

During the California portion of filming "Do You Speak American?" I drove a car equipped with an elaborate voice-recognition system. I speak a version of standard broadcast American English, and I tried to enunciate clearly. Occasionally, it worked, but often it did not and the car kept saying, "Pardon me? Pardon me?" and I gave it up.

Everything in the American experience, each new frontier encountered—geographical, spiritual, technological—has altered our language. What kind of a frontier are we crossing by teaching computers our most fundamental human skill, that of the spoken word?

ROBERT MACNEIL, former co-anchor of PBS's Emmy Award-winning "MacNeil/Lehrer NewsHour," is a member of the Television Academy Hall of Fame and the author of several books.

46

Cell Phones, Sharing, and Social Status in an African Society

Daniel Jordan Smith

Contemporary processes of globalization have stimulated many anthropologists to begin asking new research questions. One important area of innovative research pertains to the global spread of technology and its influence on local people, practices, values, and behaviors. Globalization involves the worldwide transfer of technology, capital, industry, people, and cultural ideas. It has made the world a smaller place, but it has also increased social inequalities across the "digital divide."

In the twentieth century, radio and television played powerful roles in creating linkages between previously disconnected areas of the world. Without a doubt, new mass media brought the signs, symbols, images, and cultural values of the industrialized "First World" to people and communities in poorer "Third World" regions. The globalization of technology is not a top-down, unidirectional process. New technologies create new ways in which small groups of people can shape the ideas, values, political opinions, and even the actions of large groups of people within a particular town, district, country, or world region.

Recent technological developments are influencing people and communities in new ways, raising new research questions for anthropologists. One such development is the Internet, although on a global scale fewer people have access to that technology than the topic of this selection: cell phones. Like radio and television before them, cell phones create new and unprecedented opportunities for communication across distances. As this selection vividly demonstrates, the ways in which people use cell phones are powerfully influenced by local ideas, values, customs, and practices. In other words, global processes always take place within local contexts. Both the symbolic meaning and the social rules for using cell phones change in different cultural contexts.

As you read this selection, ask yourself the following questions:

- Why do so many Nigerians who can barely afford life's basic necessities go to such great lengths to acquire a cell phone?
- The author notes that in Nigeria "affluent people are meant to demonstrate and share their prosperity, but in ways that do not humiliate their peers." How is this social ethic expressed in terms of cell phone use?
- What are the basic social rules associated with the "politics of sharing cell phone credit?"
- Why is the author told, "This phone doesn't fit you?" What does this comment tell us about the sociopolitics of cell phones in Nigeria?
- How, and why, has the symbolic significance of cell phone as status symbol changed in the past decade?

The following terms discussed in this selection are included in the Glossary at the back of the book:

consumable commodity
microeconomics
micropolitics of social inequality
reciprocity
social status

INTRODUCTION

On July 19, 2004, the popular BBC Africa Service morning news program, *Network Africa,* carried a curious story from its Nigeria correspondent. He described a recent epidemic of rumors circulating in the country, purporting that anyone who answered calls on their cellular telephones originating from several specific numbers risked madness, and even death. I had heard a similar story in the previous few days from dozens of friends and acquaintances in and around the towns of

Smith, Daniel Jordan. "Cell Phones, Sharing, and Social Status in African Society." Reprinted with permission of the author.

Owerri and Umuahia in southeastern Nigeria, where I was conducting research. Ironically, cell phone usage around the country surged in the wake of the rumors, as people phoned and sent text messages to friends and relatives, warning them of the "killer numbers."

Once the popular rumors circulated widely, Nigerian newspapers carried stories printing some of the suspected numbers and incorporating quotations from citizens who allegedly witnessed the effects of these sinister calls (Akinsuyi 2004). But the newspapers also published statements from spokespersons for the country's major mobile telephone service providers, denying that such killer numbers existed (Ikhemuemhe 2004). Further, they published interviews with government authorities and university scientists disputing the technological feasibility of transmitting witchcraft through cell phones. Radio call-in programs and television talk shows buzzed with debate about the story, mesmerizing the nation for the better part of two weeks. Eventually, popular attention faded, as it had with regard to a previous rumor suggesting that men who carried cell phones in their pockets or strapped them to their belts risked becoming infertile.

The rumors that mobile phones might be implicated in infertility, madness, and murder are a testament to how dramatically this new technology has affected Nigeria. A few elite Nigerians had access to older cellular telephone technologies beginning in the 1990s, but the number of such phones was minuscule. The introduction of the Global System for Mobile Communications (GSM) technology to Nigeria in 2001 and the liberalization of Nigeria's previously government-controlled telecommunications industry transformed cell phones from an extreme rarity into an everyday technology to which literally millions of ordinary citizens have access. When GSM technology was first introduced in Nigeria, the country had only approximately 500,000 landlines for over 100 million people (Obadare 2004), a number which had not increased significantly in many years. By the end of 2004, less than four years after the first GSM cellular phones and services went on sale to the Nigerian public, the country had over seven million subscribers (Mobile Africa 2005), with some recent estimates putting the number of mobile phones users in Nigeria at over eleven million (PANA 2005).

In addition, millions more people without their own phones were provided easy access to cell phone service, as individual cell phone owners became small-scale entrepreneurs, converting their personal phones into informal businesses. By the time the BBC story was broadcast, thousands of call centers, most with just one or two phones and a single attendant, dotted Nigeria's landscape. Every major city and many small towns are now connected, and countless rural and urban communities that have no running water and little or no electricity service are integrated into the country's vast and expanding mobile telephone network.

Cell phones have produced dramatic changes in communication in Nigeria, with many positive effects. Mobile phones have been integrated into long-standing patterns of social relationship, enabling Nigerians separated by great distances to continue to interact based on expectations of sharing and reciprocity. But just as important, they have become symbols of social status. Nigerians assert and express modern identities by purchasing, using, and publicly displaying the latest consumer commodities. Mastery of the new phone technology is a marker of being middle class, educated, and urban. Yet the reality is that cell phones represent a level of economic achievement that is out of reach to most Nigerians. The majority of new cell phone consumers experience the costs of usage as exorbitant, reinforcing the sense that middle-class status remains elusive. Thus, while the burgeoning popularity of cell phones in Nigeria, and throughout sub-Saharan Africa, represents the aspirations of ordinary people for better lives, this new technology exposes the pronounced and enduring nature of social inequality.

CELL PHONE ECONOMICS

Owning and using a cell phone in Nigeria requires three primary investments: (1) buying a phone; (2) accessing service from one of the country's four major providers through the purchase of a SIM (Subscriber Identity Module) card that is installed in the back of the phone to connect it to the service network; and (3) procuring "recharge cards," through which call time is paid for by loading a unique pin number each time one wants to add credit to an individual account. While the phone and the SIM card are onetime acquisitions, access to service depends on the regular purchase of the recharge cards to load call time as previously purchased amounts are exhausted.

In 2005, new phones are available in Nigeria for as little as 6,000 naira (approximately forty-five U.S. dollars), and as much as 60,000 naira (over U.S. $450), depending on the brand, the model, and the complexity of features offered on the phone. The price of SIM cards declined dramatically in the past several years, to about five to ten dollars, with companies sometimes offering free SIM cards as part of periodic marketing campaigns. The vast majority of customers use the "pay as you go" recharge card system.

Most crucial from the perspective of ordinary Nigerians is the cost of calls themselves. As with every other feature of cell phone service, the cost of calls has declined significantly over the four years since GSM service was introduced. But the price of calls per minute and per second (a choice between these rates is now available to most consumers) is still expensive, relative to both Nigerians' purchasing power and the cost of cell phone service in other countries (Obadare 2004). Importantly, although incoming calls are free, every outgoing call is charged—there are no free minutes per month or at night and on weekends, though lower rates apply in off-peak hours. Further, recharge cards expire. Credit not utilized within a specified period of time is forever lost. For example, ten dollars of credit would typically need to be used within about two weeks.

Initially, when GSM cell phone service was first introduced, domestic calls cost approximately fifty naira (thirty-seven U.S. cents) per minute. Recently, the cost has declined to about twenty-five naira (nineteen cents) per minute, with the precise amount depending upon the volume of calls per month, whether the call is in or out of network, the time of day, and so on. Each of the country's four main service providers (Glomobile, Mtel, MTN, and Vmobile) offers a diverse range of service packages and special deals, but most consumers cannot afford to make enough calls to qualify for the plans that offer the cheapest calling rates. Indeed, an entire discourse of complaint about the high cost of cell phone calls has emerged in Nigeria (Obadare 2004). Popular reaction to the economics of personal cell phone use has generated a new lexicon and a growing repertoire of behaviors designed to mitigate the financial burdens of cell phone ownership.

"THE FIRE THAT CONSUMES MONEY"

In southeastern Nigeria, where I work, and where the predominant language is Igbo, the vernacular name for a cell phone is *oku na iri ego,* which translates literally as "the fire that consumes money." This popular local name reflects ordinary citizens' frustrations with the perceived exorbitant costs of cell phone calls. New linguistic turns of phrase and innovative social practices that have evolved with the proliferation of cell phone technology build on people's aggravation over the strain of cell phone ownership, but they also indicate the degree to which cell phone culture has taken root in everyday life.

Nigerians have adapted their cell phone usage to suit their economic circumstances, and some aspects of the service plans offered by the country's main providers are clearly designed to attract and keep customers who cannot afford to make a high volume of phone calls. For example, the Short Messaging Systems (SMS), through which customers can send "text messages," is extremely popular in Nigeria and typically costs only fifteen naira (about ten U.S. cents) per message. Text messages must be limited in size, usually no more than 160 characters. Text messaging is particularly popular with younger customers and it has generated its own lexicon of abbreviations, an economy of language that has also become part of Nigeria's youth culture, as it has in other settings (for literature on text messaging generally see Fox 2001; Dooring 2002; and Sylvia and Hady 2004).

Text messaging has become a common way for Nigerians who cannot afford regular phone calls to communicate using the new technology. But for older people, and even among young folks, using text messages too frequently without also calling can be interpreted as sign of unwillingness to spend money on a particular relationship—reflecting either stinginess or a lack of deep concern about the relationship or both. As a consequence, although text messaging is extremely popular, people are careful not to rely on it too exclusively, lest they become objects of criticism. In times of economic hardship, the willingness to spend money on a phone call is evidence of interest or commitment to a relationship, whether it is a friendship, a family tie, a business partnership, or a romance. The consequences of the microeconomics of cell phone use reflect the importance and the complexity of how issues of wealth, inequality, and status are negotiated in human relationships.

"FLASH ME, I FLASH YOU"

Other common practices besides text messaging illustrate the economics and micropolitics of cell phone behavior, and the importance of these behaviors in navigating issues of inequality in social relationships. For example, a major consequence of the fact that many cell phone owners cannot afford to maintain credit on a regular basis is the innovation of what Nigerians call "flashing." To "flash" someone means to call the recipient's line and allow the phone to ring just once, so that the incoming number is displayed to the recipient, but the caller hangs up before the recipient answers. This way, the recipient knows the number of the person trying to reach him or her, and hopefully has enough credit to call back. Flashing is possible because one can make a call without paying for it as long as no one picks up. Under the prevailing plans in Nigeria, it is possible to receive incoming calls even when one does not have any credit.

From my experience observing scores of friends and acquaintances receiving flashes, whether or not the recipient of the flash could identify the caller from the incoming number was not necessarily a good predictor of a callback. Sometimes knowledge of the identity of the incoming caller created the incentive to call back immediately, perhaps out of obligation, affection, or some prior awareness about the reason for the call. Conversely, on other occasions, knowledge of the identity of the caller had the opposite effect, the attitude being that anyone who had something important to communicate would find a way to pay for a call, even if only for a minute or two. People often refused to call back after a flash out of suspicion that the caller wanted the recipient to bear the cost of the conversation. Nevertheless, unidentified flashes often sparked curiosity, and people frequently responded to them.

Given that countless Nigerians who own cell phones are often in a position where credit is exhausted or very low, and therefore very precious, flashing can sometimes become a comical exchange in which no one wants to bear the costs of a call. In the Pidgin English that is often the lingua franca in Nigeria, people expressed the phenomenon of reciprocal flashing, in which no one was willing to pay for a call, with the phrase "flash me, I flash you." Mostly in good humor, friends frequently suspected each other of trying to transfer and defray the costs of communication through flashing. As a consequence, people sometimes tried to answer their phones before the end of the first ring, engaging the call before the flasher could hang up. This practice was particularly common when someone flashed more than once, giving the recipient time to prepare for a quick answer. Over the past couple of years I witnessed numerous comic scenes where people plotted to "catch" flashers before they could hang up, making them pay for the connection.

SHARING CREDIT: INEQUALITY AND SOCIALITY

Of course most people who communicate by telephone eventually see each other in person, and past episodes of flashing are often topics of discussion. A typical face-to-face conversation about flashing might include a query by the flasher as to why the recipient did not call back, followed by an admission (or assertion) by the recipient that he or she did not have any credit. The recipient, in turn, may accuse the flasher of having credit and being unwilling to use it. These mostly good-natured conversations reproduce some of the complexity of how people in Nigeria navigate the social representation of wealth more generally. On the one hand, using and sharing one's cell phone liberally are clear signals of wealth, and, like many kinds of conspicuous consumption in Nigeria, seemingly carefree cell phone usage can be rewarded with recognition and prestige. On the other hand, in Nigeria's current economic climate, in which most people are struggling to make ends meet, a strong ethos prevails in which even the relatively affluent portray themselves as just getting by, particularly among people who are otherwise their peers.

These contradictory dimensions of people's public representations of wealth play out constantly in the arena of cell phone socioeconomics. For those who really are struggling, claiming one has no credit can be a strategy for protecting a precious and dwindling resource. Conversely, using one's cell phone generously even when one cannot actually afford it can be a way of portraying or maintaining social status that is threatened by economic hardship. For those who are better off, claiming not to have credit can be a form of humility, representing oneself as just as much of a victim of Nigeria's unjust political economy as one's peers. But the balance can be precarious. Humility can easily be interpreted as stinginess if a wealthy person persists too long in feigning hardship. However, acting too carefree can be seen as ostentatious or arrogant. Ultimately, affluent people are meant to demonstrate and share their prosperity, but in ways that do not humiliate their peers. The proliferation of cell phones has created a very prominent sphere in which the micropolitics of social inequality in Nigeria are enacted (for other examples see Barber 1995; Cornwall 2002; and Smith 2004).

Although Nigerians' cell phone–related social behaviors illustrate the importance of economics in how people manage their phone usage, including strategizing about the social representation of one's wealth, it would be a mistake to emphasize only the economic dimensions of Nigeria's emerging cell phone culture and its associated behavior. A good deal of cell phone–related behavior requires a social rather than an economic interpretation.

Perhaps the most striking example is the way that Nigerians conceptualize cell phone credit. Clearly, everyone who uses cell phones knows how much phone calls cost, and people are aware of the exact amounts in which recharge cards are sold. Further, as the discussion above regarding the phenomenon of flashing suggests, there is a considerable degree of conscious jockeying with regard to sharing and spending one's credit. However, to a remarkable extent, Nigerians seem to think of cell phone credit in much different terms than they think of money. Once money is transformed into cell phone credit through the purchase and loading of recharge cards, cell phone credit becomes much more like food or drink than money, in the sense that people feel more entitled to share in it without the strict incursion of a debt that would be the case if one asked to borrow money. As with food or drink, there is a strong social expectation that cell phone credit should be shared if one has it.

My awareness of the difference between Nigerian and Western (or at least American) sensibilities in this matter was driven home to me by the experience of an American student who worked as my summer research assistant. She lived with a Nigerian family and found them amazingly hospitable and generous, to the point where they refused to allow her to pay rent or contribute to the household budget for food. She felt guilty about this, knowing the family's limited means, and we devised ways that she could contribute without offending her hosts. But when it came to the student's cell phone, the situation was quite the opposite. She had acquired a cell phone mainly so that her parents could call her at any time from the United States. Over the course of the summer, she found that people in the household had no compunctions about asking if she had credit, and, if she did, they had no hesitation in asking to use her phone to make calls. One young woman in the household asked to use her phone so often that the student finally became exasperated and reported it to me. She could not understand how the same family that was so generous and so unwilling to accept her money could expect to use her cell phone in ways that, from her perspective, seemed so insensitive.

Conceived of as a consumable commodity, cell phone credit was easily incorporated into long-standing traditions of sharing, gift giving, and reciprocity, in which people are expected and often genuinely desire to share without incurring the equivalent of a monetary debt. Of course money too is highly implicated in social relationships, and it can be gifted and shared as well as borrowed, lent, or spent, but it was clear from my student's experience, and from numerous similar interactions that I have since participated in and observed, that cell phone credit is transformed into a medium of social exchange that is much different from money once it is loaded into a phone. Nigerians routinely ask their friends and family, and even acquaintances of less intimacy, whether or not they have credit, in ways they would rarely, if ever, ask so openly about money.

The politics of sharing cell phone credit is nonetheless complicated, both because forms of nonmonetary sharing and reciprocity have their own moral economy, with numerous unspoken rules and expectations, and because cell phone credit is, in fact, in some ways more like money than are consumable commodities like food or drink. Even in the sharing of food and drink, in which Nigerians, like people in many societies, are extremely generous and social, there are expectations of generalized reciprocity (Bearman 1997). Although one does not incur a quantifiable debt by sharing someone's food, if, over time, one only takes and never gives, this will be recognized and admonished in some way. Similarly, with the sharing of cell phone credit, someone asking to make calls on another's phone cannot expect indefinite cooperation if favors are not eventually reciprocated.

However, cell phone credit is still more like money than is a beer or a plate of cooked meat. Although ordinary Nigerians have obviously participated in the conversion of cell phone credit from money into a commodity that carries a more social definition, this transformation is not complete. People routinely lied to their friends about their credit, and I observed countless instances in which people were "caught" misrepresenting their credit. At a club in Nigeria where I play tennis, men would commonly pick up a person's phone while he was on the court to check how much credit was available. Someone caught underreporting his credit would almost certainly have to relent and share his phone. Through such actions people contribute to the demonetization of cell phone credit. But this demonetization did not occur without ambivalence. Indeed, the social expectation that one must share phone credit contributed further to the notion that cell phones are a "fire that consumes money."

As these anecdotes suggest, sociality is at least as important a dynamic in Nigerian social life as inequality, and not just in terms of sharing, but also with regard to the importance of regularly greeting and communicating with people in one's social network. The preeminent value of sociality has greatly influenced cell phone usage, in ways that have significant economic implications, even if economic calculations are not always foremost in the minds of cell phone users. Although much of what I have described above demonstrates that Nigerians are highly conscious of the economics of cell phone use and deeply aware of the social implications of cell phone behavior, it is also true that people's penchant for regular communication for purely social purposes means that people make many calls just to say hello and to be in touch. To have a phone and not use it to reach out to family and friends is similar to the idea of living alone or preferring solitude and privacy to social interaction. For most Nigerians it is not only unconscionable, it is unthinkable (Uchendu 1965). As a consequence, although many Nigerians rightly extol the virtues of the country's new cell phone services for promoting business and facilitating a more effective and productive commercial sector, my observations suggest that the vast majority of ordinary customers use a good deal of their credit making calls that are the cellular telephone version of a friendly visit. All this suggests that while cell phone technology has sparked some changes in social life, in many ways the new technology has also adapted to and been incorporated into longer-standing behavioral customs.

"GLO WITH PRIDE:" CELL PHONES AS STATUS SYMBOLS

As I sat down in the parlor of my friend's house in the southeastern town of Owerri, her twenty-three-year-old son, Uzoma, inquired whether I owned a cell phone. I said I did, and he asked to see it. After a quick inspection of my very simple and obviously low-end Motorola phone, Uzoma declared dismissively: "This phone doesn't fit you." He meant that a person of my status should have a fancier and more expensive phone, preferably the type currently most popular in Nigeria, where the face flips open, the phone has numerous elaborate technical features, and the screen looks like a computer LCD. I defended my simple phone, but I was not surprised at Uzoma's evaluation. I had encountered this reaction to my phone many times before in a society where cell phones have become important markers of social status.[1]

The relatively educated, mostly urban, and at least marginally economically successful Nigerians who own the majority of the country's more than ten million cell phones are acutely aware of the status distinctions conferred by different models. People are constantly noting the quality of their peers' phones, openly conveying approval or disapproval in ways that consciously connect cell phones to social status. Even where people cannot afford to upgrade their phones, the quality of one's cell phone cover and the type and number of accessories owned can be the subject of more fine-grained attempts to assert both status and fashion. Indeed, as status symbols, the cell phones operate at the cusp between economics and fashion, marking both financial position and sense of style. Uzoma assumed I could afford a more expensive phone, so he concluded that I was either too cheap to own a phone fit for a man of my means or too fashion-challenged to know that my phone was a disgrace.

In a huge country like Nigeria, where many people migrate from their villages of origin to cities and towns in search of education, employment, and economic advancement (Geschiere and Gugler 1998; Gugler 2002), the advent of cell phones in a context where landlines served less than 1 percent of the population has revolutionized communication between family and friends separated by long distances. It is little wonder that so many people want cell phones, or that people who can barely afford some of the basic necessities of everyday life make extraordinary efforts to acquire one. But aside from the practical advantages of cell phone ownership, there is no doubt that cell phones have become an important form of symbolic capital, and that the social status conferred by owning a cell phone is a major motivation for many people (Bourdieu 1984). The cell phone companies cultivate and exploit the symbolic dimensions of cell phone ownership in their advertising, and the pressure of seeing peers enjoy the benefits and social recognition of cell phone ownership induces ever larger numbers of consumers to take the leap.

Whereas just ten years ago, before the advent of GSM technology in Nigeria, cell phones were the exclusive province of the superelite, by 2004 many Nigerians who were not wealthy enough to own their own houses and could not afford to buy a used car were able to acquire the latest marker of modernity. The transition from an elite exoticism to an almost essential accessory for an aspiring middle class happened remarkably fast. Just two years ago, Umuahia, a small city of less than 200,000 that is the capital of Abia State, had not yet been linked to the network of any of the four main service providers. However, for those who really wanted cell phone service, a regional company called Baudex provided a mostly effective but very expensive service.

At the social club where I frequently played tennis, a playground for the town's elite, approximately fifteen to twenty men owned these Baudex phones in the summer of 2003. To call further attention to the status they displayed by owning and sporting these expensive phones, the owners formed a club within the club. They called themselves "*Ofo* United." "*Ofo*" refers to a mystical staff that is the emblem of traditional authority in Igbo society, a symbol that implies supernatural backing. "United" presumably refers to the name of famous football teams, most notably the world-famous Manchester United, but also to teams in Nigeria that use "United" in their names. The members of *Ofo* United sometimes further separated themselves from other members of the larger club, sharing a roasted goat and several cartons of beer, greeting each other saying "*Ofo* United," and brandishing their phones like some sort of secret society symbol. Just a year later, all this changed dramatically, as both MTN and Glomobile had established full service in Umuahia. By the time I left Nigeria in December of 2004, literally every member of the tennis club had a phone, as did the club's receptionists, one of the bar girls, and some of the kitchen staff. *Ofo* United was no more.

As cell phones have come within the reach of more ordinary citizens, their availability has only intensified the status competition associated with the new technology. Just as the poorest Nigerians have for many years worn watches that do not keep time in order to appear better off than they are, one now sees many young people carrying cell phones that are just shells—though being exposed in such a deception is worse than having no phone at all. Because so many people can aspire to having a cell phone, the distinctions noticed with regard to brands, models, and accessories have become even more fine-grained. Many wealthier people now own multiple phones, with one line for each provider, and they carry them wherever they go. Having a cell phone is no longer so distinctive, but having two or three is still notable. Similarly, making calls to friends or relatives in London or New York, seemingly without a care about the higher cost, can still impress one's peers. In late 2004, camera phones were just hitting the Nigerian market, and I have no doubt they will be all the rage in a very short time.

CONCLUSION

Although it is impossible to pinpoint the origin of the "killer numbers" rumors described at the start of this article, I suggest that their currency and appeal were related to popular discontents about the role of cell phones in highlighting and sometimes aggravating social inequality. Some speculated that the rumors were the work of one provider trying to undermine the business of another (the killer numbers were first associated with the phone numbers of one company, though, in time, it spread to them all). Others argued that the rumors were a form of consumer revenge, with the allegations meant to damage the reputation and profits of companies toward which customers felt increasing anger. Still others suggested that the rumors were started by some among the vast majority of Nigerians who still cannot afford to own cell phones, in order to strike fear into those who were intimidating their economic inferiors with their ostentatious use of this flashy new technology. More important than these theories about origin is the speed with which the rumors spread and the extent to which they captured popular imagination. The fascination they generated reflects the fact that, as happy as most Nigerians are for their newfound access to a modern communications technology, ordinary citizens remain extremely discontented over the extent of inequality in their society. The new technology is being interpreted, to a large extent, in relation to these discontents.

NOTE

1. In 2000, the *New York Times* published an article suggesting the importance of cell phones not only for displaying social status generally, but for the attraction of mates. The newspaper account drew on an article in the journal *Human Nature*, entitled "Mobile Phones as Lekking Devices among Human Males" (Lycett and Dunbar 2000). Regardless of whether one finds a sociobiological argument convincing, the association of cell phones with social status seems to strike a chord across many societies.

REFERENCES

Akinsuyi, Yemi. 2004. Anxiety Over 'Satanic' GSM Phone Numbers. *This Day* (Nigeria), July 23.

Barber, Karin. 1995. Money, Self-Realization, and the Person Yoruba Texts. In *Money Matters: Instability, Values and Social Payments in the Modern History of West African Communities*, ed. J. Guyer, 205–224. Portsmouth, NH: Heinemann.

Bearman, Peter. 1997. Generalized Exchange. *American Journal of Sociology* 102(5): 1383–1415.

Bourdieu, Pierre. 1984. *Distinction: A Social Critique of the Judgement of Taste.* Translated by Richard Nice. Cambridge: Harvard University Press.

Cornwall, Andrea. 2002. Spending Power: Love, Money, and the Reconfiguration of Gender Relations in Ado-Odo, Southwestern Nigeria. *American Ethnologist* 29(4): 963–980.

Dooring, Nicolas. 2002. 'Kurzm-wird-gesendet'—Abbreviations and Acronyms in SMS Communication (Short-Message-Service). *Muttersparche.*

Fox, Barry. 2001. No 2MORO for Text Messaging Lingo. *New Scientist* 171(2298): 24.

Geschiere, Peter, and Josef Gugler. 1998. The Urban-Rural Connection: Changing Issues of Belonging and Identification. *Africa* 68(3): 309–319.

Gugler, Josef. 2002. The Son of a Hawk Does Not Remain Abroad: The Urban-Rural Connection in Africa. *African Studies Review* 45(1): 21–41.

Ikhemuemhe, Godfrey. 2004. The Killer Phone Rumour—Operators Cry Foul. *Vanguard* (Nigeria), July 26, 2004.

Lycett, John, and Dunbar, Robin. 2000. Mobile Phones as Lekking Devices among Human Males. *Human Nature* 11(1): 93–104.

Mobile Africa. 2005. Cellular/Mobile Phone Networks in Africa. http://www.mobileafrica.net/mobile-phone-networks-in-africa.php. (Accessed June 7, 2005).

Obadare, Ebenezer. 2004. "The Great GSM (cell phone) Boycott: Civil Society, Big Business and the State in Nigeria." Dark Roast Occasional Paper Series, No. 18. Cape Town: South Africa: Isandla Institute.

PANA (Pan African News Agency). 2005. Nigeria's Phone Subscriber Base Hits 12 Million. *PanAfrican News Agency Daily Newswire,* May 4.

Smith, Daniel Jordan. 2004. Burials and Belonging in Nigeria: Rural-Urban Relations and Social Inequality in a Contemporary African Ritual. *American Anthropologist* 106(3): 569–579.

Sylvia, K. N., and Hady, S. W. 2004. Communication Pattern with SMS: Short Message Service and MMS: Multimedia Message Service as a Trend of Conduct of Modern Teenagers. *International Journal of Psychology* 39 (5–6): 289.

Uchendu, Victor. 1965. *The Igbo of Southeast Nigeria.* Fort Worth, TX: Holt, Reinhart, Winston.

Eating Christmas in the Kalahari

RICHARD BORSHAY LEE

The !Kung Bushmen's knowledge of Christmas is third-hand. The London Missionary Society brought the holiday to the southern Tswana tribes in the early nineteenth century. Later, native catechists spread the idea far and wide among the Bantu-speaking pastoralists, even in the remotest corners of the Kalahari Desert. The Bushmen's idea of the Christmas story, stripped to its essentials, is "praise the birth of white man's god-chief"; what keeps their interest in the holiday high is the Tswana-Herero custom of slaughtering an ox for his Bushmen neighbors as an annual goodwill gesture. Since the 1930's, part of the Bushmen's annual round of activities has included a December congregation at the cattle posts for trading, marriage brokering, and several days of trance-dance feasting at which the local Tswana headman is host.

As a social anthropologist working with !Kung Bushmen, I found that the Christmas ox custom suited my purposes. I had come to the Kalahari to study the hunting and gathering subsistence economy of the !Kung, and to accomplish this it was essential not to provide them with food, share my own food, or interfere in any way with their food-gathering activities. While liberal handouts of tobacco and medical supplies were appreciated, they were scarcely adequate to erase the glaring disparity in wealth between the anthropologist, who maintained a two-month inventory of canned goods, and the Bushmen, who rarely had a day's supply of food on hand. My approach, while paying off in terms of data, left me open to frequent accusations of stinginess and hard-heartedness. By their lights, I was a miser.

The Christmas ox was to be my way of saying thank you for the cooperation of the past year; and since it was to be our last Christmas in the field, I determined to slaughter the largest, meatiest ox that money could buy, insuring that the feast and trance-dance would be a success.

Through December I kept my eyes open at the wells as the cattle were brought down for watering. Several animals were offered, but none had quite the grossness that I had in mind. Then, ten days before the holiday, a Herero friend led an ox of astonishing size and mass up to our camp. It was solid black, stood five feet high at the shoulder, had a five-foot span of horns, and must have weighed 1,200 pounds on the hoof. Food consumption calculations are my specialty, and I quickly figured that bones and viscera aside, there was enough meat—at least four pounds—for every man, woman, and child of the 150 Bushmen in the vicinity of /ai/ai who were expected at the feast.

Having found the right animal at last, I paid the Herero £20 ($56) and asked him to keep the beast with his herd until Christmas day. The next morning word spread among the people that the big solid black one was the ox chosen by /ontah (my Bushman name; it means, roughly, "whitey") for the Christmas feast. That afternoon I received the first delegation. Ben!a, an outspoken sixty-year-old mother of five, came to the point slowly.

"Where were you planning to eat Christmas?"

"Right here at /ai/ai," I replied.

"Alone or with others?"

"I expect to invite all the people to eat Christmas with me."

"Eat what?"

"I have purchased Yehave's black ox, and I am going to slaughter and cook it."

"That's what we were told at the well but refused to believe it until we heard it from yourself."

"Well, it's the black one," I replied expansively, although wondering what she was driving at.

"Oh, no!" Ben!a groaned, turning to her group. "They were right." Turning back to me she asked, "Do you expect us to eat that bag of bones?"

"Bag of bones! It's the biggest ox at /ai/ai."

"Big, yes, but old. And thin. Everybody knows there's no meat on that old ox. What did you expect us to eat off it, the horns?"

Everybody chuckled at Ben!a's one-liner as they walked away, but all I could manage was a weak grin.

That evening it was the turn of the young men. They came to sit at our evening fire. /gaugo, about my age, spoke to me man-to-man.

"/ontah, you have always been square with us," he lied. "What has happened to change your heart? That sack of guts and bones of Yehave's will hardly feed one camp, let alone all the Bushmen around ai/ai." And he proceeded to enumerate the seven camps in the /ai/ai vicinity, family by family. "Perhaps you have forgotten that we are not few, but many. Or are you too blind to tell the difference between a proper cow and an old wreck? That ox is thin to the point of death."

"Look, you guys," I retorted, "that is a beautiful animal, and I'm sure you will eat it with pleasure at Christmas."

"Of course we will eat it; it's food. But it won't fill us up to the point where we will have enough strength to dance. We will eat and go home to bed with stomachs rumbling."

That night as we turned in, I asked my wife, Nancy: "What did you think of the black ox?"

"It looked enormous to me. Why?"

"Well, about eight different people have told me I got gypped; that the ox is nothing but bones."

"What's the angle?" Nancy asked. "Did they have a better one to sell?"

"No, they just said that it was going to be a grim Christmas because there won't be enough meat to go around. Maybe I'll get an independent judge to look at the beast in the morning."

Bright and early, Halingisi, a Tswana cattle owner, appeared at our camp. But before I could ask him to give me his opinion on Yehave's black ox, he gave me the eye signal that indicated a confidential chat. We left the camp and sat down.

"/ontah, I'm surprised at you: you've lived here for three years and still haven't learned anything about cattle."

"But what else can a person do but choose the biggest, strongest animal one can find?" I retorted.

"Look, just because an animal is big doesn't mean that it has plenty of meat on it. The black one was a beauty when it was younger, but now it is thin to the point of death."

"Well I've already bought it. What can I do at this stage?"

"Bought it already? I thought you were just considering it. Well, you'll have to kill it and serve it, I suppose. But don't expect much of a dance to follow."

My spirits dropped rapidly. I could believe that Ben!a and /gaugo just might be putting me on about the black ox, but Halingisi seemed to be an impartial critic. I went around that day feeling as though I had bought a lemon of a used car.

In the afternoon it was Tomazo's turn. Tomazo is a fine hunter, a top trance performer . . . and one of my most reliable informants. He approached the subject of the Christmas cow as part of my continuing Bushman education.

"My friend, the way it is with us Bushmen," he began, "is that we love meat. And even more than that, we love fat. When we hunt we always search for the fat ones, the ones dripping with layers of white fat: fat that turns into a clear, thick oil in the cooking pot, fat that slides down your gullet, fills your stomach and gives you a roaring diarrhea," he rhapsodized.

"So, feeling as we do," he continued, "it gives us pain to be served such a scrawny thing as Yehave's black ox. It is big, yes, and no doubt its giant bones are good for soup, but fat is what we really crave and so we will eat Christmas this year with a heavy heart."

The prospect of a gloomy Christmas now had me worried, so I asked Tomazo what I could do about it.

"Look for a fat one, a young one . . . smaller, but fat. Fat enough to make us *//gom* ('evacuate the bowels'), then we will be happy."

My suspicions were aroused when Tomazo said that he happened to know of a young, fat, barren cow that the owner was willing to part with. Was Tomazo working on commission, I wondered? But I dispelled this unworthy thought when we approached the Herero owner of the cow in question and found that he had decided not to sell.

The scrawny wreck of a Christmas ox now became the talk of the /ai/ai water hole and was the first news told to the outlying groups as they began to come in from the bush for the feast. What finally convinced me that real trouble might be brewing was the visit from u!au, an old conservative with a reputation for fierceness. His nickname meant spear and referred to an incident thirty years ago in which he had speared a man to death. He had an intense manner; fixing me with his eyes, he said in clipped tones:

"I have only just heard about the black ox today, or else I would have come here earlier. /ontah, do you honestly think you can serve meat like that to people and avoid a fight?" He paused, letting the implications sink in. "I don't mean fight you, /ontah; you are a white man. I mean a fight between Bushmen. There are many fierce ones here, and with such a small quantity of meat to distribute, how can you give everybody a fair share? Someone is sure to accuse another of taking too much or hogging all the choice pieces. Then you will see what happens when some go hungry while others eat."

The possibility of at least a serious argument struck me as all too real. I had witnessed the tension that surrounds the distribution of meat from a kudu or gemsbok kill, and had documented many arguments that sprang up from a real or imagined slight in meat distribution. The owners of a kill may spend up to two hours arranging and rearranging the piles of meat under the gaze of a circle of recipients before handing them out. And I also knew that the Christmas feast at /ai/ai would be bringing together groups that had feuded in the past.

Convinced now of the gravity of the situation, I went in earnest to search for a second cow; but all my inquiries failed to turn one up.

The Christmas feast was evidently going to be a disaster, and the incessant complaints about the meagerness of the ox had already taken the fun out of it for me. Moreover, I was getting bored with the wisecracks, and after losing my temper a few times, I resolved to serve the beast anyway. If the meat fell short, the hell with it. In the Bushmen idiom, I announced to all who would listen:

"I am a poor man and blind. If I have chosen one that is too old and too thin, we will eat it anyway and see if there is enough meat there to quiet the rumbling of our stomachs."

On hearing this speech, Ben!a offered me a rare word of comfort. "It's thin," she said philosophically, "but the bones will make a good soup."

At dawn Christmas morning, instinct told me to turn over the butchering and cooking to a friend and take off with Nancy to spend Christmas alone in the bush. But curiosity kept me from retreating. I wanted to see what such a scrawny ox looked like on butchering and if there *was* going to be a fight, I wanted to catch every word of it. Anthropologists are incurable that way.

The great beast was driven up to our dancing ground, and a shot in the forehead dropped it in its tracks. Then, freshly cut branches were heaped around the fallen carcass to receive the meat. Ten men volunteered to help with the cutting. I asked /gaugo to make the breast bone cut. This cut, which begins the butchering process for most large game, offers easy access for removal of the viscera. But it also allows the hunter to spot-check the amount of fat on the animal. A fat game animal carries a white layer up to an inch thick on the chest, while in a thin one, the knife will quickly cut to bone. All eyes fixed on his hand as /gaugo, dwarfed by the great carcass, knelt to the breast. The first cut opened a pool of solid white in the black skin. The second and third cut widened and deepened the creamy white. Still no bone. It was pure fat; it must have been two inches thick.

"Hey /gau," I burst out, "that ox is loaded with fat. What's this about the ox being too thin to bother eating? Are you out of your mind?"

"Fat?" /gau shot back, "You call that fat? This wreck is thin, sick, dead!" And he broke out laughing. So did everyone else. They rolled on the ground, paralyzed with laughter. Everybody laughed except me; I was thinking.

I ran back to the tent and burst in just as Nancy was getting up. "Hey, the black ox. It's fat as hell! They were kidding about it being too thin to eat. It was a joke or something. A put-on. Everyone is really delighted with it!"

"Some joke," my wife replied. "It was so funny that you were ready to pack up and leave /ai/ai."

If it had indeed been a joke, it had been an extraordinarily convincing one, and tinged, I thought, with more than a touch of malice as many jokes are. Nevertheless, that it was a joke lifted my spirits considerably, and I returned to the butchering site where the shape of the ox was rapidly disappearing under the axes and knives of the butchers. The atmosphere had become festive. Grinning broadly, their arms covered with blood well past the elbow, men packed chunks of meat into the big cast-iron cooking pots, fifty pounds to the load, and muttered and chuckled all the while about the thinness and worthlessness of the animal and /ontah's poor judgment.

We danced and ate that ox two days and two nights; we cooked and distributed fourteen potfuls of meat and no one went home hungry and no fights broke out.

But the "joke" stayed in my mind. I had a growing feeling that something important had happened in my relationship with the Bushmen and that the clue lay in the meaning of the joke. Several days later, when most of the people had dispersed back to the bush camps, I raised the question with Hakekgose, a Tswana man who had grown up among the !Kung, married a !Kung girl, and who probably knew their culture better than any other non-Bushman.

"With us whites," I began, "Christmas is supposed to be the day of friendship and brotherly love. What I can't figure out is why the Bushmen went to such lengths to criticize and belittle the ox I had bought for the feast. The animal was perfectly good and their jokes and wisecracks practically ruined the holiday for me."

"So it really did bother you," said Hakekgose. "Well, that's the way they always talk. When I take my rifle and go hunting with them, if I miss, they laugh at me for the rest of the day. But even if I hit and bring one down, it's no better. To them, the kill is always too small or too old or too thin; and as we sit down on the kill site to cook and eat the liver, they keep grumbling, even with their mouths full of meat. They say things like, 'Oh this is awful! What a worthless animal! Whatever made me think that this Tswana rascal could hunt!' "

"Is this the way outsiders are treated?" I asked.

"No, it is their custom; they talk that way to each other too. Go and ask them."

/gaugo had been one of the most enthusiastic in making me feel bad about the merit of the Christmas ox. I sought him out first.

"Why did you tell me the black ox was worthless, when you could see that it was loaded with fat and meat?"

"It is our way," he said smiling. "We always like to fool people about that. Say there is a Bushman who has been hunting. He must not come home and announce like a braggard, 'I have killed a big one in the bush!' He must first sit down in silence until I or someone else comes up to his fire and asks, 'What did you see today?' He replies quietly, 'Ah, I'm no good for hunting. I saw nothing at all [pause] just a little tiny one.' Then I smile to myself," /gaugo continued, "because I know he has killed something big."

"In the morning we make up a party of four or five people to cut up and carry the meat back to the camp. When we arrive at the kill we examine it and cry out, 'You mean to say you have dragged us all the way out here in order to make us cart home your pile of bones? Oh, if I had known it was this thin I wouldn't have come.' Another one pipes up, 'People, to think I gave up a nice day in the shade for this. At home we may be hungry but at least we have nice cool water to drink.' If the horns are big, someone says, 'Did you think that somehow you were going to boil down the horns for soup?'

"To all this you must respond in kind. 'I agree,' you say, 'this one is not worth the effort; let's just cook the liver for strength and leave the rest for the hyenas. It is not too late to hunt today and even a duiker or a steenbok would be better than this mess.'

"Then you set to work nevertheless; butcher the animal, carry the meat back to the camp and everyone eats," /gaugo concluded.

Things were beginning to make sense. Next, I went to Tomazo. He corroborated /gaugo's story of the obligatory insults over a kill and added a few details of his own.

"But," I asked, "why insult a man after he has gone to all that trouble to track and kill an animal and when he is going to share the meat with you so that your children will have something to eat?"

"Arrogance," was his cryptic answer.

"Arrogance?"

"Yes, when a young man kills much meat he comes to think of himself as a chief or a big man, and he thinks of the rest of us as his servants or inferiors. We can't accept this. We refuse one who boasts, for someday his pride will make him kill somebody. So we always speak of his meat as worthless. This way we cool his heart and make him gentle."

"But why didn't you tell me this before?" I asked Tomazo with some heat.

"Because you never asked me," said Tomazo, echoing the refrain that has come to haunt every field ethnographer.

The pieces now fell into place. I had known for a long time that in situations of social conflict with Bushmen I held all the cards. I was the only source of tobacco in a thousand square miles, and I was not incapable of cutting an individual off for non-cooperation. Though my boycott never lasted longer than a few days, it was an indication of my strength. People resented my presence at the water hole, yet simultaneously dreaded my leaving. In short I was a perfect target for the charge of arrogance and for the Bushmen tactic of enforcing humility.

I had been taught an object lesson by the Bushmen; it had come from an unexpected corner and had hurt me in a vulnerable area. For the big black ox was to be the one totally generous, unstinting act of my year at /ai/ai, and I was quite unprepared for the reaction I received.

As I read it, their message was this: There are no totally generous acts. All "acts" have an element of calculation. One black ox slaughtered at Christmas does not wipe out a year of careful manipulation of gifts given to serve your own ends. After all, to kill an animal and share the meat with people is really no more than Bushmen do for each other every day and with far less fanfare.

In the end, I had to admire how the Bushmen had played out the farce—collectively straight-faced to the end. Curiously, the episode reminded me of the *Good Soldier Schweik* and his marvelous encounters with authority. Like Schweik, the Bushmen had retained a thorough-going skepticism of good intentions. Was it this independence of spirit, I wondered, that had kept them culturally viable in the face of generations of contact with more powerful societies, both black and white? The thought that the Bushmen were alive and well in the Kalahari was strangely comforting. Perhaps, armed with that independence and with their superb knowledge of their environment, they might yet survive the future.

Richard Borshay Lee is a full professor of anthropology at the University of Toronto. He has done extensive fieldwork in southern Africa, is coeditor of *Man the Hunter* (1968) and *Kalahari Hunter-Gatherers* (1976), and author of *The !Kung San: Men, Women, and Work in a Foraging Society.*

Ties That Bind

Hopi gift culture and its first encounter with the United States.

Peter M. Whiteley

In 1852, shortly after the United States had nominally annexed Hopi country, in northern Arizona, the Hopi people arranged for a diplomatic packet to reach President Millard Fillmore at the White House. Part message and part magical gift, the packet was delivered by a delegation of five prominent men from another Pueblo tribe, the Tewas of Tesuque Pueblo in New Mexico, who wanted to gain legal protection from Anglo and Hispanic settlers who were encroaching on their lands. The delegation traveled for nearly three months, on horseback, steamboat, and train, from Santa Fe to Washington, D.C., more than 2,600 miles away. The five men spoke fluent Spanish, the dominant European language of the region at the time—which made them ideally suited to convey the gift packet and its message to the president.

At the time, no U.S. government official had visited the Hopi (and few would do so before the 1890s). Their "unique diplomatic pacquet," in the words of the nineteenth-century ethnologist Henry Rowe Schoolcraft, offered "friendship and intercommunication . . . opening, symbolically, a road from the Moqui [Hopi] country to Washington." The packet was in two parts. The first part comprised two *pahos,* or prayer-sticks, at either end of a long cotton cord, dyed for part of its length. Separating the dyed from the undyed part of the cord were six varicolored feathers, knotted into a bunch. The *pahos* "represent the Moqui [Hopi] people and the President [respectively]," Schoolcraft wrote; "the cord is the road which separates them; the [bunch of feathers] tied to the cord is the meeting point."

As well as encoding a message, the *pahos* were an offering of a kind that Hopi deities such as Taawa, the Sun god, traditionally like to receive. By giving the president *pahos* worthy of the Sun, the Hopi signaled their expectation that he would reciprocate. Just as the Sun, on receiving the appropriate offerings, would send rain clouds for sustaining life and growth, so, too, the president would send protection for Hopi lives and lands—in this instance, protection from assaults by neighboring tribes such as the Navajo.

The second part of the packet comprised a cornstalk cigarette filled with tobacco ("to be smoked by the president") and a small cornhusk package that enclosed honey-soaked cornmeal. According to the Tesuque delegation, the honey-meal package was "a charm to call down rain from heaven." When the president smoked the cigarette, he would exhale clouds of smoke, which would sympathetically attract the clouds of the sky. Then, when he chewed the cornmeal and spat the wild honey on ground that needed rain, the Tesuque statement concluded, "the Moquis assure him that it [the rain] will come."

In sum, the packet was three things at once: message, offering, and gift of magical power. In conveying those elements, the Hopi sought to open diplomatic relations with the U.S.

But their intent appears to have been lost on their recipient. As so often happens when two cultures make contact, deep misunderstandings can arise: What does a gift mean? What, if anything, does the gift giver expect in return? Do the giver and the recipient both assign the same value to the gift? In twenty-five years of ethnographic fieldwork with the Hopi, it has been my goal to learn something of their history and culture. Recently I turned my attention to certain important events, such as the Millard Fillmore episode, that might shed light on how Hopi society changed as the U.S. developed. In that context Hopi gift giving and the ways it functions as a pillar of Hopi social organization have been central to my studies. One lesson of my work shines through: When nations exchange gifts, all the parties would do best to keep in mind the old adage, "It's the thought that counts."

Given the differences between Hopi and Western traditions and culture, perhaps it is not surprising that the Hopi idea of "gift" is only loosely equivalent to the Western one. In 1852 the Hopi people were still little affected by outside populations, and Hopi land use spread across much of northern Arizona and even into southern Utah. At that time, the Hopi lifestyle was traditional, based on farming, foraging, and some pastoralism. Even today, important elements of the subsistence economy persist, though wage labor and small business provide supplemental income.

The Hopi typically divide their work according to gender. Work done by men (such as farming and harvesting of crops) is perceived as a gift to the women; work done by women (such as gardening, gathering of piñion nuts, grasses, wild fruits, berries, and the like) is perceived as a gift to the men. Women also own and manage the distribution of their household's goods and crops. In fact, Hopi women control most of the material economic life, whereas Hopi men largely control the ritual and spiritual aspects.

The Hopi take part in an elaborate cycle of religious ceremonies, to which a range of specialized offices and privileges is attached. But individuals gain those distinctive social positions not through material wealth but rather through gender and kinship relations, which are ordered in a matrilineal manner. In fact, clan heads and chiefs of religious societies are typically worse off materially than the average member of the clan. Hopi leaders are supposed to be materially poor, and a wealthy individual is often criticized as *qahopi,* un-Hopi, for failing to share. Wealth and status among the Hopi is thus phrased in ritual terms: a poor person is one without ceremonial prerogatives, not one without money. So averse are the Hopi to material accumulation that in May 2004, for the second time, they voted against casino gambling, despite substantial poverty on the reservation.

Does such a primacy of value placed on ceremonial roles explain the evanescent nature of the gift given to President Fillmore? In what world of meaning did the packet represent great value? Indeed, what's in a gift?

Anthropologists have been making hay of that last question ever since 1925, when the French anthropologist Marcel Mauss published his groundbreaking *Essai sur le Don* (translated into English as "The Gift"). Mauss convincingly argued that in small-scale societies (10,000 or fewer persons) gifts are "total social facts." What he meant is that, in gift- or barter-based social systems, divisions of social life into discrete domains—such as economy, politics, law, or religion—are meaningless; each sphere interpenetrates and overlaps the others.

As in strict barter, an exchange in Hopi culture that begins by making a gift to someone does not involve money, but it does require reciprocity. Thus goods, services, or knowledge "given" to an individual or a group are answered with something of equivalent value. "Gifts" develop an interconnectedness between Hopi individuals in a way that outright purchases cannot. Furthermore, the Hopi offer gifts in a much broader range of circumstances than people in Western cultures do, and the value of those gifts extends to the religious realm, tying individuals and groups to each other and to the realm of the spirits.

Probably the key to understanding a gift-based system such as that of the Hopi is to recognize that such systems are built on kinship. "Kinship"—the godzilla that has driven multitudes of college students screaming from anthropology 101—is, in this regard at least, straightforward. It means simply that the great majority of human social activity is framed in terms of reciprocal family ties. Where all personal relationships are cast within the "kinship idiom" there are no members of the society who are not kin to me, nor I to them.

Kinship terms encode behavioral expectations as well as familial role. As anthropologists never tire of saying, such terms are primarily social, not biological: obviously if I call fifteen women "mother," as the average Hopi can do, I do not assume that each woman physically gave birth to me. But my "mothers" all have rights and duties in relation to me. And, reciprocally, I have duties and rights with respect to them: in fact, their duties are my rights, and my duties are their rights in the relationship. That is what reciprocity is all about. You give me food, I plant your cornfield, to give a crude example. But, in a kinship society, such a basic structure of mutual expectations forms the foundation for an entire apparatus of courtesy and manners, deference and respect, familiarity or distance. Those expectations are concretely expressed by gifts—spontaneous and planned, routine and special, trivial and grand. Gifts are thus communications in a language of social belonging.

So averse are the Hopi to material accumulation that in May 2004 they voted against casino gambling.

So-called gift economies entail a certain kind of sociality, or sense of what it means to belong to a community. In such an economy, one gives a gift to mark social relations built on kinship and altruism, but without the expectation of direct repayment. According to some arguments, gifts are also given to foster a sense of community, as well as sustainable interrelations with the local environment. In fact, in some respects the giver still "owns" some part of the gift, and it is the intangible connection between the two parties, mediated by the gift, that forms the basis of interpersonal relationships.

In contrast, in exchange economies, commodities dominate social interchange. Competitive markets, governed by the profit motive, connect buyer and seller, and social relations are characterized by individualism. A gift, once given, belongs entirely to the recipient; only when the item given has sentimental value does it keep the bond between giver and recipient alive.

That is not to say the Hopi did not engage in the more impersonal, "Western" forms of material exchange. In the Hopi language, as in English, several words describe how an item is transferred from one person to another: *maqa* ("to give"); *hùuya* ("to barter or trade"); and *tu'i* ("to buy"). Those words all antedate the arrival of Europeans—and anthropological classifications. Barter and purchase, as well as gifts, have all long been present in Hopi life. Furthermore, gift exchange in the West can also function as it does among the Hopi, as part of kinship obligations or ordinary social life.

What is distinctive about Hopi custom is the fact that the gift economy is responsible for the great majority of exchanges. Furthermore, there is no such thing as a free gift. The strong interpersonal bonds created by a gift make giving almost de rigueur at ceremonial events. Gifts, particularly gifts of food or utensils, are transmitted during ceremonies of personal milestones (at a birth or a marriage), as well as at public gatherings.

For example, at the annual so-called basket dances, girls and women distribute a variety of objects they have collected for the occasion. The dances illustrate the Hopi lack of acquisitiveness. The women form a semicircle and dance and sing; after each song two girls fling gifts into the crowd of men assembled outside the circle. Among the gifts are valuable baskets and buckskins, though inexpensive utensils and manufactured items are also popular. Each man zealously grabs for the flying objects, and if two men happen to catch the same item, both wrestle with the object, often until it has been totally destroyed.

Although gift giving has been a pillar of Hopi society, trade has also flourished in Hopi towns since prehistory, with a network that extended from the Great Plains to the Pacific Coast, and from the Great Basin, centered on present-day Nevada and Utah, to the Valley of Mexico. Manufactured goods, raw materials, and gems drove the trade, supplemented by exotic items such as parrots. The Hopis were producers as well, manufacturing large quantities of cotton cloth and ceramics for the trade. To this day, interhousehold trade and barter, especially for items of traditional manufacture for ceremonial use (such as basketry, bows, cloth, moccasins, pottery, and rattles), remain vigorous.

For hundreds of years, at least, the Hopi traded with the Rio Grande Pueblos to acquire turquoise, *heishi* (shell necklaces), and buckskins; one long string of *heishi,* for instance, was worth two Hopi woven cotton mantas. Similarly, songs, dances, and other ritual elements were often exchanged for an agreed-upon equivalent.

The high value the Hopi placed on the items they acquired by trade correlate, in many respects, with the value Europeans placed on them. Silver, for instance, had high value among both Westerners and Native Americans as money and as jewelry. *Siiva,* the Hopi word both for "money" and for "silver jewelry" was borrowed directly from the English word "silver" Paper money itself was often treated the way traditional resources were: older Hopi men bundled it and stored it in trunks, stacked by denomination.

It was not until the 1890s, however, that silver jewelry began to be produced by the Hopi. A man named Sikyatala learned silversmithing from a Zuni man, and his craftsmanship quickly made silver jewelry into treasured adornments. Those among the Hopi who cared for it too much, though, were criticized for vanity; one nickname, Siisiva ("[wearing] a lot of silver"), characterized a fop.

Some jewels, such as turquoise, traditionally had a sacred value, beyond adornment. Even today, flakes of turquoise are occasionally offered to the spirits in religious ceremonies. Turquoise and shell necklaces appear in many ritual settings, frequently adorning the costumes of *katsinas* (ceremonial figures) and performers in the social dances.

How much the Hopi value turquoise becomes apparent toward the close of a ritual enactment known as the Clown Ceremony. The "clowns"—more than mere entertainers—represent unbridled human impulses. Warrior *katsinas* arrive to punish the clowns for licentious behavior and teach them good Hopi behavior: modest and quiet in conduct, careful and decorous in speech, abstemious and sharing about food, and unselfish about other things. The clowns fail miserably (and hilariously) at their lessons. Eventually the warrior chief presents an ultimatum: stop flaunting chaos or die. The clown chief then offers him a turquoise necklace as a "mortgage" on the clowns' lives. The warrior chief accepts, the downs receive a lesser punishment, and community life goes on—not with perfection, but with a human mixture of the virtuous and the flawed.

In Hopi tradition, the first clan among the Hopi, and the one that supplied the *kikmongwi,* or village chief, was Bear. When other clans arrived, their leaders approached the *kikmongwi* to request entry into the village. He asked what they had to contribute, such as a beneficial ceremony. So challenged, each clan performed its ceremony, and if successful, say, in producing rain, its members were invited to live in the village, assigned an area for housing, and granted agricultural lands to work in the valley below. In return, the clan agreed to perform its ceremony, as part of a cycle of ceremonies throughout the year, and to intermarry with the other clans of the community, a practice called exogamous marriage. In that way, the Snake clan brought the Snake Dance, the Badger clan introduced principal katsina ceremonies, and the Fire clan brought the Warriors' society to the Hopi village. The villages thus came to be made up of mutually interdependent clans.

One of the essential principles expressed here, and the very cornerstone of Hopi society and sociality, is the exchange of mutually beneficial gifts—ceremonies for land, people in exogamous marriage—and the relationships reconfigured by those exchanges. And the same model is extended to the supernatural world: the gods must be propitiated with offerings of ritual gifts, and thus reminded of their dependence upon and obligations to mortal people.

The items sent to President Fillmore conform to the archetypal Hopi offering. Seeking to incorporate the president into the Hopi world, the appropriate strategy was to give him valuable presents that sought something in return, and to make sure he understood what that meant. Addressing him with prayer-sticks the way they might address the Sun father, the delegation sought to engage him within the gifting and kinship idiom. The instructions delivered with the packet—even across a succession of translations—spoke clearly of the Hopi intent. As with the turquoise mortgage of the *katsina* clowns, the idea of reciprocity is central. If the president wants more of, say, rain-magic, he must give back: he must receive the gift and its political proposal, and provide something in return.

Alas, the magico-religious sensibility of the Hopi worldview and the offer of serial reciprocity clashed with Manifest Destiny and the assimilationist ideology of Fillmore's presidency. Historical records make it clear that he did not smoke the cigarette, nor chew nor spit the honey-meal, and, so far as we know, he sent no formal reply. None of the objects has survived.

What the five men of the Tesuque delegation received no doubt perplexed them as much as the packet they delivered perplexed the president: Each man was given a Millard Fillmore peace medal, a Western-style business suit, and a daguerreotype portrait (all now lost, as well). They also got a tour of standard destinations in Washington, including the Patent Office and the Smithsonian Institution, where they were introduced to the "wonders of electricity," according to a contemporary newspaper account in the *Daily National Intelligencer.* In their meeting with Fillmore they heard the president say he "hoped the Great Spirit would bless and sustain them till they again returned to the bosom of their families."

Certainly Fillmore expressed the goodwill of the U.S. toward the Pueblos in general and to the Tesuque party in particular—who, in all probability, conveyed that sentiment to the Hopi. But the dissonance between gift and exchange economies helps explain why the Hopis did not achieve their goals. (The U.S. did not protect the Hopi from intrusions by the Navajo or by anyone else.)

The Hopi sought to embrace the president in their own sphere of sociality and mutuality—to extend kinship to him. But in a social system like the president's, where gifts are not total social facts, the political belongs in a separate domain from the religious or the economic, and kinship is secondary. The gift of a jeweled sword, for instance, might have impressed Fillmore more, but for the Hopi, its strictly symbolic value—as an item for display, but with no political, religious, or social value—would not have ensured a return, a social connection built on mutual exchange. More, by Hopi standards, presenting such a gift might have seemed inhospitable and materialistic, indeed, undiplomatic and even selfish. Thus does understanding fail between nations.

42

The Kpelle Moot

James L. Gibbs, Jr.

Some scholars argue that law, like marriage, is a major institution found in all societies, although in widely divergent forms. Others argue that law exists only where some individual or group possesses the authority to impose punishments. Debates about what is and what isn't law aside, conflict exists in all societies. Further, all societies have culturally defined mechanisms by which people attempt to settle their differences.

Conflict-management procedures must be geared to meet the needs of particular social systems. In the urban centers of Western society, people live in faceless anonymity. Relations between people can be characterized as single interest. For example, generally a person's landlord is neither kin nor neighbor. The landlord-tenant relationship is not complicated by any other social bonds. A person who has a car accident is unlikely to have run into a friend or a relative. Our legal system, with its narrow focus on the grievance itself, fits our social system of one-dimensional relationships.

In small-scale social systems, people are often involved with one another on multiple levels. A landlord may also be a neighbor and a relative. In such settings, people are born, grow up, grow old, and die in the same community. Because their social relationships are long-term and highly valued, people in such communities need to resolve disputes in a way that maintains good relations.

Today in the United States, government agencies and grassroots organizations are establishing programs—Neighborhood Justice Centers or Dispute Resolution Centers—based on models of consensus and conciliation. According to the *Citizen's Dispute Resolution Handbook,* the potential of local-level conflict resolution was originally recognized in the work of an anthropologist who had described these processes in Africa.

As you read this selection, ask yourself the following questions:

- How are formal courtroom hearings different from moots?
- In what kinds of cases is the formal court effective and in what kinds is it ineffective?
- How is a mediator different from a judge?
- What is the function of the blessing at the beginning of the moot?
- In contrast to the official court, how does the procedure used during the moot facilitate harmony and reconciliation?
- Why does the author consider the moot therapeutic?

The following terms discussed in this selection are included in the Glossary at the back of the book:

clan	*multiplex relationship*
culture area	*palaver*
extended family	*patrilineal*
mediator	*single-interest relationship*
moot	*social control*

Africa as a major culture area has been characterized by many writers as being marked by a high development of law and legal procedures.[1] In the past few years research on African law has produced a series of highly competent monographs such as those on law among the Tiv, the Barotse, and the Nuer.[2] These and related shorter studies have focused primarily on formal processes for the settlement of disputes, such as those which take place in a courtroom, or those which are, in some other way, set apart from simpler measures of social control. However, many African societies have informal, quasi-legal, dispute-settlement procedures, supplemental to formal ones, which have not been as well studied, or—in most cases—adequately analysed.

Gibbs, Jr. James. L. "The Kpelle Moot." Africa, 33 (1963), no. 1.
Reprinted with permission of the author.

In this paper I present a description and analysis of one such institution for the informal settlement of disputes, as it is found among the Kpelle of Liberia; it is the moot, the *bɛrɛi mu meni saa* or "house palaver." Hearings in the Kpelle moot contrast with those in a court in that they differ in tone and effectiveness. The genius of the moot lies in the fact that it is based on a covert application of the principles of psychoanalytic theory which underlie psychotherapy.

The Kpelle are a Mande-speaking, patrilineal group of some 175,000 rice cultivators who live in Central Liberia and the adjoining regions of Guinea. This paper is based on data gathered in a field study which I carried out in 1957 and 1958 among the Liberian Kpelle of Panta Chiefdom in north-east Central Province.

Strong corporate patrilineages are absent among the Kpelle. The most important kinship group is the virilocal polygynous family which sometimes becomes an extended family, almost always of the patrilineal variety. Several of these families form the core of a residential group, known as a village quarter, more technically, a clan-barrio.[3] This is headed by a quarter elder who is related to most of the household heads by real or putative patrilineal ties.

Kpelle political organization is centralized although there is no single king or paramount chief, but a series of chiefs of the same level of authority, each of whom is superordinate over district chiefs and town chiefs. Some political functions are also vested in the tribal fraternity, the Poro, which still functions vigorously. The form of political organization found in the area can thus best be termed the polycephalous associational state.

The structure of the Kpelle court system parallels that of the political organization. In Liberia the highest court of a tribal authority and the highest tribal court chartered by the Government is that of a paramount chief. A district chief's court is also an official court. Disputes may be settled in these official courts or in unofficial courts, such as those of town chiefs or quarter elders. In addition to this, grievances are settled informally in moots, and sometimes by associational groupings such as church councils or cooperative work groups.

In my field research I studied both the formal and informal methods of dispute settlement. The method used was to collect case material in as complete a form as possible. Accordingly, immediately after a hearing, my interpreter and I would prepare verbatim transcripts of each case that we heard. These transcripts were supplemented with accounts—obtained from respondents—of past cases or cases which I did not hear litigated. Transcripts from each type of hearing were analysed phrase by phrase in terms of a frame of reference derived from jurisprudence and ethno-law. The results of the analysis indicate two things: first, that courtroom hearings and moots are quite different in their procedures and tone, and secondly, why they show this contrast.

Kpelle courtroom hearings are basically coercive and arbitrary in tone. In another paper[4] I have shown that this is partly the result of the intrusion of the authoritarian values of the Poro into the courtroom. As a result, the court is limited in the manner in which it can handle some types of disputes. The court is particularly effective in settling cases such as assault, possession of illegal charms, or theft where the litigants are not linked in a relationship which must continue after the trial. However, most of the cases brought before a Kpelle court are cases involving disputed rights over women, including matrimonial matters which are usually cast in the form of suits for divorce. The court is particularly inept at settling these numerous matrimonial disputes because its harsh tone tends to drive spouses farther apart rather than to reconcile them. The moot, in contrast, is more effective in handling such cases. The following analysis indicates the reasons for this.[5]

The Kpelle *bɛrɛi mu meni saa*, or "house palaver," is an informal airing of a dispute which takes place before an assembled group which includes kinsmen of the litigants and neighbors from the quarter where the case is being heard. It is a completely ad hoc group, varying greatly in composition from case to case. The matter to be settled is usually a domestic problem: alleged mistreatment or neglect by a spouse, an attempt to collect money paid to a kinsman for a job which was not completed, or a quarrel among brothers over the inheritance of their father's wives.

In the procedural description which follows I shall use illustrative data from the Case of the Ousted Wife:

> Wama Nya, the complainant, had one wife, Yua. His older brother died and he inherited the widow, Yokpo, who moved into his house. The two women were classificatory sisters. After Yokpo moved in, there was strife in the household. The husband accused her of staying out late at night, of harvesting rice without his knowledge, and of denying him food. He also accused Yokpo of having lovers and admitted having had a physical struggle with her, after which he took a basin of water and "washed his hands of her."
>
> Yokpo countered by denying the allegations about having lovers, saying that she was accused falsely, although she had in the past confessed the name of one lover. She further complained that Wama Nya had assaulted her and, in the act, had committed the indignity of removing her headtie, and had expelled her from the house after the ritual hand-washing. Finally, she alleged that she had been thus cast out of the house at the instigation of the other wife who, she asserted, had great influence over their husband.

> Kɔlɔ Waa, the Town Chief and quarter elder, and the brother of Yokpo, was the mediator of the moot, which decided that the husband was mainly at fault, although Yua and Yokpo's children were also in the wrong. Those at fault had to apologize to Yokpo and bring gifts of apology as well as local rum[6] for the disputants and participants in the moot.

The moot is most often held on a Sunday—a day of rest for Christians and non-Christians alike—at the home of the complainant, the person who calls the moot. The mediator will have been selected by the complainant. He is a kinsman who also holds an office such as town chief or quarter elder, and therefore has some skill in dispute settlement. It is said that he is chosen to preside by virtue of his kin tie, rather than because of his office.

The proceedings begin with the pronouncing of blessings by one of the oldest men of the group. In the Case of the Ousted Wife, Gbenai Zua, the elder who pronounced the blessings, took a rice-stirrer in his hand and, striding back and forth, said:

> This man has called us to fix the matter between him and his wife. May ɣala (the supreme, creator deity) change his heart and let his household be in good condition. May ɣala bless the family and make them fruitful. May He bless them so they can have food this year. May He bless the children and the rest of the family so they may always be healthy. May He bless them to have good luck. When Wama Nya takes a gun and goes in the bush, may he kill big animals. May ɣala bless us to enjoy the meat. May He bless us to enjoy life and always have luck. May ɣala bless all those who come to discuss this matter.

The man who pronounces the blessings always carries a stick or a whisk (*kpung*) which he waves for effect as he paces up and down chanting his injunctions. Participation of spectators is demanded, for the blessings are chanted by the elder (*kpung namu* or "*kpung* owner") as a series of imperatives, some of which he repeats. Each phrase is responded to by the spectators who answer in unison with a formal response, either *e ka ti* (so be it), or a low, drawn-out *eeee.* The *kpung namu* delivers his blessings faster and faster, building up a rhythmic interaction pattern with the other participants. The effect is to unite those attending in common action before the hearing begins. The blessing focuses attention on the concern with maintaining harmony and the well-being of the group as a whole.

Everyone attending the moot wears their next-to-best clothes or, if it is not Sunday, everyday clothes. Elders, litigants, and spectators sit in mixed fashion, pressed closely upon each other, often overflowing onto a veranda. This is in contrast to the vertical spatial separation between litigants and adjudicators in the courtroom. The mediator, even though he is a chief, does not wear his robes. He and the oldest men will be given chairs as they would on any other occasion.

The complainant speaks first and may be interrupted by the mediator or anyone else present. After he has been thoroughly quizzed, the accused will answer and will also be questioned by those present. The two parties will question each other directly and question others in the room also. Both the testimony and the questioning are lively and uninhibited. Where there are witnesses to some of the actions described by the parties, they may also speak and be questioned. Although the proceedings are spirited, they remain orderly. The mediator may fine anyone who speaks out of turn by requiring them to bring some rum for the group to drink.

The mediator and others present will point out the various faults committed by both the parties. After everyone has been heard, the mediator expresses the consensus of the group. For example, in the Case of the Ousted Wife, he said to Yua: "The words you used towards your sister were not good, so come and beg her pardon."

The person held to be mainly at fault will then formally apologize to the other person. This apology takes the form of the giving of token gifts to the wronged person by the guilty party. These may be an item of clothing, a few coins, clean hulled rice, or a combination of all three. It is also customary for the winning party in accepting the gifts of apology to give, in return, a smaller token such as a twenty-five cent piece[7] to show his "white heart" or good will. The losing party is also lightly "fined;" he must present rum or beer to the mediator and the others who heard the case. This is consumed by all in attendance. The old man then pronounces blessings again and offers thanks for the restoration of harmony within the group, and asks that all continue to act with good grace and unity.

An initial analysis of the procedural steps of the moot isolates the descriptive attributes of the moot and shows that they contrast with those of the courtroom hearing. While the airing of grievances is incomplete in courtroom hearings, it is more complete in the moot. This fuller airing of the issues results, in many marital cases, in a more harmonious solution. Several specific features of the house palaver facilitate this wider airing of grievances. First, the hearing takes place soon after a breach has occurred, before the grievances have hardened. There is no delay until the complainant has time to go to the paramount chief's or district chief's headquarters to institute suit. Secondly, the hearing takes place in the familiar surroundings of a home. The robes, writs, messengers, and other symbols of power which subtly intimidate and inhibit the parties in the courtroom, by reminding them of the physical force which underlies the procedures, are absent. Thirdly, in the courtroom the conduct of the hearing is firmly in the hands of the judge but in the moot the investigatory initiative rests much more with the parties themselves. Jurisprudence suggests that, in such a case, more of the grievances lodged between the parties are likely to be aired and adjusted. Finally, the range of relevance applied to matters which are brought out is extremely broad. Hardly anything mentioned is held to be irrelevant. This too leads to a more thorough ventilation of the issues.

There is a second surface difference between court and moot. In a courtroom hearing, the solution is, by and large, one which is imposed by the adjudicator. In the moot the solution is more consensual. It is, therefore, more likely to be accepted by both parties and hence more durable. Several features of the moot contribute to the consensual solution: first, there is no unilateral ascription of blame, but an attribution of fault to both parties. Secondly, the mediator, unlike the chief in the courtroom, is not backed by political authority and the physical force which underlies it. He cannot jail parties, nor can he levy a heavy fine. Thirdly, the sanctions which are imposed are not so burdensome as to cause hardship to the losing party or to give him or her grounds for a new grudge against the other party. The gifts for the winning party and the potables for the spectators are not as expensive as the fines and the court costs in a paramount chief's court. Lastly, the ritualized apology of the moot symbolizes very concretely the consensual nature of the solution.[8] The public offering and acceptance of the tokens of apology indicate that each party has no further grievances and that the settlement is satisfactory and mutually acceptable. The parties and spectators drink together to symbolize the restored solidarity of the group and the rehabilitation of the offending party.

This type of analysis describes the courtroom hearing and the moot, using a frame of reference derived from jurisprudence and ethno-law which is explicitly comparative and evaluative. Only by using this type of comparative approach can the researcher select features of the hearings which are not only unique to each of them, but theoretically significant in that their contribution to the social-control functions of the proceedings can be hypothesized. At the same time, it enables the researcher to pin-point in procedures the cause for what he feels intuitively: that the two hearings contrast in tone, even though they are similar in some ways.

However, one can approach the transcripts of the trouble cases with a second analytical framework and emerge with a deeper understanding of the implications of the contrasting descriptive attributes of the court and the house palaver. Remember that the coercive tone of the courtroom hearing limits the court's effectiveness in dealing with matrimonial disputes, especially in effecting reconciliations. The moot, on the other hand, is particularly effective in bringing about reconciliations between spouses. This is because the moot is not only conciliatory, but *therapeutic*. Moot procedures are therapeutic in that, like psychotherapy, they re-educate the parties through a type of social learning brought about in a specially structured interpersonal setting.

Talcott Parsons[9] has written that therapy involves four elements: support, permissiveness, denial of reciprocity, and manipulation of rewards. Writers such as Frank,[10] Klapman,[11] and Opler[12] have pointed out that the same elements characterize not only individual psychotherapy, but group psychotherapy as well. All four elements are writ large in the Kpelle moot.

The patient in therapy will not continue treatment very long if he does not feel support from the therapist or from the group. In the moot the parties are encouraged in the expression of their complaints and feelings because they sense group support. The very presence of one's kinsmen and neighbors demonstrates their concern. It indicates to the parties that they have a real problem and that the others are willing to help them to help themselves in solving it. In a parallel vein, Frank, speaking of group psychotherapy, notes that: "Even anger may be supportive if it implies to a patient that others take him seriously enough to get angry at him, especially if the object of the anger feels it to be directed toward his neurotic behavior rather than himself as a person."[13] In the moot the feeling of support also grows out of the pronouncement of the blessings which stress the unity of the group and its harmonious goal, and it is also undoubtedly increased by the absence of the publicity and expressive symbols of political power which are found in the courtroom.

Permissiveness is the second element in therapy. It indicates to the patient that everyday restrictions on making anti-social statements or acting out anti-social impulses are lessened. Thus, in the Case of the Ousted Wife, Yua felt free enough to turn to her ousted co-wife (who had been married leviratically) and say:

> You don't respect me. You don't rely on me any more. When your husband was living, and I was with my husband, we slept on the farm. Did I ever refuse to send you what you asked me for when you sent a message? Didn't I always send you some of the meat my husband killed? Did I refuse to send you anything you wanted? When your husband died and we became co-wives, did I disrespect you? Why do you always make me ashamed? The things you have done to me make me sad.

Permissiveness in the therapeutic setting (and in the moot) results in catharsis, in a high degree of stimulation of feelings in the participants and an equally high tendency to verbalize these feelings.[14] Frank notes that:

"Neurotic responses must be expressed in the therapeutic situation if they are to be changed by it."[15] In the same way, if the solution to a dispute reached in a house palaver is to be stable, it is important that there should be nothing left to embitter and undermine the decision. In a familiar setting, with familiar people, the parties to the moot feel at ease and free to say *all* that is on their minds. Yokpo, judged to be the wronged party in the Case of the Ousted Wife, in accepting an apology, gave expression to this when she said:

> I agree to everything that my people said, and I accept the things they have given me—I don't have *anything else* about them on my mind. *(My italics.)*

As we shall note below, this thorough airing of complaints also facilitates the gaining of insight into and the unlearning of idiosyncratic behaviour which is socially disruptive. Permissiveness is rooted in the lack of publicity and the lack of symbols of power. But it stems, too, from the immediacy of the hearing, the locus of investigatory initiative with the parties, and the wide range of relevance.

Permissiveness in therapy is impossible without the denial of reciprocity. This refers to the fact that the therapist will not respond in kind when the patient acts in a hostile manner or with inappropriate affection. It is a type of privileged indulgence which comes with being a patient. In the moot, the parties are treated in the same way and are allowed to hurl recriminations that, in the courtroom, might bring a few hours in jail as punishment for the equivalent of contempt of court. Even though inappropriate views are not responded to in kind, neither are they simply ignored. There is denial of *congruent* response, not denial of *any* response whatsoever. In the *bɛrɛi mu meni saa,* as in group psychotherapy, "private ideation and conceptualization are brought out into the open and all their facets or many of their facets exposed. The individual gets a 'reading' from different bearings on the compass, so to speak,[16] and perceptual patterns . . . are joggled out of their fixed positions. . . ."[17]

Thus, Yua's outburst against Yokpo quoted above was not responded to with matching hostility, but its inappropriateness was clearly pointed out to her by the group. Some of them called her aside in a huddle and said to her:

> You are not right. If you don't like the woman, or she doesn't like you, don't be the first to say anything. Let her start and then say what you have to say. By speaking, if she heeds some of your words, the wives will scatter, and the blame will be on you. Then your husband will cry for your name that you have scattered his property.

In effect, Yua was being told that, in view of the previous testimony, her jealousy of her co-wife was not justified. In reality testing, she discovered that her view of the situation was not shared by the others and, hence, was inappropriate. Noting how the others responded, she could see why her treatment of her co-wife had caused so much dissension. Her interpretation of her new co-wife's actions and resulting premises were not shared by the co-wife, nor by the others hearing a description of what had happened. Like psychotherapy, the moot is gently corrective of behavior rooted in such misunderstandings.

Similarly, Wama Nya, the husband, learned that others did not view as reasonable his accusing his wife of having a lover and urging her to go off and drink with the suspected paramour when he passed their house and wished them all a good evening. Reality testing for him taught him that the group did not view this type of mildly paranoid sarcasm as conducive to stable marital relationships.

The reaction of the moot to Yua's outburst indicates that permissiveness in this case was certainly not complete, but only relative, being much greater than in the courtroom. But without this moderated immunity the airing of grievances would be limited, and the chance for social relearning lessened. Permissiveness in the moot is incomplete because, even there, prudence is not thrown to the winds. Note that Yua was not told not to express her feelings at all, but to express them only after the co-wife had spoken so that, if the moot failed, she would not be in an untenable position. In court there would be objection to her blunt speaking out. In the moot the objection was, in effect, to her speaking *out of turn.* In other cases the moot sometimes fails, foundering on this very point, because the parties are *too* prudent, all waiting for the others to make the first move in admitting fault.

The manipulation of rewards is the last dimension of therapy treated by Parsons. In this final phase of therapy[18] the patient is coaxed to conformity by the granting of rewards. In the moot one of the most important rewards is the group approval which goes to the wronged person who accepts an apology and to the person who is magnanimous enough to make one.

In the Case of the Ousted Wife, Kɔlɔ Waa, the mediator, and the others attending decided that the husband and the co-wife, Yua, had wronged Yokpo. Kɔlɔ Waa said to the husband:

> From now on, we don't want to hear of your fighting. You should live in peace with these women. If your wife accepts the things which the people have brought you should pay four chickens and ten bottles of rum as your contribution.

The husband's brother and sister also brought gifts of apology, although the moot did not explicitly hold them at fault.

By giving these prestations, the wrong-doer is restored to good grace and is once again acting like an "upright Kpelle" (although, if he wishes, he may refuse to accept the decision of the moot). He is eased into this position by being grouped with others to whom blame is also allocated, for, typically, he is not singled out and isolated in being labelled deviant. Thus, in the Case of the Ousted Wife, the children of Yokpo were held to be at fault in "being mean" to their step-father, so that blame was not only shared by one "side," but ascribed to the other also.

Moreover, the prestations which the losing party is asked to hand over are not expensive. They are significant enough to touch the pocketbook a little; for the Kpelle say that if an apology does not cost something other than words, the wrong-doer is more likely to repeat the offending action. At the same time, as we noted above, the tokens are not so costly as to give the loser additional reason for anger directed at the other party which can undermine the decision.

All in all, the rewards for conformity to group expectations and for following out a new behaviour pattern are kept within the deviant's sight. These rewards are positive, in contrast to the negative sanctions of the courtroom. Besides the institutionalized apology, praise and acts of concern and affection replace fines and jail sentences. The mediator, speaking to Yokpo as the wronged party, said:

> You have found the best of the dispute. Your husband has wronged you. All the people have wronged you. You are the only one who can take care of them because you are the oldest. Accept the things they have given to you.

The moot in its procedural features and procedural sequences is, then, strongly analogous to psychotherapy. It is analogous to therapy in the structuring of the role of the mediator also. Parsons has indicated that, to do his job well, the therapist must be a member of two social systems: one containing himself and his patient; and the other, society at large.[19] He must not be seduced into thinking that he belongs only to the therapeutic dyad, but must gradually pull the deviant back into a relationship with the wider group. It is significant, then, that the mediator of a moot is a kinsman who is also a chief of some sort. He thus represents both the group involved in the dispute and the wider community. His task is to utilize his position as kinsman as a lever to manipulate the parties into living up to the normative requirements of the wider society, which, as chief, he upholds. His major orientation must be to the wider collectivity, not to the particular goals of his kinsmen.

When successful, the moot stops the process of alienation which drives two spouses so far apart that they are immune to ordinary social-control measures such as a smile, a frown, or a pointed aside.[20] A moot is not always successful, however. Both parties must have a genuine willingness to cooperate and a real concern about their discord. Each party must be willing to list his grievances, to admit his guilt, and make an open apology. The moot, like psychotherapy, is impotent without well-motivated clients.

The therapeutic elements found in the Kpelle moot are undoubtedly found in informal procedures for settling disputes in other African societies also; some of these are reported in literature and others are not. One such procedure which seems strikingly parallel to the Kpelle *bɛrɛi mu meni saa* has been described by J. H. M. Beattie.[21] This is the court of neighbors or *rukurato rw'enzarwa* found in the Banyoro kingdom of Uganda. The group also meets as an ad hoc assembly of neighbors to hear disputes involving kinsmen or neighbors.[22]

The intention of the Nyoro moot is to "reintegrate the delinquent into the community and, if possible, to achieve reconciliation without causing bitterness and resentment; in the words of an informant, the institution exists 'to finish off people's quarrels and to abolish bad feeling.'"[23] This therapeutic goal is manifested in the manner in which the dispute is resolved. After a decision is reached the penalty imposed is always the same. The party held to be in the wrong is asked to bring beer (four pots, modified downwards according to the circumstances) and meat, which is shared with the other party and all those attending the *rukurato*. The losing party is also expected to "humble himself, not only to the man he has injured but to the whole assembly."[24]

Beattie correctly points out that, because the council of neighbors has no power to enforce its decision, the shared feast is *not* to be viewed primarily as a penalty, for the wrong-doer acts as a host and also shares in the food and drink. "And it is a praiseworthy thing; from a dishonourable status he is promoted to an honourable one . . ."[25] and reintegrated into the community.[26]

Although Beattie does not use a psychoanalytic frame of reference in approaching his material, it is clear that the communal feast involves the manipulation of rewards as the last step in a social-control measure which breaks the progressive alienation of the deviance cycle. The description of procedures in the *rukurato* indicates that it is highly informal in nature, convening in a room in a house with everyone "sitting around." However, Beattie does not provide enough detail to enable one to determine whether or not the beginning and intermediate steps in the Nyoro moot show the permissiveness, support, and denial of reciprocity which characterize the Kpelle moot. Given the structure and outcome of most Nyoro councils, one would surmise that a close examination of their proceedings[27] would reveal the implicit operation of therapeutic principles.

The fact that the Kpelle court is basically coercive and the moot therapeutic does not imply that one is dysfunctional while the other is eufunctional. Like Beattie, I conclude that the court and informal dispute-settlement procedures have separate but complementary functions. In marital disputes the moot is oriented to a couple as a dyadic social system and serves to reconcile them wherever possible. This is eufunctional from the point of view of the couple, to whom divorce would be dysfunctional. Kpelle courts customarily treat matrimonial matters by granting a divorce. While this may be dysfunctional from the point of view of the couple, because it ends their marriage, it may be eufunctional from the point of view of society. Some marriages, if forced to continue, would result in adultery or physical violence at best, and improper socialization of children at worst. It is clear that the Kpelle moot is to the Kpelle court as the domestic and family relations courts (or commercial and labour arbitration boards) are to ordinary courts in our own society. The essential point is that both formal and informal dispute-settlement procedures serve significant functions in Kpelle society and neither can be fully understood if studied alone.[28]

NOTES

1. The fieldwork on which this paper is based was carried out in Liberia in 1957 and 1958 and was supported by a grant from the Ford Foundation, which is, of course, not responsible for any of the views presented here. The data were analyzed while the writer was the holder of a pre-doctoral National Science Foundation Fellowship. The writer wishes to acknowledge, with gratitude, the support of both foundations. This paper was read at the Annual Meeting of the American Anthropological Association in Philadelphia, Pennsylvania, in November 1961.

   The dissertation, in which this material first appeared, was directed by Philip H. Gulliver, to whom I am indebted for much stimulating and provocative discussion of many of the ideas here. Helpful comments and suggestions have also been made by Robert T. Holt and Robert S. Merrill.

   Portions of the material included here were presented in a seminar on African Law conducted in the Department of Anthropology at the University of Minnesota by E. Adamson Hoebel and the writer. Members of the seminar were generous in their criticisms and comments.
2. Paul J. Bohannan, *Justice and Judgment among the Tiv,* Oxford University Press, London, 1957; Max Gluckman, *The Judicial Process among the Barotse of Northern Rhodesia,* Manchester University Press, 1954; P. P. Howell, *A Handbook of Nuer Law,* Oxford University Press, London, 1954.
3. Cf. George P. Murdock, *Social Structure,* Macmillan, New York, 1949, p. 74.
4. James L. Gibbs, Jr., "Poro Values and Courtroom Procedures in a Kpelle Chiefdom," *Southwestern Journal of Anthropology* (in press) [1963, 18:341–350]. A detailed analysis of Kpelle courtroom procedures and of procedures in the moot together with transcripts appears in: James L. Gibbs, Jr., *Some Judicial Implications of Marital Instability among the Kpelle* (unpublished Ph.D. Dissertation, Harvard University, Cambridge, Mass., 1960).
5. What follows is based on a detailed case study of moots in Panta Chiefdom and their contrast with courtroom hearings before the paramount chief of that chiefdom. Moots, being private, are less susceptible to the surveillance of the anthropologist than courtroom hearings; thus I have fewer transcripts of moots than of court cases. The analysis presented here is valid for Panta Chiefdom and also valid, I feel, for most of the Liberian Kpelle area, particularly the north-east where people are, by and large, traditional.
6. This simple distilled rum, bottled in Monrovia and retailing for twenty-five cents a bottle in 1958, is known in the Liberian Hinterland as "cane juice" and should not be confused with imported varieties.
7. American currency is the official currency of Liberia and is used throughout the country.
8. Cf. J. F. Holleman, "An Anthropological Approach to Bantu Law (with special reference to Shona law)" in the *Journal of the Rhodes-Livingstone Institute,* vol. x, 1950, pp. 27–41. Holleman feels that the use of tokens for effecting apologies—or marriages—shows the proclivity for reducing events of importance to something tangible.
9. Talcott Parsons, *The Social System,* The Free Press, Glencoe, Ill., 1951, pp. 314–319.
10. Jerome D. Frank, "Group Methods in Psychotherapy," in *Mental Health and Mental Disorder: A Sociological Approach,* edited by Arnold Rose, W. W. Norton Co., New York, pp. 524–535.
11. J. W. Klapman, *Group Psychotherapy: Theory and Practice,* Grune & Stratton, New York, 1959.
12. Marvin K. Opler, "Values in Group Psychotherapy," *International Journal of Social Psychiatry,* vol. iv, 1959, pp. 296–298.
13. Frank, op. cit., p. 531.
14. Ibid.
15. Ibid.
16. Klapman, op. cit., p. 39.
17. Ibid., p. 15.
18. For expository purposes the four elements of therapy are described as if they always occur serially. They may, and do, occur simultaneously also. Thus, all four of the factors may be implicit in a single short behavioural sequence. Parsons (op. cit.) holds that these four elements

are common not only to psychotherapy but to all measures of social control.

19. Parsons, op. cit., p. 314. Cf. loc. cit., chap. 10.
20. Cf. Parsons, op. cit., chap. 7. Parsons notes that in any social-control action the aim is to avoid the process of alienation, that "vicious-cycle" phenomenon whereby each step taken to curb the non-conforming activity of the deviant has the effect of driving him further into his pattern of deviance. Rather, the need is to "reach" the deviant and bring him back to the point where he is susceptible to the usual everyday informal sanctions.
21. J. H. M. Beattie, "Informal Judicial Activity in Bunyoro," *Journal of African Administration*, vol. ix, 1957, pp. 188–195.
22. Disputes include matters such as a son seducing his father's wives, a grown son disobeying his father, or a husband or wife failing in his or her duties to a spouse. Disputes between unrelated persons involve matters like quarrelling, abuse, assault, false accusations, petty theft, adultery, and failure to settle debts. (Ibid., p. 190.)
23. Ibid., p. 194.
24. Beattie, op. cit., p. 194.
25. Ibid., p. 193.
26. Ibid., p. 195. Moreover, Beattie also recognizes the functional significance of the Nyoro moots, for he notes that: "It would be a serious error to represent them simply as clumsy, 'amateur' expedients for punishing wrong-doers or settling civil disputes at an informal, sub-official level." (Ibid.)
27. The type of examination of case materials that is required demands that fieldworkers should not simply record cases that meet the "trouble case" criterion (cf. K. N. Llewellyn and E. A. Hoebel, *The Cheyenne Way*, Norman, Okla., University of Oklahoma Press, 1941; and E. A. Hoebel, *The Law of Primitive Man*, Cambridge, Mass., Harvard University Press, 1954), but that cases should be recorded in some transcript-like form.
28. The present study has attempted to add to our understanding of informal dispute-settlement procedures in one African society by using an eclectic but organized collection of concepts from jurisprudence, ethno-law, and psychology. It is based on the detailed and systematic analysis of a few selected cases, rather than a mass of quantitative data. In further research a greater variety of cases handled by Kpelle moots should be subjected to the same analysis to test its merit more fully.

The Berdache Tradition

Walter L. Williams

Because it is such a powerful force in the world today, the Western Judeo-Christian tradition is often accepted as the arbiter of "natural" behavior of humans. If Europeans and their descendant nations of North America accept something as normal, then anything different is seen as abnormal. Such a view ignores the great diversity of human existence.

This is the case of the study of gender. How many genders are there? To a modern Anglo-American, nothing might seem more definite than the answer that there are two: men and women. But not all societies around the world agree with Western culture's view that all humans are either women or men. The commonly accepted notion of "the opposite sex," based on anatomy, is itself an artifact of our society's rigid sex roles.

Among many cultures, there have existed different alternatives to "man" or "woman." An alternative role in many American Indian societies is referred to by anthropologists as *berdache*. . . . The role varied from one Native American culture to another, which is a reflection of the vast diversity of aboriginal New World societies. Small bands of hunter-gatherers existed in some areas, with advanced civilizations of farming peoples in other areas. With hundreds of different languages, economies, religions, and social patterns existing in North America alone, every generalization about a cultural tradition must acknowledge many exceptions.

This diversity is true for the berdache tradition as well, and must be kept in mind. My statements should be read as being specific to a particular culture, with generalizations being treated as loose patterns that might not apply to peoples even in nearby areas.

Briefly, a berdache can be defined as a morphological male who does not fill a society's standard man's role, who has a non-masculine character. This type of person is often stereotyped as effeminate, but a more accurate characterization is androgyny. Such a person has a clearly recognized and accepted social status, often based on a secure place in the tribal mythology. Berdaches have special ceremonial roles in many Native American religions, and important economic roles in their families. They will do at least some women's work, and mix together much of the behavior, dress, and social roles of women and men. Berdaches gain social prestige by their spiritual, intellectual, or craftwork/artistic contributions, and by their reputation for hard work and generosity. They serve a mediating function between women and men, precisely because their character is seen as distinct from either sex. They are not seen as men, yet they are not seen as women either. They occupy an alternative gender role that is a mixture of diverse elements.

In their erotic behavior berdaches also generally (but not always) take a nonmasculine role, either being asexual or becoming the passive partner in sex with men. In some cultures the berdache might become a wife to a man. This male-male sexual behavior became the focus of an attack on berdaches as "sodomites" by the Europeans who, early on, came into contact with them. From the first Spanish conquistadors to the Western frontiersmen and the Christian missionaries and government officials, Western culture has had a considerable impact on the berdache tradition. In the last two decades, the most recent impact on the tradition is the adaptation of a modern Western gay identity.

To Western eyes berdachism is a complex and puzzling phenomenon, mixing and redefining the very concepts of what is considered male and female. In a culture with only two recognized genders, such individuals are gender nonconformist, abnormal, deviant. But to American Indians, the institution of another gender role means that berdaches are not deviant—indeed, they do conform to the requirements of a custom in which their culture tells them they fit. Berdachism is a way for society to recognize and assimilate some atypical individuals without imposing a change on them or stigmatizing them as deviant. This cultural institution confirms their legitimacy for what they are.

Societies often bestow power upon that which does not neatly fit into the usual. Since no cultural system can explain everything, a common way that many cultures deal with these inconsistencies is to imbue them with negative power, as taboo, pollution, witchcraft, or sin. That which is not understood is seen as a threat. But an alternative method of dealing with such things, or people, is to take them out of the realm of threat and to sanctify them.[1] The berdaches' role as mediator is thus not just between women and men, but also between the physical and the spiritual. American Indian cultures have taken what Western culture calls negative, and made it a positive; they have successfully utilized the different skills and insights of a class of people that Western culture has stigmatized and whose spiritual powers have been wasted.

Many Native Americans also understood that gender roles have to do with more than just biological sex. The standard

Western view that one's sex is always a certainty, and that one's gender identity and sex role always conform to one's morphological sex is a view that dies hard. Western thought is typified by such dichotomies of groups perceived to be mutually exclusive: male and female, black and white, right and wrong, good and evil. Clearly, the world is not so simple; such clear divisions are not always realistic. Most American Indian worldviews generally are much more accepting of the ambiguities of life. Acceptance of gender variation in the berdache tradition is typical of many native cultures' approach to life in general.

Overall, these are generalizations based on those Native American societies that had an accepted role for berdaches. Not all cultures recognized such a respected status. Berdachism in aboriginal North America was most established among tribes in four areas: first, the Prairie and western Great Lakes, the northern and central Great Plains, and the lower Mississippi Valley; second, Florida and the Caribbean; third, the Southwest, the Great Basin, and California; and fourth, scattered areas of the Northwest, western Canada, and Alaska. For some reason it is not noticeable in eastern North America, with the exception of its southern rim. . . .

American Indian Religions

Native American religions offered an explanation for human diversity by their creation stories. In some tribal religions, the Great Spiritual Being is conceived as neither male nor female but as a combination of both. Among the Kamia of the Southwest, for example, the bearer of plant seeds and the introducer of Kamia culture was a man-woman spirit named Warharmi.[2] A key episode of the Zuni creation story involves a battle between the kachina spirits of the agricultural Zunis and the enemy hunter spirits. Every four years an elaborate ceremony commemorates this myth. In the story a kachina spirit called *ko'lhamana* was captured by the enemy spirits and transformed in the process. This transformed spirit became a mediator between the two sides, using his peacemaking skills to merge the differing lifestyles of hunters and farmers. In the ceremony, a dramatic reenactment of the myth, the part of the transformed *ko'lhamana* spirit, is performed by a berdache.[3] The Zuni word for berdache is *lhamana,* denoting its closeness to the spiritual mediator who brought hunting and farming together.[4] The moral of this story is that the berdache was created by the deities for a special purpose, and that this creation led to the improvement of society. The continual reenactment of this story provides a justification for the Zuni berdache in each generation.

In contrast to this, the lack of spiritual justification in a creation myth could denote a lack of tolerance for gender variation. The Pimas, unlike most of their Southwestern neighbors, did not respect a berdache status. *Wi-kovat,* their derogatory word, means "like a girl," but it does not signify a recognized social role. Pima mythology reflects this lack of acceptance, in a folk tale that explains male androgyny as due to Papago witchcraft. Knowing that the Papagos respected berdaches, the Pimas blamed such an occurrence on an alien influence.[5] While the Pimas' condemnatory attitude is unusual, it does point out the importance of spiritual explanations for the acceptance of gender variance in a culture.

Other Native American creation stories stand in sharp contrast to the Pima explanation. A good example is the account of the Navajos, which presents women and men as equals. The Navajo origin tale is told as a story of five worlds. The first people were First Man and First Woman, who were created equally and at the same time. The first two worlds that they lived in were bleak and unhappy, so they escaped to the third world. In the third world lived two twins, Turquoise Boy and White Shell Girl, who were the first berdaches. In the Navajo language the world for berdache is *nadle,* which means "changing one" or "one who is transformed." It is applied to hermaphrodites—those who are born with the genitals of both male and female—and also to "those who pretend to be *nadle,*" who take on a social role that is distinct from either men or women.[6]

In the third world, First Man and First Woman began farming, with the help of the changing twins. One of the twins noticed some clay and, holding it in the palm of his/her hand, shaped it into the first pottery bowl. Then he/she formed a plate, a water dipper, and a pipe. The second twin observed some reeds and began to weave them, making the first basket. Together they shaped axes and grinding stones from rocks, and hoes from bone. All these new inventions made the people very happy.[7]

The message of this story is that humans are dependent for many good things on the inventiveness of *nadle.* Such individuals were present from the earliest eras of human existence, and their presence was never questioned. They were part of the natural order of the universe, with a special contribution to make.

Later on in the Navajo creation story, White Shell Girl entered the moon and became the Moon Bearer. Turquoise Boy, however, remained with the people. When First Man realized that Turquoise Boy could do all manner of women's work as well as women, all the men left the women and crossed a big river. The men hunted and planted crops. Turquoise Boy ground the corn, cooked the food, and weaved cloth for the men. Four years passed with the women and men separated, and the men were happy with the *nadle.* Later, however the women wanted to learn how to grind corn from the *nadle,* and both the men and women had decided that it was not good to continue living separately. So the women crossed the river and the people were reunited.[8]

They continued living happily in the third world, until one day a great flood began. The people ran to the highest mountaintop, but the water kept rising and they all feared they would be drowned. But just in time, the ever-inventive Turquoise Boy found a large reed. They climbed upward inside the tall hollow reed, and came out at the top into the fourth world. From there, White Shell Girl brought another reed, and they climbed again to the fifth world, which is the present world of the Navajos.[9]

These stories suggest that the very survival of humanity is dependent on the inventiveness of berdaches. With such a mythological belief system, it is no wonder that the Navajos held *nadle* in high regard. The concept of the *nadle* is well formulated in the creation story. As children were educated by these stories, and all Navajos believed in them, the high status accorded to gender variation was passed down from generation to generation. Such stories also provided instruction for *nadle* themselves to live by. A spiritual explanation guaranteed a special place for a person who was considered different but not deviant.

For American Indians, the important explanations of the world are spiritual ones. In their view, there is a deeper reality than the here-and-now. The real essence or wisdom occurs when one finally gives up trying to explain events in terms of "logic" and "reality." Many confusing aspects of existence can better be explained by actions of a multiplicity of spirits. Instead of a concept of a single god, there is an awareness of "that which we do not understand." In Lakota religion, for example, the term *Wakan Tanka* is often translated as "god." But a more proper translation, according to the medicine people who taught me, is "The Great Mystery."[10]

While rationality can explain much, there are limits to human capabilities of understanding. The English language is structured to account for cause and effect. For example, English speakers say, "It is raining," with the implication that there is a cause "it" that leads to rain. Many Indian languages, on the other hand, merely note what is most accurately translated as "raining" as an observable fact. Such an approach brings a freedom to stop worrying about causes of things, and merely to relax and accept that our human insights can go only so far. By not taking ourselves too seriously, or overinflating human importance, we can get beyond the logical world.

The emphasis of American Indian religions, then, is on the spiritual nature of all things. To understand the physical world, one must appreciate the underlying spiritual essence. Then one can begin to see that the physical is only a faint shadow, a partial reflection, of a supernatural and extrarational world. By the Indian view, everything that exists is spiritual. Every object—plants, rocks, water, air, the moon, animals, humans, the earth itself—has a spirit. The spirit of one thing (including a human) is not superior to the spirit of any other. Such a view promotes a sophisticated ecological awareness of the place that humans have in the larger environment. The function of religion is not to try to condemn or to change what exists, but to accept the realities of the world and to appreciate their contributions to life. Everything that exists has a purpose.[11]

One of the basic tenets of American Indian religion is the notion that everything in the universe is related. Nevertheless, things that exist are often seen as having a counterpart: sky and earth, plant and animal, water and fire. In all of these polarities, there exist mediators. The role of the mediator is to hold the polarities together, to keep the world from disintegrating. Polarities exist within human society also. The most important category within Indian society is gender. The notions of Woman and Man underlie much of social interaction and are comparable to the other major polarities. Women, with their nurtural qualities, are associated with the earth, while men are associated with the sky. Women gatherers and farmers deal with plants (of the earth), while men hunters deal with animals.

The mediator between the polarities of woman and man, in the American Indian religious explanation, is a being that combines the elements of both genders. This might be a combination in a physical sense, as in the case of hermaphrodites. Many Native American religions accept this phenomenon in the same way that they accept other variations from the norm. But more important is their acceptance of the idea that gender can be combined in ways other than physical hermaphroditism. The physical aspects of a thing or a person, after all, are not nearly as important as its spirit. American Indians use the concept of a person's *spirit* in the way that other Americans use the concept of a person's *character.* Consequently, physical hermaphroditism is not necessary for the idea of gender mixing. A person's character, their spiritual essence, is the crucial thing.

The Berdache's Spirit

Individuals who are physically normal might have the spirit of the other sex, might range somewhere between the two sexes, or might have a spirit that is distinct from either women or men. Whatever category they fall into, they are seen as being different from men. They are accepted spiritually as "Not Man." Whichever option is chosen, Indian religions offer spiritual explanations. Among the Arapahos of the Plains, berdaches are called *haxu'xan* and are seen to be that way as a result of a supernatural gift from birds or animals. Arapaho mythology recounts the story of Nih'a'ca, the first *haxu'xan.* He pretended to be a woman and married the mountain lion, a symbol for masculinity. The myth, as recorded by ethnographer Alfred Kroeber about 1900, recounted that "These people had the natural desire to become women, and as they grew up gradually became women. They gave up the desires of men. They were married to men. They had miraculous power and could do supernatural things. For instance, it was one of them that first made an intoxicant from rainwater."[12] Besides the theme of inventiveness, similar to the Navajo creation story, the berdache role is seen as a product of a "natural desire." Berdaches "gradually became women," which underscores the notion of woman as a social category rather than as a fixed biological entity. Physical biological sex is less important in gender classification than a person's desire—one's spirit.

They myths contain no prescriptions for trying to change berdaches who are acting out their desires of the heart. Like many other cultures' myths, the Zuni origin myths simply sanction the idea that gender can be transformed independently of biological sex.[13] Indeed, myths warn of dire consequences when interference with such a transformation is attempted. Prince Alexander Maximilian of the German state of Wied, traveling in the northern Plains in the 1830s, heard a myth about a warrior who once tried to force a berdache to avoid women's clothing. The berdache resisted, and the warrior shot him with an arrow. Immediately the berdache disappeared, and the warrior saw only a pile of stones with his arrow in them. Since then, the story concluded, no intelligent person would try to coerce a berdache.[14] Making the point even more directly, a Mandan myth told of an Indian who tried to force *mihdake* (berdaches) to give up their distinctive dress and status, which led the spirits to punish many people with death. After that, no Mandans interfered with berdaches.[15]

With this kind of attitude, reinforced by myth and history, the aboriginal view accepts human diversity. The creation story of the Mohave of the Colorado River Valley speaks of a time when people were not sexually differentiated. From this perspective, it is easy to accept that certain individuals might combine elements of masculinity and femininity.[16] A respected Mohave elder, speaking in the 1930s, stated this viewpoint simply: "From the very beginning of the world it was meant that there should be [berdaches], just as it was instituted that there should be shamans. They were intended for that purpose."[17]

This elder also explained that a child's tendencies to become a berdache are apparent early, by about age nine to twelve, before the child reaches puberty: "That is the time when young persons become initiated into the functions of their sex. . . . None but young people will become berdaches as a rule."[18] Many tribes have a public ceremony that acknowledges the acceptance of berdache status. A Mohave shaman related the ceremony for his tribe: "When the child was about ten years old his relatives would begin discussing his strange ways. Some of them disliked it, but the more intelligent began envisaging an initiation ceremony." The relatives prepare for the ceremony without letting the boy know if it. It is meant to take him by surprise, to be both an initiation and a test of his true inclinations. People from various settlements are invited to attend. The family wants the community to see it and become accustomed to accepting the boy as an *alyha.*

On the day of the ceremony, the shaman explained, the boy is led into a circle: "If the boy showed a willingness to remain standing in the circle, exposed to the public eye, it was almost certain that he would go through with the ceremony. The singer, hidden behind the crowd, began singing the songs. As soon as the sound reached the boy he began to dance as women do." If the boy is unwilling to assume *alyha* status, he would refuse to dance. But if his character—his spirit—is *alyha,* "the song goes right to his heart and he will dance with much intensity. He cannot help it. After the fourth song he is proclaimed." After the ceremony, the boy is carefully bathed and receives a woman's skirt. He is then led back to the dance ground, dressed as an *alyha,* and announces his new feminine name to the crowd. After that he would resent being called by his old male name.[19]

Among the Yuman tribes of the Southwest, the transformation is marked by a social gathering, in which the berdache prepares a meal for the friends of the family.[20] Ethnographer Ruth Underhill, doing fieldwork among the Papago Indians in the early 1930s, wrote that berdaches were common among the Papago Indians, and were usually publicly acknowledged in childhood. She recounted that a boy's parents would test him if they noticed that he preferred female pursuits. The regular pattern, mentioned by many of Underhill's Papago informants, was to build a small brush enclosure. Inside the enclosure they placed a man's bow and arrows, and also a woman's basket. At the appointed time the boy was brought to the enclosure as the adults watched from outside. The boy was told to go inside the circle of brush. Once he was inside, the adults "set fire to the enclosure. They watched what he took with him as he ran out and if it was the basketry materials, they reconciled themselves to his being a berdache."[21]

What is important to recognize in all of these practices is that the assumption of a berdache role was not forced on the boy by others. While adults might have their suspicions, it was only when the child made the proper move that he was considered a berdache. By doing woman's dancing, preparing a meal, or taking the woman's basket he was making an important symbolic gesture. Indian children were not stupid, and they knew the implications of these ceremonies beforehand. A boy in the enclosure could have left without taking anything, or could have taken both the man's and the woman's tools. With the community standing by watching, he was well aware that his choice would mark his assumption of berdache status. Rather than being seen as an involuntary test of his reflexes, this ceremony may be interpreted as a definite statement by the child to take on the berdache role.

Indians do not see the assumption of berdache status, however, as a free will choice on the part of the boy. People felt that the boy was acting out his basic character. The Lakota shaman Lame Deer explained:

> They were not like other men, but the Great Spirit made them *winktes* and we accepted them as such. . . . We think that if a woman has two little ones growing inside her, if she is going to have twins, sometimes instead of giving birth to two babies they have formed up in her womb into just one, into a half-man/half-woman kind of being. . . . To us a man is what nature, or his dreams, make him. We accept him for what he wants to be. That's up to him.[22]

While most of the sources indicate that once a person becomes a berdache it is a lifelong status, directions from the spirits determine everything. In at least one documented case, concerning a nineteenth-century Klamath berdache named Lele'ks, he later had a supernatural experience that led him to leave the berdache role. At that time Lele'ks began dressing and acting like a man, then married women, and eventually became one of the most famous Klamath chiefs.[23] What is important is that both in assuming berdache status and in leaving it, supernatural dictate is the determining factor.

Dreams and Visions

Many tribes see the berdache role as signifying an individual's proclivities as a dreamer and a visionary. . . .

Among the northern Plains and related Great Lakes tribes, the idea of supernatural dictate through dreaming—the vision quest—had its highest development. The goal of the vision quest is to try to get beyond the rational world by sensory deprivation and fasting. By depriving one's body of nourishment, the brain could escape from logical thought and connect with the higher reality of the supernatural. The person doing the quest simply sits and waits for a vision. But a vision might not come easily; the person might have to wait for days.

The best way that I can describe the process is to refer to my own vision quest, which I experienced when I was living on a Lakota reservation in 1982. After a long series of prayers and blessings, the shaman who had prepared me for the ceremony took me out to an isolated area where a sweat lodge had been set up for my quest. As I walked to the spot, I worried that I might not be able to stand it. Would I be overcome by hunger?

Could I tolerate the thirst? What would I do if I had to go to the toilet? The shaman told me not to worry, that a whole group of holy people would be praying and singing for me while I was on my quest.

He had me remove my clothes, symbolizing my disconnection from the material would, and crawl into the sweat lodge. Before he left me I asked him, "What do I think about?" He said, "Do not think. Just pray for spiritual guidance." After a prayer he closed the flap tightly and I was left in total darkness. I still do not understand what happened to me during my vision quest, but during the day and a half that I was out there, I never once felt hungry or thirsty or the need to go to the toilet. What happened was an intensely personal experience that I cannot and do not wish to explain, a process of being that cannot be described in rational terms.

When the shaman came to get me at the end of my time, I actually resented having to end it. He did not need to ask if my vision quest was successful. He knew that it was even before seeing me, he explained, because he saw an eagle circling over me while I underwent the quest. He helped interpret the signs I had seen, then after more prayers and singing he led me back to the others. I felt relieved, cleansed, joyful, and serene. I had been through an experience that will be a part of my memories always.

If a vision quest could have such an effect on a person not even raised in Indian society, imagine its impact on a boy who from his earliest years had been waiting for the day when he could seek his vision. Gaining his spiritual power from his first vision, it would tell him what role to take in adult life. The vision might instruct him that he is going to be a great hunter, a craftsman, a warrior, or a shaman. Or it might tell him that he will be a berdache. Among the Lakotas, or Sioux, there are several symbols for various types of visions. A person becomes *wakan* (a sacred person) if she or he dreams of a bear, a wolf, thunder, a buffalo, a white buffalo calf, or Double Woman. Each dream results in a different gift, whether it is the power to cure illness or wounds, a promise of good hunting, or the exalted role of a *heyoka* (doing things backward).

A white buffalo calf is believed to be a berdache. If a person has a dream of the sacred Double Woman, this means that she or he will have the power to seduce men. Males who have a vision of Double Woman are presented with female tools. Taking such tools means that the male will become a berdache. The Lakota word *winkte* is composed of *win,* "woman," and *kte,* "would become."[24] A contemporary Lakota berdache explains, "To become a *winkte,* you have a medicine man put you up on the hill, to search for your vision. "You can become a *winkte* if you truly are by nature. You see a vision of the White Buffalo Calf Pipe. Sometimes it varies. A vision is like a scene in a movie."[25] Another way to become a *winkte* is to have a vision given by a *winkte* from the past.[26]. . .

By interpreting the result of the vision as being the work of a spirit, the vision quest frees the person from feeling responsible for his transformation. The person might even claim that the change was done against his will and without his control. Such a claim does not suggest a negative attitude about berdache status, because it is common for people to claim reluctance to fulfill their spiritual duty no matter what vision appears to them. Becoming any kind of sacred person involves taking on various social responsibilities and burdens.[27]. . .

A story was told among the Lakotas in the 1880s of a boy who tried to resist following his vision from Double Woman. But according to Lakota informants "few men succeed in this effort after having taken the strap in the dream." Having rebelled against the instructions given him by the Moon Being, he committed suicide.[28] The moral of that story is that one should not resist spiritual guidance, because it will lead only to grief. In another case, an Omaha young man told of being addressed by a spirit as "daughter," whereupon he discovered that he was unconsciously using feminine styles of speech. He tried to use male speech patterns, but could not. As a result of this vision, when he returned to his people he resolved himself to dress as a woman.[29] Such stories function to justify personal peculiarities as due to a fate over which the individual has no control.

Despite the usual pattern in Indian societies of using ridicule to enforce conformity, receiving instructions from a vision inhibits others from trying to change the berdache. Ritual explanation provides a way out. It also excuses the community from worrying about the cause of that person's difference, or the feeling that it is society's duty to try to change him.[30] Native American religions, above all else, encourage a basic respect for nature. If nature makes a person different, many Indians conclude, a mere human should not undertake to counter this spiritual dictate. Someone who is "unusual" can be accommodated without being stigmatized as "abnormal." Berdachism is thus not alien or threatening; it is a reflection of spirituality.

Notes

1. Mary Douglas, *Purity and Danger* (Baltimore: Penguin, 1966), p. 52. I am grateful to Theda Perdue for convincing me that Douglas's ideas apply to berdachism. For an application of Douglas's thesis to berdaches, see James Thayer, "The Berdache of the Northern Plains: A Socioreligious Perspective," *Journal of Anthropological Research 36* (1980): 292–93.
2. E. W. Gifford, "The Kamia of Imperial Valley," *Bureau of American Ethnology Bulletin 97* (1931): 12.
3. By using present tense verbs in this text, I am not implying that such activities are necessarily continuing today. I sometimes use the present tense in the "ethnographic present," unless I use the past tense when I am referring to something that has not continued. Past tense implies that all such practices have disappeared. In the absence of fieldwork to prove such disappearance, I am not prepared to make that assumption, on the historic changes in the berdache tradition.
4. Elsie Clews Parsons, "The Zuni La' Mana," *American Anthropologist* 18 (1916): 521; Matilda Coxe Stevenson, "Zuni Indians," *Bureau of American Ethnology Annual Report 23* (1903): 37; Franklin Cushing, "Zuni Creation Myths," *Bureau of American Ethnology Annual Report 13* (1894): 401–3. Will Roscoe clarified this origin story for me.
5. W. W. Hill, "Note on the Pima Berdache," *American Anthropologist 40* (1938): 339.
6. Aileen O'Bryan, "The Dine': Origin Myths of the Navaho Indians," *Bureau of American Ethnology Bulletin 163* (1956): 5;

W. W. Hill, "The Status of the Hermaphrodite and Transvestite in Navaho Culture,"*American Anthropologist 37* (1935): 273.

7. Martha S. Link, *The Pollen Path: A Collection of Navajo Myths* (Stanford: Stanford University Press, 1956).
8 O'Bryan, "Dine'," pp. 5, 7, 9–10.
9. Ibid.
10. Lakota informants, July 1982. See also William Powers, *Oglala Religion* (Lincoln: University of Nebraska Press, 1977).
11. For this admittedly generalized overview of American Indian religious values, I am indebted to traditionalist informants of many tribes, but especially those of the Lakotas. For a discussion of native religions see Dennis Tedlock, *Finding the Center* (New York: Dial Press, 1972); Ruth Underhill, *Red Man's Religion* (Chicago: University of Chicago Press, 1965); and Elsi Clews Parsons, *Pueblo Indian Religion* (Chicago: University of Chicago Press, 1939).
12. Alfred Kroeber, "The Arapaho," *Bulletin of the American Museum of Natural History 18* (1902–7): 19.
13. Parsons, "Zuni La' Mana," p. 525.
14. Alexander Maximilian, *Travels in the interior of North America, 1832–1834,* vol. 22 of *Early Western Travels,* ed. Reuben Gold Thwaites, 32 vols. (Cleveland: A. H. Clark, 1906), pp. 283–84, 354. Maximilian was quoted in German in the early homosexual rights book by Ferdinand Karsch-Haack, *Das Gleichgeschlechtliche Leben der Naturvölker* (The same-sex life of nature peoples) (Munich: Verlag von Ernst Reinhardt, 1911; reprinted New York: Arno Press, 1975), pp. 314, 564.
15. Oscar Koch, *Der Indianishe Eros* (Berlin: Verlag Continent, 1925), p. 61.
16. George Devereux, "Institutionalized Homosexuality of the Mohave Indians," *Human Biology 9* (1937): 509.
17. Ibid., p. 501
18. Ibid.
19. Ibid., pp. 508–9.
20. C. Daryll Forde, "Ethnography of the Yuma Indians," *University of California Publications in American Archaeology and Ethnology 28* (1931): 157.
21. Ruth Underhill, *Social Organization of the Papago Indians* (New York: Columbia University Press, 1938), p. 186. This story is also mentioned in Ruth Underhill, ed., *The Autobiography of a Papago Woman* (Menasha, Wisc.: American Anthropological Association, 1936), p. 39.
22. John Fire and Richard Erdoes, *Lame Deer, Seeker of Visions* (New York: Simon and Schuster, 1972), pp. 117, 149.
23. Theodore Stern, *The Klamath Tribe: A People and Their Reservation* (Seattle: University of Washington Press, 1965), pp. 20, 24; Theodore Stern, "Some Sources of Variability in Klamath Mythology,"*Journal of American Folklore 69* (1956): 242ff; Leshe Spier, *Klamath Ethnography* (Berkeley: University of California Press, 1930), p. 52.
24. Clark Wissler, "Societies and Ceremonial Associations in the Oglala Division of the Teton Dakota," *Anthoropological Papers of the american Museum of Natural History 11,* pt. 1 (1916): 92; Powers, *Oglala Religion,* pp. 57–59.
25. Ronnie Loud Hawk, Lakota informant 4, July 1982.
26. Terry Calling Eagle, Lakota informant 5, July 1982.
27. James S. Thayer, "The Berdache of the Northern Plains: A Socioreligious Perspective," *Journal of Anthropological Research 36* (1980): 289.
28. Fletcher, "Elk Mystery," p. 281.
29. Alice Fletcher and Francis La Flesche, "The Omaha Tribe," *Bureau of American Ethnology Annual Report 27* (1905–6): 132.
30. Harriet Whitehead offers a valuable discussion of this element of the vision quest in "The Bow and the Burden Strap: A New Look at Institutionalized Homosexuality in Native North America," in *Sexual Meanings,* ed. Sherry Ortner and Harriet Whitehead (Cambridge: Cambridge University Press, 1981), pp. 99–102. See also Erikson, "Childhood," p. 329.

A Woman's Curse?

Why do cultures the world over treat menstruating women as taboo? An anthropologist offers a new answer—and a challenge to Western ideas about contraception

MEREDITH F. SMALL

The passage from girlhood to womanhood is marked by a flow of blood from the uterus. Without elaborate ceremony, often without discussion, girls know that when they begin to menstruate, their world is changed forever. For the next thirty years or so, they will spend much energy having babies, or trying not to, reminded at each menstruation that either way, the biology of reproduction has a major impact on their lives.

Anthropologists have underscored the universal importance of menstruation by documenting how the event is interwoven into the ideology as well as the daily activities of cultures around the world. The customs attached to menstruation take peculiarly negative forms: the so-called menstrual taboos. Those taboos may prohibit a woman from having sex with her husband or from cooking for him. They may bar her from visiting sacred places or taking part in sacred activities. They may forbid her to touch certain items used by men, such as hunting gear or weapons, or to eat certain foods or to wash at certain times. They may also require that a woman paint her face red or wear a red hip cord, or that she segregate herself in a special hut while she is menstruating. In short, the taboos set menstruating women apart from the rest of their society, marking them as impure and polluting.

Anthropologists have studied menstrual taboos for decades, focusing on the negative symbolism of the rituals as a cultural phenomenon. Perhaps, suggested one investigator, taking a Freudian perspective, such taboos reflect the anxiety that men feel about castration, an anxiety that would be prompted by women's genital bleeding. Others have suggested that the taboos serve to prevent menstrual odor from interfering with hunting, or that they protect men from microorganisms that might otherwise be transferred during sexual intercourse with a menstruating woman. Until recently, few investigators had considered the possibility that the taboos—and the very fact of menstruation—might instead exist because they conferred an evolutionary advantage.

In the mid-1980s the anthropologist Beverly I. Strassmann of the University of Michigan in Ann Arbor began to study the ways men and women have evolved to accomplish (and regulate) reproduction. Unlike traditional anthropologists, who focus on how culture affects human behavior, Strassmann was convinced that the important role played by biology was being neglected. Menstruation, she suspected, would be a key for observing and understanding the interplay of biology and culture in human reproductive behavior.

To address the issue, Strassmann decided to seek a culture in which making babies was an ongoing part of adult life. For that she had to get away from industrialized countries, with their bias toward contraception and low birthrates. In a "natural-fertility population," she reasoned, she could more clearly see the connection between the physiology of women and the strategies men and women use to exploit that physiology for their own reproductive ends.

Strassmann ended up in a remote corner of West Africa, living in close quarters with the Dogon, a traditional society whose indigenous religion of ancestor worship requires that menstruating women spend their nights at a small hut. For more than two years Strassmann kept track of the women staying at the hut, and she confirmed the menstruations by testing urine samples for the appropriate hormonal changes. In so doing, she amassed the first long-term data describing how a traditional society appropriates a physiological event—menstruation—and refracts that event through a prism of behaviors and beliefs.

What she found explicitly challenges the conclusions of earlier investigators about the cultural function of menstrual taboos. For the Dogon men, she discovered, enforcing visits to the menstrual hut serves to channel parental resources into the upbringing of their own children. But more, Strassmann, who also had training as a reproductive physiologist, proposed a new theory of why menstruation itself evolved as it did—and again, the answer is essentially a story of conserving resources. Finally, her observations pose provocative questions about women's health in industrialized societies, raising serious doubts about the tactics favored by Western medicine for developing contraceptive technology.

Menstruation is the visible stage of the ovarian cycle, orchestrated primarily by hormones secreted by the ovaries: progesterone and a family of hormones called estrogens. At the beginning of each cycle (by convention, the first day of a woman's period) the levels of the estrogens begin to rise. After about five days, as their concentrations increase, they cause the blood- and nutrient-rich inner lining of the uterus, called the endometrium, to thicken and acquire a densely branching network of blood vessels. At about the middle of the cycle, ovulation takes place, and an egg makes its way from one of the two ovaries down one of the paired fallopian tubes to the uterus. The follicle from which the egg was released in the ovary now begins to secrete progesterone as well as estrogens, and the progesterone causes the endometrium to swell and become even richer with blood vessels—in short, fully ready for a pregnancy, should conception take place and the fertilized egg become implanted.

If conception does take place, the levels of estrogens and progesterone continue to rise throughout the pregnancy. That keeps the endometrium thick enough to support the quickening life inside the uterus. When the baby is born and the new mother begins nursing, the estrogens and progesterone fall to their initial levels, and lactation hormones keep them suppressed. The uterus thus lies quiescent until frequent lactation ends, which triggers the return to ovulation.

If conception does not take place after ovulation, all the ovarian hormones also drop to their initial levels, and menstruation—the shedding of part of the uterine lining—begins. The lining is divided into three layers: a basal layer that is constantly maintained, and two superficial layers, which shed and regrow with each menstrual cycle. All mammals undergo cyclical changes in the state of the endometrium. In most mammals the sloughed-off layers are resorbed into the body if fertilization does not take place. But in some higher primates, including humans, some of the shed endometrium is not resorbed. The shed lining, along with some blood, flows from the body through the vaginal opening, a process that in humans typically lasts from three to five days.

Of course, physiological facts alone do not explain why so many human groups have infused a bodily function with symbolic meaning. And so in 1986 Strassmann found herself driving through the Sahel region of West Africa at the peak of the hot season, heading for a sandstone cliff called the Bandiagara Escarpment, in Mali. There, permanent Dogon villages of mud or stone houses dotted the rocky plateau. The menstrual huts were obvious: round, low-roofed buildings set apart from the rectangular dwellings of the rest of the village.

The Dogon are a society of millet and onion farmers who endorse polygyny, and they maintain their traditional culture despite the occasional visits of outsiders. In a few Dogon villages, in fact, tourists are fairly common, and ethnographers had frequently studied the Dogon language, religion and social structure before Strassmann's arrival. But her visit was the first time someone from the outside wanted to delve into an intimate issue in such detail.

It took Strassmann a series of hikes among villages, and long talks with male elders under the thatched-roof shelters where they typically gather, to find the appropriate sites for her research. She gained permission for her study in fourteen villages, eventually choosing two. That exceptional welcome, she thinks, emphasized the universality of her interests. "I'm working on all the things that really matter to [the Dogon]—fertility, economics—so they never questioned my motives or wondered why I would be interested in these things," she says. "It seemed obvious to them." She set up shop for the next two and a half years in a stone house in the village, with no running water or electricity. Eating the daily fare of the Dogon, millet porridge, she and a research assistant began to integrate themselves into village life, learning the language, getting to know people and tracking visits to the menstrual huts.

Following the movements of menstruating women was surprisingly easy. The menstrual huts are situated outside the walled compounds of the village, but in full view of the men's thatched-roof shelters. As the men relax under their shelters, they can readily see who leaves the huts in the morning and returns to them in the evening. And as nonmenstruating women pass the huts on their way to and from the fields or to other compounds, they too can see who is spending the night there. Strassmann found that when she left her house in the evening to take data, any of the villagers could accurately predict whom she would find in the menstrual huts.

The huts themselves are cramped, dark buildings—hardly places where a woman might go to escape the drudgery of work or to avoid an argument with her husband or a co-wife. The huts sometimes become so crowded that some occupants are forced outside—making the women even more conspicuous. Although babies and toddlers can go with their mothers to the huts, the women consigned there are not allowed to spend time with the rest of their families. They must cook with special pots, not their usual household possessions. Yet they are still expected to do their usual jobs, such as working in the fields.

> Why, Strassmann wondered, would anyone put up with such conditions?

The answer, for the Dogon, is that a menstruating woman is a threat to the sanctity of religious altars, where men pray and make sacrifices for the protection of their fields, their families and their village. If menstruating women come near the altars, which are situated both indoors and outdoors, the Dogon believe that their aura of pollution will ruin the altars and bring calamities upon the village. The belief is so ingrained that the women themselves have internalized it, feeling its burden of responsibility and potential guilt. Thus violations of the taboo are rare, because a menstruating woman who breaks the rules knows that she is personally responsible if calamities occur.

Nevertheless, Strassmann still thought a more functional explanation for menstrual taboos might also exist, one closely related to reproduction. As she was well aware, even before her studies among the Dogon, people around the world have a fairly sophisticated view of how reproduction works. In general, people everywhere know full well that menstruation signals the absence of a pregnancy and the possibility of another one. More precisely, Strassmann could frame her hypothesis by reasoning as follows: Across cultures, men and women recognize that a lack of menstrual cycling in a woman implies she is either pregnant, lactating or menopausal. Moreover, at least among natural-fertility cultures that do not practice birth control, continual cycles during peak reproductive years imply to people in those cultures that a woman is sterile. Thus, even though people might not be able to pinpoint ovulation, they can easily identify whether a woman will soon be ready to conceive on the basis of whether she is menstruating. And that leads straight to Strassmann's insightful hypothesis about the role of menstrual taboos: information about menstruation can be a means of tracking paternity.

"There are two important pieces of information for assessing paternity," Strassmann notes: timing of intercourse and timing of menstruation. "By forcing women to signal menstruation, men are trying to gain equal access to one part of that critical information." Such information, she explains, is crucial to Dogon men, because they invest so many resources in their own offspring. Descent is marked through the male line; land and the food that comes from the land is passed down from fathers to sons. Information about paternity is thus crucial to a man's entire lineage. And because each man has as many as four wives, he cannot possibly track them all. So forcing women to signal their menstrual periods, or lack thereof, helps men avoid cuckoldry.

To test her hypothesis, Strassmann tracked residence in the menstrual huts for 736 consecutive days, collecting data on 477 complete cycles. She noted who was at each hut and how long each woman stayed. She also collected urine from ninety-three women over a ten-week period, to check the correlation between residence in the menstrual hut and the fact of menstruation.

The combination of ethnographic records and urinalyses showed that the Dogon women mostly play by the rules. In 86 percent of the hormonally detected menstruations, women went to the hut. Moreover, none of the tested women went to the hut when they were not menstruating. In the remaining 14 percent of the tested menstruations, women stayed home from the hut, in violation of the taboo, but some were near menopause and so not at high risk for pregnancy. More important, none of the women who violated the taboo did it twice in a row. Even they were largely willing to comply.

Thus, Strassmann concluded, the huts do indeed convey a fairly reliable signal, to men and to everyone else, about the status of a woman's fertility. When she leaves the hut, she is considered ready to conceive. When she stops going to the hut, she is evidently pregnant or menopausal. And women of prime reproductive age who visit the hut on a regular basis are clearly infertile.

It also became clear to Strassmann that the Dogon do indeed use that information to make paternity decisions. In several cases a man was forced to marry a pregnant woman, simply because everyone knew that the man had been the woman's first sexual partner after her last visit to the menstrual hut. Strassmann followed one case in which a child was being brought up by a man because he was the mother's first sexual partner after a hut visit, even though the woman soon married a different man. (The woman already knew she was pregnant by the first man at the time of her marriage, and she did not visit the menstrual hut before she married. Thus the truth was obvious to everyone, and the real father took the child.)

In general, women are cooperative players in the game because without a man, a woman has no way to support herself or her children. But women follow the taboo reluctantly. They complain about going to the hut. And if their husbands convert from the traditional religion of the Dogon to a religion that does not impose menstrual taboos, such as Islam or Christianity, the women quickly cease visiting the hut. Not that such a religious conversion quells a man's interest in his wife's fidelity: far from it. But the rules change. Perhaps the sanctions of the new religion against infidelity help keep women faithful, so the men can relax their guard. Or perhaps the men are willing to trade the reproductive advantages of the menstrual taboo for the economic benefits gained by converting to the new religion. Whatever the case, Strassmann found an almost perfect correlation between a husband's religion and his wives' attendance at the hut. In sum, the taboo is established by men, backed by supernatural forces, and internalized and accepted by women until the men release them from the belief.

But beyond the cultural machinations of men and women that Strassmann expected to find, her data show something even more fundamental—and surprising—about female biology. On average, she calculates, a woman in a natural-fertility population such as the Dogon has only about 110 menstrual periods in her lifetime. The rest of the time she will be prepubescent, pregnant, lactating or menopausal. Women in industrialized cultures, by contrast, have more than three times as many cycles: 350 to 400, on average, in a lifetime. They reach menarche (their first menstruation) earlier—at age twelve and a half, compared with the onset age of sixteen in natural-fertility cultures. They have fewer babies, and they lactate hardly at all. All those factors lead women in the industrialized world to a lifetime of nearly continuous menstrual cycling.

The big contrast in cycling profiles during the reproductive years can be traced specifically to lactation. Women in more traditional societies spend most of their reproductive years in lactation amenorrhea, the state in which the hormonal changes required for nursing suppress ovulation and inhibit menstruation. And it is not just that the Dogon bear more children (eight to nine on average); they also nurse each child on demand rather than in scheduled bouts, all through the night as well as the day, and intensely enough that ovulation simply stops for about twenty months per child. Women in industrialized societies typically do not breast-feed as intensely (or at all), and rarely breast-feed each child for as long as the Dogon women do. (The average for American women is four months.)

The Dogon experience with menstruation may be far more typical of the human condition over most of evolutionary history than is the standard menstrual experience in industrialized nations. If so, Strassmann's findings alter some of the most closely held beliefs about female biology. Contrary to what the Western medical establishment might think, it is not particularly "normal" to menstruate each month. The female body, according to Strassmann, is biologically designed to spend much more time in lactation amenorrhea than in menstrual cycling. That in itself suggests that oral contraceptives, which alter hormone levels to suppress ovulation and produce a bleeding, could be forcing a continual state of cycling for which the body is ill-prepared. Women might be better protected against reproductive cancers if their contraceptives mimicked lactation amenorrhea and depressed the female reproductive hormones, rather than forcing the continual ebb and flow of menstrual cycles.

Strassmann's data also call into question a recently popularized idea about menstruation: that regular menstrual cycles might be immunologically beneficial for women. In 1993 the controversial writer Margie Profet, whose ideas about evolutionary and reproductive biology have received vast media attention, proposed in *The Quarterly Review of Biology* that menstruation could have such an adaptive value. She noted that viruses and bacteria regularly enter the female body on the backs of sperm, and she hypothesized that the best way to get them out is to flush them out. Here, then, was a positive, adaptive role for something unpleasant, an evolutionary reason for suffering cramps each month. Menstruation, according to Profet, had evolved to rid the body of pathogens. The "anti-pathogen" theory was an exciting hypothesis, and it helped win Profet a MacArthur Foundation award. But Strassmann's work soon showed that Profet's ideas could not be supported because of one simple fact: under less-industrialized conditions, women menstruate relatively rarely.

Instead, Strassmann notes, if there is an adaptive value to menstruation, it is ultimately a strategy to conserve the body's resources. She estimates that maintaining the endometrial lining during the second half of the ovarian cycle takes substantial metabolic energy. Once the endometrium is built up and ready to receive a fertilized egg, the tissue requires a sevenfold metabolic increase to remain rich in blood and ready to support a pregnancy. Hence, if no pregnancy is forthcoming, it makes a lot of sense for the body to let part of the endometrium slough off and then regenerate itself, instead of maintaining that rather costly but unneeded tissue. Such energy conservation is common among vertebrates: male rhesus monkeys have shrunken testes during their nonbreeding season, Burmese pythons shrink their guts when they are not digesting, and hibernating animals put their metabolisms on hold.

Strassmann also suggests that periodically ridding oneself of the endometrium could make a difference to a woman's long-term survival. Because female reproductive hormones affect the brain and other tissues, the metabolism of the entire body is involved during cycling. Strassmann estimates that by keeping hormonal low through half the cycle, a woman can save about six days' worth of energy for every four nonconceptive cycles. Such caloric conservation might have proved useful to early hominids who lived by hunting and gathering, and even today it might be helpful for women living in less affluent circumstances than the ones common in the industrialized West.

But perhaps the most provocative implications of Strassmann's work have to do with women's health. In 1994 a group of physicians and anthropologists published a paper, also in *The Quarterly Review of Biology*, suggesting that the reproductive histories and lifestyles of women in industrialized cultures are at odds with women's naturally evolved biology, and that the differences lead to greater risks of reproductive cancers. For example, the investigators estimated that women in affluent cultures may have a hundredfold greater risk of breast cancer than do women who subsist by hunting and gathering. The increased risk is probably caused not only by low levels of exercise and a high-fat diet, but also by a relatively high number of menstrual cycles over a lifetime. Repeated exposure to the hormones of the ovarian cycle—because of early menarche, late menopause, lack of pregnancy and little or no breast-feeding—is implicated in other reproductive cancers as well.

Those of us in industrialized cultures have been running an experiment on ourselves. The body evolved over millions of years to move across the landscape looking for food, to live in small kin-based groups, to make babies at intervals of four years or so and to invest heavily in each child by nursing intensely for years. How many women now follow those traditional patterns? We move little, we rely on others to get our food, and we rarely reproduce or lactate. Those culturally initiated shifts in lifestyles may pose biological risks.

Our task is not to overcome that biology, but to work with it. Now that we have a better idea of how the female body was designed, it may be time to rework our lifestyles and change some of our expectations. It may be time to borrow from our distant past or from our contemporaries in distant cultures, and treat our bodies more as nature intended.

Meredith F. Small is a professor of anthropology at Cornell University in Ithaca, New York. Her latest book, *Our Babies, Ourselves: How Biology And Culture Shape The Way We Parent,* was published in May 1998 [see Laurence A. Marschall's review in *Books in Brief*, November/December 1998].

When Brothers Share a Wife

Among Tibetans, the good life relegates many women to spinsterhood.

MELVYN C. GOLDSTEIN

Eager to reach home, Dorje drives his yaks hard over the 17,000-foot mountain pass, stopping only once to rest. He and his two older brothers, Pema and Sonam, are jointly marrying a woman from the next village in a few weeks, and he has to help with the preparations.

Dorje, Pema, and Sonam are Tibetans living in Limi, a 200-square-mile area in the northwest corner of Nepal, across the border from Tibet. The form of marriage they are about to enter—fraternal polyandry in anthropological parlance—is one of the world's rarest forms of marriage but is not uncommon in Tibetan society, where it has been practiced from time immemorial. For many Tibetan social strata, it traditionally represented the ideal form of marriage and family.

The mechanics of fraternal polyandry are simple. Two, three, four, or more brothers jointly take a wife, who leaves her home to come and live with them. Traditionally, marriage was arranged by parents, with children, particularly females, having little or no say. This is changing somewhat nowadays, but it is still unusual for children to marry without their parents' consent. Marriage ceremonies vary by income and region and range from all the brothers sitting together as grooms to only the eldest one formally doing so. The age of the brothers plays an important role in determining this: very young brothers almost never participate in actual marriage ceremonies, although they typically join the marriage when they reach their midteens.

The eldest brother is normally dominant in terms of authority, that is, in managing the household, but all the brothers share the work and participate as sexual partners. Tibetan males and females do not find the sexual aspect of sharing a spouse the least bit unusual, repulsive, or scandalous, and the norm is for the wife to treat all the brothers the same.

Offspring are treated similarly. There is no attempt to link children biologically to particular brothers, and a brother shows no favoritism toward his child even if he knows he is the real father because, for example, his other brothers were away at the time the wife became pregnant. The children, in turn, consider all of the brothers as their fathers and treat them equally, even if they also know who is their real father. In some regions children use the term "father" for the eldest brother and "father's brother" for the others, while in other areas they call all the brothers by one term, modifying this by the use of "elder" and "younger."

Unlike our own society, where monogamy is the only form of marriage permitted, Tibetan society allows a variety of marriage types, including monogamy, fraternal polyandry, and polygyny. Fraternal polyandry and monogamy are the most common forms of marriage, while polygyny typically occurs in cases where the first wife is barren. The widespread practice of fraternal polyandry, therefore, is not the outcome of a law requiring brothers to marry jointly. There is choice, and in fact, divorce traditionally was relatively simple in Tibetan society. If a brother in a polyandrous marriage became dissatisfied and wanted to separate, he simply left the main house and set up his own household. In such cases, all the children stayed in the main household with the remaining brother(s), even if the departing brother was known to be the real father of one or more of the children.

The Tibetans' own explanation for choosing fraternal polyandry is materialistic. For example, when I asked Dorje why he decided to marry with his two brothers rather than take his own wife, he thought for a moment, then said it prevented the division of his family's farm (and animals) and thus facilitated all of them achieving a higher standard of living. And when I later asked Dorje's bride whether it wasn't difficult for her to cope with three brothers as husbands, she laughed and echoed the rationale of avoiding fragmentation of the family and land, adding that she expected to be better off economically, since she would have three husbands working for her and her children.

Exotic as it may seem to Westerners, Tibetan fraternal polyandry is thus in many ways analogous to the way primogeniture functioned in nineteenth-century England. Primogeniture dictated that the eldest son inherited the family estate, while younger sons had to leave home and seek their own employment—for example, in the military or the clergy. Primogeniture maintained family estates intact over generations by permitting only one heir per generation. Fraternal polyandry also accomplishes this but does so by keeping all the brothers together with just one wife so that there is only one *set* of heirs per generation.

While Tibetans believe that in this way fraternal polyandry reduces the risk of family fission, monogamous marriages among brothers need not necessarily precipitate the division of the family estate: brothers could continue to live together, and the family land could continue to be worked jointly. When I asked Tibetans about this, however, they invariably responded that such joint families are unstable because each wife is primarily oriented to her own children and interested in their success and well-being over that of the children of the other wives. For example, if the youngest brother's wife had three sons while the eldest brother's wife had only one daughter, the wife of the youngest brother might begin to demand more resources for her children since, as males, they represent the future of the family. Thus, the children from different wives in the same generation are competing sets of heirs, and this makes such families inherently unstable. Tibetans perceive that conflict will spread from the wives to their husbands and consider this likely to cause family fission. Consequently, it is almost never done.

Although Tibetans see an economic advantage to fraternal polyandry, they do not value the sharing of a wife as an end in itself. On the contrary, they articulate a number of problems inherent in the practice. For example, because authority is customarily exercised by the eldest brother, his younger male siblings have to subordinate themselves with little hope of changing their status within the family. When these younger brothers are aggressive and individualistic, tensions and difficulties often occur despite there being only one set of heirs.

In addition, tension and conflict may arise in polyandrous families because of sexual favoritism. The bride normally sleeps with the eldest brother, and the two have the responsibility to see to it that the other males have opportunities for sexual access. Since the Tibetan subsistence economy requires males to travel a lot, the temporary absence of one or more brothers facilitates this, but there are also other rotation practices. The cultural ideal unambiguously calls for the wife to show equal affection and sexuality to each of the brothers (and vice versa), but deviations from this ideal occur, especially when there is a sizable difference in age between the partners in the marriage.

Dorje's family represents just such a potential situation. He is fifteen years old and his two older brothers are twenty-five and twenty-two years old. The new bride is twenty-three years old, eight years Dorje's senior. Sometimes such a bride finds the youngest husband immature and adolescent and does not treat him with equal affection; alternatively, she may find his youth attractive and lavish special attention on him. Apart from that consideration, when a younger male like Dorje grows up, he may consider his wife "ancient" and prefer the company of a woman his own age or younger. Consequently, although men and women do not find the idea of sharing a bride or bridegroom repulsive, individual likes and dislikes can cause familial discord.

Two reasons have commonly been offered for the perpetuation of fraternal polyandry in Tibet: that Tibetans practice female infanticide and therefore have to marry polyandrously, owing to a shortage of females; and that Tibet, lying at extremely high altitudes, is so barren and bleak that Tibetans would starve without resort to this mechanism. A Jesuit who lived in Tibet during the eighteenth century articulated this second view: "One reason for this most odious custom is the sterility of the soil, and the small amount of land that can be cultivated owing to the lack of water. The crops may suffice if the brothers all live together, but if they form separate families they would be reduced to beggary."

Both explanations are wrong, however. Not only has there never been institutionalized female infanticide in Tibet, but Tibetan society gives females considerable rights, including inheriting the family estate in the absence of brothers. In such cases, the woman takes a bridegroom who comes to live in her family and adopts her family's name and identity. Moreover, there is no demographic evidence of a shortage of females. In Limi, for example, there were (in 1974) sixty females and fifty-three males in the fifteen- to thirty-five-year age category, and many adult females were unmarried.

The second reason is also incorrect. The climate in Tibet is extremely harsh, and ecological factors do play a major role perpetuating polyandry, but polyandry is not a means of preventing starvation. It is characteristic, not of the poorest segments of the society, but rather of the peasant landowning families.

In the old society, the landless poor could not realistically aspire to prosperity, but they did not fear starvation. There was a persistent labor shortage throughout Tibet, and very poor families with little or no land and few animals could subsist through agricultural labor, tenant farming, craft occupations such as carpentry, or by working as servants. Although the per person family income could increase somewhat if brothers married polyandrously and pooled their wages, in the absence of inheritable land, the advantage of fraternal polyandry was not generally sufficient to prevent them from setting up their own households. A more skilled or energetic younger brother could do as well or better alone, since he would completely control his income and would not have to share it with his siblings. Consequently, while there was and is some polyandry among the poor, it is much less frequent and more prone to result in divorce and family fission.

An alternative reason for the persistence of fraternal polyandry is that it reduces population growth (and thereby reduces the pressure on resources) by relegating some females to lifetime spinsterhood. Fraternal polyandrous marriages in Limi (in 1974) averaged 2.35 men per woman, and not surprisingly, 31 percent of the females of child-bearing age (twenty to forty-nine) were unmarried. These spinsters either continued to live at home, set up their own households, or worked as servants for other families. They could also become Buddhist nuns. Being unmarried is not synonymous with exclusion from the reproductive pool. Discreet extramarital relationships are tolerated, and actually half of the adult unmarried women in Limi had one or more children. They raised these children as single mothers, working for wages or weaving cloth and blankets for sale. As a group, however, the unmarried woman had far fewer offspring than the married women, averaging only 0.7 children per woman, compared with 3.3 for married women, whether polyandrous, monogamous, or polygynous. While polyandry helps regulate population, this function of polyandry is not consciously perceived by Tibetans and is not the reason they consistently choose it.

If neither a shortage of females nor the fear of starvation perpetuates fraternal polyandry, what motivates brothers, particularly younger brothers, to opt for this system of marriage? From the perspective of the younger brother in a landholding family, the main incentive is the attainment or maintenance of the good life. With polyandry, he can expect a more secure and higher standard of living, with access not only to this family's land and animals but also to its inherited collection of clothes, jewelry, rugs, saddles, and horses. In addition, he will experience less work pressure and much greater security because all responsibility does not fall on one "father." For Tibetan brothers, the question is whether to trade off the greater personal freedom inherent in monogamy for the real or potential economic security, affluence, and social prestige associated with life in a larger, labor-rich polyandrous family.

A brother thinking of separating from his polyandrous marriage and taking his own wife would face various disadvantages. Although in the majority of Tibetan regions all brothers theoretically have rights to their family's estate, in reality Tibetans are reluctant to divide their land into small fragments. Generally, a younger brother who insists on leaving the family will receive only a small plot of land, if that. Because of its power and wealth, the rest of the family usually can block any attempt of the younger brother to increase his share of land through litigation. Moreover, a younger brother may not even get a house and cannot expect to receive much above the minimum in terms of movable possessions, such as furniture, pots, and pans. Thus, a brother contemplating going it on his own must plan on achieving economic security and the good life not through inheritance but through his own work.

The obvious solution for younger brothers—creating new fields from virgin land—is generally not a feasible option. Most Tibetan populations live at high altitudes (above 12,000 feet), where arable land is extremely scarce. For example, in Dorje's village, agriculture ranges only from about 12,900 feet, the lowest point in the area, to 13,300 feet. Above that altitude, early frost and snow destroy the staple barley crop. Furthermore, because of the low rainfall caused by the Himalayan rain shadow, many areas in Tibet and northern Nepal that are within the appropriate altitude range for agriculture have no reliable sources of irrigation. In the end, although there is plenty of unused land in such areas, most of it is either too high or too arid.

Even where unused land capable of being farmed exists, clearing the land and building the substantial terraces necessary for irrigation constitute a great undertaking. Each plot has to be completely dug out to a depth of two to two and half feet so that the large rocks and boulders can be removed. At best, a man might be able to bring a few new fields under cultivation in the first years after separating from his brothers, but he could not expect to acquire substantial amounts of arable land this way.

In addition, because of the limited farmland, the Tibetan subsistence economy characteristically includes a strong emphasis on animal husbandry. Tibetan farmers regularly maintain cattle, yaks, goats, and sheep, grazing them in the areas too high for agriculture. These herds produce wool, milk, cheese, butter, meat, and skins. To obtain these resources, however, shepherds must accompany the animals on a daily basis. When first setting up a monogamous household, a younger brother like Dorje would find it difficult to both farm and manage animals.

In traditional Tibetan society, there was an even more critical factor that operated to perpetuate fraternal polyandry—a form of hereditary servitude somewhat analogous to serfdom in Europe. Peasants were tied to large estates held by aristocrats, monasteries, and the Lhasa government. They were allowed the use of some farmland to produce their own subsistence but were required to provide taxes in kind and corvée (free labor) to their lords. The corvée was a substantial hardship, since a peasant household was in many cases required to furnish the lord with one laborer daily for most of the year and more on specific occasions such as the harvest. This enforced labor, along with the lack of new land and ecological pressure to pursue both agriculture and animal husbandry, made polyandrous families particularly beneficial. The polyandrous family allowed an internal division of adult labor, maximizing economic advantage. For example, while the wife worked the family fields, one brother could perform the lord's corvée, another could look after the animals, and a third could engage in trade.

Although social scientists often discount other people's explanations of why they do things, in the case of Tibetan fraternal polyandry, such explanations are very close to the truth. The custom, however, is very sensitive to changes in its political and economic milieu and, not surprisingly, is in decline in most Tibetan areas. Made less important by the elimination of the traditional serf-based economy, it is disparaged by the dominant non-Tibetan leaders of India, China, and Nepal. New opportunities for economic and social mobility in these countries, such as the tourist trade and government employment, are also eroding the rationale for polyandry, and so it may vanish within the next generation.

Melvyn C. Goldstein, now a professor of anthropology at Case Western Reserve University in Cleveland, has been interested in the Tibetan practice of fraternal polyandry (several brothers marrying one wife) since he was a graduate student in the 1960s.

29

How Many Fathers Are Best for a Child?

Meredith F. Small

Anthropologists study systems of kinship and marriage in many societies for three reasons: first, these issues are very important to the people themselves; second, kinship and marriage are keys for understanding how contemporary cultures work; and finally, because they give us clues as to what patterns of family organization may have existed over the course of human history. As a great deal of anthropological research has revealed, diverse cultures have many different ways of organizing families.

In the United States, we often think of the "traditional" family as a nuclear family: two married parents with their children. Many people ethnocentrically believe that this is the normal or natural family system. Other types of family organization, such as "blended" families, are often described as recent variants. But in fact, the nuclear family model is just one of the many types of kinship organization humans have used at present and in the past—and it is only a relatively recent development in the broader context of human history.

This selection describes a pattern in some South American societies, in which a woman has intercourse with two or more men during her pregnancy and the resulting child is considered as having multiple fathers. This kinship system, like many others across the world, is quite different from the American model of a "traditional" family. However, as this selection argues, this arrangement helps improve children's likelihood of survival in Barí social communities. In the United States, social scientists have shown that having a father present is beneficial for children's development.

As you read this selection, ask yourself the following questions:

- If one father is good, are two or more better? How many fathers are best for a child?
- Why do the Barí believe a child can have more than one father?
- How do Barí women justify taking lovers during pregnancy?
- From an evolutionary perspective, what is the ideal number of fathers for a child to have in Barí society? Why?
- How is the Barí system similar to and different from the system of frequent divorce and court-enforced "child support" payments in modern American society?

The following terms discussed in this selection are included in the Glossary at the back of the book:

multiple paternity
nuclear family
paleoanthropology

Anthropologist Stephen Beckerman was well into his forties before he finally understood how babies are made. He had thought, as most people do, that a sperm from one man and an egg from one woman joined to make a child. But one summer day, as he and his colleague Roberto Lizarralde lounged around in hammocks, chatting with Rachel, an elderly woman of the Barí tribe of Venezuela, she pointed out his error. Babies, she explained, can easily have more than one biological father. "My first husband was the father of my first child, my second child, and my third child," Rachel said, recalling her life. "But the fourth child, actually, he has two fathers." It was clear that Rachel didn't mean there was a stepfather hanging around or a friendly uncle who took the kid fishing every weekend. She was simply explaining the Barí version of conception to these ignorant anthropologists: A fetus is built up over time with repeated washes of sperm—which means, of course, that more than one man can contribute to the endeavor.

Small, Meredith F. "How Many Fathers Are Best for a Child?" Discover Magazine (March 2003):54–61. Reprinted with permission of the author.

This interview changed not only the way Beckerman and Lizarralde viewed Barí families but also brought into question the very way that anthropologists portray human coupling. If biological fatherhood can be shared—an idea accepted by many indigenous groups across South America and in many other cultures across the globe—then the nuclear family with one mom and one dad might not be the established blueprint for a family that we have been led to expect. If so, the familiar story of traditional human mating behavior, in which man the hunter brings home the bacon to his faithful wife, loses credibility. And if the Barí and other groups work perfectly well with more flexible family styles, the variety of family structures that are increasingly common in Western culture these days—everything from single-parent households to blended families—may not be as dangerous to the social fabric as we are led to believe. People in this culture may simply be exercising the same family options that humans have had for millions of years, options that have been operating in other cultures while the West took a stricter view of what constitutes a family.

Stephen Beckerman folds his 6-foot-4-inch frame into a chair and turns to the mountainous topography of papers on his desk at Pennsylvania State University. Once he manages to locate a map under all the piles, he points to a spot on the border between Venezuela and Colombia where he spent 20 years, off and on, with the indigenous Barí Indians.

The traditional Barí culture, Beckerman explains, has come under attack by outside forces, starting with the conquistadors who arrived in the early sixteenth century. Today Catholic missionaries interact with the Barí, coal and oil companies are trying to seize their land, and drug traffickers and guerrillas are threats. Western influences are apparent: Most families have moved from traditional longhouses to single-family dwellings, and everyone wears modern Western clothes and uses Western goods. However, the Barí continue to practice their traditions of manioc farming, fishing, and hunting, according to Roberto Lizarralde, an anthropologist at the Central University of Venezuela who has been visiting the Barí regularly since 1960. Lizarralde also says that the Barí still have great faith in traditional spirits and ancestral wisdom, including their notion that a child can have multiple biological fathers.

The Barí believe that the first act of sex, which should always be between a husband and wife, plants the seed. Then the fledgling fetus must be nourished by repeated anointings of semen; the woman's body is viewed as a vessel where men do all the work. "One of the reasons women give you for taking lovers is that they don't want to wear out their husbands," Beckerman says. "They claim it's hard work for men to support a pregnancy by having enough sex, and so lovers can help." Just look, the Barí say. Women grow fat during a pregnancy, while men grow thin from all their work.

Anthropologists study a culture's ideas about conception because those ideas have a profound impact on the way people run their lives. In our culture, for example, conceiving children incurs long-term economic responsibility for both the mother and father. We take this obligation so seriously that when a parent fails to provide for a child, it is usually a violation of law. In the Barí system, when a man is named as a secondary biological father he is also placed under an obligation to the mother and the child. In addition, he is expected to give gifts of fish and game. These gifts are a significant burden because the man must also provide for his own wife and primary children.

Beckerman and his colleagues have discovered that naming secondary fathers has evolutionary consequences. A team of ethnographers led by Beckerman, Roberto Lizarralde, and his son Manuel, an anthropologist at Connecticut College who has been visiting the Barí since he was 5 years old, interviewed 114 Barí women past childbearing years and asked them about their full reproductive histories. "These interviews were a lot of fun," Beckerman says, laughing. "Randy old ladies talking about their lovers." In total, the researchers recorded claims of 916 pregnancies, an average of eight pregnancies for each woman. But child mortality was high—about one-third of the children did not survive to age 15. Naming secondary fathers was a critical factor in predicting which babies made it to adulthood. Secondary fathers were involved in 25 percent of pregnancies, and the team determined that two fathers were the ideal number. Children with one father and one secondary father made it to their teens most often; kids with only one father or those with more than two fathers didn't fare as well. The researchers also found that this decrease in mortality occurred not during the child's life but during fetal development: Women were less likely to have a miscarriage or stillbirth if they had a husband and an additional male contributing food. This result was a surprise because researchers had expected that help during childhood would be more important. "The Barí are not hungry; they are not close to the bone. But it must be the extra fat and protein that they get from secondary fathers during gestation that makes the difference," Beckerman explains as he points to photographs of Barí women who look well nourished, even downright plump.

Barí women seem to use this more flexible system of paternity when they need it. Within families, some children have secondary fathers, while their siblings belong to the husband alone. The team discovered that mothers are more likely to take on a secondary father when a previous child has died in infancy. Manuel Lizarralde claims the strategy makes perfect sense, given the Barí belief that the best way to cure a sick child is for the father to blow tobacco smoke over the child's body. "It is easy to imagine a bereaved mother thinking to herself that if she had only provided a secondary father and so more smoke for her dead child, she might have saved him—and vowing to provide that benefit for her next child."

Beckerman says extra fathers may have always been insurance for uncertain times: "Because the Barí were once hunted as if they were game animals—by other Indians, conquistadors, oilmen, farmers, and ranchers—the odds of a woman being widowed when she still had young children were one in three, according to data we gathered about the years 1930 to 1960. The men as well as the women knew this. None of these guys can go down the street to Mutual of Omaha and buy a life insurance policy. By allowing his wife to take a lover, the husband is doing all he can to ensure the survival of his children."

Barí women are also freer to do as they wish because men need their labor—having a wife is an economic necessity because women do the manioc farming, harvesting, and cooking, while men hunt and fish. "The sexual division of labor is such that you can't make it without a member of the opposite sex," says Beckerman. Initially, the researchers worried that jealousy on the part of husbands would make Barí women reticent about discussing multiple sexual partners. "In our first interviews, we would wait until the husband was out of the house," says Beckerman. "But one day we interviewed an old couple who were enjoying thinking about their lives; they were lying in their hammocks, side by side, and it was obvious he wasn't going anywhere. So we went down the list of her children and asked about other fathers. She said no, no, no for each child, and then the husband interrupted when we got to one and said, 'That's not true, don't you remember, there was that guy . . .' And the husband was grinning."

Not all women take lovers. Manuel Lizarralde has discovered through interviews that one-third of 122 women were faithful to their husbands during their pregnancies. "These women say they don't need it, or no one asked, or they have enough support from family and don't require another father for their child," Lizarralde says. "Some even admit that their husbands were not that happy about the idea." Or it may be a sign of changing times. Based on his most recent visits to the Barí, Lizarralde thinks that under the influence of Western values, the number of people who engage in multiple fatherhood may be decreasing. But his father, who has worked with the Barí for more than 40 years, disagrees. He says the practice is as frequent but that the Barí discuss it less openly than before, knowing that Westerners object to their views. After all, it took the anthropologists 20 years to hear about other fathers, and today the Barí are probably being even more discreet because they know Westerners disapprove of their beliefs.

"What this information adds up to," Beckerman says, "is that the Barí may be doing somewhat less fooling around within marriage these days but that most of them still believe that a child can have multiple fathers."

More important, the Barí idea that biological paternity can be shared is not just the quirky custom of one tribe; anthropologists have found that this idea is common across South America. The same belief is shared by indigenous groups in New Guinea and India, suggesting that multiple paternity has been part of human behavior for a long time, undermining all previous descriptions of how human mating behavior evolved.

Since the 1960s, when anthropologists began to construct scenarios of early human mating, they had always assumed that the model family started with a mom and dad bonded for life to raise the kids, a model that fit well with acceptable Western behavior. In 1981 in an article titled "The Origin of Man," C. Owen Lovejoy, an anthropologist at Kent State University, outlined the standard story of human evolution as it was used in the field—and is still presented in textbooks today: Human infants with their big brains and long periods of growth and learning have always been dependent on adults, a dependence that separates the humans from the apes. Mothers alone couldn't possibly find enough food for these dependent young, so women have always needed to find a mate who would stick close to home and bring in supplies for the family. Unfortunately for women, as evolutionary psychologists suggest, men are compelled by their biology to mate with as many partners as possible to pass along their genes. However, each of these men might be manipulated into staying with one woman who offered him sex and a promise of fidelity. The man, under those conditions, would be assured of paternity, and he might just stay around and make sure his kids survived.

This scenario presents humans as naturally monogamous, forming nuclear families as an evolutionary necessity. The only problem is that around the world families don't always operate this way. In fact, as the Barí and other cultures show, there are all sorts of ways to run a successful household.

The Na of Yunnan Province in China, for example, have a female-centric society in which husbands are not part of the picture. Women grow up and continue to live with their mothers, sisters, and brothers; they never marry or move away from the family compound. As a result, sisters and brothers rather than married pairs are the economic unit that farms and fishes together. Male lovers in this system are simply visitors. They have no place or power in the household, and children are brought up by their mothers and by the mothers' brothers. A father is identified only if there is a resemblance between him and the child, and even so, the father has no responsibilities toward the child. Often women have sex with so many partners that the biological father is unknown. "I have not found any term that would cover the notion of father in the Na language," writes Chinese anthropologist Cai Hua in his book *A Society Without Fathers or Husbands: The Na of China*. In this case, women have complete control over their children, property, and sexuality.

Across lowland South America, family systems vary because cultures put their beliefs into practice in different ways. Among some native people, such as the Canela, Mehinaku, and Araweté, women control their sex lives and their fertility, and most children have several fathers. Barí women are also sexually liberated from an early age. "Once she has completed her puberty ritual, a Barí girl can have sex with anyone she wants as long as she doesn't violate the incest taboo," Beckerman explains. "It's nobody's business, not even Mom's and Dad's business." Women can also turn down prospective husbands.

In other cultures in South America, life is not so free for females, although members of these cultures also believe that babies can have more than one father. The Curripaco of Amazonia, for instance, acknowledge multiple fatherhood as a biological possibility and yet frown on women having affairs. Paul Valentine, a senior lecturer in anthropology at the University of East London who has studied the Curripaco for more than 20 years, says, "Curripaco women are in a difficult situation. The wives come into the village from different areas, and it's a very patrilineal system." If her husband dies, a widow is allowed to turn only to his brothers or to clan members on his side of the family for a new husband.

The relative power of women and men over their sex lives has important consequences. "In certain social and economic systems, women are free to make mate choices," says Valentine. In these cultures women are often the foundation of society, while men have less power in the community. Sisters tend to stay in the same household as their mothers. The women, in other words, have power to make choices. "At the other extreme, somehow, it's the men who try to maximize their evolutionary success at the expense of the women," says Valentine.

Men and women often have a conflict of interest when it comes to mating, marriage, and who should invest most in children, and the winners have sometimes been the men, sometimes the women. As Beckerman wryly puts it, "Anyone who believes that in a human mating relationship the man's reproductive interests always carry the day has obviously never been married."

The Barí and others show that human systems are, in fact, very flexible, ready to accommodate any sort of mating system or type of family. "I think that human beings are capable of making life extremely complicated. That's our way of doing business," says Ian Tattersall, a paleoanthropologist and curator in the division of anthropology at the American Museum of Natural History in New York City. Indeed, such flexibility suggests there's no reason to assume that the nuclear family is the natural, ideal, or even most evolutionarily successful system of human grouping. As Beckerman says, "One of the things this research shows is that human beings are just as clever and creative in assembling their kin relations as they are putting together space shuttles or symphonies."

Arranging a Marriage in India

Serena Nanda

> Sister and doctor brother-in-law invite correspondence from North Indian professionals only, for a beautiful, talented, sophisticated, intelligent sister, 5'3", slim, M.A. in textile design, father a senior civil officer. Would prefer immigrant doctors, between 26–29 years. Reply with full details and returnable photo. A well-settled uncle invites matrimonial correspondence from slim, fair, educated South Indian girl, for his nephew, 25 years, smart, M.B.A., green card holder, 5'6". Full particulars with returnable photo appreciated.
>
> *Matrimonial Advertisements,*
> India Abroad

In India, almost all marriages are arranged. Even among the educated middle classes in modern, urban India, marriage is as much a concern of the families as it is of the individuals. So customary is the practice of arranged marriage that there is a special name for a marriage which is not arranged: It is called a "love match."

On my first field trip to India, I met many young men and women whose parents were in the process of "getting them married." In many cases, the bride and groom would not meet each other before the marriage. At most they might meet for a brief conversation, and this meeting would take place only after their parents had decided that the match was suitable. Parents do not compel their children to marry a person who either marriage partner finds objectionable. But only after one match is refused will another be sought.

Young men and women do not date and have very little social life involving members of the opposite sex.

As a young American woman in India for the first time, I found this custom of arranged marriage oppressive. How could any intelligent young person agree to such a marriage without great reluctance? It was contrary to everything I believed about the importance of romantic love as the only basis of a happy marriage. It also clashed with my strongly held notions that the choice of such an intimate and permanent relationship could be made only by the individuals involved. Had anyone tried to arrange my marriage, I would have been defiant and rebellious!

At the first opportunity, I began, with more curiosity than tact, to question the young people I met on how they felt about this practice. Sita, one of my young informants, was a college graduate with a degree in political science. She had been waiting for over a year while her parents were arranging a match for her. I found it difficult to accept the docile manner in which this well-educated young woman awaited the outcome of a process that would result in her spending the rest of her life with a man she hardly knew, a virtual stranger, picked out by her parents.

"How can you go along with this?" I asked her, in frustration and distress. "Don't you care who you marry?"

"Of course I care," she answered." This is why I must let my parents choose a boy for me. My marriage is too important to be arranged by such an inexperienced person as myself. In such matters, it is better to have my parents' guidance."

I had learned that young men and women in India do not date and have very little social life involving members of the opposite sex. Although I could not disagree with Sita's reasoning, I continued to pursue the subject.

"But how can you marry the first man you have ever met? Not only have you missed the fun of meeting a lot of different people, but you have not given yourself the chance to know who is the right man for you."

"Meeting with a lot of different people doesn't sound like any fun at all," Sita answered. "One hears that in America the girls are spending all their time worrying about whether they will meet a man and get married. Here we have the chance to enjoy our life and let our parents do this work and worrying for us."

She had me there. The high anxiety of the competition to "be popular" with the opposite sex certainly was the most prominent feature of life as an American teenager in the late fifties. The endless worrying about the rules that governed our behavior and about our popularity ratings sapped both our self-esteem and our enjoyment of adolescence. I reflected that absence of this competition in India most certainly may have contributed to the self-confidence and natural charm of so many of the young women I met.

And yet, the idea of marrying a perfect stranger, whom one did not know and did not "love," so offended my American ideas of individualism and romanticism, that I persisted with my objections.

"I still can't imagine it," I said. "How can you agree to marry a man you hardly know?"

"But of course he will be known. My parents would never arrange a marriage for me without knowing all about the boy's family background. Naturally we will not rely only on what the family tells us. We will check the particulars out ourselves. No one will want their daughter to marry into a family that is not good. All these things we will know beforehand."

Impatiently, I responded, "Sita, I don't mean know the family, I mean, know the man. How can you marry someone you don't know personally and don't love? How can you think of spending your life with someone you may not even like?"

"If he is a good man, why should I not like him?" she said. "With you people, you know the boy so well before you marry, where will be the fun to get married? There will be no mystery and no romance. Here we have the whole of our married life to get to know and love our husband. "This way is better, is it not?"

Her response made further sense, and I began to have second thoughts on the matter. Indeed, during months of meeting many intelligent young Indian people, both male and female, who had the same ideas as Sita, I saw arranged marriages in a different light. I also saw the importance of the family in Indian life and realized that a couple who took their marriage into their own hands was taking a big risk, particularly if their families were irreconcilably opposed to the match. In a country where every important resource in life—a job, a house, a social circle—is gained through family connections, it seemed foolhardy to cut oneself off from a supportive social network and depend solely on one person for happiness and success.

Six years later I returned to India to again do fieldwork, this time among the middle class in Bombay, a modern, sophisticated city. From the experience of my earlier visit, I decided to include a study of arranged marriages in my project. By this time I had met many Indian couples whose marriages had been arranged and who seemed very happy. Particularly in contrast to the fate of many of my married friends in the United States who were already in the process of divorce, the positive aspects of arranged marriages appeared to me to outweigh the negatives. In fact, I thought I might even participate in arranging a marriage myself. I had been fairly successful in the United States in "fixing up" many of my friends, and I was confident that my matchmaking skills could be easily applied to this new situation, once I learned the basic rules. "After all," I thought, "how complicated can it be? People want pretty much the same things in a marriage whether it is in India or America."

An opportunity presented itself almost immediately. A friend from my previous Indian trip was in the process of arranging for the marriage of her eldest son. In India there is a perceived shortage of "good boys," and since my friend's family was eminently respectable and the boy himself personable, well educated, and nice looking, I was sure that by the end of my year's fieldwork, we would have found a match.

The basic rule seems to be that a family's reputation is most important. It is understood that matches would be arranged only within the same caste and general social class, although some crossing of subcastes is permissible if the class positions of the bride's and groom's families are similar. Although dowry is now prohibited by law in India, extensive gift exchanges took place with every marriage. Even when the boy's family do not "make demands," every girl's family nevertheless feels the obligation to give the traditional gifts, to the girl, to the boy, and to the boy's family. Particularly when the couple would be living in the joint family—that is, with the boy's parents and his married brothers and their families, as well as with unmarried siblings—which is still very common even among the urban, upper-middle class in India, the girls' parents are anxious to establish smooth relations between their family and that of the boy. Offering the proper gifts, even when not called "dowry," is often an important factor in influencing the relationship between the bride's and groom's families and perhaps, also, the treatment of the bride in her new home.

In a society where divorce is still a scandal and where, in fact, the divorce rate is exceedingly low, an arranged marriage is the beginning of a lifetime relationship not just between the bride and groom but between their families as well.

In a society where divorce is still a scandal and where, in fact, the divorce rate is exceedingly low, an arranged marriage is the beginning of a lifetime relationship not just between the bride and groom but between their families as well. Thus, while a girl's looks are important, her character is even more so, for she is being judged as a prospective daughter-in-law as much as a prospective bride. Where she would be living in a joint family, as was the case with my friend, the girls's ability to get along harmoniously in a family is perhaps the single most important quality in assessing her suitability.

My friend is a highly esteemed wife, mother, and daughter-in-law. She is religious, soft-spoken, modest, and deferential. She rarely gossips and never quarrels, two qualities highly desirable in a woman. A family that has the reputation for gossip and conflict among its womenfolk will not find it easy to get good wives for their sons. Parents will not want to send their daughter to a house in which there is conflict.

My friend's family were originally from North India. They had lived in Bombay, where her husband owned a business, for forty years. The family had delayed in seeking a match for their eldest son because he had been an Air Force pilot for several years, stationed in such remote places that it had seemed fruitless to try to find a girl who would be willing to accompany him.

In their social class, a military career, despite its economic security, has little prestige and is considered a drawback in finding a suitable bride. Many families would not allow their daughters to marry a man in an occupation so potentially dangerous and which requires so much moving around.

The son had recently left the military and joined his father's business. Since he was a college graduate, modern, and well traveled, from such a good family, and, I thought, quite handsome, it seemed to me that he, or rather his family, was in a position to pick and choose. I said as much to my friend.

While she agreed that there were many advantages on their side, she also said, "We must keep in mind that my son is both short and dark; these are drawbacks in finding the right match." While the boy's height had not escaped my notice, "dark" seemed to me inaccurate; I would have called him "wheat" colored perhaps, and in any case, I did not realize that color would be a consideration. I discovered, however, that while a boy's skin color is a less important consideration than a girl's, it is still a factor.

An important source of contacts in trying to arrange her son's marriage was my friend's social club in Bombay. Many of the women had daughters of the right age, and some had already expressed an interest in my friend's son. I was most enthusiastic about the possibilities of one particular family who had five daughters, all of whom were pretty, demure, and well educated. Their mother had told my friend, "You can have your pick for your son, whichever one of my daughters appeals to you most."

I saw a match in sight. "Surely," I said to my friend, "we will find one there. Let's go visit and make our choice." But my friend held back; she did not seem to share my enthusiasm, for reasons I could not then fathom.

When I kept pressing for an explanation of her reluctance, she admitted, "See, Serena, here is the problem. The family has so many daughters, how will they be able to provide nicely for any of them? We are not making any demands, but still, with so many daughters to marry off, one wonders whether she will even be able to make a proper wedding. Since this is our eldest son, it's best if we marry him to a girl who is the only daughter, then the wedding will truly be a gala affair." I argued that surely the quality of the girls themselves made up for any deficiency in the elaborateness of the wedding. My friend admitted this point but still seemed reluctant to proceed.

"Is there something else," I asked her, "some factor I have missed?" "Well," she finally said, "there is one other thing. They have one daughter already married and living in Bombay. The mother is always complaining to me that the girl's in-laws don't let her visit her own family often enough. So it makes me wonder, will she be that kind of mother who always wants her daughter at her own home? This will prevent the girl from adjusting to our house. It is not a good thing." And so, this family of five daughters was dropped as a possibility.

Somewhat disappointed, I nevertheless respected my friend's reasoning and geared up for the next prospect. This was also the daughter of a woman in my friend's social club. There was clear interest in this family and I could see why. The family's reputation was excellent; in fact, they came from a subcaste slightly higher than my friend's own. The girl, who was an only daughter, was pretty and well educated and had a brother studying in the United States. Yet, after expressing an interest to me in this family, all talk of them suddenly died down and the search began elsewhere.

"What happened to that girl as a prospect?" I asked one day. "You never mention her any more. She is so pretty and so educated, what did you find wrong?"

"She is too educated. We've decided against it. My husband's father saw the girl on the bus the other day and thought her forward. A girl who 'roams about' the city by herself is not the girl for our family." My disappointment this time was even greater, as I thought the son would have liked the girl very much. But then I thought, my friend is right, a girl who is going to live in a joint family cannot be too independent or she will make life miserable for everyone. I also learned that if the family of the girl has even a slightly higher social status than the family of the boy, the bride may think herself too good for them, and this too will cause problems. Later my friend admitted to me that this had been an important factor in her decision not to pursue the match.

The next candidate was the daughter of a client of my friend's husband. When the client learned that the family was looking for a match for their son, he said, "Look no further, we have a daughter." This man then invited my friends to dinner to see the girl. He had already seen their son at the office and decided that "he liked the boy." We all went together for tea, rather than dinner—it was less of a commitment—and while we were there, the girl's mother showed us around the house. The girl was studying for her exams and was briefly introduced to us.

After we left, I was anxious to hear my friend's opinion. While her husband liked the family very much and was impressed with his client's business accomplishments and reputation, the wife didn't like the girl's looks. "She is short, no doubt, which is an important plus point, but she is also fat and wears glasses." My friend obviously thought she could do better for her son and asked her husband to make his excuses to his client by saying that they had decided to postpone the boy's marriage indefinitely.

"If a mistake is made we have not only ruined the life of our son or daughter, but we have spoiled the reputation of our family as well."

By this time almost six months had passed and I was becoming impatient. What I had thought would be an easy matter to arrange was turning out to be quite complicated. I began to believe that between my friend's desire for a girl who was modest enough to fit into her joint family, yet attractive and educated enough to be an acceptable partner for her son, she would not find anyone suitable. My friend laughed at my impatience: "Don't be so much in a hurry," she said. "You Americans want everything done so quickly. You get married quickly and then

Appendix
Further Reflections on Arranged Marriage . . .

This essay was written from the point of view of a family seeking a daughter-in-law. Arranged marriage looks somewhat different from the point of view of the bride and her family. Arranged marriage continues to be preferred, even among the more educated, Westernized sections of the Indian population. Many young women from these families still go along, more or less willingly, with the practice, and also with the specific choices of their families. Young women do get excited about the prospects of their marriage, but there is also ambivalence and increasing uncertainty, as the bride contemplates leaving the comfort and familiarity of her own home, where as a "temporary guest" she had often been indulged, to live among strangers. Even in the best situation she will now come under the close scrutiny of her husband's family. How she dresses, how she behaves, how she gets along with others, where she goes, how she spends her time, her domestic abilities—all of this and much more—will be observed and commented on by a whole new set of relations. Her interaction with her family of birth will be monitored and curtailed considerably. Not only will she leave their home, but with increasing geographic mobility, she may also live very far from them, perhaps even on another continent. Too much expression of her fondness for her own family, or her desire to visit them, may be interpreted as an inability to adjust to her new family, and may become a source of conflict. In an arranged marriage the burden of adjustment is clearly heavier for a woman than for a man. And that is in the best of situations.

In less happy circumstances, the bride may be a target of resentment and hostility from her husband's family, particularly her mother-in-law or her husband's unmarried sisters, for whom she is now a source of competition for the affection, loyalty, and economic resources of their son or brother. If she is psychologically, or even physically abused, her options are limited, as returning to her parents' home, or divorce, are still very stigmatized. For most Indians, marriage and motherhood are still considered the only suitable roles for a woman, even for those who have careers, and few women can comfortably contemplate remaining unmarried. Most families still consider "marrying off" their daughters as a compelling religious duty and social necessity. This increases a bride's sense of obligation to make the marriage a success, at whatever cost to her own personal happiness.

The vulnerability of a new bride may also be intensified by the issue of dowry, which although illegal, has become a more pressing issue in the consumer conscious society of contemporary urban India. In many cases, where a groom's family is not satisfied with the amount of dowry a bride brings to her marriage, the young bride will be constantly harassed to get her parents to give more. In extreme cases, the bride may even be murdered, and the murder disguised as an accident or suicide. This also offers the husband's family an opportunity to arrange another match for him, thus bringing in another dowry. This phenomena, called dowry death, calls attention not just to the "evils of dowry" but also to larger issues of the powerlessness of women as well.

—Serena Nanda
March 1998

just as quickly get divorced. Here we take marriage more seriously. We must take all the factors into account. It is not enough for us to learn by our mistakes. This is too serious a business. If a mistake is made we have not only ruined the life of our son or daughter, but we have spoiled the reputation of our family as well. And that will make it much harder for their brothers and sisters to get married. So we must be very careful."

What she said was true and I promised myself to be more patient, though it was not easy. I had really hoped and expected that the match would be made before my year in India was up. But it was not to be. When I left India my friend seemed no further along in finding a suitable match for her son than when I had arrived.

Two years later, I returned to India and still my friend had not found a girl for her son. By this time, he was close to thirty, and I think she was a little worried. Since she knew I had friends all over India, and I was going to be there for a year, she asked me to "help her in this work" and keep an eye out for someone suitable. I was flattered that my judgment was respected, but knowing now how complicated the process was, I had lost my earlier confidence as a matchmaker. Nevertheless, I promised that I would try.

It was almost at the end of my year's stay in India that I met a family with a marriageable daughter whom I felt might be a good possibility for my friend's son. The girl's father was related to a good friend of mine and by coincidence came from the same village as my friend's husband. This new family had a successful business in a medium-sized city in central India and were from the same subcaste as my friend. The daughter was pretty and chic; in fact, she had studied fashion design in college. Her parents would not allow her to go off by herself to any of the major cities in India where she could make a career, but they had compromised with her wish to work by allowing her to run a small dress-making boutique from their home. In spite of her desire to have a career, the daughter was both modest and home-loving and had had a traditional, sheltered upbringing. She had only one other sister, already married, and a brother who was in his father's business.

I mentioned the possibility of a match with my friend's son. The girl's parents were most interested. Although their daughter was not eager to marry just yet, the idea of living in Bombay—a sophisticated, extremely fashion-conscious city where she could continue her education in clothing design—was a great inducement. I gave the girl's father my friend's address and suggested that when they went to Bombay on some business or whatever, they look up the boy's family.

Returning to Bombay on my way to New York, I told my friend of this newly discovered possibility. She seemed to feel there was potential but, in spite of my urging, would not make any moves herself. She rather preferred to wait for the girl's family to call upon them. I hoped something would come of this introduction, though by now I had learned to rein in my optimism.

A year later I received a letter from my friend. had indeed come to visit Bombay, and their daughter friend's daughter, who were near in age, had become very g friends. During that year, the two girls had frequently visite each other. I thought things looked promising.

Last week I received an invitation to a wedding: My friend's son and the girl were getting married. Since I had found the match, my presence was particularly requested at the wedding. I was thrilled. Success at last! As I prepared to leave for India, I began thinking, "Now, my friend's younger son, who do I know who has a nice girl for him . . .?"

Edited by Philip R. DeVita.

34

Law, Custom, and Crimes against Women

The Problem of Dowry Death in India

John van Willigen and V. C. Channa

Anthropologists find many societies with unusual customs, beliefs, and behaviors. Usually they discover, after careful study and reflection, that these perform some useful function within the society, as discussed in Goldstein's *When Brothers Share a Wife.* But is this always the case? Must we assume that simply because a custom exists it is healthy for the members of society? We think not, and the Christians who were fed to lions and the Aztec slaves who were sacrificed to a bloodthirsty god would most likely agree.

Times change; hunters and gatherers plant crops, tribal people rush headlong into peasantry, and small-scale farmers become urban wage earners. Traditions that helped maintain a healthy society in one context may become dysfunctional in another. For better or worse, traditions and beliefs run deep and are almost impossible to unlearn. It is the nature of culture to resist change.

As you will read, the practice of dousing a bride with kerosene and creating a human torch certainly indicates that the payment of dowry is a traditional practice gone awry. That said, what can be done? Laws, even those that carry serious penalties, are light ammunition against the armor of strongly held cultural beliefs. Governments will solve such problems only through public policy based on in-depth cultural understanding.

As you read this selection, ask yourself the following questions:

- What do you think the authors mean when they suggest that dowry death presents a problem for ethnologists because of ethnological theory's functional cast?
- Why does the institution of dowry make college education problematic for some young women?
- What are the present-day approaches to solving the dowry death problem?
- How can women's access to production roles and property, delocalization of social control, and economic transformation affect the problem of dowry death?
- Dowry-related violence in India is related to the economic value of women. What might be said about the relationship between the economic position and the social status of women in America?

The following terms discussed in this selection are included in the Glossary at the back of the book:

caste	*ethnology*
cultural materialism	*peasants*
demography	*sex roles*
dowry	

A 25-year-old woman was allegedly burnt to death by her husband and mother-in-law at their East Delhi home yesterday. The housewife, Mrs. Sunita, stated before her death at the Jaya Prakash Narayana Hospital that members of her husband's family had been harassing her for bringing inadequate dowry.

The woman told the Shahdara subdivisional magistrate that during a quarrel over dowry at their Pratap Park house yesterday, her husband gripped her from behind while the mother-in-law poured kerosene over her clothes.

Her clothes were then set ablaze. The police have registered a case against the victim's husband, Suraj Prakash, and his mother.

—*Times of India,* February 19, 1988

van Willigen, John and Channa, V.C. "Law, Custom, and Crimes against Women: The Problem of Dowry Deaths in India." Reproduced by permission of the Society for Applied Anthropology (SfAA) from Human Organization 50 (1991) no. 4:369–377.

This routinely reported news story describes what in India is termed a "bride-burning" or "dowry death." Such incidents are frequently reported in the newspapers of Delhi and other Indian cities. In addition, there are cases in which the evidence may be ambiguous, so that deaths of women by fire may be recorded as kitchen accidents, suicides, or murders. Dowry violence takes a characteristic form. Following marriage and the requisite giving of dowry, the family of the groom makes additional demands for the payment of more cash or the provision of more goods. These demands are expressed in unremitting harassment of the bride, who is living in the household of her husband's parents, culminating in the murder of the woman by members of her husband's family or by her suicide. The woman is typically burned to death with kerosene, a fuel used in pressurized cook stoves, hence the use of the term "bride-burning" in public discourse.

Dowry death statistics appear frequently in the press and parliamentary debates. Parliamentary sources report the following figures for married women 16 to 30 years of age in Delhi: 452 deaths by burning for 1985; 478 for 1986 and 300 for the first six months of 1987 (Bhatia 1988). There were 1,319 cases reported nationally in 1986 (*Times of India,* January 10, 1988). Police records do not match hospital records for third degree burn cases among younger married women; far more violence occurs than the crime reports indicate (Kumari 1988).

There is other violence against women related both directly and indirectly to the institution of dowry. For example, there are unmarried women who commit suicide so as to relieve their families of the burden of providing a dowry. A recent case that received national attention in the Indian press involved the triple suicide of three sisters in the industrial city of Kanpur. A photograph was widely published showing the three young women hanging from ceiling fans by their scarves. Their father, who earned about 4,000 Rs. [rupees] per month, was not able to negotiate marriage for his oldest daughter. The grooms were requesting approximately 100,000 Rs. Also linked to the dowry problem is selective female abortion made possible by amniocentesis. This issue was brought to national attention with a startling statistic reported out of a seminar held in Delhi in 1985. Of 3,000 abortions carried out after sex determination through amniocentesis, only one involved a male fetus. As a result of these developments, the government of the state of Maharashtra banned sex determination tests except those carried out in government hospitals.

The phenomenon of dowry death presents a difficult problem for the ethnologist. Ethnological theory, with its residual functionalist cast, still does not deal effectively with the social costs of institutions of what might be arguably referred to as custom gone bad, resulting in a culturally constituted violence syndrome.

This essay examines dowry and its violent aspects, and some of the public solutions developed to deal with it in India. Our work consists of a meta-analysis of some available literature. We critique the legal mechanisms established to regulate the cultural institution of dowry and the resultant social evils engendered by the institution, and argue that policies directed against these social evils need to be constructed in terms of an underlying cause rather than of the problem itself. We consider cause, an aspect of the problem infrequently discussed in public debate. As Saini asserts, "legal academicians have shown absolutely no interest in the causal roots of dowry as practiced in contemporary India" (1983:143).

THE INSTITUTION

Since ancient times, the marriage of Hindus has required the transfer of property from the family of the bride to the family of the groom. Dowry or *daan dehej* is thought by some to be sanctioned by such religious texts as the *Manusmriti.* Seen in this way, dowry is a religious obligation of the father of a woman and a matter of *dharma* (religious duty) whereby authority over a woman is transferred from her father to her husband. This transfer takes different forms in different communities in modern India (Tambiah 1973). In public discussion, the term "dowry" covers a wide range of traditional payments and expenses, some presented to the groom's family and others to be retained by the bride. Customs have changed through time. The financial burdens of gifts and the dowry payments per se are exacerbated by the many expenses associated with the marriage celebration itself, but dowry payment is especially problematic because of its open-ended nature. As Tambiah notes, "marriage payments in India usually comprise an elaborate series of payments back and forth between the marrying families" and "this series extends over a long period of time and persists after marriage" (1973:92). Contemporary cases such as the death of Mrs. Sunita, often revolve around such continued demands.

A daughter's marriage takes a long time to prepare and involves the development of an adaptive strategy on the part of her family. An important part of the strategy is the preparation for making dowry payments; family consumption may be curtailed so as to allow accumulation of money for dowry. Seeing to marriage arrangements may be an important aspect of retirement planning. The dowries that the family receives on behalf of their sons may be "rolled over" to deal with the daughter's requirements. Families attempt to cultivate in both their sons and daughters attributes that will make them more attractive in marriage negotiations. Many things besides dowry are considered in negotiations: "non-economic" factors have demonstrable effect on the expectations for dowry and the family's strategy concerning the dowry process.

Education is a variable to be considered in the negotiation process. Education of young women is somewhat problematic because suitable husbands for such women must also be college educated. The parents of such young men demand more dowry for their sons. A consideration in sending a young woman to college will therefore be her parents' capacity to dower her adequately so as to obtain an appropriate groom. In any case, education is secondary to a man's earning power and the reputation of a woman's family. Education is, however, important in the early stages of negotiation because of the need to coordinate the level of the education of the men and women. Education qualifications are also less ambiguously defined than other dimensions of family reputation. Physical attractiveness is a consideration, but it is thought somewhat unseemly to emphasize this aspect of the decision.

Advertisements in newspapers are used for establishing marriage proposals (Aluwalia 1969; Niehoff 1959; Weibe and Ramu 1971), but contacts are more typically established through kin and other networks. Some marriages may be best termed "self-arranged," and are usually called "love marriages." In these cases, young men and women may develop a relationship independent of their families and then ask that negotiations be carried out on their behalf by family representatives.

Analysis of matrimonial advertisements shows some of the attributes considered to be important. Listed in such advertisements are education, age, income and occupation, physical attributes, *gotra* (a kind of unilineal descent group) membership, family background, place of residence, personality features, consideration of dowry, time and type of marriage, and language.

Consideration of dowry and other expenditures are brought out early in the negotiations and can serve as a stumbling block. Dowry negotiations can go on for some time. The last stage is the actual "seeing of the groom" and the "seeing of the bride," both rather fleeting encounters whose position at the end of the process indicates their relative lack of importance.

Marriage is a process by which two families mutually evaluate each other. The outcome of the negotiations is an expression of the relative worth of the two persons, a man and a woman, and, by extension, the worth of their respective families. This estimation of worth is expressed in marriage expenditures, of which dowry is but a part. There are three possible types of expenditures: cash gifts, gifts of household goods, and expenditures on the wedding celebration itself. The cash gift component of the dowry goes to the groom's father and comes to be part of his common household fund. The household goods are for use by the groom's household, although they may be used to establish a separate household for the newlyweds. When separate accommodations are not set up, the groom's family may insist that the goods do not duplicate things they already have.

Dates for marriages are set through consideration of horoscopes; horoscopy is done by professional astrologers *(pandits)*. This practice leads to a concentration of marriage dates and consequent high demand for marriage goods and services at certain times of the year. During marriage seasons, the cost of jewelry, furniture, clothes, musicians' services, and other marriage related expenditures goes up, presumably because of the concentration of the demand caused by the astrologers.

The expenditures required of the woman's family for the wedding in general and the dowry in particular are frequently massive. Paul reports, for a middle-class Delhi neighborhood, that most dowries were over 50,000 Rs. (1986). Srinivas comments that dowries over 200,000 Rs. are not uncommon (1984).[1]

ETHNOLOGICAL THEORIES ABOUT DOWRY

Dowry had traditionally been discussed by ethnologists in the context of the functionalist paradigm, and much theorizing about dowry appears to be concerned with explaining the "contribution" that the institution makes to social adaptation. The early theoretician Westermarck interpreted dowry as a social marker of the legitimacy of spouse and offspring, and as a mechanism for defining women's social roles and property rights in the new household (Westermarck 1921:428). Murdock suggests that dowry may confirm the contract of marriage (1949). Dowry is interpreted by Friedl as a means to adjust a woman to her affinal home as it rearranges social relationships including the social separation of the man from his parents (1967). Dowry payments are public expressions of the new relationship between the two families, and of the social status of the bride and groom.

Dowry is seen in the social science literature as a kind of antemortem or anticipated inheritance by which a widow is assured of support, and provision for her offspring (Friedl 1967; Goody 1973, 1976). It transfers money to where the women will be and where they will reproduce; as a result, resources are also placed where the children will benefit, given the practice of patrilineal inheritance of immovable, economically valuable property like farm land.

In India, dowry is also seen as an expression of the symbolic order of society. According to Dumont, dowry expresses the hierarchal relations of marriage in India and lower status of the bride (Dumont 1957). The amount of dowry given is an expression of prestige. The capacity to buy prestige through dowry increases the potential for social mobility (Goody 1973). Dowry is a kind of delayed consumption used to demonstrate or improve social rank (Epstein 1960).

There is a significant discontinuity between discussions of dowry in the ethnological theory and in public discourse. Certainly the dowry problem does appear in the writing of contemporary ethnologists, but it is simply lamented and left largely uninterpreted and unexplained.

THE EXTANT SOLUTIONS TO THE PROBLEM

The Dowry Prohibition Act of 1961, as amended in 1984 and 1986, is the primary legal means for regulating the dowry process and controlling its excesses. The laws against dowry are tough. Dowry demand offenses are "cognizable" (require no warrant) and nonbailable, and the burden of proof is on the accused. There are, in fact, convictions under the law.

The act defines dowry as "any property of valuable security given or agreed to be given either directly or indirectly—(a) by one party to a marriage to the other party to a marriage; or (b) by parents of either party to a marriage or by any other person, to either party to the marriage or to any other person" (Government of India 1986:1). The act makes it illegal to give or take dowry, "If any person after the commencement of this act, gives or takes or abets the giving or taking of dowry, he shall be punishable with imprisonment for a term which shall not be less than five years; and with fine which shall not be less than fifteen thousand rupees or the amount of the value of such dowry which ever is more" (Government of India 1986:1). While this section unambiguously prohibits dowry, the third section allows wedding presents to be freely given. Thus the law does not apply to "presents which are given at the time of marriage to the bride (without demand having been made in that behalf)" (Government of India 1986:1). Identical provisions apply to the groom. Furthermore, all such presents must be listed on a document before the consummation of the marriage. The list is to contain a brief description and estimation of the value of the gifts, name of presenting person, and the relationship that person has with the bride and groom. This regulation also provides "that where such presents are made by or on the behalf of the bride or any other person related to the bride, such presents are of a customary nature and the value thereof is not excessive having regard to the financial status of the person by whom, or on whose behalf, such presents are given" (Government of India 1986:2). Amendments made in 1984 make it illegal for a person to demand dowry with the same penalty as under the earlier "giving and taking" provision. It was also declared illegal to advertise for dowry, such an offense being defined as not bailable, with the burden of proof on the accused person.

This legislation was coupled with some changes in the Indian Penal Code that legally established the concept of "dowry death." That is, "where the death of a woman is caused by any burns or bodily injury or occurs otherwise than under normal circumstances within seven years of her marriage and it is shown that soon before her death she was subjected to cruelty or harassment by her husband or any relative of her husband for, or in connection with, any demand for dowry, such death shall be called 'dowry death,' and such husband or relative shall be deemed to have caused her death" (Government of India 1987:4). The Indian Evidence Act of 1871 was changed so as to allow for the presumption of guilt under the circumstances outlined above. Changes in the code allowed for special investigation and reporting procedures of deaths by apparent suicide of women within seven years of marriage if requested by a relative. There were also newly defined special provisions for autopsies.

To this point, however, these legal mechanisms have proved ineffective. According to Sivaramayya, the "act has signally failed in its operation" (1984:66). Menon refers to the "near total failure" of the law (1988:12). A similar viewpoint is expressed by Srinivas, who wrote, "The Dowry Prohibition Act of 1961 has been unanimously declared to be an utterly ineffective law" (1984:29).

In addition to the legal attack on dowry abuses, numerous public groups engage in public education campaigns. In urban settings, the most noteworthy of these groups are specialized research units such as the Special Cell for Women of the Tata Institute of Social Sciences (Bombay), and the Center for Social Research (New Delhi). Also involved in the effort are private voluntary organizations such as the Crimes Against Women Cell, Karmika, and Sukh Shanti.

These groups issue public education advertising on various feminist issues. The anti-dowry advertisement of the Federation of Indian Chambers of Commerce and Industry Ladies Organization exemplifies the thrust of these campaigns. In the following advertisement, which was frequently run in the winter of 1988 in newspapers such as the *Times of India*, a photograph of a doll dressed in traditional Indian bridal attire was shown in flames.

> Every time a young bride dies because of dowry demands, we are all responsible for her death. Because we allow it to happen. Each year in Delhi hospitals alone, over 300 brides die of third degree burns. And many more deaths go unreported. Most of the guilty get away. And we just shrug helplessly and say, "what can we do?" We can do a lot.
>
> Help create social condemnation of dowry. Refuse to take or give dowry. Protest when you meet people who condone the practice. Reach out and help the girl being harassed for it. Act now.
>
> Let's fight it together.
>
> As parents, bring up educated, self-reliant daughters. Make sure they marry only after 18. Oppose dowry; refuse to even discuss it. If your daughter is harassed after marriage stand by her.
>
> As young men and women, refuse marriage proposals where dowry is being considered. As friends and neighbors, ostracize families who give or take dowry. Reach out to help victims of dowry harassment.
>
> As legislators and jurists, frame stronger laws. Ensure speedy hearings, impose severe punishments. As associations, give help and advice. Take up the challenge of changing laws and attitudes of society. Let us all resolve to fight the evil. If we fight together we can win.
>
> SAY NO TO DOWRY.

Also engaged in anti-dowry work are peasant political action groups such as Bharatiya Kisan Union (BKU). BKU consists of farmers from western Uttar Pradesh whose political program is focused more generally on agricultural issues. The group sponsored a massive 25-day demonstration at Meerut, Uttar Pradesh, in 1988. The leadership used the demonstration to announce a social reform program, most of it dealing with marriage issues. According to news service reports, "The code of social reforms includes fixing the maximum number of persons in a marriage party at 11, no feasts relating to marriage, and no dowry except 10 grams of gold and 30 grams of silver" (*Times of India*, February 11, 1988). Buses plying rural roads in western Uttar Pradesh are reported to have been painted with the slogan "The bride is the dowry." Private campaigns against dowry occur in the countryside as well as among the urban elites, although it is likely that the underlying motivations are quite different.

POLICY ANALYSIS

Our argument is based on the assumption that social problems are best dealt with by policies directed at the correction of causative factors, rather than at the amelioration of symptoms. While current legal remedies directly confront dowry violence, the linkage between cause and the problematic behavior is not made. Here we develop an argument consisting of three components: women's access to production roles and property; delocalization of social control; and economic transformation of society. The pattern of distribution of aspects of the institution of dowry and its attendant problems is important to this analysis. Although dowry practices and the related crimes against women are distributed throughout Indian society, the distribution is patterned in terms of geography, caste rank, socioeconomic rank, urban/rural residence, and employment status of the women. In some places and among some people there are demonstrably more violence, more intensity of dowry practices, and more commitment to dowry itself. Much of the distributional data are problematic in one way or another. The most frequent problem is that the studies are not based on national samples. Furthermore, the interpretation of results is often colored by reformist agendas. There is a tendency to deemphasize differences in frequency from one segment of the population to another so as to build support of dowry death as a general social reform issue. Nevertheless, while the data available for these distributions are of inconsistent quality, they are interpretable in terms of our problem.

Women's Access to Production Roles and Property

Dowry violence is most frequent in north India. Some say that it is an especially severe problem in the Hindi Belt (i.e., Uttar Pradesh, Haryana, Punjab, Delhi, Bihar) (Government of India 1974:75). It is a lesser, albeit increasing problem in the south. There is also a north/south difference in the marriage institution itself. To simplify somewhat, in the north hypergamy is sought after in marriage alliances, in which case brides seek grooms from higher rank descent groups within their caste group (Srinivas 1984). In the south, marriages are more typically isogamous.

The literature comparing north and south India indicates important contrasts at both the ecological and the institutional levels. Based on conceptions developed by Boserup (1970) in a cross-cultural comparative framework on the relationship between the farming system and occupational role of women, Miller (1981) composed a model for explaining the significant north-south differences in the juvenile sex ratio [the ratio of males to females ten years of age and below]. The farming systems of the north are based on "dry-field plow cultivation," whereas in the south the farming systems are dominated by "swidden and wet-rice cultivation" (Miller 1981:28). These two systems make different labor demands. In the wet rice or swidden systems of the south, women are very important sources of labor. In the north, women's involvement in agricultural production is limited. According to Miller, women in the north are excluded from property holding and receive instead a "dowry of movables." In the south, where women are included in the production activities, they may receive "rights to land" (Miller 1981:28). In the north, women are high-cost items of social overhead, while in the south, women contribute labor and are more highly valued. In the north there is a "high cost of raising several daughters" while in the south there is "little liability in raising several daughters." There is thus "discrimination against daughters" and an "intense preference for sons" in the north, and "appreciation for daughters" and "moderate preference for sons" in the south. Miller thus explains the unbalanced-toward-males juvenile sex ratios of the north and the balanced sex ratios of the south (Miller 1981:27–28). The lower economic value of women in the north is expressed in differential treatment of children by sex. Females get less food, less care, and less attention, and therefore they have a higher death rate. In general the Boserup and Miller economic argument is consistent with Engels's thesis about the relationship between the subordination of women and property (Engels 1884; Hirschon 1984:1).

Miller extended her analysis of juvenile sex ratios to include marriage costs (including dowry), female labor participation, and property owning, and found that property owning was associated with high marriage costs and low female labor force participation, both of which were associated with high juvenile sex ratios. That is, the death rate of females is higher when marriage costs are high and women are kept from remunerative employment. Both of these patterns are associated with the "propertied" segment of the population (Miller 1981:156–159). Her data are derived from the secondary analysis of ethnographic accounts. The literature concerning the distribution of dowry practices and dowry death is consistent with these results.

Miller's analysis shows a general pattern of treatment of females in India. Their access to support in various forms is related to their contribution to production (Miller 1981). This analysis does not explain the problem of dowry violence, but it does demonstrate a fundamental pattern within which dowry violence can be interpreted.

The distribution of dowry varies by caste. In her study of dowry violence victims in Delhi, Kumari found that members of the lower ranking castes report less "dowry harassment" than do those in higher ranking castes (Kumari 1988:31). These results are consistent with Miller's argument since the pattern of exclusion of women from economic production roles varies by caste. Women of lower castes are less subject to restrictions concerning employment outside the realm of reproduction within the household. These women are often poor and uneducated, and are subject to other types of restrictions.

In the framework of caste, dowry practices of higher caste groups are emulated by lower caste groups. This process is known as "Sanskritization" and it may relate to the widely held view that dowry harassment is increasing in lower ranking castes. Sanskritization is the process by which lower ranked caste groups attempt to raise their rank through the emulation of higher rank castes. The emulation involves discarding certain behaviors (such as eating meat or paying bride price) and adopting alternatives (Srinivas 1969). Attitudinal research shows that people of the lower socio-economic strata have a greater commitment to dowry than do those of higher strata (Hooja 1969; Khanna and Verghese 1978; Paul 1986). Although the lower and middle classes are committed to dowry, the associated violence, including higher death rates, is more typically a middle class problem (Kumari 1988).

Employment status of women has an effect on dowry. In her survey of dowry problems in a south Delhi neighborhood, Paul (1986) found that the amount of dowry was less for employed middle class women than it was for the unemployed. This pattern is also suggested by Verghese (1980) and van der Veen (1972:40), but disputed by others (Murickan 1975). This link is also manifested among tribal people undergoing urbanization. Tribal people, ranked more toward the low end of the social hierarchy, typically make use of bride price (i.e., a payment to the bride's family) rather than dowry (Karve 1953). As these groups become more integrated into national life, they will shift to dowry practices to emulate high castes while their women participate less in gainful employment (Luthra 1983). Croll finds a similar relationship in her analysis of post-revolutionary China. She says, "it is the increased value attributed to women's labor which is largely responsible for the decline in the dowry" (1984:58).

Both Kumari (1988) and Srinivas (1984) developed arguments based on non-economic factors. Kumari in effect indicated that if dowry could be explained in economic terms, marriage would be simply a calculation of the value of a woman: if the value were high, bride price would be paid, and if the value were low, dowry transactions would occur. This formulation was presented as a refutation of Madan's dowry-as-compensation argument (Kumari 1988). We agree that reducing this practice to purely economic terms is an absurdity. The argument is not purely economic, but it is certainly consistent with a cultural materialist perspective (Harris 1979) in which symbolic values are shaped by an underlying material relationship that is the basis for the construction of cultural reality.

Delocalization of Social Control

Dowry violence is more frequent in cities (Saini 1983). Delhi has the reputation of having a high frequency of problems of dowry (Srinivas 1984:7). The urban-rural distribution pattern may be a manifestation of the effects of the delocalization of dowry. Dowry, when operative in the relationships among local caste groups in related villages, was to an extent self-regulating through caste *panchayats* (councils) and by the joint families themselves. These groups easily reach into peoples' lives. By contrast, the national level laws have inadequate reach and cannot achieve regulation. While in some areas caste groups continue to function to limit abuses, these groups are less effective in urban settings. Population movements and competition with state level social control mechanisms limit the effectiveness of self-regulation. A government commission study of women's status argues "that because of changed circumstances in which a son generally has a separate establishment and has a job somewhere away from home, the parents cannot expect much help from him, and so they consider his marriage as the major occasion on which their investment in his education can be recovered" (Government of India 1974:74). These views are consistent with the research results reported by Paul, who demonstrates that dowry amounts are higher among people who have migrated to Delhi and those who live in nuclear families, because the families in general and the women in particular are less subject to social constraints (Paul 1986). New brides do not seem to have adequate support networks in urban settings.

Economic Transformation of Society

The custom of dowry has been thrown into disarray by inflationary pressures. The consumer price index for urban non-manual workers has increased from its reference year of 1960 value of 100 to 532 for 1984–85 (Government of India 1987). The media of dowry exchange have changed dramatically because of the increasing availability of consumer goods. It has become increasingly difficult to prepare for giving dowry for a daughter or a sister. Sharma argues that, in part, dowry problems are caused by rapid change in the nature of consumer goods which made it no longer possible to accumulate gift goods over a long period as the latest styles in material goods could not be presented (1984: 70–71).

The current regime of individual dowry seeking and giving is constituted as a kind of rational behavior. That is, it is achieved through choice, is consistent with certain values, and serves to increase someone's utility. There are a number of things sought by the groom's family in these transactions. Wealth and family prestige are especially important. The family prestige "bought" with marriage expenditures, which is relevant to both the bride and groom's side in the transaction, is no doubt very much worth maximizing in the Indian context. From the perspective of the bride's family, dowry payments involve trading present consumption for future earning power for their daughter through acquiring a groom with better qualities and connections. In a two-tier, gender segregated, high unemployment, inflationary economy such as that of India, one can grasp the advantage of investing in husbands with high future earning potential. It is also possible to argue that in societies with symbolic mechanisms of stratification, it is expected that persons will attempt to make public displays of consumption in order to improve their overall performance and so to take advantage of the ambiguities of the status hierarchy system. The demand for both symbolic goods and future earnings is highly elastic. Family connections, education, and wealth seem especially important in India, and they all serve as hedges against inflation and poverty. With women having limited access to jobs and earning lower pay, it is rational to invest in a share of the groom's prospects. If you ask people why they give dowry when their daughters are being married they say, "because we love them." On the other hand, grooms' families will find the decision to forgo dowry very difficult.

SUMMARY

The distributional data indicate that the relationship between the way females are treated in marriage and their participation in economic production is consistent with Miller's development of the Boserup hypothesis. It is assumed that the pattern of maltreatment of females has been subject to various controls operating at the levels of family, caste, and community. Urbanization reduces the effectiveness of these mechanisms, thus increasing the intensity of the problem. This trend is exacerbated by the economic transformations within contemporary Indian society. It is our viewpoint that policies developed to reduce dowry-related violence will fail if they do not increase the economic value of women.

The criminalization of dowry may have been a politically useful symbol, but it has not curtailed the practice. As dowry is attacked, the state has not adequately dealt with the ante-mortem inheritance aspect of the custom. If dowry continues to provide a share of the family wealth to daughters before the death of the parents, then legally curtailing the practice is likely to damage the economic interests of women in the name of protecting them. One might argue that the primary legal remedy for the dowry problem actually makes it worse because it limits the transfer of assets to women. Perhaps this is why research on attitudes toward dowry indicates a continued positive commitment to the institution (Mathew 1987). India is a society in which most people (most particularly the elite) have given and received dowry; most people are even today giving and taking dowries. Declaring dowry a crime creates a condition in which the mass of society are technically criminals. The moral-legal basis of society suffers, and communal, parochial, and other fissiparous forces are encouraged.

To be effective, anti-dowry legislation must make sure that the social utility provided by dowry practices be displaced to practices that are less problematic, and that the apparent causes of the practice be attacked. To do so would mean that attempts to eradicate the social evils produced by the dowry institution need to be based on an examination of women's property rights so as to increase their economic access. Traditional Hindu customs associated with inheritance give sons the right from birth to claim the so-called ancestral properties. This principle is part of the Mitakshara tradition of Hindu law, which prevails throughout India except in Bengal, Kerala, Assam, and northern parts of Orissa. These properties are obtained from father, paternal grandfather, or paternal great-grandfather. According to Sivaramayya (1984:71), "The Hindu Succession Act (the law which controls inheritance) did not abrogate this right by birth which exists in favor of a son, paternal grandson, and paternal great grandson. The availability of the right in favor of these male descendants only is a discrimination against daughters." The right is derived from ancient texts. According to Tambiah (1973:95), the Dharmasastras provide that it is "essentially males who inherit the patrimony while women are entitled to maintenance, marriage expenses and gifts." While the Hindu Succession Act abrogates much traditional law, it specifically accepts the principle of male birthright to the property of the joint family. That is, "When a male Hindu dies after the commencement of the Act, having at the time of death an interest in a Mitakshara coparcenary property, his interest in the property shall devolve by survivorship upon the surviving members of the coparcenary and not in accordance with this Act" (Government of India 1985:3). The Hindu Succession Act in its most recent form provides for the intestate or testamentary inheritance of a female of a share of the family property. Yet the prior right of males at birth is not abrogated. Hindu males own a share of the family rights at birth; females can inherit it. Testamentary succession overrides the principle of intestate succession, and therefore the interests of females can be usurped simply by writing a will. The other procedures for a female to renounce an interest in family property are very simple. Moreover, according to Sivaramayya (1984:58), "no specific formality is required for the relinquishment of the interest beyond the expression of a clear intention to that effect." Instruments of relinquishment can be and are forged.

The antemortem inheritance function of dowry has been eroded or perhaps supplanted by transfer of goods to the groom's family for their consumption and the expression of the so-called prestige of the family. Indeed social science commentary on dowry in India suggests that this aspect of dowry is relatively unimportant in any case because only a small portion of the total marriage expenditure is under the bride's control. There is evidence that even the clothing and ornaments and other personal property of the bride are being usurped (Verghese 1980). Implementation of a gender-neutral inheritance law as advocated by the Government of India Committee on the Status of Women may serve to increase the economic value of women in general, while it serves as an alternative to the ante-mortem inheritance aspect of dowry. Since dowry constitutes a kind of ante-mortem inheritance, it is logical to change the inheritance laws in conjunction with the restrictions on dowry behavior. Sisters as well as brothers need to have a share in the family wealth from birth, and that right should be associated with legal procedures that increase the difficulty of alienation of property rights. There is no question that such a procedure would serve to erode the stability of the patrilineal family by diluting its economic base.

The Government of India has passed legislation such as the Hindu Succession Act (1956) and the Hindu Adoption and Maintenance Act (1956), both of which inter-alia provide for a woman's right of inheritance from her father. For example, under the Adoption and Maintenance Act, a woman has a claim of rights of maintenance from her husband's father in case she is widowed. Moreover, she has the right to claim inheritance from her deceased husband's estate. In spite of these changes, inheritance provisions are quite different for males and females. The Chief Justice of the Supreme Court of India, Honorable Mr. Justice Y. V. Chandrachud, wrote that in spite of changes, "some inequalities like the right of birth in favor of a son, paternal grandson, and paternal great grandson still persist" (1984:vii). Provision of females with equal rights to inherit ancestral property from birth, or from a bequest, or at the death may reduce dowry problems.

Furthermore, property that is allowed to remain in the name of the deceased for any length of time, as is frequently the case in India, should revert to the state. As it stands, property may remain in the name of a deceased ancestor, while his descendants divide it informally among themselves.

The establishment of a gender-neutral inheritance law represents a significant shift in public policy. We argue that there is a link between pro-male property laws and violence toward women. While we assert this position, we also need to recognize that the property laws give coherence and stability to an essential Indian institution, the joint family. The Mitakshara principle of male inheritance rights is both a reflection and a cause of family solidarity. Modifying this principle in an attempt to reduce violence toward women could have a deleterious effect on family coherence. In addition, the fundamental nature of these institutions makes it inconceivable that there would be substantial resistance to these changes. Yet if one considers this issue in historic terms, it is apparent that during the twentieth century, legal change is in the direction of gender neutrality, a process that started with the Hindu Law of Inheritance (Amendment) Act (1929) and the Hindu Succession Act (1956), and continues through judicial decisions to the present (Diwan 1988:384). As Diwan notes in reference to the changes brought by the Hindu Succession Act of 1956, "the Mitakshara bias towards preference of males over females and of agnates over cognates has been considerably whittled down" (1988:358). Such change is not easy. The changes brought with the Hindu Succession Act in 1956 were achieved only after overcoming "stiff resistance from the traditionalists" (Government of India 1974:135). The same report states, "The hold of tradition, however, was so strong that even while introducing sweeping changes, the legislators compromised and retained in some respects the inferior position of women" (Government of India 1974:135). It must be remembered that the texts that are the foundations of contemporary law include legislation (such as the Hindu Succession Act itself), case law, and religious texts, so that the constitutional question is also a question for religious interpretation, despite the constitutional commitment to secularism.

We are advocating further steps toward gender neutrality of the inheritance laws so that women and men will receive an equal share under intestate succession, and have an equal chance to be testamentary heirs. The law should thus be gender-neutral while still permitting a range of decisions allowing property to stay in a male line if the holder of the property so chooses. The required social adjustment could be largely achieved through the decisions of a family, backed by the power of the state. Families could express their preferences, but the state would not serve to protect the economic interests of males. The process could involve the concept of birthright as well as succession at death. We do not choose to engage those arguments, but do point out that the rapid aging of the Indian population may suggest that a full abrogation of the Mitakshara principle of birthright would be the best social policy because doing so would give older people somewhat greater control over their property in an economy virtually devoid of public investment in social services for older people (Bose and Gangrade 1988, Sharma and Dak 1987).

There are precedents for such policy at the state level. In Andhra Pradesh, the Hindu Succession Act was amended to provide for a female's birthright interest in the Mitakshara property. In Kerala, the Mitakshara property concept was legally abrogated altogether. Other gender asymmetries in the laws of India need to be attacked. The overall goal of policy should be to increase the economic value of women.

Ethnological theory directs our attention to social recognition of marriage and property transfer as functionally important features of the institution. The state can provide a means of socially recognizing marriage through registration and licensure. The law expresses no explicit preference for traditional marriage ritual, and it is possible to have a civil marriage under the provisions of the Special Marriage Act (1954) through registration with a magistrate. Nevertheless, this system co-exists parallel with the traditional system of marriage, which is beyond the reach of state control. Other marriages may be registered under this act if the persons involved so choose, and if a ceremony has been carried out. These special marriages are an alternative to an unregistered marriage.

We conclude that a useful mechanism for state control of dowry problems is the establishment of universal marriage registration, which does not exist at the present time. Marriage registration is also called for by the first Round Table on Social Audit of Implementation of Dowry Legislation (Bhatia 1988), which may serve to provide some monitoring of dowry abuses and perhaps to manifest the state's interest in an effective marriage institution. It would be naive to assume that such a policy would be widely honored, but as it is, low-income persons do not get married because they do not have the resources for marriage under the traditional non-state controlled regime. There are numerous reform groups that organize mass marriage ceremonies of village people so as to help them escape the burden of marriage expenditures. The point is that compliance is a large problem even under current circumstances.

In conclusion, we feel that the causes of the dowry problems are a product of the low economic value of women, loss of effective social control of abuse through delocalization, and pressures caused by economic transformation. The traditional family, caste group, and community controls which have been reduced in effectiveness should be replaced by state functions. The foundation of state control is universal marriage registration and licensure. The impact of the economic value of women on the problem is indicated by the transition from bride price to dowry among tribal people. It is also associated with a reduction in the extent of gainful employment and lower dowry amounts demonstrated for employed women. A broad program to increase the economic value of women would be the most useful means of dealing with the problem of dowry. Further restrictions on dowry without providing for a radically different property right for females is probably not in the interests of Indian women, since dowry represents ante-mortem inheritance. This underlying paradox may explain the commitment to dowry revealed in attitudinal research with Indian women, even though it is also an important feminist issue. The alternatives include the abolishment of the legal basis for the joint family as a corporate unit as has been done in Kerala, or the legal redefinition of the joint family as economically duolineal, as has occurred in Andhra Pradesh.

NOTE

1. For purposes of comparison, a mid-career Indian academic might be paid 60,000 Rs. per year.

REFERENCES

Aluwalia, H. 1969. Matrimonial Advertisements in Panjab. *Indian Journal of Social Work* 30:55–65.

Bhatia, S. C. 1988. Social Audit of Dowry Legislation. Delhi: Legal Literacy Project.

Bose, A. B., and K. D. Gangrade. 1988. *The Aging in India, Problems and Potentialities.* New Delhi: Abhinav.

Boserup, Ester. 1970. *Women's Role in Economic Development.* New York: St. Martin's Press.

Chandrachud, Y. V. 1984. Foreword. In *Inequalities and the Law.* B. Sivaramayya, ed. Pp. iv–vi. Lucknow: Eastern Book Company.

Croll, Elisabeth. 1984. The Exchange of Women and Property: Marriage in Post-revolutionary China. In *Women and Property—Women as Property,* ed. Renee Hirschon, 44–61. London/New York: Croom Helm/St. Martin's Press.

Diwan, Paras. 1988. *Modern Hindu Law, Codified and Uncodified.* Allahabad: Allahabad Law Agency.

Dumont, Louis. 1957. *Hierarchy and Marriage Alliance in South Indian Kinship.* London: Royal Anthropological Institute.

Engels, Fredrich. 1884. *The Origin of Family, Private Property and the State.* New York: International.

Epstein, T. Scarlett. 1960. Peasant Marriage in South India. *Man in India* 40: 192–232.

Friedl, Ernestine. 1967. *Vasilika, A Village in Modern Greece.* New York: Holt, Rinehart and Winston.

Goody, Jack. 1973. Bridewealth and Dowry in Africa and Eurasia. In *Bridewealth and Dowry,* eds. Jack Goody and S. J. Tambiah, 1–58. Cambridge: Cambridge University Press.

______. 1976. *Production and Reproduction, A Comparative Study of the Domestic Domain.* Cambridge: Cambridge University Press.

Government of India. 1974. *Towards Equality: Report of the Committee on the Status of Women.* New Delhi: Government of India, Ministry of Education and Social Welfare.

______. 1985. The Hindu Succession Act. New Delhi: Government of India.

______. 1986. The Dowry Prohibition Act, 1961 (Act No. 28 of 1961) and Connected Legislation (as on 15th January, 1986). New Delhi: Government of India.

______. 1987. *India 1986, A Reference Manual.* Delhi: Ministry of Information and Broadcasting.

Harris, Marvin. 1979. *Cultural Materialism: The Struggle for a Science of Culture.* New York: Random House.

Hirschon, Renee. 1984. Introduction: Property, Power and Gender Relations. In *Women and Property—Women as Property,* ed. Renee Hirschon, 1–22. London/New York: Croom Helm/St. Martin's Press.

Hooja, S. L. 1969. *Dowry System in India.* New Delhi: Asia Press.

Karve, Irawati. 1953. *Kinship Organization in India.* Bombay: Asia Publishing.

Khanna, G., and M. Verghese. 1978. *Indian Women Today.* New Delhi: Vikas Publishing House.

Kumari, Ranjana. 1988. Practice and Problems of Dowry: A Study of Dowry Victims in Delhi. In *Social Audit of Dowry Legislation,* ed. S. C. Bhatia, 27–37. Delhi: Legal Literacy Project.

Luthra, A. 1983. Dowry Among the Urban Poor, Perception and Practice. *Social Action* 33: 207.

Mathew, Anna. 1987. Attitudes Toward Dowry. *Indian Journal of Social Work* 48: 95–102.

Menon, N. R. Madhava. 1988. The Dowry Prohibition Act: Does the Law Provide the Solution or Itself Constitute the Problem? In *Social Audit of Dowry Legislation,* ed. S. C. Bhatia, 11–26. Delhi: Legal Literacy Project.

Miller, Barbara D. 1981. *The Endangered Sex, Neglect of Female Children in Rural North India.* Ithaca, NY: Cornell University Press.

Murdock, George P. 1949. *Social Structure.* New York: Macmillan.

Murickan, J. 1975. Women in Kerala: Changing Socio-economic Status and Self Image. In *Women in Contemporary India,* ed. A. de Souza, 73–95. Delhi: Manohar.

Niehoff, Arthur H. 1959. A Study of Matrimonial Advertisements in North India. *Eastern Anthropologist* 12: 37–50.

Paul, Madan C. 1986. *Dowry and the Position of Women in India. A Study of Delhi Metropolis.* New Delhi: Inter India Publishers.

Saini, Debi. 1983. Dowry Prohibition Law, Social Change and Challenges in India. *Indian Journal of Social Work* 44(2): 143–147.

Sharma, M. L., and T. Dak. 1987. *Aging in India, Challenge for the Society.* Delhi: Ajanta Publications.

Sharma, Ursula. 1984. Dowry in North India: Its Consequences for Women. In *Women and Property—Women as Property,* ed. Renee Hirschon, 62–74. London/New York: Croom Helm/St. Martin's Press.

Sivaramayya, B. 1984. *Inequalities and the Law.* Lucknow: Eastern Book Company.

Srinivas, M. N. 1969. *Social Change in Modern India.* Berkeley, CA: University of California Press.

______. 1984. *Some Reflections on Dowry.* Delhi: Oxford University Press.

Tambiah, S. J. 1973. Dowry and Bridewealth and the Property Rights of Women in South Asia. In *Bridewealth and Dowry,* eds. Jack Goody and S. J. Tambiah, 59–169. Cambridge: Cambridge University Press.

van der Veen, Klaus W. 1972. *I Give Thee My Daughter—A Study of Marriage and Hierarchy Among the Anavil Brahmins of South Gujarat.* Assen: Van Gorcum.

Verghese, Jamila. 1980. *Her Gold and Her Body.* New Delhi: Vikas Publishing House.

Weibe, P. O., and G. N. Ramu. 1971. A Content Analysis of Matrimonial Advertisements. *Man in India* 51: 119–120.

Westermarck, Edward. 1921. *The History of Human Marriage.* London: MacMillan and Co.

The Adaptive Value of Religious Ritual

Rituals promote group cohesion by requiring members to engage in behavior that is too costly to fake.

RICHARD SOSIS

I was 15 years old the first time I went to Jerusalem's Old City and visited the 2,000-year-old remains of the Second Temple, known as the Western Wall. It may have foreshadowed my future life as an anthropologist, but on my first glimpse of the ancient stones I was more taken by the people standing at the foot of the structure than by the wall itself. Women stood in the open sun, facing the Wall in solemn worship, wearing long-sleeved shirts, head coverings and heavy skirts that scraped the ground. Men in their thick beards, long black coats and fur hats also seemed oblivious to the summer heat as they swayed fervently and sang praises to God. I turned to a friend, "Why would anyone in their right mind dress for a New England winter only to spend the afternoon praying in the desert heat?" At the time I thought there was no rational explanation and decided that my fellow religious brethren might well be mad.

Of course, "strange" behavior is not unique to ultraorthodox Jews. Many religious acts appear peculiar to the outsider. Pious adherents the world over physically differentiate themselves from others: Moonies shave their heads, Jain monks of India wear contraptions on their heads and feet to avoid killing insects, and clergy almost everywhere dress in outfits that distinguish them from the rest of society. Many peoples also engage in some form of surgical alteration. Australian aborigines perform a ritual operation on adolescent boys in which a bone or a stone is inserted into the penis through an incision in the urethra. Jews and Muslims submit their sons to circumcision, and in some Muslim societies daughters are also subject to circumcision or other forms of genital mutilation. Groups as diverse as the Nuer of Sudan and the latmul of New Guinea force their adolescents to undergo ritual scarification. Initiation ceremonies, otherwise known as rites of passage, are often brutal. Among Native Americans, Apache boys were forced to bathe in icy water, Luiseno initiates were required to lie motionless while being bitten by hordes of ants, and Tukuna girls had their hair plucked out.

How can we begin to understand such behavior? If human beings are rational creatures, then why do we spend so much time, energy and resources on acts that can be so painful or, at the very least, uncomfortable? Archaeologists tell us that our species has engaged in ritual behavior for at least 100,000 years, and every known culture practices some form of religion. It even survives covertly in those cultures where governments have attempted to eliminate spiritual practices. And, despite the unparalleled triumph of scientific rationalism in the 20th century, religion continued to flourish. In the United States a steady 40 percent of the population attended church regularly throughout the century. A belief in God (about 96 percent), the afterlife (about 72 percent), heaven (about 72 percent) and hell (about 58 percent) remained substantial and remarkably constant. Why do religious beliefs, practices and institutions continue to be an essential component of human social life?

Such questions have intrigued me for years. Initially my training in anthropology did not provide an answer. Indeed, my studies only increased my bewilderment. I received my training in a subfield known as human behavioral ecology, which studies the adaptive design of behavior with attention to its ecological setting. Behavioral ecologists assume that natural selection has shaped the human nervous system to respond successfully to varying ecological circumstances. All organisms must balance trade-offs: Time spent doing one thing prevents them from pursuing other activities that can enhance their survival or reproductive success. Animals that maximize the rate at which they acquire resources, such as food and mates, can maximize the number of descendants, which is exactly what the game of natural selection is all about.

Behavioral ecologists assume that natural selection has designed our decision-making mechanisms to optimize the rate at which human beings accrue resources under diverse ecological conditions—a basic prediction of *optimal foraging theory.* Optimality models offer predictions of the "perfectly adapted" behavioral response, given a set of environmental constraints. Of course, a perfect fit with the environment is almost never achieved because organisms rarely have perfect information and because environments are always changing. Nevertheless, this assumption has provided a powerful framework to analyze a variety of decisions, and most research (largely conducted among foraging populations) has shown that our species broadly conforms to these expectations.

If our species is designed to optimize the rate at which we extract energy from the environment, why would we engage in religious behavior that seems so counterproductive? Indeed, some religious practices, such as ritual sacrifices, are a conspicuous display of wasted resources. Anthropologists can explain why foragers regularly share their food with others in the group, but why would anyone share their food with a dead ancestor by burning it to ashes on an altar? A common response to this question is that people believe in the efficacy of the rituals and the tenets of the faith that give meaning to the ceremonies. But this response merely begs the question. We must really ask why natural selection has favored a psychology that believes in the supernatural and engages in the costly manifestations of those beliefs.

Ritual Sacrifice

Behavioral ecologists have only recently begun to consider the curiosities of religious activities, so at first I had to search other disciplines to understand these practices. The scholarly literature suggested that I wasn't the only one who believed that intense religious behavior was a sign of madness. Some of the greatest minds of the past two centuries, such as Marx and Freud, supported my thesis. And the early anthropological theorists also held that spiritual beliefs were indicative of a primitive and simple mind. In the 19th century, Edward B. Tylor, often noted as one of the founding fathers of anthropology, maintained that religion arose out of a misunderstanding among "primitives" that dreams are real. He argued that dreams about deceased ancestors might have led the primitives to believe that spirits can survive death.

Eventually the discipline of anthropology matured, and its practitioners moved beyond the equation that "primitive equals irrational." Instead, they began to seek functional explanations of religion. Most prominent among these early 20th-century theorists was the Polish-born anthropologist Bronislaw Malinowski. He argued that religion arose out of "the real tragedies of human life, out of the conflict between human plans and realities." Although religion may serve to allay our fears of death, and provide comfort from our incessant search for answers, Malinowski's thesis did not seem to explain the origin of rituals. Standing in the midday desert sun in several layers of black clothing seems more like a recipe for increasing anxiety than treating it. The classical anthropologists didn't have the right answers to my questions. I needed to look elsewhere.

Fortunately, a new generation of anthropologists has begun to provide some explanations. It turns out that the strangeness of religious practices and their inherent costs are actually the critical features that contribute to the success of religion as a universal cultural strategy and why natural selection has favored such behavior in the human lineage. To understand this unexpected benefit we need to recognize the adaptive problem that ritual behavior solves. William Irons, a behavioral ecologist at Northwestern University, has suggested that the universal dilemma is the promotion of cooperation within a community. Irons argues that the primary adaptive benefit of religion is its ability to facilitate cooperation within a group—while hunting, sharing food, defending against attacks and waging war—all critical activities in our evolutionary history. But, as Irons points out, although everyone is better off if everybody cooperates, this ideal is often very difficult to coordinate and achieve. The problem is that an individual is even better off if everyone else does the cooperating, while he or she remains at home enjoying an afternoon siesta. Cooperation requires social mechanisms that prevent individuals from free riding on the efforts of others. Irons argues that religion is such a mechanism.

The key is that religious rituals are a form of communication, which anthropologists have long maintained. They borrowed this insight from ethologists who observed that many species engage in patterned behavior, which they referred to as "ritual." Ethologists recognized that ritualistic behaviors served as a form of communication between members of the same species, and often between members of different species. For example, the males of many avian species engage in courtship rituals—such as bowing, head wagging, wing waving and hopping (among many other gestures)—to signal their amorous intents before a prospective mate. And, of course, the vibration of a rattlesnake's tail is a powerful threat display to other species that enter its personal space.

Irons's insight is that religious activities signal commitment to other members of the group. By engaging in the ritual, the member effectively says, "I identify with the group and I believe in what the group stands for." Through its ability to signal commitment, religious behavior can overcome the problem of free riders and promote cooperation within the group. It does so because trust lies at the heart of the problem: A member must assure everyone that he or she will participate in acquiring food or in defending the group. Of course, hunters and warriors may make promises—"you have my word, I'll show up tomorrow"—but unless the trust is already established such statements are not believable.

It turns out that there is a robust way to secure trust. Israeli biologist Amotz Zahavi observes that it is often in the best interest of an animal to send a dishonest signal—perhaps to fake its size, speed, strength, health or beauty. The only signal that can be believed is one that is too costly to fake, which he referred to as a "handicap." Zahavi argues that natural selection has favored the evolution of handicaps. For example, when a springbok antelope spots a predator it often *stots*—it jumps up and down. This extraordinary behavior puzzled biologists for years: Why would an antelope waste precious energy that could be used to escape the predator? And why would the animal make itself more visible to something that wants to eat it? The reason is that the springbok is displaying its quality to the predator—its ability to escape, effectively saying, "Don't bother chasing me. Look how strong my legs are, you won't be able to catch me." The only reason a predator believes the springbok is because the signal is too costly to fake. An antelope that is not quick enough to escape cannot imitate the signal because it is not strong enough to repeatedly jump to a certain height. Thus, a display can provide honest information if the signals are so costly to perform that lower quality organisms cannot benefit by imitating the signal.

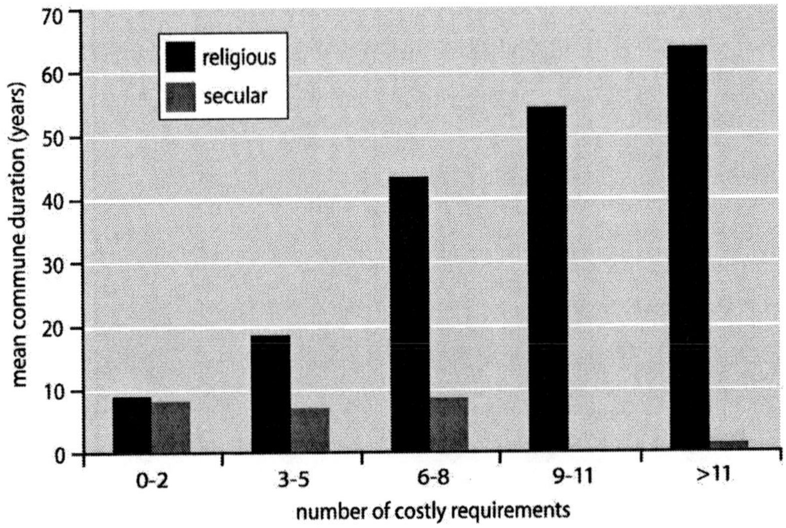

behaviors that are constrained

consumption of:
coffee, alcohol, tobacco, meat, other foods or beverages

use and ownership of:
photographs, jewelry, certain technology, other material items

activities:
monogamous marriage, gambling, communication with the outside, living as a nuclear family, maintaining rights to biological children

behaviors that are required

trial period for membership, surrender of material belongings, learn a body of knowledge, endure public sessions of criticism, certain clothing styles, certain hairstyles, fasting

In much the same way, religious behavior is also a costly signal. By donning several layers of clothing and standing out in the midday sun, ultraorthodox Jewish men are signaling to others: "Hey! Look, I'm a *haredi* Jew. If you are also a member of this group you can trust me because why else would I be dressed like this? No one would do this *unless* they believed in the teachings of ultraorthodox Judaism and were fully committed to its ideals and goals." The quality that these men are signaling is their level of commitment to a specific religious group.

Adherence to a set of religious beliefs entails a host of ritual obligations and expected behaviors. Although there may be physical or psychological benefits associated with some ritual practices, the significant time, energy and financial costs involved serve as effective deterrents for anyone who does not believe in the teachings of a particular religion. There is no incentive for nonbelievers to join or remain in a religious group, because the costs of maintaining membership—such as praying three times a day, eating only kosher food, donating a certain part of your income to charity and so on—are simply too high.

Those who engage in the suite of ritual requirements imposed by a religious group can be trusted to believe sincerely in the doctrines of their respective religious communities. As a result of increased levels of trust and commitment among group members, religious groups minimize costly monitoring mechanisms that are otherwise necessary to overcome free-rider problems that typically plague communal pursuits. Hence, the adaptive benefit of ritual behavior is its ability to promote and maintain cooperation, a challenge that our ancestors presumably faced throughout our evolutionary history.

Benefits of Membership

One prediction of the "costly signaling theory of ritual" is that groups that impose the greatest demands on their members will elicit the highest levels of devotion and commitment. Only committed members will be willing to dress and behave in ways that differ from the rest of society. Groups that maintain more-committed members can also offer more because it's easier for them to attain their collective goals than groups whose members are less committed. This may explain a paradox in the religious marketplace: Churches that require the most of their adherents are experiencing rapid rates of growth. For example, the Church of Jesus Christ of Latter-day Saints (Mormons), Seventh-day Adventists and Jehovah's Witnesses, who respectively abstain from caffeine, meat and blood transfusions (among other things), have been growing at exceptional rates. In contrast, liberal Protestant denominations such as the Episcopalians, Methodists and Presbyterians have been steadily losing members.

Economist Lawrence Iannaccone, of George Mason University, has also noted that the most demanding groups also have the greatest number of committed members. He found that the more distinct a religious group was—how much the group's lifestyle differed from mainstream America—the higher its attendance rates at services. Sociologists Roger Finke and Rodney Stark, of Penn State and the University of Washington, respectively, have argued that when the Second Vatican Council in 1962 repealed many of the Catholic Church's prohibitions and reduced the level of strictness in the church, it initiated a decline in church attendance among American Catholics and reduced the enrollments in seminaries. Indeed, in the late 1950s almost 75 percent of American Catholics were attending Mass weekly, but since the Vatican's actions there has been a steady decline to the current rate of about 45 percent.

The costly signaling theory of ritual also predicts that greater commitment will translate into greater cooperation within groups. My colleague Eric Bressler, a graduate student at McMaster University, and I addressed this question by looking at data from the records of 19th-century communes. All communes face an inherent problem of promoting and sustaining cooperation because individuals can free ride on the efforts of others. Because cooperation is key to a commune's survival, we employed commune longevity as a measure of cooperation. Compared to their secular counterparts, the religious communes did indeed demand more of their members, including such behavior as celibacy, the surrender of all material possessions and vegetarianism. Communes that demanded more of their members survived longer, overcoming the fundamental challenges of cooperation. By placing greater demands on their

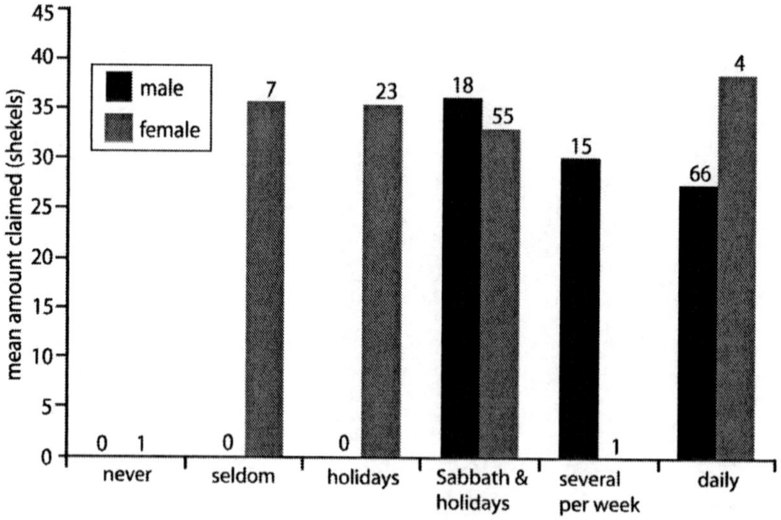

members, they were presumably able to elicit greater belief in and commitment toward the community's common ideology and goals.

I also wanted to evaluate the costly signaling theory of ritual within modern communal societies. The kibbutzim I had visited in Israel as a teenager provided an ideal opportunity to examine these hypotheses. For most of their 100-year history, these communal societies have lived by the dictum, "From each according to his abilities, to each according to his needs." The majority of the more than 270 kibbutzim are secular (and often ideologically antireligious); fewer than 20 are religiously oriented. Because of a massive economic failure—a collective debt of more than $4 billion—the kibbutzim are now moving in the direction of increased privatization and reduced communality. When news of the extraordinary debt surfaced in the late 1980s, it went largely unnoticed that the religious kibbutzim were financially stable. In the words of the Religious Kibbutz Movement Federation, "the economic position of the religious kibbutzim is sound, and they remain uninvolved in the economic crisis."

The success of the religious kibbutzim is especially remarkable given that many of their rituals inhibit economic productivity. For example, Jewish law does not permit Jews to milk cows on the Sabbath. Although rabbinic rulings now permit milking by kibbutz members to prevent the cows from suffering, in the early years none of this milk was used commercially. There are also significant constraints imposed by Jewish law on agricultural productivity. Fruits are not allowed to be eaten for the first few years of the tree's life, agricultural fields must lie fallow every seven years, and the corners of fields can never be harvested—they must be left for society's poor. Although these constraints appear detrimental to productivity, the costly signaling theory of ritual suggests that they may actually be the key to the economic success of the religious kibbutzim.

I decided to study this issue with economist Bradley Ruffle of Israel's Ben Gurion University. We developed a game to determine whether there were differences in how the members of secular and religious kibbutzim cooperated with each other. The game involves two members from the same kibbutz who remain anonymous to each other. Each member is told there are 100 shekels in an envelope to which both members have access. Each participant decides how many shekels to withdraw and keep. If the sum of both requests exceeds 100 shekels, both members receive no money and the game is over. However, if the requests are less than or equal to 100 shekels, the money remaining in the envelope is increased by 50 percent and divided evenly among the participants. Each member also keeps the original amount he or she requested. The game is an example of a common-pool resource dilemma in which publicly accessible goods are no longer available once they are consumed. Since the goods are available to more than one person, the maintenance of the resources requires individual self-restraint; in other words, cooperation.

After we controlled for a number of variables, including the age and size of the kibbutz and the amount of privatization, we found not only that religious kibbutzniks were more cooperative with each other than secular kibbutzniks, but that male religious kibbutz members were also significantly more cooperative than female members. Among secular kibbutzniks we found no sex differences at all. This result is understandable if we appreciate the types of rituals and demands imposed on religious Jews. Although there are a variety of requirements that are imposed equally on males and females, such as keeping kosher and refraining from work on the Sabbath, male rituals are largely performed in public, whereas female rituals are generally pursued privately. Indeed, none of the three major requirements imposed exclusively on women—attending a ritual bath, separating a portion of dough when baking bread and lighting Shabbat and holiday candles—are publicly performed. They are not rituals that signal commitment to a wider group; instead they appear to signal commitment to the family. Men, however, engage in highly visible rituals, most notably public prayer, which they are expected to perform three times a day. Among male religious kibbutz members, synagogue attendance is positively correlated with cooperative behavior. There is no similar correlation among females. This is not surprising given that women are not required to attend services, and so their presence does not signal commitment to the group. Here the costly signaling theory of ritual provides a unique explanation of these findings. We expect that further work will provide even more insight into the ability of ritual to promote trust, commitment and cooperation.

We know that many other species engage in ritual behaviors that appear to enhance trust and cooperation. For example, anthropologists John Watanabe of Dartmouth University and Barbara Smuts at the University of Michigan have shown that greetings between male olive baboons serve to signal trust and commitment between former rivals. So why are human rituals often cloaked in mystery and the supernatural? Cognitive anthropologists Scott Atran of the University of Michigan and Pascal Boyer at Washington University in St. Louis have pointed out that the counterintuitive nature of supernatural concepts are more easily remembered than mundane ideas, which facilitates their cultural transmission. Belief in supernatural agents such as gods, spirits and ghosts also appears to be critical to religion's ability to promote long-term cooperation. In our study of 19th-century communes, Eric Bressler and I found that the strong positive relationship between the number of costly requirements imposed on members and commune longevity only held for religious communes, not secular ones. We were surprised by this result because secular groups such as militaries and fraternities appear to successfully employ costly rituals to maintain cooperation. Cultural ecologist Roy Rappaport explained, however, that although religious and secular rituals can both promote cooperation, religious rituals ironically generate greater belief and commitment because they sanctify unfalsifiable statements that are beyond the possibility of examination. Since statements containing supernatural elements, such as "Jesus is the son of God," cannot be proved or disproved, believers verify them "emotionally." In contrast to religious propositions, the kibbutz's guiding dictum, taken from Karl Marx, is not beyond question; it can be evaluated by living according to its directives by distributing labor and resources appropriately. Indeed, as the economic situation on the kibbutzim has worsened, this fundamental proposition of kibbutz life has been challenged and is now disregarded by many who are pushing their communities to accept differential pay scales. The ability of religious rituals to evoke emotional experiences that can be associated with enduring supernatural concepts and symbols differentiates them from both animal and secular rituals and lies at the heart of their efficiency in promoting and maintaining long-term group cooperation and commitment.

Evolutionary research on religious behavior is in its infancy, and many questions remain to be addressed. The costly signaling theory of ritual appears to provide some answers, and, of course, it has given me a better understanding of the questions I asked as a teenager. The real value of the costly signaling theory of ritual will be determined by its ability to explain religious phenomena across societies. Most of us, including ultraorthodox Jews, are not living in communes. Nevertheless, contemporary religious congregations that demand much of their members are able to achieve a close-knit social community—an impressive accomplishment in today's individualistic world.

Religion has probably always served to enhance the union of its practitioners; unfortunately, there is also a dark side to this unity. If the intragroup solidarity that religion promotes is one of its significant adaptive benefits, then from its beginning religion has probably always played a role in intergroup conflicts. In other words, one of the benefits for individuals of intragroup solidarity is the ability of unified groups to defend and compete against other groups. This seems to be as true today as it ever was, and is nowhere more apparent than the region I visited as a 15-year-old boy—which is where I am as I write these words. As I conduct my fieldwork in the center of this war zone, I hope that by appreciating the depth of the religious need in the human psyche, and by understanding this powerful adaptation, we can learn how to promote cooperation rather than conflict.

Bibliography

Atran, S. 2002. *In Gods We Trust.* New York: Oxford University Press.

Iannaccone, L. 1992. Sacrifice and stigma: Reducing free-riding in cults, communes, and other collectives. *Journal of Political Economy* 100:271–291.

Iannaccone, L. 1994. Why strict churches are strong. *American Journal of Sociology* 99:1180–1211.

Irons, W. 2001. Religion as a hard-to-fake sign of commitment. In *Evolution and the Capacity for Commitment,* ed. R. Nesse, pp. 292–309. New York: Russell Sage Foundation.

Rappaport, R. 1999. *Ritual and Religion in the Making of Humanity.* Cambridge: Cambridge University Press.

Sosis, R. 2003. Why aren't we all Hutterites? Costly signaling theory and religious behavior. *Human Nature* 14:91–127.

Sosis, R., and C. Alcorta. 2003. Signaling, solidarity, and the sacred: The evolution of religious behavior. *Evolutionary Anthropology* 12:264–274.

Sosis, R., and E. Bressler. 2003. Cooperation and commune longevity: A test of the costly signaling theory of religion. *Cross-Cultural Research* 37:211–239.

Sosis, R., and B. Ruffle. 2003. Religious ritual and cooperation: Testing for a relationship on Israeli religious and secular kibbutzim. *Current Anthropology* 44:713–722.

Zahavi, A., and A. Zahavi. 1997. *The Handicap Principle.* New York: Oxford University Press.

Richard Sosis is an assistant professor of anthropology at the University of Connecticut. His research interests include the evolution of cooperation, utopian societies and the behavioral ecology of religion. Address: Department of Anthropology, U-2176, University of Connecticut, Storrs, CT 06269–2176. Internet: richard.sosis@uconn.edu

The Secrets of Haiti's Living Dead

A Harvard botanist investigates mystic potions, voodoo rites, and the making of zombies.

Gino Del Guercio

Five years ago, a man walked into l'Estère, a village in central Haiti, approached a peasant woman named Angelina Narcisse, and identified himself as her brother Clairvius. If he had not introduced himself using a boyhood nickname and mentioned facts only intimate family members knew, she would not have believed him. Because, eighteen years earlier, Angelina had stood in a small cemetery north of her village and watched as her brother Clairvius was buried.

The man told Angelina he remembered that night well. He knew when he was lowered into his grave, because he was fully conscious, although he could not speak or move. As the earth was thrown over his coffin, he felt as if he were floating over the grave. The scar on his right cheek, he said, was caused by a nail driven through his casket.

The night he was buried, he told Angelina, a voodoo priest raised him from the grave. He was beaten with a sisal whip and carried off to a sugar plantation in northern Haiti where, with other zombies, he was forced to work as a slave. Only with the death of the zombie master were they able to escape, and Narcisse eventually returned home.

Legend has it that zombies are the living dead, raised from their graves and animated by malevolent voodoo sorcerers, usually for some evil purpose. Most Haitians believe in zombies, and Narcisse's claim is not unique. At about the time he reappeared, in 1980, two women turned up in other villages saying they were zombies. In the same year, in northern Haiti, the local peasants claimed to have found a group of zombies wandering aimlessly in the fields.

But Narcisse's case was different in one crucial respect; it was documented. His death had been recorded by doctors at the American-directed Schweitzer Hospital in Deschapelles. On April 30, 1962, hospital records show, Narcisse walked into the hospital's emergency room spitting up blood. He was feverish and full of aches. His doctors could not diagnose his illness, and his symptoms grew steadily worse. Three days after he entered the hospital, according to the records, he died. The attending physicians, an American among them, signed his death certificate. His body was placed in cold storage for twenty hours, and then he was buried. He said he remembered hearing his doctors pronounce him dead while his sister wept at his bedside.

At the Centre de Psychiatrie et Neurologie in Port-au-Prince, Dr. Lamarque Douyon, a Haitian-born, Canadian-trained psychiatrist, has been systematically investigating all reports of zombies since 1961. Though convinced zombies were real, he had been unable to find a scientific explanation for the phenomenon. He did not believe zombies were people raised from the dead, but that did not make them any less interesting. He speculated that victims were only made to *look* dead, probably by means of a drug that dramatically slowed metabolism. The victim was buried, dug up within a few hours, and somehow reawakened.

The Narcisse case provided Douyon with evidence strong enough to warrant a request for assistance from colleagues in New York. Douyon wanted to find an ethnobotanist, a traditional-medicines expert, who could track down the zombie potion he was sure existed. Aware of the medical potential of a drug that could dramatically lower metabolism, a group organized by the late Dr. Nathan Kline—a New York psychiatrist and pioneer in the field of psychopharmacology—raised the funds necessary to send someone to investigate.

The search for that someone led to the Harvard Botanical Museum, one of the world's foremost institutes of ethnobiology. Its director, Richard Evans Schultes, Jeffrey professor of biology, had spent thirteen years in the tropics studying native medicines. Some of his best-known work is the investigation of curare, the substance used by the nomadic people of the Amazon to poison their darts. Refined into a powerful muscle relaxant called D-tubocurarine, it is now an essential component of the anesthesia used during almost all surgery.

Schultes would have been a natural for the Haitian investigation, but he was too busy. He recommended another Harvard ethnobotanist for the assignment, Wade Davis, a 28-year-old Canadian pursuing a doctorate in biology.

Davis grew up in the tall pine forests of British Columbia and entered Harvard in 1971, influenced by a *Life* magazine story on the student strike of 1969. Before Harvard, the only Americans he had known were draft dodgers, who seemed very exotic. "I used to fight forest fires with them," Davis says. "Like everybody else, I thought America was where it was at. And I wanted to go to Harvard because of that Life article. When I got there, I realized it wasn't quite what I had in mind."

Davis took a course from Schultes, and when he decided to go to South America to study plants, he approached his professor for guidance. "He was an extraordinary figure," Davis remembers. "He was a man who had done it all. He had lived alone for years in the Amazon." Schultes sent Davis to the rain forest with two letters of introduction and two pieces of advice: wear a pith helmet and try ayahuasca, a powerful hallucinogenic vine. During that expedition and others, Davis proved himself an "outstanding field man," says his mentor. Now, in early 1982, Schultes called him into his office and asked if he had plans for spring break.

"I always took to Schultes's assignments like a plant takes to water," says Davis, tall and blond, with inquisitive blue eyes. "Whatever Schultes told me to do, I did. His letters of introduction opened up a whole world." This time the world was Haiti.

Davis knew nothing about the Caribbean island—and nothing about African traditions, which serve as Haiti's cultural basis. He certainly did not believe in zombies. "I thought it was a lark," he says now.

Davis landed in Haiti a week after his conversation with Schultes, armed with a hypothesis about how the zombie drug—if it existed—might be made. Setting out to explore, he discovered a country materially impoverished, but rich in culture and mystery. He was impressed by the cohesion of Haitian society; he found none of the crime, social disorder, and rampant drug and alcohol abuse so common in many of the other Caribbean islands. The cultural wealth and cohesion, he believes, spring from the country's turbulent history.

During the French occupation of the late eighteenth century, 370,000 African-born slaves were imported to Haiti between 1780 and 1790. In 1791, the black population launched one of the few successful slave revolts in history, forming secret societies and overcoming first the French plantation owners and then a detachment of troops from Napoleon's army, sent to quell the revolt. For the next hundred years Haiti was the only independent black republic in the Caribbean, populated by people who did not forget their African heritage. "You can almost argue that Haiti is more African than Africa," Davis says. "When the west coast of Africa was being disrupted by colonialism and the slave trade, Haiti was essentially left alone. The amalgam of beliefs in Haiti is unique, but it's very, very African."

Davis discovered that the vast majority of Haitian peasants practice voodoo, a sophisticated religion with African roots. Says Davis, "It was immediately obvious that the stereotypes of voodoo weren't true. Going around the countryside, I found clues to a whole complex social world." Vodounists believe they communicate directly with, indeed are often possessed by, the many spirits who populate the everyday world. Vodoun society is a system of education, law, and medicine; it embodies a code of ethics that regulates social behavior. In rural areas, secret vodoun societies, much like those found on the west coast of Africa, are as much or more in control of everyday life as the Haitian government.

Although most outsiders dismissed the zombie phenomenon as folklore, some early investigators, convinced of its reality, tried to find a scientific explanation. The few who sought a zombie drug failed. Nathan Kline, who helped finance Davis's expedition, had searched unsuccessfully, as had Lamarque Douyon, the Haitian psychiatrist. Zora Neale Hurston, an American black woman, may have come closest. An anthropological pioneer, she went to Haiti in the Thirties, studied vodoun society, and wrote a book on the subject, *Tell My Horse,* first published in 1938. She knew about the secret societies and was convinced zombies were real, but if a power existed, she too failed to obtain it.

Davis obtained a sample in a few weeks.

He arrived in Haiti with the names of several contacts. A BBC reporter familiar with the Narcisse case had suggested he talk with Marcel Pierre. Pierre owned the Eagle Bar, a bordello in the city of Saint Marc. He was also a voodoo sorcerer and had supplied the BBC with a physiologically active powder of unknown ingredients. Davis found him willing to negotiate. He told Pierre he was a representative of "powerful but anonymous interests in New York," willing to pay generously for the priest's services, provided no questions were asked. Pierre agreed to be helpful for what Davis will only say was a "sizable sum." Davis spent a day watching Pierre gather the ingredients—including human bones—and grind them together with mortar and pestle. However, from his knowledge of poison, Davis knew immediately that nothing in the formula could produce the powerful effects of zombification.

Three weeks later, Davis went back to the Eagle Bar, where he found Pierre sitting with three associates. Davis challenged him. He called him a charlatan. Enraged, the priest gave him a second vial, claiming that this was the real poison. Davis pretended to pour the powder into his palm and rub it into his skin. "You're a dead man," Pierre told him, and he might have been, because this powder proved to be genuine. But, as the substance had not actually touched him, Davis was able to maintain his bravado, and Pierre was impressed. He agreed to make the poison and show Davis how it was done.

The powder, which Davis keeps in a small vial, looks like dry black dirt. It contains parts of toads, sea worms, lizards, tarantulas, and human bones. (To obtain the last ingredient, he and Pierre unearthed a child's grave on a nocturnal trip to the cemetery.) The poison is rubbed into the victim's skin. Within hours he begins to feel nauseated and has difficulty breathing. A pins-and-needles sensation afflicts his arms and legs, then progresses to the whole body. The subject becomes paralyzed; his lips turn blue for lack of oxygen. Quickly—sometimes within six hours—his metabolism is lowered to a level almost indistinguishable from death.

As Davis discovered, making the poison is an inexact science. Ingredients varied in the five samples he eventually acquired, although the active agents were always the same. And the poison came with no guarantee. Davis speculates that sometimes instead of merely paralyzing the victim, the compound kills him. Sometimes the victim suffocates in the coffin before he can be resurrected. But clearly the potion works well enough often enough to make zombies more than a figment of Haitian imagination.

Analysis of the powder produced another surprise. "When I went down to Haiti originally," says Davis, "my hypothesis was that the formula would contain *concombre zombi,* the 'zombie's cucumber,' which is a *Datura* plant. I thought somehow *Datura*

Richard Schultes

His students continue his tradition of pursuing botanical research in the likeliest of unlikely places.

Richard Evans Schultes, Jeffrey professor of biology emeritus, has two homes, and they could not be more different. The first is Cambridge, where he served as director of the Harvard Botanical Museum from 1970 until last year, when he became director emeritus. During his tenure he interested generations of students in the exotic botany of the Amazon rain forest. His impact on the field through his own research is worldwide. The scholarly ethnobotanist with steel-rimmed glasses, bald head, and white lab coat is as much a part of the Botanical Museum as the thousands of plant specimens and botanical texts on the museum shelves.

In his austere office is a picture of a crew-cut, younger man stripped to the waist, his arms decorated with tribal paint. This is Schultes's other persona. Starting in 1941, he spent thirteen years in the rain forests of South America, living with the Indians and studying the plants they use for medicinal and spiritual purposes.

Schultes is concerned that many of the people he has studied are giving up traditional ways. "The people of so-called primitive societies are becoming civilized and losing all their forefathers' knowledge of plant lore," he says. "We'll be losing the tremendous amounts of knowledge they've gained over thousands of years. We're interested in the practical aspects with the hope that new medicines and other things can be developed for our own civilization."

Schultes's exploits are legendary in the biology department. Once, while gathering South American plant specimens hundreds of miles from civilization, he contracted beri-beri. For forty days he fought creeping paralysis and overwhelming fatigue as he paddled back to a doctor. "It was an extraordinary feat of endurance," says disciple Wade Davis. "He is really one of the last nineteenth-century naturalists."

Hallucinogenic plants are one of Schultes's primary interests. As a Harvard undergraduate in the Thirties, he lived with Oklahoma's Kiowa Indians to observe their use of plants. He participated in their peyote ceremonies and wrote his thesis on the hallucinogenic cactus. He has also studied other hallucinogens, such as morning glory seeds, sacred mushrooms, and ayahuasca, a South American vision vine. Schultes's work has led to the development of anesthetics made from curare and alternative sources of natural rubber.

Schultes's main concern these days is the scientific potential of plants in the rapidly disappearing Amazon jungle. "If chemists are going to get material on 80,000 species and then analyze them, they'll never finish the job before the jungle is gone," he says. "The short cut is to find out what the [native] people have learned about the plant properties during many years of living in the very rich flora."

—G.D.G.

was used in putting people down." *Datura* is a powerful psychoactive plant, found in West Africa as well as other tropical areas and used there in ritual as well as criminal activities. Davis had found *Datura* growing in Haiti. Its popular name suggested the plant was used in creating zombies.

But, says Davis, "there were a lot of problems with the *Datura* hypothesis. Partly it was a question of how the drug was administered. *Datura* would create a stupor in huge doses, but it just wouldn't produce the kind of immobility that was key. These people had to appear dead, and there aren't many drugs that will do that."

One of the ingredients Pierre included in the second formula was a dried fish, a species of puffer or blowfish, common to most parts of the world. It gets its name from its ability to fill itself with water and swell to several times its normal size when threatened by predators. Many of these fish contain a powerful poison known as tetrodotoxin. One of the most powerful non-protein poisons known to man, tetrodotoxin turned up in every sample of zombie powder that Davis acquired.

Numerous well-documented accounts of puffer fish poisoning exist, but the most famous accounts come from the Orient, where *fugu* fish, a species of puffer, is considered a delicacy. In Japan, special chefs are licensed to prepare *fugu*. The chef removes enough poison to make the fish nonlethal, yet enough remains to create exhilarating physiological effects—tingles up and down the spine, mild prickling of the tongue and lips, euphoria. Several dozen Japanese die each year, having bitten off more than they should have.

"When I got hold of the formula and saw it was the *fugu* fish, that suddenly threw open the whole Japanese literature," says Davis. Case histories of *fugu* poisoning read like accounts of zombification. Victims remain conscious but unable to speak or move. A man who had "died" after eating *fugu* recovered seven days later in the morgue. Several summers ago, another Japanese poisoned by *fugu* revived after he was nailed into his coffin. "Almost all of Narcisse's symptoms correlated. Even strange things such as the fact that he said he was conscious and could hear himself pronounced dead. Stuff that I thought had to be magic, that seemed crazy. But, in fact, that is what people who get *fugu*-fish poisoning experience."

Davis was certain he had solved the mystery. But far from being the end of his investigation, identifying the poison was, in fact, its starting point. "The drug alone didn't make zombies," he explains. "Japanese victims of puffer-fish poisoning don't become zombies, they become poison victims. All the drug could do was set someone up for a whole series of psychological pressures that would be rooted in the culture. I wanted to know why zombification was going on," he says.

He sought a cultural answer, an explanation rooted in the structure and beliefs of Haitian society. Was zombification simply a random criminal activity? He thought not. He had discovered that Clairvius Narcisse and "Ti Femme," a second victim he interviewed, were village pariahs. Ti Femme was regarded as a thief. Narcisse had abandoned his children and deprived his brother of land that was rightfully his. Equally suggestive, Narcisse claimed that his aggrieved brother had sold him to a *bokor,* a voodoo priest who dealt in black magic; he made cryptic reference to having been tried and found guilty by the "masters of the land."

Gathering poisons from various parts of the country, Davis had come into direct contact with the vodoun secret societies. Returning to the anthropological literature on Haiti and pursuing his contacts with informants, Davis came to understand the social matrix within which zombies were created.

Davis's investigations uncovered the importance of the secret societies. These groups trace their origins to the bands of escaped slaves that organized the revolt against the French in the late eighteenth century. Open to both men and women, the societies control specific territories of the country. Their meetings take place at night, and in many rural parts of Haiti the drums and wild celebrations that characterize the gatherings can be heard for miles.

Davis believes the secret societies are responsible for policing their communities, and the threat of zombification is one way they maintain order. Says Davis, "Zombification has a material basis, but it also has a societal logic." To the uninitiated, the practice may appear a random criminal activity, but in rural vodoun society, it is exactly the opposite—a sanction imposed by recognized authorities, a form of capital punishment. For rural Haitians, zombification is an even more severe punishment than death, because it deprives the subject of his most valued possessions: his free will and independence.

The vodounists believe that when a person dies, his spirit splits into several different parts. If a priest is powerful enough, the spiritual aspect that controls a person's character and individuality, known as *ti bon ange,* the "good little angel," can be captured and the corporeal aspect, deprived of its will, held as a slave.

From studying the medical literature on tetrodotoxin poisoning, Davis discovered that if a victim survives the first few hours of the poisoning, he is likely to recover fully from the ordeal. The subject simply revives spontaneously. But zombies remain without will, in a trance-like state, a condition vodounists attribute to the power of the priest. Davis thinks it possible that the psychological trauma of zombification may be augmented by *Datura* or some other drug; he thinks zombies may be fed a *Datura* paste that accentuates their disorientation. Still, he puts the material basis of zombification in perspective: "Tetrodotoxin and *Datura* are only templates on which cultural forces and beliefs may be amplified a thousand times."

Davis has not been able to discover how prevalent zombification is in Haiti. "How many zombies there are is not the question," he says. He compares it to capital punishment in the United States: "It doesn't really matter how many people are electrocuted, as long as it's a possibility." As a sanction in Haiti, the fear is not of zombies, it's of becoming one.

Davis attributes his success in solving the zombie mystery to his approach. He went to Haiti with an open mind and immersed himself in the culture. "My intuition unhindered by biases served me well," he says. "I didn't make any judgments." He combined this attitude with what he had learned earlier from his experiences in the Amazon. "Schultes's lesson is to go and live with the Indians as an Indian." Davis was able to participate in the vodoun society to a surprising degree, eventually even penetrating one of the Bizango societies and dancing in their nocturnal rituals. His appreciation of Haitian culture is apparent. "Everybody asks me how did a white person get this information? To ask the question means you don't understand Haitians—they don't judge you by the color of your skin."

As a result of the exotic nature of his discoveries, Davis has gained a certain notoriety. He plans to complete his dissertation soon, but he has already finished writing a popular account of his adventures. To be published in January by Simon and Schuster, it is called *The Serpent and the Rainbow,* after the serpent that vodounists believe created the earth and the rainbow spirit it married. Film rights have already been optioned; in October Davis went back to Haiti with a screenwriter. But Davis takes the notoriety in stride. "All this attention is funny," he says. "For years, not just me, but all Schultes's students have had extraordinary adventures in the line of work. The adventure is not the end point, it's just along the way of getting the data. At the Botanical Museum, Schultes created a world unto itself. We didn't think we were doing anything above the ordinary. I still don't think we do. And you know," he adds, "the Haiti episode does not begin to compare to what others have accomplished—particularly Schultes himself."

Gino Del Guercio is a national science writer for United Press International.

33

Using Cultural Skills for Cooperative Advantage in Japan

Richard H. Reeves-Ellington

Cultural awareness and sensitivity have significant payoffs, helping people avoid major mistakes resulting from cultural ignorance or cultural misunderstanding. In addition, businesspeople who are more culturally aware are also more successful. In this selection, Reeves-Ellington describes a cross-cultural training program that he designed and implemented for an American company doing business in Japan. About fifty employees participated in the on-site cross-cultural training. The long-term results of their training are impressive. Project managers who took the cultural training program were able to cut project completion time nearly in half and increase the financial returns from the projects threefold (see Table 7). After the training program, managers felt much more comfortable and confident about conducting business in Japan on their own.

What might account for this dramatic success? Do the trained managers make no cultural mistakes, and are there no communication misunderstandings? Obviously, some cultural "horror stories" are instructive, like the case of the nervous American who publicly folded and then tore up a Japanese counterpart's business card during a meeting. But there is also evidence that the American efforts to learn Japanese customs and cultural rules of politeness engendered much goodwill and increased trust between employees involved in multinational business cooperation.

Reeves-Ellington teaches businesspeople to use the basic methods developed by cultural anthropologists to describe and analyze cultural settings. In this selection, he describes the cultural values and behavioral rituals implicit in day-to-day business interactions. In many ways, it is more important to recognize the different ways to observe and interpret cultural patterns than to remember the particular details of the cultural rules of business described here. There are practical advantages to being a participant observer rather than a nonobserving participant.

As you read this selection, ask yourself the following questions:

- What Japanese cultural values are illustrated in the stories about business cards and identity?
- Given the cultural expectations for business entertainment described, do you think there may be special challenges facing American women doing business in Japan?
- What are aspects of American culture that Japanese people might find particularly perplexing?
- In what ways do the rules of a business meeting seem to be ritualized?
- How would you convince an American company of the value of intercultural training?

The following terms discussed in this selection are included in the Glossary at the back of the book:

artifact
intercultural communication
participant observation
ritual
values

Through trial and error, American managers who do business in Japan have learned to gain insight into the Japanese culture. Nonetheless, most American managers remain uneasy dealing with their Japanese counterparts, and "home office" continues to be suspicious of Japanese business practices. This situation produces ineffective business relationships and poor business results. The paradigm of discomfort and suspicion must be replaced by one of confidence and trust if American business is to succeed in Japan.

Reproduced by permission of the Society for Applied Anthropology, from Reeves-Ellington, Richard H., Using Cultural Skills for Comparative Advantage in Japan, SfAA 1993, *Human Organization*, Vol. 52, No. 2, pp. 203–215.

Pharmco, a pharmaceutical subsidiary of a major United States multinational, was saddled with this "home office" attitude of suspicion. Having done business in Japan for more than 20 years, it was dissatisfied with the relationships and financial arrangements with its Japanese licensees. The advent of innovative pharmaceutical technologies provided an opportunity to develop a new strategic alliance with a major Japanese company, Diversity KK. Pharmco anticipated that the alliance would facilitate rapid introduction of its technology in Japan, yield tenfold greater financial returns, and furnish the framework for learning to operate more successfully in Japan. Senior managers in the company understood that they and their staff needed to work effectively at many levels with Japanese managers and scientists in both the Japanese and American cultural environments. They had, however, no plan for learning about Japanese culture; the initial meetings between employees of the two companies resulted in more "damage control" than was desirable. The Pharmco senior manager responsible for Japanese operations, a trained anthropologist, proposed a program offering United States-based managers and scientists assistance in learning about Japanese culture. As a result of the program, American-Japanese relations at Pharmco improved considerably and business operations are running smoothly.

This paper . . . demonstrates how individuals used a cultural understanding process, ethnographic data, and participant observation (PO) to get through a business day in Japan, build their own database, and eventually, predict Japanese social behavior in different settings. Empirical evidence is provided to demonstrate the value the program had for one company.

UNDERPINNINGS OF THE PROGRAM

Employee Needs

The purpose of education in the business setting is to resolve problems. . . . Within the Pharmco context, the people who needed cultural information were based in the United States, worked in a variety of functions, and had to operate in several different cultures, not only Japan. Two common learning methods were thereby excluded, i.e., general reading and the use of culture-specific training courses. The manager-anthropologist had to devise another method.

To determine the educational needs, he set up small-group and one-on-one meetings with managers and scientists who would be required to work on the Japanese strategic alliance. He discovered that two questions deterred employees from wanting to work with Japanese in particular and all non-Americans in general: "What do I do during a business day?" and "How can I learn to respond to the various situations I might find myself in while travelling in foreign cultures?" The initial training objective, therefore, was to offer assistance in getting through a Japanese business day while at the same time providing the tools and processes to enable employees to gain cultural understanding and apply their learning to other cultural contexts.

Involvement of an Insider Anthropologist

The manager-anthropologist responsible for Japan operations provided all training that took place over a five-year period and involved ten sets of employees. Training content included "horror" stories of what goes wrong in U.S.-Japanese relationships, examples of successful activities and processes for increasing the chances of success, and practice in using all the material discussed and presented. Material selection depended on the previous experience of members of the group in multicultural settings. Initial sessions were timed approximately two weeks before contacts with Japanese counterparts. This timing coincided with the peak interest employees had in learning the information. All training was done at the employees' work site, allowing them a greater comfort level. The manager-anthropologist was present at all initial meetings between U.S. employees and their Japanese contacts, and he continued to be present until the Americans expressed confidence that he was not needed at future meetings. . . .

The goal of training was that, through better understanding of Japan, employees would change their normal behavior patterns when working with Japanese counterparts. All improved their ability to work cross-culturally, but not all applied the material learned equally. Managers, in particular, had less patience to learn "how to do things," but rather just wanted to know "what to do." Scientists, on the other hand, tended to apply the models and processes in a much more diligent manner. . . .

Application of the "Understanding and Predicting Culture Process" in Japan

Pharmco employees started gaining understanding of Japanese culture by gathering and understanding cultural generalities. . . . Employees became more involved in the learning process by working on the tools to be used as well as applying them in a Japanese context.

Employees gathered information through visits, while in Japan, to museums, theaters, shrines, baseball games, and business meetings. . . . The initial work session was led by the manager-anthropologist but the trainees at the session participated in data entry. . . . After the introduction of the model, the anthropologist made no effort to suggest data classification according to anthropological criteria. Rather, Pharmco employees using the model defined classifications acceptable to and understood by them. For example, in the case of "insider-outsider," discussed under "artifacts" below, the visual artifact was the way people sat at business and dinner tables, with the concept rightly belonging in the cultural logic. Employees, however, skipped the visual and placed the cultural logic in the artifacts section. The point is that they understood what they meant.

The following analysis of Japanese culture used by Pharmco as baseline data is:

Artifacts *How are things classified or what are the artifacts of an agreed classification system?* In Japan there are two basic classification systems commonly used: (1) insider-outsider and (2) front-rear. The insider is determined in the first instance by what Nakane (1970) refers to as a "frame." By frame, she means criteria that classify and identify individuals as part of a group. In business, the most obvious is the identification by company. When introducing oneself, one says, for example, "I am Pharmco's Reeves-Ellington." Japanese frames can also be determined by locality, such as the city in which one is born or family or household affiliations. In all cases frame indicates a criterion that sets a boundary and gives a common basis to a group of individuals who are located or involved in it. Outsiders are all those who are excluded from the frame. Hence, the use of the word "foreigner" (*gaijin*) is frequent in Japan. If one is not part of the frame, i.e., Japanese (insider), then one is a foreigner (outsider) (Nakane 1970).

Front and rear in the Japanese concept are not linear, as in the western world, but circular. The front, which embodies the concept of *tatamae,* is what is seen or what is commonly known, or frontstage, whereas the rear is what is hidden or backstage. This rear embodies the concept of *honne,* commonly referred to as what is "true." In the western world, these two concepts are the flip sides of a coin existing in a dichotomous relationship, but in Japan, the two concepts are a circular continuum. One folds into the next as do the rooms of a house as one walks through it. Outsiders are always kept to the front, whereas insiders are introduced to the rear (Matsumoto 1988).

The artifacts of the classifications are always determined by the situation in which people come together (Hall and Hall 1987). For example, in the inside-outside relationship, obvious manifestations are the family, localities, schools, companies, and associations. Tour groups are formed to make a group of people insiders. Outsiders are those not in a particular group, e.g., family members are outsiders to the company inside group. On the other hand, fellow employees are typically outsiders to a colleague's family group. In another context, such as going on a trip together, the family and business colleagues could both be insiders, as members of the XYZ tour group. The artifacts of the front and rear classifications can be exemplified by business meetings. Humans typically belong to a complex of groups that can be concentrically layered and are variably mutually inclusive and exclusive. The front artifacts are expressed in how people are arranged at a table and the courtesy that is extended to guests. The rear artifacts are expressed in terms of who is attending and the body language that occurs.

Social Knowledge *(values). What are proper principles for behavior? What are the values that drive the categories and artifacts described above?* In Japan, adoption of the classification systems discussed above keeps as many people on the outside as possible. One keeps one's social obligations to a level that encourages self gain but eliminates all that offer less gain than one is required to give. One sees this principle in action in the Tokyo subway system. The proverbial Japanese politeness is totally absent, replaced with a "survival of the fittest" behavior pattern, which is accomplished, in part, by avoiding eye contact, thereby assuring that everyone around stays on the outside.

Keeping people on the outside embodies another principle: Minimize obligations to others. The personal value that drives this principle is the desire and need for personal relationships of a meaningful nature. If too many people are insiders, personal relationships would be weakened and a fundamental value diluted.

There is a third human principle at work: Everyone needs to be an insider somewhere. All Japanese are striving to be an insider in situations that will provide personal gain. In companies, they have a strong sense of being inside: On tour groups, they all do things together as insiders in a travel experience. The driving value that leads Japanese to strive for insider status is the value of acknowledging and accepting mutual interdependencies with others *(amae)* (Doi 1990).

Cultural Logic Social knowledge or values are based on underlying cultural logic around relationships to the environment, the nature of reality, truth, human nature, human activities, human relationships, and use of time. Within a culture, these are all taken for granted, rarely understood, and almost never expressible by

TABLE 1 Cultural Logic

Environmental relationships

Japanese, as well as other Asians, view the physical environment and human environment as intertwined and not in opposition as do most Christians (Campbell 1960, 1989; Pelzel 1974). As exemplified in Japanese gardens, humans control and shape the environment in ways that suit the artistic feeling of people. The garden denotes the desire for environmental harmony and orderliness.

Nature of truth and reality

Truth and reality are determined by situations and social contexts in which people find themselves (Hall and Hall 1987; Lebra 1976). In a social group, only the insiders determine what is true and real. The accuracy of this determination is based on the degree of harmony and orderliness obtained within the insider group.

Nature of human nature

Humans are driven by emotion and not by logic (Doi 1990b). Mutuality of love and obligation (within the context of the concept of obligation) ties closely with that of hate (Ishida 1974). This mutuality in human relations forces the concept of consensus into human society organization. Since human nature is not believed to be inherently "bad," it is assumed this behavior is caused by ignorance and not evil intent.

Nature of human relationships

Using the concept of relational value orientation (Kluckhohn and Strodbeck 1961), collaterality in human relationships is highly valued. Within this concept is the perception that uncertainty is to be avoided and much effort is put into avoiding it. Within the basic collateral value, there exists a strong power distance within organizations and generational structures (Hofstede 1980).

Nature of human activities

Activity is focused on working toward ideals of harmonious relationships and involves an orientation toward human interdependency (Doi 1990; Lebra 1976; Hayashi 1988). Activity is necessarily done in groups and by groups.

Use of time

Time is polychronic (Hall and Hall 1987). The time system is characterized by the simultaneous occurrence of many things and by a deep involvement with people. There is more emphasis on completing transactions than holding to a schedule. A person confronted with too many subjects to be covered in too short a time chooses to expand the time available to complete the tasks rather than reduce the number of tasks.

those living in the culture, but they are of utmost importance to foreigners wishing to live and work in that culture. An explanation of Japanese cultural logic is contained in Table 1. . . .

THEORY INTO PRACTICE

To get theory into practice, Pharmco decided to learn how to do introductions, meetings, leavings, dinner, and drinking in Japan.

This analysis brings to life Pharmco's learning by relating incidents about just how badly things can go wrong when there is no basis for successful behaviors leading to appropriate judgements in the course of cross-cultural activities. In spite of the mistakes made, Diversity employees were gracious and appreciative of the efforts made to behave properly. They understand that Pharmco, being foreign, will never get it exactly right in Japan—just as the Japanese will never get it exactly right in the United States. Pharmco employees constantly remind themselves that they are involved in a continuous process they may never get entirely "right." There are always new and more subtle nuances to learn.

The Business Card (*meishi*)

During the initial meeting with the Japanese, the first item of business is introductions. (See Table 2.) Proper introductions require proper business cards (*meishi*). The word *meishi* is used by all people in Japan, including foreigners because the two words, business card and *meishi*, refer to the same card but the meaning behind the card is substantially different. For this reason, *meishi* should be prepared in Japan and be ready upon arrival to do business. At the time of presenting the *meishi*, the Japanese expect the viewer of the *meishi* to examine it carefully and to remember both name and title.

TABLE 2 Introductions at Business Meetings

Artifacts	Social Knowledge	Cultural Logic
Technology • Business cards • *Meishi* Visual behavior • Presentation of *meishi* by presenting card, facing recipient. • Senior people present *meishi* first. • Guest presents first, giving name, company affiliation and bowing. • Host presents *meishi* in same sequence. • Upon sitting at conference table, all *meishi* are placed in front of recipient to assure name use.	• Once given a card is kept—not discarded. • *Meishi* are not exchanged a second time unless there is a position change. • Before the next meeting between parties, the *meishi* are reviewed for familiarization with the people attending the meeting. • The *meishi* provides status for the owner.	Human relations • *Meishi* provide understanding of appropriate relations between parties. • *Meishi* take uncertainty out of relationships. Environment • *Meishi* establish insider/outsider environment. • *Meishi* help establish possible obligations to environment. Human activity • *Meishi* help to establish human activities.

Mistreatment of a Japanese businessman's *meishi* will ruin a relationship, whether new or established. Since the *meishi* is an extension of self, damage to the card is damage to the individual. Explaining this to Pharmco staff was not sufficient. They did not understand the implications of the *meishi* until two stories were told to help their understanding.

The importance of this point is demonstrated in the following story. A major U.S. company was having problems with one of its distributors, and the parties seemed unable to resolve their differences. The president of the U.S. company decided to visit Japan, meet with his counterpart in the wholesaler organization, and attempt to resolve their differences. The two had not met previously and, upon meeting, each followed proper *meishi* ritual. The American, however, did not put the Japanese counterpart's *meishi* on the table; instead he held on to it. As the conversation became heated, the American rolled up the *meishi* in his hand. Horror was recorded on the face of the Japanese businessman. The American then tore the *meishi* into bits. This was more than the Japanese could stand; he excused himself from the meeting. Shortly afterward the two companies stopped doing business with each other.

How Japanese use the *meishi* also helped Pharmco staff understand its importance. Japanese companies value a high degree of consistency in those with whom they work and in the handling of personnel within a company. Failure to demonstrate consistency toward internal employees indicates a probable inconsistency in relationships outside the company. The *meishi* can provide the Japanese executive with some indication of a company's attitude toward its employees. The Pharmco employees learned this lesson with a particularly painful outcome at a meeting with a senior Japanese executive. After the Pharmco team explained the purpose of the visit, this executive took a number of *meishi* from his desk. As he turned each of them up, he asked, "I see that I met with Mr. Hansen of your company ten years ago. Where is he now?" Then came the next card. "I see I met with Mr. Harman of your company eight years ago. Where is he now?" The questioning went through eight separate *meishi*. The Pharmco team leader responded each time that the particular person was no longer with the company. At the end, the Japanese executive said, "People are not treated well in your company. In our company, people do not leave until retirement." The meeting was not successful.

With this background, Pharmco staff visiting Japan have a good understanding of the *meishi* and treat it and its presentation with the respect Japanese expect.

The Conference Table

As soon as introductions are complete both sides take a seat at the conference table. In Japan, there are no round tables at business meetings. The expression "head of the table" is meaningless in a Japanese context. Understanding conference table arrangements (Table 3) leads to a successful meeting.

Seating is highly ritualistic and stylized. The power position is flanked by advisors; next come suppliers of data and information, should they be requested; and

TABLE 3 Conference Seating Arrangements

Artifacts	Social Knowledge	Cultural Logic
Technology • Rectangular table Visual behavior • Hosts on one side of the table and guests on the other. • Guests are framed by most attractive background. • The power seat is in the middle of the table. • Junior people are closest to the door.	• Set seating allows all parties social/business understanding. • Person responsible for success has the authority. • Guests are treated as customers.	Human relations • Seating arrangements allow established order to be known, allowing a proper order and power structure to function between people. Reality and truth • Responsibility and authority are combined for success. • The inside and outside are maintained at the conference table. Environment • Used to honor customers and guests. • Used to maintain inside-outside definitions.

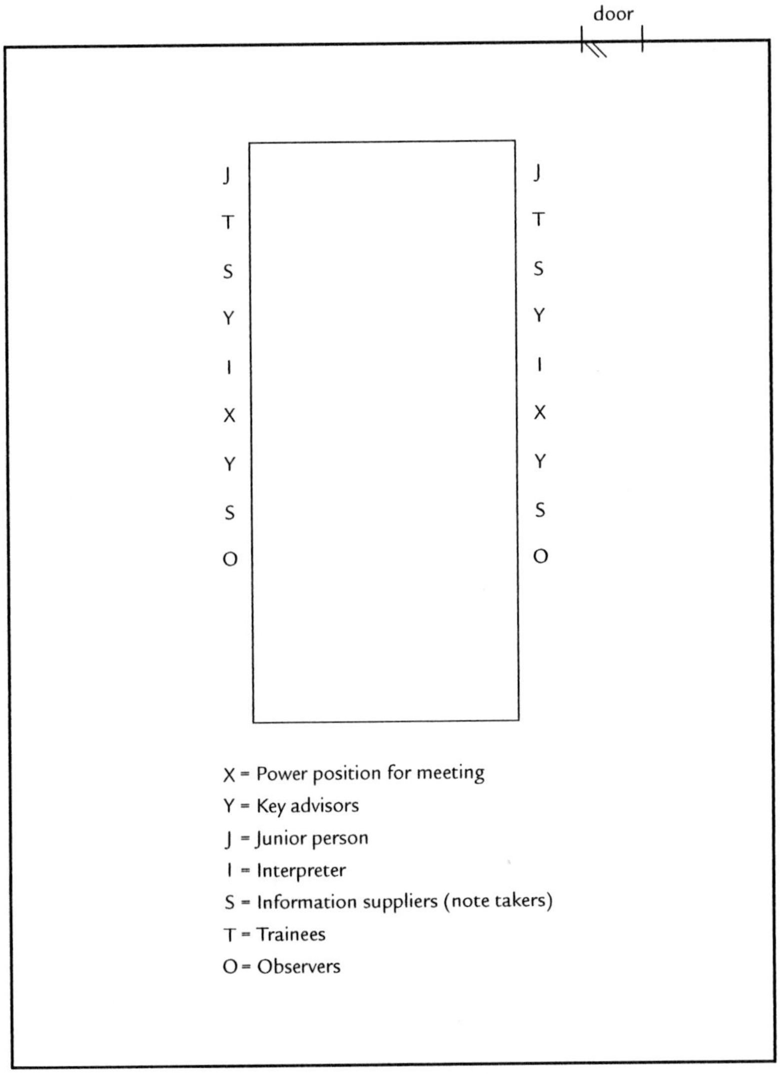

FIGURE 1 Meeting room

TABLE 4 Leaving the Conference

Artifacts	Social Knowledge	Cultural Logic
Visual behavior • Ritualistic thank yous end the meeting while all are seated. • Conclusion of exchange means guests initiate standing. All arise. • Power person stays with guests until they are off company premises. • Bows start upon arising and continue each time one of either side leaves.	• Politeness demands guests be treated as though they were visiting the Japanese at home.	Environment • Guests are under control while in the insider environment. They are left only when they achieve the outside environment. Truth and reality • All exchanges assure a smooth transition from one status to another. Human relations • All structured interactions require a host and a guest role.

finally interested parties are seated at the extremities of the conference table (Figure 1). The person in the power seat performs all ritualistic duties for the side represented. That person directs all comments or questions to particular members of his team who are best qualified to answer them and also functions as the go-between for his team and the other side.

Contrary to usual western practice, the person in the power seat is not necessarily the most senior person present. Rather, the person designated as the official contact for his company or the person most knowledgeable about the subject matter to be discussed takes the seat. The Japanese want the powerful person to be the one who can accomplish the business at hand.

Not understanding this point led to Pharmco embarrassment. Pharmco managers believed at first that the senior person present always occupied the power seat. This assumption was based on meetings between senior managers of the companies who were addressing subject matter only they could decide. When Pharmco's R&D senior manager led Pharmco's initial discussions with Diversity regarding research philosophy and programs, he correctly took the power seat. At a subsequent meeting, called to address program execution, the senior R&D manager again took the power seat. The Japanese body language indicated he should not be there. A new lesson was learned that day: expertise and subject matter, not status, determine the occupant of the power seat. In the case of program execution, the Pharmco power seat occupant should have been the senior scientist for toxicology, not the head of R&D. By taking the power seat, the R&D manager offended the Japanese scientist because he had less status and therefore felt ineffectual. The meeting was inconclusive.

Knowing who is in the power seat offers insights to the other side's agenda. At a negotiating meeting between Diversity KK and Pharmco, the Pharmco team expected the meeting to be a confirmation of work done. When the meeting started, however, the Diversity power seat was occupied by an attorney, not the familiar businessman known by Pharmco. Pharmco immediately excused themselves for a few minutes. In private caucus, the team discussed the change of people and decided that major changes in the contract under negotiation were about to be introduced. This proved to be a correct interpretation. Even this short notice helped the Pharmco team stay in control of unfolding events. At the conclusion of the meeting, leaving is as ritualistic as arriving. Table 4 provides a grasp of the ritual.

At the conclusion of a business meeting, both sides stand up to leave; the host leads the guests out of the conference room; the host's team escorts the guests to the elevator; the entire team, excluding the host, leaves the guests as the elevator doors close, both sides bowing profusely; the host joins his guests in the elevator. The remaining host and his guests then go to the front door of the office, where, if a car has been arranged, the host will get into the car if there is room and accompany his guests back to their hotel. If no car is arranged, the host will stay with the guests until a taxi is found and the guests are safely in it and driving off. The host will remain at the curb, bowing, until the taxi is well into the traffic. The guests keep eye contact, heads nodding and arms waving until the car leaves the curb.

The respect ritualistically shown is based on the status of the individual's company, not on that of the individual. By showing this level of courtesy, the hosts expect the guests to recognize that they have an obligation to reciprocate in the future, when he is on their turf.

Once Pharmco staff understood the social importance of what the Japanese were doing in seeing them off, they immediately instituted the same policy of courtesy for the Japanese when they visited the Pharmco facilities.

Going out to Dinner

When foreigners are invited to dinner, they must be prepared to express a preference for the nationality of food to be eaten; in Japan, a preference for Japanese is obligatory because it demonstrates a willingness to engage in things "Japanese." The Japanese restaurant is likely to be more comfortable and offer more privacy than others, thus creating a better relationship. A Japanese menu includes raw fish. The Japanese host will inevitably ask "Do you like raw fish?" The answer is "yes." Accepting what is offered is a necessity for relationship building in Japan, but it does not include the necessity of eating everything. Being a guest is a simple task as all that is necessary is responding to what the Japanese host suggests or discusses. The intricacies of the organization are the responsibility of the hosts.

Hosting a dinner is much more difficult than being a guest. The host is responsible for assuring a successful relationship-building event. Hosting requires an understanding of Japanese social knowledge if the event is to be successful. Three principles of social knowledge are at work in dinner meetings: (1) have an environment that permits individual members of the companies to start to become acquainted and either start building a relationship or support and maintain one; (2) provide a setting and a meal befitting the guests' social position and thereby show that the host respects this position; and (3) send indirect signals of the status of the relationship in terms of the locale and quality of food. The meal can offer a form of celebration, a basis of apology[1] or just a feeling of comfort. The atmosphere created at dinner should be relaxed and enjoyable. The host is responsible for the comfort of the guests and, should that comfort be threatened for any reason, the host must make certain that conviviality is restored.

Execution of these social values requires one to know when to host, how to select the right guests, how to select a proper restaurant, how to assure that the meal is a proper one, how to keep the conversation in an acceptable mood and assure that the event starts and ends within a culturally acceptable time frame.

Determination of who hosts must be settled well in advance of the date of the dinner. The decision should not be left open until the close of a formal business meeting. If one side has an apology to make or if they have a difficult request, then they should certainly offer to host. For dinners following routine meetings, Pharmco works on the basis that if the meetings are in Japan, then the Japanese host, and if they are in the United States, Pharmco hosts. This works well. If, however, the Japanese are insistent upon acting as host, it is best to follow their lead.

The attendees of any particular dinner must correlate to reciprocal status of individuals from both companies. Therefore the attendees must be agreed upon well in advance of the dinner. Any changes of attendee by one side must be announced well in advance of the dinner. For one side to change the status level of attendance at the last minute causes problems for the other. If the side making changes lowers the level of attendance, the other side has two problems to sort out. First, is a *honne* message being sent and why? For example, Japanese companies have been known to use this type of last-minute change as a way to tell the other company that they want to downgrade the existing relationship between the two companies. Second, how can a Japanese manager explain such changes to his superior? If, on the other hand, the level of attendance is increased at the last minute, the other might not be able to reciprocate, leading to embarrassment and a weakening of friendly relations. Attendance, once set, should not change.

The class of the restaurant must be in keeping with the status of the senior member of the party being invited, for Japanese executives have a clear understanding of where their status allows them to dine. Selection of a restaurant considered below a Japanese guest's status results in the guest losing face with his colleagues. Anticipation of this problem makes the Japanese uncomfortable during the meal, precluding the building of good social relationships. An example demonstrates the point.

Pharmco headquarters decided that the cost of entertaining in Tokyo was too high and dictated that cheaper places be found. The dictum was followed and, on the occasion of the next business meeting with a middle manager of Diversity, disaster resulted. When the guest arrived, his first comment was that one of his subordinates often brought suppliers to the restaurant. Pharmco had clearly insulted him in the choice of eating establishment, causing Pharmco managers to spend the rest of the night apologizing. Trying to rectify the situation, the next time they hosted the manager, Pharmco managers went to a very exclusive place. The first comment received was, "the president of our company likes this restaurant but I have never been here." This time, Pharmco embarrassed the Diversity manager by taking him to a location beyond his status, causing him to explain to his colleagues the next day why he was there.

Avoiding these problems requires only that foreigners ask a Japanese for a restaurant preference. The answer will be "no," followed by a comment indicating a restaurant in which he has never eaten but would like to do so. If this approach fails, a visit to the social

TABLE 5 Going to Dinner

Artifacts	Social Knowledge	Cultural Logic
Physical • Guests • Restaurant • Meals • Transportation Visual behavior • Hosting • Guesting • Timing to eat	• Relationship building is purpose of eating. • Status is honored by correct dinners. • Dinner group has some "insider" attributes.	Use of time • Time at dinners is effective use of time for relations. Relationships • Identifies how two companies view people's position in hierarchy. • Confirms status matching through acceptance or nonacceptance of invitations.

director of the hotel in which the foreigner is staying will yield dividends. By showing the director the card of the individual to be entertained, she will make appropriate selections, based on the *meishi* information of the name of the company and the title of the person. She never errs in judgement.

Selection of the restaurant leads to the selection of a suitable menu, which is done by the host in advance and must reflect the status of the guests and the nature of the occasion. For example, if it is a dinner just to end the day, a simple meal is in order. If the relationship is particularly strong, a stop in a noodle shop can be totally appropriate. If the dinner is one of celebration or a form of apology, however, a more elaborate meal is required. As with the choice of a restaurant, use Japanese expertise. A visit to the restaurant with the guest's business card and a discussion of the room and the meal with the majordomo of the restaurant (a discussion that should also cover who will attend and the purpose of the meal) assures a proper menu and setting.

When Pharmco management decided to enter a strategic alliance with Diversity KK, they had to inform Nippon Pharmaceutical, a potential partner, that they had decided not to work with them. The business aspects of the decision were discussed with Nippon Pharma at their offices, but then at dinner the relationship aspects of the decision were covered. The choice of location and meal was more elaborate than would normally be the case, given the state of the relationship. At the end of the meal, the Nippon Pharma representatives complimented Pharmco on their ability to be a good Japanese host.

Conversation at dinners does not include heavy business negotiations under any but the most unusual circumstances. Talk focuses on recreational activities, current politics, travel, or other "cocktail party" chat. The point of conversation, as well as of the food, is to put everyone at ease. Failure to follow this principle can cause discomfort.

At a dinner hosted by Diversity management, a Pharmco manager discussed matters relating to fundamental changes in the Japanese health care system. He did not notice that the Japanese were becoming upset until one of them exploded that "these matters were not the business of foreigners and they should not express opinions. Rather they should wait to be taught the right way to do business by the Japanese." While the foreigner thought himself at fault by not avoiding the delicate subject matter, he received an extensive apology by a colleague of the Japanese who expressed such a forceful opinion. He said "As host, I should not permit such things to happen!"

In Japan, dinners are arranged for the end of the business day, which is around 6:30 p.m. The foreign host should plan to invite his guests for a 7 p.m. dinner, as doing so will give them a half an hour to get to the restaurant. Always offer an exact time. The American habit of "let's make it around 6:30 to 7" is not acceptable. The host always should arrive a few minutes early and be there to greet his guests. At the close of the meal, the host walks the guest to the front of the restaurant, where he has had the restaurant arrange transportation. The host stands at the curb and stays there, preferably bowing or waving, until the guests have been driven off. Table 5 summarizes the critical cultural factors concerning dinner engagements.

Drinking in Bars

Going out to drink after dinner is the first opportunity for colleagues of different companies to have the chance to behave as a set of "insiders." It also provides a setting in which anyone of the group can express a *honne* sentiment. Drinking provides the foreigner a sense of how relationship-building is progressing between his company, himself and his Japanese

TABLE 6 Going Out Drinking

Artifacts	Social Knowledge	Cultural Logic
Physical • Karaoke bars • Tabs • Female social managers Visual behavior • Singing • Joking • Honest opinion	• Freedom of speech acceptable. • Drunken behavior acceptable. • Place to get things "off the chest." • Everyone can be an "insider."	Human relations • Provides a time for *honne* talk. • Fills the need for business associates to be a set of "insiders." Environment • Setting is outside a traditional "insider" setting, allowing a new set of "insiders" to be formed on "neutral" ground. Reality and truth • Feelings (reality) must be expressed and understood (truth) by an insider group.

counterparts. Therefore, ethnographic understanding of ritual drinking is imperative (Table 6).

"Know how to sing," was the key learned by Pharmco management before going out drinking after dinner. Drinking in Karaoke bars is the ultimate socializing and relationship-building mechanism with and among Japanese. Power and social distance are almost completely broken down at the bars. The president as well as the most junior person present will sing, tell jokes, and generally relax. Although there is still not a round table, all the people together act as though they are at one. The environment has also changed substantially from that of the office. The bar is smaller than the office, and women are an important addition as they are to provide conversation and pour the drinks.[2] The tables are laid out so that there is little structure in the physical environment. A basic assumption is that this is the one place in the entire social milieu where uncertainty is acceptable. The assumption is that, with drink, it is totally acceptable to say what is on your mind to whomever you want. A further assumption is that whatever is said cannot be held against a person after leaving the bar.

Being there makes one an insider for the time spent together in the bar. "Insidership" is created only if the proper bar is chosen—one befitting the status of the group. Unlike choosing a restaurant, however, the foreigner must ask his Japanese associates for advice as to where to go, for they know that the foreigner lacks the knowledge to make a proper selection. A Pharmco executive experienced near-disaster the one time he selected a bar without consulting a Japanese businessman. He had found the hotel social relations director helpful with restaurants so [he] thought that person would be a good source of information for bars. He was not. As soon as he walked in the bar recommended by the director, he knew there was a problem: Except for one or two Japanese, only foreigners were present; the bar was almost empty; and the hostesses ranged in age from 40 to 50—far too old for the tastes of the Japanese guests. Fortunately, relationships between the Pharmco executive and his Japanese guests [were] strong enough for everyone to get a good laugh from the situation. He is still periodically reminded of the incident.

Business is usually not done at the bar, where drinking offers the Japanese an opportunity to express *honne* opinions about his relationships with colleagues, both foreign and Japanese. These opinions are tolerable as they are expressed when the person expressing them is acceptably drunk. Within the drinking context, everyone is in the same social circle. For this reason, one must constantly be alert for signals that might indicate something is on a colleague's mind. At one drinking session, a Pharmco manager felt that something was bothering his Japanese counterpart but, as the evening wore on, nothing was said. Just before it ended, the Japanese manager put his face down on the table and muttered that he had something important to say. The American leaned forward and asked what it was. All the Japanese said was "Your Johns-san is an asshole." Nothing more was said and the subject was never raised again. The American assumed that just stating the opinion was enough to relieve the tension the Japanese had. The opinion was not reported to Johns. The next business day discussions with the Japanese gentlemen were more relaxed than had been previously experienced.

TABLE 7 Critical Factors Outcome

Effective working relationships

1. Pharmco employees are more self-assured when meeting Japanese in Japan.
2. Their Japanese counterparts state they prefer working with Pharmco over other foreign companies.

Shortened project times

1. Prior to introducing the cultural material, projects between Pharmco and Diversity averaged 15 months to completion.
2. Projects run by executives applying cultural methodologies shortened project completion times to an average of 8 months, while all others remain at 15 months.

Improved financial returns

1. Financial returns based on contracts negotiated by personnel not exposed to the cultural material average gross income of 6% of sales.
2. Financial returns of contracts negotiated by personnel applying the anthropological techniques provide gross income equal to 18% of sales.

PHARMCO BUSINESS IMPROVEMENTS

Three critical factors were deemed necessary for the program to be judged a success: (1) effective working relationships with Japanese executives; (2) shortened project times; and (3) improved financial returns. The project is successful based on these factors (Table 7) and is in the process of being applied to other countries.

Before learning the methodologies and skills outlined in this paper, Pharmco executives avoided travel to Japan and working with Japanese whenever possible. Fifty Pharmco executives have been through the training program. Before the program, they were asked to evaluate their comfort level of working with Japanese and their enjoyment of business trips to Japan. The rating scale was 1 to 10 with 1 expressing no comfort and no enjoyment to 10 expressing total comfort and enjoyment. The average score was 3 with a range of 1 to 5. After exposure to the concepts, tools, and material, the average score increased to 6, with a range of 5 to 9. The final measurement was based on 15 executives who used the concepts and tools in their next series of meetings. The average score of this group was 8, with a low score of 5 and a high score of 10. Before the program, most employees wanted to be accompanied to Japan by a person experienced in Japan. After the exposure, almost all are comfortable making these trips on their own. This willingness to work in and with Japan has improved the personal effectiveness of all these employees working on Japanese projects.

Late delivery of projects was costly to Pharmco and discouraged Diversity managers from working with their Pharmco counterparts. In one case the delays were estimated to cost Pharmco $90 million over a ten-year period. The delays were of a nature that a competitor entered the market with a similar product, thereby denying innovator status to Pharmco. The improved delivery times are helping both Diversity and Pharmco in gaining valuable marketing time over their key competitors.

SUMMARY

The ability to work with and within a foreign culture requires an organization to adopt and implement an interpretive strategy that permits its practitioners to set out to work proactively within the perceived meaning of the foreign environment. This strategy requires managers to become transformational in order to operate successfully in other social and institutional environments. Successful implementation of such a strategy demands the use of both business and anthropological tools and skills. By creating a base of these skills and providing a training environment in which employees individually could learn and implement such a strategy, Pharmco achieved dramatic improvements in its Japanese business relationships and business results. This success has led to adapting the training to other countries.

NOTES

1. In Japan, the concept of apology involves a great shame for not having behaved correctly or done something in the right way. To apologize is traumatic for a Japanese.
2. Apologies are necessary to my female colleagues for this chauvinistic viewpoint. It is how things are in Japan, however. I would like to point out that should a female

colleague be part of the group visiting the bar, she would be treated as a colleague by her peers and be well received by the employees in the bar.

REFERENCES

Brislin, Richard W., Kenneth Cushner, Craig Cherrie, and Mehalahi Yong. 1986. *Intercultural Interactions: A Practical Guide.* Beverly Hills, CA: Sage.

Campbell, Joseph. 1960. *The Masks of God: Primitive Mythology.* New York: Viking Press.

______. 1989. *The Hero with a Thousand Faces.* New York: Viking Press.

David, Kenneth. 1985. *Participant Observation in Pharmaceutical Field Selling.* Norwich, CT: Norwich Eaton Pharmaceutical Co., Inc.

Doi, Takeo. 1990a. *The Anatomy of Dependence.* Tokyo: Kodansha International.

______. 1990b. *The Anatomy of Self.* Tokyo: Kodansha International.

Hall, Edward T., and Mildred R. Hall. 1987. *Hidden Differences.* New York: Anchor Press.

Hamada, Tomoko. 1991. *American Enterprise in Japan.* Albany: SUNY Press.

Hayashi, Shuji. 1988. *Culture and Management in Japan.* Tokyo: University of Tokyo Press.

Hofstede, Geert. 1980. *Culture's Consequences: International Differences in Work-Related Values.* Beverly Hills, CA: Sage.

Ishida, Eiichiro. 1974. A Culture of Love and Hate. In *Japanese Culture and Behavior,* Takie Sugiyama Lebra and William P. Lebra, eds. Pp. 27–36. Honolulu: University Press of Hawaii.

Kluckhohn, F. R., and F. L. Strodbeck. 1961. *Variations in Value Orientations.* Westport, CT: Greenwood Press.

Lebra, Takie Sugiyama. 1976. *Japanese Patterns of Behavior.* Honolulu: University Press of Hawaii.

Matsumoto, Michihiro. 1988. *The Unspoken Way.* Tokyo: Kodansha International.

Nakane, Chie. 1970. *Japanese Society.* Tokyo: Charles E. Tuttle Co.

Pelzel, John C. 1974. Human Nature in the Japanese Myths. In *Japanese Culture and Behavior,* Takie Sugiyama Lebra and William P. Lebra, eds. Pp. 3–26. Honolulu: University Press of Hawaii.

Reeves-Ellington, Richard H. 1988. Relationships Between Multinationals and Peasants. Paper presented at the annual meeting of the American Anthropological Association, Chicago.

Reeves-Ellington, Richard H., and Paul Steidlmeier. 1991. *Total Quality, Institutionalism and the Retooling of American Business.* Binghamton, NY: SUNY-Binghamton, School of Management.

12

The Domestication of Wood in Haiti

A Case Study in Applied Evolution

Gerald F. Murray

In its annual report on the state of the planet, the Worldwatch Institute describes the growing shortage of wood for fuel and construction throughout the Third World. The problem is most acute in densely populated areas with a long history of agriculture. In these areas, peasant farmers or members of their families can spend several hours each day finding firewood. Because forests take such a long time to grow and such a short time to cut down, reforestation is a worldwide ecological challenge.

As described in this selection, Haiti has a severe deforestation problem that is closely related to wider issues of poverty and overpopulation. In this context, traditional reforestation projects, with ponderous educational components on the value of trees, had failed miserably. Anthropologist Gerald Murray, who had done research on land tenure among rural Haitian peasants, had the rare opportunity to design and implement an alternative project in forestry and agricultural development. His anthropological understanding of the economic system and culture of the Haitian people clearly paid off. The project represents applied cultural anthropology at its best.

As you read this selection, ask yourself the following questions:

- Why does Haiti have a deforestation problem?
- How was Gerald Murray's anthropological alternative project different from traditional reforestation programs?
- Why was using particular kinds of trees important for the project?
- What accounted for the Haitian peasants' enthusiasm for the idea of trees as a cash crop?
- What is meant by the title of this piece?

The following terms discussed in this selection are included in the Glossary at the back of the book:

arable land
cadastral
domestication of plants and animals
horticulture
population pressure
reforestation
swidden cultivation
usufruct rights

PROBLEM AND CLIENT

Expatriate tree lovers, whether tourists or developmental planners, often leave Haiti with an upset stomach. Though during precolonial times the island Arawaks had reached a compromise with the forest, their market-oriented colonial successors saw trees as something to be removed. The Spaniards specialized in exporting wood from the eastern side of the island, whereas the French on the western third found it more profitable to clear the wood and produce sugar cane, coffee, and indigo for European markets. During the nineteenth century, long after Haiti had become an independent republic, foreign lumber companies cut and exported most of the nation's precious hardwoods, leaving little for today's peasants.

The geometric increase in population since colonial times—from an earlier population of fewer than half a million former slaves to a contemporary population of more than six million—and the resulting shrinkage of average family holding size have led to the evolution of a land use system devoid of systematic fallow periods. A vicious cycle has set in—one that seems to have targeted the tree for ultimate destruction. Not only has land pressure eliminated a regenerative fallow phase in the local agricultural cycle; in addition the catastrophic declines in per hectare food yields have forced peasants into alternative income-generating strategies. Increasing numbers crowd into the capital city, Port-au-Prince, creating a market for construction wood and charcoal. Poorer sectors of the peasantry in the rural areas respond to this market by racing each other with axes and machetes to cut down the few natural tree stands remaining in remoter regions of the republic. The proverbial snowball in Hades is at less risk than a tree in Haiti.

Unable to halt the flows either of wood into the cities or of soil into the oceans, international development organizations finance studies to measure the volume of these flows (50 million trees cut per year is one of the round figures being bandied about) and to predict when the last tree will be cut from Haiti. Reforestation projects have generally been entrusted by their well-meaning but short-sighted funders to Duvalier's Ministry of Agriculture, a kiss-of-death resource channeling strategy by which the Port-au-Prince jobs created frequently outnumber the seedlings produced. And even the few seedlings produced often died in the nurseries because the peasants were understandably reluctant to cover their scarce holdings with state-owned trees. Project managers had been forced to resort to "food for work" strategies to move seedlings out of nurseries onto hillsides. And peasants have endeavored where possible to plant the trees on somebody else's hillsides and to enlist their livestock as allies in the subsequent removal of this dangerous vegetation.

This generalized hostility to tree projects placed the U.S. Agency for International Development (AID)/Haiti mission in a bind. After several years of absence from Haiti in the wake of expulsion by Francois Duvalier, AID had reestablished its presence under the government of his son Jean Claude. But an ambitious Integrated Agricultural Development Project funded through the Ministry of Agriculture had already given clear signs of being a multimillion-dollar farce. And an influential congressman chairing the U.S. House Ways and Means Committee—consequently exercising strong control over AID funds worldwide—had taken a passionate interest in Haiti. In his worldwide travels this individual had become adept at detecting and exposing developmental charades. And he had been blunt in communicating his conviction that much of what he had seen in AID/Haiti's program was precisely that. He had been touched by the plight of Haiti and communicated to the highest AID authorities his conviction about the salvific power of contraceptives and trees and his determination to have AID grace Haiti with an abundant flow of both. And he would personally visit Haiti (a convenient plane ride from Washington, D.C.) to inspect for himself, threatening a worldwide funding freeze if no results were forthcoming. A chain reaction of nervous "yes sirs" speedily worked its way down from AID headquarters in Washington to a beleaguered Port-au-Prince mission.

The pills and condoms were less of a problem. Even the most cantankerous congressman was unlikely to insist on observing them in use and would probably settle for household distribution figures. Not so with the trees. He could (and did) pooh-pooh nursery production figures and asked to be taken to see the new AID forests, a most embarrassing request in a country where peasants creatively converted daytime reforestation projects into nocturnal goat forage projects. AID's reaction was twofold—first, to commission an immediate study to explain to the congressman and others why peasants refused to plant trees (for this they called down an AID economist); and second, to devise some program strategy that would achieve the apparently unachievable: to instill in cash-needy, defiant, pleasant charcoalmakers a love, honor, and respect for newly planted trees. For this attitudinal transformation, a task usually entrusted to the local armed forces, AID/Haiti invited an anthropologist to propose an alternative approach.

PROCESS AND PLAYERS

During these dynamics, I completed a doctoral dissertation on the manner in which Haitian peasant land tenure had evolved in response to internal population growth. The AID economist referred to above exhaustively reviewed the available literature, also focusing on the issue of Haitian peasant land tenure, and produced for the mission a well-argued monograph (Zuvekas 1978) documenting a lower rate of landlessness in Haiti than in many other Latin American settings but documenting as well the informal, extralegal character of the relationship between many peasant families and their landholdings. This latter observation was interpreted by some in the mission to mean that the principal determinant of the failure of tree planting projects was the absence among peasants of legally secure deeds over their plots. Peasants could not be expected to invest money on land improvements when at mildest the benefits could accrue to another and at worst the very improvements themselves could lead to expropriation from their land. In short, no massive tree planting could be expected, according to this model, until a nationwide cadastral reform granted plot-by-plot deeds to peasant families.

This hypothesis was reputable but programmatically paralyzing because nobody dreamed that the

Duvalier regime was about to undertake a major cadastral reform for the benefit of peasants. Several AID officers in Haiti had read my dissertation on land tenure (Murray 1977), and I received an invitation to advise the mission. Was Haitian peasant land tenure compatible with tree planting? Zuvekas' study had captured the internally complex nature of Haitian peasant land tenure. But the subsequent extrapolations as to paralyzing insecurity simply did not seem to fit with ethnographic evidence. In two reports (Murray 1978a, 1978b) I indicated that peasants in general feel secure about their ownership rights over their land. Failure to secure plot-by-plot surveyed deeds is generally a cost-saving measure. Interclass evictions did occur, but they were statistically rare; instead most land disputes were intrafamilial. A series of extralegal tenure practices had evolved—preinheritance land grants to young adult dependents, informal inheritance subdivisions witnessed by community members, fictitious sales to favored children, complex community-internal share-cropping arrangements. And though these practices produced an internally heterogeneous system with its complexities, there was strong internal order. Any chaos and insecurity tended to be more in the mind of observers external to the system than in the behavior of the peasants themselves. There was a danger that the complexities of Haitian peasant land tenure would generate an unintended smokescreen obscuring the genuine causes of failure in tree planting projects.

What then were these genuine causes? The mission, intent on devising programming strategies in this domain, invited me to explore further, under a contract aimed at identifying the "determinants of success and failure" in reforestation and soil conservation projects. My major conclusion was that the preexisting land tenure, cropping, and livestock systems in peasant Haiti were perfectly adequate for the undertaking of significant tree planting activities. Most projects had failed not because of land tenure or attitudinal barriers among peasants but because of fatal flaws in one or more key project components. Though my contract called principally for analysis of previous or existing projects, I used the recommendation section of the report to speculate on how a Haiti-wise anthropologist would program and manage reforestation activities if he or she had the authority. In verbal debriefings I jokingly challenged certain young program officers in the mission to give me a jeep and carte blanche access to a $50,000 checking account, and I would prove my anthropological assertions about peasant economic behavior and produce more trees in the ground than their current multimillion-dollar Ministry of Agriculture charade. We had a good laugh and shook hands, and I departed confident that the report would be as dutifully perused and as honorably filed and forgotten as similar reports I had done elsewhere.

To my great disbelief, as I was correcting Anthro 101 exams some two years later, one of the program officers still in Haiti called to say that an Agroforestry Outreach Project (AOP) had been approved chapter and verse as I had recommended it; and that if I was interested in placing my life where my mouth had been and would leave the ivory tower to direct the project, my project bank account would have not $50,000, but $4 million. After several weeks of hemming and hawing and vigorous negotiating for leave from my department, I accepted the offer and entered a new (to me) role of project director in a strange upside-down world in which the project anthropologist was not a powerless cranky voice from the bleachers but the chief of party with substantial authority over general project policy and the allocation of project resources. My elation at commanding resources to implement anthropological ideas was dampened by the nervousness of knowing exactly who would be targeted for flak and ridicule if these ideas bombed out, as most tended to do in the Haiti of Duvalier.

The basic structural design of AOP followed a tripartite conceptual framework that I proposed for analyzing projects. Within this framework a project is composed of three essential systemic elements: a technical base, a benefit flow strategy, and an institutional delivery strategy. Planning had to focus equally on all three; I argued that defects in one would sabotage the entire project.

Technical Strategy

The basic technical strategy was to make available to peasants fast-growing wood trees (*Leucaena leucocephala, Cassia siamea, Azadirachta indica, Casuarina equisetifolia, Eucalyptus camaldulensis*) that were not only drought resistant but also rapid growing, producing possible four-year harvest rotations in humid lowland areas (and slower rotations and lower survival rates in arid areas) and that were good for charcoal and basic construction needs. Most of the species mentioned also restore nutrients to the soil, and some of them coppice from a carefully harvested stump, producing several rotations before the need for replanting.

Of equally critical technical importance was the use of a nursery system that produced lightweight microseedlings. A project pickup truck could transport over 15,000 of these microseedlings (as opposed to 250 traditional bag seedlings), and the average peasant could easily carry over 500 transportable seedlings at one time, planting them with a fraction of the ground preparation time and labor required for bulkier bagged seedlings. The anthropological implications of this nursery system were critical. It constituted a technical breakthrough that reduced to a fraction the fossil-fuel and human energy expenditure required to transport and plant trees.

But the technical component of the project incorporated yet another element: the physical juxtaposition of trees and crops. In traditional reforestation models, the trees are planted in large unbroken monocropped stands. Such forests or woodlots presuppose local land tenure and economic arrangements not found in Haiti. For the tree to make its way as a cultivate into the economy of Haitian peasants and most other tropical cultivators, reforestation models would have to be replaced by agroforestry models that entail spatial or temporal juxtaposition of crops and trees. Guided by prior ethnographic knowledge of Haitian cropping patterns, AOP worked out with peasants various border planting and intercropping strategies to make tree planting feasible even for small holding cultivators.

Benefit Flow Strategies

With respect to the second systemic component, the programming of benefit flows to participants, earlier projects had often committed the fatal flaw of defining project trees planted as *pyebwa leta* (the state's trees). Authoritarian assertions by project staff concerning sanctions for cutting newly planted trees created fears among peasants that even trees planted on their own land would be government property. And several peasants were frank in reporting fears that the trees might eventually be used as a pretext by the government or the "Company" (the most common local lexeme used to refer to projects) for eventually expropriating the land on which peasants had planted project trees.

Such ambiguities and fears surrounding benefit flows paralyze even the technically soundest project. A major anthropological feature of AOP was a radical frontal attack on the issue of property and usufruct rights over project trees. Whereas other projects had criticized tree cutting, AOP promulgated the heretical message that trees were meant to be cut, processed, and sold. The only problem with the present system, according to project messages, was that peasants were cutting nature's trees. But once the landowner "mete fos li deyo" (expends his resources) and plants and cares for his or her own wood trees on his or her own land, the landowner has the same right to harvest and sell wood as corn or beans.

I was inevitably impressed at the impact that this blunt message had when I delivered it to groups of prospective peasant tree planters. Haitian peasants are inveterate and aggressive cash-croppers; many of the crops and livestock that they produce are destined for immediate consignment to local markets. For the first time in their lives, they were hearing a concrete proposal to make the wood tree itself one more marketable crop in their inventory.

But the message would ring true only if three barriers were smashed.

1. The first concerned the feared delay in benefits. Most wood trees with which the peasants were familiar took an impractically long time to mature. There fortunately existed in Haiti four-year-old stands of leucaena, cassia, eucalyptus, and other project trees to which we could take peasant groups to demonstrate the growth speed of these trees.
2. But could they be planted on their scanty holdings without interfering with crops? Border and row planting techniques were demonstrated, as well as intercropping. The average peasant holding was about a hectare and a half. If a cultivator planted a field in the usual crops and then planted 500 seedlings in the same field at 2 meters by 2 meters, the seedlings would occupy only a fifth of a hectare. And they would be far enough apart to permit continued cropping for two or three cycles before shade competition became too fierce. That is, trees would be planted on only a fraction of the peasant's holdings and planted in such a way that they would be compatible with continued food growing even on the plots where they stood. We would then calculate with peasants the potential income to be derived from these 500 trees through sale as charcoal, polewood, or boards. In a best-case scenario, the gross take from the charcoal of these trees (the least lucrative use of the wood) might equal the current annual income of an average rural family. The income potential of these wood trees clearly would far offset any potential loss from decreased food production. Though it had taken AID two years to decide on the project, it took about twenty minutes with any group of skeptical but economically rational peasants to generate a list of enthusiastic potential tree planters.
3. But there was yet a third barrier. All this speculation about income generation presupposed that the peasants themselves, and not the government or the project, would be the sole owners of the trees and that the peasants would have unlimited rights to the harvest of the wood whenever they wished. To deal with this issue, I presented the matter as an agreement between cultivator and the project: We would furnish the free seedlings and technical assistance; the cultivators would agree to plant 500 of these seedlings on their own

land and permit project personnel to carry out periodic survival counts. We would, of course, pay no wages or "Food for Work" for this planting. But we would guarantee to the planters complete and exclusive ownership of the trees. They did not need to ask for permission from the project to harvest the trees whenever their needs might dictate, nor would there be any penalties associated with early cutting or low survival. If peasants changed their minds, they could rip out their seedlings six months after planting. They would never get any more free seedlings from us, but they would not be subject to any penalties. There are preexisting local forestry laws, rarely enforced, concerning permissions and minor taxes for tree cutting. Peasants would have to deal with these as they had skillfully done in the past. But from our project's point of view, we relinquish all tree ownership rights to the peasants who accept and plant the trees on their property.

Cash-flow dialogues and ownership assurances such as these were a far cry from the finger-wagging ecological sermons to which many peasant groups had been subjected on the topic of trees. Our project technicians developed their own messages; but central to all was the principle of peasant ownership and usufruct of AOP trees. The goal was to capitalize on the preexisting fuel and lumber markets, to make the wood tree one more crop in the income-generating repertoire of the Haitian peasant.

Institutional Strategy

The major potential fly in the ointment was the third component, the institutional component. To whom would AID entrust its funds to carry out this project? My own research had indicated clearly that Haitian governmental involvement condemned a project to certain paralysis and possible death, and my report phrased that conclusion as diplomatically as possible. The diplomacy was required to head off possible rage, less from Haitian officials than from certain senior officers in the AID mission who were politically and philosophically wedded to an institution-building strategy. Having equated the term "institution" with "government bureaucracy," and having defined their own career success in terms, not of village-level resource flows, but of voluminous and timely bureaucracy-to-bureaucracy cash transfers, such officials were in effect marshaling U.S. resources into the service of extractive ministries with unparalleled track records of squandering and/or pilfering expatriate donor funds.

To the regime's paradoxical credit, however, the blatant openness and arrogance of Duvalierist predation had engendered an angry willingness in much of Haiti's development community to explore other resource flow channels. Though the nongovernmental character of the proposal provoked violent reaction, the reactionaries in the Haiti mission were overridden by their superiors in Washington, and a completely nongovernmental implementing mode was adopted for this project.

The system, based on private voluntary organizations (PVOs), worked as follows.

1. AID made a macrogrant to a Washington-based PVO (the Pan American Development Foundation, PADF) to run a tree-planting project based on the principles that had emerged in my research. At the Haiti mission's urging, PADF invited me to be chief of party for the project and located an experienced accountant in Haiti to be financial administrator. PADF in addition recruited three American agroforesters who, in addition to MA-level professional training, had several years of overseas village field experience under their belts. Early in the project they were supplemented by two other expatriates, a Belgian and a French Canadian. We opened a central office in Port-au-Prince and assigned a major region of Haiti to each of the agroforesters, who lived in their field regions.
2. These agroforesters were responsible for contacting the many village-based PVOs working in their regions to explain the project, to emphasize its microeconomic focus and its difference from traditional reforestation models, to discuss the conditions of entry therein, and to make technical suggestions as to the trees that would be appropriate for the region.
3. If the PVO was interested, we drafted an agreement in which our mutual contributions and spheres of responsibility were specified. The agreements were not drafted in French (Haiti's official language) but in Creole, the only language spoken by most peasants.
4. The local PVO selected *animateurs* (village organizers) who themselves were peasants who lived and worked in the village where trees would be planted. After receiving training from us, they contacted their neighbors and kin, generated lists of peasants interested in planting a specified number of trees, and informed us when the local rains began to fall. At the proper moment we packed the seedlings in boxes customized to the particular region and shipped them on our trucks to the farmers, who would be waiting at specified drop-off points at a specified time. The trees were to be planted within twenty-four hours of delivery.

5. The animateurs were provided with Creole language data forms by which to gather ecological, land use, and land tenure data on each plot where trees would be planted and certain bits of information on each peasant participant. These forms were used to follow up, at periodic intervals, the survival of trees, the incidence of any problems (such as livestock depredation, burning, disease), and—above all—the manner in which the farmer integrated the trees into cropping and livestock patterns, to detect and head off any unintended substitution of food for wood.

RESULTS AND EVALUATION

The project was funded for four years from October 1981 through November 1985. During the writing of the project paper we were asked by an AID economist to estimate how many trees would be planted. Not knowing if the peasants would in fact plant any trees, we nervously proposed to reach two thousand peasant families with a million trees as a project goal. Fiddling with his programmed calculator, the economist informed us that that output would produce a negative internal rate of return. We would need at least two million trees to make the project worth AID's institutional while. We shrugged and told him cavalierly to up the figure and to promise three million trees on the land of six thousand peasants. (At that time I thought someone else would be directing the project.)

Numbers of Trees and Beneficiaries

Though I doubted that we could reach this higher goal, the response of the Haitian peasants to this new approach to tree planting left everyone, including myself, open mouthed. Within the first year of the project, one million trees had been planted by some 2,500 peasant households all over Haiti. My fears of peasant indifference were now transformed into nervousness that we could not supply seedlings fast enough to meet the demand triggered by our wood-as-a-cash-crop strategy. Apologetic village animateurs informed us that some cultivators who had not signed up on the first lists were actually stealing newly planted seedlings from their neighbors' fields at night. They promised to catch the scoundrels. If they did, I told them, give the scoundrels a hug. Their pilfering was dramatic proof of the bull's-eye nature of the anthropological predictions that underlie the project.

By the end of the second year (when I left the project), we had reached the four-year goal of three million seedlings and the project had geared up and decentralized its nursery capacity to produce several million seedlings per season (each year having two planting seasons). Under the new director, a fellow anthropologist, the geometric increase continued. By the end of the fourth year, the project had planted, not its originally agreed-upon three million trees, but twenty million trees. Stated more accurately, some 75,000 Haitian peasants had enthusiastically planted trees on their own land. In terms of its quantitative outreach, AOP had more than quintupled its original goals.

Wood Harvesting and Wood Banking

By the end of its fourth year the project had already received an unusual amount of professional research attention by anthropologists, economists, and foresters. In addition to AID evaluations, six studies had been released on one or another aspect of the project (Ashley 1986; Balzano 1986; Buffum and King 1985; Conway 1986; Grosenick 1985; McGowan 1986). As predicted, many peasants were harvesting trees by the end of the fourth year. The most lucrative sale of the wood was as polewood in local markets, though much charcoal was also being made from project trees.

Interestingly, however, the harvesting was proceeding much more slowly than I had predicted. Peasants were "clinging" to their trees and not engaging in the clear cutting that I hoped would occur, as a prelude to the emergence of a rotational system in which peasants would alternate crops with tree cover that they themselves had planted. This technique would have been a revival, under a "domesticated" mode, of the ancient swidden sequence that had long since disappeared from Haiti. Though such a revival would have warmed anthropological hearts, the peasants had a different agenda. Though they had long ago removed nature's tree cover, they were extremely cautious about removing the tree cover that they had planted. Their economic logic was unassailable. Crop failure is so frequent throughout most of Haiti, and the market for wood and charcoal so secure, that peasants prefer to leave the tree as a "bank" against future emergencies. This arboreal bank makes particular sense in the context of the recent disappearance from Haiti of the peasant's traditional bank, the pig. A governmentally mandated (and U.S. financed) slaughter of all pigs because of fears of African swine fever created a peasant banking gap that AOP trees have now started to fill.

THE ANTHROPOLOGICAL DIFFERENCE

Anthropological findings, methods, and theories clearly have heavily influenced this project at all stages. We are dealing, not with an ongoing project affected by anthropological input, but with a project whose very existence was rooted in anthropological research and whose very character was determined by ongoing anthropological direction and anthropologically informed managerial prodding.

My own involvement with the project spanned several phases and tasks:

1. Proposal of a theoretical and conceptual base of AOP, and concept of "wood as a cash crop."
2. Preliminary contacting of local PVOs to assess preproject interest.
3. Identification of specific program measures during project design.
4. Preparation of social soundness analysis for the AID project paper.
5. Participation as an outside expert at the AID meetings in Washington at which the fate of the project was decided.
6. Participation in the selection and in-country linguistic and cultural training of the agroforesters who worked for the project.
7. Direction and supervision of field operations.
8. Formative evaluation of preliminary results and the identification of needed midcourse corrections.
9. Generation of several hundred thousand dollars of supplemental funding from Canadian and Swiss sources and internationalization of the project team.
10. Preparation of publications about the project (Murray 1984, 1986).

In addition to my own participation in the AOP, four other anthropologists have been involved in long-term commitments to the project. Fred Conway did a preliminary study of firewood use in Haiti (Conway 1979). He subsequently served for two years as overall project coordinator within AID/Haiti. More recently he has carried out revealing case study research on the harvesting of project trees (Conway 1986). Glenn Smucker likewise did an early feasibility study in the northwest (Smucker 1981) and eventually joined the project as my successor in the directorship. Under his leadership, many of the crucial midcourse corrections were introduced. Ira Lowenthall took over the AID coordination of the project at a critical transitional period and has been instrumental in forging plans for its institutional future. And Anthony Balzano has carried out several years of case study fieldwork on the possible impact of the tree-planting activities on the land tenure in participating villages. All these individuals have PhDs, or are PhD candidates, in anthropology. And another anthropologist in the Haiti mission, John Lewis, succeeded in adapting the privatized umbrella agency outreach model for use in a swine repopulation project. With the possible exception of Vicos, it would be hard to imagine a project that has been as heavily influenced by anthropologists.

But how specifically has anthropology influenced the content of the project? There are at least three major levels at which anthropology has impinged on the content of AOP.

1. *The Application of Substantive Findings.* The very choice of "wood as a marketable crop" as the fundamental theme of the project stemmed from ethnographic knowledge of the cash-oriented foundations of Haitian peasant horticulture and knowledge of current conditions in the internal marketing system. Because of ethnographic knowledge I was able to avoid succumbing to the common-sense inclination to emphasize fruit trees (whose perishability and tendency to glut markets make them commercially vulnerable) and to choose instead a fast-growing wood tree. There is a feverishly escalating market for charcoal and construction wood that cannot be dampened even by the most successful project. And there are no spoilage problems with wood. The peasants can harvest it when they want. Furthermore, ethnographic knowledge of Haitian peasant land tenure—which is highly individualistic—guided me away from the community forest schemes that so many development philosophers seem to delight in but that are completely inappropriate to the social reality of Caribbean peasantries.
2. *Anthropological Methods.* The basic research that led up to the project employed participant observation along with intensive interviewing with small groups of informants to compare current cost/benefit ratios of traditional farming with projected cash yields from plots in which trees are intercropped with food on four-year rotation cycles. A critical part of the project design stage was to establish the likelihood of increased revenues from altered land use behaviors. During project design I also applied ethnographic techniques to the behavior of institutional personnel. The application of anthropological notetaking on 3-by-5 slips, not only with peasants but also with technicians, managers, and officials, exposed the institutional roots of earlier project failures and stimulated the proposal of alternative institutional routes. Furthermore, ethno-scientific elicitation of folk taxonomies led to the realization that whereas fruit trees are classified as a crop by Haitian peasants, wood trees are not so classified. This discovery exposed the need for the creation

of explicit messages saying that wood can be a crop, just as coffee, manioc, and corn can. Finally, prior experience in Creole-language instrument design and computer analysis permitted me to design a baseline data gathering system.

3. *Anthropological Theory.* My own thinking about tree planting was heavily guided by cultural-evolutionary insights into the origins of agriculture. The global tree problem is often erroneously conceptualized in a conservationist or ecological framework. Such a perspective is very short-sighted for anthropologists. We are aware of an ancient food crisis, when humans still hunted and gathered, that was solved, not by the adoption of conservationist practices, but rather by the shift into a domesticated mode of production. From hunting and gathering we turned to cropping and harvesting. I found the analogy with the present tree crisis conceptually overpowering. Trees will reemerge when and only when human beings start planting them aggressively as a harvestable crop, not when human consciousness is raised regarding their ecological importance. This anthropological insight (or bias), nourished by the aggressive creativity of the Haitian peasants among whom I had lived, swayed me toward the adoption of a dynamic "domestication" paradigm in proposing a solution to the tree problem in Haiti. This evolutionary perspective also permitted me to see that the cash-cropping of wood was in reality a small evolutionary step, not a quantum leap. The Haitian peasants already cut and sell natural stands of wood. They already plant and sell traditional food crops. It is but a small evolutionary step to join these two unconnected streams of Haitian peasant behavior, and this linkage is the core purpose of the Agroforestry Outreach Project.

Broader anthropological theory also motivated and justified a nongovernmental implementing mode for AOP. Not only AID but also most international development agencies tend to operate on a service model of the state. This idealized model views the basic character of the state as that of a provider of services to its population. Adherence to this theoretically naive service model has led to the squandering of untold millions of dollars in the support of extractive public bureaucracies. This waste is justified under the rubric of institution building—assisting public entities to provide the services that they are supposed to be providing.

But my anthropological insights into the origins of the state as a mechanism of extraction and control led me to pose the somewhat heretical position that the predatory behavior of Duvalier's regime was in fact not misbehavior. Duvalier was merely doing openly and blatantly what other state leaders camouflage under rhetoric. AID's search of nongovernmental implementing channels for AOP, then, was not seen as a simple emergency measure to be employed under a misbehaving regime but rather as an avenue of activity that might be valid as an option under many or most regimes. There is little justification in either ethnology or anthropological theory for viewing the state as the proper recipient of developmental funds. This theoretical insight permitted us to argue for a radically nongovernmental mode of tree-planting support in AOP. In short, sensitivity to issues in anthropological theory played a profound role in the shaping of the project.

Would AOP have taken the form it did without these varied types of anthropological input? Almost certainly not. Had there been no anthropological input, a radically different scenario would almost certainly have unfolded with the following elements.

1. AID would probably have undertaken a reforestation project—congressional pressure alone would have ensured that. But the project would have been based, not on the theme of "wood as a peasant cash-crop," but on the more traditional approach to trees as a vehicle of soil conservation. Ponderous educational programs would have been launched to teach the peasants about the value of trees. Emphasis would have been placed on educating the ignorant and on trying to induce peasants to plant commercially marginal (and nutritionally tangential) fruit trees instead of cash-generating wood trees.
2. The project would have been managed by technicians. The emphasis would probably have been on carrying out lengthy technical research concerning optimal planting strategies and the combination of trees with optimally effective bench terraces and other soil conservation devices. The outreach problem would have been given second priority. Throughout Haiti hundreds of thousands of dollars have been spent on numerous demonstration projects to create terraced, forested hillsides, but only a handful of cooperative local peasants have been induced to undertake the same activities on their own land.
3. The project would almost certainly have been run through the Haitian government. When after several hundred thousand dollars of expenditures few trees were visible, frustrated young AID program officers would have gotten finger-wagging lectures about the sovereign right of local officials to use donor money as they see fit. And the few trees planted would have been defined as *pyebwa leta* (the government's trees), and peasants would

have been sternly warned against ever cutting these trees, even the ones planted on their own land. And the peasants would soon turn the problem over to their most effective ally in such matters, the free-ranging omnivorous goat, who would soon remove this alien vegetation from the peasants' land.

Because of anthropology, the Agroforestry Outreach Project has unfolded to a different scenario. It was a moving experience for me to return to the village where I had done my original fieldwork (and which I of course tried to involve in the tree-planting activities) to find several houses built using the wood from leucaena trees planted during the project's earliest phases. Poles were beginning to be sold, although the prices had not yet stabilized for these still unknown wood types. Charcoal made from project trees was being sold in local markets. For the first time in the history of this village, people were "growing" part of their house structures and their cooking fuel. I felt as though I were observing (and had been a participant in) a replay of an ancient anthropological drama, the shift from an extractive to a domesticated mode of resource procurement. Though their sources of food energy had been domesticated millennia ago, my former village neighbors had now begun replicating this transition in the domain of wood and wood-based energy. I felt a satisfaction at having chosen a discipline that could give me the privilege of participating, even marginally, in this very ancient cultural-evolutionary transition.

REFERENCES

Ashley, Marshall D. 1986. *A Study of Traditional Agroforestry Systems in Haiti and Implications for the USAID/Haiti Agroforestry Outreach Project.* Port-au-Prince: University of Maine Agroforestry Outreach Research Project.

Balzano, Anthony. 1986. *Socioeconomic Aspects of Agroforestry in Rural Haiti.* Port-au-Prince: University of Maine Agroforestry Outreach Research Project.

Buffum, William, and Wendy King. 1985. *Small Farmer Decision Making and Tree Planting: Agroforestry Extension Recommendations.* Port-au-Prince: Haiti Agroforestry Outreach Project.

Conway, Frederick. 1979. *A Study of the Fuelwood Situation in Haiti.* Port-au-Prince: USAID.

——. 1986. *The Decision Making Framework for Tree Planting Within the Agroforestry Outreach Project.* Port-au-Prince: University of Maine Agroforestry Outreach Research Project.

Grosenick, Gerald. 1985. *Economic Evaluation of the Agroforestry Outreach Project.* Port-au-Prince: University of Maine Agroforestry Outreach Research Project.

McGowan, Lisa A. 1986. *Potential Marketability of Charcoal, Poles, and Planks Produced by Participants in the Agroforestry Outreach Project.* Port-au-Prince: University of Maine Agroforestry Outreach Research Project.

Murray, Gerald F. 1977. *The Evolution of Haitian Peasant Land Tenure: A Case Study in Agrarian Adaptation to Population Growth.* Ph.D. dissertation, Columbia University, New York.

——. 1978a. *Hillside Units, Wage Labor, and Haitian Peasant Land Tenure: A Strategy for the Organization of Erosion Control.* Port-au-Prince: USAID.

——. 1978b. *Informal Subdivisions and Land Insecurity: An Analysis of Haitian Peasant Land Tenure.* Port-au-Prince: USAID.

——. 1979. *Terraces, Trees, and the Haitian Peasant: An Assessment of 25 Years of Erosion Control in Rural Haiti.* Port-au-Prince: USAID.

——. 1984. "The Wood Tree as a Peasant Cash-Crop: An Anthropological Strategy for the Domestication of Energy." In A. Valdman and R. Foster, eds., *Haiti—Today and Tomorrow: An Interdisciplinary Study.* New York: University Press of America.

——. 1986. "Seeing the Forest While Planting the Trees: An Anthropological Approach to Agroforestry in Rural Haiti." In D. W. Brinkerhoff and J. C. Garcia-Zamor, eds., *Politics, Projects, and Peasants: Institutional Development in Haiti.* New York: Praeger, pp. 193–226.

Smucker, Glenn R. 1981. *Trees and Charcoal in Haitian Peasant Economy: A Feasibility Study.* Port-au-Prince: USAID.

Zuvekas, Clarence. 1978. *Agricultural Development in Haiti: An Assessment of Sector Problems, Policies, and Prospects under Conditions of Severe Soil Erosion.* Washington, D.C.: USAID.

The Price of Progress

JOHN BODLEY

In aiming at progress . . . you must let no one suffer by too drastic a measure, nor pay too high a price in upheaval and devastation, for your innovation.

Maunier, 1949: 725

Until recently, government planners have always considered economic development and progress beneficial goals that all societies should want to strive toward. The social advantage of progress—as defined in terms of increased incomes, higher standards of living, greater security, and better health—are thought to be positive, *universal* goods, to be obtained at any price. Although one may argue that tribal peoples must sacrifice their traditional cultures to obtain these benefits, government planners generally feel that this is a small price to pay for such obvious advantages.

In earlier chapters [in *Victims of Progress,* 3rd ed.], evidence was presented to demonstrate that autonomous tribal peoples have not *chosen* progress to enjoy its advantages, but that governments have *pushed* progress upon them to obtain tribal resources, not primarily to share with the tribal peoples the benefits of progress. It has also been shown that the price of forcing progress on unwilling recipients has involved the deaths of millions of tribal people, as well as their loss of land, political sovereignty, and the right to follow their own life style. This chapter does not attempt to further summarize that aspect of the cost of progress, but instead analyzes the specific effects of the participation of tribal peoples in the world-market economy. In direct opposition to the usual interpretation, it is argued here that the benefits of progress are often both illusory and detrimental to tribal peoples when they have not been allowed to control their own resources and define their relationship to the market economy.

Progress and the Quality of Life

One of the primary difficulties in assessing the benefits of progress and economic development for any culture is that of establishing a meaningful measure of both benefit and detriment. It is widely recognized that *standard of living,* which is the most frequently used measure of progress, is an intrinsically ethnocentric concept relying heavily upon indicators that lack universal cultural relevance. Such factors as GNP, per capita income, capital formation, employment rates, literacy, formal education, consumption of manufactured goods, number of doctors and hospital beds per thousand persons, and the amount of money spent on government welfare and health programs may be irrelevant measures of actual *quality* of life for autonomous or even semiautonomous tribal cultures. In its 1954 report, the Trust Territory government indicated that since the Micronesian population was still largely satisfying its own needs within a cashless subsistence economy, "Money income is not a significant measure of living standards, production, or well-being in this area" (TTR, 1953: 44). Unfortunately, within a short time the government began to rely on an enumeration of certain imported consumer goods as indicators of a higher standard of living in the islands, even though many tradition-oriented islanders felt that these new goods symbolized a lowering of the quality of life.

A more useful measure of the benefits of progress might be based on a formula for evaluating cultures devised by Goldschmidt (1952: 135). According to these less ethnocentric criteria, the important question to ask is: Does progress or economic development increase or decrease a given culture's ability to satisfy the physical and psychological needs of its population, or its stability? This question is a far more direct measure of quality of life than are the standard economic correlates of development, and it is universally relevant. Specific indication of this *standard* of living could be found for any society in the nutritional status and general physical and mental health of its population, the incidence of crime and delinquency, the demographic structure, family stability, and the society's relationship to its natural resource base. A society with high rates of malnutrition and crime, and one degrading its natural environment to the extent of threatening its continued existence, might be described as at a lower standard of living than is another society where these problems did not exist.

Careful examination of the data, which compare, on these specific points, the former condition of self-sufficient tribal peoples with their condition following their incorporation into the world-market economy, leads to the conclusion that their standard of living is *lowered,* not raised, by economic progress—and often to a dramatic degree. This is perhaps the most outstanding and inescapable fact to emerge from the years of research that anthropologists have devoted to the study of culture change and modernization. Despite the best intentions of those who have promoted change and improvement, all too often the results have been poverty, longer working hours, and much greater physical exertion, poor health, social disorder, discontent, discrimination, overpopulation, and environmental deterioration—combined with the destruction of the traditional culture.

Diseases of Development

Perhaps it would be useful for public health specialists to start talking about a new category of diseases. . . . Such diseases could be called the "diseases of development" and would consist of those pathological conditions which are based on the usually unanticipated consequences of the implementation of developmental schemes.

Hughes & Hunter, 1972: 93

Economic development increases the disease rate of affected peoples in at least three ways. First, to the extent that development is successful, it makes developed populations suddenly become vulnerable to all of the diseases suffered almost exclusively by "advanced" peoples. Among these are diabetes, obesity, hypertension, and a variety of circulatory problems. Second, development disturbs traditional environmental balances and may dramatically increase certain bacterial and parasite diseases. Finally, when development goals prove unattainable, an assortment of poverty diseases may appear in association with the crowded conditions of urban slums and the general breakdown in traditional socioeconomic systems.

Outstanding examples of the first situation can be seen in the Pacific, where some of the most successfully developed native peoples are found. In Micronesia, where development has progressed more rapidly than perhaps anywhere else, between 1958 and 1972 the population doubled, but the number of patients treated for heart disease in the local hospitals nearly tripled, mental disorder increased eightfold, and by 1972 hypertension and nutritional deficiencies began to make significant appearances for the first time (TTR, 1959, 1973, statistical tables).

Although some critics argue that the Micronesian figures simply represent better health monitoring due to economic progress, rigorously controlled data from Polynesia show a similar trend. The progressive acquisition of modern degenerative diseases was documented by an eight-member team of New Zealand medical specialists, anthropologists, and nutritionists, whose research was funded by the Medical Research Council of New Zealand and the World Health Organization. These researchers investigated the health status of a genetically related population at various points along a continuum of increasing cash income, modernizing diet, and urbanization. The extremes on this acculturation continuum were represented by the relatively traditional Pukapukans of the Cook Islands and the essentially Europeanized New Zealand Maori, while the busily developing Rarotongans, also of the Cook Islands, occupied the intermediate position. In 1971, after eight years of work, the team's preliminary findings were summarized by Dr. Ian Prior cardiologist and leader of the research, as follows:

We are beginning to observe that the more an islander takes on the ways of the West, the more prone he is to succumb to our degenerative diseases. In fact, it does not seem too much to say our evidence now shows that the farther the Pacific natives move from the quiet, carefree life of their ancestors, the closer they come to gout, diabetes, atherosclerosis, obesity, and hypertension.

Prior, 1971: 2

In Pukapuka, where progress was limited by the island's small size and its isolated location some 480 kilometers from the nearest port, the annual per capita income was only about thirty-six dollars and the economy remained essentially at a subsistence level. Resources were limited and the area was visited by trading ships only three or four times a year; thus, there was little opportunity for intensive economic development. Predictably, the population of Pukapuka was characterized by relatively low levels of imported sugar and salt intake, and a presumably related low level of heart disease, high blood pressure, and diabetes. In Rarotonga, where economic success was introducing town life, imported food, and motorcycles, sugar and salt intakes nearly tripled, high blood pressure increased approximately ninefold, diabetes two- to threefold, and heart disease doubled for men and more than quadrupled for women, while the number of grossly obese women increased more than tenfold. Among the New Zealand Maori, sugar intake was nearly eight times that of the Pukapukans, gout in men was nearly double its rate on Pukapuka, and diabetes in men was more than fivefold higher, while heart disease in women had increased more than sixfold. The Maori were, in fact, dying of "European" diseases at a greater rate than was the average New Zealand European.

Government development policies designed to bring about changes in local hydrology, vegetation, and settlement patterns and to increase population mobility, and even programs aimed at reducing certain diseases, have frequently led to dramatic increases in disease rates because of the unforeseen effects of disturbing the preexisting order. Hughes and Hunter (1972) published an excellent survey of cases in which development led directly to increased disease rates in Africa. They concluded that hasty development intervention in relatively balanced local cultures and environments resulted in "a drastic deterioration in the social and economic conditions of life."

Traditional populations in general have presumably learned to live with the endemic pathogens of their environments, and in some cases they have evolved genetic adaptations to specific diseases, such as the sickle-cell trait, which provided an immunity to malaria. Unfortunately, however, outside intervention has entirely changed this picture. In the late 1960s, sleeping sickness suddenly increased in many areas of Africa and even spread to areas where it did not formerly occur, due to the building of new roads and migratory labor, both of which caused increased population movement. Large-scale relocation schemes, such as the Zande Scheme, had disastrous results when natives were moved from their traditional disease-free refuges into infected areas. Dams and irrigation developments inadvertently created ideal conditions for the rapid proliferation of snails carrying schistosomiasis (a liver fluke disease), and major epidemics suddenly occurred in areas where this disease had never before been a problem. DDT spraying programs have been temporarily successful in controlling malaria, but there is often a rebound effect that increases the problem when spraying is discontinued, and the malarial mosquitoes are continually evolving resistant strains.

Urbanization is one of the prime measures of development, but it is a mixed blessing for most former tribal peoples. Urban health standards are abysmally poor and generally worse than in rural areas for the detribalized individuals who have crowded into the towns and cities throughout Africa, Asia, and Latin America seeking wage employment out of new economic necessity. Infectious diseases related to crowding and poor sanitation are rampant in urban centers, while greatly increased stress and poor nutrition aggravate a variety of other health problems. Malnutrition and other diet-related conditions are, in fact, one of the characteristic hazards of progress faced by tribal peoples and are discussed in the following sections.

The Hazards of Dietary Change

The traditional diets of tribal peoples are admirably adapted to their nutritional needs and available food resources. Even though these diets may seem bizarre, absurd, and unpalatable to outsiders, they are unlikely to be improved by drastic modifications. Given the delicate balances and complexities involved in any subsistence system, change always involves risks, but for tribal people the effects of dietary change have been catastrophic.

Under normal conditions, food habits are remarkably resistant to change, and indeed people are unlikely to abandon their traditional diets voluntarily in favor of dependence on difficult-to-obtain exotic imports. In some cases it is true that imported foods may be identified with powerful outsiders and are therefore sought as symbols of greater prestige. This may lead to such absurdities as Amazonian Indians choosing to consume imported canned tunafish when abundant high-quality fish is available in their own rivers. Another example of this situation occurs in tribes where mothers prefer to feed their infants expensive nutritionally inadequate canned milk from unsanitary, but *high status,* baby bottles. The high status of these items is often promoted by clever traders and clever advertising campaigns.

Aside from these apparently voluntary changes, it appears that more often dietary changes are forced upon unwilling tribal peoples by circumstances beyond their control. In some areas, new food crops have been introduced by government decree, or as a consequence of forced relocation or other policies designed to end hunting, pastoralism, or shifting cultivation. Food habits have also been modified by massive disruption of the natural environment by outsiders—as when sheepherders transformed the Australian Aborigines' foraging territory or when European invaders destroyed the bison herds that were the primary element in the Plains Indians' subsistence patterns. Perhaps the most frequent cause of diet change occurs when formerly self-sufficient peoples find that wage labor, cash cropping, and other economic development activities that feed tribal resources into the world-market economy must inevitably divert time and energy away from the production of subsistence foods. Many developing peoples suddenly discover that, like it or not, they are unable to secure traditional foods and must spend their newly acquired cash on costly, and often nutritionally inferior, manufactured foods.

Overall, the available data seem to indicate that the dietary changes that are linked to involvement in the world-market economy have tended to *lower* rather than raise the nutritional levels of the affected tribal peoples. Specifically, the vitamin, mineral, and protein components of their diets are often drastically reduced and replaced by enormous increases in starch and carbohydrates, often in the form of white flour and refined sugar.

Any deterioration in the quality of a given population's diet is almost certain to be reflected in an increase in deficiency diseases and a general decline in health status. Indeed, as tribal peoples have shifted to a diet based on imported manufactured or processed foods, there has been a dramatic rise in malnutrition, a massive increase in dental problems, and a variety of other nutritional-related disorders. Nutritional physiology is so complex that even well-meaning dietary changes have had tragic consequences. In many areas of Southeast Asia, government-sponsored protein supplementation programs supplying milk to protein-deficient populations caused unexpected health problems and increased mortality. Officials failed to anticipate that in cultures where adults do not normally drink milk, the enzymes needed to digest it are no longer produced and milk *intolerance* results (Davis & Bolin, 1972). In Brazil, a similar milk distribution program caused an epidemic of permanent blindness by aggravating a preexisting vitamin A deficiency (Bunce, 1972).

Teeth and Progress

> *There is nothing new in the observation that savages, or peoples living under primitive conditions, have, in general, excellent teeth. . . . Nor is it news that most civilized populations possess wretched teeth which begin to decay almost before they have erupted completely, and that dental caries is likely to be accompanied by periodontal disease with further reaching complications.*
>
> Hooton, 1945: xviii

Anthropologists have long recognized that undisturbed tribal peoples are often in excellent physical condition. And it has often been noted specifically that dental caries and the other dental abnormalities that plague industrialized societies are absent or rare among tribal peoples who have retained their traditional diets. The fact that tribal food habits may contribute to the development of sound teeth, whereas modernized diets may do just the opposite, was illustrated as long ago as 1894 in an article in the *Journal of the Royal Anthropological Institute* that described the results of a comparison between the teeth of ten Sioux Indians were examined when they came to London as members of Buffalo Bill's Wild West Show and were found to be completely free of caries and in possession of all their teeth, even though half of the group were over thirty-nine years of age. Londoners' teeth were conspicuous for both their caries and their steady reduction in number with advancing age. The difference was attributed primarily to the wear and polishing caused by the traditional Indian diet of coarse food and the fact that they chewed their food longer, encouraged by the absence of tableware.

One of the most remarkable studies of the dental conditions of tribal peoples and the impact of dietary change was conducted in the 1930s by Weston Price (1945), an American dentist who was interested in determining what caused normal, healthy teeth. Between 1931 and 1936, Price systematically explored tribal areas throughout the world to locate and examine the most isolated peoples who were still living on traditional foods. His fieldwork covered Alaska, the Canadian Yukon, Hudson Bay, Vancouver Island, Florida, the Andes, the Amazon, Samoa, Tahiti, New Zealand, Australia, New Caledonia, Fiji, the Torres Strait, East Africa, and the Nile. The study demonstrated both the superior quality of aboriginal dentition and the devastation that occurs as modern diets are adopted. In nearly every area where traditional foods were still being eaten, Price found perfect teeth with normal dental arches and virtually no decay, whereas caries and abnormalities increased steadily as new diets were adopted. In many cases the change was sudden and striking. Among Eskimo groups subsisting entirely on traditional food he found caries totally absent, whereas in groups eating a considerable quantity of store-bought food approximately 20 percent of their teeth were decayed. This figure rose to more than 30 percent with Eskimo groups subsisting almost exclusively on purchased or government-supplied food, and reached an incredible 48 percent among the Vancouver Island Indians. Unfortunately for many of these people, modern dental treatment did not accompany the new food, and their suffering was appalling. The loss of teeth was, of course, bad enough in itself, and it certainly undermined the population's resistance to many new diseases, including tuberculosis. But new foods were also accompanied by crowded, misplaced teeth, gum diseases, distortion of the face, and pinching of the nasal cavity. Abnormalities in the dental arch appeared in the new generation following the change in diet, while caries appeared almost immediately even in adults.

Price reported that in many areas the affected peoples were conscious of their own physical deterioration. At a mission school in Africa, the principal asked him to explain to the native schoolchildren why they were not physically as strong as children who had had no contact with schools. On an island in the Torres Strait the natives knew exactly what was causing their problems and resisted—almost to the point of bloodshed—government efforts to establish a store that would make imported food available. The government prevailed, however, and Price was able to establish a relationship between the length of time the government store had been established and the increasing incidence of caries among a population that showed an almost 100 percent immunity to them before the store had been opened.

In New Zealand, the Maori, who in their aboriginal state are often considered to have been among the healthiest, most perfectly developed of people, were found to have "advanced" the furthest. According to Price:

> *Their modernization was demonstrated not only by the high incidence of dental caries but also by the fact that 90 percent of the adults and 100 percent of the children had abnormalities of the dental arches.*
>
> Price, 1945: 206

Malnutrition

Malnutrition, particularly in the form of protein deficiency, has become a critical problem for tribal peoples who must adopt new economic patterns. Population pressures, cash cropping, and government programs all have tended to encourage the replacement of traditional crops and other food sources that were rich in protein with substitutes, high in calories but low in protein. In Africa, for example, protein-rich staples such as millet and sorghum are being replaced systematically by high-yielding manioc and plantains, which have insignificant amounts of protein. The problem is increased for cash croppers and wage laborers whose earnings are too low and unpredictable to allow purchase of adequate amounts of protein. In some rural areas, agricultural laborers have been forced systematically to deprive nonproductive members (principally children) of their households of their minimal nutritional requirements to satisfy the need of the productive members. This process has been documented in northeastern Brazil following the introduction of large-scale sisal plantations (Gross & Underwood, 1971). In urban centers the difficulties of obtaining nutritionally adequate diets are even more serious for tribal immigrants, because costs are higher and poor quality foods are more tempting.

One of the most tragic, and largely overlooked, aspects of chronic malnutrition is that it can lead to abnormally undersized brain development and apparently irreversible brain damage; it has been associated with various forms of mental impairment or retardation. Malnutrition has been linked clinically with mental retardation in both Africa and Latin America (see, for example, Mönckeberg, 1968), and this appears to be a worldwide phenomenon with serious implications (Montagu, 1972).

Optimistic supporters of progress will surely say that all of these new health problems are being overstressed and that the introduction of hospitals, clinics, and the other modern health institutions will overcome or at least compensate for all of these difficulties. However, it appears that uncontrolled population growth and economic impoverishment probably will keep most of these benefits out of reach for many tribal peoples, and the intervention of modern medicine has at least partly contributed to the problem in the first place.

The generalization that civilization frequently has a broad negative impact on tribal health has found broad empirical support (see especially Kroeger & Barbira-Freedman [1982] on Amazonia; Reinhard [1976] on the Arctic; and Wirsing

[1985] globally), but these conclusions have not gone unchallenged. Some critics argue that tribal health was often poor before modernization, and they point specifically to tribals' low life expectancy and high infant mortality rates. Demographic statistics on tribal populations are often problematic because precise data are scarce, but they do show a less favorable profile than that enjoyed by many industrial societies. However, it should be remembered that our present life expectancy is a recent phenomenon that has been very costly in terms of medical research and technological advances. Furthermore, the benefits of our health system are not enjoyed equally by all members of our society. High infant mortality could be viewed as a relatively inexpensive and egalitarian tribal public health program that offered the reasonable expectation of a healthy and productive life for those surviving to age fifteen.

Some critics also suggest that certain tribal populations, such as the New Guinea highlanders, were "stunted" by nutritional deficiencies created by tribal culture and are "improved" by "acculturation" and cash cropping (Dennett & Connell, 1988). Although this argument does suggest that the health question requires careful evaluation, it does not invalidate the empirical generalizations already established. Nutritional deficiencies undoubtedly occurred in densely populated zones in the central New Guinea highlands. However, the specific case cited above may not be widely representative of other tribal groups even in New Guinea, and it does not address the facts of outside intrusion or the inequities inherent in the contemporary development process.

Ecocide

"How is it," asked a herdsman . . . "how is it that these hills can no longer give pasture to my cattle? In my father's day they were green and cattle thrived there; today there is no grass and my cattle starve." As one looked one saw that what had once been a green hill had become a raw red rock.

Jones, 1934

Progress not only brings new threats to the health of tribal peoples, but it also imposes new strains on the ecosystems upon which they must depend for their ultimate survival. The introduction of new technology, increased consumption, lowered mortality, and the eradication of all traditional controls have combined to replace what for most tribal peoples was a relatively stable balance between population and natural resources, with a new system that is imbalanced. Economic development is forcing *ecocide* on peoples who were once careful stewards of their resources. There is already a trend toward widespread environmental deterioration in tribal areas, involving resource depletion, erosion, plant and animal extinction, and a disturbing series of other previously unforeseen changes.

After the initial depopulation suffered by most tribal peoples during their engulfment by frontiers of national expansion, most tribal populations began to experience rapid growth. Authorities generally attribute this growth to the introduction of modern medicine and new health measures and the termination of intertribal warfare, which lowered morality rates, as well as to new technology, which increased food production. Certainly all of these factors played a part, but merely lowering mortality rates would not have produced the rapid population growth that most tribal areas have experienced if traditional birth-spacing mechanisms had not been eliminated at the same time. Regardless of which factors were most important, it is clear that all of the natural and cultural checks on population growth have suddenly been pushed aside by culture change, while tribal lands have been steadily reduced and consumption levels have risen. In many tribal areas, environmental deterioration due to overuse of resources has set in, and in other areas such deterioration is imminent as resources continue to dwindle relative to the expanding population and increased use. Of course, population expansion by tribal peoples may have positive political consequences, because where tribals can retain or regain their status as local majorities they may be in a more favorable position to defend their resources against intruders.

Swidden systems and pastoralism, both highly successful economic systems under traditional conditions, have proved particularly vulnerable to increased population pressures and outside efforts to raise productivity beyond its natural limits. Research in Amazonia demonstrates that population pressures and related resource depletion can be created indirectly by official policies that restrict swidden peoples to smaller territories. Resource depletion itself can then become a powerful means of forcing tribal people into participating in the world-market economy—thus leading to further resource depletion. For example, Bodley and Benson (1979) showed how the Shipibo Indians in Peru were forced to further deplete their forest resources by cash cropping in the forest area to replace the resources that had been destroyed earlier by the intensive cash cropping necessitated by the narrow confines of their reserve. In this case, certain species of palm trees that had provided critical housing materials were destroyed by forest clearing and had to be replaced by costly purchased materials. Research by Gross (1979) and others showed similar processes at work among four tribal groups in central Brazil and demonstrated that the degree of market involvement increases directly with increases in resource depletion.

The settling of nomadic herders and the removal of prior controls on herd size have often led to serious overgrazing and erosion problems where these had not previously occurred. There are indications that the desertification problem in the Sahel region of Africa was aggravated by programs designed to settle nomads. The first sign of imbalance in a swidden system appears when the planting cycles are shortened to the point that garden plots are reused before sufficient forest regrowth can occur. If reclearing and planting continue in the same area, the natural patterns of forest succession may be disturbed irreversibly and the soil can be impaired permanently. An extensive tract of tropical rainforest in the lower Amazon of Brazil was reduced to a semiarid desert in just fifty years through such a process (Ackermann, 1964). The soils in the Azande area are also now seriously threatened with laterization and other problems as a result of the government-promoted cotton development scheme (McNeil, 1972).

The dangers of overdevelopment and the vulnerability of local resource systems have long been recognized by both anthropologists and tribal peoples themselves. But the pressures for change have been overwhelming. In 1948 the Maya villagers of Chan Kom complained to Redfield (1962) about the shortening of their swidden cycles, which they correctly attributed to increasing population pressures. Redfield told them, however, that they had no choice but to go "forward with technology" (Redfield, 1962: 178). In Assam, swidden cycles were shortened from an average of twelve years to only two or three within just twenty years, and anthropologists warned that the limits of swiddening would soon be reached (Burling, 1963: 311–312). In the Pacific, anthropologists warned of population pressures on limited resources as early as the 1930s (Keesing, 1941: 64–65). These warnings seemed fully justified, considering the fact that the crowded Tikopians were prompted by population pressures on their tiny island to suggest that infanticide be legalized. The warnings have been dramatically reinforced since then by the doubling of Micronesia's population in just the fourteen years between 1958 and 1972, from 70,600 to 114,645, while consumption levels have soared. By 1985 Micronesia's population had reached 162,321.

The environmental hazards of economic development and rapid population growth have become generally recognized only since worldwide concerns over environmental issues began in the early 1970s. Unfortunately, there is as yet little indication that the leaders of the new developing nations are sufficiently concerned with environmental limitations. On the contrary, governments are forcing tribal peoples into a self-reinforcing spiral of population growth and intensified resource exploitation, which may be stopped only by environmental disaster or the total impoverishment of the tribals.

The reality of ecocide certainly focuses attention on the fundamental contrasts between tribal and industrial systems in their use of natural resources, who controls them, and how they are managed. Tribal peoples are victimized because they control resources that outsiders demand. The resources exist because tribals managed them conservatively. However, as with the issue of the health consequences of detribalization, some anthropologists minimize the adaptive achievements of tribal groups and seem unwilling to concede that ecocide might be a consequence of cultural change. Critics attack an exaggerated "noble savage" image of tribals living in perfect harmony with nature and having no visible impact on their surroundings. They then show that tribals do in fact modify the environment, and they conclude that there is no significant difference between how tribals and industrial societies treat their environments. For example, Charles Wagley declared that Brazilian Indians such as the Tapirape

> *are not "natural men." They have human vices just as we do. . . . They do not live "in tune" with nature any more than I do; in fact, they can often be as destructive of their environment, within their limitations, as some civilized men. The Tapirape are not innocent or childlike in any way.*
>
> Wagley, 1977: 302

Anthropologist Terry Rambo demonstrated that the Semang of the Malaysian rain forests have a measurable impact on their environment. In his monograph *Primitive Polluters,* Rambo (1985) reported that the Semang live in smoke-filled houses. They sneeze and spread germs, breathe, and thus emit carbon dioxide. They clear small gardens, contributing "particulate matter" to the air and disturbing the local climate because cleared areas proved measurably warmer and drier than the shady forest. Rambo concluded that his research "demonstrates the essential functional similarity of the environmental interactions of primitive and civilized societies" (1985: 78) in contrast to a "noble savage" view (Bodley, 1983) which, according to Rambo (1985: 2), mistakenly "claims that traditional peoples almost always live in essential harmony with their environment."

This is surely a false issue. To stress, as I do, that tribals tend to manage their resources for sustained yield within relatively self-sufficient subsistence economies is not to make them either innocent children or natural men. Nor is it to deny that tribals "disrupt" their environment and may never be in absolute "balance" with nature.

The ecocide issue is perhaps most dramatically illustrated by two sets of satellite photos taken over the Brazilian rain forests of Rôndonia (Allard & McIntyre, 1988: 780–781). Photos taken in 1973, when Rôndonia was still a tribal domain, show virtually unbroken rain forest. The 1987 satellite photos, taken after just fifteen years of highway construction and "development" by outsiders, show more than 20 percent of the forest destroyed. The surviving Indians were being concentrated by FUNAI (Brazil's national Indian foundation) into what would soon become mere islands of forest in a ravaged landscape. It is irrelevant to quibble about whether tribals are noble, childlike, or innocent, or about the precise meaning of balance with nature, carrying capacity, or adaptation, to recognize that for the past 200 years rapid environmental deterioration on an unprecedented global scale has followed the wresting of control of vast areas of the world from tribal groups by resource-hungry industrial societies.

Deprivation and Discrimination

> *Contact with European culture has given them a knowledge of great wealth, opportunity and privilege, but only very limited avenues by which to acquire these things.*
>
> Crocombe, 1968

Unwittingly, tribal peoples have had the burden of perpetual relative deprivation thrust upon them by acceptance—either by themselves or by the governments administering them—of the standards of socioeconomic progress set for them by industrial civilizations. By comparison with the material wealth of industrial societies, tribal societies become, by definition, impoverished. They are then forced to transform their cultures and work to achieve what many economists now acknowledge to be unattainable goals. Even though in many cases the modest GNP goals set by development planners for the developing nations during the "development decade" of the 1960s were often met, the results were hardly noticeable for most of the tribal people involved. Population growth, environmental limitations, inequitable distribution of wealth, and the continued rapid growth of the industrialized nations have all meant that both the absolute and the relative gap between the rich and poor in the world is steadily widening. The prospect that tribal peoples will actually be able to attain the levels of resource consumption to which they are being encouraged to aspire is remote indeed except for those few groups who have retained effective control over strategic mineral resources.

Tribal peoples feel deprivation not only when the economic goals they have been encouraged to seek fail to materialize, but also when they discover that they are powerless, second-class citizens who are discriminated against and exploited by the dominant society. At the same time, they are denied the satisfactions of their traditional cultures, because these have been sacrificed in the process of modernization. Under the impact of major economic change family life is disrupted, traditional social controls are often lost, and many indicators of social anomie such as alcoholism, crime, delinquency, suicide, emotional disorders, and despair may increase. The inevitable frustration resulting from this continual deprivation finds expression in the cargo cults, revitalization movements, and a variety of other political and religious movements that have been widespread among tribal peoples following their disruption by industrial civilization.

Bibliography

Ackermann, F. L. 1964. *Geologia e Fisiografia da Região Bragantina, Estado do Pará.* Manaus, Brazil: Conselho Nacional de Pesquisas, Instituto Nacional de Pesquisas da Amazonia.

Allard, William Albert, and Loren McIntyre. 1988. Rondônia's settlers invade Brazil's imperiled rain forest. *National Geographic* 174(6):772–799.

Bodley, John H. 1970. *Campa Socio-Economic Adaptation.* Ann Arbor: University Microfilms.

______. 1983. *Der Weg der Zerstörung: Stammesvölker und die industrielle Zivilization.* Munich: Trickster-Verlag. (Translation of *Victims of Progress.*)

Bodley, John H., and Foley C. Benson. 1979. Cultural ecology of Amazonian palms. *Reports of Investigations,* no. 56. Pullman: Laboratory of Anthropology, Washington State University.

Bunce, George E. 1972. Aggravation of vitamin A deficiency following distribution of non-fortified skim milk: An example of nutrient interaction. In *The Careless Technology: Ecology and International Development,* ed. M. T. Farvar and John P. Milton, pp. 53–60. Garden City, N.Y.: Natural History Press.

Burling, Robbins. 1963. *Rengsanggri: Family and Kinship in a Garo Village.* Philadelphia: University of Pennsylvania Press.

Davis, A. E., and T. D. Bolin. 1972. Lactose intolerance in Southeast Asia. In *The Careless Technology: Ecology and International Development,* ed. M. T. Farvar and John P. Milton, pp. 61–68. Garden City, N.Y.: Natural History Press.

Dennett, Glenn, and John Connell. 1988. Acculturation and health in the highlands of Papua New Guinea. *Current Anthropology* 29(2):273–299.

Goldschmidt, Walter R. 1972. The interrelations between cultural factors and the acquisition of new technical skills. In *The Progress of Underdeveloped Areas,* ed. Bert F. Hoselitz, pp. 135–151. Chicago: University of Chicago Press.

Gross, Daniel R., et al. 1979. Ecology and acculturation among native peoples of Central Brazil. *Science* 206(4422): 1043–1050.

Hughes, Charles C., and John M. Hunter. 1972. The role of technological development in promoting disease in Africa. In *The Careless Technology: Ecology and International Development,* ed. M. T. Farvar and John P. Milton, pp. 69–101. Garden City, N.Y.: Natural History Press.

Keesing, Felix M. 1941. *The South Seas in the Modern World.* Institute of Pacific Relations International Research Series. New York: John Day.

Kroeger, Axel, and François Barbira-Freedman. 1982. *Culture Change and Health: The Case of South American Rainforest Indians.* Frankfurt am Main: Verlag Peter Lang. (Reprinted in Bodley, 1988a:221–236.)

McNeil, Mary. 1972. Lateritic soils in distinct tropical environments: Southern Sudan and Brazil. In *The Careless Technology: Ecology an International Development,* ed. M. T. Farvar and John P. Milton, pp. 591–608. Garden City, N.Y.: Natural History Press.

Mönckeberg, F. 1968. Mental retardation from malnutrition. *Journal of the American Medical Association* 206:30–31.

Montagu, Ashley. 1972. Sociogenic brain damage. *American Anthropologist* 74(5):1045–1061.

Rambo, A. Terry. 1985. *Primitive Polluters: Semang Impact on the Malaysian Tropical Rain Forest Ecosystem.* Anthropological Papers no. 76, Museum of Anthropology, University of Michigan.

Redfield, Robert. 1953. *The Primitive World and Its Transformations.* Ithaca, N.Y.: Cornell University Press.

______. 1962. *A Village That Chose Progress: Chan Kom Revisited.* Chicago: University of Chicago Press, Phoenix Books.

Smith, Wilberforce. 1894. The teeth of ten Sioux Indians. *Journal of the Royal Anthropological Institute* 24:109–116.

TTR: *See under* United States.

United States, Department of the Interior, Office of Territories. 1953. *Report on the Administration of the Trust Territory of the Pacific Islands* (by the United States to the United Nations) for the Period July 1, 1951, to June 30, 1952.

______. 1954. *Annual Report, High Commissioner of the Trust Territory of the Pacific Islands to the Secretary of the Interior* (for 1953).

United States, Department of State. 1955. *Seventh Annual Report to the United Nations on the Administration of the Trust Territory of the Pacific Islands* (July 1, 1953, to June 30, 1954).

______. 1959. *Eleventh Annual Report to the United Nations on the Administration of the Trust Territory of the Pacific Islands* (July 1, 1957, to June 30, 1958).

______. 1964. *Sixteenth Annual Report to the United Nations on the Administration of the Trust Territory of the Pacific Islands* (July 1, 1962 to June 30, 1963).

______. 1973. *Twenty-Fifth Annual Report to the United Nations on the Administration of the Trust Territory of the Pacific Islands* (July 1, 1971, to June 30, 1972).

Why Can't People Feed Themselves?

FRANCES MOORE LAPPÉ AND JOSEPH COLLINS

Question: You have said that the hunger problem is not the result of overpopulation. But you have not yet answered the most basic and simple question of all: Why can't people feed themselves? As Senator Daniel P. Moynihan put it bluntly, when addressing himself to the Third World, "Food growing is the first thing you do when you come down out of the trees. The question is, how come the United States can grow food and you can't?"

Our Response: In the very first speech I, Frances, ever gave after writing *Diet for a Small Planet,* I tried to take my audience along the path that I had taken in attempting to understand why so many are hungry in this world. Here is the gist of that talk that was, in truth, a turning point in my life:

> When I started I saw a world divided into two parts: a *minority* of nations that had "taken off" through their agricultural and industrial revolutions to reach a level of unparalleled material abundance and a *majority* that remained behind in a primitive, traditional, undeveloped state. This lagging behind of the majority of the world's peoples must be due, I thought, to some internal deficiency or even to several of them. It seemed obvious that the underdeveloped countries must be deficient in natural resources—particularly good land and climate—and in cultural development, including modern attitudes conducive to work and progress.
>
> But when looking for the historical roots of the predicament, I learned that my picture of these two separate worlds was quite false. My two separate worlds were really just different sides of the same coin. One side was on top largely because the other side was on the bottom. Could this be true? How were these separate worlds related?
>
> Colonialism appeared to me to be the link. Colonialism destroyed the cultural patterns of production and exchange by which traditional societies in "underdeveloped" countries previously had met the needs of the people. Many precolonial social structures, while dominated by exploitative elites, had evolved a system of mutual obligations among the classes that helped to ensure at least a minimal diet for all. A friend of mine once said: "Precolonial village existence in subsistence agriculture was a limited life indeed, but it's certainly not Calcutta."
>
> The misery of starvation in the streets of Calcutta can only be understood as the end-point of a long historical process—one that has destroyed a traditional social system.
>
> "Underdeveloped," instead of being an adjective that evokes the picture of a static society, became for me a verb (to "underdevelop") meaning the *process* by which the minority of the world has transformed—indeed often robbed and degraded—the majority.

That was in 1972. I clearly recall my thoughts on my return home. I had stated publicly for the first time a world view that had taken me years of study to grasp. The sense of relief was tremendous. For me the breakthrough lay in realizing that today's "hunger crisis" could not be described in static, descriptive terms. Hunger and underdevelopment must always be thought of as a *process.*

To answer the question "why hunger?" it is counterproductive to simply *describe* the conditions in an underdeveloped country today. For these conditions, whether they be the degree of malnutrition, the levels of agricultural production, or even the country's ecological endowment, are not static factors—they are not "givens." They are rather the *results* of an ongoing historical process. As we dug ever deeper into that historical process for the preparation of this book, we began to discover the existence of scarcity-creating mechanisms that we had only vaguely intuited before.

We have gotten great satisfaction from probing into the past since we recognized it is the only way to approach a solution to hunger today. We have come to see that it is the *force* creating the condition, not the condition itself, that must be the target of change. Otherwise we might change the condition today, only to find tomorrow that it has been recreated—with a vengeance.

Asking the question "Why can't people feed themselves?" carries a sense of bewilderment that there are so many people in the world not able to feed themselves adequately. What astonished us, however, is that there are not *more* people in the world who are hungry—considering the weight of the centuries of effort by the few to undermine the capacity of the majority to feed themselves. No, we are not crying "conspiracy!" If these forces were entirely conspiratorial, they would be easier to detect and many more people would by now have risen up to resist. We are talking about something more subtle and insidious; a heritage of a colonial order in which people with the advantage of considerable power sought their own self-interest, often arrogantly believing they were acting in the interest of the people whose lives they were destroying.

The Colonial Mind

The colonizer viewed agriculture in the subjugated lands as primitive and backward. Yet such a view contrasts sharply with documents from the colonial period now coming to light. For example, A. J. Voelker, a British agricultural scientist assigned to India during the 1890s wrote:

> Nowhere would one find better instances of keeping land scrupulously clean from weeds, of ingenuity in device of water-raising appliances, of knowledge of soils and their capabilities, as well as of the exact time to sow and reap, as one would find in Indian agriculture. It is wonderful too, how much is known of rotation, the system of "mixed crops" and of fallowing. . . . I, at least, have never seen a more perfect picture of cultivation."[1]

None the less, viewing the agriculture of the vanquished as primitive and backward reinforced the colonizer's rationale for destroying it. To the colonizers of Africa, Asia, and Latin America, agriculture became merely a means to extract wealth—much as gold from a mine—on behalf of the colonizing power. Agriculture was no longer seen as a source of food for the local population, nor even as their livelihood. Indeed the English economist John Stuart Mill reasoned that colonies should not be thought of as civilizations or countries at all but as "agricultural establishments" whose sole purpose was to supply the "larger community to which they belong." The colonized society's agriculture was only a subdivision of the agricultural system of the metropolitan country. As Mill acknowledged, "Our West India colonies, for example, cannot be regarded as countries. . . . The West Indies are the place where England *finds it convenient* to carry on the production of sugar, coffee and a few other tropical commodities."[2]

Prior to European intervention, Africans practiced a diversified agriculture that included the introduction of new food plants of Asian or American origin. But colonial rule simplified this diversified production to single cash crops—often to the exclusion of staple foods—and in the process sowed the seeds of famine.[3] Rice farming once had been common in Gambia. But with colonial rule so much of the best land was taken over by peanuts (grown for the European market) that rice had to be imported to counter the mounting prospect of famine. Northern Ghana, once famous for its yams and other foodstuffs, was forced to concentrate solely on cocoa. Most of the Gold Coast thus became dependent on cocoa. Liberia was turned into a virtual plantation subsidiary of Firestone Tire and Rubber. Food production in Dahomey and southeast Nigeria was all but abandoned in favor of palm oil; Tanganyika (now Tanzania) was forced to focus on sisal and Uganda on cotton.

The same happened in Indochina. About the time of the American Civil War the French decided that the Mekong Delta in Vietnam would be ideal for producing rice for export. Through a production system based on enriching the large landowners, Vietnam became the world's third largest exporter of rice by the 1930s; yet many landless Vietnamese went hungry.[4]

Rather than helping the peasants, colonialism's public works programs only reinforced export crop production. British irrigation works built in nineteenth-century India did help increase production, but the expansion was for spring export crops at the expense of millets and legumes grown in the fall as the basic local food crops.

Because people living on the land do not easily go against their natural and adaptive drive to grow food for themselves, colonial powers had to force the production of cash crops. The first strategy was to use physical or economic force to get the local population to grow cash crops instead of food on their own plots and then turn them over to the colonizer for export. The second strategy was the direct takeover of the land by large-scale plantations growing crops for export.

Forced Peasant Production

As Walter Rodney recounts in *How Europe Underdeveloped Africa,* cash crops were often grown literally under threat of guns and whips.[5] One visitor to the Sahel commented in 1928: "Cotton is an artificial crop and one the value of which is not entirely clear to the natives . . . " He wryly noted the "enforced enthusiasm with which the natives . . . have thrown themselves into . . . planting cotton."[6] The forced cultivation of cotton was a major grievance leading to the Maji Maji wars in Tanzania (then Tanganyika) and behind the nationalist revolt in Angola as late as 1960.[7]

Although raw force was used, taxation was the preferred colonial technique to force Africans to grow cash crops. The colonial administrations simply levied taxes on cattle, land, houses, and even the people themselves. Since the tax had to be paid in the coin of the realm, the peasants had either to grow crops to sell or to work on the plantations or in the mines of the Europeans.[8] Taxation was both an effective tool to "stimulate" cash cropping and a source of revenue that the colonial bureaucracy needed to enforce the system. To expand their production of export crops to pay the mounting taxes, peasant producers were forced to neglect the farming of food crops. In 1830, the Dutch administration in Java made the peasants an offer they could not refuse; if they would grow government-owned export crops on one fifth of their land, the Dutch would remit their land taxes.[9] If they refused and thus could not pay the taxes, they lost their land.

Marketing boards emerged in Africa in the 1930s as another technique for getting the profit from cash crop production by native producers into the hands of the colonial government and international firms. Purchases by the marketing boards were well below the world market price. Peanuts bought by the boards from peasant cultivators in West Africa were sold in Britain for more than *seven times* what the peasants received.[10]

The marketing board concept was born with the "cocoa hold-up" in the Gold Coast in 1937. Small cocoa farmers refused to sell to the large cocoa concerns like United Africa Company (a subsidiary of the Anglo-Dutch firm, Unilever—which we know as Lever Brothers) and Cadbury until they got a higher price. When the British government stepped in and agreed to buy the cocoa directly in place of the big business concerns, the smallholders must have thought they had scored at least a minor victory. But had they really? The following year the British formally set up the West African Cocoa Control Board. Theoretically, its purpose was to pay the peasants a reasonable price for their crops. In practice, however, the board, as sole purchaser, was able to hold down the prices paid the peasants for their crops when the world prices were rising. Rodney sums up the real "victory":

> None of the benefits went to Africans, but rather to the British government itself and to the private companies. . . . Big companies like the United African Company and John Holt were given . . . quotas to fulfill on behalf of the boards. As agents of the government, they were no longer exposed to direct attack, and their profits were secure.[11]

These marketing boards, set up for most export crops, were actually controlled by the companies. The chairman of the Cocoa Board was none other than John Cadbury of Cadbury Brothers (ever had a Cadbury chocolate bar?) who was part of a buying pool exploiting West African cocoa farmers.

The marketing boards funneled part of the profits from the exploitation of peasant producers indirectly into the royal treasury. While the Cocoa Board sold to the British Food Ministry at low prices, the ministry upped the price for British manufacturers, thus netting a profit as high as 11 million pounds in some years.[12]

These marketing boards of Africa were only the institutionalized rendition of what is the essence of colonialism—the extraction of wealth. While profits continued to accrue to foreign interests and local elites, prices received by those actually growing the commodities remained low.

Plantations

A second approach was direct takeover of the land either by the colonizing government or by private foreign interests. Previously self-provisioning farmers were forced to cultivate the plantation fields through either enslavement or economic coercion.

After the conquest of the Kandyan Kingdom (in present day Sri Lanka), in 1815, the British designated all the vast central part of the island as crown land. When it was determined that coffee, a profitable export crop, could be grown there, the Kandyan lands were sold off to British investors and planters at a mere five shillings per acre, the government even defraying the cost of surveying and road building.[13]

Java is also a prime example of a colonial government seizing territory and then putting it into private foreign hands. In 1870, the Dutch declared all uncultivated land—called waste land—property of the state for lease to Dutch plantation enterprises. In addition, the Agrarian Land Law of 1870 authorized foreign companies to lease village-owned land. The peasants, in chronic need of ready cash for taxes and foreign consumer goods, were only too willing to lease their land to the foreign companies for very modest sums and under terms dictated by the firms. Where land was still held communally, the village headman was tempted by high cash commissions offered by plantation companies. He would lease the village land even more cheaply than would the individual peasant or, as was frequently the case, sell out the entire village to the company.[14]

The introduction of the plantation meant the divorce of agriculture from nourishment, as the notion of food value was lost to the overriding claim of "market value" in international trade. Crops such as sugar, tobacco, and coffee were selected, not on the basis of how well they feed people, but for their high price value relative to their weight and bulk so that profit margins could be maintained even after the costs of shipping to Europe.

Suppressing Peasant Farming

The stagnation and impoverishment of the peasant food-producing sector was not the mere by-product of benign neglect, that is, the unintended consequence of an overemphasis on export production. Plantations—just like modern "agro-industrial complexes"—needed an abundant and readily available supply of low-wage agricultural workers. Colonial administrations thus devised a variety of tactics, all to undercut self-provisioning agriculture and thus make rural populations dependent on plantation wages. Government services and even the most minimal infrastructure (access to water, roads, seeds, credit, pest and disease control information, and so on) were systematically denied. Plantations usurped most of the good land, either making much of the rural population landless or pushing them onto marginal soils. (Yet the plantations have often held much of their land idle simply to prevent the peasants from using it—even to this day. Del Monte owns 57,000 acres of Guatemala but plants only 9000. The rest lies idle except for a few thousand head of grazing cattle.)[15]

In some cases a colonial administration would go even further to guarantee itself a labor supply. In at least twelve countries in the eastern and southern parts of Africa the exploitation of mineral wealth (gold, diamonds, and copper) and the establishment of cash-crop plantations demanded a continuous supply of low-cost labor. To assure this labor supply, colonial administrations simply expropriated the land of the African communities by violence and drove the people into small reserves.[16] With neither adequate land for their traditional slash-and-burn methods nor access to the means—tools, water, and fertilizer—to make continuous farming of such limited areas viable, the indigenous population could scarcely meet subsistence needs, much less produce surplus to sell in order to cover the colonial taxes. Hundreds of thousands of Africans were forced to become the cheap labor source so "needed" by the colonial plantations. Only by laboring on plantations and in the mines could they hope to pay the colonial taxes.

The tax scheme to produce reserves of cheap plantation and mining labor was particularly effective when the Great Depression hit and the bottom dropped out of cash crop economies. In 1929 the cotton market collapsed, leaving peasant cotton producers, such as those in Upper Volta, unable to pay their colonial taxes. More and more young people, in some years as many as 80,000, were thus forced to migrate to the Gold Coast to compete with each other for low-wage jobs on cocoa plantations.[17]

The forced migration of Africa's most able-bodied workers—stripping village food farming of needed hands—was a recurring feature of colonialism. As late as 1973 the Portuguese "exported" 400,000 Mozambican peasants to work in South Africa in exchange for gold deposited in the Lisbon treasury.

The many techniques of colonialism to undercut self-provisioning agriculture in order to ensure a cheap labor supply are no better illustrated than by the story of how, in the mid-nineteenth century, sugar plantation owners in British Guiana coped with the double blow of the emancipation of slaves and the crash in the world sugar market. The story is graphically recounted by Alan Adamson in *Sugar Without Slaves.*[18]

Would the ex-slaves be allowed to take over the plantation land and grow the food they needed? The planters, many ruined by the sugar slump, were determined they would not. The planter-dominated government devised several schemes for thwarting food self-sufficiency. The price of crown land was kept artificially high, and the purchase of land in parcels smaller than 100 acres was outlawed—two measures guaranteeing that newly organized ex-slave cooperatives could not hope to gain access to much land. The government also prohibited cultivation on as much as 400,000 acres—on the grounds of "uncertain property titles." Moreover, although many planters held part of their land out of sugar production due to the depressed world price, they would not allow any alternative production on them. They feared that once the ex-slaves started growing food it would be difficult to return them to sugar production when world market prices began to recover. In addition, the government taxed peasant production, then turned around and used the funds to subsidize the immigration of laborers from India and Malaysia to replace the freed slaves, thereby making sugar production again profitable for the planters. Finally, the government neglected the infrastructure for subsistence agriculture and denied credit for small farmers.

Perhaps the most insidious tactic to "lure" the peasant away from food production—and the one with profound historical consequences—was a policy of keeping the price of imported food low through the removal of tariffs and subsidies. The policy was double-edged: first, peasants were told they need not grow food because they could always buy it cheaply with their plantation wages; second, cheap food imports destroyed the market for domestic food and thereby impoverished local food producers.

Adamson relates how both the Governor of British Guiana and the Secretary for the Colonies Earl Grey favored low duties on imports in order to erode local food production and thereby release labor for the plantations. In 1851 the governor rushed through a reduction of the duty on cereals in order to "divert" labor to the sugar estates. As Adamson comments, "Without realizing it, he [the governor] had put his finger on the most mordant feature of monoculture: . . . its convulsive need to destroy any other sector of the economy which might compete for 'its' labor."[19]

Many colonial governments succeeded in establishing dependence on imported foodstuffs. In 1647 an observer in the West Indies wrote to Governor Winthrop of Massachusetts: "Men are so intent upon planting sugar that they had rather buy food at very dear rates than produce it by labour, so infinite is the profitt of sugar workes. . . ."[20] By 1770, the West Indies were importing most of the continental colonies' exports of dried fish, grain, beans, and vegetables. A dependence on imported food made the West Indian colonies vulnerable to any disruption in supply. This dependence on imported food stuffs spelled disaster when the thirteen continental colonies gained independence and food exports from the continent to the West Indies were interrupted. With no diversified food system to fall back on, 15,000 plantation workers died of famine between 1780 and 1787 in Jamaica alone.[21] The dependence of the West Indies on imported food persists to this day.

Suppressing Peasant Competition

We have talked about the techniques by which indigenous populations were forced to cultivate cash crops. In some countries with large plantations, however, colonial governments found it necessary to *prevent* peasants from independently growing cash crops not out of concern for their welfare, but so that they would not compete with colonial interests growing the same crop. For peasant farmers, given a modicum of opportunity, proved themselves capable of outproducing the large plantations not only in terms of output per unit of land but, more important, in terms of capital cost per unit produced.

In the Dutch East Indies (Indonesia and Dutch New Guinea) colonial policy in the middle of the nineteenth century forbade the sugar refineries to buy sugar cane from indigenous growers and imposed a discriminatory tax on rubber produced by native smallholders.[22] A recent unpublished United Nations study of agricultural development in Africa concluded that large-scale agricultural operations owned and controlled by foreign commercial interests (such as the rubber plantations of Liberia, the sisal estates of Tanganyika [Tanzania], and the coffee estates of Angola) only survived the competition of peasant producers because "the authorities actively supported them by suppressing indigenous rural development."[23]

The suppression of indigenous agricultural development served the interests of the colonizing powers in two ways. Not only did it prevent direct competition from more efficient native producers of the same crops, but it also guaranteed a labor force to work on the foreign-owned estates. Planters and foreign investors were not unaware that peasants who could survive economically by their own production would be under less pressure to sell their labor cheaply to the large estates.

The answer to the question, then, "Why can't people feed themselves?" must begin with an understanding of how colonialism actively prevented people from doing just that.

Colonialism

- forced peasants to replace food crops with cash crops that were then expropriated at very low rates;
- took over the best agricultural land for export crop plantations and then forced the most able-bodied workers to leave the village fields to work as slaves or for very low wages on plantations;

- encouraged a dependence on imported food;
- blocked native peasant cash crop production from competing with cash crops produced by settlers or foreign firms.

These are concrete examples of the development of underdevelopment that we should have perceived as such even as we read our history schoolbooks. Why didn't we? Somehow our schoolbooks always seemed to make the flow of history appear to have its own logic—as if it could not have been any other way. I, Frances, recall, in particular, a grade-school, social studies pamphlet on the idyllic life of Pedro, a nine-year-old boy on a coffee plantation in South America. The drawings of lush vegetation and "exotic" huts made his life seem romantic indeed. Wasn't it natural and proper that South America should have plantations to supply my mother and father with coffee? Isn't that the way it was *meant* to be?

Notes

1. Radha Sinha, *Food and Poverty* (New York: Holmes and Meier, 1976), p. 26.
2. John Stuart Mill, *Political Economy,* Book 3, Chapter 25 (emphasis added).
3. Peter Feldman and David Lawrence, "Social and Economic Implications of the Large-Scale Introduction of New Varieties of Foodgrains," Africa Report, preliminary draft (Geneva: UNRISD, 1975), pp. 107–108.
4. Edgar Owens, *The Right Side of History,* unpublished manuscript, 1976.
5. Walter Rodney, *How Europe Underdeveloped Africa* (London: Bogle-L'Ouverture Publications, 1972), pp. 171–172.
6. Ferdinand Ossendowski, *Slaves of the Sun* (New York: Dutton, 1928), p. 276.
7. Rodney, *How Europe Underdeveloped Africa,* pp. 171–172.
8. bid., p. 181.
9. Clifford Geertz, *Agricultural Involution* (Berkeley and Los Angeles: University of California Press, 1963), pp. 52–53.
10. Rodney, *How Europe Underdeveloped Africa,* p. 185.
11. Ibid., p. 184.
12. Ibid., p. 186.
13. George L. Beckford, *Persistent Poverty: Underdevelopment in Plantation Economies of the Third World* (New York: Oxford University Press, 1972), p. 99.
14. Ibid., p. 99, quoting from Erich Jacoby, *Agrarian Unrest in Southeast Asia* (New York: Asia Publishing House, 1961), p. 66.
15. Pat Flynn and Roger Burbach, North American Congress on Latin America, Berkely, California, recent investigation.
16. Feldman and Lawrence, "Social and Economic Implications," p. 103.
17. Special Sahelian Office Report, Food and Agriculture Organization, March 28, 1974, pp. 88–89.
18. Alan Adamson, *Sugar Without Slaves: The Political Economy of British Guiana, 1838–1904* (New Haven and London: Yale University Press, 1972).
19. Ibid., p. 41.
20. Eric Williams, *Capitalism and Slavery* (New York: Putnam, 1966), p. 110.
21. Ibid., p. 121.
22. Gunnar Myrdal, *Asian Drama,* vol. 1 (New York: Pantheon, 1966), pp. 448–449.
23. Feldman and Lawrence, "Social and Economic Implications," p. 189.

Frances Moore Lappé and **Dr. Joseph Collins** are founders and directors of the Institute for Food and Development Policy, located in San Francisco and New York.

The Arrow of Disease

When Columbus and his successors invaded the Americas, the most potent weapon they carried was their germs. But why didn't deadly disease flow in the other direction, from the New World to the Old?

JARED DIAMOND

The three people talking in the hospital room were already stressed out from having to cope with a mysterious illness, and it didn't help at all that they were having trouble communicating. One of them was the patient, a small, timid man, sick with pneumonia caused by an unidentified microbe and with only a limited command of the English language. The second, acting as translator, was his wife, worried about her husband's condition and frightened by the hospital environment. The third person in the trio was an inexperienced young doctor, trying to figure out what might have brought on the strange illness. Under the stress, the doctor was forgetting everything he had been taught about patient confidentiality. He committed the awful blunder of requesting the woman to ask her husband whether he'd had any sexual experiences that might have caused the infection.

As the young doctor watched, the husband turned red, pulled himself together so that he seemed even smaller, tried to disappear under his bed sheets, and stammered in a barely audible voice. His wife suddenly screamed in rage and drew herself up to tower over him. Before the doctor could stop her, she grabbed a heavy metal bottle, slammed it onto her husband's head, and stormed out of the room. It took a while for the doctor to elicit, through the man's broken English, what he had said to so enrage his wife. The answer slowly emerged: he had admitted to repeated intercourse with sheep on a recent visit to the family farm; perhaps that was how he had contracted the mysterious microbe.

This episode, related to me by a physician friend involved in the case, sounds so bizarrely one of a kind as to be of no possible broader significance. But in fact it illustrates a subject of great importance: human diseases of animal origins. Very few of us may love sheep in the carnal sense. But most of us platonically love our pet animals, like our dogs and cats; and as a society, we certainly appear to have an inordinate fondness for sheep and other livestock, to judge from the vast numbers of them that we keep.

Some of us—most often our children—pick up infectious diseases from our pets. Usually these illnesses remain no more than a nuisance, but a few have evolved into far more. The major killers of humanity throughout our recent history—smallpox, flu, tuberculosis, malaria, plague, measles, and cholera—are all infectious diseases that arose from diseases of animals. Until World War II more victims of war died of microbes than of gunshot or sword wounds. All those military histories glorifying Alexander the Great and Napoleon ignore the ego-deflating truth: the winners of past wars were not necessarily those armies with the best generals and weapons, but those bearing the worst germs with which to smite their enemies.

The grimmest example of the role of germs in history is much on our minds this month, as we recall the European conquest of the Americas that began with Columbus's voyage of 1492. Numerous as the Indian victims of the murderous Spanish conquistadores were, they were dwarfed in number by the victims of murderous Spanish microbes. These formidable conquerors killed an estimated 95 percent of the New World's pre-Columbian Indian population.

Why was the exchange of nasty germs between the Americas and Europe so unequal? Why didn't the reverse happen instead, with Indian diseases decimating the Spanish invaders, spreading back across the Atlantic, and causing a 95 percent decline in *Europe's* human population?

Similar questions arise regarding the decimation of many other native peoples by European germs, and regarding the decimation of would-be European conquistadores in the tropics of Africa and Asia.

Naturally, we're disposed to think about diseases from our own point of view: What can we do to save ourselves and to kill the microbes? Let's stamp out the scoundrels, and never mind what *their* motives are!

In life, though, one has to understand the enemy to beat him. So for a moment, let's consider disease from the microbes' point of view. Let's look beyond our anger at their making us sick in bizarre ways, like giving us genital sores or diarrhea, and ask why it is that they do such things. After all, microbes are as much a product of natural selection as we are, and so their actions must have come about because they confer some evolutionary benefit.

Basically, of course, evolution selects those individuals that are most effective at producing babies and at helping those babies find suitable places to live. Microbes are marvels at this latter requirement. They have evolved diverse ways of spreading from one person to another, and from animals to people. Many of our symptoms of disease actually represent ways in which some clever bug modifies our bodies or our behavior such that we become enlisted to spread bugs.

The most effortless way a bug can spread is by just waiting to be transmitted passively to the next victim. That's the strategy practiced by microbes that wait for one host to be eaten by the next—salmonella bacteria, for example, which we contract by eating already-infected eggs or meat; or the worm responsible for trichinosis, which waits for us to kill a pig and eat it without properly cooking it.

As a slight modification of this strategy; some microbes don't wait for the old host to die but instead hitchhike in the saliva of an insect that bites the old host and then flies to a new one. The free ride may be provided by mosquitoes, fleas, lice, or tsetse flies, which spread malaria, plague, typhus, and sleeping sickness, respectively. The dirtiest of all passive-carriage tricks is perpetrated by microbes that pass from a woman to her fetus—microbes such as the ones responsible for syphilis, rubella (German measles), and AIDS. By their cunning these microbes can already be infecting an infant before the moment of its birth.

Other bugs take matters into their own hands, figuratively speaking. They actively modify the anatomy or habits of their host to accelerate their transmission. From our perspective, the open genital sores caused by venereal diseases such as syphilis are a vile indignity. From the microbes' point of view, however, they're just a useful device to enlist a host's help in inoculating the body cavity of another host with microbes. The skin lesions caused by smallpox similarly spread microbes by direct or indirect body contact (occasionally very indirect, as when U.S. and Australian whites bent on wiping out "belligerent" native peoples sent them gifts of blankets previously used by smallpox patients).

More vigorous yet is the strategy practiced by the influenza, common cold, and pertussis (whooping cough) microbes, which induce the victim to cough or sneeze, thereby broadcasting the bugs toward prospective new hosts. Similarly the cholera bacterium induces a massive diarrhea that spreads bacteria into the water supplies of potential new victims. For modification of a host's behavior, though, nothing matches the rabies virus, which not only gets into the saliva of an infected dog but drives the dog into a frenzy of biting and thereby infects many new victims.

Thus, from our viewpoint, genital sores, diarrhea, and coughing are "symptoms" of disease. From a bug's viewpoint, they're clever evolutionary strategies to broadcast the bug. That's why it's in the bug's interests to make us "sick." But what does it gain by killing us? That seems self-defeating, since a microbe that kills its host kills itself.

Though you may well think it's of little consolation, our death is really just an unintended by-product of host symptoms that promote the efficient transmission of microbes. Yes, an untreated cholera patient may eventually die from producing diarrheal fluid at a rate of several gallons a day. While the patient lasts, though, the cholera bacterium profits from being massively disseminated into the water supplies of its next victims. As long as each victim thereby infects, on average, more than one new victim, the bacteria will spread, even though the first host happens to die.

So much for the dispassionate examination of the bug's interests. Now let's get back to considering our own selfish interests: to stay alive and healthy, best done by killing the damned bugs. One common response to infection is to develop a fever. Again, we consider fever a "symptom" of disease, as if it developed inevitably without serving any function. But regulation of body temperature is under our genetic control, and a fever doesn't just happen by accident. Because some microbes are more sensitive to heat than our own bodies are, by raising our body temperature we in effect try to bake the bugs to death before we get baked ourselves.

We and our pathogens are now locked in an escalating evolutionary contest, with the death of one contestant the price of defeat, and with natural selection playing the role of umpire.

Another common response is to mobilize our immune system. White blood cells and other cells actively seek out and kill foreign microbes. The specific antibodies we gradually build up against a particular microbe make us less likely to get reinfected once we are cured. As we all know there are some illnesses, such as flu and the common cold, to which our resistance is only temporary; we can eventually contract the illness again. Against other illnesses, though—including measles, mumps, rubella, pertussis, and the now-defeated menace of smallpox—antibodies stimulated by one infection confer lifelong immunity. That's the principle behind vaccination—to stimulate our antibody production without our having to go through the actual experience of the disease.

Alas, some clever bugs don't just cave in to our immune defenses. Some have learned to trick us by changing their antigens, those molecular pieces of the microbe that our antibodies recognize. The constant evolution or recycling of new strains of flu, with differing antigens, explains why the flu you got two years ago didn't protect you against the different strain that arrived this year. Sleeping sickness is an even more slippery customer in its ability to change its antigens rapidly.

Among the slipperiest of all is the virus that causes AIDS, which evolves new antigens even as it sits within an individual patient, until it eventually overwhelms the immune system.

Our slowest defensive response is through natural selection, which changes the relative frequency with which a gene appears from generation to generation. For almost any disease some people prove to be genetically more resistant than others. In an epidemic, those people with genes for resistance to that particular microbe are more likely to survive than are people lacking such genes. As a result, over the course of history human populations repeatedly exposed to a particular pathogen tend to be made up of individuals with genes that resist the appropriate microbe just because unfortunate individuals without those genes were less likely to survive to pass their genes on to their children.

Fat consolation, you may be thinking. This evolutionary response is not one that does the genetically susceptible dying individual any good. It does mean, though, that a human population as a whole becomes better protected.

In short, many bugs have had to evolve tricks to let them spread among potential victims. We've evolved counter-tricks, to which the bugs have responded by evolving counter-counter-tricks. We and our pathogens are now locked in an escalating evolutionary contest, with the death of one contestant the price of defeat, and with natural selection playing the role of umpire.

The form that this deadly contest takes varies with the pathogens: for some it is like a guerrilla war, while for others it is a blitzkrieg. With certain diseases, like malaria or hookworm, there's a more or less steady trickle of new cases in an affected area, and they will appear in any month of any year. Epidemic diseases, though, are different: they produce no cases for a long time, then a whole wave of cases, then no more cases again for a while.

Among such epidemic diseases, influenza is the most familiar to Americans, this year having been a particularly bad one for us (but a great year for the influenza virus). Cholera epidemics come at longer intervals, the 1991 Peruvian epidemic being the first one to reach the New World during the twentieth century. Frightening as today's influenza and cholera epidemics are, through, they pale beside the far more terrifying epidemics of the past, before the rise of modern medicine. The greatest single epidemic in human history was the influenza wave that killed 21 million people at the end of the First World War. The black death, or bubonic plague, killed one-quarter of Europe's population between 1346 and 1352, with death tolls up to 70 percent in some cities.

The infectious diseases that visit us as epidemics share several characteristics. First, they spread quickly and efficiently from an infected person to nearby healthy people, with the result that the whole population gets exposed within a short time. Second, they're "acute" illnesses: within a short time, you either die or recover completely. Third, the fortunate ones of us who do recover develop antibodies that leave us immune against a recurrence of the disease for a long time, possibly our entire lives. Finally, these diseases tend to be restricted to humans; the bugs causing them tend not to live in the soil or in other animals. All four of these characteristics apply to what Americans think of as the once more-familiar acute epidemic diseases of childhood, including measles, rubella, mumps, pertussis, and smallpox.

It is easy to understand why the combination of those four characteristics tends to make a disease run in epidemics. The rapid spread of microbes and the rapid course of symptoms mean that everybody in a local human population is soon infected, and thereafter either dead or else recovered and immune. No one is left alive who could still be infected. But since the microbe can't survive except in the bodies of living people, the disease dies out until a new crop of babies reaches the susceptible age—and until an infectious person arrives from the outside to start a new epidemic.

A classic illustration of the process is given by the history of measles on the isolated Faeroe Islands in the North Atlantic. A severe epidemic of the disease reached the Faeroes in 1781, then died out, leaving the islands measles-free until an infected carpenter arrived on a ship from Denmark in 1846. Within three months almost the whole Faeroes population—7,782 people—had gotten measles and then either died or recovered, leaving the measles virus to disappear once again until the next epidemic. Studies show that measles is likely to die out in any human population numbering less than half a million people. Only in larger populations can measles shift from one local area to another, thereby persisting until enough babies have been born in the originally infected area to permit the disease's return.

Rubella in Australia provides a similar example, on a much larger scale. As of 1917 Australia's population was still only 5 million, with most people living in scattered rural areas. The sea voyage to Britain took two months, and land transport within Australia itself was slow. In effect, Australia didn't even consist of a population of 5 million, but of hundreds of much smaller populations. As a result, rubella hit Australia only as occasional epidemics, when an infected person happened to arrive from overseas and stayed in a densely populated area. By 1938, though, the city of Sydney alone had a population of over one million, and people moved frequently and quickly by air between London, Sydney, and other Australian cities. Around then, rubella for the first time was able to establish itself permanently in Australia.

What's true for rubella in Australia is true for most familiar acute infectious diseases throughout the world. To sustain themselves, they need a human population that is sufficiently numerous and densely packed that a new crop of susceptible children is available for infection by the time the disease would otherwise be waning. Hence the measles and other such diseases are also known as "crowd diseases."

Crowd diseases could not sustain themselves in small bands of hunter-gatherers and slash-and-burn farmers. As tragic recent experience with Amazonian Indians and Pacific Islanders confirms, almost an entire tribelet may be wiped out by an epidemic brought by an outside visitor, because no one in the tribelet has any antibodies against the microbe. In addition, measles and some other "childhood" diseases are more likely to kill infected adults than children, and all adults in the tribelet are susceptible. Having killed most of the tribelet, the epidemic then disappears. The small population size explains why tribelets can't sustain epidemics introduced from the outside; at the same time it explains why they could never evolve epidemic diseases of their own to give back to the visitors.

That's not to say that small human populations are free from all infectious diseases. Some of their infections are caused by microbes capable of maintaining themselves in animals or in soil, so the disease remains constantly available to infect people. For example, the yellow fever virus is carried by African wild monkeys and is constantly available to infect rural human populations of Africa. It was also available to be carried to New World monkeys and people by the transAtlantic slave trade.

Other infections of small human populations are chronic diseases, such as leprosy and yaws, that may take a very long time to kill a victim. The victim thus remains alive as a reservoir of microbes to infect other members of the tribelet. Finally, small human populations are susceptible to nonfatal infections against which we don't develop immunity, with the result that the same person can become reinfected after recovering. That's the case with hookworm and many other parasites.

All these types of diseases, characteristic of small, isolated populations, must be the oldest diseases of humanity. They were the ones that we could evolve and sustain through the early millions of years of our evolutionary history, when the total human population was tiny and fragmented. They are also shared with, or are similar to the diseases of, our closest wild relatives, the African great apes. In contrast, the evolution of our crowd diseases could only have occurred with the buildup of large, dense human populations, first made possible by the rise of agriculture about 10,000 years ago, then by the rise of cities several thousand years ago. Indeed, the first attested dates for many familiar infectious diseases are surprisingly recent: around 1600 B.C. for smallpox (as deduced from pockmarks on an Egyptian mummy), 400 B.C. for mumps, 1840 for polio, and 1959 for AIDS.

Agriculture sustains much higher human population densities than do hunting and gathering—on average, 10 to 100 times higher. In addition, hunter-gatherers frequently shift camp, leaving behind their piles of feces with their accumulated microbes and worm larvae. But farmers are sedentary and live amid their own sewage, providing microbes with a quick path from one person's body into another person's drinking water. Farmers also become surrounded by disease-transmitting rodents attracted by stored food.

The explosive increase in world travel by Americans, and in immigration to the United States, is turning us into another melting pot—this time of microbes that we'd dismissed as causing disease in far-off countries.

Some human populations make it even easier for their own bacteria and worms to infect new victims, by intentionally gathering their feces and urine and spreading it as fertilizer on the fields where people work. Irrigation agriculture and fish farming provide ideal living conditions for the snails carrying schistosomes, and for other flukes that burrow through our skin as we wade through the feces-laden water.

If the rise of farming was a boon for our microbes, the rise of cities was a veritable bonanza, as still more densely packed human populations festered under even worse sanitation conditions. (Not until the beginning of the twentieth century did urban populations finally become self-sustaining; until then, constant immigration of healthy peasants from the countryside was necessary to make good the constant deaths of city dwellers from crowd diseases.) Another bonanza was the development of world trade routes, which by late Roman times effectively joined the populations of Europe, Asia, and North Africa into one giant breeding ground for microbes. That's when smallpox finally reached Rome as the "plague of Antonius," which killed millions of Roman citizens between A.D. 165 and 180.

Similarly, bubonic plague first appeared in Europe as the plague of Justinian (A.D. 542–543). But plague didn't begin to hit Europe with full force, as the black death epidemics, until 1346, when new overland trading with China provided rapid transit for flea-infested furs from plague-ridden areas of Central Asia. Today our jet planes have made even the longest intercontinental flights briefer than the duration of any human infectious disease. That's how an Aerolíneas Argentinas airplane, stopping in Lima, Peru, earlier this year, managed to deliver dozens of cholera-infected people the same day to my city of Los Angeles, over 3,000 miles away. The explosive increase in world travel by Americans, and in immigration to the United States, is turning us into another melting pot—this time of microbes that we previously dismissed as just causing exotic diseases in far-off countries.

When the human population became sufficiently large and concentrated, we reached the stage in our history when we could at last sustain crowd diseases confined to our species. But that presents a paradox: such diseases could never have existed before. Instead they had to evolve as new diseases. Where did those new diseases come from?

Evidence emerges from studies of the disease-causing microbes themselves. In many cases molecular biologists have identified the microbe's closest relative. Those relatives also prove to be agents of infectious crowd diseases—but ones confined to various species of domestic animals and pets! Among animals too, epidemic diseases require dense populations, and they're mainly confined to social animals that provide the necessary large populations. Hence when we domesticated social animals such as cows and pigs, they were already afflicted by epidemic diseases just waiting to be transferred to us.

For example, the measles virus is most closely related to the virus causing rinderpest, a nasty epidemic disease of cattle and many wild cud-chewing mammals. Rinderpest doesn't affect humans. Measles, in turn, doesn't affect cattle. The close similarity of the measles and rinderpest viruses suggests that the rinderpest virus transferred from cattle to humans, then became the measles virus by changing its properties to adapt to us. That transfer isn't surprising, considering how closely many peasant farmers live and sleep next to cows and their accompanying feces, urine, breath, sores, and blood. Our intimacy with cattle has been going on for 8,000 years since we domesticated them—ample time for the rinderpest virus to discover us nearby. Other familiar infectious diseases can similarly be traced back to diseases of our animal friends.

Given our proximity to the animals we love, we must constantly be getting bombarded by animal microbes. Those invaders get winnowed by natural selection, and only a few succeed in establishing themselves as human diseases. A quick survey of current diseases lets us trace four stages in the evolution of a specialized human disease from an animal precursor.

In the first stage, we pick up animal-borne microbes that are still at an early stage in their evolution into specialized human pathogens. They don't get transmitted directly from one person to another, and even their transfer from animals to us remains uncommon. There are dozens of diseases like this that we get directly from pets and domestic animals. They include cat scratch fever from cats, leptospirosis from dogs, psittacosis from chickens and parrots, and brucellosis from cattle. We're similarly susceptible to picking up diseases from wild animals, such as the tularemia that hunters occasionally get from skinning wild rabbits.

In the second stage, a former animal pathogen evolves to the point where it does get transmitted directly between people and causes epidemics. However, the epidemic dies out for several reasons—being cured by modern medicine, stopping when everybody has been infected and died, or stopping when everybody has been infected and become immune. For example, a previously unknown disease termed *o'nyong-nyong* fever appeared in East Africa in 1959 and infected several million Africans. It probably arose from a virus of monkeys and was transmitted to humans by mosquitoes. The fact that patients recovered quickly and became immune to further attack helped cause the new disease to die out quickly.

The annals of medicine are full of diseases that sound like no known disease today but that once caused terrifying epidemics before disappearing as mysteriously as they had come. Who alive today remembers the "English sweating sickness" that swept and terrified Europe between 1485 and 1578, or the "Picardy sweats" of eighteenth- and nineteenth-century France?

A third stage in the evolution of our major diseases is represented by former animal pathogens that establish themselves in humans and that do not die out; until they do, the question of whether they will become major killers of humanity remains up for grabs. The future is still very uncertain for Lassa fever, first observed in 1969 in Nigeria and caused by a virus probably derived from rodents. Better established is Lyme disease, caused by a spirochete that we get from the bite of a tick. Although the first known human cases in the United States appeared only as recently as 1962, Lyme disease is already reaching epidemic proportions in the Northeast, on the West Coast, and in the upper Midwest. The future of AIDS, derived from monkey viruses, is even more secure, from the virus's perspective.

The final stage of this evolution is represented by the major, long-established epidemic diseases confined to humans. These diseases must have been the evolutionary survivors of far more pathogens that tried to make the jump to us from animals—and mostly failed.

Diseases represent evolution in progress, as microbes adapt by natural selection to new hosts. Compared with cows' bodies, though, our bodies offer different immune defenses and different chemistry. In that new environment, a microbe must evolve new ways to live and propagate itself.

The best-studied example of microbes evolving these new ways involves myxomatosis, which hit Australian rabbits in 1950. The myxoma virus, native to a wild species of Brazilian rabbit, was known to cause a lethal epidemic in European domestic rabbits, which are a different species. The virus was intentionally introduced to Australia in the hopes of ridding the continent of its plague of European rabbits, foolishly introduced in the nineteenth century. In the first year, myxoma produced a gratifying (to Australian farmers) 99.8 percent mortality in infected rabbits. Fortunately for the rabbits and unfortunately for the farmers, the death rate then dropped in the second year to 90 percent and eventually to 25 percent, frustrating hopes of eradicating rabbits completely from Australia. The problem was that the myxoma virus evolved to serve its own interest, which differed from the farmers' interests and those of the rabbits. The virus changed to kill fewer rabbits and to permit lethally infected ones to live longer before dying. The result was bad for Australian farmers but good for the virus: a less lethal myxoma virus spreads baby viruses to more rabbits than did the original, highly virulent myxoma.

For a similar example in humans, consider the surprising evolution of syphilis. Today we associate syphilis with genital sores and a very slowly developing disease, leading to the death of untreated victims only after many years. However, when syphilis was first definitely recorded in Europe in 1495, its pustules often covered the body from the head to the knees, caused flesh to fall off people's faces, and led to death within a few months. By 1546 syphilis had evolved into the disease with the symptoms known to us today. Apparently, just as with myxomatosis, those syphilis spirochetes evolved to keep their victims alive longer in order to transmit their spirochete offspring into more victims.

How, then, does all this explain the outcome of 1492—that Europeans conquered and depopulated the New World, instead of Native Americans conquering and depopulating Europe?

In the century or two following Columbus's arrival in the New World, the Indian population declined by about 95 percent. The main killers were European germs, to which the Indians had never been exposed.

Part of the answer, of course, goes back to the invaders' technological advantages. European guns and steel swords were more effective weapons than Native American stone axes and wooden clubs. Only Europeans had ships capable of crossing the ocean and horses that could provide a decisive advantage in battle. But that's not the whole answer. Far more Native Americans died in bed than on the battlefield—the victims of germs, not of guns and swords. Those germs undermined Indian resistance by killing most Indians and their leaders and by demoralizing the survivors.

The role of disease in the Spanish conquests of the Aztec and Inca empires is especially well documented. In 1519 Cortés landed on the coast of Mexico with 600 Spaniards to conquer the fiercely militaristic Aztec Empire, which at the time had a population of many millions. That Cortés reached the Aztec capital of Tenochtitlán, escaped with the loss of "only" two-thirds of his force, and managed to fight his way back to the coast demonstrates both Spanish military advantages and the initial naïveté of the Aztecs. But when Cortés's next onslaught came, in 1521, the Aztecs were no longer naïve; they fought street by street with the utmost tenacity.

What gave the Spaniards a decisive advantage this time was smallpox, which reached Mexico in 1520 with the arrival of one infected slave from Spanish Cuba. The resulting epidemic proceeded to kill nearly half the Aztecs. The survivors were demoralized by the mysterious illness that killed Indians and spared Spaniards, as if advertising the Spaniards' invincibility. By 1618 Mexico's initial population of 20 million had plummeted to about 1.6 million.

Pizarro had similarly grim luck when he landed on the coast of Peru in 1531 with about 200 men to conquer the Inca Empire. Fortunately for Pizarro, and unfortunately for the Incas, smallpox had arrived overland around 1524, killing much of the Inca population, including both Emperor Huayna Capac and his son and designated successor, Ninan Cuyoche. Because of the vacant throne, two other sons of Huayna Capac, Atahuallpa and Huáscar, became embroiled in a civil war that Pizarro exploited to conquer the divided Incas.

When we in the United States think of the most populous New World societies existing in 1492, only the Aztecs and Incas come to mind. We forget that North America also supported populous Indian societies in the Mississippi Valley. Sadly, these societies too would disappear. But in this case conquistadores contributed nothing directly to the societies' destruction; the conquistadores' germs, spreading in advance, did everything. When De Soto marched through the Southeast in 1540, he came across Indian towns abandoned two years previously because nearly all the inhabitants had died in epidemics. However, he was still able to see some of the densely populated towns lining the lower Mississippi. By a century and a half later, though, when French settlers returned to the lower Mississippi, almost all those towns had vanished. Their relics are the great mound sites of the Mississippi Valley. Only recently have we come to realize that the mound-building societies were still largely intact when Columbus arrived, and that they collapsed between 1492 and the systematic European exploration of the Mississippi.

When I was a child in school, we were taught that North America had originally been occupied by about one million Indians. That low number helped justify the white conquest of what could then be viewed as an almost empty continent. However, archeological excavations and descriptions left by the first European explorers on our coasts now suggest an initial number of around 20 million. In the century or two following Columbus's arrival in the New World, the Indian population is estimated to have declined by about 95 percent.

The main killers were European germs, to which the Indians had never been exposed and against which they therefore had neither immunologic nor genetic resistance. Smallpox, measles, influenza, and typhus competed for top rank among the killers. As if those were not enough, pertussis, plague, tuberculosis, diphtheria, mumps, malaria, and yellow fever came close behind. In countless cases Europeans were actually there to witness the decimation that occurred when the germs arrived. For example, in 1837 the Mandan Indian tribe, with one of the most elaborate cultures in the Great Plains, contracted smallpox thanks to a steamboat traveling up the Missouri River from St. Louis. The population of one Mandan village crashed from 2,000 to less than 40 within a few weeks.

The one-sided exchange of lethal germs between the Old and New Worlds is among the most striking and consequence-laden facts of recent history. Whereas over a dozen major infectious diseases of Old World origins became established in the New World, not a single major killer reached Europe from the Americas. The sole possible exception is syphilis, whose area of origin still remains controversial.

That one-sidedness is more striking with the knowledge that large, dense human populations are a prerequisite for the evolution of crowd diseases. If recent reappraisals of the pre-Columbian New World population are correct, that population was not far below the contemporaneous population of Eurasia. Some New World cities, like Tenochtitlán, were among the world's most populous cities at the time. Yet Tenochtitlán didn't have awful germs waiting in store for the Spaniards. Why not?

One possible factor is the rise of dense human populations began somewhat later in the New World than in the Old. Another is that the three most populous American centers—the Andes, Mexico, and the Mississippi Valley—were never connected by regular fast trade into one gigantic breeding ground for microbes, in the way that Europe, North Africa, India, and China became connected in late Roman times.

The main reason becomes clear, however, if we ask a simple question: From what microbes could any crowd diseases of the Americas have evolved? We've seen that Eurasian crowd diseases evolved from diseases of domesticated herd animals. Significantly, there were many such animals in Eurasia. But there were only five animals that became domesticated in the Americas: the turkey in Mexico and parts of North America, the guinea pig and llama/alpaca (probably derived from the same original wild species) in the Andes, and Muscovy duck in tropical South America, and the dog throughout the Americas.

That extreme paucity of New World domestic animals reflects the paucity of wild starting material. About 80 percent of the big wild mammals of the Americas became extinct at the end of the last ice age, around 11,000 years ago, at approximately the same time that the first well-attested wave of Indian hunters spread over the Americas. Among the species that disappeared were ones that would have yielded useful domesticates, such as American horses and camels. Debate still rages as to whether those extinctions were due to climate changes or to the impact of Indian hunters on prey that had never seen humans. Whatever the reason, the extinctions removed most of the basis for Native American animal domestication—and for crowd diseases.

The few domesticates that remained were not likely sources of such diseases. Muscovy ducks and turkeys don't live in enormous flocks, and they're not naturally endearing species (like young lambs) with which we have much physical contact. Guinea pigs may have contributed a trypanosome infection like Chagas' disease or leishmaniasis to our catalog of woes, but that's uncertain.

Initially the most surprising absence is of any human disease derived from llamas (or alpacas), which are tempting to consider as the Andean equivalent of Eurasian livestock. However, llamas had three strikes against them as a source of human pathogens: their wild relatives don't occur in big herds as do wild sheep, goats, and pigs; their total numbers were never remotely as large as the Eurasian populations of domestic livestock, since llamas never spread beyond the Andes; and llamas aren't as cuddly as piglets and lambs and aren't kept in such close association with people. (You may not think of piglets as cuddly, but human mothers in the New Guinea highlands often nurse them, and they frequently live right in the huts of peasant farmers.)

The importance of animal-derived diseases for human history extends far beyond the Americas. Eurasian germs played a key role in decimating native peoples in many other parts of the world as well, including the Pacific islands, Australia, and southern Africa. Racist Europeans used to attribute those conquests to their supposedly better brains. But no evidence for such better brains has been forthcoming. Instead, the conquests were made possible by Europeans' nastier germs, and by the technological advances and denser populations that Europeans ultimately acquired by means of their domesticated plants and animals.

So on this 500th anniversary of Columbus's discovery, let's try to regain our sense of perspective about his hotly debated achievements. There's no doubt that Columbus was a great visionary, seaman, and leader. There's also no doubt that he and his successors often behaved as bestial murderers. But those facts alone don't fully explain why it took so few European immigrants to initially conquer and ultimately supplant so much of the native population of the Americas. Without the germs Europeans brought with them—germs that were derived from their animals—such conquests might have been impossible.

Jared Diamond is a contributing editor of *Discover,* a professor of physiology at the UCLA School of Medicine, a recipient of a MacArthur genius award, and a research associate in ornithology at the American Museum of Natural History. Expanded versions of many of his *Discover* articles appear in his book *The Third Chimpanzee: The Evolution and Future of the Human Animal,* which won Britain's 1992 COPUS prize for best science book. Not least among his many accomplishments was his rediscovery in 1981 of the long-lost bowerbird of New Guinea. Diamond wrote about pseudo-hermaphrodites for *Discover's* special June issue on the science of sex.